DEPRESSION

A PSYCHOBIOLOGICAL SYNTHESIS

DEPRESSION

A PSYCHOBIOLOGICAL SYNTHESIS

PAUL WILLNER
City of London Polytechnic
London, England

A Wiley-Interscience Publication
JOHN WILEY & SONS
New York • Chichester • Brisbane • Toronto • Singapore

Library of Congress Cataloging in Publication Data:

Willner, Paul.
  Depression: a psychobiological synthesis.

  "A Wiley-Interscience publication."
  Bibliography: p.
  Includes index.
  1. Depression, Mental.   2. Psychobiology.   I. Title.

RC537.W554 1985   616.85'27   84-29100
ISBN 0-471-80671-4

Printed in the United States of America

10 9 8 7 6 5 4 3 2 1

This book is dedicated to the memory of my parents
Emil and Susi

PREFACE

The 1980s are an exciting time to be working on the psychobiology of depression. Not a month goes by without reports of clinical trials of a novel experimental antidepressant, the description of a new animal model of depression, or the discovery of yet another biochemical or endocrine abnormality in depressed patients. The publication of symposia devoted to these advances is hardly less frequent. Yet what is conspicuously lacking in all this activity is a coherent theoretical framework within which to assess the significance and potential importance of each new finding. That is what I have attempted to provide.

This book presents a way of organizing evidence from many diverse disciplines, and it shows that much of what has been uncovered empirically about the psychobiology of depression may be readily understood in terms of what we already know about the brain. By examining the evidence within an organized framework, the relationships between the contributions from different disciplines become apparent, and a set of yardsticks is constructed against which to measure new discoveries. Above all, I have tried to build a mirror in which workers involved in any aspect of the psychobiology of depression can see exactly where they stand in relation to everyone else.

In order to produce a comprehensive survey of the psychobiology of depression, I have been forced to enter a number of territories with which I was previously unfamiliar. I think that the map I have drawn of these areas does not suffer greatly on account of the recency of my visit, but there must inevitably be inaccuracies in places, and for this I apologize. Although the end product is a theory of the causes, symptoms, and treatment of depression, I like to think that the book presents an objective assessment of the work described, rather than an attempt to force the literature to conform to my own theoretical preconceptions. I freely admit that at the outset I did have a number of prejudices; however, all but one of them collapsed on encountering the evidence. The survivor was a preference for producing a clear conclusion wherever it was at all possible, rather than leaving loose ends (and there are certainly enough of those).

The bulk of this book was written while on sabbatical leave from the City of London Polytechnic for the academic year 1982–1983. I am extremely grateful to Larry Currie and Stephen Jones for giving me this opportunity and to Tom Walsh for his help during my absence and after my return. The first few weeks of writing were spent in the Department of Pharmacology at the University of Goteborg, Sweden, and the remainder in the Department of Psychiatry at the University of California, San Diego; I am deeply indebted to Professors Arvid Carlsson and Lewis Judd for extending me their hospitality and for the use of their excellent facilities. I should also like to thank the many friends and colleagues who gave up their time to discuss ideas or read sections of the manuscript: in Sweden, David Clark, Elias Eriksson, and Torgny Svensson; in California, Christian Gillin, David Janowsky, Alan Kraft, George Mandler, David Segal, James Tepper, and Steven Young; and in England, Graham Holder, Sebastian Lazareno, Richard Muscat, and Anthony Towell. I am also grateful to Alec and Kath Reid, whose assistance in caring for Matthew and Jessica was invaluable, and to Martin Lyon and Maxine Winter, who prepared the figures. My greatest debt is to Heather Reid, without whose constant support, encouragement, and patience this book would still be unfinished.

PAUL WILLNER

London
February 1985

CONTENTS

SYNOPSIS

PART 2   FOUNDATIONS

PART 3   PSYCHOBIOLOGY

PART 4   SYNTHESIS

ABBREVIATIONS

ACh	Acetylcholine
ACTH	Adrenocorticotrophic hormone
AMPT	Alpha-methylparatyrosine
cAMP	Cyclic adenosine monophosphate
COMT	Catechol-O-methyltransferase
CRF	Corticotrophin releasing factor
CSF	Cerebrospinal fluid
DA	Dopamine
DBEE	Dorsal bundle extinction effect
DBH	Dopamine-beta-hydroxylase
DDC	Diethyldithiocarbamate
DHA	Dihydroalprenolol
DHE	Dihydroergocryptine
5,6-DHT	5,6-Dihydroxytryptamine
5,7-DHT	5,7-Dihydroxytryptamine
DMI	Desmethylimipramine
DOPA	Dihydroxyphenylalanine
DOPAC	Dihydroxyphenylacetic acid
DOPS	Dihydroxyphenylserine
DSM-III	*Diagnostic and Statistical Manual of Psychiatric Disorders*, 3rd ed.
DST	Dexamethasone suppression test
ECS	Electroconvulsive shock
EEG	Electroencephalogram
EMG	Electromyogram
GABA	Gamma-aminobutyric acid
GAD	Glutamic acid decarboxylase
GBI	General behavior inventory
GH	Growth hormone
GHRF	Growth hormone releasing factor
5-HIAA	5-Hydroxyindoleacetic acid
HPA	Hypothalamic–pituitary–adrenal

5-HT	5-Hydroxytryptamine
5-HTP	5-Hydroxytryptophan
HVA	Homovanillic acid
ICD	International classification of disease
ICSS	Intracranial self-stimulation
LGN	Lateral geniculate nucleus
LHRH	Luteinizing hormone releasing factor
LSD	Lysergic acid diethylamide
MAO	Monoamine oxidase
MAOI	Monoamine oxidase inhibitor
5-MeO-DMT	5-Methoxydimethyltryptamine
MFB	Medial forebrain bundle
MHPG	Methoxyhydroxyphenylethyleneglycol
MIF	Melanocyte stimulating hormone inhibiting factor
MMPI	Minnesota multiple personality inventory
MRF	Midbrain reticular formation
MSH	Melanocyte stimulating hormone
NA	Noradrenaline
NRM	Nucleus raphe magnus
6-OHDA	6-Hydroxydopamine
PAG	Periaqueductal grey
PCPA	Parachlorophenylalanine
PVN	Paraventricular nucleus
QNB	Quinuclinidyl benzilate
RDC	Research diagnostic criteria
REM	Rapid eye movements
SPA	Stimulation produced analgesia
T3	Triiodothyronine
TRH	Thyroid stimulating hormone releasing factor
TSH	Thyroid stimulating hormone
VEP	Visual evoked potential
VMA	Vanillylmandelic acid
VTA	Ventral tegmental area
WAIS	Wechsler adult intelligence scale

DEPRESSION

A PSYCHOBIOLOGICAL SYNTHESIS

1

Ground Rules

one

STARTING POINTS

In 1952, the drug reserpine was isolated from *Rauwolfia serpentia*, a plant used for hundreds of years in Indian folk medicine for a variety of purposes (Bein, 1982). Reserpine was introduced into Western medicine as an antihypertensive agent, and shortly thereafter the first of many papers appeared reporting that depression was a frequent side effect (Fries, 1954). At about the same time, iproniazid, a monoamine oxidase-inhibiting drug, which was developed from a successful antitubercular agent, isoniazid, and was undergoing tests for the same purpose, was observed to produce euphoria and hyperactivity in some patients. The results of controlled trials confirming that iproniazid was an effective antidepressant were published in 1957 (Crane, 1957; Loomer et al., 1957). A similar accident led to the discovery of the tricyclic antidepressants. Chlorpromazine, the first neuroleptic (antischizophrenic) drug, was introduced in 1953, and imipramine, synthesized as long ago as 1899, was noted to have a similar chemical structure (including three interlocking rings—hence the name tricyclic). Trials of imipramine in schizophrenia were unsuccessful, but antidepressant effects were observed, and in 1957, the results of a controlled trial of imipramine in depression (Kuhn, 1958) were communicated at the second International Congress of Psychiatry to an audience of about 12 people (Ayd & Blackwell, 1970).

There is nothing new about a biological approach to depression (the ancient Greeks called depression "melancholia," in the belief that it was caused by an excess of black bile), but from these inauspicious beginnings, the past 25 years have seen an explosion of research into the mechanisms of action of antidepressant agents and the biochemical bases of depression. The ascendency of the biological perspective in recent years can be attributed to the success of antidepressant drugs, set alongside the failure of traditional psychologically based therapies, and accompanied by a conviction that as the secrets of the brain finally succumbed to the relentless onslaught of modern science, depression and other mental disorders would be eradicated as surely as smallpox.

The pendulum is swinging once again. Some progress has been made in understanding the social and psychological origins of depression, and successful psychotherapies do now exist (see, e.g., Kovacs, 1980). However, the biological literature on depression is currently lacking in any sense of direction, and the prevailing mood is one of pessimism. It would not be fair to suggest that the emperor has no clothes, but it is becoming increasingly apparent that those clothes he does possess are ragged and full of holes.

I set out to write this book in the belief that, if there ever was a time when it was profitable to pursue a biological approach to depression in isolation from psychological considerations, that time is now past. Psychological and biological perspectives on depression can and should complement one another. At present, however, the divorce between these two areas of research is almost total. It can only be advantageous to end this state of affairs, and that is what I have attempted to do.

It is my hope that the model developed in this book will form an acceptable psychobiological framework within which workers in any of the contributing disciplines may communicate with one another and evaluate the importance and relevance of new research. To a great extent, the shape of the book has been determined by the need to review large volumes of literature from disparate sources, which made it impractical to attempt to develop a theory in a linear fashion. Instead, Parts 2 and 3 review the "state of the art" in many different areas of research, and the conclusions form a basis on which a psychobiological theory of depression is constructed in Part 4. While it was not intended that chapters in Parts 2 and 3 should be fully self-contained, a reader interested in a specific problem will only rarely need to refer to earlier or later chapters. A more detailed account of the structure of the book may be found at the end of Chapter 2.

The likelihood of solving any problem is greatly enhanced by knowing in general terms what kinds of solutions are possible. For historical reasons, biological theories of depression have concentrated largely on biochemical events in the brain. It is my belief that this emphasis is misplaced, in that biochemical theories of depression do not fall within the general class of possible solutions. Before embarking on an investigation of the psychobiology of depression, it is therefore necessary to outline some of the more influential biochemical theories of depression (this chapter) and examine their shortcomings (Chapter 2). This leads to an account of some general properties of acceptable psychobiological explanations, which makes explicit the philosophical standpoint from which this book is written.

1.1. THE MONOAMINE HYPOTHESES OF DEPRESSION

Much of the biological literature on depression concerns the monoamine neurotransmitters noradrenaline (NA), dopamine (DA), and serotonin (5-hydroxytryptamine, 5-HT); NA and DA are catecholamines, and 5-HT is an indoleamine. As ideas about the role of these compounds in depression have been extremely influential in determining the directions of research, it is appropriate to begin by charting the history of the "monoamine hypotheses of depression." A brief account of the neurochemistry of monoamine terminals provides a basis for understanding their early success.

Dopamine is synthesized from the amino acid tyrosine, via the intermediate compound dihydroxyphenylalanine (DOPA). Under most circumstances, the first enzyme in this pathway, tyrosine hydroxylase, is saturated; consequently, the synthesis of DA can be increased by DOPA, but not by tyrosine. A further enzymatic step produces NA, and the presence or absence of this third enzyme, dopamine-beta-hydroxylase (DBH) defines the difference between DA and NA neurons (Fig. 1.1). The catecholamines are degraded by two enzymes, monoamine oxidase (MAO) and catechol-O-methyltransferase (COMT), which produce a bewildering variety of breakdown products even more extensive than those shown in Fig. 1.1 (Sharman, 1973).

Like DA, 5-HT is also synthesized in two enzymatic steps from another amino acid, tryptophan, and in fact, the same enzyme is probably responsible for the second step in both of these pathways (Fig. 1.1). The degradation of 5-HT is much simpler than that of the catecholamines. One enzyme (MAO) is involved, rather than two, and as a result, there is a single major breakdown product, 5-hydroxyindoleacetic acid (5-HIAA) (Fig. 1.1).

Stores of catecholamines and 5-HT are maintained in synaptic vesicles, and because MAO is present within nerve terminals, any transmitter that is not stored in vesicles will be destroyed (Fig. 1.2). A proportion of the synaptic vesicles form a "functional pool" from which the transmitter is released when a nerve impulse invades the terminal (Glowinski, 1973). Although MAO and COMT are both present in the region of the synapse, the major mechanism for clearing the transmitter from the synapse is a process of physical re-uptake, rather than enzymatic degradation (Fig. 1.2). Following re-uptake, transmitter is recycled back into the functional pool.

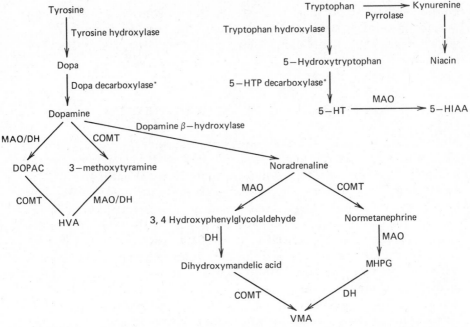

Fig. 1.1. Simplified diagram of tryptophan and tyrosine metabolism. *Probably same enzyme; 5-HT, 5-hydroxytryptamine; 5-HIAA, 5-hydroxyindoleacetic acid; DH dehydrogenase; MAO monamine oxidase; COMT, catechol-*O*-methyltransferase; VMA, 3-methoxy-4-hydroxymandelic acid (vanillyl mandelic acid); HVA, homovanillic acid; MHPG, 3-methoxy-4-hydroxyphenylethylene glycol. From A. R. Green and D. W. Costain, "The Biochemistry of Depression." Reprinted by permission of the Oxford University Press. In E. S. Paykel and A. Coppen, eds. *Psychopharmacology of Depression.* Oxford University Press, Oxford, 1979.

1.1.1. The Catecholamine Hypothesis

In the late 1950s, a number of workers discussed the possibility that catecholamines might be involved in the regulation of mood states (Everett & Tolman, 1959; Jacobsen, 1964; Rosenblatt et al., 1960). However, two articles published in 1965, one by Schildkraut, the other by Bunney and Davis, brought the catecholamine hypothesis of depression firmly into prominence. These papers reviewed the evidence, provided a comprehensive framework, and presented a formal statement of the hypothesis that

> some, if not all, depressions are associated with an absolute or relative deficiency of catecholamines, particularly noradrenaline, at functionally important receptor sites in the brain. Elation, conversely, may be associated with an excess of such amines. (Schildkraut, 1965, p. 509)

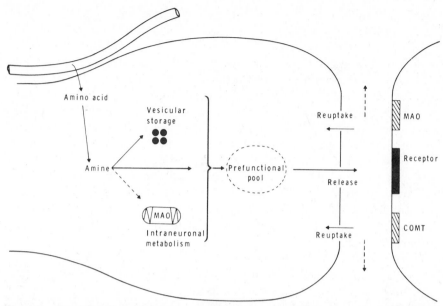

Fig. 1.2. Simplified diagrammatic representation of a monoamine nerve terminal. From A. R. Green and D. W. Costain, "The Biochemistry of Depression." In E. S. Paykel and A. Coppen, eds. *Psychopharmacology of Depression.* Oxford University Press, Oxford, 1979. Reprinted by permission of the Oxford University Press.

The evidence reviewed in these seminal papers came from a variety of sources. It became clear in the late 1950s that reserpine, and also tetrabenazine, another drug reported to cause depression as a side effect (Lingjaerde, 1963), cause a profound depletion of NA in various tissues, including the brain. The mechanism of this action appears to be that reserpine and tetrabenazine interfere with the binding of NA by storage granules. As a result, NA diffuses freely within the cell, and is exposed to MAO and broken down (Carlsson, 1961; Shore, 1962). Significantly, iproniazid, the first clinically effective antidepressant, was an inhibitor of MAO; subsequently, other monoamine oxidase inhibitors (MAOIs) of different chemical structure were also shown to possess antidepressant activity. Not only did MAOIs elevate NA levels and, at high doses, produce behavioral excitation in experimental animals (Spector et al., 1963), but pretreatment with MAOIs also prevented the sedative and NA-depleting effects of reserpine (Carlsson, 1961).

So, too, did tricyclic antidepressants (Sulser et al., 1964). The action of tricyclic antidepressants was at first a mystery:

> Where the effect of imipramine stands . . . is still a complete riddle which must await elucidation. Here our pres-

ent ignorance is such that not even a preliminary hypothesis can be offered. (Jacobsen, 1964, p. 212)

Within a very short time, however, the riddle had been solved. It was
known that noradrenergic neurons possess the machinery to take up NA
from the extracellular fluid. It was soon discovered that imipramine enhances the peripheral effects of sympathetic nerve stimulation and of
exogenously applied NA, and it was established that these effects of imipramine were brought about by blockade of the uptake mechanism, with
a consequent prolongation of the synaptic effects of NA (Hertting et al.,
1961). Blockade of NA uptake by tricyclic antidepressants was also demonstrated in the brain (Glowinski & Axelrod, 1964), and this finding,
taken together with the known actions of reserpine and of MAOI antidepressants, led directly to the formulation of the catecholamine hypothesis of depression.

Other strands of evidence were also available. First, amphetamine,
which prior to the introduction of MAOIs and tricyclic antidepressants,
was frequently used as an antidepressant, was known to potentiate the
synaptic effects of NA by promoting its release and inhibiting uptake
(Iversen, 1964). Second, DOPA, the precursor of NA, had been tested in
depression, and while results were generally equivocal, one study reported mood elevation (Turner & Merlis, 1964). Finally, a number of
biochemical changes consistent with the hypothesis were observed in the
urine of depressed or manic patients (Schildkraut, 1965). Although analysis of urine specimens to determine changes in brain chemistry has been
likened to analyzing the waters of the Potomac to find out what the Pres-
ident ate for dinner, these studies were subsequently supplemented by
the observation that the urine of depressed patients was low in
methoxyhydroxyphenylethyleneglycol (MHPG), a metabolite of NA. Unlike NA and its various other metabolites, MHPG in urine appeared to
derive largely from the brain (Maas et al., 1968).

1.1.2. The Dopamine Hypothesis

At the time the catecholamine hypothesis was first put forward, the major
catecholamines considered were NA and adrenaline, and because there
is very little adrenaline in the brain, the hypothesis was formulated primarily in terms of NA. Dopamine was known to be a precursor of NA in
sympathetic nerve terminals. The differences in regional distribution of
NA and DA and the relatively specific depletion of DA found postmortem
in the brains of patients suffering from Parkinson's disease (Hornykiewicz, 1966) suggested that, in the central nervous system, DA might function as a neurotransmitter in its own right. However, in 1965 this had
not yet been firmly established.

In the late 1960s, Swedish workers developed histological methods for visualizing catecholamine-containing cell bodies, axons, and terminals. Initially, formaldehyde vapor was used, which reacts with catecholamines to create fluorescent condensation products; this technique, and later refinements, allowed the mapping of catecholamine pathways (Falck et al., 1962; Lindvall & Bjorklund, 1974; Ungerstedt, 1971). Subsequently, an immunological method was developed, which used specific antibodies to label DBH, the enzyme which synthesizes NA from DA (B. Hartman, 1973). Application of these techniques, combined with pharmacological methods for distinguishing NA- and DA-containing neurons left no doubt that the brain contains independent NA and DA pathways.

Much of the evidence put forward in support of the catecholamine (NA) hypothesis of depression implicates DA as well as, or in some cases better than, NA. Both are metabolized by MAO, and consequently, protected by MAOIs (Molinoff & Axelrod, 1971). As in NA terminals, reserpine also blocks the storage, and consequently hastens the destruction, of DA (Carlsson, 1961). Indeed, in animals, stimulation of DA receptors was found to reverse reserpine-induced sedation, but stimulation of NA receptors alone was ineffective (Carlsson et al., 1957; Anden et al., 1973). Similarly, in animals, the stimulant effects of amphetamine appear to be mediated by DA, rather than NA (Kelly et al., 1975). Moreover, some depressed patients were found to show evidence of reduced central DA function, as judged by the concentration of the DA metabolite, homovanillic acid (HVA), in the cerebrospinal fluid (CSF) (Goodwin et al., 1973a).

A major discrepancy, however, was that tricyclic antidepressants were found to be relatively ineffective as blockers of DA uptake, as compared with their effects at NA synapses (Carlsson, 1970). As a result, DA was omitted for several years from serious consideration as a biochemical mediator of depression. However, in 1975, Randrup and co-workers advanced a "dopamine hypothesis of depression," citing the additional evidence that depression was associated with a number of conditions known to reduce DA function, including Parkinson's disease, neuroleptic drug treatment, and withdrawal from chronic amphetamine use (Randrup et al., 1975).

1.1.3. The Indoleamine Hypothesis

Much of the early evidence could also be interpreted as supporting an involvement of the indoleamine 5-HT in depression. Indeed, depletion of brain 5-HT by reserpine was reported a year earlier than the analogous effect on NA (Pletscher et al., 1956). Like the catecholamines, 5-HT is broken down by MAO, and in consequence, 5-HT levels are also elevated by MAOIs, although in animals, behavioral activation by MAOIs did appear to be rather more closely related to the elevation of catecholamine levels (Spector et al., 1963). Additionally, tricyclics block the uptake of both NA and 5-HT by roughly equal amounts, though the relative potencies vary somewhat from drug to drug (Carlsson et al., 1969a,b).

In the United States, the catecholamine hypothesis dominated the early literature, possibly owing to the demonstration that in animals, the sedative effects of reserpine could be reversed by the catecholamine precursor DOPA, but not by the 5-HT precursor 5-hydroxytryptophan (5-HTP) (Carlsson et al., 1957). In Europe, however, an "indoleamine hypothesis of depression" (Lapin & Oxenkrug, 1969) was more popular. Despite the lack of activity of 5-HTP in reserpinized animals, there was evidence dating back as far as the mid-1950s, which suggested that tryptophan, another 5-HT precursor, might have antidepressant properties, particularly in combination with the MAOIs (Coppen et al., 1963). It had also been reported in 1960 that the CSF of depressed patients showed a reduced level of substances related to 5-HT (Ashcroft & Sharman, 1960) and a deficiency of 5-HIAA, the major metabolite of 5-HT, was subsequently confirmed (Ashcroft et al., 1966).

1.1.4. Troubled Times

By the end of the 1960s, only 12 years after the first antidepressant drug trial, it seemed that an understanding of the biochemistry of depression would soon be forthcoming. True, most of the literature adduced in support of the catecholamine and indoleamine hypotheses failed to distinguish between them. Nonetheless, there was little reason to suspect that 10 years later, the literature would be in a state of utter chaos.

One strong prediction of the monoamine hypotheses was that treatments that interfere with monoaminergic transmission should induce depression. However, attempts to test this hypothesis by pharmacological blockade of catecholamine or 5-HT synthesis found minimal evidence that depression could be induced by either treatment (Engelman et al., 1967, 1968). Additionally, the reality of reserpine depression, which historically was the first and most important observation implicating monoamines in depression, was itself questioned: a review of the extensive literature on reserpine depression concluded that the majority of cases actually consisted of a "pseudo-depression" syndrome of sedation and lethargy; the incidence of true depressions was only 5–9%, and the vast majority of these cases appeared to be people with a prior history of depression (Goodwin et al., 1972). Although these findings are not really as crucial to the monoamine hypotheses as they appeared at the time (see Section 9.2.1), by the mid-1970s, critical reviews questioning the usefulness of the catecholamine hypothesis were beginning to appear (Baldessarini, 1975a; Shopsin et al., 1974).

Evidence derived from antidepressant treatments was also extremely equivocal. Although prior to the introduction of antidepressant drugs, amphetamine, for want of an alternative, had been widely used for this purpose, there is little evidence that it was an effective treatment, other than in the short term (Ban, 1969; Klerman, 1972). Similarly, controlled trials of DOPA did not support its promise as an antidepressant: although there were clear psychomotor activating effects, depressed patients treated with DOPA showed only minimal mood elevation (Goodwin et al., 1970; van Praag & Korf, 1975).

Additionally, it became clear that the antidepressant effect of MAOIs was difficult to demonstrate, and more seriously, it could not with any certainty be attributed to monoamine oxidase inhibition. A review of controlled studies found that tranylcypromine and phenelzine were superior to placebo in 3/4 and 5/9 studies, respectively, but isocarboxazid, an effective MAOI, was superior to placebo in only one study out of eight (Morris & Beck, 1974). A further problem for any theory which assumes that MAOIs and tricyclics share a common action, is that MAOIs appear to be effective in a very restricted group of patients with mixed anxiety/depression conditions ("atypical depressions") (West & Dally, 1959; Robinson et al., 1973; Ravaris et al., 1976). These patients do not, however, respond particularly well to tricyclics (Paykel, 1972). As Tyrer later commented

> The amine theory of affective disorders is still an important influence in research and it would be so much more convenient if MAOIs were useful in psychotic depression as this would be consistent with the theory. By inhibiting monoamine oxidase and thereby raising concentrations of amines at cerebral receptor sites a relative deficiency of the amines would be overcome and depression reversed. Unfortunately, the clinical facts do not support this theory. (Tyrer, 1979, p. 165)

Of the various lines of evidence adduced in support of the monoamine hypotheses, the mechanism of action of tricyclic antidepressants has been the subject of the greatest critical attention. Two problems, in particular, surfaced in the early 1970s. The first was the question of whether their therapeutic actions could actually be explained by inhibition of NA and/or 5-HT uptake. This question was stimulated by the discovery of the so-called "second-generation" antidepressants, which are chemically dissimilar from the tricyclics and MAOIs. The atypical drug iprindole (Gluckman & Baum, 1969) was particularly problematic. Although it is apparently an effective antidepressant, iprindole appeared to be almost totally ineffective as an amine uptake inhibitor; some uptake-blocking potential was subsequently demonstrated, but iprindole is several orders of magnitude weaker than the tricyclics, and for all practical purposes, the effect might as well be nonexistent.

Actually, a recent review of controlled studies concluded that the efficacy of iprindole in depression is not well established (Zis & Goodwin, 1979), but even if it were, the discovery of an antidepressant that did not potentiate NA or 5-HT activity would not in any way reflect adversely on the monoamine hypotheses. There is no necessary reason to suppose that an effective treatment operates directly on the system that is causing the problem. A fever may be controlled by a cold sponge or hypertension by diuretics, without any implication that fever is a disorder of the skin or that blood pressure is controlled by the kidneys. For many years, Parkinson's disease has been controlled by anticholinergic drugs, which compensate for the decreased DA activity which we now know to be responsible. The more critical question is not whether drugs can be found that are effective antidepressants without blocking monoamine uptake mechanisms, but rather, whether there are uptake blockers that are not effective clinically. Nonetheless, many workers did use the discovery of iprindole as evidence to add to the atmosphere of growing disillusionment with the monoamine hypothesis. Indeed, the importance of iprindole has been inflated to the point where theories are now put to the "iprindole test," and are judged, in part, by whether or not they can provide a satisfactory account of how this drug works.

The second issue was the time course of antidepressant drug action. Blockade of monoamine uptake occurs within a short time after tricyclic administration, but the clinical effects do not usually appear for two to four weeks. The significance of this discrepancy remains unclear. The delayed clinical action could, for example, reflect a delay in reaching steady state plasma levels of the drug, which usually takes a matter of weeks (Risch et al., 1981b); a number of studies have reported that if intravenous administration is used, antidepressant effects may be observed as early as the second day of treatment (Becker, 1971). It is therefore rather premature to conclude, as many workers have, that the discrepant time course rules out amine uptake blockade as the mechanism of clinical action of tricyclics. However, consideration of the delayed onset of clinical action prompts the question of whether antidepressant drugs do have actions that can be observed only following prolonged administration. Studies which attempted to address this issue produced answers that were directly contrary to those predicted by the catecholamine hypothesis: far from increasing NA function, chronic tricyclic treatment in rats actually caused a decrease in the amount of NA in the brain (Schildkraut et al., 1971), which was a result of a decrease in NA synthesis (Segal et al., 1974).

On the basis of these observations, in 1974 Segal and co-workers proposed the radically new hypothesis that depression resulted not from "too little" NA, but rather from "too much," a state of affairs corrected by chronic antidepressant treatment. By this time, of the evidence put forward in support of the original catecholamine hypothesis of depression, the only piece remaining intact was the observation that, in some depressed patients NA activity appeared to be low, as indicated by their reduced excretion of the NA metabolite MHPG (Maas et al., 1968). In the new hypothesis, this observation was interpreted rather differently. It was suggested that in depression, postsynaptic receptors to NA were supersensitive. The resulting overstimulation brought into play a negative feedback mechanism, which reduced the activity of NA neurons, causing a decrease in NA synthesis and the observed reduction in MHPG excretion. It was further postulated that this mechanism could only partially compensate for the supersensitive receptors, and the system still remained in a state of overstimulation. The effect of tricyclics would be to increase receptor stimulation once more, which would further activate the negative feedback system, and finally, would reduce the activity of NA neurons sufficiently to compensate fully for abnormal receptor activity (Segal et al., 1974).

This paper, which was the starting point for a second wave of research into monoamines and depression, introduced three important aspects of later theories. One is the counterintuitive logic, in which phenomena that seem to mean one thing are taken to mean the opposite. A second is the recognition that the brain is a dynamic system, in which changes imposed exogenously are counteracted by processes of adaptive regulation. The third is the focus on receptors as a possible target for antidepressant drug action. This was an extremely timely suggestion, since a number of methods for studying receptors had very recently been developed and were now available for use.

1.2. MONOAMINE RECEPTORS

1.2.1. Methods

Neurotransmitter receptors are sometimes likened to a lock to which the transmitter is the key. The receptor is a membrane-bound protein; combination with the transmitter is thought to change the conformational shape of the protein, resulting in a variety of intracellular events. These events include changes in ionic permeability of the membrane, which increase or decrease the likelihood that an action potential will be generated. Until recently, the receptor has been a convenient fiction, its existence deduced from indirect pharmacological evidence. In a classic example, Ahlqvist studied the effects of five sympathetomimetic drugs and observed that for some actions, NA was the most potent agent and isoprenaline the least, whereas other actions showed a different ordering of potencies. From these results, it was inferred that there were two different receptors, with different structural requirements, which were labeled alpha and beta (Ahlqvist, 1948).

During the past few years, the strategy of studying receptors indirectly, by studying the effects consequent on stimulating them, has been successfully applied to the central nervous system. A diversity of paradigms are available, using drugs that specifically mimic (receptor agonists) or block (receptor antagonists) neurotransmitter function. Techniques used include the measurement of neuroendocrine effects, which reflect the fact that neurotransmitters in the brain control (via the hypothalamus) the functioning of the pituitary gland (e.g., Risch et al., 1981d); the recording of electrophysiological responses from single neurons, which may be located by stereotaxic surgery once the anatomy of the pathway of interest has been determined (e.g., Bloom et al., 1981); and the observation of behavioral effects (e.g., Davis, 1982). A fourth technique exploits the fact that, in some systems, receptor activation stimulates the intracellular synthesis of the compound cyclic AMP (cAMP), which functions as an intracellular hormone, or "second messenger," to control a variety of aspects of cellular function (Greengard, 1976). Unlike other methods for studying receptor function, which usually require an intact brain, the cAMP technique can also be used in vitro. All of these techniques have been used extensively to study aspects of antidepressant drug action; it is worthwhile to reflect that none of them were available when the original catecholamine hypothesis of depression was formulated in 1965.

Another methodology, which for the first time allows receptors to be studied directly, is the biochemical technique of "receptor binding." This is probably the most significant of the recent developments in this area (though it must be added that like all experimental techniques, it is limited in the information that it can provide). In order to study receptor binding, a drug which is known to interact specifically with the receptor must first be prepared in a radioactive form. Membranes are isolated from a homogenate of brain by centrifugation techniques and are incubated with the radioactive drug; the amount of the drug bound to the membranes at the end of the experiment is then measured. By using ligands (literally: that which binds) which are very highly radioactive and can therefore be used at very low concentrations, and by using some technical tricks, the contribution of nonspecific binding to sites other than the receptor is minimized. By examining binding at different ligand concentrations, it is possible to calculate two quantities, B_{max}, the number of available receptor sites, and K_D, the dissociation constant, which describes the affinity of the ligand for the receptor (Snyder et al., 1978). A logical extension of the receptor binding method is the widely used radioreceptor assay, in which the interaction of cold (i.e., nonradioactive) ligand with the receptor is assessed by its ability to compete with (displace) a standard radioactive ligand (Innis & Snyder, 1981).

1.2.2. Receptor Modulation

In recent years, traditional ways of thinking about the brain have been transformed by the discovery that the sensitivity of neuroreceptors can change over time. The fact that receptor sensitivity is not static was actually first demonstrated 25 years ago in studies of the neuromuscular junction: muscle fibers are normally only sensitive to the transmitter acetylcholine (ACh) in the immediate vicinity of the motor end-plate; however, following denervation, sensitivity to ACh could be recorded over a much wider region (Thesleff, 1960). In the early 1970s, similar phenomena were demonstrated in the central nervous system. It was observed, for example, that the neurotoxin 6-hydroxydopamine (6-OHDA), which selectively destroys catecholaminergic neurons, increases sensitivity to the locomotor stimulant effects of the receptor agonist apomorphine (Kelly et al., 1975). The study of receptor modulation in the central nervous system immediately became a focus of immense interest.

Contrary to the predictions of the catecholamine hypothesis of depression, but consistent with the reformulated hypothesis of Segal and coworkers, it was observed that chronic treatment (2–3 weeks) with tricyclic and other antidepressants reduced the physiological sensitivity of central beta-receptors, as assessed by the ability of NA to stimulate cAMP production (Vetulani & Sulser, 1975). Chronic antidepressant treatment also reduced the number of beta-receptors, as assessed by the receptor binding method (Banerjee et al., 1977). It quickly became clear that most antidepressants reduced the density of beta-receptors, and the ability to reduce beta-receptor function (cAMP formation) was a property of virtually all effective or suspected antidepressant treatments, including tricyclics, MAOIs, iprindole and other atypical antidepressants, electro-convulsive shock, and sleep deprivation. The theory that "down-regulation" of beta-receptors was the mechanism of antidepressant action (Sulser, 1978), with the corollary that depression was a state of noradrenergic hyperactivity (Segal et al., 1974), rapidly moved into a leading position.

In general, receptors are found to function homeostatically, "down-regulating" when their input increases, and "up-regulating" when their input decreases. The paradoxical nature of the reformulated catecholamine hypothesis requires that receptors behave nonhomeostatically: in order for the theory to work, treatments that initially enhance NA function must produce a sufficient receptor "down-regulation" not only to compensate for their acute effects but also to produce a further decrease in synaptic transmission. Although this seems an unlikely result, over-compensation of this kind has also been postulated to explain other phenomena. Neuroleptic-induced tardive dyskinesias are one example: involuntary facial movements in patients treated chronically with neuroleptic drugs are assumed to reflect a hypersensitivity of DA receptors that results from long-term receptor blockade (Rubovits & Klawans, 1972)—though direct clinical support for this hypothesis has not been forthcoming (Tamminga, 1981). Curiously, the problem of which effect predominates after chronic antidepressant treatment was never discussed in the early (1977–1979) literature on antidepressant-induced receptor "down-regulation," and indeed, it has only rarely been addressed subsequently (Maas, 1979; Waldmeier, 1981; Willner & Montgomery, 1980a). This question, which is obviously of central importance in assessing the role of monoaminergic transmission in depression, will be considered in more detail in later chapters (see Chapters 13, 16).

1.2.3. Autoreceptors

One immediate consequence of the development of methods for studying central receptors was a proliferation of receptor subtypes, which might have been anticipated from the general principle that technical developments tend to generate new problems. Quite unexpected, however, was the discovery that in addition to the classical postsynaptic receptors, neurons also have receptors situated presynaptically on nerve endings, which are sensitive to their own transmitter and are therefore known as *autoreceptors*. Moreover, in addition to the classical release of transmitter from axon terminals, transmitter is also released from dendrites, and it affects autoreceptors situated on dendrites and cell bodies. In general, autoreceptors appear to mediate inhibitory functions and to serve as negative feedback systems, which act to minimize changes in the activity of the cell (Usdin & Bunney, 1975).

In addition to their effects on postsynaptic beta-receptors, electrophysiological recording from NA cells revealed that some antidepressant drugs also decreased the sensitivity of presynaptic autoreceptors (Svensson & Usdin, 1978). This finding adds another dimension of complexity to the problem, since "down-regulation" of inhibitory autoreceptors by antidepressants would tend to increase NA function overall, an effect opposite to that of postsynaptic "down-regulation." An alternative interpretation would be that alleviation of negative feedback reduces constraints on the range of permitted activity. Needless to say, changes in autoreceptor sensitivity have also occupied a central position in some recent accounts of depression and antidepressant drug action.

1.3. ON THE LIMITS OF BIOCHEMICAL HYPOTHESES

This brief introductory review has considered some of the major developments in the biochemistry and pharmacology of depression up to approximately 1978. By the end of the 1970s, what had seemed to be a problem on the verge of solution 10 years previously had become a welter

TABLE 1.1. SOME BIOCHEMICAL "THEORIES" OF DEPRESSION

NA low in depression, high in mania (the catecholamine hypothesis: Schildkraut, 1965; Bunney & Davis, 1965).

NA high in depression (the reformulated catecholamine hypothesis: Segal et al., 1974; Sulser, 1978).

NA overconstrained in depression, underconstrained in mania (Cohen et al., 1980).

5-HT low in depression, high in mania (the indoleamine hypothesis: Lapin & Oxenkrug, 1969).

5-HT high in depression (the hypersensitive serotonin receptor hypothesis: Aprison et al., 1978).

Low 5-HT predisposes to depression and mania (Mendels et al., 1972).

Low 5-HT and low NA in depression; low 5-HT and high NA in mania (the permissive 5-HT hypothesis: Prange et al., 1974).

Two types of depression: low NA or low 5-HT (Maas, 1975).

DA low in depression, high in mania (Randrup et al., 1975).

Catecholamines low in depression, or acetylcholine high (the adrenergic/cholinergic balance hypothesis: Janowsky et al., 1972a).

---

of conflicting hypotheses. Some of the more prominent theoretical positions, including those already described, and a number of others, which have not yet been discussed, are outlined in Table 1.1. Until very recently, with the exception of a small literature on acetylcholine (ACh), research has concentrated almost exclusively on the catecholamines and 5-HT, which necessarily, therefore, form the major focus of this book.

Each of the positions summarized in Table 1.1 has its adherents, and though allegiances shift as the evidence changes, it is commonly believed that in principle, any one of these hypotheses could be correct. In fact, in a very important sense, they must all be wrong. In addition to the empirical issues, there is a further problem, which the monoamine hypotheses of depression share with the majority of hypotheses in biological psychiatry: their conceptual structure is not adequate to provide satisfactory solutions to the problems that they address.

In presenting the catecholamine hypothesis, Schildkraut stressed

> that this is undoubtedly, at best, a reductionist oversimplification of a very complex biological state and that the simultaneous effects of the indoleamines, other biogenic amines, hormones and ionic changes will ultimately have to be included in any comprehensive formulation of the biochemistry of the affective disorders." (Schildkraut, 1965, p. 517)

Unfortunately, the issue is not simply one of complexity. At one level, the statement is undoubtedly true, but a more basic problem lies in the very concept of a "comprehensive biochemical formulation." The underlying assumption is that depression can be understood in biochemical terms. However, it is not immediately apparent how including any number of chemicals in a "comprehensive biochemical formulation" would help us to understand why it is that a depressed patient feels worthless or tries to commit suicide. In fact, as shown in the following chapter, any theory of depression that concentrates on biochemical variables to the exclusion of any detailed consideration of the specific neural pathways implicated and their role in normal brain function is fundamentally flawed. As a result, any "biochemical hypothesis of depression," however comprehensive, is deficient in a crucial area.

two

ON THE NATURE OF PSYCHOBIOLOGICAL EXPLANATIONS

At present it is difficult to explain why increased concentrations of NE in the synaptic cleft attenuates the depression symptoms. It is probable that increased activity of NE neurons by interaction with other transmitter systems induces a mosaic of changes in neuronal mechanisms that finally compensates pathological processes and consequently, attenuates depression. (Kostowski, 1981, p. 317)

2.1. CONSTRUCTING A PSYCHOBIOLOGICAL EXPLANATION

What is the relationship between biochemical events in the brain and the experiences that people have when they are depressed? Although the literature on neurotransmitters and depression now runs to several thousand papers and numerous symposia, this is a question about which there is a stunning silence. The above quotation is a little out of the ordinary, but only because it acknowledges that the problem exists. The fact that it does not actually say anything is not at all unusual.

The prevailing attitude that governs the kinds of issues about which people working in the field allow themselves to theorize seems to be that "it is still too early . . . to question the precise mechanism whereby the action of a chemical or drug on the brain is ultimately translated into behavioral, psychological and emotional changes" (Sourkes, 1980). This view is both short-sighted and mistaken. It is short-sighted because a hypothesis of brain function that omits any reference to the structure or operating principles of the brain is unlikely to be of more than heuristic value: a biochemical theory of depression may be useful for the development of new antidepressant drugs but is unlikely to provide any further insight into why antidepressants work. It is mistaken because, in principle, we do in fact know a great deal about the mechanisms whereby the actions of chemicals and drugs are translated into physiological, behavioral, and emotional changes. Our understanding of the brain mechanisms underlying behavior is progressing by leaps and bounds, and by adopting an appropriate theoretical perspective, these achievements may be brought to bear on psychiatric problems.

2.1.1. Bridging the Gap

A recent theory of the action of antianxiety drugs (Gray, 1982) will serve as an illustration of how this might be done. It is now known that the most widely used class of antianxiety drugs, the benzodiazepines, act at specific receptors in the brain (Squires & Braestrup, 1977), which appear to be linked to receptors for the neurotransmitter gamma-aminobutyric acid (GABA) (Braestrup & Nielsen, 1980). This observation can form the basis for a "GABA hypothesis of anxiety", which states that anxiety results from a deficiency of GABA-ergic transmission. As in the catecholamine hypothesis of depression, this hypothesis is a conceptual vacuum: there is no attempt to define the relationship between the neurotransmitter and the state of mind that it supposedly controls. Gray's theory of anxiety attempts to bridge this gap. First, the relevant set of receptors is specified, and the physiological consequences of anxiolytic drug action are spelled out: by interacting with the GABA–benzodiazepine receptor complex, antianxiety drugs disrupt the flow of impulses in neural circuits in the hippocampus and subiculum. Next, the manner in which this system operates as an information processor is described: the information carried in the hippocampal–subicular circuits is used to make a comparison between actual and expected events; a mismatch activates a "behavioral inhibition system," which suppresses ongoing activity and increases arousal and attention to the environment. Third, the relationship to the subjective experience of anxiety is clarified: anxiety is experienced when activity in the "behavioral inhibition system" is excessive. The theory also addresses the relationship between the conditions under which this state arises and the symptoms of anxiety (Gray, 1982). The crude "GABA hypothesis of anxiety" has been unpacked to specify the relevant set of benzodiazepine receptors, the neural pathways involved, their role in normal brain function, and the relationship betwen functional changes and changes in experience. Irrespective of its empirical merits, which are controversial (Gray et al., 1982), the conceptual structure of this expanded theory is clearly superior to that of the "GABA hypothesis of anxiety" or, for that matter, to the catecholamine hypothesis of depression.

An important point which does not emerge from this example is that the relationship between functional changes and the resulting experience can be rather complex. Hallucinogenic drugs provide the most persuasive illustration. A few micrograms of lysergic acid diethylamide (LSD) can produce a major psychological experience, usually described as an *altered state of consciousness*, which can sometimes be the most powerful experience a person has ever had. "Explanations" of these phenomena usually involve a discussion of the neurotransmitter 5-HT (Freedman & Halaris, 1978; Watson, 1977). Clearly, however, a description of biochemical phenomena in no sense explains the LSD experience, because no account is offered of how the biochemical changes give rise to altered states of consciousness.

Many features of the "acid trip" may, however, be understood as resulting from a breakdown of sensory information processing. In addition to sending the drug taker on a "fantastic voyage," which may reach heights of delight or terror (or both), these drugs produce striking perceptual effects, distortions of reality rather than true hallucinations, in which perceptual dimensions and intensities change constantly and unpredictably "like reflections in choppy water" (Hofmann, 1970). However, a high proportion of subjects who were given LSD while in sensory deprivation failed to experience any effects (Cohen, 1970). This suggests that the perceptual effects might mediate the LSD experience. How? Perception is not an automatic process, but rather, it proceeds by the formation of hypotheses about what might be "out there." These hypotheses are tested by seeking further sensory information (Lindsay & Norman, 1971). In the conditions of degraded sensory input, which characterize the LSD state, reality testing breaks down: it is no longer possible to read small but important perceptual cues, such as facial expressions, from which we deduce the nature and significance of events around us. These are conditions in which fantasies may be played out on the stage of the world, unchecked by those sensory ties that normally bind us to reality. It is possible, in other words, that hallucinogenic drugs simply set the conditions under which a "trip" may occur, and the user then provides his or her own itinerary (Willner, 1984b).

If sensory chaos underlies the acid trip, what mediates the sensory effects? LSD has also been found to cause totally unpredictable changes in the way that single cells in the lateral geniculate nucleus (LGN) responded to visual stimulation (McKay and Horn, 1971). 5-HT fibers terminate in the LGN (as well as other thalamic nuclei) and modulate the transmission of visual information (Strahlendorf et al., 1982). It is therefore quite possible that the physiological chaos which LSD wreaks on the visual system might be caused by biochemical effects at 5-HT synapses, which brings us back to the traditional "explanation" of hallucinogenic drug effects. It is not suggested that this is a total explanation of the LSD experience: in some people, the perceptual effects are relatively minor (Barr et al., 1972), and LSD may also have effects at DA synapses (Da Prada et al, 1975). The object is rather to indicate that psychological effects which are seemingly of inordinate complexity could derive in large part from an almost trivial change in sensory information processing.

2.1.2. Levels of Explanation

Like Gray's theory of anxiety, the foregoing account of hallucinogenic drug action attempts to provide an explanation of the relationship between a biochemical effect (interaction with 5-HT receptors) and the complex experiential change that results, by interposing two intermediate levels of analysis. The first is a specification of the particular pathway involved (the 5-HT projection to thalamic sensory nuclei) and the effect of perturbing it (increased "noise" in the transmission of sensory input). The second is a description of the resulting changes in information processing (failure of reality testing), and the way in which the consequence depends upon the psychological context.

It is possible, in other words, to bridge the conceptual gap between neurochemistry and subjective experience by seeking explanations of psychobiological phenomena in four independent explanatory domains: biochemical, physiological, cognitive, and experiential (using the word *cognitive* in the information processing sense in which it is now used in cognitive psychology, rather than as a synonym for *conscious*). In terms of a computer analogy, these four domains include two levels of hardware and two of software, which correspond (roughly) to components, wiring, programming, and editing (Willner 1983, 1984b).

In describing the psychological consequences of a change at the level of neurochemistry, it is important to consider not only the intervening levels of explanation, but also the nature of the transitions between adjacent levels. The generation of changes in neural firing (level 2) from the biochemical effect of a drug (level 1) depends upon the integration of that biochemical effect into a context of other ongoing biochemical processes, which include adaptive regulation resulting from the primary drug effect. The effect of tricyclic antidepressants at NA synapses is a good example of this problem. As outlined in Chapter 1, it is well established that in addition to potentiating neurotransmission by blocking NA reuptake, chronic administration of tricyclics also decreases neurotransmission by reducing the sensitivity of postsynaptic beta-receptors. The important issue, however, is the net effect of these and other effects on the traffic of nerve impulses in postsynaptic structures, and as noted earlier (Section 1.2.2), the existence of this problem is rarely acknowledged.

Similar considerations apply to the transition from physiology (level 2) to cognitive processes (level 3). Parkinson's disease, which has a high incidence of depression associated with it (Robins, 1976), is a relevant example: degeneration of a dopaminergic pathway (Hornykiewicz, 1966) causes an inability to initiate voluntary movements, which may, however, be partially compensated for by drugs that antagonize receptors for a different neurotransmitter—acetylcholine. Conversely, drugs that stimulate cholinergic receptors induce feelings of fatigue and, in some instances, depression; these effects may be antagonized by methylphenidate, a drug that activates catecholaminergic transmission (Janowsky et al., 1973b). It is to some extent a truism to point out that the brain is a complex system, in which effects of one kind may be neutralized by antagonistic actions at a different site. However, this self-evident fact has a very imporant consequence, which is easily forgotten or ignored: understanding the mode of action of an effective treatment tells us little or nothing about the underlying pathology. As far as possible in this book, the physiology of depression and the actions of antidepressants are discussed separately, in order not to confuse these two issues.

2.2. SOME PSYCHOLOGICAL AND PHILOSOPHICAL ISSUES

Although, in the early days of neuropharmacology, there was a tendency to treat the brain as though it consisted of a uniform soup of neurotransmitters, it is now universally accepted that the brain has structure and that neurotransmitters are localized within defined (or at least definable) pathways. Consequently, the proposal that a physiological level of analysis should intervene between biochemistry and psychology is not at all controversial (even though, as outlined in the preceding paragraphs, some of the consequences are frequently overlooked).

The need for a cognitive level of analysis to mediate between physiology and experience is much less self-evident, largely because cognitive psychology is a relatively new discipline that is not particularly accessible to most neuroscientists. There are in fact two issues here. One is a parochial problem which psychology: why do we need two separate levels of psychological analysis—cognitive and experiential? But for many neuroscientists, there is a much more fundamental problem: the need for psychological models of any kind is far from obvious.

2.2.1. The Reductionist Fallacy

There is a pervasive assumption among nonpsychologists that in the fullness of time, when there is a better and more complete understanding of how the brain works, psychology will wither away, to be replaced by physiological explanations of the phenomena that psychologists currently study; the fact that it is possible to use drugs to treat mental disorders lends credence to this position. Although the vigorous assault on the physiological correlates of mental disorders (which follows from the belief that psychological problems are "really" physiological problems) has led to progress in certain areas, there are also a number of disturbing con-

nces. To researchers in biological psychiatry, depression is an en-
ｌe problem, a sleep disorder, a defect of receptor regulation, or an
abnormality of any one of a variety of neurotransmitter systems; in fact,
almost anything other than feelings of misery and despair. Almost invariably, however, the belief that depression is a physiological disorder
is not accompanied by a theoretical framework that explains why this
particular mental state results from the physiological phenomenon in
question. Consequently, there is no basis for adjudicating between the
multitude of physiological "theories": anything goes. At best, this state
of intellectual anarchy is counterproductive. At worst, the absence of any
integrated psychobiological perspective can be extremely dangerous, for
if psychological problems are "really" physiological, then there can be no
objection to treating them as such, hence the excessive, indiscriminate,
and in many instances mindless use of psychiatric drugs.

The belief in the ultimate reducibility of psychology to physiology is
based on a misunderstanding of the nature of reductionism. The reduction
of one theory to another may take a variety of forms, and in one variant,
which is known as eliminative reduction (Clark, 1980), the theory that
is reduced does indeed become obsolete. This happened when, for example,
the theory of relativity superseded Newtonian mechanics: the old theory
was abandoned because the new theory could handle everything that the
old theory could explain, and also a number of additional phenomena
which the old theory could not. However, in other forms of reduction, the
new theory does not supersede the old theory, but only provides an alternative set of explanations. Thus, the laws of statistical mechanics,
which describe the behavior of gases as aggregates of moving particles,
do not invalidate the earlier laws of thermodynamics, which use terms
such as "temperature" and "pressure" to describe the same phenomena
(Nagel, 1961). In examples of this kind, the elucidation of an alternative,
more basic set of explanatory terms does not imply that research and
theorizing at the higher level should forthwith be abandoned. This would
be

> analogous to claiming that because the thermodynamic
> gas laws reduce to theories in statistical mechanics, ther-
> modynamic research into gases is thereafter inappro-
> priate, and our calculations for designing furnaces and
> radiators must thereafter be made in statistical mechan-
> ical terms. (Clark, 1980, p. 6).

There are three major reasons why physiological modes of explanation
do not, and cannot, replace psychological theories. The first is that replacing an account of phenomena at one level of explanation with an
account at a more basic level will usually involve an increase in the
complexity of the explanation. This is very likely to be true of the rela-

tionship between psychology and physiology. It is possible, for example, that in the not-too-distant future we might possess a reasonable understanding of the physiological mechanisms of visual perception. However, it seems very probable that to apply this understanding to describe any particular instance of "seeing" would involve enumerating the state of activity of many thousands of neurons—far in excess of the monitoring ability of present, or foreseeable, technology. This is not a problem that is specific to the relationship between psychology and physiology. We understand the molecular basis of the action potential reasonably well, but when we want to talk about the rate of firing of a cell, it would become extremely tedious to insist that the conversation must be confined to discussing ionic fluxes.

The second problem is that a number of the central constructs of psychological theories are simply not reducible. Chief among these is the concept of information. Information does not exist in a vacuum, but only in a transaction between a transmitter and a receiver. The information content of the message "Today is Thursday," for example, would be different for person A who knows that today is Thursday, person B who is uncertain whether today is Thursday or Friday, person C who has just awoken from a coma, and person D who knows that today is Monday (Hill, 1982). The information resides neither in the transmitter nor in the receiver, but rather, in the relationship between them. Consequently, when a system that involves the transfer of information is broken down into its constituent parts, the information content disappears.

The third, and most significant factor, is that with increasing complexity of organization, properties emerge that are not apparent in more simple systems. It may soon become possible to describe in some detail the sequence of events in the nervous system which underlie the performance of a piece of goal-directed behavior. However, it is difficult to see how a study of the laws of neuronal functioning, however exhaustive, could possibly have revealed the fact that an animal has a "cognitive map" of its environment and an expectation of its goal (Tolman, 1932).

Again, there is nothing special about the relationship between psychology and physiology: the emergent properties of complex systems are even apparent at the molecular level. Nothing in the physical properties of carbon, hydrogen and oxygen can explain the asymmetry of sugar molecules found in living systems, all of which spiral in the same direction. Sugar molecules obey the laws of physics, but there is no way in which it would have been possible to start from those laws and predict the observed asymmetry (Anderson, 1972). The genetic code is another very clear example. Given the discovery that a protein is constructed by reading out the sequence of triplets of bases in the RNA molecule (Crick et al., 1961), it becomes possible to adduce the physical principles governing protein synthesis. However, the converse, the deduction of the genetic code from the laws of physics, is unthinkable (Anderson, 1972).

In other words, "The ability to reduce everything to simple fundamental laws does not imply the ability to start from those laws and reconstruct the universe" (Anderson, 1972, p. 393). In general, the reductionist approach works well for most analytical problems: the isolation of a functional element at one level of explanation renders that element susceptible to explanation at a lower level. However, as it does not work in the opposite direction, "a reductionist analysis is premature until the analysis of behavioural phenomena has identified suitable behavioral units and determined the principles to which the physiological processes underlying those units must adhere" (Gallistel, 1981, p. 610). Furthermore, for this reason, the psychological component must not only precede the physiological component of a psychobiological investigation, but it also takes precedence, because "If the psychological component . . . [is] . . . wrong, there can be no success in finding neural processes to match its supposed function" (Gray, 1982, p. 4).

To summarize, psychological processes must be explained by psychological theories, for three reasons. They are likely to be more efficient; the information content of psychological processes defies reduction; and most important, this is the only way in which it is possible to specify the questions about mental processes that require physiological answers. To say that psychology is not reducible to physiology is not to say that psychological phenomena do not arise out of physiology—obviously they must. It is only to claim that eliminative reductionism is an inappropriate theoretical model to describe the relationship between these two disciplines. Nadel and O'Keefe summarized the relationship in the following terms:

> A theory in physiological psychology does not explain behavior by reducing it to physiological processes or vice versa. Rather, each domain is related to an intermediate level by a different dictionary. For example, on one side the theory would specify which behaviors, or aspects of behavior, the model was involved in, and how it was involved, while on the other side it would specify how the model was realized in terms of anatomy and physiology. (Nadel & O'Keefe, 1974, p. 371)

If a psychological theory can be shown to explain a certain set of data and an account can also be given of physiological processes that are responsible for the same phenomena, the latter account does not invalidate the former. On the contrary, it explains why it is correct.

2.2.2. Subjective Experience and Cognitive Processes

Given that psychobiology needs well developed psychological models, why distinguish two levels of psychological analysis? It might be useful, at this point, to clarify the way in which I am using the terms *cognitive* and *experiential*. Cognitive processes are those which describe the way in which the brain handles information and controls behavior—arousal, attention, perception, action, motivation, memory, and so on, and all the smaller functions into which these categories are subdivided. The analysis of these processes is the major business of experimental psychology. Aspects of some cognitive processes, such as memory and perception, are accessible to conscious experience. In general, these are the processes involved in controlling the selection of actions and the direction of attention (Shallice, 1978).

It is paradoxical that despite our intimate familiarity with subjective experience, few methods are available for describing it with precision. Some methods have been developed to tap aspects of mental structure, such as repertory grid techniques (Bannister & Mair, 1968) and multi-dimensional scaling (Shepard, 1980), but with very few exceptions (e.g., Parrott & Kentridge, 1982), these tools have not been applied to problems of psychobiology and would, in any case, be inappropriate for answering many questions. For most purposes, therefore, subjective experience can be described only in everyday language. As a result, there is a degree of imprecision in discussing subjective experience, which is unfortunate, but for the moment, unavoidable.

It seems possible that in due course, the scope of cognitive psychology will so expand that a unified theoretical framework will suffice to explain both the functional constraints on information processing and also the contents of consciousness as they are experienced from moment to moment (Mandler, 1983). At the present time, however, and particularly in the context of a psychobiological investigation, it is useful to draw a distinction, for the following reason: it seems that endogenous or drug-induced changes in the activity of a neurotransmitter system do not affect consciousness directly, by promoting or suppressing particular thoughts or feelings. Rather, they act indirectly by altering the constraints under which information is processed (Willner, 1984b).

This principle has already been illustrated in the example of the effects of the drug LSD. It may seem that mood states are simpler, more unitary phenomena than the LSD experience, but in fact the clinical syndrome of depression encompasses a wide variety of symptoms (see Chapter 3). Furthermore, the effects of drugs on mood are far from simple. Amphetamine is usually considered to be a euphoriant. However, although amphetamine is sometimes reported to improve mood in experimental studies of nondepressed volunteers (e.g., Johanson & Uhlenluth, 1980; Jonsson et al., 1969), it frequently does not. In one study, for example, in which amphetamine was infused intravenously up to a dose which induced a psychotic reaction, it was reported that none of the subjects showed any signs of euphoria at any dose (Griffith et al., 1972).

Some light is thrown on this discrepancy by the classic experiment of Schachter and Singer (1962). In this study, subjects were first injected with adrenaline, then left in the company of an actor, who had been instructed to behave in a euphoric or an angry manner. The subjects interpreted their increased arousal levels either as euphoria or as anger, depending upon the behavior of their companion. Subjects who had been informed what physiological changes to expect did not report feeling any emotion, and neither did subjects in other studies (Maranon, 1924) who were given adrenaline but left by themselves. Clearly, the development of an emotional state depended upon two factors: a drug-induced increase in arousal and a psychological context within which to make sense of feeling aroused. When both were present, subjects attributed emotions to themselves, and they felt and behaved appropriately.

This analysis is not confined to stimulant drugs. A variety of other drugs, of varying pharmacology—alcohol, opiates, cannabis, and others— can produce euphoric effects, but a common feature of all euphoriants is that euphoria is extremely rare on first exposure. One must learn to enjoy a drug, and this process, first described for cannabis, appears to consist of first learning to recognize the effects, and then learning to interpret the effects as pleasant and desirable, usually under the instruction of friends who are already initiated (Becker, 1953).

It is possible that drug-induced depressions may also be amenable to an attributional analysis. As noted in Section 1.1.4, the classic depression-inducing drug, reserpine, appears to precipitate true depressions in only a small proportion (5–9%) of subjects, and, significantly, almost all of the people who became depressed on reserpine had been depressed before (Goodwin et al., 1972). The reason for this selective action has not been investigated, but a plausible explanation is that patients with a prior clinical history were able to understand their drug-induced lethargy by labeling it "depression." In fact, by the end of this book it will be clear that no drugs are known that unequivocally induce depression in people who are not already depressed and never have been. This finding is fatal to any theory that equates depressed mood with the level of functioning of a neurotransmitter system. It does not affect the status of a theory in which the neurotransmitter system regulates an underlying cognitive process (arousal level, in the case of reserpine-induced depressions), while other factors, such as personal history and current environmental conditions, determine the affective quality of the ensuing experience.

2.2.3. The Mind–Body Question

The subject of this chapter, the question of how to reconcile mental events to the brain is, of course, the mind–body problem (Bindra, 1980), which has plagued philosophers and scientists since Descartes declared that there was no solution, a view recently echoed by Popper and Eccles (1977).

The dualist perspective underwrites the popular misconception that some depressions are "psychological" and others are "biological."

A number of authors have pointed out that the mind–body problem is actually no more problematic than the relationship between other pairs of disciplines; the earlier discussion of reductionism provides examples of some similarities. Such problems arise when there is a lack of an adequate theory in one or both domains (Hill, 1982; Mandler, 1975). I have tried to show in this chapter that the distinction between psychological and biological depressions is a false dichotomy. All depressions are necessarily both. They are psychological by virtue of being mental phenomena and biological because all mental phenomena must have a physical basis in the brain. What is needed is a set of parallel descriptions of psychological and physiological phenomena, together with a set of principles for relating the two sets of constructs (Nagel, 1961).

The factor largely responsible for the continued survival of the mind–body problem is the difficulty in establishing connecting principles to form a link between the constructs used in theoretical accounts of subjective experience and those of neuroscience. One interesting aspect of the present approach is that it does not attempt to make direct connections between experience and physiology. Instead, each of these domains is related to an intervening level of analysis. As a result the mind–body problem recedes into the distance, to be replaced by two sets of empirical issues. The transition from level 3 (cognition) to level 4 (experience) is not the mind–body interface, but rather, a mind–mind interface, which is beginning to succumb to assault by cognitive psychologists. The mind–body interface lies elsewhere, between level 2 (physiology) and level 3 (cognition). This area is the traditional province of physiological psychology, and while the attempt to uncover the machinery by which the brain processes information is far from easy, most of the difficulties are practical, rather than metaphysical.

2.3. ABOUT THIS BOOK

In addition to finessing the mind–body problem, the explanatory framework outlined in this chapter is of heuristic value in expanding the scope of psychobiological investigation into depression. It becomes possible to integrate research in the psychology of depression, in the area of animal models, and in behavioral neuroscience, with traditional biochemical and pharmacological concerns. As the theoretical perspective has determined the way in which material has been organized in the remainder of the book, this forms a convenient juncture at which to summarize its contents.

The point was made earlier that without an adequate understanding of the psychological issues, it is unclear exactly what it is that a psychobiological analysis is trying to explain. Accordingly, the second part of the book (the next five chapters) deals with the psychology of depression. Rather than presenting a general review of this subject, I have attempted to extract those aspects that are amenable to physiological analysis. This material, which from the present perspective is crucial, is not usually considered relevant to the psychobiology of depression, and is largely absent from most reviews and symposia.

The starting point (Chapter 3) is an examination of the various ways in which the word depression is used, particularly in clinical contexts. Chapter 4 then addresses the major issue of the changes in information processing which underlie the experience of depression. In a sense, this analysis, which is primarily in terms of responsiveness to pleasant and unpleasant events, is central to the book as a whole. The reason is that unlike descriptions of subjective experience, the constructs used to describe information processing (the cognitive level of analysis) are also applicable to animal subjects. A discussion of whether the lateralization of emotional function in the human brain renders work in other species irrelevant concludes that it does not (Chapter 5). Having cleared aside this obstacle, the final two chapters of Part 2 (Chapters 6 and 7) address the question of the validity of animal models of depression, on the assumption that valid models can be a valuable research tool, but invalid models will only mislead.

Part 3 of the book (Chapters 8–19), which reviews what we know about the physiological basis of depression, is organized by neurotransmitter systems. There are three chapters each on DA, NA, and 5-HT, a chapter on ACh, a chapter on four other systems, and a final chapter which examines neurotransmitter interactions. For each system, there are three separate reviews. The first, which represents another major departure from the pattern of most books of this kind, deals with basic behavioral neuroscience. Two issues are addressed. One is the extent to which the system in question is implicated in those animal models of depression that appear to have some degree of validity. The other is more wide ranging: given that we know (from Chapter 4) something about the nature of cognitive changes in depression, does the physiological system in question have behavioral properties which make it a likely candidate to mediate any of them?

The second set of problems discussed in Part 3 concerns the more mainstream question of the empirical involvement of each neurotransmitter system in the clinical phenomena of depression. Again, there are two separate issues. One concerns the effects on mood of pharmacological agents known to increase or decrease the level of functioning in the neurotransmitter system under discussion. These pharmacological questions are relatively easy to answer. Interpretation of these studies is not entirely straightforward, but they do provide reasonably direct evidence. The other issue is the state of activity of the system in depressed people. This problem is more fundamental, but also more recondite. Although a variety of techniques are available for studying aspects of brain bio-chemistry in clinical conditions, all are indirect, and to a greater or lesser degree, unsatisfactory. In contrast to some workers who see such phe-nomena as hormonal changes and sleep disorders as primary symptoms of depression, I have chosen to treat these biological markers as being of interest primarily as indicators of central neurotransmitter function. Consequently, this book has no chapter on psychoendocrinology, for ex-maple, but the use of endocrinological markers as analytical tools is doc-umented extensively in each of the clinical chapters.

The effects on each neurotransmitter system of antidepressant drugs and other antidepressant agents, such as electroconvulsive shock (ECS), form the subject of the third set of reviews in Part 3. Because chronic drug regimes are used clinically, the major emphasis in reviewing the pharmacology of antidepressants is on the effects of chronic treatment. The object is to attempt to enumerate all of the biochemical effects of a given agent on a particular system and to estimate how they operate together to affect the integrated functioning of the system as a whole (see Section 1.2.1). The answers to these questions have important conse-quences for theories of depression. Although the actions of antidepres-sants taken in isolation carry no implications as to the underlying pa-thology (see Section 2.1.3), they do play a crucial role in assessing hypotheses about the pathophysiology of depression derived from other sources.

Chapter 19 (which, incidentally, includes a novel theory of the function of dreaming) considers the interactions between different neurotrans-mitter systems and describes some potentially significant relationships. And finally, in Part 4, I have attempted to develop a psychobiological synthesis of the conclusions of earlier chapters. Chapter 20 includes a review of the etiology of depression, which is not considered in detail in earlier chapters, and uses the relationships described in Chapter 19 as a basis on which to build a psychobiological theory of depression—its causes, symptomatology and treatment. An outline of the theory, which takes the form of a summary of the major conclusions of this investigation into the psychobiology of depression, will be found in Chapter 21.

2

Foundations

three

WHAT DO WE MEAN BY "DEPRESSION"?

To those who suffer its severe forms, depression can be a living hell. I
must therefore begin with a word of explanation and apology, for nothing
in this book will even begin to capture the quality of their torment. The
flavor of how it feels to be depressed—the misery, the feelings of emp-
tiness and worthlessness, the despair, and often the conviction that only
death can bring release—have been described with great sensitivity and
compassion by a number of authors, for both professional and lay audi-
ences (e.g., Alvarez, 1971; Rowe, 1978). Although the section which follows is entitled *The Experience of Depression*, it is not my intention to
reproduce these accounts or to present case studies. It is rather to try to
derive certain underlying common themes, which can be used as a bridge
to reach the brain. As such, the discussion is more academic than the
title might suggest.

3.1. THE EXPERIENCE OF DEPRESSION

We use the word *depression* to refer both to a clinical condition and to
the brief, mild, downward mood swings that we all experience as part of
daily living. In the clinical context, the term depression refers not simply
to a state of depressed mood, but to a syndrome comprising mood disorder,
psychomotor changes, and a variety of somatic and vegetative disturb-

ances. All of these changes may be present, but none, including depressed mood, is essential. Indeed, to make a diagnosis of major depression, the only essential criterion is that the syndrome be present for at least two weeks (American Psychiatric Association, 1980).

It is possible that in its everyday language usage and in its clinical usage, the word depression is being used to label similar mental states, which differ only in intensity. However, there is no necessary reason to assume that this is so. Words frequently have different meanings in different contexts: there is a great difference between feeling cold and the feeling of having a cold; and what we do in aeroplanes is only remotely analogous to what birds do when they fly. It is therefore important to examine what we mean when we say that someone is depressed.

3.1.1. Depression As a Mood State

Although, for most purposes, language provides the only means of systematically investigating experience, this does not mean that the study of experience must rely on poetry, literature, and anecdote, invaluable as these sources are for providing insights into the psychological world of other people. A study of the ways in which words are used and the relationships between them can uncover underlying dimensions of meaning and, by inference, dimensions of experience. The most pertinent example is an investigation of the language of emotion by Davitz (1969), which merits description in some detail. Although this study was not directed at any one emotion, it does throw light on the way that the word depression is used in everyday language.

In a preliminary study, 1200 subjects were asked to describe in writing a variety of emotional situations. From these descriptions, a check-list was constructed, consisting of several hundred phrases applicable to emotional situations. A further list of 50 emotional states was compiled from Roget's *Thesaurus* to represent a wide and varied range of emotions. Fifty new subjects were recruited for the main study; all were highly educated (college graduates) and were volunteers; none had any training or professional interest in psychology. The procedure required them to think of a time when they had experienced each of the 50 emotions and to indicate whether each of the 556 phrases on the check list was an applicable description.

From these heroic efforts a dictionary was compiled showing the phrases that were used to describe each emotional state. The statistical technique of cluster analysis was then applied to the 50 definitions; this technique groups together clusters of items that tend to appear together. The analysis produced the 12 clusters shown in Table 3.1. Next, a score was computed showing the extent to which each cluster was represented in the description of each emotion. Depression was characterized by five

**TABLE 3.1.   TYPICAL PHRASES IN EACH OF DAVITZ' CLUSTERS OF
EMOTION-RELATED STATEMENTS**[a]

Activation	Sense of vitality, aliveness; acute awareness of pleasurable things; a strong sense of interest and involvement.
Hypoactivation:	I feel empty, drained, hollow; I feel heavy, sluggish; understimulated, undercharged.
Hyperactivation:	There's an excitement, a sense of being keyed up, overstimulated; my heart pounds.
Moving toward:	I want to be tender and gentle with another person; a sense of trust and appreciation; being wanted, needed.
Moving away:	I want to withdraw, disappear, be alone; a sense of unrelatedness to others; out of contact.
Moving against:	An impulse to strike out, to do something that will hurt; I keep thinking of getting even.
Comfort:	A sense of harmony and comfort within; I'm optimistic and cheerful; I feel like smiling.
Discomfort:	A clutching, sinking feeling in the middle of my chest; an inner ache; a sense of loss, of deprivation.
Tension:	I'm wound up inside; a tight knotted feeling in my stomach; ready to snap.
Enhancement:	I feel taller, stronger, bigger; a sense of accomplishment, fulfillment; a feeling that I can do anything.
Incompetence/ dissatisfaction:	Seems that nothing I do is right; I keep blaming myself; there's a yearning, a desire for change.
Inadequacy:	A sense of being totally unable to cope; not knowing where to go, what to do; I feel vulnerable and totally helpless.

[a] From Davitz, 1969, Table 4.1.

of the clusters: "hypoactivity," "moving away" (withdrawal), "discomfort," "incompetence–dissatisfaction," and "inadequacy."

In order to use the approach to mind–brain relations outlined in Chapter 2, it is necessary to extract from changes in subjective experience an analysis in terms of underlying dimensions of cognition. This was achieved in the Davitz study by examining interrelationships between the 12 clusters. The three groups of clusters shown in Fig. 3.1. were the outcome of a factor analysis of the cluster scores. One factor separates four emotionally positive clusters from eight emotionally negative clusters, and a second factor (passive–active) divides the latter into two further groups of four. As shown in Table 3.2, the 12 clusters may conveniently be stratified into what Davitz suggested might be four basic dimensions of emotional experience: "activation," "social relatedness," "hedonic tone," and "perceived competence." Within this framework, the original five descriptors of depression reduce to three; the experience of

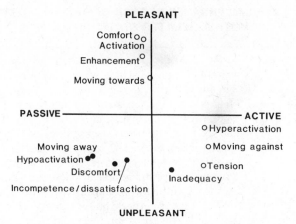

Fig. 3.1. Factor analysis of clusters of emotion-related statements (drawn from data in Davitz, 1969). The five clusters that contributed significantly to the experience of depression are shown in black.

depression is characterized by hypoactivity–withdrawal, discomfort, and an absence of perceived competence (Table 3.2).

The results of Davitz' study describe the emotional memories of a group of subjects who were highly selected by their articulate use of language and by their motivation to complete the rigorous experimental protocol. Nonetheless, the picture of depression that emerges from this study prefigures to a remarkable degree the results of studies of cognitive

TABLE 3.2.   A STRUCTURAL ANALYSIS OF EMOTIONAL MEANING[a]

		Clusters[b,c]	
Dimension	Positive	Negative: type I (passive)	Negative: type II (active)
Activation	Activation	Hypoactivation [49]	Hyperactivation
Relatedness	Moving toward	Moving away [38]	Moving against
Hedonic tone	Comfort	Discomfort [42]	Tension
Competence	Enhancement	Incompetence– dissatisfaction [19]	Inadequacy [35]

[a] After Davitz, 1969.

[b] The numbers in brackets are the scores of the five clusters that contributed significantly to the experience of depression; the maximum score attainable was 100, but score of greater than 50 were extremely rare.

[c] The occurrence of "hypoactivation" in relation to depression was highly correlated with the occurrence of "moving away" ($r = 0.9$); consequently, these two clusters reduce to a single descriptor. Similarly, "incompetence–dissatifaction" and "inadequacy" could be taken together as the negative pole of the "competence" dimension.

functioning in clinically depressed patients, which are described in Chapter 4.

Davitz' study did not single out any one emotional state for particular attention. For present purposes, however, it is of interest to examine the relationship between depression and other emotions. In performing this further analysis on Davitz' data, I have employed the following criterion to determine relatedness. Since the lowest of the five cluster scores associated with depression was 19 (a score of 54 for a sixth cluster, "tension," was deemed to be inconsequential), an emotion was considered to be related to depression if it had a score of 19 or more on any of the five depression-related clusters. Application of this criterion revealed that 12 of the 50 emotions were related to depression; the profiles of their cluster scores are shown in Table 3.3.

Table 3.3 tells an interesting story. The two terms most similar to depression were grief and sadness, which had high scores on "discomfort" and, to a lesser extent, "inadequacy". However, their scores on "withdrawal" and "hypoactivity" were very much lower than for depression. A second group of emotions—shame, remorse, guilt, and embarrassment—had a rather different profile, characterized primarily by "incompetence–dissatisfaction." Fear, panic, frustration, and anxiety were different in another way, with high scores on "inadequacy," and also, high scores on "tension" and/or "hyperactivity." The surprise, however, is that of the 50 emotional terms in the list, the only two with significant scores on "withdrawal" and "hypoactivity," other than depression, were apathy and boredom. This analysis suggests that in the lay usage of the term, depression appears to be experienced as a unique combination of misery (grief, sadness) and lethargy (apathy, boredom). As will be seen, this account of the experience of depression in nondepressed volunteers could apply equally well to some forms of severe melancholia.

3.1.2.   Depression As a Clinical Syndrome

No study comparable to Davitz' analysis of the language of emotion has been carried out on psychiatric patients; the extremely heavy demands of the experimental protocol would render such a study impossible during a depressive episode, though studies of depressed patients following recovery might be feasible. Insight into the mental state of depressed patients therefore comes primarily from three other sources: the intuitions derived from psychiatric interviews, the responses of depressed patients to short symptom checklists or similar devices, and a number of more formal questionnaire-based rating scales.

A distillation of these insights is embodied in the diagnostic criteria for depression. Diagnostic criteria were developed during the 1970s as part of an attempt to achieve a reliable and objective system of psychiatric diagnosis. Until recently, psychiatric diagnosis has been notoriously un-

TABLE 3.3. DEPRESSION COMPARED WITH TWELVE RELATED EMOTIONS[a]

Emotions	Descriptive Clusters											
	Hypo-activation	Moving Away	Discomfort	Incompetence—Dissatisfaction	Inadequacy	Activation	Hyper-activation	Moving Toward	Moving Against	Comfort	Tension	Enhancement
Depression	49	38	42	19	35	0	0	0	0	0	5	0
Grief	14	8	38	11	20	0	0	0	0	0	4	0
Sadness	14	0	36	8	11	0	0	0	0	0	0	0
Remorse	12	0	15	46	11	0	0	0	0	0	4	0
Guilt	3	0	10	35	5	0	0	0	0	0	15	0
Shame	3	6	0	48	5	0	0	0	0	0	9	0
Embarrassment	0	10	3	34	7	0	21	0	0	0		0
Fear	0	5	0	5	45	0	47	0	0	0	26	0
Panic	0	5	4	0	45	0	48	0	0	0	11	0
Frustration	5	0	4	13	22	0	5	0	7	0	46	0
Anxiety	0	0	7	4	20	0	0	0	8	0	18	0
Apathy	37	38	0	0	0	0	0	0	0	0	0	0
Boredom	52	28	0	12	0	0	0	0	0	0	9	0

[a] Data extracted from Davitz, 1969.

reliable, in the sense of giving a low level of inter-rater agreement and a high level of cross-cultural variability (Heltzer et al., 1977; Spitzer & Williams, 1980; Ward et al., 1962; Zubin, 1967). The effort to improve this position led to the development of the Feighner criteria (Feighner et al., 1972) and Research Diagnostic Criteria (RDC) (Spitzer et al., 1978), which did give reliable diagnoses, and culminated in the publication of DSM-III: *The Diagnostic and Statistical Manual of Psychiatric Diagnosis,* 3rd Ed. (American Psychiatric Association, 1980).

The DSM-III description of a major depression does show some similarity to the everyday use of the term depression, as defined above, and there are also some differences.

> The essential feature is either a dysphoric mood, usually depression, or loss of interest or pleasure in all or almost all usual activities and pastimes. This disturbance is prominent, relatively persistent, and associated with other symptoms of the depressive syndrome. These symptoms include appetite disturbance, changes in weight, sleep disturbance, psychomotor agitation or retardation, decreased energy, feelings of worthlessness or guilt, difficulty concentrating or thinking, and thoughts of death or suicide or suicidal attempts.
>
> An individual with a depressive syndrome will usually describe his or her mood as depressed, sad, hopeless, discouraged, down in the dumps, or in terms of some other colloquial variant. Sometimes, however, the mood disturbance may not be expressed as a synonym for depressive mood, but rather as a complaint of "not caring anymore," or as a painful inability to experience pleasure. . . .
>
> Loss of interest or pleasure is probably always present in a major depressive episode to some degree, but the individual may not complain of this or even be aware of the loss, although family members may notice it. Withdrawal from friends and family and neglect of avocations that were previously a source of pleasure are common. . . .
>
> Psychomotor agitation takes the form of inability to sit still, pacing, hand-wringing, pulling or rubbing of hair, skin, clothing, or other objects, outbursts of complaining or shouting, or pressure of speech. Psychomotor retardation may take the form of slowed speech, increased pauses before answering, low or monotonous speech, slowed body movements, a markedly decreased amount of speech (poverty of speech) or muteness. A decrease in energy level is almost invariably present, and is experi-

enced as sustained fatigue even in the absence of physical exertion. The smallest task may seem difficult or impossible to accomplish. . . . Difficulty in concentrating, slowed thinking, and indecisiveness are frequent. The individual may complain of memory difficulty and appear easily distracted.

The sense of worthlessness varies from feelings of inadequacy to completely unrealistic negative evaluations of one's worth. The individual may reproach himself or herself for minor failings that are exaggerated and search the environment for cues confirming the negative self-evaluation. Guilt may be expressed as an excessive reaction to either current or past failings or as exaggerated responsibility for some untoward or tragic event. The sense of worthlessness or guilt may be of delusional proportions. . . .

Thoughts of death or suicide are common. There may be fear of dying, the belief that the individual or others would be better off dead, wishes to die, or suicidal plans or attempts. (American Psychiatric Association, 1980, pp. 210–211)

The actual DSM-III criteria for a major depression are the presence for at least two weeks of either a dysphoric mood, or loss of interest or pleasure, plus four of the following eight symptoms (three if both cardinal symptoms are present): psychomotor agitation or retardation; feelings of worthlessness, self-reproach, or excessive or inappropriate guilt; suicidal ideation; decreased ability to concentrate; loss of energy; decreased sex drive; sleep disturbance; appetite disturbance. The most noteworthy feature of this definition is that while dysphoric mood and loss of interest or pleasure will usually both be present, either alone will suffice. In some cases ("masked depression"), the diagnosis of depression may be conferred even though the patient denies feeling unhappy.

3.2. THE CLASSIFICATION OF DEPRESSION

The full DSM-III diagnostic system for affective disorders is shown in Fig. 3.2. DSM-III classifies depression at a phenomenological level and was designed to make the minimum of theoretical assumptions. However, even at this level, it is clear that depression may take a variety of forms. Before beginning an exploration of the psychobiology of depression, it is therefore necessary to attempt to establish how many distinct clinical entities or dimensions the term "depression" subsumes. Additionally, in order to be able to compare studies carried out using earlier classification

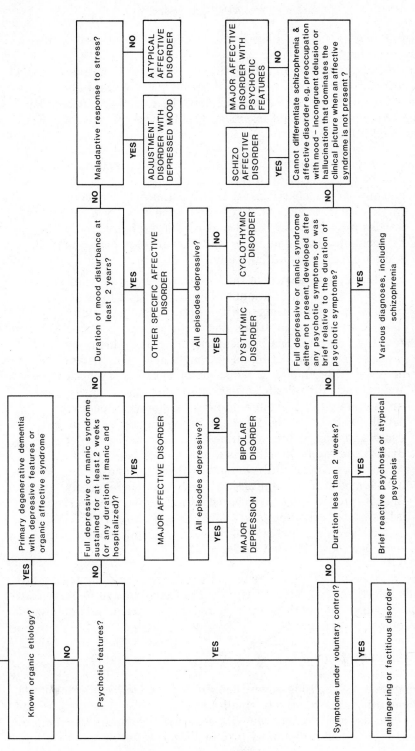

Fig. 3.2. The differential diagnosis of affective disorders according to DSM-III. An affective disorder is defined as one in which depressed, irritable, or expansive mood is the predominant clinical feature. The figure combines the DSM-III decision tree for affective disorders with the relevant parts of the decision tree for the differential diagnosis of psychotic features. Entry is at the top left.

schemes, it is necessary to address the problem of the extent to which the various taxonomies overlap.

There seems little point in attempting a comprehensive review of the classification of depression, because in addition to being unreliable, many aspects of classification have a very insubstantial empirical basis. Commenting on the International Classification of Disease (ICD) system, Kendell observed ruefully that

> It is difficult to see much connection between the changes that have taken place in the successive revisions of ICD and any of the research on the classification of depressions carried out in the last twenty years. None of the new categories introduced in ICD-8 and ICD-9 can be regarded as adequately validated and most have never been the subject of any substantial study.
>
> The fundamental cause of this unsatisfactory state of affairs is that the International Classification has to be acceptable to psychiatrists in fifty different countries, with their divergent orientations and traditions. . . . Depressive illness presents a particularly difficult problem because so many conflicting and strongly held opinions are involved. There has to be a distinction between psychotic and neurotic illnesses to satisfy those who regard the distinction as vital; there has to be a category for reactive psychoses to meet the needs of Scandinavian psychiatrists; a ragbag "depressive illness" category is needed for British and other psychiatrists who do not believe that depressions can usefully be subdivided, . . . and so on. ICD-9 meets these conflicting needs more adequately than its predecessors. In the process of doing so, however, it has lost all coherence and all pretense of unity, and has in fact become a melange of different and incompatible classifications. (Kendell, 1976, p. 25)

In these circumstances, there seems little point in ploughing once more over this infertile soil. Instead, the present discussion will be restricted to a brief consideration of those taxonomies that are frequently employed in psychobiological research.

3.2.1. Unipolar–Bipolar

Following an initial episode, severe depressions tend to recur at intervals throughout life. In a relatively small proportion of patients, these depressive episodes are interspersed with episodes of mania or hypomania. Unipolar depressions are defined by the absence of prior manic or hypomanic episodes, whereas bipolar depressions are defined by their presence. Further divisions of the bipolar category have also been proposed: bipolar I illness is defined by the presence of manic episodes, which require treatment, and usually hospitalization; bipolar II by manic or (more usually) hypomanic episodes, which have never required hospitalization; and bipolar III by the presence of depressive episodes only, but in the context of a family history of mania or hypomania (Depue & Monroe, 1978, 1979). The usefulness of the bipolar III category has not yet been established. Unipolar mania is sometimes seen, but these patients are usually placed in the bipolar I group, because they do not differ from the latter in terms of manic symptomatology, demographic variables, or family history (Abrams & Taylor, 1974; Depue & Monroe, 1979; Pfohl et al., 1983).

The general acceptance of the unipolar–bipolar distinction followed primarily from a study by Perris (1966), which showed that the two groups differed in family history: a family history of bipolarity was almost never seen in unipolar patients, and vice versa. However, subsequent studies have only partially confirmed these findings. A family history of bipolar illness is very rarely found in unipolars, but the converse does not hold. Bipolars are, if anything, more likely to have a family history of unipolar than of bipolar illness. As these data suggest, comparisons between the two groups reveal that bipolars are more likely than unipolars to have a family history of affective disorder (of either polarity) (Angst, 1966; Dunner et al., 1976a; Gershon et al., 1975; Smeraldi et al., 1977; Taylor & Abrams, 1980; Taylor et al., 1980; Tsuang, 1978).

Although the family history data no longer compel the view that unipolar and bipolar depressions constitute separate disorders (Gershon et al., 1975; Smeraldi et al., 1977; Taylor & Abrams, 1980), the distinction remains a useful one, insofar as the bipolar group are relatively homogeneous, but the unipolars are not. In particular, there is strong evidence for genetic transmission of bipolar disorder, with a concordance rate for monozygotic twins of 72%, as compared with 11% for dizygotic twins (Allen, 1976). Some evidence, such as an association between bipolar illness and color blindness (Mendelwicz & Fliess, 1974) suggested that the mode of transmission may be dominant and linked to the X-chromosome (reviewed by Depue & Monroe, 1979). However, under an X-linked mode of transmission father–son transmission of bipolar illness could not occur; the fact that it does has led to the development of alternative theories of genetic heterogeneity (Depue & Monroe, 1979; Winokur, 1975). The evidence for genetic transmission of unipolar disorder is much weaker, with only 40% concordance for monozygotic twins, as against 17% for dizygotic twins (Allen, 1976), and there is no evidence for any particular mode of transmission (Depue & Monroe, 1979).

Unipolar and bipolar depressed patients do not appear to differ markedly in the quality of their mental state. Some potentially interesting differences have been described, but the unipolar group are far more heterogeneous, which makes meaningful comparisons difficult. Bipolar patients are more likely to exhibit psychomotor retardation during depressive episodes, and unipolars, psychomotor agitation (Beigel & Murphy, 1971; Kupfer et al., 1974), with bipolars showing a considerably greater change in motor activity on recovery (Kupfer et al., 1974). Additionally, bipolar patients were more likely to exhibit hypersomnia (>8 hours-sleep/ night) and unipolars hyposomnia (< 6 hours sleep/night) (Detre et al., 1972; Hartman, 1968; Kupfer et al., 1972). It has also been observed that bipolars show very low levels of anger and anxiety (Beigel & Murphy, 1971). However, a high proportion of unipolars are similar to bipolars in exhibiting psychomotor retardation and hypersomnia (Kupfer et al., 1975a,b). This suggests that the apparent differences between unipolar and bipolar patients actually reflect the greater variability within the unipolar group, rather than a true unipolar–bipolar difference.

Similarly, there is little evidence that unipolar and bipolar depressions show a differential response to treatment. For example, five studies concur in finding no difference in response to ECS (Avery et al., 1983). One apparent exception is lithium, which is extremely well extablished as an antimanic agent and also has antidepressant properties. On the basis of the early clinical literature, it has been claimed that lithium is a more effective antidepressant in bipolar patients (Dunner and Fieve, 1978). However, many bipolar depressed patients simultaneously show manic symptoms. When clinical features have been controlled for, lithium has not been found to differ in its effects on unipolar and bipolar depressions (Donnelly et al., 1978; Mendels, 1976; Watanabe et al., 1975). Furthermore, prophylactic treatment with lithium appears to be equally effective in the two cases (reviewed by Taylor & Abrams, 1980).

In fact, when the heterogeneity of unipolar depressions is taken into account, there seems little reason to see bipolar depression as a distinct category. The major difference between bipolar and unipolar patients is in what happens to them when they are not depressed. There is, however, a further manifestation of the underlying tendency to mania in bipolar patients, which is of diagnostic and clinical significance. In a substantial proportion of bipolar depressions, hypomanic episodes are induced by tricyclic antidepressants (Akiskal et al., 1979; Bunney, 1978; Klein, 1968; Prien & Caffey, 1977) or by DOPA (Bunney et al., 1970; Murphy et al., 1971). This response appears to be a biological marker for bipolar illness, since it is very rarely seen in unipolar depressions (Akiskal et al., 1979; Bunney, 1978). Indeed, those rare instances of "pharmacological hypomania" in unipolars may actually indicate a misdiagnosis, since the induction of "pharmacological hypomania" is highly predictive of the future occurrence of spontaneous hypomanic or manic episodes (Akiskal et al., 1979).

The possibility that some unipolar patients might "really" be bipolars, on the basis of their pharmacological response to tricyclics or their family history (i.e., the bipolar III group), raises the question of the reliability of this classification scheme. In practice, this becomes a potentially serious issue in relation to patients presenting with a single episode of depression, which may or may not be followed by mania. Some authors have dealt with this problem by withholding the diagnosis "unipolar" until a patient has had three episodes of depression with no manic episode, and using the label "undifferentiated" in the meanwhile (Perris, 1975). In fact, bipolars constitute a very small proportion of the total population of depressed patients (bipolar 1 less than 5% and bipolar II 5–15%) (Akiskal et al., 1979; Boyd & Weissman, 1981; Dunner et al., 1976c; Winokur & Morrison, 1973). Since most bipolars have their first manic attack before or within six months of their first hospitalization for depression, it has been estimated that the "contamination" of a unipolar group by unrecognized bipolars is probably less than 5% (Dunner et al., 1976c).

3.2.2. Primary–Secondary

Like the unipolar–bipolar distinction, the primary–secondary classification is also based on considerations external to the depression. The main object of this classification scheme, which was a forerunner of the RDC and DSM-III systems, was to define for research purposes a group of primary depressed patients, uncontaminated by other psychiatric disorders (Feighner et al., 1972; Robins & Guze, 1972). A depressive episode was defined stringently by a depressed mood lasting at least one month, combined with at least five from a list of eight other symptoms (as in DSM-III). The diagnosis of primary depression, which may be unipolar or bipolar, requires that there be no concurrent psychiatric disorder or severe physical illness and no previous history of any other psychiatric disorder. Frequently, secondary depressions arise in the context of an ongoing non-affective disorder, but the definition does not require this temporal contiguity. Many patients with "neurotic depressions" would be excluded as a result of previously diagnosed neuroses. However, a substantial proportion of patients meeting RDC criteria for major affective disorder also fail to meet the criterion for primary depression-—40% in one study (Spitzer et al., 1978).

Given that the distinction between primary and secondary depression is not based on clinical features of the depression, it is hardly surprising that patterns of symptoms have not been found to differ (Guze et al., 1971; G. Murphy et al., 1974; Weissman et al., 1977; Winokur, 1972; Wood et al., 1977; Woodruff et al., 1967). Furthermore, the distinction does not map particularly well on to other classifications. In one study, for example, among patients meeting RDC criteria for major depression, of 59 with primary depression, 64% were also diagnosed as endogenous, 29%

as psychotic, and 51% as situational; the corresponding figures for 31 secondary depressives were hardly different: 45, 19, and 48% (Spitzer et al., 1978). The one significant exception is that secondary depression is almost never seen in bipolar patients (Akiskal et al., 1979; Spitzer et al., 1978). Consistent with this observation, it has also been reported that two predictors associated with bipolarity, a family history of bipolarity and a switch into hypomania during tricyclic antidepressant treatment, were seen almost exclusively in primary depression (Akiskal et al., 1979).

In the context of "neurotic depression" (see below), some evidence suggests that the primary–secondary distinction may have prognostic value, since it has been observed that whereas primary depressions run episodically, with a generally good outcome, the course of secondary depressions tends to depend more on the associated nonaffective disorder, with, in many cases, a poor outcome (Akiskal et al., 1978).

3.2.3. Endogenous–Reactive

The unipolar–bipolar and primary–secondary dichotomies classify depressions according to whether the patient suffers only from depression or also suffers from other disorders. However, the major problem in the classification of depression has always been that of deciding how many disorders the term "depression" actually subsumes. The issue is one of immense complexity, which arises from the fact that although there is a consensus that there are two types of depression, until recently there has been very little agreement over how they differ.

The essential features of this debate may be covered by considering three of the many proposed dichotomies: autonomous–reactive, endogenous–psychogenic, and psychotic–neurotic. Although these three dichotomies all refer to roughly the same two groups of patients, they have radically different meanings. The autonomous–reactive distinction describes the course of the depression. Autonomous depressions follow a predetermined course and do not respond to psychosocial interventions, whereas reactive depressions are those that do respond to treatment. This usage of the word "reactive" is the original usage and is the sense in which it is used in this book. It is a source of some considerable confusion, however, that over the years, usage of the term "reactive depression" has changed; it is now often used interchangeably with "psychogenic," which means something quite different. The endogenous–psychogenic distinction concerns etiology; unlike psychogenic depressions, it is supposed that endogenous depressions have no clear psychological precipitants. The third distinction, psychotic–neurotic, concerns clinical symptomatology. Different authors have used the terms in different ways, which reflect their various theoretical predilections, though often no more is implied than a difference in severity.

Considering the differences in meaning between the three sets of terms, it is astonishing that, in practice, they often have been used more or less interchangeably. A number of reviews have examined this issue in more detail and discussed the origins of this remarkable state of affairs (Fowles & Gersh, 1979; Kendell, 1976; Klerman, 1972; Mendels & Cochrane, 1968; Rosenthal & Klerman, 1966; Schatzberg, 1978). As a result of these terminological conflations, the endogenous/autonomous/psychotic–psychogenic/neurotic/reactive distinction raises two questions. Is there a valid distinction, and if so, which sets of terminology are appropriate?

As will be shown below, there are, in fact, good grounds for distinguishing two groups of depressions on the basis of their "reactivity"—defined here as reactivity of symptoms. The classic "endogenous" or "autonomous" (i.e., nonreactive) depression is recognized in DSM-III by the diagnosis major depression with melancholia. The defining feature of melancholia is an inability to experience pleasure, even when something good happens: the bereaved person can usually raise a smile to a kind word; the melancholic cannot. In addition to this lack of "reactivity," the DSM-III diagnosis of melancholia requires at least three of the following: distinct quality of mood (i.e., distinctly different from the feeling of, for example, grief), excessive or inappropriate guilt, marked psychomotor change (retardation or agitation), anorexia, early morning awakening, or diurnal variation with greater intensity of depression in the morning. The validity of these criteria will be examined below.

As discussed by Kendell (1976), whether or not the terms "psychotic" and "neurotic" are used to label the autonomous–reactive dimension is largely a matter of how the terms are defined. In the European literature, melancholia has frequently been defined as a psychosis and is therefore, by definition, psychotic. In the American literature, however, the term "psychotic" has usually been reserved for more unequivocal forms of thought disorder—delusions and hallucinations. The DSM-III position (Fig. 3.2) is closer to the latter usage: Psychotic features, which may be part of a major affective disorder, are defined as a gross impairment of reality testing (delusions or hallucinations) or depressive stupor (mute and unresponsive). It is unclear why the framers of DSM-III thought it appropriate to lump together delusional depression with depressive stupor. However, for present purposes this question can remain unanswered, as the latter condition is almost never referred to in the biological literature. Note that in the DSM-III usage, psychotic depression is not one end of a psychotic–neurotic dimension: nonpsychotic is not equivalent to neurotic, since melancholia is also nonpsychotic. Because of the many discrepancies, the term *delusional depression* will be used in this book, as far as possible, rather than psychotic depression. When the term *psychotic* is used, it will be in the restricted DSM-III sense, rather than as a synonym for melancholia.

These terminological issues are confused even further by the fact that the word *reactive* has two quite different meanings. As discussed above, the term *reactive depression* originally meant a depression which "reacted" to treatment. By the 1920s, however, reactive had taken on the additional meaning of psychogenic. In this new meaning, which is now the more common usage, "reactive depression" means a depression precipitated by environmental stress. Because of this ambiguity, the term *situational* (Spitzer et al., 1978) is preferable to *reactive* as a way of describing depressions with clear environmental precipitants.

So far, this discussion has been about the use of words. However, there is also a very important empirical question: Do depressions that respond to psychosocial interventions (reactive depressions) and those that do not (autonomous or endogenous depressions) differ in their etiology? The widespread belief that reactive depressions are precipitated and endogenous depressions are not is the source of the confusion described in the previous paragraph. In fact, many recent studies have demonstrated that this assumption is false; both types of depression are equally likely to be preceded by psychosocial stressors. The apparent presence of precipitants in one group and their absence in the other arises from two complementary artifacts. On the one hand, neurotic/reactive depressives are likely to report events as precipitants, which may appear to an observer to be no more than trivial inconveniences. On the other hand, endogenous/autonomous depressives are likely to fail to report serious precipitating incidents as causes of their depression, in part because they see themselves as having been responsible. In studies that have assessed the frequency and severity of precipitating events following recovery, no differences are observed between the two groups (Brown & Harris, 1978; Leff et al., 1970; Lewinsohn et al., 1977; Matussek et al., 1981; Paykel, 1979b; Paykel et al., 1969). A possible reason for the difference in the way in which endogenous and reactive depressives view the causes of their depression will be discussed in Section 4.4.2.

3.3. THE EMPIRICAL APPROACH TO CLASSIFICATION

The empirical approach to the classification of depression begins not with a predetermined criterion, as in the taxonomies discussed above, but with the signs and symptoms displayed by populations of depressed patients. Multivariate statistical analyses are used to reveal underlying relationships and generate diagnostic labels (Kiloh & Garside, 1963). The analytic techniques most frequently employed are factor analysis and cluster analysis. Factor analysis separates patients along one or more dimensions (factors), to which different symptoms are more or less strongly related; cluster analysis identifies groups of patients with similar patterns of symptoms. These techniques and others have consistently produced evidence supporting the reality of endogenous depression (DSM-III major depression with melancholia) as a distinct diagnostic category.

3.3.1. The Reality of "Endogenous Depression"

Nelson and Charney (1981) reviewed 13 factor-analytic studies, which identified an endogenous-neurotic factor; the symptoms most strongly associated with the endogenous pole of this dimension were retardation, lack of reactivity, and severity of depressed mood, followed by delusions, self-reproach, loss of interest, and distinct quality of mood. They also reviewed eight cluster–analytic studies; symptoms associated with the endogenous cluster were retardation, lack of reactivity, severity of depressed mood, and self-reproach, followed by agitation, delusions, loss of interest, diurnal worsening, and early morning awakening. This general picture was also seen in more recent cluster analytic studies (Andreasen & Grove, 1982; Mutussek et al., 1982). Overall, combining the results of factor analytic, cluster analytic and a variety of other types of study, Nelson and Charney concluded, perhaps surprisingly, that the symptom most strongly associated with endogenous depression was not severity of depressed mood, or even lack of reactivity, but psychomotor change— particularly retardation but also agitation. Severity of depressed mood and lack of reactivity were strongly associated with the syndrome, as expected, as were depressive delusions, self-reproach, and loss of interest. Some other symptoms traditionally thought to be an important part of the endogenous profile were less strongly supported; these included "distinct quality of mood" and diurnal morning worsening. Furthermore, while there is no doubt that neurovegetative symptoms such as early morning awakening and appetite loss are prominent in depression, these did not distinguish well between endogenous and nonendogenous depressions.

The picture of melancholia that emerges from these studies is supported by a number of more recent studies of the validity of RDC or DSM-III criteria (Feinberg & Carroll, 1982; Matussek et al., 1981, 1982; Nelson et al., 1981). These included a W.H.O. multicultural collaborative study, which, like the Nelson and Charney review, found that the symptom most characteristic of melancholia was psychomotor retardation (Jablensky et al., 1981). A further validation was that the DSM-III criteria for melancholia successfully identified patients who failed to respond to psychotherapy (Nelson et al., 1981).

Severe depression is not synonymous with melancholia. As noted above, most studies which have examined this question have found an association between severity of depression and lack of reactivity (e.g., Nelson & Charney, 1981), but some studies have found evidence of equally severe nonmelancholic depressions (Bech, 1981; Feinberg & Carroll, 1982). What gives these nonmelancholic depressions their severity is the presence of depressive delusions. The possibility that delusional depression may be a separate syndrome (psychotic depression in the DSM-III sense) is suggested by studies showing a differential treatment response. Unlike nondelusional depressions, which respond well to tricyclic antidepressants, delusional depressions tend to respond poorly to tricyclics, but do appear to respond well to tricyclic–neuroleptic combinations or to ECT (Charney & Nelson, 1981; Nelson & Bowers, 1978).

The DSM-III system forces a diagnostic choice between melancholia and psychotic depression; it is not permitted to apply both of these labels simultaneously. However, the empirical evidence suggests a considerable overlap between these two categories. No difference has been found between severely depressed patients who were delusional and those who are not in demographic variables, family history, or course of the illness (Frangos et al,. 1983), and apart from the presence or absence of delusions, there is apparently only one symptomatic variable that distinguishes these groups: delusional patients show a higher incidence of psychomotor agitation (Frances et al., 1981; Frangos et al., 1983; Nelson & Bowers, 1978). However, as noted above, agitation is one of the symptoms most strongly diagnostic of melancholia, and depressive delusions are also a prominent feature (Nelson & Charney, 1981).

Given this overlap and given the importance of psychomotor change in both melancholic and delusional depressions, it might be better to begin with psychomotor change and work back. In their review of empirical studies of endogenous depression, Nelson and Charney (1981) reported that both psychomotor retardation and psychomotor agitation were strongly associated with severely depressed mood and lack of reactivity. However, retardation and agitation were differentially associated with some other symptoms. As noted above, delusional thinking and also self-reproach were especially prominent in agitated depressions. By contrast, loss of interest in usually pleasurable activities was more prominent in retarded depressions (Nelson & Charney, 1981). This same pattern has also been reported in two more recent studies (Andreasen & Grove, 1982; Glassman & Roose, 1981).

These findings may be summarized by saying that psychomotor change almost invariably signifies that a depression is severe. Psychomotor retardation is a reliable diagnostic indication of endogenous depression (melancholia). Psychomotor agitation is a good indication of delusional thinking; melancholia is a likely concomitant, but delusional reactive depressions are also possible.

3.3.2. Biological Markers

A further validation of the concept of endogenous depression is the association of this condition with biological markers. The most widely studied is the dexamethasone suppression test (DST), which probes the integrity of the hypothalamic–pituitary–adrenal (HPA) system. In some depressed patients, there is evidence that HPA activity is abnormally high: cortisol levels are elevated in plasma (reviewed by Carroll 1977, 1978) and in cerebrospinal fluid (Carroll et al., 1976; Traskman et al., 1980), in some cases to an extent comparable to that seen in Cushing's disease. The cause of this abnormality appears to be the failure of the brain to inhibit the release of adrenocorticotrophic hormone (ACTH) (Carroll & Mendels, 1976). Dexamethasone is a synthetic corticosteroid which suppresses ACTH release. Depressed patients usually show a normal suppression of blood cortisol level in response to dexamethasone; however, in the standardized version of the DST, they escape from suppression significantly earlier than normal and therefore do not show suppression of plasma cortisol levels when tested 17 to 24 hours later (Carroll, 1982). A number of studies have demonstrated that normalization of the DST accompanies or precedes clinical recovery from depression (Greden et al., 1980; Holsboer et al,. 1982; Papakostas et al., 1980). It has also been observed that a patient who appears to have recovered from depression, but fails to suppress cortisol after dexamethasone, has a high risk of relapse (Holsboer et al., 1982; Targum, 1983a).

A potential confounding factor in interpreting the significance of the DST is that dexamethasone nonsuppression is associated with loss of weight. Negative (i.e., nonsuppressing) DSTs are associated with malnutrition (Smith et al., 1975), and nonsuppression is also seen in a high proportion of anorexia nervosa patients (Doerr et al., 1980; Gerner & Gwirtsman, 1981). Negative DSTs can be induced in healthy obese volunteers by dieting (Edelstein et al., 1983), and it has been reported that in depressed patients, the likelihood of a negative DST was increased in proportion to weight loss (Berger et al., 1982a; Targum, 1983b). Despite these observations, however, it seems clear that in a substantial proportion of depressed patients, abnormal DST responses are seen in the absence of recent weight loss (Berger et al., 1982a; Targum, 1983b).

The observation of abnormal DST responses in the apparent absence of any psychopathology poses some difficulty for the view that depression is primarily an endocrinological disorder. From the more catholic perspective adopted in this book, the implication is that those systems in the brain which are dysfunctional in depression may also be involved in the control of body weight.

Abnormal DST responses are not shown indiscriminately by all psychiatric patients. Negative DSTs are very uncommon, for example, in panic disorders and in agorophobia, two conditions that are sometimes thought to be related to depression because they can be treated effectively with some antidepressant drugs (Curtis et al., 1982). It has been reported that negative DSTs were more frequent in delusional than in nondelusional depressions (Mendlewicz et al., 1982a; Rudorfer et al., 1982), but this probably reflects their severity rather than the presence of psychosis as such, since patients with "psychotic (i.e., delusional) depressions" have substantially higher postdexamethasone cortisol levels than other groups of psychotic patients (Rothschild et al., 1982). Negative DSTs are occasionally seen in psychiatric conditions other than depression, such as mania (Graham et al., 1982), obsessive–compulsive neuroses (Insel et al., 1982), and schizophrenia (Stokes et al., 1976), as well as in normal subjects with (Edelstein et al., 1983) and without (Amsterdam et al., 1982a) weight loss, but their frequency is substantially lower than in depression.

Among depressed patients, DST nonsuppression appears to be specific to endogenous and/or primary depressions. Carroll and co-workers, in a series of studies, reported that escape from dexamethasone suppression was seen in 43% of endogenous depressions but in only 4% of nonendogenous depressions (Carroll et al., 1981a; Carroll, 1982). Although there have been some negative findings (Berger et al., 1982a; Coryell et al., 1982; Holsboer et al., 1980), many independent studies have confirmed this observation (W. Brown et al., 1979; Dotti et al., 1980, cited in Carroll, 1982; Carroll, 1982; Mendlewicz et al., 1982a; Nuller & Ostroumova, 1980; Papakostas et al., 1980; Rush et al., 1982). An abnormal DST is also seen in approximately 45% of primary affective disorders, compared with a 9% incidence in secondary depressions (W. Brown et al., 1979; Brown & Schuey, 1980; Carroll, 1982; Carroll et al., 1981a; Mendlewicz et al., 1982a; Papakostas et al., 1980; Rush et al., 1982; Schlesser et al., 1980). A rather lower proportion of abnormal DST responses is seen in depressed outpatients than in inpatients, possibly because their depressions are less severe, and in one study, the DST response was not found to be abnormal in primary affective disorder patients, compared with healthy controls (Amsterdam et al., 1982a). More recently, however, a higher frequency of abnormal DST responses has also been reported in primary depressed outpatients, particularly in an endogenous subgroup (Peselow et al., 1983b).

A second biological marker of importance, which like the DST appears to be specific for primary and/or endogenous depression, is a decrease in the latency to enter rapid eye movement (REM) sleep. There are actually a number of sleep abnormalities that reliably distinguish endogenous depressives from nonendogenous depressives and normal subjects (Kupfer & Thase, 1983), of which REM latency has been the most extensively studied. In normal subjects, the mean REM latency, defined as the latency from the onset of sleep to the first REM period, is 90 minutes. REM latency is unaffected by transient dysphoria in normal volunteers (Cohen, 1979), but in the majority of patients suffering from endogenous and/or primary depression, REM latency is halved to 40–50 minutes (Akiskal, 1980; Duncan et al., 1979; Feinberg et al., 1982; Kupfer, 1976; Kupfer & Foster, 1975; Kupfer & Thase, 1983; Kupfer et al., 1978; Rush et al., 1982). Like the DST, abnormal REM latencies normalize with clinical recovery (Kupfer et al., 1983). Unlike the DST, REM latency does not appear to be influenced by changes in body weight (Berger et al., 1982a).

The endogenous–reactive distinction appears to discriminate those patients with abnormally short REM latencies better than the primary–secondary distinction, because shortened REM latencies are seen in some patients with depressions "secondary" to a variety of other psychiatric conditions; this point is sometimes obscured by the fact that in many studies, most patients with primary depression also meet diagnostic criteria for endogenous depression (Kupfer & Thase, 1983). However, the primary–secondary distinction remains useful. Although many secondary depressions show reduced REM latencies after one or more nights adaptation to the sleep laboratory, it appears that on the first night, only primary depressives show the abnormality (Akiskal et al., 1982). REM latencies do not distinguish between unipolar and bipolar endogenous depressions (Duncan et al., 1979; Feinberg et al., 1982), and REM latencies may also be reduced in mania and hypomania (Kupfer and Thase, 1983). However, short REM latencies are very rarely seen in normal volunteers or in patients with medical or nonaffective psychiatric diagnoses (Kupfer & Thase, 1983).

Considering the amount of research on each of these biological markers, it is surprising how few studies have addressed the question of whether the two abnormalities co-exist in the same patients. However, two recent studies have reported that REM latency was inversely related to plasma cortisol level (Rush et al., 1982) and to dexamethasone non-suppression (Asnis et al., 1983). This suggests that these very different measures may reflect a common physiological substrate and further supports the validity of endogenous depression as a diagnostic entity.

3.3.3. Severity of Depression As a Continuum

A question of some considerable importance arises from the validation of the concepts of major depression with melancholia and/or psychotic features. Do these severe depressions differ from milder forms of depression only in their intensity, or is there also a qualitative difference? It might seem that this issue is resolved, in favor of a qualitative difference by the fact that cluster analysis studies nearly always find evidence for a group of patients with endogenous depressions, who cluster together but differ from other depressed patients. The problem in accepting this conclusion is that in a very real sense, cluster analysis, like other multivariate analytical techniques finds what it looks for. The method is designed to produce clusters of patients, so that is what it does.

Evidence from other sources suggests that there is not, in fact, a qualitative difference, and that major depressions differ from mild depressions and normal mood swings primarily in their intensity. For example, some patients suffering from chronic mild depressions appear to suffer from a mild version of endogenous (possible bipolar) depression. This is indicated by their favorable response to tricyclic antidepressants or lithium, short REM latencies, the occasional pharmacologically induced hypomanic episode, family histories positive for bipolar disorder (Akiskal et al., 1981; Rosenthal et al., 1981), and abnormal DST results (Carroll et al., 1981c).

The evidence for continuity between major and minor depressions is strongest in the case of bipolar depression. Cyclothymia (chronic mild bipolar disorder) resembles full syndromal bipolar disorder in two very characteristic respects (see Section 3.2.1.). Both groups of patients have family histories of bipolarity, and in both groups, tricyclic antidepressants can induce "pharmacological hypomania." Cyclothymic patients did not differ in these respects from bipolar I patients, but neither feature was seen in a control group of patients with personality disorders (Akiskal et al., 1977). It is clear from these results that in the case of bipolar disorders, the difference between mild and severe forms is quantitative rather than qualitative.

There is also evidence that this continuum extends beyond mild clinical depressions into normal day-to-day mood swings in nonclinical populations. Depue and co-workers constructed a qustionnaire, the general behavior inventory (GBI), which was designed to assess the frequency and intensity of mood swings and behavioral changes characteristic of bipolar disorder. When the GBI was administered to a student population, 53% of subjects scoring higher than a predetermined cut-off score had at least one first-degree relative with a history of depression, compared to only one subject (3%) scoring below the cut-off score. These results strongly suggest that a population of subclinical affective disorder cases was being identified. A further interesting feature of these results was that subjects scoring high on the GBI were also characterized by more frequent and severe within-day mood swings, suggesting the intriguing possibility of defective inhibitory modulation of normal moment to moment or circadian mood fluctuations (Depue et al., 1981).

3.3.4. The Heterogeneity of "Neurotic Depression"

In contrast to the broad level of agreement regarding endogenous depression (melancholia) and psychotic depression, there exists considerable disagreement over the features that characterize nonmelancholic, nonpsychotic depressions (i.e., neurotic depressions). In DSM-III, these conditions may be variously diagnosed as unipolar major depressions without melancholia or psychotic features, dysthymic disorders, cyclothymic disorders, atypical depressions, or adjustment disorders with depressed mood (Fig. 3.2).

This heterogeneity is not consistent with the idea of neurotic depression as one end of an endogenous-neurotic dimension, but is consistent with the view expressed by some authors that "neurotic depression" is simply a residual category diagnosed by the exclusion of depressions with clear endogenous features (e.g., Foulds, 1975; Kiloh et al., 1972; Mendels & Cochrane, 1968). The DSM-III diagnosis *dysthymic disorder* alone appears to subsume a variety of separate diagnoses: chronic primary depressions which are often the aftermath of a major depressive episode, chronic secondary dysphorias, and characterological depressions, which can be further subdivided into subaffective dysthymic disorders (mild melancholia, described above), and character spectrum disorders (Akiskal, 1983).

This impression of heterogeneity is supported by empirical studies. Cluster analytic studies frequently identify two or three nonendogenous clusters, but while there is good agreement over the characterization of the endogenous cluster, descriptions of the nonendogenous clusters vary greatly from study to study (Andreasen & Grove, 1982; Blashfield & Morey, 1979; Matussek et al., 1982; Nelson & Charney, 1981). Furthermore, the diagnosis of neurotic depression is unstable over time. During a three to four year follow-up period, 40% of the patients so diagnosed developed unipolar (22%) or bipolar (18%) major affective disorders, and two-thirds of the remainder were found to be suffering from nonaffective disorders (Akiskal et al., 1978).

Within the spectrum of neurotic depressions, there is some support for the idea that atypical depression (Paykel et al., 1983a,b; Quitkin et al., 1979, 1983) may be a distinct diagnostic entity. In DSM-III, this condition, also known as "anxious depression" (Paykel, 1971; Kendell, 1976) or "secondary dysphoria" (Akiskal, 1983), is the major diagnostic label for episodes of mild depression which have lasted less than two years. Although anxiety is not uncommon among endogenously depressed patients, usually in association with psychomotor agitation (e.g., Hamilton, 1967; Hollister & Overall, 1965), the results of cluster analytic studies support the identification of a distinct, nonendogenous, anxious subgroup (Gersh & Fowles, 1979; Matussek et al., 1982). However, the label "atypical" is probably inappropriate. This term refers to an *atypical functional shift*: a pattern of evening worsening of mood, increased sleep, and weight increase, all of which, supposedly, are opposite to the changes observed in endogenous depressions. However, a recent study has reported that these atypical symptoms are not strongly associated either with anxiety or with reactivity (Paykel et al., 1983a,b).

Probably the most significant observation concerning anxious depressions is that they respond to treatment with MAOIs; as noted earlier (Section 1.1.4), MAOIs have proved to be of little value in endogenous depressions (Avery et al., 1983; Quitkin et al., 1979; Tyrer, 1979). What is not clear is whether MAOIs are more effective than other treatments in anxious depressions. Although traditionally it has been believed that tricyclic antidepressants are ineffective in anxious depressions (Raskin & Crook, 1976; Quitkin et al., 1983), some studies have reported that tricyclics were equally effective in their antidepressant effects (Paykel, 1979a; Paykel et al., 1983b; Ravaris et al., 1980). MAOIs may, however, have a greater antianxiety effect than tricyclics (Ravaris et al., 1980), giving them an overall clinical superiority. The reason that MAOIs work in anxious depressions but not in endogenous depressions may simply be that MAOIs are weak antidepressants with added antianxiety effects, and anxious depressions are mild depressions with added anxiety.

Another substantial group of depressions which fall outside the DSM-III diagnosis of major affective disorder are the so-called characterological depressions. These are chronic and persistent states of intermittent or mild depression which usually begin early in life. Characterological depressions appear to take two forms. One is the group of *subaffective dysthymic disorder* patients referred to above (Section 3.3.3), who appear to suffer from a mild version of endogenous depression, as indicated, inter alia, by their favorable response to tricyclic antidepressants and short REM latencies (Akiskal et al., 1981; Rosenthal et al., 1981). These patients had a classic *depressive character* (Schneider, 1958; Standage, 1979): passive, gloomy, self-derogatory, complaining, self-disciplining, brooding, and preoccupied with inadequacy and failure (Akiskal, 1983).

By contrast, a second group of chronically depressed patients, those labeled *character spectrum disorders*, did not respond to antidepressant medication and had normal REM latencies; their depressions were associated with polydrug and alcohol abuse and family histories of alcoholism (Akiskal et al., 1981; Rosenthal et al., 1981; Winokur et al., 1971). These patients are characterized by histrionic, antisocial, or schizoid features (Akiskal et al., 1981; Rosenthal et al., 1981; Tyrer & Alexander, 1979); their *hysteroid dysphoria* (Klein, 1974) appears to result from early exposure to an alcoholic or sociopathic home environment (Rosenthal et al., 1981; Winokur, 1979). The term *neurotic depression* is appropriate here: these cases are best conceptualized as a chronic overreaction to disappointment, resulting in dysphoria, anger, and feelings of helplessness. However, the depressions are not melancholic. Despite their irritability, the patients maintain the capacity for pleasure and interest, given the appropriate situation (Akiskal, 1983; Klein, 1974; Liebowitz & Klein, 1979).

3.4. CONCLUSIONS: VARIETIES OF DEPRESSION

It is plain from the foregoing discussion that clinically, depression takes a variety of forms. The most clearly delineated is "endogenous depression" (melancholia), the defining feature of which is not a lack of environmental precipitation, but rather, an inability to experience pleasure; the term *autonomous depression* (Gillespie, 1929) is more appropriate. Melancholia, characterized by severely depressed mood, the inability to experience pleasure, and loss of interest in previously pleasurable activities, most closely approximates the everyday language term "depression," as defined by the Davitz study (Section 3.1.1). Bipolar patients almost invariably show an endogenous profile during a depressive episode (Klein, 1974; Spitzer et al., 1978).

Nonendogenous depressions are much more varied. Some severe delusional depressions escape melancholia, but nonendogenous depressions usually are less severe, as exemplified by the category of atypical or anxious depressions. Indeed, some authors have suggested that in the final analysis, the various dichotomous classifications of depression put forward during the past 50 years largely come down to a distinction between severe and mild depressions (Kendell, 1976).

Klein (1974) suggested a dichotomy that puts the dividing line in a rather different place. In Klein's model, the distinction is made on the basis of whether or not the depression has endogenous features. The class of "endogenomorphic depressions" comprises the classic endogenous depression (DSM-III major depressions with melancholia), and in addition, these minor depressions in which the capacity for pleasure is diminished, such as the subaffective dysthymic disorders discussed above. The class of nonendogenomorphic depressions, which Klein termed "chronic overreactive dysphorias" is correspondingly smaller and more homogenous than the traditional category of "neurotic depression," and the term *neurotic* is now more applicable: this group comprises mainly anxious depressions and the character spectrum disorder type of characterological depression.

The potential importance of this distinction was the proposal that endogenomorphic depressions result from an inhibited or unresponsive "pleasure center," whereas neurotic depressions arise from an inability to tolerate frustration (a third category of acute reactive dysphorias will not be discussed here). This hypothesis of a difference in the underlying psychological mechanisms sets Klein's model apart from all other dichotomous classification schemes and forms a suitable point at which to move on to a consideration of the psychology of depression.

four

COGNITIVE FUNCTIONING IN DEPRESSION

In considering the relationship between psychiatric classification and psychological theory, it is apparent that there are two conspicuous omissions. On one hand, psychological theories of depression have almost always ignored the diagnostic heterogeneity of the clinical phenomena. On the other, psychiatric classification schemes have made virtually no attempt to explain the fact that within diagnostic categories, there is considerable variability of clinical symptomatology.

Klein's 1974 paper was a notable exception on both counts. In traditional accounts of the endogenous–nonendogenous distinction, endogenous depressions are assumed to be "physiological" and therefore not to need any further psychological analysis. The falsity of this view was discussed in Chapter 2. Klein's distinction between endogenomorphic depressions, which result from an inhibited or unresponsive "pleasure center," and neurotic depressions, which arise out of an inability to tolerate frustration, recognizes not only that are there two types of depression, but also that both of them require a psychological theory. This alone represents a considerable advance over other classification schemes. However, there is another feature of the model that makes it radically different. In addition to the hypothesized underlying dysfunctions of reward mechanisms and responsiveness to stress, the model also postulates a nexus of intervening variables through which these underlying processes give rise to manifest symptoms.

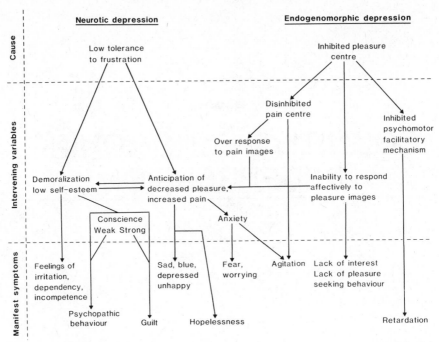

Fig. 4.1. A simplified version of Klein's model of the interrelationships between depressive symptoms (after Klein, 1974, Fig. 2). From Willner, 1984d.

A simplified version of the model is shown in Fig. 4.1. Three broad classes of symptom may be distinguished, which are related in different ways to the underlying causes. One major intervening variable is a shift in the anticipated balance of pleasure and pain, which causes subjective feelings of depression, sadness, hopelessness, and so on; a second is a loss of self-esteem, which results in feelings of incompetence and guilt. These mechanisms may be activated, by different routes, in both forms of depression. Because the third group of symptoms, retardation and lack of interest, stem from underactivity in the "pleasure center" and there is no point of entry from the left-hand side of the model, these symptoms are only seen in the endogenomorphic form (Klein, 1974).

The model not only explains the many similarities between endogenomorphic and neurotic depressions, but it also has considerable flexibility to account for different patterns of manifest symptoms, since the particular symptoms displayed will depend on the relative predominance of the different intervening variables. The flexibility arises out of the fact that the intervening variables may be influenced by other factors, such as personality charateristics. Guilt, for example, is a symptom that some theories of depression have difficulty in explaining (Abramson & Sackheim, 1977). Klein's model sees guilt as arising in people with a strong conscience; this relationship has recently been confirmed empirically (Prosen et al., 1983).

Apart from the word *endogenomorphic*, which has passed into general, if limited, use, Klein's model has been almost totally ignored. However, the three divisions of the model (Fig. 4.1) form a convenient backdrop against which to systematize the literature on cognitive processing in depression and to examine the interrelationships between the various areas of theory and research. This chapter reviews recent attempts to understand the changes in thinking and behavior that accompany depression and the relationship between these changes and depressed mood. The first section covers studies demonstrating a deterioration on tests of psychomotor performance, learning, and memory. These changes are related to the clinical symptom of psychomotor retardation, and they appear to result primarily from an inability to sustain effort or concentration. The second section reviews the evidence that there is also a qualitative shift in the way in which information is processed by depressed pepole or by volunteers subjected to an experimental mood-induction procedure. This change may be characterized as a relative increase in the prominence of unpleasant material. The third section discusses research dealing with the contribution of attitudinal factors to the causation and maintenance of depressed mood.

For the most part, the psychological literature has not taken account of the clinical distinction between endogenomorphic and reactive depressions. This does not automatically invalidate the results to be described, as the two extreme syndromes do not differ greatly in their manifest symptoms (Nelson & Charney, 1981). As will be seen, however, there are a number of areas in which important results may have been obscured by an inadequate specification of the diagnostic status of the subject population.

4.1. PSYCHOMOTOR RETARDATION

4.1.1. Motor Behavior and Test Performance

Although psychomotor retardation is the most prominent clinical feature of endogenous depression (Nelson & Charney, 1981; see Sections 3.3.1), experimental demonstration of retardation, a prerequisite to any further investigation, proves to be surprisingly difficult. In part, this problem arises from the fact that clinical retardation scores usually derive from the patient's response to questionnaire items; a number of studies have shown that depressed patients perceive themselves as being slower than they actually are (Friedman, 1964; Loeb et al., 1971). Objective demonstration of retardation is not impossible, however. For example, increases in reaction time have been observed in a number of studies (reviewed by Miller, 1975).

The study of whole body activity in depression has not progressed far beyond the demonstration of decreased activity in bipolar patients (Kupfer et al., 1974), despite a number of recent technological advances (Greden & Carroll, 1981). However, experimental studies of speech production have confirmed the clinical observation that depressed patients talk slowly (Hinchcliffe et al., 1971; Pope et al., 1970); additionally, changes in the structure of spontaneous speech have been observed. Pope and co-workers (1970) reported that on days when patients were rated as "highly depressed" their speech was characterized by a high proportion of silence in comparison to "high anxiety, low depression" days; increased pause time has since been confirmed using more accurate recording techniques (Greden & Carroll, 1980; Szabadi et al., 1976). The change was observed among both unipolar and bipolar endogenous depressives and normalized on clinical recovery (Greden et al., 1981a). The fact that pause times were elongated in these studies, whereas phonation times were unchanged, suggests a decrease in the initiation of activity, rather than its performance. This phenomenon may account for the observation that depressed college students made few verbal interjections in conversations with other depressed and nondepressed students (Libet & Lewinsohn, 1973).

In addition to a difficulty in initiating responses, depressed patients also appear to have difficulty in maintaining them for protracted periods. For example, the last of a series of reaction time trials was slower in depressed patients than the first; this change did not occur in controls (Friedman, 1964; Martin & Rees, 1966). An inability to sustain motor effort has also been demonstrated (Cohen et al., 1982c). As discussed in the following section, the inability to sustain effort or concentration has pervasive consequences.

Tests of intellectual speed in depressed patients have given rather equivocal results. Some studies have observed slower performance in endogenous, but not in neurotic, depressed patients (Furneaux, 1956; Martin & Rees, 1966; Payne & Hewlett, 1960), and also in depressed college students (Miller, 1974). However, there have also been a number of reports of normal performance in depressed patients (Colbert & Harrow, 1968; Donnelly et al., 1982; Tucker & Spielberg, 1958). These discrepancies are only to be expected. The evidence suggests that depressed people have difficulty in getting started, then perform normally for a time, until their concentration runs out. In these circumstances, the likelihood of observing a deficit would be high in very short or in protracted tests, but lower in tasks of intermediate length.

4.1.2. Learning and Memory Tasks

Memory problems are a common complaint of depressed people, and a number of studies have reported that the severity of memory impairments is correlated with the severity of depression (Cohen et al., 1982c; Harness et al., 1977; Henry et al., 1973; Sternberg & Jarvik, 1976; Stromgren, 1977). However, there is evidence that these deficits are not primarily problems of learning or memory but, like psychomotor performance deficits, arise out of an inability to sustain effort or concentration. Some studies, for example, have reported impaired learning of the later items in a list, but not of the earlier items (Henry et al., 1973), or impairments on delayed recall, but not on immediate recall (Cohen et al., 1982c; Stromgren, 1977). Furthermore, depressed patients are more likely to demonstrate impairment when memory is tested by free recall than when tested by the ability to recognize previously presented items (Stromgren, 1977); performance on free recall, but not on recognition, depends to some extent on the subjects' willingness to continue dredging through memory for those last few difficult-to-remember items. In a similar vein, depressed subjects were most impaired in learning lists of randomly chosen words, but did not differ from normal controls under conditions where the material to be learned was highly organized (Weingartner & Silberman, 1982).

An alternative account of these results might be that depressed patients fail on more difficult memory tasks. However, this hypothesis runs foul of a number of observations. For example, depressed students were slower than controls to learn a multidimensional discrimination problem when this was the last of a series of tasks but performed normally when the same task was presented earlier in the testing session (Miller et al., 1974, cited in Miller, 1975). In another study, depressed patients performed normally in a task in which the material to be learned was presented incidentally, with no instructions that it was to be memorized, and at the same time performed poorly in memorizing material they had been instructed to learn (Weingartner et al., 1981); again, these results cannot be explained by invoking differences in task difficulty.

Perhaps the most instructive finding in this area is the observation that depressed patients did not differ from controls in remembering lists of words which were clustered in semantically related groups, but they performed significantly worse when the same material was presented in a random order (control subjects found the two conditions equally difficult) (Weingartner et al., 1981). Given the body of evidence already cited, the most likely explanation is that the depressed subjects were unwilling or unable to do the extra work of sorting out the material for themselves. This explanation is also suggested by the observations that depressed subjects impose less order (clustering) on recalled material (Russell & Beekhuis, 1976) and appear to devote less effort to rehearsal of material to be remembered (Hasher and Zacks, 1979).

One study also provides direct evidence that the learning and memory problems of depressed patients stem from an inability to sustain effort or concentration. Cohen and co-workers (1982c) observed that in a group of depressed subjects the intensity of their memory impairment, their ability to sustain motor effort and the severity of their depression were all highly intercorrelated (Cohen et al., 1982c). It is unclear whether, like changes in speech time, this more subtle form of psychomotor retardation is also confined to endogenous depression. Also in need of clarification is the question of whether a causal relationship exists between psychomotor retardation and the inability to experience pleasure, and if so, in which direction.

4.2. PLEASURE AND PAIN

4.2.1. Pleasure

In addition to their general psychomotor retardation endogenous depressives also show a specific decrease in pleasure seeking ("loss of interest") (American Psychiatric Association, 1980; Nelson & Charney, 1981; see Section 3.3.1). This aspect of depression has generated relatively little research, but to compensate, there is a considerable body of theory, which deals with the possibility that the behavior of depressives produces situations in which they experience a reduced frequency of pleasurable events, with a consequent loss of the incentive to engage in pleasure seeking (Eastman, 1976).

One suggestion is that depressives fail to engage in actions that lead to pleasant consequences because their behavior is dominated by actions directed at escaping from or avoiding unpleasant situations (Ferster, 1973; Lewinsohn et al., 1969). A second factor is that when depressed people do produce behaviors that should be rewarded, they frequently are not. Depressed patients have been observed, for example, to receive fewer positive responses from other participants in pair or group interactions (Youngren & Lewinsohn, 1980). Additionally, in self-reinforcement experiments, in which subjects are permitted to judge their own performance by pressing buttons labeled "R" for reward or "P" for punishment, depressed subjects give themselves fewer of the former and more of the latter (Nelson & Craighead, 1977; Lobitz & Post, 1979; Rozensky et al., 1977). A third factor, which applies to situational depressions, is that the consequences of the loss of a major source of gratification will depend on the availability of alternatives; the greater the proportional investment, the more catastrophic the loss (Ferster, 1965; Lazarus, 1968). Some support for this position comes from studies showing that the likelihood of severe depression following bereavement is increased if there are no alternative sources of social support (Clayton et al., 1968; Maddison & Walker, 1967).

More generally, Lewinsohn has suggested that a variety of reinforcement-reducing contingencies may apply in depression. Few events may be reinforcing; of these few may be available in the immediate environment; and for lack of social skill, those responses that would be reinforced are made infrequently (Lewinsohn, 1974; Lewinsohn et al., 1979). Moreover, the situation may be exacerbated by the fact that others find depressed people such bad company that they avoid them, reducing their opportunities for social reinforcement still further (Lewinsohn et al., 1969).

A number of studies have, in fact, furnished empirical demonstrations of an association between reduced frequency of occurrence of pleasant events and severity of depressed mood (Grosscup & Lewinsohn, 1980; Harmon et al., 1980; Lewinsohn & Libet, 1972; Lewinsohn & Graf, 1973; Rehm, 1978). It is unclear, however, what, if any, is the nature of the causal relationship between this environmental impoverishment and depression. Depressed people are found to have fewer and less supportive social relationships (Billings et al., 1983), and in a prospective study, this factor was found to predict the occurrence of depression in response to stress (Monroe et al., 1983). In general, however, there is little support for the idea that a mere reduction in the frequency of pleasant events is depressing. A number of studies have found that a decreased participation in pleasant activities on one day did not result in a depressed mood on the following days (Lewinsohn & Libet, 1972; Lewinsohn & Graf, 1973; Rehm, 1978), and a similar lack of relationship has been observed between level of satisfaction and whether or not subjects were depressed two months later (Tanner et al., 1975). Conversely, inducing depressed patients to increase their participation in pleasant activities has not led to significant clinical improvements (Hammen & Glass, 1975; Padfield, 1976).

Given the observation that depressed people have less pleasure in their lives, a decreased expectation of future enjoyment, leading to a decrease in pleasure seeking, is perfectly understandable. Furthermore, it is not difficult to see how a decrease in motivation could lead to a failure to sustain concentration or effort, as described above. However, the melancholic's inability to experience pleasure when the circumstances do arise is not explained by a decrease in the frequency of such circumstances. A decrease in the enjoyability of potentially pleasant events does not follow inevitably from a decrease in their frequency: Lewinsohn and Mac-Phillamy (1974) found that in old people, the frequency of potentially pleasant events was reduced, but there was no loss of enjoyment when good things did happen. In younger depressed subjects, however, both the frequency and the enjoyability of pleasant events were low. This latter finding has subsequently been replicated (Grosscup & Lewinsohn, 1980); in both of these studies, the subjects were neurotic depressives. This finding does not support Klein's hypothesis that a decreased ability to experience pleasure is categorically associated with endogenomorphic depression (Klein, 1974).

Few theorists have attempted to deal with the problem of the origin of this reduced reinforcer effectiveness. Costello (1972) proposed that it could be a consequence of the disruption of a behavioral chain: if the reward for the final element of a chain is omitted, this is hypothesized to devalue the reinforcers for all the preceding elements, and removal of a reward which terminates many behavioral chains (the "all the eggs in one basket" condition) should have correspondingly widespread consequences. Unfortunately, the theory was not very explicitly stated (the foregoing account is an interpretation), and no experimental research has followed from it. Klinger (1975) reviewed evidence suggesting that loss of reinforcer effectiveness following the loss of a major source of reward was part of an "incentive disengagement cycle," consisting of successive phases of anger, protest, quiescence, and eventual recovery. This also seems a hypothesis worthy of investigation, which it has not yet received.

In fact, there is some evidence that a decrease in the ability to enjoy pleasant activities may be a direct consequence of being in a state of depression, rather than the reverse. Velten (1968) introduced a procedure in which states of elation or depression are induced experimentally, by having subjects read positive or negative self-evaluative statements; numerous studies have demonstrated the success of this mood-induction technique, both in normal subjects (e.g., Aderman, 1972; Natale, 1977; Velten, 1968) and in depressed patients, in whom the preexisting depression may be experimentally exacerbated or attenuated (Coleman, 1975; Raps et al., 1980). Using this method, Carson and Adams (1980) found that the induction of a negative mood state decreased ratings of the enjoyability of pleasant activities, whereas induction of a positive mood state had the opposite effect.

There is little evidence that reduced participation in pleasant events causes depression. However, as discussed in the following section, there is more evidence that an increased exposure to unpleasant events does adversely affect mood. Could it be that the frequency of unpleasant events modulates the ability to experience pleasure? In an empirical approach to this problem, Grosscup and Lewinsohn (1980) observed that in a group of depressed patients studied daily over a six-week period, severity of depression was associated with both a decrease in the frequency of pleasant events and an increase in the frequency of unpleasant events; this dual relationship has also been observed in the day-to-day mood swings of normal subjects (Rehm, 1978). In the Grosscup and Lewinsohn study, a significant inverse relationship was observed between the pleasantness of pleasant events and the frequency of unpleasant events. This observation suggests that reinforcer effectiveness may indeed be reduced in depression as a direct consequence of an increase in punishment. However, a reciprocal interaction between the frequency of pleasant events and the perceived unpleasantness of unpleasant events was also reported, leaving the direction of causality uncertain. As noted above, subjects in this study were mainly neurotic depressives; it is not known whether the same relationships between pleasant and unpleasant events also hold in endogenous depression.

4.2.2. Pain

Like depression, chronic pain states are also associated with sleep disturbances, loss of appetite and libido, inability to concentrate, and loss of interest. Indeed, the phenomenological similarities are so striking that it has frequently been suggested that depression and chronic pain states may represent alternative manifestations of a common underlying pathology. Although most reviewers tend to conclude against this position (e.g., Maruta et al., 1976; Pilowsky & Bassett, 1982), it does appear that the incidence of depressive disorders is elevated among first degree relatives of chronic pain patients (Schaffer et al., 1980).

Conversely, depressed patients are likely to complain of somatic distress, such as headaches or stomache aches (G. Davis et al., 1979). Although there are some exceptions (Joseph & Reus, 1981; Lewinsohn et al., 1973), most studies have found that some depressed patients are actually relatively insensitive to experimentally induced pain (G. Davis et al., 1979; Hall & Stride, 1954; Hemphill et al., 1952; von Knorring, 1975). It is likely that to some extent, these results were artefactual, since the methods used confound changes in sensitivity to the pain with changes in deciding whether to report it or not; however, it is clear that not all of the results can be explained away as changes in the response criterion (G. Davis et al., 1979).

In contrast to this insensitivity to physical pain, which may reflect the body's attempt to cope with high levels of somatic distress (see Section 18.1), depressed patients appear to have a greatly increased sensitivity to unpleasant events of other kinds; indeed, it seems likely that their somatic complaints may reflect their high level of psychic pain. Depressed patients rated specific stressful life events as more unpleasant than did controls (Lewinsohn & Tarkington, 1979; Schless et al., 1974), and, significantly, depressed people were more upset by recent stressful life events than a control group who had been equally stressed but had not become depressed (Hammen & Cochran, 1981). In social situations, depressed people are particularly slow to respond following a negative social reaction, such as disagreement or criticism, and such reactions lead to a greater suppression of behavior in depressed patients than in controls (Grosscup & Lewinsohn, 1980). In these circumstances, it is perhaps not surprising that the frequency of unpleasant events is correlated with severity of depressed mood (Grosscup & Lewinsohn, 1980; Rehm, 1978).

Increased sensitivity to aversive events is in fact but one facet of a more general change in information processing, in the direction of an increased response to negative events and a decreased response to positive events. The tendency of depressed patients to award themselves fewer merits and more demerits has already been commented upon. Similarly, when rating videotapes of their own behavior, depressed subjects overestimated negative behaviors and underestimated positive behaviors (Roth & Rehm, 1980), and they were also found to underestimate their performance on (supposedly) a "social intelligence" test (Wener & Rehm, 1975). These findings are complemented by the observation that depressed people see themselves as less socially competent (Kanfer & Zeiss, 1983; Lewinsohn et al., 1980). Compared with nondepressed controls, depressed patients underestimated the amount of positive feedback they had received in an experimental task, but recalled negative feedback accurately, although equal feedback was provided to both groups (de Monbreun & Craighead, 1977; Nelson & Craighead, 1977). Even in a situation in which depressed patients really had received fewer rewards and more punishments, they still underestimated the former and overestimated the latter (Gotlib, 1981).

This information processing bias is also seen in memory experiments. Following a test in which subjects had been asked whether or not they were described by each of a list of adjectives, depressed subjects remembered more "depression-related" words, whereas controls remembered more neutral words (Derry & Kuiper, 1981). Compared with nondepressed controls, depressed patients also recalled fewer of the positive themes of a story, while showing normal recall of negative or neutral themes (Breslow et al., 1981). Moreover, these effecs do not apply simply to memories related to the experimental situation; depressed patients also appear to have a memory for events out of their own personal history which is qualitatively different from that of nondepressed subjects. They recall more unpleasant and fewer pleasant events (Fogarty & Hemsley, 1983; Lishman, 1972), and they recall unpleasant events faster, and pleasant events more slowly (Lloyd & Lishman, 1975), although the latter effect is somewhat unreliable (Clark & Teasdale, 1982).

These results could mean one of two things: either that people for whom unpleasant events are highly salient are likely to become depressed, or, more interestingly, that depressed mood actually biases the retrieval of information from memory, and other related aspects of information processing. The former explanation receives some support from the finding that unpleasant self-referent information is particularly salient for neurotic individuals (Martin et al., 1983; Young & Martin, 1981), coupled with the observation that women with high levels of neuroticism during pregnancy were more likely to develop postnatal depressions (Meares et al., 1976). However, two lines of evidence suggest that the latter explanation is also correct: depressed mood does cause a systematic information-processing bias. First, a number of studies have demonstrated that the accessibility of information in memory is biased toward the retrieval of unpleasant memories when a state of depressed mood is induced experimentally in nondepressed subjects; conversely, retrieval of pleasant memories is facilitated by a state of experimentally induced elation. A variety of mood induction procedures have been used to demonstrate these effects, including hypnosis (Bower, 1981), success or failure on a computer game (Isen et al., 1978), and the Velten (1968) procedure of reading joyful or dismal statements (Teasdale & Fogarty, 1979; Teasdale & Taylor, 1981; Teasdale et al., 1980). Second, in a study of a group of depressed patients who showed marked diurnal variations in their depressed mood, Clark and Teasdale (1982) observed the same set of biases: within the same subject, memories of unhappy events were more likely to be retrieved when severely depressed, and memories of happy events were more likely to be retrieved when they were less depressed. There studies demonstrate that at least in part, increased prominence of aversive information is a direct consequence of depressed mood, rather than a preexisting personality trait of depressed people.

The mechanisms by which a depressed mood selectively primes the accessibility in memory of unpleasant memories have not yet been fully determined. To some extent, the increased recall of unpleasant personal memories by depressed people may reflect state-dependent learning. This explanation assumes that unpleasant events are more likely to have been experienced in the context of an unhappy mood and as the context forms a part of the memory trace, an unhappy mood will subsequently serve as a cue to prime the recall of these memories (Bower, 1981). However, this is not the whole story. A depressed mood has been found to prime the selective recall of unpleasant items among a mixture of pleasant, unpleasant, and neutral items persented in the same previous mood state (Teasdale, 1983). It appears, therefore, that a depressed mood biases information processing towards unpleasant memories over and above any state dependent effects that might be present.

4.3. ATTITUDES

4.3.1. Self-Esteem

The results outlined in the previous section show that a systematic negative bias in information processing permeates the thinking of depressed people. These results provide strong support for an account of depression put forward by Beck (1967, 1974), in which depressed pepole are characterized by a negative "cognitive set," comprising a negative view of themselves, the world, and the future. This cognitive triad permeates their thinking, their fantasies, and even their dreams. According to Beck's theory, cognitive distortions arise from early traumatic experiences, such as parental loss or deprivation, or peer group rejection, which condition responses to stress in later life (Brown & Harris, 1978; Lloyd,

1980a). Studies described above attest to a negative set in relation to the world and the self; in addition, a number of studies have confirmed that depressed people are indeed hopeless, in the sense of having a pessimistic view of the future (Minkoff et al., 1973; Prociuk et al., 1976). Of the three members of the cognitive triad, a negative view of the self is central; low self-esteem causes depressives to see themselves as unworthy of pleasure and, consequently, to view the world as barren and overdemanding, and to project "pseudolosses" into the future so that possible unpleasant events are experienced as inevitable (Beck, 1967, 1974). Numerous other accounts of depression concur in attributing major importance to the concept of low self-esteem (reviewed by Becker, 1979).

As a description of depression, Beck's theory is uncontroversial. However, the theory goes beyond description and attributes causal significance to the depressive cognitive style. With the possible exception of bipolar depression and severe endogenous unipolar depressions, depression is viewed as being primarily a thought disorder, of which dysphoric mood is a secondary manifestation, in contrast to the traditional view of depression as a primary mood disorder, which may also influence thinking. Apparently strong support for Beck's position comes from studies demonstrating the experimental induction of mood states by cognitive manipulations. Ludwig (1975), for example, found that depression could be introduced in women students by giving them the (falsified) results of psychological tests, which indicated that they were immature and uncreative. Similarly, many studies, some of which were cited above, demonstrate mood induction by the Velten (1968) procedure of reading statements aloud, under instructions to attempt to believe them.

The adequacy of the Velten technique has recently been questioned by two studies which suggest that subjects in these experiments may simply be responding to the "demand characteristics" of the task. In these studies, it was found that subjects who were instructed to "act as if" they were depressed or elated did not differ in their questionnaire and test performance from subjects exposed to the mood-induction procedure (Buchwald et al., 1981; Polivy & Doyle, 1980). These results could mean that in mood-induction experiments, subjects do not change their mood, but only produce the responses that they think the experimenter wants to hear. Alternatively, they could mean that asking a subject to simulate depression or elation is itself an effective mood-induction procedure; essentially, this is what is involved in hypnotic mood-induction (Bower, 1981).

There is some support for this latter position: both mood-induction subjects and demand-characteristic controls reported in a debriefing session that they had actually felt the appropriate emotion (Polivy & Doyle, 1980). Additionally, some of the results of mood induction experiments can not easily be explained away as subject compliance. For example, Teasdale and Fogarty (1979) found that the retrieval of a pleasant memory in response to a prompting word was slower for "sad" subjects, whereas unhappy memories took longer for "happy" subjects; in both cases, the instructions were to respond as quickly as possible. Furthermore, mood induction procedures have also been shown to produce several of the behavioral changes associated with depression, such as an increase in speech pause time (Goodwin & Williams, 1983; Natale, 1977). It therefore seems likely that the Velten procedure and similar techniques of "mood-induction" really do induce mood. However, whether they do so via a belief in the information provided, as required by Beck's theory, or by some other means, such as reinstating a sad memory, remains uncertain.

A convincing demonstration that depressive thinking can induce depressed mood in these short-term experiments would not, in any case, answer the question of whether depressed people do in fact have a preexisting depressive "cognitive style," which predisposes them to become depressed, as assumed by Beck and by many other theorists. One study has attempted to address this issue by surveying depression-related attitudes in a large community sample, who were then followed for up to a year (average 8 months) and reassessed. Although subjects who were depressed at the time of the initial assessment showed various signs of depressive thinking, including low self-esteem, subjects who became depressed during the course of the study did not differ on initial assessment from those who did not become depressed (Lewinsohn et al., 1981).

These findings suggest that depressive thinking is not a personality characteristic of to-be-depressed people. However, they do not rule out a causal role of depressive thinking (for example, low self-esteem) in the onset of a depressive episode. Many clinical accounts have emphasized that the important feature of people who become depressed is not so much that their self-esteem is low but that their self-esteem is vulnerable and is liable to evaporate in the face of stresses with which others would cope adequately (Arieti & Bemporad, 1980; Becker, 1979). (This position is, of course, compatible with the behavioral hypotheses described above, which emphasize the risk of placing too great a reliance on a major source of gratification.) As the two assessments in the study by Lewinsohn and co-workers (1981) were separated by several months, the study did not address the possibility that depressive thinking may be an immediate antecedent of depressed mood.

A further problem in assessing these results is that their generality to other depressed populations is uncertain. The study found that people who had been depressed previously but were not depressed at the first assessment did not differ from people who had never been depressed (Lewinsohn et al., 1981). Another recent study also found evidence for a depressive cognitive style in severely depressed patients, which normalized on clinical recovery (Hamilton & Abramson, 1983). However, others have found marked differences between previously depressed subjects and those who had never been depressed, including an unhappy outlook and low self-esteem (Altman & Wittenborn, 1980; Cofer & Wittenborn, 1980).

Another approach to the problem of whether depressive thinking precedes or merely accompanies depressive episodes is via the concept of "schema"—an organized and structured body of information stored in memory (Rumelhart & Ortony, 1977). In most people, the self-schema serves as a powerful organizer of information. For example, following a task in which subjects were required to make judgments about the semantic (Does this word mean the same as . . . .?) or self-referent (Does this word refer to you?) status of a list of adjectives, substantially better recall was found for self-referring words than for potentially self-referring words that were rejected or for adjectives that were the subject of a semantic judgment (Derry & Kuiper, 1981; Rodgers et al., 1977). Using a similar technique, Davis and Unruh (1981) found that the strength of the self-schema, as measured by the degree of organization of words in memory, was weak in short-term depressives (5 months), as compared to nondepressed controls and to long-term depressives (3 years). These results were interpreted as meaning that at the onset of depression, the self-concept undergoes a radical reorganization. A considerable time elapses before it reassumes its preeminent organizing position, and then the "new self" is different from the "old self"; as noted above, the depressive self-schema differs from normal in containing a high proportion of self-derogatory material (Derry & Kuiper, 1981). The implication is that depressive thinking develops during rather than before the depression.

In a similar vein, depressed patients newly admitted to hospital were found to have high scores on a scale measuring "temporal disintegration" (Kirstein & Bukberg, 1979). The significance of this observation is that scores on the temporal disintegration scale have been found to correlate highly with feelings of depersonalization (Freeman & Melges, 1977, 1978). These findings suggest that acutely depressed patients experience a discontinuity in the way in which they perceive themselves, which argues against depression simply being an intensification of preexisting personality structures.

4.3.2. Learned Helplessness

A second cognitive approach to depression, which in recent years has generated an unprecedented volume of research (see, e.g., Garber & Seligman, 1980), is the learned helplessness hypothesis (Seligman, 1975). Based originally on animal experiments, which will be described in Chapter 7, this hypothesis proposed that depression is the outcome of learning that one is unable to control the outcome of ongoing events; aversive events as such do not engender depression unless they are perceived as being uncontrollable (Seligman, 1975). Learning that one is helpless was held to have consequences in three areas: motivational (retarded initiation of voluntary responses, a consequence of the expectation that responses will be without effect), cognitive (difficulty in learning that responses do produce outcomes), and emotional (depressed mood).

Most early studies of learned helplessness in humans concentrated on the cognitive rather than the affective manifestations. In a typical experiment, Hiroto (1974) exposed one group of student volunteers to loud noises, which they could terminate by pressing a button four times; for a second group, the noise was uncontrollable, because it started and stopped independently of anything they did; a third group were not exposed to noise. Subsequently, all subjects were tested on a "finger shuttle box," an apparatus in which noise could be terminated by moving a finger from one side of the box to the other. Unlike the other groups, the subjects who had experienced uncontrollable noise failed to solve this extremely simple problem. Similar results have been reported in many other studies, employing a wide range of uncontrollable aversive events ranging from strong electric shocks to popular music, though most frequently loud noise or insoluble anagram problems have been used. Typically, performance deficits have been demonstrated in the finger shuttle box or in anagram solving, though other tests have also been employed (reviewed by Abramson et al., 1980; Garber et al., 1979; Seligman, 1978).

Although the design of these studies does suggest that uncontrollability is the critical element that gives rise to the performance deficits, this interpretation has not gone unchallenged. One alternative explanation suggests that uncontrollable events may simply be more stressful than controllable events (Costello, 1978). However, while there is evidence from animal studies to support this idea (e.g., Weiss, 1968), it seems rather implausible as an explanation of human helplessness effects, given that performance is impaired following exposure to insoluble discrimination problems, but that performance is normal following exposure to controllable high-intensity electric shock (Seligman, 1978). A more serious problem is that although uncontrollable aversive events, such as noise or insoluble anagrams, do usually produce subsequent performance deficits, often there are no impairments (Buchwald et al., 1978; Seligman, 1978), and performance may even be facilitated (Roth & Kubal, 1976; Thornton & Jacobs, 1972). In general, impairments are seen when subjects are forced to experience failure in a task, but not when they know from the outset that success will not be possible (Buchwald et al., 1978). This suggests that the perception of noncontingency between response and outcome, which is the central construct in helplessness theory, may be less important than the experience of failure on problems that the subject has been led to believe are soluble (Coyne et al., 1980b). A further problem concerns the generality of helplessness effects. Cole and Coyne (1977), for example, found that failure to escape from noise interfered with subsequent performance on anagram solving if subjects saw the latter task as part of the same experiment, but not if they were given to believe that the second task was part of a different experiment.

Although the significance of much of the human helplessness research is questionable, because it was carried out on mildly depressed college students rather than on depressed patients (Costello, 1978; Depue & Monroe, 1978), a number of studies have demonstrated that severely depressed patients show performance deficits similar to those seen in nondepressed volunteers subjected to a helplessness induction procedure (Abramson et al., 1978a; Price et al., 1978; Raps et al., 1980). A similar point applies to studies of mood induction in relation to Beck's cognitive triad. In general, experimental mood induction procedures in nondepressed subjects produce results similar to those obtained in clinical populations (see previous section, and Goodwin & Williams, 1983).

However, the learned helplessness hypothesis of depression makes some very specific predictions regarding the circumstances in which performance deficits would be expected among depressed subjects, and although many of these predictions have been confirmed (Seligman, 1978), others have not (Buchwald et al., 1978; McNitt & Thornton, 1978; Rizley, 1978; Willis & Blaney, 1978). Additionally, in the minority of studies that investigated the effects of helplessless induction procedures on mood, rather than on performance, increases in depression are sometimes seen, but this finding is far from universal, and increases in anxiety and hostility are equally common (Blaney, 1977; Buchwald et al., 1978).

A particular problem for the learned helplessness hypothesis is to explain why depressed people feel such intense guilt over situations over which they have no control; many authors have seen the coexistence of helplessness and guilt as a major paradox. Why, if depressed people feel unable to control events, do they feel an inordinate responsibility for bad situations? A number of potential resolutions were discussed and rejected by Abramson and Sackheim (1977), including the possibility that these symptoms are present in different groups of depressed patients. This seems unlikely; although there is some evidence that helplessness and guilt are relatively independent phenomena (Blatt et al., 1976, 1982), they do occur together in a significant proportion of depressed patients (Abramson & Sackheim, 1977; Beck, 1967; Blatt et al., 1982). It should be noted that the coexistence of guilt and helplessness is not a problem for Beck's account of depression, in which depressives see themselves in the worst possible light, in relation to both past events (guilt) and future events (helplessness).

4.3.3. The Reformulated Learned Helplessness Hypothesis

As a result of the growing number of discrepancies between the theory and the clinical and experimental evidence, the theory of learned helplessness was reformulated in 1978, within an attributional farmework

(Abramson et al., 1978b). The reformulated hypothesis is based on the assumption that "when a person finds that he is helpless, he asks himself why" (Abramson et al., 1978b, p. 50). It is asserted that subjects come to see themselves as helpless if they perceive a lack of contingency between their responses and the outcome (as in the earlier version), but only if they make an appropriate attribution as to the cause of their failure. Attributions may be specific to the particular situation or global, they may be stable or unstable in time, and they may be internal or external to the person. An example of a global, stable and internal attribution might be "I failed the test because I am stupid," whereas "I failed the test because the examiner was in a bad mood today" would be a specific, unstable, external attribution. These three factors determine, respectively, whether performance failures will be broad or narrow, whether they will be chronic or acute, and whether or not self-esteem will be damaged (Abramson et al., 1978b).

Somewhat oddly for a theory of depression, depressed mood is largely outside the scope of the reformulated learned helplessness hypothesis: it is postulated that depressed mood is the result of "the expectation that bad outcomes will occur, not from their expected uncontrollabilty" (Abramson et al., 1978b, p. 65), which, of course, does not differ significantly from Beck's formulation. In addition, "intensity of depressed affect may depend on whether the person views his helplessness as universal or personal . . . failure attributed to internal factors, such as lack of ability, produces greater negative affect than failure attributed to external factors such as task difficulty. The intensity of cognitive and motivational components of depression, however, does not depend on whether helplessness is universal or personal" (Abramson et al., 1978b, p. 65).

According to Abramson and co-workers (1978b, p. 66) the emphasis on internal attributions resolves the paradox of guilt and helplessness (although the reformulated theory still does not actually explain why depressed people should feel guilty). Additionally, the reformulated theory is able to explain many of the discrepant findings of helplessness induction experiments. However, a number of empirical findings are not explained. One example is a study by Coyne and co-workers, in which the disruptive effects of helplessness induction on later performance were alleviated by "attentional redeployment," in the form of an imagination excercise; it was suggested that interference effects are caused not by attributions of helplessness, but by the high levels of anxiety generated by the induction procedure (Coyne et al., 1980b).

In addition to empirical difficulties, the reformulated hypothesis also begs many theoretical questions, such as whether the model uses the appropriate attributional dimensions. One study, for example, suggests that attributions about the consequences of events may be more relevant to depression than attributions about their causes (Hammen & DeMayo, 1982). Some other issues are whether subjects in helplessness experiments all use the same kind of strategy (Diener & Dweck, 1978), whether the concept of noncontingency is actually an easy one for people to use (Buchwald et al., 1978), and whether attributions are systematically related to behavior (Wortman & Dintzer, 1978). Additionally, the theory fails to specify the conditions under which particular attributions will be made (Huesmann, 1978; Wortman & Dintzer, 1978), which considerably weakens its explanatory power.

Despite these failings, the reformulated learned helplessness hypothesis has been extremely influential in generating large amounts of research, in a variety of different areas (see Garber & Seligman, 1980). In relation to depression, the main focus has been the question of whether depressed people do actually make the attributions ascribed to them by the model.

Although there are some exceptions (Golin et al., 1981; Seligman et al., 1979), most studies have not supported the idea that depressives attribute their failures to causes that are global and stable (Hammen & Cochran, 1981; Harvey, 1981; Kuiper, 1978; Manly et al., 1982; Pasahow, 1980; Rizley, 1978). Arguably, the internal–external dimension provides a more important test of the hypothesis, because it is held that the attribution of failure to personal (internal) causes has specific effects on depressed mood (see above). Results in this area are inconclusive. Laboratory studies using uncontrollable situations manipulated by the experimenter have found that depressives do tend to attribute their failures to internal causes, such as lack of ability (Klein et al., 1976; Kuiper, 1978; Litman-Adizes, 1978; Rizley, 1978), though attributions about success are made less consistently (Kuiper, 1978; Rizley, 1978). Some studies in more naturalistic settings have also supported the concept of a depressive "attributional style" in mildly (Harvey, 1981; Golin et al., 1981; Seligman et al., 1979) and severely (Raps et al., 1982) depressed subjects. However, rather more of the real-world studies fail to support this relationship (Coyne et al., 1980a; Feather & Barber, 1983; Hammen & Cochran, 1981; Hammen & DeMayo, 1982; Lewinsohn et al., 1981; Manly et al., 1982).

The question of whether depressive thinking antedates depression has already been touched upon. Like Beck's theory, the learned helplessness hypothesis also postulates that depressive thinking causes and therefore should antedate the onset of episodes of depression. Peterson and co-workers (1983) reported that changes in attributional style did precede mood swings in a single rapidly cycling bipolar patient. Three other studies have not observed this relationship, however. One was the prospective community study by Lewinsohn and co-workers, which has already been described (Lewinsohn et al., 1981); a second was a study of postpartum depression, in which depression and attributional style were assessed during the third trimester of pregnancy, and again on the third day postpartum (Manly et al., 1982); the third was a study of college students assessed on two occasions separated by one month (Golin et al., 1981).

Two further problems must be noted. First, not only are increases in anxiety and hostility as frequent as increases in depression in response to helplessness induction procedures (Blaney, 1977; Buchwald et al., 1978), but similar manipulations have also been used to study a remarkable range of psychological conditions, including repression, anxiety, stress, frustration, achievement motivation, and even schizophrenia (Coyne et al., 1980b). Second, it is unclear to whom the learned helplessness hypothesis of depression is supposed to apply (Depue & Monroe, 1978). Originally, the hypothesis was proposed to account for reactive depression (Seligman, 1975). However, as discussed in the Section 3.2.3, reactive depression, in the sense of depression precipitated by environmental events, does not seem to be a particularly valid concept, because environmental events are found to precipitate both endogenous and neurotic (reactive) depressions equally (Brown & Harris, 1978; Lewinsohn et al. 1977; Paykel, 1979b). More recently, it has been proposed that learned helplessness is the causal factor in "helplessness depressions" (Seligman, 1978), but no criteria have been proposed to break the circularity of this argument (but see Section 4.4.2).

4.4. THE PSYCHOLOGY OF DEPRESSION

4.4.1. Theory and Research

Since the early 1970s, it has become increasingly clear that depression can no longer be viewed as a circumscribed disorder of mood, with no other attendant alterations in cognitive functioning. The most significant findings concern the processing of affective information. Not only are pleasant events less frequent in depression, and unpleasant events more frequent, but also, the affective quality of both is biased in the aversive direction; there are also reciprocal interrelationships between the frequency of one type of event and the affective quality of the other. The descriptive features of depression are consistent with the ideas of Beck and Lewinsohn, which are shown to be complementary. However, the learned helplessness hypothesis, both in its original version (Seligman, 1975) and in its later reformulation (Abramson et al., 1978b), has received much less support. Furthermore, the primacy of depressive thinking, assumed by Beck (1967, 1974) and by the learned helplessness theorists, is challenged by studies demonstrating that depressed mood biases the processing of affective information; it seems unlikely that these results can be written off as "experimenter effects."

Irrespective of the extent to which the evidence supports any particular theory, it is clear that there is a diversity of traps though which a mildly depressed person might fall and spiral downwards. Depressed mood produces cognitive distortions, which increase the salience of unpleasant events, which further depresses mood. Sad thoughts increase the accessibility of unpleasant memories, which further increase sad thoughts. A high level of unpleasant events will decrease the pleasantness of pleasant events, leading to a decrease in pleasure seeking, a reduction in the frequency of pleasant events, and a consequent increase in the unpleasantness of unpleasant events. Other similar amplification processes may be readily identified. Once a state of depression is established, the literature is replete with mechanisms which would tend to maintain it.

In contrast to the consensus emerging over the nature of cognitive and behavioral changes in depression, research into the psychological antecedents of depression has been less successful. The occurrence of unpleasant events does appear to influence mood adversely. Although the effect of major life events, such as bereavement, has not yet been considered in detail (see Section 20.1), it is worth noting the possibility that chronic low-grade stresses and strains may be potent antecedents of depression, perhaps outweighing major life stresses (Billings et al., 1983; Kanner et al., 1981). However, there is little support in the literature either for the position that depression arises out of a lack of opportunity to engage in pleasant activities or for the hypotheses of Beck and Seligman that depression arises out of a set of preexisting depressive attitudes.

One psychological attribute that does appear to predispose to depression is introversion (Akiskal et al., 1983; Hirschfeld & Klerman, 1979). More specifically, introversion may be a characteristic of endogenomorphic depressions, as high introversion scores are associated with nonsuppression of serum cortisol in the dexamethasone suppression test (DST: Section 3.3.2) (Bryer et al., 1983). Gray (1970) has proposed that the introversion–extraversion dimension is in fact derived from two underlying dimensions of susceptibility to rewards and to punishments. In conditioning experiments, introverts are found to perform worse than extraverts when rewards (e.g., approval) are used, but they perform better than extraverts in response to punishment (e.g., disapproval) (Gray 1970, 1981; McCord & Wakefield, 1981). As discussed above, although depressed people tend to be relatively insensitive to physical pain, they are hypersensitive to secondary aversive stimuli, such as disapproval; endogenous depressives are also insensitive to rewards. As far as these two dimensions are concerned, therefore, endogenous depression could be viewed as an intensification of the processes already occurring in introverts.

4.4.2. On the Heterogeneity of Depression (Again)

It is possible that the general inconclusiveness of most studies that attempt to identify other psychological antecedents of depression may simply reflect the heterogeneity of depressive syndromes. Although the learned helplessness hypothesis, in particular, has been pilloried in the literature for failing to take account of this diversity, the same criticism may be levelled at the great majority of the studies surveyed in this chapter. It is important therefore to reiterate that there is good reason to differentiate between endogenomorphic and reactive (Klein, 1974) forms of both mild (Akiskal et al., 1979) and severe (Nelson & Charney, 1981) depression.

However, the overlap is considerable, Klein (1974) suggested that endogenomorphic depressions are characterized by an underactive "pleasure center," possibly, but not necessarily, accompanied by depressive thinking; reactive depressions, on the other hand, are heavily invested with depressive thoughts, arising from an overreaction to frustration, but involve no change in the ability to experience pleasure. This categorical separation is untenable. In a rare study that did compare well-defined diagnostic groups, Giles and Rush (1981) found that depressive thinking was equally as frequent in endogenous as in reactive depressions (although there was a more subtle difference: only in the reactive group was there a correlation between depressive attitudes and severity of depression). Conversely, an increase in unpleasant events, which was proposed as the cause of reactive depression, has been demonstrated in three studies to reduce the pleasantness of pleasant events, which in Klein's scheme should only occur in endogenomorphic depressions (Grosscup & Lewinsohn, 1980; Rehm, 1978; Carson & Adams, 1980). In the light of these studies, it seems possible that an increase in unpleasant events could be responsible for both forms of depression. This conclusion accords with the observation that environmental precipitants are no less common in endogenous than in reactive depressions (Brown & Harris, 1978; Lewinsohn et al., 1977; Paykel, 1979b).

If, as seems likely, an explanation for the differences between endogenous and reactive depressions is not to be found in their etiology, it must be sought elsewhere. Clearly, the psychological impact of stressful life events is more important than their occurrence: even in bereavement, the progression to prolonged depression only happens in some 5% of cases (Parkes, 1972). Beck recently expanded the cognitive perspective by suggesting that personality differences may be the major determinant. Two extreme personality types are described. *Autonomous* people set their own standards and obtain pleasure from "doing" and reaching goals; their depressions are permeated by themes of defeat or failure. *Socially dependent* people rely for their satisfaction on the approval of others, and when depressed are preoccupied with themes of deprivation and rejection. Autonomous people have autonomous, or endogenous, depressions: they have failed in their own terms, and so lose their motivation. They are unable to gain satisfaction or experience pleasure, and blaming themselves for their failure, they minimize the importance of environmental precipitants. Socially dependent people have reactive depressions: believing that nobody cares, they will show temporary mood improvements if they receive a strong input of attention and reassurance. Because relationships with the outside world are central to the socially dependent person, precipitants are much more obvious and may be exaggerated in a desparate clinging attempt to regain love or affection (Beck, 1983).

Although the validity of this typology has yet to be determined, it does appear to offer a much-needed framework for future research. One interesting feature of Beck's clinical picture of the autonomous depression is the extent to which this condition resembles learned helplessness, both in its symptomatology and in the conditions that cause it. This suggests that future tests of the learned helplessness hypothesis might be more consistently successful if confined to subjects with endogenous depressions. In general, it would seem to be important that future psychological research recognizes the heterogeneous nature of depression. At the very least, the characteristics of the subject population on the endogenous–nonendogenous dimension should be described, and some attempt should be made to assess the contribution of this variable when discrepancies in the literature arise.

4.4.3. The Cognitive Bridge

A recent review of cognitive changes in depression concluded that "although we have learned a great deal about the biology of mood disorder and about the psychology of disordered mood, surprisingly little research has been accomplished that would bring these two types of research endeavours together in a systematic manner. This may be most effectively accomplished in considering cognitive processes in the mood disorders" (Weingartner & Silberman, 1982, p. 40). As anticipated in Chapter 2, this research opens up for discussion two important and neglected areas of research. First, the concepts of reward (pleasure) and punishment (pain), which assume a central importance in the analysis of the cognitive underpinnings of depression, have been the subject of extensive neuropsychological investigation in experimental animals, along with other related issues in the psychology of motivation. Consequently, a rich source of evidence may be brought to bear on the problem of depression. The prospecting of this mine is one of the major concerns to be addressed in Part 3 of this book. Second, the identification of these underlying processes provides a platform from which to assess systematically the validity of animal models of depression. This review is carried out in Chapters 6 and 7.

Before investing time in looking at animal research, however, it is as well to address the question of whether there might be something uniquely human about depression which would preclude the admissibility of evidence from animal sources. This debate is usually conducted around the question of whether animals are capable of experiencing depression, which is invariably sterile because, for all practical purposes, we have no access to the subjective experience of animals. Another, more pertinent, question is whether the human brain is sufficiently similar to that of other species to allow useful comparisons to be made. The particular problem is that the development of language has led to an unprecedented degree of specialization in the human brain. The next chapter examines the consequences of these developments.

five

▬

SOME NEUROPSYCHOLOGICAL CONSIDERATIONS

A general feature of the brain of all vertebrate species is that the left side of the brain controls the right side of the body, and vice versa. In addition to this lateralization of perceptual and motor function, in the human brain there are also functional differences betwen the two cerebral hemispheres. Traditionally, lateralization of function has been conceptualized in terms of differences in abilities and in cognitive style: the left hemisphere is specialized for analytic, sequential functions, exemplified by language, and the right for holistic, parallel functions, exemplified by the processing of visuospatial information. These relationships tend to be more marked in right-handed subjects, and in some left-handers, the right hemisphere may be dominant for language (see Harnad et al., 1977; Kinsbourne, 1978a).

5.1. THE LATERALIZATION OF EMOTIONAL FUNCTION

In addition to these intellectual specializations, there is also evidence that the right hemisphere plays a special role in the perception and expression of emotion, and particularly in the negative emotions (Galin,

1974; Flor-Henry, 1979). This chapter reviews evidence from a variety of different convergent sources which support the conclusion that depressed mood is associated with increased activation of the right frontal lobe, in relation to that of the left frontal lobe and of posterior regions of the right hemisphere. These changes appear to be specific for depression; a different pattern of hemispheric function, activation of the left hemisphere, is seen in anxiety and schizophrenia (reviewed by Flor-Henry, 1976, 1979; Tucker, 1981).

5.1.1. The Perception and Expression of Emotions

Studies in normal (i.e., nondepressed) subjects strongly indicate that the perception and expression of emotions is primarily a function of the right hemisphere. Right hemisphere involvement in the perception of emotion has been demonstrated by using the fact that stimuli presented to one ear or to one visual hemifield are preferentially transmitted to the other hemisphere. For example, it has been found that emotion in faces is easier to recognize if they are presented to the left half of the field of vision (Campbell, 1978; Lavadas et al., 1980; Suberi & McKeever, 1977), and similarly, there is a left ear superiority in evaluating the emotional quality of voices (Carmon & Nachson, 1973; Haggard and Parkinson, 1971; Safer & Leventhal, 1977). Additionally, clinical studies have found that damage to the right, but not the left, temporo-parietal region impairs the comprehension of the affective components of speech, without disrupting comprehension of the verbal content (Heilman et al., 1975; Tucker et al., 1977).

Similarly, right hemisphere damage has been found to impair the ability to express emotions through inflection of the tone of voice (Ross & Mesulam, 1979). Right hemisphere control of the expression of emotions is also implied by the finding that in normal subjects, emotions are expressed more strongly on the left side of the face, which is controlled from the right side of the brain (Borod & Caron, 1979; Borod et al., 1981; Chaurasia & Goswami, 1975; Ekman et al., 1981; Moscovitch & Olds, 1979, cited by Ekman et al., 1981). In an interesting extension of these studies, subjects were asked about the strategy they used to generate emotional expressions. The majority reported visualizing an image or situation; this was usually located on the left, sometimes straight ahead, and hardly ever on the right (Koff et al., 1983).

In addition to these studies demonstrating a major involvement of the right hemisphere in the perception and expression of emotions, there is also evidence that the left hemisphere has a role in processing positively charged material. Dimond and co-workers used a contact lens system to restrict input to one half of the visual field, while subjects watched a Tom and Jerry cartoon, a travel film, or a film of a major surgical operation. In agreement with the studies described above, material viewed by the left visual hemifield (right hemisphere) was rated as more "unpleasant" and "horrific," and under these viewing conditions, the surgery film also produced a greater increase in heart rate. The cartoon, however, produced a greater increase in heart rate when viewed by the right visual hemifield, suggesting a greater involvement of the left hemisphere in this more pleasant experience (Dimond et al., 1976; Dimond & Farrington, 1977).

There is also evidence implicating the left and right hemispheres in the expression of positive and negative emotions, respectively. Sackheim and co-workers found that composite pictures made up from two left sides of a human face were judged as showing more fear, anger, sadness, and disgust than right-side composites; however, the opposite was true for ratings of happiness (Sackheim & Gur, 1978; Sackheim et al., 1978). Left hemispheric control of happy facial expressions is also apparent in electromyographic (EMG) recordings from the facial muscles involved in smiling. Positive emotions, elicited by loaded questions or by reading positive self-referent statements, were accompanied by a more pronounced increase in EMG activity on the right side of the face (G. Schwartz et al., 1979; Sirota & Schwartz, 1982).

5.1.2. EEG Studies

Electroencephalographic (EEG) recording provides a more direct method for investigating localization of function in the cortex. Although, for most nonclinical purposes, EEG tracings are essentially uninterpretable, they can indicate whether an area of cortex is active (desynchronized, high frequency, low amplitude, beta waves) or inactive (synchronized, low frequency, high amplitude, alpha waves). Davidson and co-workers reported the results of two experiments. In the first, nondepressed subjects watched a television program and continuously recorded their emotional reactions by pressing on a response button; in the second; the subjects generated positive or negative emotional imagery. In both experiments, negative emotional states were associated with relatively greater EEG activation over the right frontal lobe, whereas positive emotional states were associated with relatively greater activation over the left frontal lobe. In addition, greater activation over the right parietal region was seen in both conditions; it is not clear whether this latter observation is related to emotion or to the visual nature of the tasks used (Davidson et al., 1979). The asymmetry of frontal, though not of parietal, activation during self-generated depressed mood has also been observed by other workers (Tucker et al., 1981). Asymmetry of emotional function appears to develop very early in life. In 10-months-old infants, the sight of a happy face has been found to activate the left frontal lobe more than the right; in these experiments, no differential response to sad facial expressions was detected, and neither was any asymmetry in the parietal EEG (Davidson & Fox, 1982). A fourth study appears to demonstrate the opposite effect—

relatively greater activation of the left hemisphere by a negative emotion and inactivation of the left hemisphere by a positive emotion (Harman & Ray, 1977). However, the relevance of these results is uncertain, because the emotions manipulated were anxiety and calmness rather than depression and happiness; the fact that the experimenter talked to the subject throughout the testing session, with a consequent activation of the left hemisphere, also makes these results very difficult to interpret.

In studies of depressed patients, D'Elia and Perris (1973, 1974) originally reported that EEG activation was increased over the left hemisphere. However, these results were obtained using posterior (parieto-occipital) electrodes; the same workers later reported an increase in right frontal activation in depressed patients (Perris & Monakhov, 1979). Two independent studies have confirmed this observation. In one experiment, depressed college students (high scorers on the Beck Depression Inventory) showed greater right frontal activation than did nondepressed subjects; there was no difference in parietal EEG (Schaffer et al., 1983). A similar increase in right frontal activation has been reported in endogenously depressed patients compared with nondepressed controls (Matousek et al., 1981). In this study, the opposite pattern of activation was observed in the parieto-occipital region, which confirms the early observations of D'Elia and Perris (1973, 1974). In another series of studies, it was reported that under resting conditions, depressed patients had a significant increase in EEG activation over the right, but not the left, temporal (Flor-Henry, 1976; Goldstein, 1979) and parietal (Flor-Henry, 1979) regions (frontal electrode placements were not used in these studies).

Although the results of these experiments are usually discussed in terms of an increase in right hemispheric activation, it shold be noted that in general, what is observed is a difference in the right–left ratio, and it is unclear whether this is brought about by an increase in the activation of the right hemisphere at the onset of depression or by a decrease in that of the left. It has been observed that recovery from depression under ECS or imipramine treatment was associated with a significant reduction in fast cortical EEG activity over the anterior part of the right hemisphere and the posterior part of the left hemisphere (Nilsson & Smith, 1965). However, in two studies in which the EEG was recorded periodically during recovery from depression, the major changes were observed in the left hemisphere EEG (D'Elia and Perris, 1973, Goldstein, 1979).

It is also important to note that the increase in right hemisphere EEG activation does not imply an increase in the efficiency of right hemispheric function. Indeed, the reverse appears to be the case. During the performance of either verbal or spatial tasks, in comparison to normal control subjects, depressed patients showed a relative shift of activity from the right to the left hemisphere. (Flor-Henry, 1976, 1979).

5.1.3. Unilateral ECS

A further indication of right hemisphere involvement in depression comes from studies comparing unilateral with bilateral electroconvulsive shock (ECS) treatment. D'Elia and Raotma (1975) reviewed 29 methodologically adequate studies and concluded that unilateral ECS delivered to the non-dominant hemisphere was as effective as bilateral ECS. Indeed, some studies found unilateral nondominant ECS to be superior (Cohen et al., 1974; Halliday et al., 1968). By contrast unilateral dominant ECS is clearly inferior to bilateral ECS, or to nondominant ECS (Halliday et al., 1968; Cronin et al., 1970). Interpretation of these results is confounded a little by the fact that memory loss, a distressing side effect of ECS, is less pronounced when ECS is applied to the nondominant hemisphere (Kendell, 1982; Weiner et al., 1984). However, this factor in itself would not explain why unilateral dominant ECS should be inferior to bilateral ECS, since these procedures equivalent degrees of amnesia.

5.1.4. Neuropsychological Testing

Another group of studies utilizes responses not directly related to emotion, such as lateral eye movements, as indices of lateralized brain activity. Lateral eye movements appear to arise in an area of the frontal lobe sometimes known as the *frontal eye fields*, since stimulation of this area evokes contralateral eye movements (Crosby et al., 1962), and voluntary eye movements are associated with a localized increase in regional cerebral blood flow (Melamed & Larsen, 1977). Schwartz and co-workers reported that when subjects were responding to emotion-laden questions, they made more leftward eye movements, and fewer rightward eye movements, indicating right hemisphere activation (Schwartz et al., 1975). In a later study, when positive and negative emotion questions were studied separately, negative questions again tended to elicit more leftward eye movements; however, the reverse was true for positive questions (though it must be added that the results of this experiment were not particularly convincing) (Ahern & Schwartz, 1979). In a similar study, depressed patients were observed to make significantly more leftward eye movements than controls (Schweitzer, 1979), unlike schizophrenics, who are found to make more rightward eye movements (Schweitzer, 1979; Schweitzer et al., 1978; Gur, 1978). These studies are consistent with the EEG picture of a relatively greater right frontal activation in depression.

Other studies strongly suggest that in depression, the right hemisphere functions inefficiently, as indicated by some of the EEG evidence (see above). Yozawitz and co-workers (1979) found that depressed patients had poor left ear (right hemisphere) scores when pairs of words, syllables, or clicks were presented to the two ears simultaneously; their performance was actually comparable to that of patients with right temporal brain damage. However, the extent of decrements in right hemisphere performance was negatively correlated with the severity of depressive symptoms; it was speculated that right hemisphere dysfunction might be associated with patients' denial of their problems (Bruder & Yozawitz, 1979).

Subsequent studies have replicated the finding that depression is associated with functional impairment of the right hemisphere in perceptual tasks (Johnson & Crockett, 1982; Strauss et al., 1979, cited by Johnson & Crockett, 1982; Wexler & Heninger, 1979). In a similar vein, Gruzelier and Venables (1974) observed a decreased electrodermal response on the right hand of depressed patients to binaurally presented tones; as this response appears to be mediated ipsilaterally, these results also indicate right hemisphere dysfunction. A similar deficit may also be observed in normal subjects. During a period of hypnotically induced depressed mood, the same tone, presented through headphones to both ears, was judged as being louder in the right ear (Tucker et al., 1981).

Formal neuropsychological testing also provides evidence of right hemisphere impairment in depression. It is well established that damage to the dominant hemisphere leads to deficits on tests of verbal ability, whereas nondominant hemisphere damage is associated with impaired performance on tests of visuospatial ability (see e.g., Kinsbourne, 1978a). A number of studies have reported that depressed patients perform poorly on the Categories Test, a test of visual concept formation (Donnelly et al., 1980; Savard et al., 1980); scores on this test are correlated with visuospatial ability as measured by the Wechsler Adult Intelligence Scale (WAIS) performance IQ score (Lansdell & Donnelly, 1977). In the first comprehensive neuropsychological study of depression, Flor-Henry and Yeudall reported that both depressed and manic patients had low WAIS performance IQ scores, and they were also impaired on a variety of other visuospatial tests, but were relatively unimpaired on tests of verbal ability and had normal verbal IQ. Schizophrenics were reported to show the opposite pattern of results (Flor-Henry & Yeudall, 1973; Flor-Henry, 1976). Subsequent studies have confirmed that when a battery of neuropsychological tests are applied, the picture presented by depressed patients is one of impairment on tests of nondominant hemisphere function but relatively normal performance on tests of dominant hemisphere function (Goldstein et al., 1977; Kronfol et al., 1978; Shipley et al., 1981; M. Taylor et al., 1979, 1981).

These results, which consistently show evidence of right hemisphere impairment in depressed patients, have led some researchers to suggest that depression might be a manifestation of underlying right hemisphere pathology (e.g., Flor-Henry, 1976). Although this possibility cannot be excluded in all cases, a number of studies have found that evidence of right hemisphere impairment was no longer present when depressed patients were tested following clinical recovery (Savard et al., 1980; Small et al.,

1972; Kronfol et al., 1978). Similarly, perceptual asymmetries in depressed patients have also been found to normalize with clinical recovery (Johnson & Crockett, 1982; Strauss et al., 1979, cited by Johnson & Crockett, 1982; Wexler & Heninger, 1979).

5.1.5. Effects of Brain Damage

Further evidence of hemispheric differences comes from studies of the effects of brain damage. Gainotti (1972), reporting on a series of 150 patients with unilateral damage, found that 62% of patients with left-sided damage, but only 10% of those with right-sided damage exhibited short-lasting "depressive-catastrophic reactions" of despair, guilt, and feelings of worthlessness; right-sided damage, by contrast, was more likely to lead to feelings of indifference, denial, or even euphoria. More recently, Sackheim and co-workers (1982) confirmed that right-sided brain damage is much more likely than left-sided damage to lead to the expression of positive emotions, whereas left-sided damage was more likely to give rise to negative emotions. While it is quite plausible that a depressive reaction could be a reaction to the speech impairments which follow left-sided injuries, it is difficult to see how the euphoric response to right sided damage could be so explained.

Similar results have been obtained in patients undergoing the carotid barbiturization test (Wada & Rasmussen, 1960), in which a small dose of sodium amytal is injected into one carotid artery, briefly anesthetizing that side of the brain. Terzian (1964) reported that anesthetization of the left hemisphere frequently caused "catastrophic reactions," whereas with right-sided injections, euphoria was equally common. Other workers have also reported this finding (Hecaen & Ajuriaguerra, 1964; Rossi & Rossadini, 1967), although no differences were observed in one study (Milner, 1967), and the opposite pattern has been seen in Japanese subjects (Tsunoda & Oka, 1976), suggesting that localization may be subject to cultural (developmental?) influences.

In many cases, left-damaged patients progress from catastrophic reactions to severe depressions. These have usually been regarded as an understandable response to disability, particularly the impairments of language function which accompany damage to the dominant hemisphere (Charatan & Fisk, 1978; Heilman et al., 1978). However, recent evidence suggests that this explanation may be insufficient, as the location of the damage seems to be more important than the severity of functional impairments. Depression is significantly more frequent in left-sided stroke patients than in orthopedic patients, even when the two groups are comparable in the severity of their functional disability (Folstein et al., 1977; Robinson & Szetela, 1981). In one study, more than 60% of left-sided stroke patients had severe depressions, compared with only 20% of patients who had suffered traumatic brain injury. Analysis of the sites of the lesions, which were localized by brain scan, revealed that the lesions were of a similar size in the two groups, but differed in their location, the stroke group having more anterior damage. For both groups, a highly significant association was found between severity of depression and closeness to the frontal pole (Robinson & Szetela, 1981; Robinson et al., 1982). This observation is in agreement with the evidence from EEG studies that depression involves a decrease in the ratio of left-to-right frontal lobe activity.

In addition to the reactions of indifference or euphoria, depression has also been reported as a consequence of damage to the right hemisphere. Lishman (1973) reviewed 670 cases of penetrating head wounds and found that indifference was related to right frontal damage, but right temporal or parietal damage was more likely to cause depression. Similarly, a high incidence of depression has been reported in association with nondominant temporal lobe epilepsy (Flor-Henry, 1974). Dominant temporal lobe epilepsy and tumors, on the other hand, are reported to be strongly associated with schizophrenia and psychopathic personality disorders and with blunting of affect (Bingley, 1958; Flor-Henry, 1974, 1979). As in the case of depressions associated with left frontal lesions, depression has been found to be significantly more frequent following right-sided strokes than in comparably disabled orthopedic patients (Folstein et al., 1977). In this case, however, brain scans revealed the opposite relationship between depression and localization within the hemisphere: the severity of depression increased with the distance from the frontal pole (Robinson et al., 1982).

This finding resolves the apparent contradiction between the reports that both euphoria and depression may occur as sequelae of nondominant brain damage, because the former is associated primarily with right frontal damage, whereas the latter is associated with damage to the right temporal and parietal regions. This picture is in agreement with the EEG evidence that depression is associated with activation of the anterior regions of the right hemisphere as compared to right posterior regions.

There are some further data that allow speculation on the relationship between psychiatric classification and these two brain loci for depression. Depression associated with right posterior strokes or with right temporal lobe epilepsy is typically associated with neurotic features such as irritability and anxiety (Bear & Fedio, 1977; Flor-Henry, 1974; Folstein et al., 1977; Taylor, 1975). Depression associated with left frontal stroke, on the other hand, appears usually to be of the endogenomorphic type, judging by the fact that 9 of 12 such patients (75%) had abnormal results on the DST, a biological marker for endogenomorphic depressions (see Sections 3.3.2) (Lipsey et al., 1982).

5.1.6. Conclusions

In all of the areas discussed, interpretation of the results is beset by severe methodological problems, including some that have not been mentioned. However, taking all of the evidence together, there are grounds for drawing some tentative conclusions. First, it is clear that the posterior parts of the right cerebral hemisphere are crucially involved in the perception and expression of emotions. Depressed people show evidence of right hemispheric dysfunction, and conversely, damage to right parietal and temporal regions causes reactive depressions. A plausible deduction is that an inability to perceive or express emotions adequately, which is related to a dysfunction of right parieto-temporal regions, could make an important contribution to the lack of social skill seen in many reactive depressives (Section 4.2.1).

Second, it appears that a decrease in left frontal EEG activation is associated with depression, and the negative DST results observed by Lipsey and co-workers (1982) in depressed patients with left frontal damage suggest an association with endogenomorphic depression specifically. As endogenomorphic depression are characterized by an inability to experience pleasure (Section 3.4), this conclusion fits very well with the observations implicating left frontal activation in positive emotional states.

5.2. THE FRONTAL LOBES

As the evidence points strongly toward an association between endogenomorphic depression and changes in frontal lobe activity, it seems appropriate to consider the role of the frontal lobes in brain function. Clinical observations of patients who have suffered damage to the frontal lobes suggest that they suffer from a reduced ability to plan and organize their lives. When required to carry out a sequence of actions, they persistently repeat early elements of the sequence, or their behavior degenerates into conventional or habitual forms. The crucial area appears to be the dorsolateral region of the frontal cortex; these difficulties are not exhibited by patients with damage to other cortical areas, including other parts of the frontal lobes (Luria, 1973; Milner, 1964). More recent studies have formally demonstrated that frontal patients, particularly those with left-sided damage, when required to perform a sequence of responses have a diminished ability to formulate a strategy or to monitor its execution by comparing the memory of responses already performed with the program of those yet to be carried out (Petrides & Milner, 1982; Shallice, 1982). A similar difficulty in performing sequences of responses has also been observed in monkeys after damage to the frontal cortex; again, this impairment appears to be specific to frontal lesions (Brody & Pribram, 1978; Pinto-Hamuy & Linck, 1965; Pribram et al., 1964).

The classic impairments shown by monkeys after frontal damage are an inability to perform in delayed response and delayed alternation tasks (Jacobsen, 1936). As with the planning difficulties experienced by frontal patients, the crucial area of the monkey frontal lobe for producing these impairments is the dorsolateral region (Iversen, 1973; Rosenkilde, 1979). In the delayed response task, the monkey is shown one of the two cups being baited with food, and following a delay during which the cups are out of sight, the monkey is then allowed to displace the cup to take the food. The delayed alternation task is similar; the animal does not see the cups being baited, but the correct response alternates from trial to trial. After frontal lobe lesions, monkeys are severely impaired on these tasks at all but very short delays. The problem is not simply one of memory, however, since in a "go–no go" task, in which the animal responds or withholds its response according to whether the cup was baited or not, frontal-lesioned animals have no difficulty in coping with time delays.

The problem therefore seems to be one of integrating information in space and time. However, this is not the whole story. In the delayed response task, if, instead of presenting the two stimuli symmetrically in front of the animal, the display was offset to one side, frontal lesioned animals performed normally. Similarly, their difficulty in the delayed alternation task could be overcome by alternating short and long delays, thereby introducing a temporal asymmetry (Pribram & Tubbs, 1967; Pribram et al., 1977). In other words, the frontal lesioned animals performed normally when the task could be solved using external cues; they fail when they must rely on their own internal resources to tell right from left or to know which of two responses they performed most recently.

Patients with frontal lobe damage are able to perform the delayed response and delayed alternation tasks. It would be astonishing if this were not the case, given the ease with which verbal strategies can be brought to bear. However, in other tests, they too show clear evidence of a reduced ability to use internal referents for space and time. In general, memory function is intact in patients with frontal lobe damage. However, they made many errors when asked which of two words or pictures they had seen more recently; memory for the relative recency of words was impaired by left frontal damage, whereas right-sided damage had a similar effect on memory for pictures (Milner, 1971, 1982). Disorders of spatial orientation have been demonstrated in a number of studies. For example, frontal patients have difficulty in adjusting a line to the vertical when their own bodies were tilted (Teuber & Mishkin, 1954). Butters and co-workers (1972) asked their subjects to imagine walking a route shown on a street map and to say whether they would turn left or right at each corner; patients with left frontal damage showed a substantial impairment. However, like monkeys with frontal lobe damage (Pohl, 1973), the same patients showed a relatively normal performance on spatial tasks where external cues were provided (Butters et al., 1972). Their difficulties are specifically problems of personal spatial orientation, that is, knowing where the body is in relation to the outside world. This is exemplified by a study of Semmes and co-workers (1963), which found that frontal patients had difficulty in pointing to parts of their own body corresponding to those designated on a diagram. It seems likely that the difficulty experienced by frontal-lobe patients in planning more than the simplest sequence of actions (Shallice, 1982) depends upon their disordered sense of personal space and time. These functions may be the fundamental abilities on which the planning functions of the frontal lobes are based.

One consequence may be that patients with frontal lobe damage might have a rather weak self-concept, given that they are relatively unaware of where they are in relation to the rest of the world and relatively unable to sort out the temporal sequence of their memories. Although the techniques for studying the self-schema outlined in Section 4.3.1 have not yet been applied to brain-damaged patients, a relationship between the sense of time and the sense of self is suggested by the strong correlation between "temporal disintegration" and "depersonalization" reported by Freeman and Melges (1977, 1978) in acute psychiatric patients. If planning abilities and self-concept have a common foundation, then this forms a basis for understanding why, in depressed people, a negative view of the future is associated with a negative self-image.

It is difficult to leave this area without asking why the brain processes emotional information differentially in the two hemispheres, and how these differences are related to the more familiar distinctions between verbal and nonverbal material or serial and parallel processing. Kinsbourne (1978b,c) has suggested that the fundamental dichotomy underlying cerebral lateralization might actually be the differential organization of approach and avoidance behaviors. Approach behaviors, which are associated with positive emotions, require precise, calculated, sequential strategies; avoidance behaviors, which appear under conditions of danger or threat, require an immediate, holistic response, which where possible is chosen from a small repertoire of prepackaged species-specific defense mechanisms (Bolles, 1972). Consequently, one hemisphere, the left, deals in approach, positive emotions, sequential information processing, and language (which is the quintessence of affiliative behavior), whereas the right hemisphere deals in avoidance, negative emotions, and parallel, holistic information processing.

In effect this account assigns primacy of place to the lateralization of emotional function, which is held to underlie the more firmly established cognitive differences. Within this framework, it could be said that the left frontal lobe, which is involved primarily in the planning of appetitively motivated behaviors, is optimistic, whereas the right frontal lobe, which plans for aversive contingencies, is pessimistic! This is, of course, a highly speculative account of cerebral lateralization, and it is not yet possible to judge its accuracy; it would be equally possible to start from the different processing styles of the two hemispheres and by the same reasoning infer the differential organization of approach and avoidance behaviors. It does, however, have the advantage of making a clear statement about what the evolutionary antecedents of hemispheric asymmetries might be.

5.3.   ANIMAL STUDIES

If hemispheric specialization does in fact reflect the differential organization of positively and negatively motivated behaviors, or indeed, any other formulation that does not assume the priority of human language, then evidence of asymmetrical organization of the brain might also be present in other species. Indeed, studies of nonhuman species may provide the only means of apprehending the roots of cerebral lateralization. Although, traditionally, it has been assumed that asymmetry of function is a unique characteristic of the human brain, it is rapidly becoming clear that this is not the case; the antecedents of lateralization do, in fact, appear much earlier in evolution.

Asymmetry of motor function has been described in rats by Glick and co-workers. The initial observation was that amphetamine induces preferential turning to one side (Glick & Jerussi, 1974), which in a suitable experimental chamber is expressed as rotational behavior (Jerussi & Glick, 1974); undrugged rats are also found to rotate, during their period of nocturnal activity, in the same direction as that induced by amphetamine (Glick & Cox, 1978). The nigrostriatal DA system is also found to be asymmetrical, with significantly higher DA concentrations on the side opposite to the preferred direction of turning (Glick & Cox, 1978; Zimmerberg et al., 1974), and it has been demonstrated that this underlies the asymmetrical behaviors (Glick & Cox, 1978). However, the behavioral asymmetries do not represent the simple arithmetical sum of two unequal driving forces, which in the present context would be relatively trivial, but rather, a genuine dominance phenomenon: amphetamine-induced turning was in the direction away from the dominant side even after depletion of up to 90% of the DA on that side (Robinson & Becker, 1982). It has also been reported that the dominant nigrostriatal DA pathway appears to be crucial for the evocation of eating by electrical stimulation of the lateral hypothalamus (Mittelman & Valenstein, 1982).

5.3.1.   Lateralization of Function

Although these studies provide evidence of functional asymmetry, the dominant side varies randomly from animal to animal. However, other studies have found significant left–right differences in brain function. One study, for example, reported that in rats, under normal conditions, the left frontal lobe and hippocampus were more active than the right, as measured by their utilization of glucose (Sokoloff, 1977), whereas following amphetamine treatment the difference was in the opposite direction (Glick et al., 1979). The best known instances of left–right asymmetry are Nottebohm's studies of bird song, which demonstrate a dependence on the left hemisphere similar to that of human language (Nottebohm, 1971, 1977). More recently, Petersen and co-workers (1978) reported left hemisphere specialization for the recognition of species-specific vocalizations in monkeys, and Rogers and Anson (1980) reported that in newborn chicks, the left hemisphere was crucial in auditory habituation and in learning visually to discriminate food grains from pebbles.

Conversely, there are some indications from a series of studies by Denenberg and co-workers that in rats, the right hemisphere might be differentially involved in aversive states. Animals that had not been handled in infancy showed little evidence of lateralization; however, early handling induced laterality differences, as shown, for example, by a leftward turning bias (Sherman et al., 1980). In animals that were handled in infancy and then kept in standard laboratory conditions, a right-sided lesion caused an increase in activity in a novel environment (open field), but left-sided lesions had no effect (Denenberg et al., 1978). In addition, it was recently reported that the total area of isocortex in rats was significantly larger on the right side than on the left and that the asymmetry in favor of the right hemisphere was negatively correlated with locomotor activity in a novel environment (Sherman & Galaburda, 1982). Because a high level of activity in a novel environment is usually taken to indicate a low level of emotionality, these results suggest a preferential right hemisphere involvement in fear. On similar lines, it was further observed that animals with a left-sided lesion (i.e., an intact right hemisphere) showed superior retention of a conditioned taste aversion (Denenberg et al., 1980).

A series of experiments by Robinson and colleagues has demonstrated that in rats, a variety of insults to the right cerebral hemisphere cause hyperactivity. Treatments studied include ligation of the middle cerebral artery (a model of stroke), suction lesions, destruction of intrinsic cortical neurons with neurotoxin kainic acid, and saggital knife cuts to destroy fibers of passage. In all cases, right-sided damage caused hyperactivity; only one left-sided treatment (kainic acid) did so, and to a significantly lesser degree than the right-sided treatment (Kubos et al., 1982a,b; Pearlson & Robinson, 1981; Robinson & Coyle, 1980). The hyperactivity was greater the closer the lesion was to the frontal pole (Pearlson et al., 1982).

The latter result show an obvious parallel to the effects of stroke in people demonstrated by the same workers. Whether the hyperactivity

induced by right frontal lesions in rats should be considered as a model
of depression associated with left frontal stroke or of euphoria associated
with right frontal stroke is at present unclear. Hyperactivity following
right frontal damage was, however, prevented by concurrent administration of a tricyclic antidepressant (DMI) (Robinson & Bloom, 1977).

5.3.2. Neurochemical Asymmetries in Animals and People

In addition to causing hyperactivity, right frontal lesions were also found
by Robinson and co-workers to produce depletions of NA and DA, but in
general, left-sided lesions did not (Robinson & Coyle, 1980; Pearlson &
Robinson, 1981; Pearlson et al., 1982; Robinson & Bloom, 1977). Like the
hyperactivity induced by right frontal lesions, the neurochemical effects
were also greater in proportion to the closeness of the lesion to the frontal
pole (Pearlson et al., 1982). Hyperactivity was also caused by right-sided
6-hydroxydopamine (6-OHDA) induced lesions of frontal catecholamine
pathways; 6-OHDA on the left only caused hyperactivity at very high
doses, which had left-sided neurochemical sequelae (Robinson & Stitt,
1981). Lesions of 5-HT neurons using the neurotoxin 5,7-dihydroxytryp-
tamine, however, did not cause hyperactivity (Black & Robinson, 1982).
The asymmetries reported by Denenberg's group may also involve catecholamines, because early handling, in addition to causing a leftward
turning bias, has also been reported to induce asymmetry of the mesolimbic DA system, with relatively higher DA levels on the right; the
nigrostriatal DA system did not show this effect (Camp et al., 1982).

There are also several indications of neurochemical asymmetry in the
human brain. Apparently, there is a higher concentration of copper in
the left hemisphere, and because copper is a co-enzyme for dopamine-
beta-hydroxylase, the enzyme which synthesizes NA, this could point to
a similar asymmetry of NA levels (Delva, 1960, cited by Myslobodsky et
al., 1979). Another study also concerns NA: in postmortem analyses of
human thalamus, NA levels were significantly higher in the left pulvinar
(part of the visual system), and in the right ventral posterolateral and
posteromedial (somatosensory) nuclei (Oke et al., 1978). One potentially
significant, if currently obscure, aspect of these findings is that the cortical projection regions of these two areas—left temporo-occipital and
right fronto-parietal—are the areas in which reductions in EEG activation
were associated with recovery from depression under ECS treatment
(Nilsson & Smith, 1965).

Another even more intriguing observation was that the amplitude of
evoked potentials in the left, but not the right, hemisphere was correlated
with DA activity, as measured by concentrations of the DA metabolite
HVA in the lumbar CSF (Gottfries et al., 1974). The implication that DA
may be preferentially involved in left hemispheric function is supported
by the results of a recent study by Wagner and co-workers (1983), in which
a brain scan carried out on a human subject showed an elevation of DA

receptors on the left side (Tucker & Williamson, 1984). Rossor and co-workers (1980) reported that DA was not lateralized in postmortem samples of human brains, but a reanalysis of these data revealed that DA levels in the globus pallidus were, in fact, higher on the left side (Glick et al., 1982). This reanalysis also found evidence of elevated synthesis of ACh in the left globus pallidus; a similar lateralization of ACh synthesis has also been reported in cortical samples (Sorbi et al., 1980).

Pharmacological evidence also supports a preferential involvement of DA in left hemispheric activity in people (Tucker & Williamson, 1984). Reus and co-workers (1979b) reported that in subjects performing a selective attention task, the slow negative component of the visual evoked potential (VEP) was enhanced by amphetamine, and this enhancement was substantially greater over the left hemisphere. Animal studies provide a basis for understanding this observation. In rats, it has been found that asymmetry in the slow negative component of the VEP is strongly correlated with the direction of rotation induced by amphetamine (Myslobodsky et al., 1979). As noted above, rotational behavior is determined by the asymmetry in DA concentrations (Glick & Cox, 1978; Zimmerberg et al., 1978). Existing asymmetries of DA concentration were almost doubled by amphetamine (Glick et al., 1974). The anatomical basis of this finding may lie in the further observation that unilateral activation of the DA system led to a decrease in DA concentration on the contralateral side, implying that there are reciprocal inhibitory pathways between the DA systems on the two sides of the brain (Nieullon et al., 1977).

In view of the fact that DA fibers innervate only the frontal areas of the cortex (Emson & Lindvall, 1979), these observations make a decrease in brain DA activity a prime candidate to mediate the left frontal deactivation seen in depression. The implications of this relationship will be explored further in Chapter 8.

Although the evidence is less extensive, two observations suggest that abnormalities of right parieto-temporal function in depression might be related to an asymmetrical 5-HT innervation. Like DA, activity in the 5-HT system is asymmetric in the rat brain; the asymmetry is reduced by lithium treatment (Mandell & Knapp, 1979). In normal human volunteers, lithium, which enhances central 5-HT function (see Chapter 17), produced greater EEG changes over the right hemisphere than the left (Flor-Henry & Koles, 1981). Second, a correlation has been reported between evoked potentials recorded from the right hemisphere and concentrations of the 5-HT metabolite 5-HIAA in the lumbar CSF (Gottfries et al., 1974).

5.3.3. Implications

The work reviewed in the first half of this chapter clearly indicates that depression is associated with asymmetry of brain function. These observations raise the rather untoward possibility that like language, depression might be a uniquely human condition; the corollary would be that animal studies could not make any but the most minimal contribution to understanding it. This specter may now be laid to rest. The antecedents of lateralization are demonstrable in subhuman species, and there is even a suggestion from the work of Denenberg and his colleagues that negative emotional states may be differentially localized on the right side of the rat brain.

The much more pronounced lateralization of emotional function in the human brain may well complicate the interpretation of clinical phenomena. However, there does not appear to be any reason why an understanding of relevant features of the rat brain, for example, might not generate testable predictions about the nature of brain function in depressed people. The important point is that unlike language, depression may be analyzed in terms of cognitive function known to be present in lower animals: responsiveness to rewards, stressors and punishments, and the consequences of these events for approach and avoidance behaviors. As reviewed in later chapters, animal studies do, in fact, provide a basis for relating the clinical manifestations of depression to the physiology of the brain.

six

ANIMAL MODELS OF DEPRESSION: EMPIRICAL OBSERVATIONS

Once the object of considerable criticism and contempt, animal models of human psychopathology have attracted favourable interest in recent years. (Suomi et al., 1978)

Nowhere is this statement more true than in the area of animal models of depression. The recognition that supposedly "endogenous" depressions may have environmental precipitants (Brown & Harris, 1978; Lloyd, 1980b) has led to vigorous attempts to use animal models to specify the relationship of stress to depression (see Anisman & Zacharko, 1982), and the discovery that chronic treatment with antidepressant drugs produces interesting and potentially significant biochemical changes, which are not apparent on acute administration (e.g., Segal et al., 1974; Sulser et al., 1978) has led to attempts to discover situations in which behavioral effects having a similar time course may be observed. Consequently, the study of animal models of depression, until recently almost nonexistent, is now a major growth area.

6.1. VALIDATING CRITERIA FOR ANIMAL MODELS

The study of animal models of human psychopathology has passed through three distinct phases. The behaviorist period of the 1920s, 1930s, and 1940s was marked by a belief that the development of animal models would be both straightforward and productive; with a few exceptions, however (see Abramson & Seligman, 1978), this optimism was based more on faith than on any tangible empirical foundation. With the eclipse of behaviorism, animal models accompanied animal learning theory into a period of decline, which in both cases lasted until the late 1960s. The turning point for animal models was 1969, when McKinney and Bunney proposed a set of ground rules by which the validity of animal models might be assessed. Some of their prescriptions were intended to introduce a much-needed objectivity into the study of animal models: there should be observable behavioral changes that can be objectively evaluated, independent observers should agree on objective criteria for drawing conclusions about subjective state, and the system should be reproducible by other investigators. Other rules concerned the relationship between the model and the condition being modeled: the two should be similar in their etiology, biochemical basis, symptomatology, and treatment (McKinney & Bunney, 1969).

Although, with minor amendments, these criteria have met with general approval (Keehn, 1979; Maser & Seligman, 1978; Serban & Kling, 1976), it should be noted that in relation to animal models of depression, similarity of etiology and biochemistry are unsuitable as validating criteria, because, they are themselves the subject of intense research and speculation. Furthermore, it has become clear that a variety of different kinds of evidence may be adduced in support of an animal model, and the use of different criteria in relation to different models frequently makes a comparison difficult.

The McKinney and Bunney criteria assess face validity—the phenomenological similarity between the model and the condition being modeled. It is also possible to assess a model in two other ways—by examining its predictive validity and its construct validity. Predictive validity concerns the success of the predictions made from the model; construct validity concerns its theoretical rationale. In fact, assessment of predictive validity is frequently used in discussions of animal models, but the ground rules have not been explicitly formulated. Similarly, questions of construct validity are often implicit in discussions of animal models (see, e.g., Everitt & Keverne, 1979), but there has been no consideration of the rules by which construct validity may be established.

The first problem therefore is to attempt to define criteria for assessing each of these forms of validity. If animals models are to be used as a basis for asking questions about the physiological basis of depression, it seems sensible to restrict the enquiry by excluding any models which can be shown to be clearly invalid.

It is clear from a cursory examination that animal models of depression are of two kinds: those that have a theoretical rationale and those that do not. Models in the latter group are based on empirical observations, and questions of construct validity obviously do not arise. The models do not have a theoretical rationale, so there is no question of examining its adequacy. The problem of assessing construct validity, and a review of the models to which this test can be applied, is taken up in Chapter 7. The present chapter deals with the principles of predictive and face validity and reviews empirically derived models. This group can be further subdivided into those models that can claim some face validity and those that do not show even a superficial resemblance to depression.

Before discussing criteria for the validation of animal models, it is worthwhile to distinguish two closely related experimental methodologies. First, animal models are not the same as drug screening tests, although the same experimental procedures may often serve for both. The only purpose of a screening test is to discover new potentially effective drugs. Hence a screening test stands or falls by its ability to detect active compounds and reject inactive compounds. As described below, although this ability would normally be expected in an animal model, it is neither necessary nor sufficient in order for the model to be valid. Additionally, the assessment of a procedure as a potential screening test involves a number of economic and logistical factors, which play no part in assessing its validity as a model. Finally, since, by definition, animal models of human mental disorders attempt to model a psychological condition, it seems more appropriate to use the term *animal model* to refer primarily to behavioral procedures. The ability of antidepressant drugs to reduce the sensitivity of beta-receptors, for example, may prove to be a useful screening test for the discovery of new antidepressants, but designating this procedure an animal model of depression would make assumptions about the biochemical basis of depression that are not justified on the basis of current knowledge (see Chapter 13).

A second methodology, which is distinct from both animal models and screening tests, involves the use of behavioral procedures as assay systems in which to test the functional state of specific brain systems. The use of behavioral responses to agonist drugs to test the sensitivity of neurotransmitter receptors, for example, is now relatively widespread (see, e.g., Davis, 1982) and will be discussed extensively in Part 3 of this book. In such experiments, the behavioral test is being used simply as a measuring device, in the same way that biochemical or physiological tests might be used for this purpose. Calling such procedures animal models, rather than recognizing them as behavioral assay systems, again makes untenable assumptions about the physiological basis of the condition being modeled. These assumptions are counterproductive, insofar as the elucidation of the physiological basis of psychopathology is probably the area in which animal models will make their major contributions.

6.2. PREDICTIVE VALIDITY

A model has predictive validity if performance on the test predicts performance in the situation being modeled (Russell, 1964). In principle, this criterion could be applied to a number of features of animal models, including their etiology. In most cases, however, little is known about the etiology of mental disorders, and this is certainly true of depression. Furthermore, ethical considerations often preclude the testing of predictions. In practice, therefore, the primary use of predictive validation is to assess the effects of potential therapeutic treatments: the model has predictive validity if it successfully discriminates between effective and ineffective treatments. This implies testing a sufficient range of effective drugs and, where they exist, other effective treatments. An animal model of depression should be tested for its response not only to tricyclic antidepressants and MAOIs, but also to electroconvulsive shock (ECS) and a variety of atypical or second-generation antidepressants. A sufficient range of treatments, which are known to be ineffective should also be examined; these should include anticholinergics and antihistamines, which frequently give false positive responses. A useful supplementary procedure is to test compounds that have been evaluated clinically as potential therapeutic agents, but were found not to work (e.g., Sanghvi et al., 1969).

The validity of a model is greatly increased if it can be shown not only that the model discriminates active from inactive compounds, but also, that potency in the model is correlated with clinical potency. The best example of this technique is the almost perfect correlation between the clinical potency of neuroleptic (antischizophrenic) drugs and their effects at dopamine receptors (Creese & Snyder, 1978). Despite its obvious power, correlation of potencies has been very infrequently studied. One problem is that antidepressants have a rather restricted range of effective doses (Table 6.1). Unlike neuroleptics, which have a range of clinical doses spanning three orders of magnitude (Creese & Snyder, 1978), all of the antidepressants shown in Table 6.1 are effective within one order of magnitude (40–400 mg), with the single exception of the experimental drug salbutamol.

In addition to this relative lack of variability, a number of other factors also militate against a perfect match between the order of potencies obtained in an animal model and the order of clinical potencies. There may, for example, be species differences in the absorption of drugs into the bloodstream or in their transport across the blood–brain barrier. It may be necessary for the drug to be converted to an active metabolite, and again there may be species differences. In some cases, the upper limit of the clinical dose range may be set by the emergence of side effects, which might be less of a consideration in an animal model. Nonetheless, it is reasonable to expect either a reasonable correspondence between the two rank orders or an explanation of major discrepancies. This will be true, however, only if the available treatments span a sufficient range of dosages; otherwise, the experimental error inherent in estimates of effective clinical dose renders the computation of correlations meaningless. In discussing the models reviewed in this and the following chapter, correlations (Spearman rank-order correlation coefficient—rho) have been cal-

TABLE 6.1. ANTIDEPRESSANT DRUGS—
APPROXIMATE CLINICAL DOSAGE
RANGE

Dosage (mg/day)[a]	Drug
300–600	Buproprion
	Trazodone
200–300	Amoxapine
	Butriptyline
	Opipramol
	Viloxazine
	Zimelidine
100–200	Desmethylimipramine
	Imipramine
	Nialamide
75–150	Amitriptyline
	Chlorimipramine
	Doxepin
	Maprotiline
	Trimipramine
50–100	Iprindole
	Iproniazid
	Mianserin
	Nomifensine
	Nortriptyline
	Phenelzine
20–50	Isocarboxazid
	Protriptyline
	Tranylcypromine
3–6	Salbutamol

[a] Dosages were compiled from information in the *Physicians' Desk Reference* (1982), Paykel and Coppen (1979), and Costa and Racagni (1982b). Information in the table is presented for correlative purposes only and without further reference to appropriate sources should not be used as a guide to prescribing.

culated between published data and the data in Table 6.1, where there is sufficient information for this to be useful.

6.3. MODELS THAT ASPIRE ONLY TO PREDICTIVE VALIDITY

6.3.1. DOPA Potentiation

Several animal models of depression depend on the interaction of antidepressant drugs with other pharmacological agents. In all of these tests, the suspicion arises that, as discussed above, the test might be a receptor assay rather than an animal model of depression. The DOPA potentiation test is a case in point; this test is essentially an assay system for detecting drugs with adrenergic stimulating activity. Following pretreatment with an MAOI to protect newly synthesized amines, administration of DOPA, the precursor of the catecholamines DA and NA (Section 1.1), causes signs of adrenergic stimulation, including piloerection, locomotor activity, irritability, and aggression. These effects are potentiated by pretreatment with tricyclic antidepressants (Everett, 1967; Sigg & Hill, 1967). However, because of its pharmacological specificity, the test does not discriminate well. By its nature, it cannot detect MAOIs; some antihistamines and anticholinergic drugs show positive results (Sigg & Hill, 1967); and newer nonadrenergic antidepressants such as mianserin (van Riezen et al., 1975) and trazodone (Silvestrini, 1982) give negative results.

6.3.2. Yohimbine Potentiation

The yohimbine potentiation test, is another model based on pharmacological interactions. Quinton (1963) observed that the lethality of yohimbine, which is an alpha$_2$-receptor antagonist, was increased in mice by tricyclic antidepressants and MAOIs, but also by a variety of other drug classes, including neuroleptics. In a recent reevaluation of this model, neuroleptics were ineffective, but antidepressants did potentiate yohimbine lethality: positive effects were seen with tricyclics, the MAOI pargyline, and a variety of newer atypical antidepressants, including iprindole, mianserin, nomifensine, buproprion, viloxazine, and zimelidine (Malick, 1981). However, ECS, administered acutely or chronically, was ineffective, and stimulants, anticholinergics, and antihistamines gave false positive responses (Lapin, 1980; Malick, 1981). In one study (Lapin, 1980), the most potent drug in this test was the experimental compound AW-151129, which was not found to be a clinically effective antidepressant (Stille et al., 1968). And, although the test does successfully identify effective antidepressant drugs, the correlation between their potency in the test and their clinical potency is only 0.2 (calculated using LD$_{50}$ values in Malick, 1981).

In a less offensive version of this test, yohimbine was administered to dogs at low doses, and the cardiovascular (increased blood pressure) and behavioral (restlessness and body tremors) changes were measured. The tricyclics imipramine, amitriptyline, and nortriptyline, and the MAOI nialamide, potentiated the effects of yohimbine (Johnsson et al., 1970; Lang & Gershon, 1962, 1963; Sanghvi et al., 1969). However, with the exception of iprindole, which was effective (Sanghvi et al., 1976), atypical antidepressants have not been tested, and neither has ECS. This model appears to be more specific for antidepressants than the yohimbine lethality test in mice. Anticholinergics and antihistamines have not been tested, but the psychostimulants amphetamine and cocaine, which, with anticholinergics and antihistamines appear as false positives in a number of other models, were ineffective (Sanghvi & Gershon, 1969). So too were three agents that had been tested clinically as potential antidepressants, but found not to work (Sanghvi & Gershon, 1969; Sanghvi et al., 1969). Thus, unlike the mouse yohimbine lethality potentiation test, which has very little predictive validity, the dog yohimbine potentiation test has a fair degree of predictive validity, which is limited, however, by the narrow range of drugs examined.

6.3.3. Predatory Behavior

Muricide (mouse killing by rats), on the face of it an improbable animal model of depression, was the earliest model not to be based on a pharmacological interaction, and vies with the yohimbine lethality test as the most distasteful animal model of depression. Horowitz (1965) first observed that muricide was blocked by the tricyclic antidepressant imipramine. Subsequent work showed that this effect was shared by MAOIs and other tricyclics (Delina-Stula & Vassout, 1979a; Horovitz, 1965; Horovitz et al., 1966; Sofia, 1969a,b; Ueki, 1982), ECS (Ueki, 1982; Vogel & Hambrich, 1973), maprotiline (Delina-Stula & Vassout, 1979a), and mianserin, an atypical antidepressant missed by many screening procedures (Ueki, 1982; van Riezen et al., 1975).

However, one study found that only four out of ten antidepressants tested blocked muricide at doses significantly lower than those that caused motor debilitation, measured by the rotarod test (Sofia, 1969b). Additionally, there are discrepancies in the relative potencies of different antidepressants. For example, iproniazid, while slightly more potent clinically than the tricyclics and equipotent with phenelzine (Table 6.1), was 20–30 times less potent than the other drugs in the muricide test. Moreover, a number of other classes of drug have also been found to block muricide, including psychomotor stimulants, and some anticholinergics and antihistamines (Barnett et al., 1969; Horovitz, 1965; Horovitz et al., 1966).

The test therefore has only moderate predictive validity. However, it is possible that if chronic drug treatment were used, the test might be more specific than it appears. In a recent study, both imipramine and the anticholinergic drug atropine blocked muricide one hour after drug administration; following chronic treatment, imipramine was also effective after a 24 hour delay, but atropine was not (Enna et al., 1981).

The antidepressants imipramine, desmethylimipramine (DMI), and chlorimipramine have also been found to block the attack on an anesthetized rat elicited by hypothalamic stimulation in cats. This effect has been much less extensively studied than muricide. The anticholinergic atropine was ineffective, but so also was the atypical antidepressant iprindole (Dubinsky & Goldberg, 1971; Dubinsky et al., 1973).

6.3.4. Kindling

A final model in this group, physiological rather than behavioral, is based on the observation that the daily application of low-intensity electrical stimulation to certain brain areas leads to the development of electrical and behavioral seizure activity, which may eventually be elicited by as little as a few seconds stimulation. This phenomenon is known as kindling (Goddard et al., 1969). Babington and Wedeking (1973) observed that seizures elicited from the amygdala were suppressed by tricyclic antidepressants at doses lower than those required to suppress cortical seizures; anticonvulsant and anxiolytic drugs also suppressed seizure activity but failed to show selectivity. However, although ECS was effective in this test, showing a greater suppression of amygdaloid than cortical seizures (Babington, 1975), MAOIs were ineffective, as were iprindole and mianserin (Babington, 1981). Moreover, Knobloch and co-workers (1982) were unable to confirm the selective action of imipramine on amygdaloid seizures, and they also found that after subacute treatment (two or five days) neither imipramine nor amitriptyline showed selectivity. There is therefore serious doubt as to the ability of this test to identify antidepressant treatments successfully and to eliminate false positives.

6.4. FACE VALIDITY

As noted above, the ground rules for face validity were laid by McKinney and Bunney (1969), who proposed that the model should resemble the condition being modeled in etiology, biochemistry, symptomatology, and treatment. In practice, uncertainty over the etiology and biochemistry of depression renders these characteristics largely unsuitable as validating criteria—indeed, they are frequently themselves the subject of study. For most purposes, this leaves similarity of symptomatology and treatment as the usable criteria for face validity.

A number of relevant questions may be asked about treatment variables. Does drug treatment change behavior in the model at reasonable doses? Are the effects seen during chronic drug treatment or only during withdrawal? Are the effects potentiated by, or only present during, chronic treatment, as is frequently the case clinically? In relation to the latter question, it should be noted that although it seems probable that a delayed onset of therapeutic response results from a slowly developing action of the drug, which would not be present on acute administration, there are a number of alternative possibilities. A delay could arise, for example, from the need to build up adequate blood levels of the drug, from the slow development of tolerance to unpleasant side effects, or from the need to relearn new habits. Since reasons for the delayed onset of drug effects have not been established, the fact that a model is responsive to acute drug challenges, in contrast to a clinical requirement for chronic treatment, does not necessarily invalidate the model.

Although examination of the details of drug treatment is important, treating a behavior as an animal model simply because it is affected by drugs that are also clinically effective involves an unacceptable degree of circularity (see Everitt & Keverne, 1979). Similarity of symptoms is therefore the more basic criterion. In practice, however, this frequently comes down, in effect, to little more than an assertion of the sort that the animal "looks depressed," usually on the basis simply of a decrease in behavioral output. Abramson and Seligman (1977) have suggested that these problems may be circumvented by making a number of comparisons between the model and the condition modeled, rather than relying on a single symptom. This approach is obviously of value, but it is not foolproof, as there is no reason to suppose that a given condition should manifest itself in identical ways in different species (Hinde, 1976). This means that a model would not necessarily be invalidated by a lack of correspondence. (By the same token, if all the symptoms do correspond, the model could still be invalid.) Where a model does demonstrate a number of similarities to a psychopathological condition, it is important to examine the coherence of the pattern of symptoms modeled. Do the symptoms in fact appear as a group in patients suffering from the disorder, or are they drawn from a variety of diagnostic subgroups?

In addition to similarity of treatment parameters and symptomatology and coherence of the pattern of symptoms, two further criteria for face validity can be added. First, there should be no major dissimilarities between the model and the condition it models. Second, as Abramson and Seligman (1977) have pointed out, the specificity of the model should be examined. Are the symptoms addressed by the model specific to the condition modeled, or are they general features of a number of different psychopathological conditions?

6.5. MODELS THAT CLAIM FACE VALIDITY

6.5.1. Reserpine Reversal

Like several of the models already considered, three of the models in this second group are based on pharmacological interactions. Reversal of the behavioral and physiological effects of reserpine was the earliest animal model of depression to be developed (Costa et al., 1960). The syndrome induced by reserpine and related agents such as tetrabenazine and Ro4-1284 is characterized by ptosis (drooping of the upper eye lid), hypothermia, and catalepsy. The reversal of ptosis and hypothermia by tricyclic antidepressants and MAOIs is very well established, and it was the first clear demonstration of a difference in pharmacological activity between tricyclic antidepressants and neuroleptics, which potentiate, rather than counteract the effects of reserpine-like drugs (Costa et al., 1960; Maxwell & Palmer, 1961; Theobald et al., 1964). Consequently, these effects have been very widely used as a screening test for potential new antidepressants (Askew, 1963; Barnett & Taber, 1971; Hill & Tedeschi, 1971; Howard et al., 1981).

However, the test fails to detect some newer antidepressants, such as mianserin (van Riezen, 1972) and trazodone (Silvestrini, 1982), which differ structurally from the tricyclics and MAOIs. Conversely, a wide range of nonantidepressants are detected by the test, including stimulants, DOPA, alpha-methyl-DOPA, alpha-adrenergic agonists, beta-adrenergic blockers, antihistamines, and LSD (Carlsson et al., 1957; Colpaert et al., 1975; Day & Rand, 1963; Duvoisin & Marsden 1974; Grabowska et al., 1974; Sigg et al., 1965; Sigg & Hill, 1967). Correlation between reserpine-reversal and clinical potency (Table 6.1) is in the right direction, but not statistically significant (rho = 0.48, 0.43, $p > 0.1$, calculated from data of Howard et al., 1981 and Colpaert et al., 1975).

If the predictive validity of this test is poor, its face validity is worse. The claim to face validity rests on two foundations: that reserpine induces depression in people and that reserpine-induced catatonia is normalized by antidepressant drugs. The first of these claims is questionable. As discussed in Section 1.1.4, despite the many published studies of supposed reserpine-induced depressions, which appeared in the 1950s and 1960s, it has been argued that the incidence of true depressions may have been as low as 5% and that these patients usually had a prior history of depression (Goodwin et al., 1972). It is possible that true depressions might be induced more frequently by very high doses of reserpine (Peterfy et al., 1976), but this remains to be confirmed.

The second claim, that reserpine-induced catatonia is normalized by antidepressants, is simply false. Reversal of the physiological effects of reserpine-like drugs is always reported, but antidepressants frequently fail to reverse the behavioral effects (Colpaert et al., 1975; Willner & Clark, 1978). When antidepressant-treated animals do awaken from their drug-induced stupor, it is to take up a highly stereotyped and abnormal behavior, consisting of continuous sniffing and incessant, inexorable forward locomotion, which continues unabated for a period of hours (Brodie et al., 1961; Sulser et al., 1964; Willner & Clark, 1978). There is no evidence that antidepressants are able to reverse the suppression by reserpine-like drugs of normal instrumental behavior (Willner & Clark, 1978). Finally, the fact that in order to work, the antidepressant must be given first, further detracts from what little face validity remains.

6.5.2. Amphetamine Potentiation

Another classic, and invalid, model is based on the observation that most antidepressants enhance most actions of amphetamine, including, among others, hypothermia (Morpurgo & Theobald, 1965), weight loss (Claasen & Davies, 1969), locomotor activity (Halliwell et al., 1964), stereotyped behavior (Halliwell et al., 1964), and enhancement of shock avoidance performance (Carlton, 1961; Scheckel & Boff, 1964). However, the mechanism for these effects is the impairment of amphetamine metabolism by the liver, which effectively increases the dose of amphetamine reaching the brain (Lewander, 1968; Sulser et al., 1966; Valzelli et al., 1967). Not surprisingly, this action is shared by representatives of many other classes of drug, including stimulants, anticholinergics, antihistamines, neuroleptics, beta-blockers, and local anesthetics. Conversely, newer antidepressant agents structurally dissimilar to the tricyclics, such as mianserin (van Riezen, 1972) and trazodone (Silvestrini, 1982), do not potentiate amphetamine.

The claim to face validity arises from the fact that in addition to the other actions of amphetamine noted above, antidepressants also potentiate the rate-increasing effect of amphetamine in animals pressing a lever to receive brain stimulation reward (Stein, 1962; Stein & Seifter, 1961). Since the effect is nonspecific, both behaviorally and pharmacologically, and artifactual in origin, the claim that this effect confers face validity is untenable.

6.5.3. 5-HTP-Induced Behavioral Depression

Another drug interaction model involves the reversal by antidepressant drugs of the behavioral depression induced by 5-HTP, the precursor of 5-HT, in rats working for milk reinforcement. Behavioral depression was attenuated by acute pretreatment with imipramine, amitriptyline, iprindole, mianserin, or trazodone (Aprison et al., 1982; Nagayama et al., 1980, 1981). However, behavioral depression was potentiated by fluoxetine, which appears to be an effective antidepressant (see Section 16.3.4); conversely, the most potent blocker of behavioral depression was the 5-HT receptor antagonist methysergide, which is not known to have antidepressant properties (Nagayama et al., 1980, 1981).

Aside from the effects of antidepressants, the decrease in activity is the only other point of resemblance between the model and depression, so the model is extremely weak in both predictive and face validity. In fact, the model was explicitly developed as a behavioral system within which to test the effects of drugs on 5-HT neurotransmission. In this role, it serves a useful function and will be discussed in more detail in Chapter

15. It is included here as another example of the way in which behavioral bioassay systems are sometimes mistaken for animal models.

6.5.4. Olfactory Bulbectomy

The remaining models in this section are based on behavioral changes induced by a variety of nonpharmacological procedures. All have their problems, but all of them are potentially useful.

Rats subjected to bilateral lesions of the olfactory bulbs show a variety of behavioral changes, including irritability, hyperactivity, and an elevation of circulating levels of plasma corticosteroids; as a result of their hyperactivity, the animals also are deficient in passive avoidance learning. All of these changes are reversed by antidepressant drugs (Cairncross et al., 1977, 1978, 1979). However, the specificity of the effects is variable. While antidepressants (amitriptyline, mianserin, and viloxazine) reversed all of the effects of bulbectomy, irritability and the hormonal changes were also reversed by the neuroleptic chlorpromazine and the anxiolytic chlordiazepoxide. Of the three changes, therefore, the passive avoidance deficit appears to be the only one that is reversed specifically by antidepressants. The effectiveness of antidepressants in the passive avoidance paradigm has been confirmed in other laboratories, and extended to imipramine, doxepin, fluoxetine, trazodone, buproprion, and zimelidine (Broekkamp et al., 1980; Leonard, 1982; Lloyd et al., 1982; Noreika et al., 1981).

In some cases (imipramine, viloxazine, mianserin), the effects of antidepressants are only seen after subchronic treatment (5–10 days) (Lloyd et al., 1982; Noreika et al., 1981). However, other drugs, (fluoxetine, zimelidine, trazodone) were effective after a single injection. Dosage relationships are difficult to assess from the published data, but what little clinical evidence is available does not suggest that the drugs that are effective acutely in this model have a more rapid clinical onset than those that require chronic treatment. Amphetamine was ineffective in reversing the olfactory bulbectomy-induced passive avoidance deficit (Cairncross et al., 1978, 1979; Noreika et al., 1981), as was the anticholinergic atropine (Lloyd et al., 1982). However, the 5-HT agonist quipazine was effective (Lloyd et al., 1982), whereas the only MAOI to have been tested, tranylcypromine, was not (Cairncross et al., 1978, 1979; Noreika et al., 1981).

With the exception of tranylcypromine, and possibly other MAOIs, the model appears sensitive to all typical and atypical antidepressants. However, a very narrow range of nonantidepressants have been tested, and two important questions—concerning the requirement for chronic drug treatment and the specificity of antidepressant effects on the hormonal changes induced by bulbectomy—remain to be answered.

In addition to the effects described, olfactory bulbectomy induces muricide in nonkiller strains of rat (Ueki, 1982). Both spontaneous and bulbectomy-induced muricide are blocked by lesions of the corticomedial portion of the amygdala (Horovitz, 1967; Ueki, 1982). Moreover, both types of muricide and the bulbectomy-induced passive avoidance deficit were blocked by injection of antidepressant drugs directly into this region of the amygdala (Horovitz, 1967; Watanabe et al., 1979; Lloyd et al., 1982). Hence, the bulbectomy model is closely related to the muricide model described above.

The muricide model can make no claim to face validity, but the bulbectomy model can do so on two counts. First, hyperactivity is a symptom shown by a significant proportion of depressed patients (Kupfer & Detre, 1978; Nelson & Charney, 1981; see Section 3.1.2). Although the learning of a passive avoidance task is the usual paradigm for studying the bulbectomized rat, it is likely that the learning deficit simply reflects hyperactivity, since it has been observed that chronic treatment with amitriptyline or mianserin reduces locomotor activity in bulbectomized animals, but not in sham-operated controls (van Riezen et al., 1977; Leonard, 1982). Second, like the bulbectomized rat, depressed people frequently have elevated circulating corticosteroid levels (Sachar et al., 1973b; Carroll et al., 1976).

These observations raise the question of what exactly is being modeled by bulbectomy. The inactivity of the MAOI tranylcypromine and the elevation of plasma corticosteroids point strongly to endogenous rather than reactive depression. Although MAOIs have been found to be effective in reactive depression, there is little or no evidence that they are efficacious in endogenous depression (Tyrer, 1979). Similarly, abnormalities of the pituitary–adrenal system are seen in the majority of endogenous depressions, but not in reactive depressions (Carroll, 1978). It would appear, therefore, that the bulbectomized rat models a specific subgroup of depressions—endogenous depressions with psychomotor agitation. As discussed in Chapter 3, factor and other multivariate analytic studies support the concept that this diagnosis is distinct from anxious depression, which also involves hyperactivity (Gersh & Fowles, 1979; Nelson & Charney, 1981). However, two discrepancies should be noted between the model and the subgroup of agitated endogenous depressives. First, elevated levels of plasma cortisol are seen in most, perhaps all, endogenous depressions (Sachar et al., 1973b; Carroll, 1978) and are not confined to agitated depressions. Second, fluoxetine and zimelidine, which are the most potent drugs in the model and act after a single administration (Lloyd et al., 1982), in clinical use may actually make psychomotor agitation worse (Shopsin et al., 1981).

A further limitation on the face validity of the model arises from the observation that following chronic treatment with a variety of antidepressants, effects on passive avoidance in bulbectomized rats were seen after 48 or 72 hours of withdrawal, but not after 4 hours of withdrawal (Noreika et al., 1981). If, as suggested by this study, it should transpire that the effects of antidepressants in the model can only be demonstrated after a period of withdrawal, then the face validity of the model would be seriously undermined.

6.5.5. Isolation-Induced Hyperactivity

Another model involving hyperactive animals is produced by rearing rats in social isolation from an early age (two to three weeks). As adults, they show a marked hyperactivity in comparison to group-reared controls (Einon et al., 1975; Sahakian et al., 1975, 1977). Unlike the olfactory bulb-lesioned animal described above, the hyperactivity is not accompanied by any signs of aggression, either toward the experimenter or toward other animals (Garzon et al., 1979; Garzon & Del Rio, 1981). The time of isolation appears to be critical to the development of this syndrome, since isolation of two-month-old animals results in aggression toward the experimenter, and muricide, but not in hyperactivity (Sofia, 1969a; Valzelli & Bernasconi, 1971).

Garzon and colleagues have reported that the activity difference between isolated and group-reared animals was abolished by acute treatment with tricyclic antidepressants (amitriptyline, chlorimipramine, desmethylimipramine (DMI) and doxepin), MAOIs (phenelzine, clorgyline), atypical antidepressants (mianserin, iprindole, nomifensine, viloxazine, trazodone), and the beta-receptor agonist salbutamol. The 5-HT receptor blocker and antihistamine cyproheptadine, which does not appear to have been tested clinically, was also effective. However, neuroleptics (chlorpromazine, haloperidol) and anxiolytics (chlordiazepoxide, diazepam) did not abolish the activity difference between isolated and group-reared animals except at neurotoxic doses. Anticholinergic drugs were not assessed. Comparison of drug potencies is difficult from the published data, but one striking result is that salbutamol was clearly the most potent drug tested (cf. Table 6.1) (Garzon et al., 1979; Garzon & Del Rio, 1981).

With two possible exceptions, the test appears to be rather specific. The effect of NA receptor antagonists is controversial. Garzon and Del Rio (1981) reported that the beta-blocker propranolol did not affect hyperactivity, but others have found that propranolol, or phenoxybenzamine, an alpha-receptor blocker, did block isolation-induced hyperactivity (Weinstock et al., 1976). The effect of amphetamine is also unclear. On acute administration, isolated animals are hypersensitive to amphetamine (Garzon et al., 1979; Sahakian et al., 1975), but chronic amphetamine administration appears to abolish the activity difference between isolated and grouped animals (Weinstock et al., 1978). As the Garzon experiments employed acute treatments, it should probably be concluded that amphetamine is ineffective in this test.

Other than the fact of hyperactivity, which is seen in a significant proportion of depressions (Kupfer & Detre, 1978), there is little information on which to judge the face validity of this model. One potential problem is that in operant tasks, isolated animals may show greater persistence (Morgan et al., 1975), which depressed people certainly do not (Weingartner & Silberman, 1982). The effects of chronic antidepressant treatment could not be determined, since the activity difference between isolated and group-reared animals was abolished by repeated daily handling and saline injections (Garzon & Del Rio, 1981), a fact which itself does not augur well for the model's face validity.

6.5.6. Exhaustion Stress

This model is the first of several, most of them considered in the next chapter, which are based on behavioral and/or physiological responses to stress. Female rats, reared in revolving cages, show a cyclical activity pattern tied to the estrous cycle. Forced running in the wheel, to the point of exhaustion, killed about half the animals. Of the survivors, half resumed running within several days. The others, however, showed a very low spontaneous locomotor activity, with no cyclicity, for several weeks, accompanied by constant diestrous. Normal activity was restored by daily imipramine treatment (Hatotani et al., 1982). There is as yet virtually no information on which to judge either the predictive validity of the model or its face validity as a model of retarded depression. However, two features of the model are potentially of interest: the effect was all-or-none, only appearing in some of the subjects, and long-lasting.

6.5.7. Circadian Rhythms

This chapter concludes with a group of models that involve effects of antidepressants on circadian activity, and at first sight bear little relationship to depression.

Rats are nocturnal animals; their locomotor activity is high at night and low during the day. Readjustment to a normal circadian cycle of locomotor activity following reversal of the light–dark cycle was expedited by moderate doses of the antidepressants imipramine, maprotiline, and pargyline, administered daily for 10 days prior to the phase-shift, and 16 days subsequently. Chlordiazepoxide, chlorpromazine, reserpine, and amphetamine were all ineffective (Baltzer & Weiskrantz, 1975). In a related paradigm, imipramine and clorgyline have been found to cause a lengthening of the circadian period in hamsters shifted from a normal light–dark cycle to constant darkness (Goodwin et al., 1982b).

Little work has been carried out using these models, and they might appear to have little face validity. However, disturbance of circadian rhythms does appear to be a characteristic feature of depression. In addition to the well-established decrease in the latency of the first period of REM sleep (Akiskal, 1980; Kupfer, 1976; see Section 3.3.2), phase-advance of most other circadian rhythms has also been reported (Goodwin et al., 1982b). The significance of these changes is obscure (but see Section 19.2.2). However, a number of authors have suggested that changes in circadian rhythms may be of etiological significance in depression (Wehr & Wirz-Justice, 1982), and there is evidence that a variety of sleep deprivation procedures are effective as antidepressant treatments (Gillin, 1983; Vogel, 1975; Vogel et al., 1980).

A related model has been advanced, based on the suppression by antidepressants of REM sleep in cats (Scherschlicht et al., 1982). Amphetamine and morphine had a similar effect but also suppressed non-REM sleep. The only other nonantidepressant for which results were reported was phenobarbital, which had an effect similar to the antidepressants. No relationship is apparent between the ability of antidepressants to suppress REM sleep and their clinical potency.

6.6. ON THE LIMITATIONS OF PURELY EMPIRICAL MODELS

A total of 12 animal models of depression have been surveyed in this chapter, and in most cases it has not been difficult to make an assessment of their predictive and face validity. It is clear, however, that the assessments can only be as reliable as the criteria, and here there are problems. The usefulness of predictive validation is limited by the fact that failure to discriminate between active and inactive agents does not necessarily mean that a test is invalid. A failure to identify a drug known to be effective, rather than invalidating the model, could be a pointer to diagnostic or pharmacological heterogeneity of the disorder. Conversely, if a model incorrectly identifies a drug known to be ineffective, this might mean only that the measuring instrument is too crude; it is possible that a false-positive response might be eliminated by a more detailed behavioral analysis (see Section 7.2.2 for an example). Similar problems exist in relation to assessment of face validity. No definite inference may be drawn from the fact that a model responds to acute antidepressant drug administration, and symptomatic dissimilarities could easily reflect species differences.

As a result, it is not possible to state definitively that any of the models considered in this chapter are necessarily invalid (with the exception of the amphetamine potentiation model, which is clearly artifactual). Nevertheless, there seems little point in spending time studying models that fail to meet a large number of criteria and pass on only a few. On this basis, 6 of the 12 models considered in this chapter appear to be thoroughly unreliable. Of the five models in the first group, only the muricide model and the canine version of the yohimbine potentiation model appear to be worth pursuing. Of the seven models in the second group, three may be rejected, leaving the olfactory bulbectomy, social isolation, exhaustion stress, and circadian rhythm models as candidates for further study.

seven

ANIMAL MODELS OF DEPRESSION: THEORY AND APPLICATIONS

Predictive validity and face validity, the subjects of the previous chapter, are concerned with the empirical status of a model; construct validity, the subject of this chapter, addresses the theoretical status of the model and is therefore more basic. For the various reasons previously discussed, including species differences, a model may fail to meet one or more criteria for predictive or face validity without necessarily being invalid, but a model could not be valid if construct validity were violated. Unfortunately, the force of this argument is weakened by the fact that few models and their related disorders are sufficiently well understood to make definitive statements about construct validity. It follows that assessment of the validity of an animal model should, wherever possible, be based on information of all three kinds.

In this chapter, six animal models of depression are described that potentially have some degree of construct validity. The first five of these models involve behavioral states generated by stressors of varying kinds. The sixth model comprises a group of studies of reward mechanisms, which it is convenient at present to examine as a group, but which might differentiate into separate models in due course.

7.1. CONSTRUCT VALIDITY

Construct validity, a term borrowed from psychological testing (Vernon, 1963), means that a procedure is based on a sound theoretical rationale. The application of this criterion to animal models presupposes that it is possible to construct theories of psychopathology which are applicable to nonhuman species. Consideration of this issue requires a brief digression to reexamine the nature of psychopharmacological theories.

The major thrust in contemporary abnormal psychology is the elucidation of the changes in cognitive processing which underlie psychopathology (see, e.g., Mandler, 1975); as in earlier chapters, *cognitive* is used to mean simply the set of constructs that describe the information processing functions of the brain. As discussed in Chapter 2, the way in which drugs or other physical manipulations affect subjective experience can similarly be understood in terms of effects on underlying cognitive processes. Consequently, interposing an analysis at the level of information processing makes it possible to bridge the gulf between accounts of mental phenomena and analysis of events in the brain.

The introduction of a cognitive level of analysis to mediate between physiology and experience permits a substantial clarification of the nature of animal models of human mental disorders: they attempt to simulate the changes in information processing that underlie the disorder rather than the resulting changes in subjective experience. For most practical purposes, the subjective experience of animals is beyond the scope of experimental investigation. In principle, therefore, the subjective aspects of psychopathology can not be modeled in animals. However, the cognitive and behavioral dysfunctions, which underlie the experience, can be modeled. This is what is being done when, for example, schizophrenia is modeled as a disorder of attention (Kornetsky & Markovitz, 1978).

From this perspective, the demonstration of construct validity requires two things. First, it must be established that homologous constructs are being studied in animals and people. This presupposes that both the model and the disorder have been sufficiently studied to make an unambiguous interpretation of the congitive changes involved. Second, it must be shown that a change at the level of the construct being modeled is in fact central to the disorder. This places a high priority on the study of the psychology of mental disorders in people as a precondition for assessing the construct validity of animal models.

It might appear that construct validity is simply a more refined version of face validity, but this is not the case. Face validity only requires the demonstration of similarity between the model and the symptoms of the disorder being modeled. Construct validity does not require superficial similarity. It does, however, require the demonstration of homology—the same theoretical constructs must be applicable in the two cases—and an empirically supported rationale for believing that the construct in question is fundamental to the disorder, rather than an epiphenomenon. These are rather stringent criteria, and it is doubtful whether any animal model could meet them fully in our current state of relative ignorance of the cognitive foundations of psychopathology. The learned helplessness model of depression, discussed in some detail in Chapter 4, has probably been investigated more thoroughly than any other animal model of mental disorder, and it has certainly had the greatest impact on clinical research and theorizing. Consequently, the learned helplessness model forms a suitable starting point for examining those animal models of depression that have a theoretical rationale.

7.2. MODELS WITH POTENTIAL CONSTRUCT VALIDITY

7.2.1. Learned Helplessness

The term learned helplessness describes a situation in which exposure to uncontrollable stress produces performance deficits in subsequent learning tasks, which are not seen in subjects exposed to the identical stressor, but able to control it. This phenomenon was first described by Seligman and co-workers in dogs and subsequently extended to a large number of other species, including people (reviewed by Garber et al., 1979; Maier & Seligman, 1976; Miller et al., 1977; Seligman, 1975). In the original experiment, dogs were subjected to electric shocks, which some animals could escape, but others could not. Exposure to shock was equalized between the two groups by using a "yoked control" design: animals were run in pairs, one of which, by performing the escape response, could terminate delivery of shock to both itself and its yoked partner; the yoked control received the same number and pattern of shocks, but was unable to do anything about them. (This has become the standard design for the great majority of learned helplessness experiments.) Subsequently, the animals were tested for their ability to escape from shock by jumping a hurdle. The animals exposed to escapable shock were not distinguishable from unshocked controls. However, approximately two-thirds of inescapably shocked animals passively accepted the shock and if, by chance, they did make a successful escape response, they failed to learn (Overmeier & Seligman, 1967). It was assumed that during exposure to inescapable shock, the animals had learned that nothing they did would be effective—in other words, that they were helpless. The controversy surrounding this interpretation will be discussed below.

The majority of recent experiments have used rats as subjects. In this species, learned helplessness is less easy to demonstrate: difficult tasks must be used, such as crossing a barrier twice or pressing a lever three times, and performance deficits are relative rather than absolute. Although some authors have found the effect difficult to replicate (e.g., Freda & Kline, 1976), under suitable conditions the learned helplessness phenomenon appears to be a robust experimental finding (Looney & Cohen, 1972; Maier & Seligman, 1976; Seligman & Beagley, 1975).

There is considerable variability in estimates of how long helplessness effects last, which to some extent depends on the severity of the uncontrollable stressor (see Section 11.3). However, in some studies effects have been reported which lasted for periods of up to several months (Bainbridge, 1973; Hannum et al., 1976). It has also been found that helplessness effects have a considerable degree of generality. Transfer is typically observed between shock and other stressors, such as frustration (Rosellini & Seligman, 1975), cold water immersion (Weiss et al., 1976), and underwater submersion (Altenor et al., 1977), and helplessness has also been induced by a "pure" psychological stress—exposure to insoluble, as opposed to soluble, visual discrimination problems (Bainbridge, 1973). Exposure to insoluble problems (typically anagrams) or to uncontrollable stress (typically, loud noise) has also been found to induce subsequent performance deficits in human subjects. As reviewed in Chapter 4, human helplessness is now the subject of an extensive research literature (Garber & Seligman, 1980; Garber et al., 1979; Miller et al., 1977).

Until recently the effects of antidepressants on "helpless" animals had not been studied. It has now been reported that learned helplessness could be reversed by subchronic treatment (4–7 days) with a variety of antidepressants, including tricyclics, MAOIs, atypical antidepressants, and ECS (Dorworth & Overmeier, 1977; Leshner et al., 1979; Petty & Sherman, 1980; Sherman et al., 1982). The effect appears to be relatively specific to antidepressants, since neuroleptics, stimulants, sedatives, and anxiolytics were ineffective (Sherman et al., 1982). Reversal of helplessness by catecholamine receptor stimulants and by the anticholinergic scopolamine have also been reported (Anisman et al., 1979b), but it is difficult to compare this study directly with the preceding literature, owing to a large number of procedural differences, including the use of acute drug treatment. Although a range of chemically distinct antidepressants have been studied in the learned helplessness model, they do not differ greatly in their clinical potency. All could reasonably be expected to show therapeutic effects in the 75–150 mg/day dose range, which is too narrow to examine the correlation between clinical potency and effects on learned helplessness.

The current position, therefore, is that the model has good predictive validity, insofar as it responds to a wide range of clinically effective treatments and there are no false negatives. However, the drugs examined do not differ greatly in their clinical potency, so the correlation test cannot be applied. Also, the effects of chronic anticholinergic treatment on learned helplesssness have not yet been assessed; neither have the effects of antihistamines.

The effects of acute antidepressant treatment on learned helplessness are controversial. Sherman and co-workers (1979) found that acute imipramine administration did not reverse helplessness. More recently, however, successful reversal of helplessness has been reported following acute administration of imipramine, DMI, or nomifensine (Kametani et al., 1983). The discrepancy may reflect the fact that different test procedures were used in the two studies; it may be important to note that the study of Sherman and co-workers used a simple escape procedure (a single bar press), in which performance deficits are not usually observed (Seligman & Beagley, 1975). It is possible that reversal of performance deficits in more standard helplessness procedures may not require chronic treatment, which would reduce the face validity of the model.

Although the issue of acute versus chronic antidepressant treatment is potentially of importance, the assessment of face validity relies primarily on the symptomatology displayed in the model, and here, apparently, the learned helplessness model is very strong. In addition to performance deficits in aversively motivated tasks, "helpless" animals show a variety of other behavioral changes, including decreased locomotor activity (Wagner et al., 1977), poor performance in appetitively motivated tasks (Anderson et al., 1968; Rosellini, 1978; Rosellini & DeCola, 1981; Zacharko et al., 1982, 1983), decreased aggression (Maier et al., 1972), early waking (Weiss et al., 1984), and loss of appetite and weight (Weiss, 1968). At first sight, the large number of symptoms induced by inescapable shock and their obvious similarities to the symptomatology of depression appear to lend the model considerable face validity. Indeed, J. Weiss and co-workers (1982) have gone so far as to suggest that animals exposed to uncontrollable electric shock satisfy DSM-III criteria for major depressive disorder.

However, when it comes to examining parallels between the two conditions in more detail, this very richness proves to be something of an embarrassment. The defining feature of learned helplessness is a lowered voluntary response initiation, which, according to Seligman, is "pervasive in depression. It produces passivity, psychomotor retardation, intellectual slowness and social unresponsiveness; in extreme depression, it can produce stupor" (Seligman, 1975, p. 84). However, it is not true that passivity and psychomotor retardation are pervasive in depressive disorders (Depue & Monroe, 1978). Psychomotor retardation is a key symptom of endogenous depression, but it is not present in reactive depressions (Nelson & Charney, 1981; see Section 3.3.1.), and among endogenous depressions, bipolar depressions are characterized by retardation, but agitation is also common in unipolar depressions (Depue & Monroe, 1978, 1979).

Similarly, aggression and hostility are absent in bipolar depressions, but are not uncommon among unipolar endogenous depressions and are usually present in neurotic depressions (Depue & Monroe, 1978, 1979; Paykel, 1971). Helplessness therefore appears to resemble bipolar endogenous depression most strongly. However, the defining feature of endogenous depressions is their failure to respond to psychosocial intervention (Depue & Monroe, 1978; Nelson & Charney, 1981). Helplessness does respond to psychosocial intervention in that performance deficits may be overcome by forcibly exposing the animal to the fact that its responding does produce shock termination (Seligman et al., 1975). Furthermore, uncontrollable shock generates significantly more anxiety than controllable shock (reviewed by Seligman, 1975), and helplessness induction in people is also accompanied by increases in anxiety and hostility (Gatchel et al., 1975; Klein et al., 1976; Miller & Seligman, 1975). However, anxiety is not associated with endogenous depressions (Nelson & Charney, 1981), and certainly not with bipolar or retarded endogenous depressions (Depue & Monroe, 1978, 1979). Conversely, anxious depressions are not characterized by passiveness and lack of hostility (Gersh & Fowles, 1979). In short, although retarded endogenomorphic depression is the strongest candidate, it is not entirely clear which type of depression learned helplessness models.

The specificity of learned helplessness as a model of depression has also been questioned. In addition to producing the performance deficits described above, exposure to inescapable, but not to escapable, shock has also been found to potentiate "animal hypnosis," a state of tonic immobility and waxy flacidity induced in many species by immobilization. Animal hypnosis has been studied as a model of human catalepsy, and interestingly, was alleviated by imipramine, which is also effective in catalepsy (Maser & Gallup, 1974). The relationship between uncontrollable stress and anxiety has already been commented upon, and further similarities between the learned helplesssness hypothesis of depression and the theories of the etiology of a number of other psychiatric disorders, including schizophrenia, paranoia, and psychopathy have also been noted (Blaney, 1977).

Despite its appeal, therefore, there are serious doubts regarding the face validity of learned helplessness as a model of depression. Its specificity is unclear, and the model appears to predict patterns of symptoms that are not found to occur in depression. Seligman (1978) has attempted to counter these conclusions by arguing that traditional classifications of depression are not well established and by advancing the concept of "helplessness depression" as a new diagnostic category. Certainly there are depressions in which helplessness is a dominant theme (Arieti & Bemporad, 1982; Beck, 1983; Blatt et al., 1976, 1982), but, as discussed in Section 4.4.2, these appear to correspond closely to endogenous depression (Beck, 1983). Consequently, the notion of helplessness depression does little to overcome the discrepant pattern of symptoms shown by the model.

The construct validity of the learned helplessness model of depression rests on three assumptions: that animals exposed to uncontrollable aversive events do become helpless; that a similar state is induced in people by uncontrollability; and that helplessness in people is the central symptom of depression. Each of these assumptions has been the source of intense controversy.

The helplessness hypothesis asserts that in animals exposed to uncontrollable events, the perception that they have no control undermines their motivation to perform in subsequent tasks, as the incentive to perform is based in large part on the expectation that responding will bring relief (Maier & Seligman, 1976; Seligman, 1975). A number of alternative, and simpler, accounts of the performance deficits shown by inescapably shocked animals have also been advanced. One group of explanations suggest that animals subjected to inescapable shock might learn to become inactive, a habit that would interfere with the learning of an active escape response (Bracewell & Black, 1974; Glazer & Weiss, 1976b; Levis, 1976). Glazer and Weiss (1976b), for example, presented evidence that in the rat, shock elicits a burst of locomotor activity that subsides after four or five seconds; there was a high probability in this experiment that shock termination would occur at approximately the same time as the onset of immobility, which would therefore be reinforced. A second group of explanations argue that inescapable shock is more stressful than escapable shock, and it therefore depletes the brain of neurochemicals essential to initiate responding (Anisman et al., 1979a,b; Miller & Weiss, 1969; Weiss et al., 1976). Although it remains unclear in these accounts why inescapable shock is more stressful than escapable shock, it has been demonstrated that, for example, inescapable shock leads to depletions of brain catecholamines but escapable shock does not, and that the effects of inescapable shock on subsequent escape performance may be mimicked by pharmacological treatments which impair catecholaminergic neurotransmission (Anisman et al., 1979a,b; see also Chapters 8 and 11).

These alternative explanations share the common feature that performance failures are said to result from inactivity rather than from learned helplessness. This explanation is difficult to apply to two experiments by Maier and Testa (1975) in which it was shown that tasks with identical performance requirements were impaired by prior exposure to uncontrollable shock if they were cognitively difficult but not if additional cues were added to simplify the cognitive requirements. More direct evidence in favor of the learned helplessness interpretation is the observation that learning deficits following inescapable shock are also seen when the escape task requires the animal to be passive or to reduce its rate of responding (Baker, 1976; Jackson et al., 1978; Maier, 1970). These results can not easily be explained by any of the alternative hypotheses, and they constitute strong (though by no means conclusive) support for the learned helplessness position (Alloy & Seligman, 1979).

It is now clear that behind this controversy lies the fact that both sides are correct: inescapable shock produces effects of both kinds, a learning difficulty and also an activity deficit (Maier & Jackson, 1979). It has also been established that an important component of the activity deficit is that exposure to inescapable shock renders animals analgesic and therefore less responsive on subsequent reexposure to shock (Jackson et al., 1979; Maier & Jackson, 1979; see also Section 18.2.1). A number of studies have demonstrated that the learning difficulty may be readily dissociated from analgesia by the use of suitable experimental procedures (Maier & Jackson, 1979; Mah et al., 1980; MacLennan et al., 1982). In practice, however, in the great majority of studies of learned helplessness, these two factors are confounded. What this means is that even though there is strong evidence that cognitive changes (helplessness) do occur when animals are exposed to inescapable shock, it can not, in general, be assumed that the subsequent performance deficits are caused by helplessness, rather than inactivity.

The answers to the other two questions about the construct validity of the model lie in the human helplessness literature. As discussed in Section 4.3.2, exposure to uncontrollable stress (typically, loud noise) or to insoluble problems (typically, anagrams) has been found to induce subsequent performance deficits in human subjects (Garber & Seligman, 1980; Garber et al., 1979; Miller et al., 1977). As in the animal studies, however, it is not clear that the performance deficits occur because the subjects perceive themselves as being helpless (Buchwald et al., 1978; Cole & Coyne, 1977). By 1978 it had also become clear that even if the hypothesis were correct, it could operate only under very restricted conditions. In the reformulated learned helplessness hypothesis (Abramson et al., 1978b; see Section 4.3.3), uncontrollability is said to induce helplessness only if an appropriate attribution is made as to the causes of failure of the experimental task. Although problems remain (Buchwald et al., 1978; Wortman & Dintzer, 1978), the reformulated theory is able to explain most of the findings of human helplessness induction experiments. However, the cost is a considerable decrease in the testability of the model and a distancing from the form of the theory applicable to animals.

The third question to be considered is the relationship between human helplessness and depression, which has also been the subject of considerable debate (see Sections 4.3.2 & 4.3.3). A number of studies have demonstrated that nondepressed volunteers subjected to a helplessness induction procedure do show performance deficits similar to those seen in severely depressed patients (Abramson et al., 1978b; Price et al., 1978; Raps et al., 1980), though some of the specific predictions have not been confirmed (Buchwald et al., 1978; Rizley, 1978; Willis & Blaney, 1978).

However, depression is no more common than anxiety or hostility in the minority of studies that have investigated the effects of helplessness induction procedures on mood rather than on performance (Blaney, 1977; Buchwald et al., 1978; Klein et al., 1976).

The reformulation of the theory dealt with some of these problems by postulating that depression would ensue only if failure in a helplessness experiment was attributed to causes that are internal, stable, and global, such as stupidity (see Section 4.3.3). However, a number of empirical problems still remain (Buchwald et al., 1978; Hammen & de Mayo, 1982; Miller et al., 1982), as do a variety of theoretical issues, including the question of whether people do generally make attributions, the relationship between attributions and behavior, the appropriateness of the dimensions of attribution selected by the theory, and the failure to specify the conditions under which particular attributions will be made (Huesmann, 1978; Wortman & Dintzer, 1978; see also Section 4.3.3).

To summarize, the "helplessness" interpretation of the animal experiments has not been conclusively established, the "helplessness" interpretation of the human experiments is even less certain, and the relationship between helplessness and depression remains elusive. Consequently, the construct validity of the model is not well established. In defence of the model, it should also be added that it is doubtful whether any animal model would stand up well under such detailed scrutiny.

7.2.2. "Behavioral Despair"

A second model is closely related to learned helplessness, conceptually and practically. If mice or rats are forced to swim in a confined space, they initially make a frenzied attempt to escape and then assume an immobile posture. On subsequent immersion, the onset of immobility is much more rapid. This state has been named "behavioral despair," on the assumption that the animals have "given up hope of escaping," as in the learned helplessness procedure (Porsolt et al., 1977a,b, 1978a,b, 1979; Porsolt, 1981). Some authors prefer to use a more value free label, such as "the swimming test."

The onset of immobility in the swimming test is delayed by pretreatment with a wide variety of antidepressants, including tricyclics (imipramine, amitriptyline, doxepin, DMI, nortriptyline), MAOIs (clorgyline, deprenyl, iproniazid, nialamide, tranylcypromine), atypical antidepressants (maprotiline, iprindole, buproprion, mianserin, nomifensine, viloxazine), ECS, and REM sleep deprivation (Browne, 1979; Ferris et al., 1982; Gorka & Wojtasik, 1980; Gorka et al., 1979; Martorana & Nitz, 1979; Porsolt, 1981; Porsolt et al., 1977a,b, 1978a, 1979; Schechter & Chance, 1979; Wallach & Hedley, 1979). There is, in fact, a significant correlation between clinical potency (Table 6.1) and potency of antidepressants in the "behavioral despair" test (rho = 0.58, p < 0.05, calculated using data in Porsolt et al., 1977b and Porsolt, 1981); this was not found in any other of the models reviewed.

The specificity of the "behavioral despair" test has been questioned: three effective antidepressants, chlorimipramine, trazodone, and salbutamol, did not reduce immobility in the rat (Porsolt et al., 1979; Porsolt, 1981). Chlorimipramine did reduce immobility in the mouse, however; its inactivity in the rat may reflect the fact that the drug is metabolized differently in rats than in mice and people (Nagy, 1977). It is possible, though unlikely, that the maximum dose of trazodone (100 mg/kg; Porsolt, 1981) was insufficient (cf. Table 6.1), and it is also possible, though even less likely, that the minimum dose of salbutamol (16 mg/kg; Porsolt et al., 1979) was too high.

A potentially more serious problem arises from the large number of nonantidepressants that also reduce immobility. Although the test successfully discriminates antidepressants from neuroleptics and anxiolytics (Porsolt et al., 1977a,b), false positives have been reported for stimulants, convulsants, anticholinergics, antihistamines, pentobarbital, opiates, and other brain peptides, and a number of other drugs (Betin et al., 1982; Browne, 1979; Kastin et al., 1978; Porsolt, 1981; Schechter & Chance, 1979; Wallach & Hedley, 1979). However, some of these effects are nonspecific. It has been demonstrated that stimulants and anticholinergics reduce immobility by an indiscriminate stimulation of motor activity rather than by delaying the onset of immobility, and they could be distinguished from antidepressants simply by prolonging the period of the test (Kitada et al., 1981). It is possible that this procedural change might eliminate many of the false positives. Additionally, it has been found that whereas responses to antidepressants were potentiated by chronic treatment, the response to an antihistamine disappeared on chronic administration (Kitada et al., 1981). However, the generality of these effects remains to be established.

The effectiveness of acute drug treatments in this model does not correspond to their time course of clinical action. This appears to detract somewhat from the face validity of the model, but the force of this argument is weakened by the observation that chronic treatment potentiates the effects (Kitada et al., 1981; Porsolt, 1981). Also, immobility is potentiated by repeated exposure to the forced swimming procedure, and this effect could be counteracted by chronic treatment with imipramine (Gorka & Wojtasik, 1980). Nonetheless, the face validity of the "behavioral despair" model is far from well established. Unlike learned helplessness, "behavioral despair" has not been subjected to extensive behavioral investigation. If it is not taken for granted that the two procedures are equivalent (see below), then the face validity of the model rests largely on the etiological effects of stress and the analogy between immobility and the passivity seen in retarded depressions. The analogy between the life stresses that precipitate depression and the stress of water immersion goes no deeper, but the analogy betwen immobility and depression may be slightly enlarged. "Behavioral despair" represents not a generalized hypoactivity but rather an inability or reluctance to maintain the effort of attempting to escape; depressed subjects have been found to show their most pronounced psychomotor impairments in tests that require the sustained expenditure of effort (Weingartner & Silberman, 1982). The model therefore has some small degree of face validity.

The construct validity of this test derives entirely from its supposed relationship to learned helplessness. Consequently, the problems discussed in the previous section in relation to the construct validity of learned helplessness apply equally to the "behavioral despair" model. In addition, it is necessary to examine the nature of the relationship between the two models. Surprisingly, the question of escapability has hardly been investigated in relation to "behavioral despair." Only one study has addressed the problem directly: immobility was induced to the same extent by escapable or inescapable swimming (O'Neill & Valentino, 1982). However, in this study, the "escapable" condition consisted of lowering a ladder into the water at the end of each three-minute trial. In effect, the situation was inescapable for most of the time, and it is questionable whether it would be perceived as escapable by the animals involved. Inescapable immersion has been shown in another study to cause deficits on subsequent water-escape and shock-escape performance, but in this case, the procedure involved total submersion rather than forced swimming (Altenor et al., 1977).

A relationship between behavioral despair and learned helplessness is supported by the observation that inescapable shock increased immobility in the "behavioral despair" test, either 30 minutes or 24 hours later, whereas escapable shock did not have this effect (Nomura et al., 1982; J. Weiss et al., 1981, 1982, 1984). In view of the consistent finding of decreased motor activity following inescapable shock (e.g., Anisman et al., 1979a,b), it would be surprising were this not the case. However, the reciprocal finding has not been demonstrated. With the exception of the submersion experiment described above (Altenor et al., 1977), forced swimming has not been found to impair subsequent escape performance in a water maze (Porsolt, 1981) or shock avoidance responding (O'Neill & Valentino, 1982). The task used in the former study may have been too easy, since it has been found that performance deficits following inescapable shock are only seen in rats when difficult tasks are used (Maier & Testa, 1975; Seligman & Beagley, 1975). However, the shock-avoidance task used by O'Neill and Valentino (pressing a lever three times) is one in which inescapable-shock-induced performance deficits are typically seen (Seligman & Beagley, 1975).

In conclusion, therefore, while it seems possible that "behavioral despair" is a milder version of learned helplessness, it remains to be demonstrated that the two procedures do, in fact, constitute different ways of measuring the same thing, and the "behavioral despair" procedure, which is rapidly gaining in popularity, cannot at present be said to have construct validity.

7.2.3. Chronic Unpredictable Stress

Another model along similar lines has recently been proposed by Katz and colleagues. During a three-week period, rats were subjected to a variety of different stressors, including, among others, electric shocks, immersion in cold water, and reversal of the light–dark cycle. At the end of this period, they received a session of exposure to loud noises and bright lights, followed immediately by an open field test. In unstressed animals, the nose–light session caused an increase in open field activity, but this effect was not seen in chronically stressed animals. The effect was, however, restored by daily antidepressant treatment during the chronic stress period. Restoration of the activating effect of an acute stress was observed with tricyclics (imipramine, amitriptyline), an MAOI (pargyline), atypical antidepressants (iprindole, mianserin, buproprion) and ECS. A neuroleptic drug (haloperidol), an anxiolytic (oxazepam), an antihistamine (tripellenamine), an anticholinergic (scopolamine), and a stimulant (amphetamine) were ineffective; so, also, however, was the MAOI tranylcypromine. In agreement with previous research (Burchfield, 1979), chronic stress was also found to increase plasma corticosteroid levels; this effect showed the same spectrum of pharmacological sensitivity, with the exception that the anticholinergic scopolamine was also effective (Katz, 1981b; Katz & Hersh, 1981; Katz et al., 1981a,b; Katz & Baldrighi, 1982; Katz & Sibel 1982a,b; Roth & Katz, 1981). Similar effects have also been reported in mice (Soblosky & Thurmond, 1982). A further effect observed after chronic stress was a failure to increase fluid consumption when saccharine was added to the drinking water; this deficit was partially restored by imipramine; no other drugs were tested (Katz, 1982).

This model would appear to have a fair degree of face validity, since the effects observed—increased corticosteroid levels, a lack of reactivity to an acute stress, and a failure to respond to a (presumably) pleasurable stimulus—are all central symptoms of endogenomorphic depression (American Psychiatric Association, 1980; Carroll et al., 1976; see Chapter 3). The observed decrease in locomotor activity is consistent with these effects. As noted in chapter 3, loss of motivation tends to characterize retarded, rather than agitated, depression (Nelson & Charney, 1981). Additionally, the stress regime employed in these experiments appears to be a somewhat more realistic analogue of the stress of living than is a single session of either electric shock or water immersion. It must be emphasized, however, that the requirements for stress to be chronic, varied, and unpredictable have not been established; a briefer and more uniform stress regime might have proved equally effective. The requirement for chronic drug treatment has been demonstrated, but only for one drug, imipramine. It should also be noted that the model involves prophylactic treatment, since drugs were administered during, rather than following, chronic stress.

There are two sources from which the model might derive construct validity. The first is the learned helplessness literature. To the extent that the model is related to learned helplessness, it is subject to the problems previously discussed in relation to the learned helplessness model. As noted, the importance of predictability in the chronic stress model has not been investigated. In fact, elevation of blood corticosteroid levels, combined with a reduced response to stress, has been observed following daily exposure to a predictable cold stress, and a conditioning model explicitly based upon predictability of the stress was advanced to explain the results (Burchfield, 1979).

The second, and more likely, source of construct validity is the literature relating depression to psychological stress. The relationship of stress to diagnostic subgroups of depression is unclear. Passiveness comparable to that shown by chronically stressed rats would be more commonly encountered in bipolar than in unipolar depressives (Donnelly & Murphy, 1973) and among unipolars in endogenomorphic rather than neurotic depressions (Nelson & Charney, 1981). However, stressful life events are equally frequent in neurotic and endogenomorphic depressions (Brown & Harris, 1978; Lewinsohn et al., 1977; Paykel, 1979b). On the other hand, there is some evidence suggesting that bipolar depressives may suffer from a higher level of chronic stress than unipolars (Depue & Monroe, 1979).

A number of theoretical approaches have been developed that attempt to explain the supposed etiological effect of stress in depression (see Anisman & Zacharko, 1982; Depue, 1979). However, the definition of stress in relation to human studies remains a topic of endless debate (Anisman & Zacharko, 1982), and a number of fundamental questions are unanswered, including the accuracy with which depressed individuals recall stressful life events (Lishman, 1972), the possibility that stress may simply provoke hospitalization in already depressed people (Hudgens et al., 1967), and the provocative thought that the life style of depressives may be responsible for many of the stresses they experience (Beck & Harrison, 1982). Indeed, there is still some doubt as to whether there is in fact a causal relationship between stress and depression, rather than simply a statistical association (Tennant et al., 1981).

Further assessment of the chronic intermittent stress model must therefore await clarification of the relationship between stress and depression in people. It must be added, however, that recent evidence suggests that chronic low grade stressors (strains) may be rather more potent precipitants of depression than severe life events (see Section

20.1.1). These observations greatly enhance the model's potential construct validity.

7.2.4. Separation Models

For many authors (e.g., Everitt & Keverne, 1979; Howard et al., 1981), the only worthwhile animal models of depression are those involving separation phenomena in nonhuman primates; the evolutionary proximity of primate species seems to afford intuitive insights into their behavior, which are lacking in less closely related animals. In fact, separation phenomena of protest followed by despair are present to some extent in many species, including cats, dogs, rodents, and precocial birds (reviewed by Katz, 1981a; McKinney & Bunney, 1969; see also Section 19.3).

Infant monkeys respond to maternal separation by an initial stage of "protest," characterized by agitation, sleeplessness, distress calls, and screaming, followed after one or two days by "despair," characterized by a decrease in activity, appetite, play, and social interaction and by the assumption of a hunched posture and "sad" facial expression (Hinde et al., 1978; Kaufman & Rosenblum, 1967; McKinney & Bunney, 1969; Reite et al., 1981; Suomi et al., 1976). The nature of the separation response is sensitive to the environment in which the experiments are carried out, however (Hinde & McGinnis, 1977; Kaufman & Stynes, 1978; Reite et al., 1981; Suomi, 1976), and the incidence of "depressive" behaviors may in some experiments be as low as 15% (Lewis et al., 1976). Similar phenomena are also observed when group-reared animals are isolated from their peers (Bowden & McKinney, 1972; Kraemer & McKinney, 1979; Suomi et al., 1970).

Only three published studies have attempted to use antidepressant treatments to modify primate separation behavior. Chronic DMI has been found to increase social contact and decrease distress vocalization and self-oriented behaviors in maternally separated infant macaques (Hrdina et al., 1979). Similarly, chronic imipramine was found to decrease self-clasping in peer-separated infant rhesus monkeys, whereas acute treatment had the opposite effect; other separation-induced behavioral changes were unaffected by imipramine (Suomi et al., 1978). A partial response to ECS in isolated rhesus monkeys has also been reported (Lewis & McKinney, 1976). Trifluoperazine, amphetamine, and diazepam were not found to affect responses to social isolation in chimpanzees (Menzel et al., 1963; Turner et al., 1969), but some therapeutic effects of chlorpromazine were seen in rhesus monkeys (McKinney et al., 1973). It should be added that although antidepressant drugs are frequently used in childhood depression, there is a conspicuous absence of methodologically sound studies demonstrating their efficacy (Kashani et al., 1981; Pearce, 1981).

The primate separation response shows a marked similarity to the state of "anaclitic depression," first described by Spitz (1946) and Robertson and Bowlby (1952). Institutionalized children showed a similar sequence of protest (agitation, crying, insomnia, and oral stereotypies) followed in approximately 15–20% of cases by despair (retardation, self-clasping, withdrawal from social contact, and an increase in the likelihood of succumbing to disease.) Although some authors have denied the possibility of depression in children (Finch, 1960; Rie, 1966), the existence of childhood depression is now generally accepted, and the symptoms appear to resemble those of adult depression, the major diagnostic criteria being dysphoria and an inability to have fun (Kashani et al., 1981; Poznanski, 1982). Unfortunately, insufficient studies employing diagnostic criteria have been carried out to assess the claim that in children "the sine qua non in acute depressive reactions is the sudden loss of a love object" (McKnew & Cytryn, 1973), which obviously has a bearing on the face validity of the separation model.

Studies of pituitary–adrenal activity in separated monkeys provides a further test of the model's face validity. Separation is accompanied during the protest phase by a rise in plasma cortisol concentrations (Smotherman et al., 1979), and the size of this elevation has been found to predict the intensity of "depressive" responses during the despair phase (Higley et al., 1982). Like endogenously depressed people (Carroll, 1982; see Section 3.3.2), some separated monkeys also fail to suppress plasma cortisol concentrations in response to dexamethasone (Kalin et al., 1982). Unfortunately, abnormal dexamethasone suppression appears to be unrelated to the severity of the "depressive response": in a group of 11 monkeys, nonsuppression was seen in four animals, two of which showed severe behavioral responses, while the other two showed no behavioral effects at all (Kalin et al., 1983).

Accepting that preadolescents are capable of being depressed is not the same as equating the despair response of separated infants with adult depression (Ainsworth, 1976; Bowlby, 1976), and this problem is likely to remain until the nature of adult depression is more fully understood. Therefore, since no consensus exists as to the relationship between infantile anaclitic depression and depression in adults (Schulterbrandt & Raskin, 1977), the construct validity of the separation model is difficult to assess, despite the apparent homology between primate "depression" and anaclitic depression. Even the assumption that separation from a loved one is a significant cause of adult depression has been questioned. A clear relationship exists in the case of bereavement, but the incidence of clinical depression following the mourning period may be as low as 5% (Parkes, 1972), and bereavement also precipitates a wide range of other psychiatric disorders (Brown et al., 1973), as well as a variety of nonpsychiatric medical conditions (Schmale, 1973), particularly coronary thrombosis (Parkes, 1972). In the case of marital breakdown, it has not been established whether separation precipitates depression or, conversely, whether a prior depression in one partner was the cause of separation (Briscoe & Smith, 1975). Thus, the theoretical formulation of depression as a phase of the protest–despair cycle, which is assumed by the model, is at present at best tenuous.

7.2.5. Incentive Disengagement

A common feature of all four of the stress-based models described above is a biphasic response—activation by acute stress superseded eventually by passiveness, the time course varying between models. Klinger and co-workers (1974) have observed that in rats trained in a runway for food rewards, and then switched to nonreward (extinction), nonrewarded trials were followed for the first week by heightened locomotor activity, but for the next few days, nonrewarded trials were followed by a reduction in locomotor activity that was below control levels. It was hypothesized that this *incentive disengagement* cycle of invigoration followed by depression is characteristic of the period following the loss of a significant source of reinforcement (Klinger, 1975); the response to separation in primates, discussed above, would be a special case of this more general mechanism.

The incentive disengagement theory can potentially explain a number of features of depression, including the autonomous course of many depressions. Autonomy is perhaps the single most perplexing characteristic of depression yet most theories are concerned primarily with the etiology of depression and do not address the issue of its course. As this theory has attracted little attention in the research literature, and in particular, as there has been only a single relevant animal experiment, the theory will not be discussed in detail. However, it is noted that the model has potential construct validity, despite having minimal face validity and no predictive validity.

7.2.6. Intracranial Self-Stimulation

In several of the models already described, one important effect of the experimental manipulation has been a decrease in the performance of rewarded behaviors (Sections 7.2.1, 7.2.4 and 7.2.5). A number of recent experiments have attempted to investigate directly the brain systems that mediate reward, by studying brain stimulation reward in animals implanted with intracranial self-stimulation (ICSS) electrodes. Three such paradigms have been described. First, it has been found that ICSS rates were reduced, and the threshold for brain stimulation reward elevated, for a period of weeks following withdrawal from chronic amphetamine treatment (Barrett & White, 1980; Kokkinidis & Zacharko, 1980; Leith & Barrett, 1976, 1980; Simpson & Annau, 1977). This effect was alleviated by two days of imipramine or amitriptyline treatment, and with continued treatment, normal responding was restored (Kok-kinidis et al., 1980). The effects of other agents have not been studied in this model. A second model utilizes the depression of ICSS produced by a lesion of the internal capsule, in the region of the telencephalic–dien-cephalic border. The deficit was alleviated by subchronic (five to nine days) treatment with tricyclics (imipramine, amitriptyline, DMI, pro-triptyline), MAOIs (tranylcypromine, iproniazid), and atypical antide-pressants (maprotiline, mianserin, zimelidine, nomifensine, nisoxetine). Morphine, which may have antidepressant properties (Emrich, 1982; see Section 18.1.2.2), was also effective; diazepam, yohimbine, propranolol and "other nonantidepressants" were not (Cornfeldt et al., 1982; Szewczak et al., 1982). In a third paradigm, brain stimulation reward is studied without any prior treatment. Wauquier (1976) reported that acute an-tidepressant treatment prolonged lever pressing for brain stimulation reward in a progressive ratio reinforcement schedule (i.e., one in which more and more responses are required for each successive reward), but these results could not be replicated (Binks et al., 1979). However, it has been found that sensitivity to brain stimulation reward was increased in "normal" rats by chronic (two weeks) administration of DMI (Fibiger & Phillips, 1981). By contrast, amphetamine has been found to decrease ICSS threshold on acute administration, but with chronic treatment, tol-erance develops to this effect (Leith & Barrett, 1976, 1980).

The first two of these paradigms can claim face validity, as a decrease in the ability to experience pleasure may be the single most important symptom of endogenomorphic depression (American Psychiatric Associ-ation, 1980; Klein, 1974; Nelson & Charney, 1981; see Chapter 3). Ad-ditionally, in the case of post-amphetamine depression of ICSS, there is an obvious parallel with the depressions that frequently follow the ces-sation of chronic amphetamine use (Schick et al., 1973; Watson et al., 1972). These parallels depend on the assumption that the changes in self-stimulation behavior are brought about by a change in the rewarding value of the brain stimulation, rather than by nonspecific sedative or other motor effects. There exist a number of "rate-free" paradigms, in which these two factors may be dissociated (Liebman, 1983); unfortu-nately, they have not yet been employed in the models under consider-ation. However, while nonspecific factors might well be responsible for changes in ICSS rates, this is less likely in the case of the reported changes in ICSS thresholds (Barrett & White, 1980; Fibiger & Phillips, 1981; Leith & Barrett, 1976, 1980).

The ICSS models also have a degree of construct validity. ICSS appears to be controlled by many of the factors that control responding for natural rewards. For example, although the precise effects vary from electrode to electrode (e.g., Gallistel & Beagley, 1971), ICSS rates may be increased by food deprivation or by a variety of hormonal manipulations (e.g., Olds, 1958) and may be decreased by preloading with food or water (e.g., Hoebel

& Teitelbaum, 1962). These and other parallels indicate that brain stimulation reward works by activating the neural systems that mediate natural rewards (Hoebel, 1976). Homology between brain stimulation reward and positive reinforcement in people is suggested by the observation that stimulation of electrodes implanted in medial forebrain sites has been found to evoke pleasurable sensations in human subjects (Heath, 1963; Heath et al., 1968; Valenstein, 1973), though a variety of other reasons for stimulating, such as curiosity, are also reported (Sem-Jacobsen, 1976; Valenstein, 1973).

As discussed in chapter 4, the hypothesis that depression results from a reduction in the activity of reward systems is central to a number of theories of depression (Costello, 1972; Ferster, 1973; Lewinsohn, 1974; Stein, 1962). As predicted by all of these theories, there is strong support for the hypothesis that depression is associated with a low frequency of positive reinforcement, particularly social reinforcement (Blaney, 1977; Lewinsohn et al., 1979). However, the direction of causality has not yet been established.

7.3. AN OVERALL ASSESSMENT

The approach to animal models adopted here departs from tradition primarily in proposing a multiplicity of validating criteria within three relatively independent categories. The introduction of explicit criteria for predictive and construct validity reflects the two ways in which the field of animal modeling has changed in recent years. First, there has been an explosion of literature dealing with the pharmacological exploitation of animal models; this area is not well served simply by asking the model to show "similarity of treatment" to the condition it models. Second, there has been significant growth in the experimental psychological study of psychopathology; examination of construct validity provides a convenient way of bringing animal models into contact with this literature.

Information on the validity of each of the 18 models reviewed is summarized in Table 7.1. In the main body of the table, judgments of the validity (+) or invalidity (−) are made on each of the 15 criteria (five for each type of validation procedure) used in this review. The four columns at the right of the table offer a summary estimate of the current status of each model, using four-point scales (0 to + + +) for each validation procedure, and a grand total (out of 9). The models that score highest are the self-stimulation (5), chronic stress (5), separation (4), and learned helplessness (4) models; the ad hoc nature of the scales should, of course be bourne in mind.

In Table 7.2, the models are divided into four groups. Group 1 contains those models that score well on the validating criteria and have few or no invalidating characteristics. Group 2 contains potentially valid models

TABLE 7.1. ASSESSMENT OF THE MODELS AGAINST VALIDATING CRITERIA[a]

Models	Predictive Validity[b]					Face Validity[c]					Construct Validity[d]					Summary			
	RtA	WRT	NFP	NFN	CoP	TC	SoS	CoS	ND	StD	CloM	CloMd	H	ERtD	TRtD	P	F	C	Total
DOPA	+			=															0
Yohimbine (mice)	+	+	=	=															0
Yohimbine (dogs)	+	++	+?	+	−											++			2
Muricide	+	++	−	−?	−?											+			1
Kindling	+			=															0
Reserpine	+	++	−	=	+?	−	+												0
Amphetamine	+	+	−	=		−	−		−										0
5-HTP	+	++	−	−		−	+												0
Bulbectomy	+	++	−	−		?	++	?		?						+	+		2
Isolation	+	++	+?	+	+?	−	+			−						+++	+		3
Exhaustion	+	+	+			+	+					+	+?			+	+		2
Rhythms	+	+	+	+?		+	+									++	+		3
Helplessness	+	++	+	+		?	+++	−?	−	−	+?	+?	+?	?	?	++	+	+	4
'Despair'	+	++	?	−?	+	+?						+?	+?	?	?	++	+		3
Chronic stress	+	++	+	−		+	++	+		−	+	+	+	+?		++	++	+	5
Separation	+	+				+	++	+		−	+	+?	+?	?	?	+	++	+	4
Disengagement							+				+?	+?	+?	+?	+	++	+	++	2
ICSS	+	+	+?			+	+			+	+	+?	+?	+?	+	++	+	++	5

[a] The models are listed (under abbreviated titles) in the order in which they appear in the text. The main body of the table estimates the extent to which a model meets each criterion (+ or ++, model does well; − or =, model does badly). The summary columns on the right estimate predictive (P), face (F), and construct (C) validity on a four-point scale (blank, +, ++, +++); these scores are summed to give a grand total at the far right. Modified from Willner, 1984a.

[b] RtA, Responsive to antidepressants; WRT, Wide range tested; NFP, No false positives; NFN, No false negatives; CoP, Correlation of potencies.

[c] TC, Time course; SoS, Similarity of symptoms; CoS, Coherence of symptoms; ND, No dissimilarities; StD, Specificity to depression.

[d] CloM, Clear interpretation of model; CloMd, Clear interpretation of modelled; H, Homology; ERtD, Empirical relationship to depression; TRtD, Theoretical relationship to depression.

TABLE 7.2.   AN OVERALL ASSESSMENT

Model	Validity		
	Predictive	Face	Construct
Group 1 (Good?)			
"Behavioral despair"	+ +	+	
Chronic stress	+ +	+ +	+
Separation	+	+ +	+
Self-stimulation	+ +	+	+ +
Group 2 (Interesting)			
Yohimbine (dogs)	+ +		
Chronic isolation	+ + +		
Exhaustion stress	+	+	
Circadian rhythms	+ +	+	
Incentive disengagement		+	+
Group 3 (Problematic)			
Muricide	+		
Olfactory bulbectomy	+	+	
Learned helplessness	+ +	+	+
Group 4 (Poor)			
Yohimbine (mice)			
Dopa potentiation			
Kindling			
Reserpine reversal			
Amphetamine potentiation			
5-HTP reversal			

that have been the subject of limited research. Potentially serious questions have been raised concerning the validity of models in group 3; these models may still be useful, but should be treated with caution. The models in group 4 appear to have little to recommend them as animal models of depression. This of itself does not necessarily render them unsuitable as drug screening tests, since models and screening tests are assessed according to different criteria (Section 6.1). It should be noted that all of the traditional models fall into groups 3 (questionable) and 4 (probably invalid), whereas the two models that have the highest overall validity are among the most recent.

The models in groups 1 and 3 are those which (i) have been relatively extensively researched and (ii) are not clearly invalid. Two of these, olfactory bulbectomy and muricide, as well as the social isolation model in group 2, appear to model agitated depression. The other five models in groups 1 and 3 model retarded depression. These latter are closely related. Four of these models—separation, helplessness, "behavioral despair," and chronic stress—involve a biphasic activation–inhibition cycle, which has been proposed as the general form of the response to prolonged stress (Burchfield, 1979; Engel, 1962); in three of them—separation, helplessness, and chronic stress—the inhibitory phase has been shown to be associated with a decrease in positively reinforced behavior, which characterizes the self-stimulation models.

The limitations of theories that treat depression as a response to stress have already been noted; at best, stressful life events appear to account for only 25–30% of the variability in the incidence of depression (Akiskal, 1979; Brown et al., 1973). Increasingly, theories of depression emphasize multidimensional causality, with stress as only one among several etiological factors (see Section 20.1); in some of these theories, the underactivity of a central reward pathway has been proposed as a "final common path" to which the diverse precipitants lead (Akiskal & McKinney, 1973, 1975; Akiskal, 1979; Lewinsohn et al., 1979). It is therefore possible that stress-based models could prove to be valid as models of a state of depression, even if they should turn out to be less accurate as models of its etiology.

The object of this review has been to apply multiple criteria to assess the validity of animal models of depression. It is clear that no one method of validation is sufficient for this purpose. Although predictive validation and face validation suffer from a number of empirical drawbacks, construct validation rests on a theory of the nature of depression, and current theories of depression are not such as to inspire confidence in their eventual vindication. In the final analysis, an animal model is a theory of interspecific homology and, like all theories, must be judged ultimately on its power to generate testable hypotheses about the human condition being modeled.

7.4. THE USE OF ANIMAL MODELS OF DEPRESSION

The areas of research in which each of the 12 models under consideration have been used are shown in Table 7.3; the relative absence of entries attests in part to the fact that the major effort to date has been directed towards development of the models, rather than their exploitation. Most of the models have been the subject of some physiological studies, which will be described in later chapters. There have also been a small number of studies relevant to etiology and treatment, which will be considered briefly here.

7.4.1. Etiology of Depression

The contribution of animal models to an understanding of the etiology of depression has been slight. Six of the models involve the induction of abnormal states by behavioral manipulations, but in three of these—

TABLE 7.3. ANIMAL MODELS OF DEPRESSION—VALIDITY AND UTILIZATION[a]

Model	Degree of Validity			Used in Studies of		
	Predictive	Face	Construct	Etiology	Treatment	Physiology
"Behavioral despair"	+ +	+		+		+
Chronic stress	+ +	+ +	+	+		
Separation	+	+ +	+	+	+	+
Self-stimulation	+ +	+	+ +			+
Yohimbine (dogs)	+ +					
Chronic isolation	+ + +			+		+
Exhaustion stress	+	+				+
Circadian rhythms	+ +	+				+
Incentive disengagement		+	+	+		
Muricide	+					+
Olfactory bulbectomy	+	+				+
Learned helplessness	+ +	+	+	+	+	+

[a] The models are grouped by their validity: Group 1, models perform well against validating criteria; Group 2, interesting but not studied extensively; Group 3, validity questionable, but not clearly invalid. The fourth group of models, which fail to score on any of the three tests for validity, has not been included.

social isolation (Section 6.5.5), chronic stress (Section 7.2.3), and incentive disengagement (Section 7.2.5)—etiological factors have not been explicitly studied. In a fourth model, "behavioral despair," the extent of its contribution to understanding etiology consists of the observation that the behavior shows strain differences (Porsolt et al., 1978b), and it is therefore under some degree of genetic control. Etiology has been extensively investigated in the context of the learned helplessness model, but as described above, the majority of these studies have been concerned with the status and interpretation of the model rather than its use to investigate the etiology of depression.

The only model in which factors relevant to the etiology of depression have been investigated is the primate separation model; the results are not particularly illuminating and there are no major surprises. The "depressive" response of infant monkeys to maternal separationn has been found, for example, to depend upon the social setting prior to separation. For example, greater "depressive" reactions are seen when tension exists in the mother–infant relationship (Hinde & Spencer-Booth, 1970; Kaufman & Rosenblum, 1967, 1969), and infants from dominant mothers show smaller separation responses (Kaufman & Rosenblum, 1969). Social factors during separation may also be important. In a mixed group of bonnet and pigtailed macaques, pigtailed macaques were severely affected by removal of the mother, but bonnets were only severely affected if both the mother and the other juvenile bonnet macaques were removed (Kaufman & Stynes, 1978). It has also been observed that sequential removal and return of each member of a four-infant group produced a gradual deterioration of group activity and a failure of the later subjects to adjust to reunion (Suomi & Harlow, 1975). Another less than earth-shattering observation is that longer separations produce greater "depressive" responses (Spencer-Booth & Hinde, 1971; Suomi, 1976).

Studies of this kind may perhaps, in due course, contribute to an understanding of the importance of social relationships for the processes of child development (Ainsworth, 1976; Bowlby, 1976). However, they have not as yet in any way advanced our understanding of the etiology of depression, and there seems little reason to expect this state of affairs to change, particularly since separation does not appear to be a major precipitant of depression in adults (Akiskal, 1979; Briscoe & Smith, 1975; Lloyd, 1980b; Parkes, 1972).

In general, in the area of etiology, animal models have been informed by human studies rather than the other way round. There is, however, one area in which models might have something to offer. Repeated peer-group separations have been found to potentiate "depressive" responses to separation; additionally, in animals with a history of separation, the drug alpha-methylparatyrosine (AMPT) induced "depressive" responses at doses substantially lower than those needed in control animals (Kraemer & McKinney, 1979; see Section 9.4). Some insight into the mechanism of these effects comes from studies showing that in rats, the neurochemical changes associated with uncontrollable electric shock could be reinstated by a relatively mild stress, which ordinarily would produce only minimal changes (Anisman & Sklar, 1979; Jackson et al., 1979) or by an environmental stimulus paired with the shock (Cassens et al., 1980; Hintgen et al., 1976). These studies raise the possibility that classical conditioning may play a role in either the increased predisposition to depression in people who have experienced stressful life events (Lloyd, 1980a) or in the recurrence of depression following the initial episode. The plausibility of this account is enhanced by the existence of many studies demonstrating classical conditioning of physiological responses in people (see Burchfield, 1979).

7.4.2. Treatment of Depression

With the exception of the obvious utility of animal models in the discovery of new antidepressant drugs, their contribution to the treatment of depression is almost nonexistent. A number of studies have demonstrated that the rehabilitation of socially isolated or peer-separated monkeys is facilitated by the opportunity to play with younger normal monkeys (reviewed by Suomi, 1976), but the only implication for the therapy of depression that follows from these observations is that a supportive social environment may be helpful, a suggestion which antedates the animal model by many years (see Dean & Lin, 1977, and Section 20.3.1).

Similarly, it is known that learned helplessness may be overcome by forcing an animal to respond and experience the fact that relief ensues (Seligman et al., 1968). A therapy based on this observation has been proposed, which consists of having the patient experience success by working through a series of problems graded in difficulty. Although some success has been reported using this technique (Klein & Seligman, 1976), its impact has been slight (see Kovacs, 1980). This is not to deny that the learned helplessness model could generate research with implications for the treatment of depression. However, it is difficult to believe that further development in this area will owe any debt to the animal studies. Much the same can be said for suggested changes in child-rearing practices (Seligman, 1975), which follow from the observation that experience in controlling stress "immunizes" rats against becoming helpless when later exposed to uncontrollable stress (Seligman et al., 1975).

7.4.3 Prospects

All things considered, it appears that animal models of depression have made remarkably little contribution to understanding of either the etiology of depression or its treatment. With the possible exception of studies modeling the role of classical conditioning in the precipitation of depression, there seems little reason to expect this position to change. This pessimistic prognosis is due in part to the recent growth in the literature on depression itself. It is now clear that the etiological and treatment variables studied in animal models may be readily investigated in people, employing a much higher level of conceptual sophistication and with none of the problems of validation.

These conclusions have serious implications for the continued use of nonhuman primates as subjects in animal models of depression. It seems unlikely that animal models will make more than a minimal contribution outside the area of physiology. However, this is precisely the area for which primates are least well suited as experimental subjects, on both ethical and financial grounds, particularly since there exist a number of rodent models of comparable validity. The main thrust of primate separation studies has been an attempt to demonstrate similarities between "depressed" primates and depressed people; work with the models has tended to ape the clinical literature, rather than the reverse. This emphasis is unfortunate, since it means that if the model can be shown to be valid, it then becomes unethical to use it. The combination of limited utility and dubious morality suggests that primate separation paradigms have little future as animal models of depression, though they may have other uses.

In contrast to this rather gloomy picture, other animal models clearly have the potential to provide valuable insights into the physiology of depression. In the chapters which follow, physiological information derived from animal models of depression is used as one of the starting points for assessing what might be occurring in the brains of severely depressed people. Successful science should involve a two-way traffic of information, in which progress in solving a problem leads also to a better understanding of the tools used. So it is in this case. A reevaluation of animal models, in the light of a clearer understanding of the psychobiology of depression, forms a part of the conclusions of this investigation (Section 20.2.5).

3

Psychobiology

eight

DOPAMINE AND DEPRESSION: THEORETICAL PERSPECTIVES

The next 12 chapters of this book review the psychobiology of depression, using as a starting point the psychological foundations developed in Part 2. The greater part of the work to be described involves investigations of the neurochemical actions of antidepressant agents, pharmacological studies using more-or-less specific neurochemical probes, and biochemical measurements in depressed people. Consequently, the most convenient approach to this vast literature is neurochemical. The different neurotransmitter systems that have been studied in relation to depression serve to organize the literature around a coherent set of common problems.

It may seem a little irregular to begin a discussion of this kind with DA, rather than NA or 5-HT, which are usually given pride of place. However, DA provides a clearer context in which to expound the underlying philosophy of this book—that basic brain research has already answered many of the problems arising out of clinical research in psychobiology. For one thing, the issues are much clearer in the case of DA; there is only one DA hypothesis of depression, but there are two diametrically opposing hypotheses about NA and 5-HT (see Table 1.1). How-

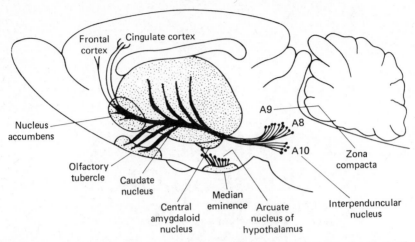

Fig. 8.1. The major DA pathways of the rat forebrain. From J. R. Cooper, F. E. Bloom, and R. H. Roth. *The Biochemical Basis of Neuropharmacology*, 4th ed. Oxford University Press, New York, 1982. Reprinted by permission of the Oxford University Press.

ever, the main reason for considering DA first is that the behavioral functions of DA are better understood than are those of NA or 5-HT. In fact, it is probably true to say that the behavioral functions of the major DA pathways are understood better than those of any other system in the brain.

8.1. FOREBRAIN DA SYSTEMS

The two major groups of DA-containing cell bodies are found in the substantia nigra (nuclei A8 and A9) and in the ventral tegmental area (VTA: nucleus A10); these nuclei lie close together in the ventral midbrain. The nigrostriatal pathway originates in the substantia nigra, runs forward through the dorso-lateral hypothalamus, and terminates in the caudate nucleus and putamen. The mesolimbic pathway originates in the VTA, projects through the lateral hypothalamus in the medial forebrain bundle, and terminates in the nucleus accumbens. Some DA fibers in the mesolimbic pathway pass through the nucleus accumbens to terminate in the frontal cortex (see Section 5.3.2); this projection is sometimes referred to as the mesocortical system (Fig. 8-1). Although the two major DA pathways are usually considered to be separate neural systems, some axons originating in the substantia nigra terminate in the nucleus accumbens, whereas some axons originating in the VTA terminate in the striatum (Fallon et al., 1978b; Simon et al., 1979). Consequently, some workers prefer to think of a single distributed forebrain DA projection system. In addition to these major DA pathways, there are also a number of smaller DA-containing cell groups. Two of these, the incertohypoth-alamic system and the tuberoinfundibular system are intrinsic to the hypothalamus. The former is probably, and the latter certainly, involved primarily in neuroendocrine regulation (Cooper et al., 1982; Lindvall & Bjorklund, 1978; Ungerstedt, 1971).

The most obvious behavioral involvement of DA systems is in the level of behavioral activation. DA activity may be reduced by a variety of other methods, including the administration of neuroleptic drugs, which are DA receptor blockers (Seeman, 1980), and selective lesions using the neurotoxin 6-hydroxydopamine (6-OHDA). Interventions which globally decrease DA function, decrease locomotor activity, and if sufficiently severe, produce a state of catatonia. Conversely, DA activity may be increased, either indirectly by drugs which release DA (e.g., amphetamine) or by direct DA receptor agonists (e.g., apomorphine). These drugs produce a dose-dependent behavioral activation, which at low doses is manifested as an increase in locomotor activity and at higher levels of stimulation is superseded by a characteristic pattern of repetitive stereotyped behavior (Costall & Naylor, 1979; Ungerstedt, 1979). The locomotor stimulant effects seen at low levels of stimulation are mediated primarily by the mesolimbic DA pathway, whereas the stereotyped behavior, which emerges at higher doses, is mediated primarily by the nigrostriatal pathway; the evidence for this dissociation comes from lesion studies (Kelly et al., 1975; Makanjuola & Ashcroft, 1982) and from experiments in which DA was injected directly into the striatum or nucleus accumbens (Fog & Pakkenburg, 1971; Makanjuola et al., 1980; Pijnenburg & van Rossum, 1973). Again, however, the distinction between the two DA systems is not absolute; it is possible to produce hyperactivity with intrastriatal injections of DA, and it may also be possible to elicit stereotyped behavior from the nucleus accumbens (Costall & Naylor, 1976, 1979).

In principle, an understanding of the psychology of depression should open up a fruitful line of psychobiological inquiry by making it possible to describe the properties that would be expected of a brain system mediating depression and to ask whether a particular system has those properties. It is clear from the clinical literature (Chapter 3) that the central feature of endogenous depressions is a decrease in the ability to experience pleasure. In the animal literature the term *reward* has been used to represent the concept of pleasure without imputing an unobservable mental state to the animal. A decrease in the level of functional activity in central reward systems is assumed by several psychological theories of depression (Chapter 4), and as seen in Chapter 7, an animal model of depression based on the concept of reward has a reasonable degree of validity (Section 7.2.6). Clearly, there could be strong grounds for thinking that a brain system which mediates the psychological impact of rewards might be dysfunctional in depression. One of the major current hypotheses for the behavioral functions of brain DA is precisely that the presence of a reward is signaled by activity in DA neurons (Wise, 1982). An evaluation of this hypothesis forms an obvious point of departure.

8.2. DA AND REWARD

8.2.1 Reward

Animal studies of the mechanism of reward have concentrated largely, though by no means exclusively, on the phenomenon of intracranial self-stimulation (ICSS) (Olds, 1956). Antidepressant drugs have been found to increase the efficacy of brain stimulation reward in three different ICSS paradigms (Section 7.2.6), one of which was the long-lasting decrease in ICSS response rates, which follow withdrawal from chronic amphetamine administration (Kokkinidis et al., 1980). Chronic amphetamine treatment is known to produce a variety of neurochemical effects, including decreases in NA (e.g., Lewander, 1974), DA (e.g., Segal, 1975), and 5-HT (e.g., Trulson & Jacobs, 1979a) function. However, the postamphetamine depression of ICSS was blocked by daily pretreatment with the DA receptor blocker haloperidol (Barrett & White, 1980), suggesting that in this case the change in ICSS was probably mediated by changes in DA function, rather than in NA or 5-HT.

A large number of studies demonstrate that neuroleptic drugs, which are DA receptor blockers (Seeman, 1980), reduce response rates in animals receiving brain stimulation reward. Since, at higher doses, neuroleptic drugs cause catalepsy, this is hardly surprising. However, evidence from a variety of sources indicates that the blockade of ICSS by reduction of DA transmission is not simply a motor deficit. The most elegant demonstration is that a unilateral reduction of DA transmission decreases performance for ICSS through an ipsilateral electrode substantially more than through a contralateral electrode, though the two tasks have identical performance requirements (Koob et al., 1978a; Mogenson et al., 1979; Phillips et al., 1976a). One very thorough study did not observe this differential impairment of ipsilateral ICSS, however (Carey, 1982). Another procedure which demonstrates that the effect of neuroleptics on ICSS is more than just a generalized decrease in motor output uses a chamber in which the animal crosses to one side to turn the brain stimulation on, and then crosses to the other side to turn the stimulation off. Neuroleptics increase the time before the stimulation is switched on, and drugs that enhance DA function have the opposite effect. However, at low doses, "off-latencies" are unaffected by manipulations of DA (Atrens et al., 1976; Liebman et al., 1982b,c).

The "shuttle-box self-stimulation" procedure has been criticized for its lack of sensitivity (Fibiger, 1979), but there is additional evidence that neuroleptics do not simply disrupt an animal's ability to perform the necessary response. Studies by Wise and his colleagues have shown that at low doses of the neuroleptic pimozide animals are capable of carrying out complex performance requirements in the early part of a training session, but they stop performing after the first few trials. This suggests that the problem is one of response maintenance rather than a simple motor deficit (Fouriezos & Wise, 1976; Fouriezos et al., 1978). Similar results are seen with natural rewards. Numerous studies have demonstrated that reducing DA transmission decreases food and water consumption; indeed, it now appears that the severe aphagia and adipsia seen after lateral hypothalamic lesions (Anand & Brobeck, 1951) are caused mainly by the interruption of ascending DA pathways (Fibiger et al., 1973). Again, however, it has been demonstrated that under low doses of pimozide, animals are perfectly capable of performing for food or saccharin rewards, but fail to maintain responding beyond the first few trials (Wise et al., 1978a,b).

In spite of these demonstrations that DA receptor antagonists abolish responding for ICSS and for natural rewards, the precise role of DA in responding for rewards is still highly controversial. It has recently been established that ICSS electrodes placed in the medial forebrain bundle (MFB), the classic ICSS site, do not directly stimulate DA axons. Rather, the substrate for MFB brain stimulation reward appears to be a system of long myelinated axons descending from the ventral forebrain to the midbrain tegmentum, the VTA in particular (Gallistel et al., 1981). However, it is likely that these axons terminate, inter alia, on the cell bodies of mesolimbic DA neurons, which are situated in the VTA. The mesolimbic DA system might, therefore, constitute a second stage in the reward process. The involvement of this pathway is suggested by the finding that self-stimulation of the VTA is blocked by injection of the DA-receptor blocker spiroperidol into the nucleus accumbens, where the DA axons terminate (Mogenson et al., 1979).

Other evidence suggests that stimulation of the mesolimbic DA system might also be responsible for the rewarding effects of opiate drugs. The VTA is the major site at which rats will self-administer opiates (Bozarth & Wise, 1981a,b). Stimulation of opiate receptors in the VTA activates DA neurons, as demonstrated by an increase in firing rate (Finnerty & Chan, 1981; Gysling & Wang, 1982; Matthews & German, 1982) and DA turnover (Moleman & Bruinvels, 1976, 1979; Smith et al., 1980) and by an increase in locomotor activity (Bozarth & Wise, 1981b; Joyce & Iversen, 1979). Although some reports disagree (Ettenberg et al., 1982; Smith & Davis, 1973), most workers have found that the rewarding effects of opiates, in a number of different behavioral paradigms, are blocked by DA receptor antagonists (Bozarth, 1983; Bozarth & Wise, 1981c; Hanson & Climini-Venema, 1972; Phillips et al., 1982; Pozuelo & Kerr, 1972; Spyraki et al., 1983) or by 6-OHDA-induced destruction of DA terminals in the nucleus accumbens (Spyraki et al., 1983).

Animals will also self-administer stimulant drugs such as amphetamine and cocaine, and these rewarding effects also appear to be mediated by DA terminals in the nucleus accumbens. 6-Hydroxydopamine-induced lesions of the nucleus accumbens have been found to block the intravenous self-administration of amphetamine and cocaine, both in the standard level-pressing paradigm (Lyness et al., 1979; Roberts et al., 1977, 1980) and in a "place preference" paradigm, which has minimal motor requirements (Spyraki et al., 1982). In the latter study, blockade of cocaine self-administration was correlated with the extent of DA depletion in the nucleus accumbens, but not with striatal DA depletion. The same correlation has also been observed following 6-OHDA lesions of the VTA (Roberts & Koob, 1982). Furthermore, it has been reported that rats will self-administer amphetamine directly into the nucleus accumbens; this effect was blocked by the simultaneous administration, through the same cannula, of the DA receptor blocker *cis*-flupenthixol, but not by the inactive isomer *trans*-flupenthixol (Hoebel et al., 1981).

These results appear to provide strong evidence for mediation of the rewarding effect of stimulant drugs by the mesolimbic DA system. However, this conclusion might be premature. Similar results are also obtained in a different paradigm, in which the drug is used not as a reward for an appropriate behavior, but rather, to provide information to the animal as to what behavior is appropriate (Winter, 1978). The ability of animals to discriminate the presence of stimulant drugs is blocked by neuroleptic drugs (Colpaert et al., 1978a,b; Silverman & Ho, 1977). This has important implications for the hypothesis that the mesolimbic DA system mediates the rewarding effect of stimulant drugs, since perception of the presence of the drug has a logical priority. In order to conclude that the rewarding effect has been blocked by neuroleptics or by nucleus accumbens lesions, it would be necessary to demonstrate that the presence of the drug could still be discriminated. This has not been done, either for stimulants or for opiates. Consequently, studies of drugs as reinforcers provide only rather weak support for the DA hypothesis of reward.

The main body of evidence for a DA hypothesis of reward comes from studies of the effects of neuroleptic drugs on operant performance rewarded by brain stimulation or by natural rewards. As described above, neuroleptic-treated animals are capable of performing rewarded responses, but have difficulty in continuing to do so. In its original form, the DA hypothesis of reward held that the reason for this deficit of response maintenance is that after neuroleptic treatment, the animal no longer finds the reward pleasant (Wise, 1982). Some findings support this interpretation. It has been observed, for example, that the pattern of responding for sucrose solutions was similarly affected by dilution, which directly reduces the reward value, and by pimozide (Xenakis & Sclafani, 1982).

However, the original form of the hypothesis is untenable, because response maintenance may be impaired even before the animal has received its first reward (Gray & Wise, 1981; Tombaugh et al., 1980). Accordingly, the hypothesis was extended to include conditioned reinforcement—the rewarding effects of stimuli associated with primary rewards (Wise, 1982). Some studies have supported this position. For example, the formation of conditioned reinforcement was impaired by pimozide (Beninger & Phillips, 1980), and responding for conditioned reward was increased by pipradol, a stimulant assumed to act through a DA mechanism (Robbins, 1975, 1976; Robbins et al., 1983). However, it is clear that under some conditions, normal acquisition is still possible under pimozide (Beninger & Phillips, 1981; Tombaugh et al., 1982a), and the apparent enhancement of conditioned reinforcement by pipradol could be interpreted as an artifact related to stereotyped behavior (Robbins, 1976).

The major problem faced by the DA hypothesis of reward, however, is that when neuroleptic-treated animals are given rewards they do not behave as though they were going unrewarded. One characteristic of extinction (i.e., the omission of expected rewards) is a transitory increase in responding (the *frustration effect*) when nonreward is first encountered (Amsel & Roussel, 1952). Such an effect has been reported in neuroleptic-treated animals responding for stimulant drugs (Yokel & Wise, 1976). However, this observation could not be replicated in another laboratory (Ettenberg et al., 1982); more important, the frustration effect has not been observed using any other form of reward (Wise, 1982). An even more serious discrepancy arises from studies in which animals are given a series of rewarded sessions under pimozide, during which responding falls to a very low level, and then are transferred to responding drug-free, but with no reward. The hypothesis predicts that they should continue to respond at the same low level. In fact, they return to their original high response rate (Mason et al., 1980; Tombaugh et al., 1980; Wise, 1982). It has been repeatedly demonstrated in experiments of this kind that neuroleptic drugs cause a decrease in the rate of responding for food rewards which is independent of extinction-like effects (Beninger, 1983).

In conclusion, the balance of the evidence at present appears to lean against the hypothesis that activity in DA neurons signals the presence of a reward. However, the mesolimbic DA system does appear to be essential for the maintenance of rewarded responding.

8.2.2. Incentive

The solution to this apparent paradox may lie in the observation that rewards have two distinct functions. The attainment of a reward serves to inform an animal that it has behaved correctly within the terms of a specific biological or experimental problem. In addition, the expectation of receiving a reward acts as a powerful source of motivation, which is known in animal learning theory as *incentive*. Incentive motivation is assumed to operate by means of a change in the properties of the environmental stimuli that predict or accompany the reward. By association with the reward, such stimuli acquire the ability to elicit behaviors appropriate to attain the reward (Bindra, 1978; Bolles, 1972). The evidence currently available suggests that neuroleptic drugs and other similar treatments interfere with the performance of rewarded behavior by altering the ability of incentives to activate behavior, rather than by changing the perception of the reward (Beninger, 1983).

The clearest demonstration is an experiment in which pimozide pretreated rats were exposed to pairings of a tone with food, and subsequently, when the animals were drug-free, the effect of the tone on lever pressing for food was examined. Presentation of the tone improved lever pressing performance, indicating that the animals had learned to associate the tone with food. However, in control animals, the improvement of lever pressing was immediately apparent. In the animals trained under pimozide, the improvement was not present in the initial transfer sessions, indicating that the tone had not acquired motivating properties (Beninger & Phillips, 1981).

One implication of the distinction between reward and incentive is that the maintenance of responding depends not solely on the expectation of reward, but also on a willingness to exert the effort required to attain it (Neill, 1982; Sinnamon, 1982). A study by Neill and Justice (1981) is particularly instructive. Rats were trained to lever press for brain stimulation in an "autotitration" paradigm, in which the intensity of brain stimulation was reduced periodically, but could be reset to its original level by pressing a second lever positioned behind a partition. The DA–reward hypothesis predicts that amphetamine should lead the rat to accept lower current intensities and should delay resetting, whereas the converse should be true for neuroleptic drugs. These results are indeed seen with systemic administration of the drugs (Schaefer & Holzman, 1979; Schaefer & Michael, 1980; Zarevics & Setler, 1979). However, these effects do not appear to be mediated by the mesolimbic DA system, because direct application to the nucleus accumbens gave exactly the opposite results: amphetamine led to resetting at higher, and haloperidol at lower, current intensities. The DA–reward hypothesis cannot explain these results. They can, however, be understood, if the drugs regulate the willingness of the animal to make the effort of going around the partition to press the reset lever (Neill & Justice, 1981), by regulating the incentive value of the reward.

Studies using progressive ratio reinforcement schedules support the position that activity in the mesolimbic DA system maintains responding by regulating the amount of effort an animal is prepared to make. In these schedules, the number of lever presses an animal must make for reward increases progressively until the animal gives up and stops responding. The "break-point" was increased by amphetamine injected into the nucleus accumbens (Neill & Justice, 1981); conversely, pimozide has been found to have its most potent suppressive effects in progressive ratio schedules when animals are performing close to their limit of tolerance (W. Rosenblatt et al., 1979).

The position that the primary function of the mesolimbic system is to disrupt not the hedonic impact of rewards, but rather their ability to arouse or activate behavior, is supported by recent anatomical and physiological studies, which suggest that the nucleus accumbens may be a "nodal point" within the brain, through which biologically significant stimuli gain access to the motor system (Swanson & Mogenson, 1981). According to this view, biologically significant stimuli converge on the VTA and influence the firing of the mesolimbic DA system (Maeda & Mogenson, 1982; Mogenson, 1982). Activity in this system modulates the transfer of information through the nucleus accumbens, which acts as a "limbic-motor interface," which receives inputs from the amygdala and other structures traditionally implicated in emotional and motivational behaviors and sends its output to the motor system (Mogenson et al., 1980; Mogenson & Yim, 1981).

8.3. RESPONSIVENESS TO THE ENVIRONMENT

This shift of emphasis from a hypothesis in which DA mediates rewarding effects to one in which DA mediates the activating effects of rewards has an important consequence. There is no obvious reason why an arousal system should specifically mediate the arousing effects of positive incentives, as opposed to other kinds of arousing stimuli. In fact, there is equally strong evidence to implicate DA in the arousing effects of negative incentives and also of stimuli that have no obvious motivational significance.

8.3.1. Negative Incentives

The role of DA in aversively motivated behaviors is extremely well-documented. The classic action of neuroleptic drugs, which has been much more extensively studied than their interactions with rewards, is to abolish the avoidance response to a stimulus which signals the imminent delivery of an electric shock (Niemegeers et al.,1969; Bignami, 1978).

The anatomical basis of this effect has received less attention. From what little evidence is available, the conditioned avoidance response appears to depend more on the nigrostriatal DA system than on the mesolimbic system. A number of studies have reported deficits of avoidance responding following microinjections of 6-OHDA in the vicinity of nigrostriatal neurons (Delacour et al., 1977; Echevarria-Mage et al., 1972; Fibiger et al., 1974; Levin & Smith, 1972; Neill et al., 1974; Zis et al., 1974) [although the only comparable study of the mesolimbic system (Koob et al., 1983) reported that impairment of avoidance performance required the destruction of both DA systems]. Second, the selective DA autoreceptor agonist 3-PPP (Hjorth et al., 1981) did not affect conditioned avoidance responding at doses substantially higher than those which greatly reduced ICSS (Liebman et al., 1982a). Changes in activity in the nigrostriatal system are strongly tempered by the activation of a descending striatonigral feedback pathway (Bunney & Aghajanian, 1976b), but these effects are much weaker in the mesolimbic system (Wang, 1981); as a result, the nigrostriatal system is less sensitive than the mesolimbic system to autoreceptor stimulation. For example, 3-PPP suppressed locomotor activity when applied to the nucleus accumbens, but it had no noticeable behavioral effects when applied to the striatum (Svensson & Ahlenius, 1983). The blockade of conditioned avoidance by neuroleptics but not by 3-PPP therefore suggests an effect on the nigrostriatal system.

The effects of neuroleptic drugs on avoidance responding appear to arise from an inability to initiate a response, because it is found that if a stronger stimulus—the electric shock—does successfully initiate a response, the subsequent performance of the escape response is unimpaired (Bignami, 1978; Niemegeers et al., 1969). The inability to initiate a response, which is, however, carried out normally if it can only be started, is one of the most prominent symptoms of Parkinson's disease. It is experienced as a "paralysis of the will," an inability to initiate an action however hard the patient might try (Sacks, 1973).

At lower doses, neuroleptics produce a gradual "extinction-like" deterioration of performance, similar to their effect on rewarded behavior (Beer & Lenard, 1975; Beninger et al., 1983; Lenard & Beer, 1976; Niemegeers et al., 1969). The disruptive effects of reducing DA transmission may be ameliorated by extensive pretraining (Fibiger et al., 1975; Zis et al., 1974). In general, the disruptive effects are inversely proportional to the ability of a signal to elicit avoidance responses, or in other words, their incentive value (Barry & Miller, 1965).

However, despite the fact that neuroleptic drugs block avoidance behavior, animals do still learn the significance of signals associated with shock, as demonstrated by their subsequent performance in the undrugged state (Beninger, 1983; Beninger et al., 1980a-c; Fibiger et al., 1975). The most graphic illustration is an experiment in which pimozide-pretreated animals and controls were shocked through an electric prod. When subsequently tested drug free, both groups were equally likely to bury the prod (Beninger et al., 1980a). As in the case of appetitively motivated behaviour, treatments which reduce DA functions disrupt aversively motivated behaviours by draining the incentive to perform.

8.3.2. Learned Helplessness

In the learned helplessness model of depression animals are exposed to uncontrollable aversive events, typically, electric shocks. Subsequently, they show poor performance in escaping from shock, and their performance of rewarded behaviors is also impaired (see Section 7.2.1). These deficits could be conceptualized as a decrease in incentive motivation, and there is evidence that a reduction in DA transmission may be at least partly responsible.

Pharmacological and neurochemical studies suggest that learned helplessness involves both dopaminergic and alpha-adrenergic systems. Exposure to unpredictable, uncontrollable electric shocks has been found to produce depletions of DA in the caudate nucleus and nucleus accumbens of rats, and NA depletions in a variety of brain areas (Blanc et al., 1980; Kvetansky et al., 1976; Schutz et al., 1979; Weiss et al., 1980, 1981). Although some studies have reported similar changes in DA irrespective of whether shocks were controllable or uncontrollable (Weiss et al., 1980, 1981), in one study the degree of DA depletion was significantly lower following exposure to shocks that were predictable, controllable, or both (Schutz et al., 1979; see also Section 11.3). A selective increase in DA turnover in frontal cortex in response to mild foot shock has also been reported (Reinhard et al., 1982). This is complemented by the observation that the number of DA receptors in the frontal cortex of rats receiving inescapable shock was reduced relative to animals receiving escapable shock (Cherek et al., 1980).

Additionally, the debilitating effects of inescapable shock on later escape performance could be mimicked or exacerbated by DA receptor blockers (pimozide, haloperidol) or by the NA synthesis inhibitor FLA-63. As with the effects of inescapable shock, these pharmacological effects were ameliorated by prior experience with escapable shock (Anisman et al., 1979a,b). Conversely, inescapable-shock-induced performance reductions were antagonized by the catecholamine precursor DOPA, the DA receptor agonist apomorphine, or the alpha-receptor agonist clonidine. The drugs were equally effective whether administered prior to inescapable shock or prior to testing (Anisman et al., 1979a,b, 1980b).

Similar results have been observed in the related "behavioral despair" model, in which rats or mice adopt an immobile posture on being forced to swim in a confined space (Section 7.2.2). Immobility was reduced by DA receptor stimulants (apomorphine, bromocryptine) or uptake blockers (mazindol, nomifensine) and was increased by DA receptor blockers (haloperidol, pimozide). Similar results were obtained with drugs acting at alpha-receptors (Porsolt et al., 1979).

The results are therefore suggestive of decreased DA (and alpha-adrenergic) function in both learned helplessness and "behavioral despair." Equally, however, it is possible that the results could be artifacts of changes in the level of general activity brought about by DA agonists and antagonists. As described in Chapter 7, techniques are available for dissociating these two effects—the use of a response suppression procedure in the learned helplessness paradigm (Baker, 1976; Jackson et al., 1978; see Section 7.2.1), and simple prolongation of the test session in the "behavioral despair" procedure (Kitada et al., 1981; see Section 7.2.2.). However, as these experiments have not yet been carried out, some uncertainty must remain as to the exact role of DA in these two behavioral conditions.

8.3.3. Responsiveness to Sensory Stimulation

The previous paragraph raised the possibility that the involvement of DA in two animal models of depression may be an artifact of locomotor effects of DA, rather than an effect on incentive motivation. However, it is also possible that the involvement of DA in locomotor activity is itself a reflection of incentive mechanisms. It may be, in other words, that the reason an increase in DA activity increases locomotor activity is that more and more environmental stimuli are able to elicit behavioral responses.

An influential theory of the behavioral actions of stimulant drugs, which activate DA receptors, has proposed just such a mechanism: an increase in the ease with which stimuli are able to elicit responses leads to more and more frequent changes of behavior, resulting in shorter and shorter sequences of behavior. This theory can explain many of the behavioral effects of stimulant drugs and might even account for stereotyped behavior (Lyon & Robbins, 1975). Beninger (1983) has recently summarized a number of other behavioral effects of stimulant drugs, which might be explained by the hypothesis of defective incentive conditioning, resulting in irrelevant environmental stimuli gaining the ability to activate responding.

Conversely, reducing DA activity decreases responsiveness to stimulation, and this applies not only to positive and negative incentive stimuli, but also to neutral stimuli, which elicit orienting and exploratory responses. Unilateral lesions of the nigro-striatal system induced by 6-OHDA cause contralateral sensory neglect: lesioned animals show well-localized orientation responses to visual or somatosensory stimuli on the same side of the body as the lesion, but fail to orient stimuli on the contralateral side (Marshall, 1979). As it can be demonstrated that such animals are not deficient in their perception of the stimulus (Siegfried & Bures, 1979) or in their ability to make the response (Feeney & Wier, 1979), the problem seems to be that stimuli contralateral to the lesion are unable to engage behavior. The converse effect has also been reported: unilateral injections of DA into the striatum cause an increase in sensorimotor responsiveness to stimuli on the contralateral side (Joyce et al., 1981).

A general conclusion is that forebrain DA pathways are responsible for the activation of behavior by environmental stimuli. Electrophysiological studies are consistent with this conclusion: the common feature of diverse stimuli which activate nigral DA neurons is that they also activate the whole animal (Chiodo et al., 1979, 1980; Steinfels et al., 1982). Within the class of arousing stimuli, there may be some differential processing by the two DA pathways. Arousal by neutral sensory stimuli is more a function of the nigrostriatal system, and arousal by positive incentives is more a function of the mesolimbic system. The anatomical basis of arousal by negative incentives is less certain: the literature appears to implicate the nigrostriatal system, but this may be to some extent a reflection of selective experimentation.

The concept of responsiveness to environmental stimulation could explain a number of effects that have been reported to develop during chronic treatment with antidepressants. In addition to antidepressant effects in the learned helplessness, "behavioral despair" and ICSS models (Section 7.2), there are also isolated reports of antidepressant-induced increases in a number of other behaviors, which include resistance to handling (Modigh, 1975; Willner et al., 1981b), fighting with a conspecific (Eichelman & Barchas, 1975; Willner et al., 1981b), stress-induced eating (Nobrega & Coscina, 1981), responding to a Pavlovian conditioned stimulus (Montgomery & Willner, 1980), and responding in advance of a conditioned stimulus (Maxwell & Palmer, 1961). The possible involvement of DA in these effects remains to be investigated.

8.4. IMPLICATIONS

Studies of the psychomotor performance of depressed patients (Section 4.1) show that they are deficient in exactly the abilities which appear to be subserved by the two DA pathways: they have greatly retarded reaction times, indicating an inability to initiate responding (Miller, 1975), and are most severely impaired in tasks requiring a sustained expenditure of effort (Weingartner & Silberman, 1982). The possibility that this could be a core symptom of depression is suggested by the observation that following a course of antidepressant treatment, patients might show a substantial alleviation of depression manifested primarily as an improvement in social functioning, without necessarily showing any marked change in their depressed mood (Friedman et al., 1966).

It follows that a decrease in DA function is a good candidate to mediate some of the major cognitive changes in depression. However, a further analysis of the clinical data allows a much more precise prediction to be made as to which group of patients might show this disorder. The concept of *endogenomorphic depression* has been proposed to describe those depressions that follow an autonomous course and are unresponsive to psychosocial intervention, but respond to tricyclic antidepressants and ECS (see Chapter 3). The defining feature of endogenomorphic depressions is an inability to experience pleasure, characterized by a failure to react with enjoyment to events which are usually pleasurable ("lack of reactivity"), and a loss of interest in seeking out pleasurable events ("loss of interest") (Klein, 1974). A recent review of the symptomatology of major depression found strong support for this concept: lack of reactivity and loss of interest were strongly associated with autonomous depression in the majority of studies examined (Nelson & Charney, 1981). Autonomous depression was almost invariably found to involve psychomotor change—either agitation or retardation; lack of reactivity and severely depressed mood were found in both subgroups, but loss of interest tended to be more strongly associated with retarded depressions (Nelson & Charney, 1981; see Sections 3.3.1).

The DA hypothesis of reward would assume that activation of DA mechanisms would mediate "reactivity" and consequently would predict that low DA activity could be responsible for all endogenomorphic depressions. However, the hypothesis is probably incorrect: DA systems mediate the activating function of rewards, rather than the way they are perceived. Although the importance of activation by significant events in the environment (incentive motivation) has long been recognized in accounts of animal behavior (Bindra, 1978), it has not featured prominently in theoretical analyses of depression. However, just as the concept of "reward" maps well onto the psychiatric symptom of "reactivity," the concept of "incentive" corresponds equally well with "interest."

If loss of interest is interpreted as a reduction in the ability of pleasurable events to arouse behavior, then there are strong grounds for predicting that this symptom might be associated with low activity in the mesolimbic DA system. A concomitant decrease in nigrostriatal activity would explain the clinical association between loss of interest and psychomotor retardation.

Before proceeding to examine the clinical literature, two further aspects of this hypothesis should be noted. In animals, DA systems appear to be involved equally in positive and negative incentive effects, but this need not necessarily be the case in people. There is some evidence that DA activity in people is more closely related to left then to right hemisphere function (see Section 5.3.2). As the left hemisphere appears to have a greater involvement in positive then in negative emotions (Chapter 5), it is possible that the asymmetry of DA function in people could mean a preferential involvement in responding to positive incentives.

It is also necessary to spell out what the consequences of a global decrease in responsiveness would be. A decrease in responding to positive incentives would mean receiving fewer rewards. However, a decrease in responding to negative incentives would not mean receiving fewer punishments, but rather, the reverse. More punishments would be received, as action would not be taken to avoid them. Consequently, a global decrease in responsiveness would be one way of producing the shift in the balance of pleasure and pain that is central to an understanding of the psychology of depression (see Chapter 4).

nine

DOPAMINE AND DEPRESSION: CLINICAL STUDIES

The idea that depression might involve a deficiency of DA transmission, in addition to or perhaps rather than an abnormality of NA and/or 5-HT systems, was first advanced in 1975 by Randrup and colleagues. In Chapter 8, we saw that to some extent the behavioral functions of brain DA systems are consistent with this hypothesis. A deficiency of DA transmission, as postulated by Randrup and co-workers, could result from exposure to uncontrollable stress, and it should correspond to a loss of incentive motivation. Given that there is an association between psychomotor retardation in depression and loss of interest, we should not be too surprised to find evidence of reduced DA functioning in retarded depressions; biochemical studies of DA turnover do indeed support such a relationship (Section 9.1.5.). Conversely, treatments that enhance DA function might act to restore the motivational deficits that are so prominent in endogenous depressions, and this hypothesis is also supported (Section 9.3).

9.1. DA FUNCTION IN DEPRESSION

9.1.1. Synthesis and Storage

Although, as discussed below, the major line of evidence for reduced DA activity in depression concerns DA turnover, there is some evidence that suggests that DA synthesis might be impaired in depressed patients by a decreased availability of the precursor amino acid tyrosine. Although there are exceptions (e.g., De Myer et al., 1981), a number of studies have reported decreased tyrosine concentrations in the blood of depressed patients as compared with normal controls, particularly during the morning, when plasma tyrosine levels are maximal in normal subjects (Benkert et al., 1971; Birkmayer & Linauer, 1970; Kishimoto & Hama, 1979). Additionally, the possibility of defective tyrosine transport to the brain has been hinted at (Gaillard & Tissot, 1979). Whatever the reason, decreased tyrosine concentrations have been found in the ventricular CSF of depressed patients undergoing psychosurgery, as compared with anxious patients (Bridges et al., 1976), and in the lumbar CSF of depressed patients as compared to normal controls (Goodnich et al., 1980).

It has also been reported that DA uptake was reduced in platelet-rich plasma of patients with endogenous depression, as compared with neurotic depressives, and normal age- and sex-matched controls (Hallstrom et al., 1976). Since platelet uptake of DA is considered to be a model for the binding of DA by amine storage granules (Stahl & Meltzer, 1978b), these results might indicate a defect of DA storage in endogenous depression. Taken together, these various observations point to a widespread disruption of DA neurochemistry.

However, it is questionable whether these changes have any functional significance, since normal regional DA concentrations have generally been found in postmortem studies of the brains of suicide victims (Beskow et al., 1976; Moses & Robins, 1975; Pare et al., 1969). In one study, low DA concentrations were reported in the striatum and red nucleus in four depressed patients who died of natural causes, but no details of the controls were given, making it impossible to assess this report (Birkmayer & Riederer, 1975).

9.1.2. Catabolism

Dopamine (as also NA) is broken down extraneuronally by COMT, and intraneuronally by MAO. It has been reported that red cell COMT activity was reduced in depressed women, as compared to normal women or women with other psychiatric or neurological diagnoses and also, that COMT was lower in bipolar than in unipolar patients (Cohn et al., 1970; Dunner et al., 1971). However, these observations are unlikely to be of etiological significance, since in animals studies, the behavioral consequences of inhibiting COMT appear to be minimal (McKenzie, 1974), and normal COMT activity has been reported in the brains of suicide victims studied postmortem (Grote et al., 1974).

A number of studies have examined MAO activity in blood platelets taken from depressed patients. Murphy and Weiss (1972) found relatively high MAO activity in unipolar patients and relatively low MAO activity in bipolar patients; subsequent studies have tended to support this relationship (reviewed by Gudeman et al., 1982). In addition, two recent studies found a significant correlation between platelet MAO activity and severity of unipolar depression (Mann, 1979; Gudeman et al., 1982). Again, however, if these findings have etiological significance, it is more likely to be in relation to peripheral NA activity than to central DA activity, because MAO in the brain appears to have a functional capacity far in excess of the demand. In one animal study, for example, no behavioral changes were seen unless the level of MAO inhibition exceeded 85% (Green et al., 1977b). And as will be seen in Chapter 12, even in relation to peripheral NA function, it is very difficult to make any sense of the literature on changes in MAO and COMT activity in depression.

9.1.3 Receptors

In the absence of postmortem studies of DA receptors in depressed patients, evidence of DA receptor function comes from neuroendocrine studies. It is now believed that DA is identical to, or closely associated with, the hypothalamic inhibitory factor for the pituitary hormone prolactin; activation of pituitary receptors by DA agonists decreases serum prolactin levels, whereas DA receptor antagonists have the opposite effect (Ettigi & Brown, 1977; Moore et al., 1980). Dopamine is also involved in the stimulation of pituitary growth hormone (GH) release (Lal et al., 1972), although in this case, the mechanism is less clear (Balldin et al., 1980a; Ettigi & Brown, 1977). Hence the stimulatory effect of DA agonist drugs on GH secretion and the inhibitory effects on prolactin secretion give an indication of the functional state of DA receptors.

Depressed patients were originally reported to have reduced GH responses to the indirectly acting DA agonists DOPA (Sachar et al., 1972, 1973a) and amphetamine (Langer et al., 1976). However, these responses depend upon age and sex. When these factors were more carefully controlled, depressed patients were found to have normal GH responses to DOPA, amphetamine, or the directly acting DA agonist apomorphine (Caspar et al., 1977; Frazer, 1975; Gold et al., 1976; Gruen et al., 1975; Halbreich et al., 1982; Maany et al., 1979; Mendels et al., 1974; Mendlewicz et al., 1977; Sachar et al., 1975). Prolactin responses to DOPA (Gold et al., 1976; Sachar et al., 1973a) and the directly acting DA agonist bromocryptine (Coppen & Ghose, 1978) were also found to be normal in unipolar patients, though an enhanced response to apomorphine in depressed men has been reported (Jimerson et al., 1980, cited by Insel & Siever, 1981). In some studies, bipolar patients were found to have a greater prolactin response to DOPA than unipolar patients (Gold et al., 1976; Sachar et al., 1973a), but the opposite result has also been reported (Mendlewicz et al., 1979a). Taken together, these findings do not suggest any major abnormality of DA receptors in depression, at least in the tuberoinfundibular DA system.

9.1.4. Turnover: Neuroendocrine Studies

To the extent that steady state levels of GH and prolactin are determined by DA, they represent a joint measure of DA release and DA receptor activation. Since responses to DA receptor activation do not appear to be abnormal in depression, the steady state levels of GH and prolactin give some indication of DA release. However, the utility of studying steady state levels of GH is considerably reduced by the large number of other factors known to be involved in the control of GH release (Ettigi & Brown, 1977) and by the presence of inhibitory influences of DA on GH release, in addition to the stimulant effect (Liuzzi et al., 1976). In depression, GH levels appear to be normal (Carroll, 1978), but it is difficult to draw any conclusions from this finding.

Studies of prolactin levels in depression are probably more reliable. The majority of studies have found no differences in prolactin levels between depressed patients and normal controls (Arana et al., 1977; Cole et al., 1976; Coppen & Ghose, 1978; Ehrensing et al., 1974; Francis et al., 1976; Gregoire et al., 1977). In some studies, increased prolactin levels have been observed in depression (Amsterdam et al., 1982b; Horrobin et al., 1976; Maeda et al., 1975; Sachar et al., 1973a, 1975), particularly in (or restricted to) bipolar patients (Amsterdam et al., 1982b; Gold et al., 1976; Sachar et al., 1973a). However, exactly the opposite result has also been reported (Judd et al., 1982; Linkowski et al., 1980b). The discrepancies may arise from the fact that prolactin secretion shows diurnal variation: two studies have found that increased prolactin secretion in depression was more marked in the evening (Halbreich et al., 1979) or at night (Mendelwicz, 1976, cited by Carroll, 1978), than at other times of day. On the other hand, one of these workers has also reported the opposite result, a lower prolactin secretion, particularly at night, in bipolar patients (Mendelwicz, 1982), and a fourth study found no alterations in the circadian pattern of prolactin secretion (Polleri et al., 1979). Additionally, prolactin levels are increased by stress and might therefore be sensitive to variations in experimental procedure. Overall, the neuroendocrine evidence for altered DA release in depression is utterly equivocal.

The lack of neuroendocrine support for changes in DA turnover or DA receptor function in depression is disappointing, because neuroendocrinological tools are easier to use and less invasive than most other approaches to the neurochemistry of the human brain. However, it is clear that these negative findings have no implications for the DA hypothesis of depression. We have no reason at present to suppose that DA-mediated neuroendocrine responses bear a functional relationship to the information processing functions of forebrain DA systems. In these circumstances a positive result would be a welcome break, but a negative result can be written off as unlucky.

9.1.5. Turnover: Biochemical Studies

Biochemical studies of DA turnover provide a more crucial test of the hypothesis, because these data do reflect the functioning of forebrain DA systems. They also present a much clearer picture. Homovanillic acid (HVA) is the major metabolite of DA. It is reasonably well-established that HVA in the CSF originates mainly—perhaps exclusively—from the turnover of DA in the central nervous system (Randrup et al., 1975), and it mainly reflects the activity of the nigrostriatal DA pathway, owing to the size of this pathway and its location adjacent to the lateral ventricles (Sourkes, 1973). Measurement of HVA in CSF is the most direct method available for studying DA turnover in the human brain (outside of a neurosurgical operating theater). If it is assumed that DA uptake mechanisms and the rate of flow of CSF do not change, then HVA concentrations measured in lumbar CSF should be proportional to DA release. Since HVA concentration also depends upon the transport of HVA out of the CSF, a better estimate of DA turnover may be obtained by measuring HVA following the administration of probenecid, a drug that blocks the transport of acid metabolites out of the CSF and produces a three- to fourfold increase in CSF HVA concentration (Goodwin et al., 1973a; Kopin, 1978).

Studies carried out without the use of probenecid have usually found reduced concentrations of HVA in the CSF of depressed patients (Bowers et al., 1969; Brodie et al., 1973; Goodwin et al., 1973a; Kasa et al., 1982; Mendels et al., 1972; Nordin et al., 1971; Papeschi & McClure, 1971; Roos & Sjostrom, 1969; Traskman et al., 1981; Wilk et al., 1972), but a number of studies have found no difference between depressed patients and normal controls (Berger et al., 1980; Sjostrom & Roos, 1972; Subramanyam, 1975; Takahashi et al., 1974; van Praag et al., 1973); in one study, there was even an increase (Vestergaard et al., 1978). However, studies that did use the probenecid technique have been unanimous in finding decreased CSF HVA accumulation in some or all depressed patients (Banki, 1977a; Berger et al., 1980; Bowers, 1972; Goodwin et al., 1973a; Sjostrom, 1973; Sjostrom & Roos, 1972; van Praag & Korf, 1971b; van Praag et al., 1973).

Decreases in CSF HVA are particularly pronounced in patients with marked psychomotor retardation; agitated patients may have normal or slightly elevated postprobenecid HVA accumulation (Banki, 1977a; Banki et al., 1981b; van Praag & Korf, 1971b; van Praag et al., 1973). In one study, the deficit was observed in bipolar but not unipolar patients (Bowers, 1972). This result may also reflect a distinction between retarded and agitated patients: the unipolar group appear to have included a high proportion of agitated patients, whereas bipolar patients usually show psychomotor retardation (Beigel & Murphy, 1971; Donnelly & Murphy, 1973; Kupfer et al., 1974). It has also been observed that nondeluded depressed patients had lower HVA accumulations that did patients with hallucinations (Sweeney et al., 1978b). It is possible that these results too represent a difference in psychomotor activation, since it has been found that in a group of psychotic patients, those with delusions and agitation had higher postprobenecid HVA accumulations than normal controls, whereas HVA was normal in those patients with delusions but no agitation (van Praag et al., 1975). As might be expected from these observations, HVA levels have usually, though not always (Bowers, 1974a), been found to be elevated in manic patients (Banki et al., 1981b; Goodwin et al., 1973a; Sjostrom & Roos, 1972; Vestergaard et al., 1978).

Most reviews of CSF studies of monoamine metabolites contrive to give the impression that there is no clear relationship between DA turnover and affective disorders. It is true that HVA levels are affected by a number of extraneous factors, such as age, height (Banki et al., 1981a), and physical activity (Post et al., 1973c; see also Section 9.4). Nevertheless, the consistent finding of decreased postprobenecid CSF HVA accumulation in depressed patients, particularly those with psychomotor retardation, is probably the most firmly established observation in the neurochemistry of depression.

9.2. TREATMENTS THAT DECREASE DA ACTIVITY

9.2.1. Reserpine

Although the drug reserpine depletes the brain of DA, NA, and 5-HT, pharmacological studies have shown that it is DA depletion that is responsible for its profound behavioral sedating effects in animals (Carlsson, 1975a). The publication in the early 1950s of a number of reports that reserpine caused depression in a high proportion of patients receiving it for the treatment of hypertension (see Chapter 1) was a major stimulus to the development of biological psychiatry (Bein, 1982) and the basis of the catecholamine hypothesis of depression (Schildkraut, 1965). In these circumstances, it is ironic that the reality of reserpine-induced depression came to be questioned. In a review of the literature on reserpine-induced depressions, which consisted of 16 studies, all published between 1952 and 1960, Goodwin and co-workers (1972) noted that depressions were reported in 20–30% of all patients on reserpine. However, only a quarter of these cases appeared to be true clinical depressions. The remainder were described as "pseudo-depression," which consisted mainly of over-tranquillization, with psychomotor retardation as the major symptom, but without feelings of helplessness, hopelessness, and guilt. The patients who did develop a "true depression" appeared largely to be those with a prior history of depression. The authors concluded that rather than caus-ing depression, reserpine might precipitate depression in susceptible in-dividuals—a very different conclusion.

This conclusion must be qualified, however, by two further observa-tions. The first is that in animals, behavioral changes are not normally observed after reserpine treatment with brain monoamine depletions of less than 80–90% (Haggendahl & Lindqvist, 1964). It is most unlikely that the doses of reserpine used clinically (up to 10 mg/day, or 0.17 mg/kg) would have such profound effects. Second, in animals chronically treated with reserpine, the initial period of sedation may be superseded after a few days by hyperactivity (Pirch, 1969), presumably as a result of the development of compensatory receptor supersensitivity; a single reserpine treatment may be sufficient to produce supersensitive receptors (Dalen et al., 1973). In clinical use, therefore, reserpine might not de-crease DA activity sufficiently for major psychological effects to become apparent. In this context, it is perhaps of interest that in the studies reviewed by Goodwin and co-workers (1972), of the 286 patients who clearly showed psychomotor retardation, 133 (47%) did develop major depressions. In a later study, a high dose of reserpine was found to induce suicidal ideation in two of nine nondepressed volunteers (Peterfy et al., 1976).

9.2.2. Other DA-Depleting Treatments

Studies of the effects on mood of the catecholamine synthesis inhibitor AMPT were reviewed by Mendels and Frazer in 1974. They concluded that "there is little evidence that AMPT has a direct effect on mood in either normal or psychiatrically disturbed persons" (Mendels and Frazer, 1974, p. 449). In the most extensive study, Engelman and co-workers (1968) gave AMPT to 52 medical patients; 44 were mildly sedated, and none became clinically depressed. However, as noted above, the lack of severity of the effects on motor function suggests that brain DA function was only mildly disabled. These negative findings can not therefore be taken as strong evidence against the DA hypothesis of depression.

Alpha-methyldopa is another drug that reduces catecholamine func-tion, probably by displacing DA from vesicles and functioning as a "false transmitter" (Sourkes et al., 1961). Severe depressions have sometimes been reported as a side effect of its use in the treatment of hypertension (McKinney & Cane, 1967). As with reserpine and AMPT, however, a recent review concluded that the evidence did not support a specific relationship between alpha-methyldopa and depression, and the precipitation of severe depressions by this drug was extremely uncommon (DeMuth & Ackerman, 1983). Again, though, it may be pertinent to raise the question of the degree of central DA impairment.

9.2.3. Parkinson's Disease

The best evidence that DA depletion can induce depression comes from studies of patients suffering from Parkinson's disease. Although there are a number of biochemical abnormalities in the brain of Parkinsonian patients, the major problem appears to be a deficiency of DA, caused by degeneration of DA-containing neurons (Hornykiewicz, 1966). The association between depression and Parkinson's disease is well-established (Randrup et al., 1975); the incidence of depression in Parkinson's disease may be as high as 90% (Asnis, 1977).

Many authors have suggested that depression may be a response to Parkinson's disease, rather than an integral part of it (Warburton, 1967). This is undoubtedly true in some cases. However, even in the early stages of Parkinson's disease when the physical disability is mild, there is a high incidence of depression (Celesia & Wanamaker, 1972), and the onset of depression may, in some cases, precede the onset of neurological symptoms (McDowell et al., 1971). Robins (1976) compared a group of 45 Parkinsonian patients with an equal number of patients suffering from chronic physical disabilities; the two groups were matched for age, sex, and psychiatric history prior to their illness. The Parkinsonian patients scored significantly higher on the Hamilton Rating Scale for depression, despite the fact that the controls had significantly more severe physical handicaps. This study demonstrates conclusively that depression is more than a reaction to the physical handicap of Parkinson's disease.

9.2.4. Neuroleptic Drugs

A large number of studies have reported depression as a side effect of neuroleptic drug treatment in schizophrenia; in some cases the states described are clearly genuine depressions (Randrup et al., 1975). Since the common feature of neuroleptic drugs is DA receptor blockade (Creese & Snyder, 1978), this finding appears to implicate DA in depression. In fact, the results are less straightforward. In the great majority of these reports, neuroleptic drugs were being used in the treatment of schizophrenia, and it is all but impossible to assess the extent to which neuroleptic-induced depressions are simply the unmasking of a preexisting depression. Dysphoric reactions have also been reported in normal subjects (Heninger et al., 1965) and in nonpsychiatric medical patients (Simonson, 1964), but the question of whether there is a specific relationship to depression does not appear to have been studied.

In contrast, there are now a large number of studies demonstrating that neuroleptics are also effective antidepressants. Reviewing double-blind therapeutic trials of neuroleptics in depression, Robertson & Trimble (1981) found neuroleptics superior to placebo in 9 out of 10 studies; neuroleptics were superior to tricyclic antidepressants in 4 studies, equally effective in 12, and inferior in 3.

These studies appear to constitute prima facie evidence against the DA hypothesis of depression. However, three further observations suggest that this would be a premature conclusion. First, the dose range for antidepressant effects appears to be considerably lower than for neuroleptic effects, particularly in the case of thioridazine and flupenthixol, the drugs that have been most extensively studied (Randrup et al., 1975; Robertson & Trimble, 1982). Indeed, for both of these drugs, it has been reported that higher blood levels were associated with a poor outcome (De Johnge & Van der Helm, 1970; Trimble & Robertson, 1983). As autoreceptors are generally responsive to much lower drug doses than postsynaptic receptors (Usdin & Bunney, 1975), it is possible that neuroleptics might act in depressed patients by selectively blocking DA autoreceptors. Such an action would activate DA neurons and would enhance, rather than suppress, DA transmission. A second possibility is that the antidepressant effects of neuroleptics may be mediated by mechanisms other than DA. Robertson and Trimble (1981; Trimble & Robertson, 1983) administered cis-flupenthixol to 16 depressed patients. Significant improvements were seen after three-days of treatment, but improvement was negatively correlated with the increase in serum prolactin level, suggesting that DA blockade might be antagonizing clinical improvement.

The most interesting data, however, come from three sets of studies which indicate that tricyclic antidepressants and neuroleptics are effective in different groups of depressed patients. In the first studies, imipramine (tricyclic) was found to be superior to thioridazine (neuroleptic) in retarded, emotionally withdrawn patients, whereas thioridazine was superior to imipramine in anxious, agitated patients (Hollister & Overall, 1965; Overall et al., 1966). In subsequent studies, similar results were obtained with the tricyclic amitriptyline and the neuroleptic perphenazine (Hollister et al., 1966, 1967). Finally, patients with psychomotor retardation and lack of interest were found to respond to imipramine but were made worse by the neuroleptic chlorpromazine, while chlorpromizine was superior to imipramine in agitated and delusional patients (Raskin et al., 1970; Raskin & Crook, 1976). These studies are unanimous in demonstrating that neuroleptics are effective primarily in agitated or delusional depressions, and in fact, the majority of double-blind trials of neuroleptics have been conducted on patients with mixed anxiety depression conditions (Robertson & Trimble, 1981, 1982). In these conditions, the most effective treatment may be a tricyclic–neuroleptic combination (Charney & Nelson, 1981; Kaskey et al., 1980). However, neuroleptics appear to be ineffective or harmful in depressed patients with psychomotor retardation (Robertson & Trimble, 1981, 1982).

9.3. TREATMENTS THAT ENHANCE DA ACTIVITY

9.3.1. Precursors

The two precursors of the catecholamine neurotransmitters are tyrosine and DOPA. The enzyme tyrosine hydroxylase, which catalyzes the conversion of tyrosine to DOPA, is rate-limiting and is normally saturated; however, there is evidence that under some circumstances tyrosine administration can increase the rate of catecholamine synthesis (Wurtman et al., 1974; Carlsson & Lindqvist, 1978b). Gelenburg and co-workers (1980) reported on a depressed patient who showed "striking improvements" on all symptoms during two double-blind periods of tyrosine treatment, with relapse on placebo substitution. This result was subsequently confirmed in a comparison of three tyrosine-treated subjects with three placebo treated controls (Gelenburg et al., 1982). Goldberg (1980) made similar observations; however, in this study evidence was also presented which suggested that the antidepressant effect of tyrosine might be mediated by NA rather than DA (see Section 12.3.2).

The majority of precursor loading studies have used DOPA to increase DA synthesis; in most studies DOPA was administered together with a peripheral decarboxylase inhibitor, to confine DA (and NA) formation to the brain. In normal subjects, DOPA appears to have a psychomotor activating effect, but minimal effects on mood (Ansel & Markham, 1970). Early studies of DOPA in depression suggested that it might have antidepressant properties (reviewed by Randrup et al., 1975). However, subsequent double-blind studies found that the antidepressant effect was confined to a relatively small group (approximately 25%) of patients, all of whom showed psychomotor retardation (Goodwin et al., 1970; van Praag & Korf, 1975). In the first of these studies, some degree of activation was seen in all patients: whereas unipolar depressed patients became agitated, 5 out of 8 patients with a prior history of hypomania (Bipolar II) showed an antidepressant response, and 10 out of 11 bipolar patients with a prior history of mania (Bipolar I) developed hypomanic episodes (Goodwin & Sack, 1974). It is possible that these results indicate improvement in both groups of bipolar patients, with overshoot in the Bipolar I group. In the second study (van Praag & Korf, 1975), results were not analyzed differentially for unipolar and bipolar patients; it was, however, found that patients who responded to DOPA had a lower DA turnover prior to treatment (measured by postprobenecid CSF HVA accumulation).

In Parkinsonian patients, DOPA therapy is usually accompanied by improvement in mood, though it is also occasionally reported to cause depression (Goodwin, 1972; Randrup et al., 1975). In both cases there are severe problems of dissociating mood changes from clinical improvement, or lack of improvement, in Parkinsonian symptoms. It is of interest, however, that in some patients improvement in mood may occur prior to any improvement in physical symptoms (Murphy, 1972).

9.3.2. Uptake Blockers

In contrast to DOPA, amphetamine, which promotes the release and inhibits the uptake of DA and NA (Sulser & Sanders-Bush, 1971), may often elicit a euphoric reaction in normal subjects (Randrup et al., 1975). Amphetamine-induced euphoria could be blocked by the catecholamine synthesis inhibitor AMPT (Jonsson et al., 1969) or by the DA receptor blocker pimozide, but not by the NA receptor blockers phenoxybenzamine and propranolol (Jonsson, 1972), so the effect appears to be mediated by DA rather than NA.

Amphetamine is not generally considered to be an effective antidepressant agent. It would be rather surprising if it were, since the stimulant effect is followed by a period of intense fatigue (Weiss & Laties, 1962), and repeated amphetamine use leads to rapid tolerance. However, short-lasting improvements in depression are frequently reported (Ban, 1969; Klerman, 1972; Randrup et al., 1975). The clinical relevance of this effect is supported by the finding that an antidepressant response to amphetamine predicts a favorable response to some tricyclic antidepressants (Fawcett et al., 1972; see Section 12.3.4). In a recent study, 20 mg of amphetamine, infused intravenously, produced a lessening of withdrawal and retardation in 94% of depressed patients and also improved mood in 50%, with elation in 61%. This latter group included all the bipolar patients but only 45% of the unipolar patients (Silberman et al., 1981).

In some patients amphetamine may produce a dysphoric reaction, as, indeed, it may in some normal subjects (Lasagna et al., 1955). In depressed patients, the dysphoric reaction usually involves a worsening in agitation (Roberts, 1959). As such, dysphoria may be secondary to a failure to cope adequately with, for example, increased sympathetic stimulation, rather than a direct effect on mood.

Clear antidepressant effects, comparable to those of tricyclic antidepressants, are seen with the DA uptake inhibitor nomifensine (Angst et al., 1974; van Scheyen et al., 1977); it is uncertain at present why nomifensine does not share the adverse side effects of amphetamine. In one study it was reported that patients who responded to nomifensine had a significantly lower DA turnover (measured by postprobenecid CSF HVA accumulation) than those who did not (van Scheyen et al., 1977).

9.3.3. Receptor Agonists

A number of studies have examined the antidepressant effects of the directly acting DA receptor agonists bromocryptine (Fuxe et al., 1978a) and piribedil (Creese, 1974). Uncontrolled studies suggested that bromocryptine might be effective in depression (Agnoli et al., 1978; Colonna et al., 1979; Nordin et al., 1981; Schubert et al., 1982), particularly in bipolar patients (Silverstone, 1978). Controlled trials have now been carried out comparing bromocryptine with imipramine, under double-blind conditions. Waerens & Gerlach (1981) found global improvement in 12 out of 13 patients on bromocryptine and 13 out of 14 on imipramine, with no significant difference between the two drugs. Interestingly, the most rapid improvement was seen in the only bipolar patient in the bromocryptine group. These results were subsequently confirmed in a large multicenter comparison of 83 patients on bromocryptine and 86 on imipramine (Theohar et al., 1981). Examination of the individual symptoms showed that the two drugs produced equal improvements in retardation and mood. However, whereas patients on imipramine also showed improvement in agitation and psychic anxiety, those on bromocryptine did not. This observation is consistent with the evidence cited above that in agitated depressions, DA receptor blockers (neuroleptic drugs) are effective as antidepressants.

Similar antidepressant effects have been reported in uncontrolled studies of piribedil (Post et al., 1978a; Reus et al., 1980; Shopsin & Gershon, 1978). Although no controlled trials of piribedil appear to have been performed, one study did find a significant correlation between the degree of improvement on piribedil and DA turnover (measured by postprobenecid CSF HVA accumulation prior to treatment). Like DOPA, piribedil has also been found to induce hypomanic episodes in some patients (Gerner et al., 1976).

9.4. CONCLUSIONS: DA AND DEPRESSION

The studies reviewed in this chapter illustrate many of the difficulties encountered in attempting to test biochemical hypotheses of depression. It is also apparent that plausible solutions to some of these problems are to be found in the animal literature.

Studies of CSF HVA using the probenecid technique show remarkable agreement in finding dereased HVA levels in some depressed patients. The evidence currently available is consistent with the conclusion that decreased DA turnover is associated with psychomotor retardation in depression; as discussed below, the relationship between psychomotor retardation and depressed mood remains uncertain. Given the possibility of deficient synthesis and/or storage of DA, the possibility of normal activity in DA neurons but decreased release of DA should not be ruled out. However, animal studies have shown that catecholamine synthesis must be decreased by approximately 50% before any changes in locomotor activity become apparent (Papeschi, 1977). This suggests that if the reduction in CSF HVA concentration in retarded depressions has functional significance, the most likely reason for the decrease in DA turnover is a decrease in the activity of DA neurons.

Since CSF HVA derives primarily from the nigrostriatal system (Sourkes, 1973), turnover studies do not provide information about functional activity in the mesolimbic DA system. Some neuroendocrine studies of the tuberoinfundibular DA system have suggested that the activity of this system might also be altered in depressed patients, which could imply a general dysfunction of DA systems, including the mesolimbic system. However, the neuroendocrine evidence is less consistent than the evidence of CSF studies, and at present, even the direction of change in tuberoinfundibular DA function is uncertain. As this evidence does not support a picture of generalized DA underactivity, the question of the functional state of the mesolimbic system in depression must therefore remain open. Since, as discussed in the previous chapter, animal studies point to the mesolimbic system as the DA system potentially most relevant to depression, the lack of any tools for assessing mesolimbic function in people is unfortunate. Perhaps, as discussed earlier (Section 5.3.2.), it may be possible to use EEG activity recorded over the left frontal lobe for this purpose.

In principle, the DA hypothesis of depression appears to make clear predictions regarding the effects of treatments that are known to affect brain DA systems. Treatments that decrease DA function should induce depression in normal subjects, and treatments that increase DA function should alleviate depression. In practice, these predictions are far less straightforward for a number of reasons. First, there is the ever-present problem of side effects. Although the use of agents acting specifically on central DA systems may make it possible to avoid unwanted peripheral effects, or effects on other transmitter systems, unwanted effects on a DA system other than the "target system" may be unavoidable. A further consequence of the need to avoid unwanted side effects is that the doses used may be too low to have the desired effect. Second, the position is greatly complicated by the fact that chronic drug treatments induce biochemical adaptations, which may ameliorate or even reverse the acute effects. These factors must be taken into account in assessing the significance of studies that fail to confirm predictions regarding drug effects on mood.

A third problem concerns the nature of mood and the relationship of mood states to the brain. Amphetamine, which is usually considered to be a euphoriant, may frequently fail to improve mood in experimental studies (e.g., Griffith et al., 1972; Jain et al., 1980). It will be recalled that in the classic experiment of Schachter and Singer (1962) subjects who had been injected with adrenaline became either angry or euphoric, depending on the behavior of their companion (Section 2.2.2). These results indicate that a state of physiological arousal may be channelled into a variety of emotional states, as determined by the cognitive "set" induced in the subject by environmental conditions. Environmental conditions, specifically the attitude of the prescribing physician to antidepressant drugs (which presumably communicates itself to the patient) have also been found to influence the efficacy of antidepressant drug therapy (Sheard, 1960). In view of these findings, it may be inappropriate to expect a one-to-one relationship between mood changes and manipulation of a particular neurotransmitter system, irrespective of environmental conditions, the psychological state of the subject at the time of testing, and of course, the neurochemical status of other neurotransmitter systems.

In addition to this indeterminacy of drug effects on mood, the relationship of depressed mood to the state of clinical depression is itself unclear. Many patients may be clinically depressed, on the basis of such symptoms as social withdrawal, sleep disturbance, and loss of energy, appetite, and libido, while scoring normally on mood scales. Conversely, clinical improvement during antidepressant drug therapy may not necessarily be accompanied by improvements in mood (Murphy & Redmond, 1975). The independence of changes in different response dimensions following amphetamine administration has frequently been commented upon (Checkley, 1978; Silberman et al., 1981).

These issues are particularly pertinent in relation to the association between psychomotor retardation in depression and low DA turnover. In an attempt to establish whether low DA function was related to depressed mood or to motor activity, Post and co-workers (1973c) asked seven moderately depressed patients to simulate mania, which they did successfully. This procedure produced a significant increase in CSF HVA accumulation. However, as most of the patients stimulating mania also experienced mood elevation, the causal relationships remain unclear. Furthermore, even in the absence of mood changes, an experiment of this kind would be unable to determine whether a change in DA turnover was caused by feedback from motor activity or from the effort to produce motor activity.

Fortunately, the animal literature is unequivocal on this point: the evidence reviewed in the previous chapter shows that manipulations of brain DA cause changes in locomotor activity. It is important to note, however, that these changes in locomotor activity are far from trivial: they arise from changes in incentive motivation and represent the extent to which behavior can be aroused by the environment. Similarly in people, psychomotor retardation is not simply a decrease in motor activity but a pervasive reduction in effort and concentration (see Section 4.1), which when present in depression is central to the syndrome and, if anything, rather more important a symptom than depression of mood (see Chapter 3). The involvement of DA in motivational processes in human subjects is illustrated by the observation that DOPA administration improved attention and memory in addition to raising locomotor activity (Murphy, 1972, 1976).

Although relatively few studies have examined the antidepressant effects of DA agonist drugs, there is a degree of unanimity among them, which may be summarized as follows:

1. All treatments produced some degree of improvement.

2. The response with DA uptake blockers and direct receptor agonists is comparable to that obtained with tricyclic antidepressants. Although the predominant effect is usually on psychomotor retardation, the drugs also appear to improve depressed mood.

3. DOPA has similar but more restricted effects. In particular, there is little evidence that DOPA can elevate mood, either in normal subjects or in depressed patients.

4. Bipolar patients appear to respond better than unipolar patients; unipolar patients with pronounced psychomotor retardation respond better than agitated patients. Since most bipolar patients show retardation (Beigel & Murphy, 1971; Donnelly & Murphy, 1973; Kupfer et al., 1974), this factor probably subsumes the bipolar–unipolar distinction.

5. The antidepressant response to DA agonist treatments is associated with a low pretreatment DA turnover; this has been demonstrated for DOPA, nomifensine, and piribedil (Post et al., 1978a; van Praag & Korf, 1975; van Scheyen et al., 1977). Only one study has failed to confirm this relationship, and in this case, the more sensitive probenecid technique for measuring CSF HVA accumulation was not used (Nordin et al., 1981). It is of interest in this context that low pretreatment CSF HVA also predicts a good antidepressant response to one night's sleep deprivation (Gerner et al., 1979); as discussed in Chapter 10, sleep deprivation enhances DA transmission.

It is unclear at present why DOPA should be efficacious in a more restricted population of patients than other DA agonist treatments. One biochemical difference of potential interest is that unlike the other drugs, DOPA decreases 5-HT function in rats (Ng et al., 1970) and people (Goodwin et al., 1970). As 5-HT depletion may be of etiological significance in depression (Murphy et al., 1978a; see Chapters 15–17), a decrease in 5-HT function could mask a mood-elevating effect of DOPA. Evidence on this point is minimal. In a study of combined treatment with DOPA and the 5-HT precursor tryptophan, two out of five patients showed slight mood improvements, while one (unipolar) patient became worse (Dunner & Fieve, 1975). Another possibility might be that in comparison to the directly acting DA agonists, DOPA might produce a relatively greater activation of nigrostriatal than of mesolimbic DA neurons. At high levels of activation, the behavioral output of the nigrostriatal system suppresses that of the mesolimbic system (Kelly et al., 1975). If, as suggested by the animal studies, the mesolimbic system is more crucially involved in mood regulation, a shift in the balance of activity in these two systems could determine whether mood will be enhanced by DA activating drugs. Whatever the reason for the relative ineffectiveness of DOPA, this may be less significant than the mood-elevating effects of other DA agonists and the DA-dependent euphoric effect of amphetamine.

Pharmacological treatments which reduce DA function may sometimes induce depression, but the incidence of true depressions following reserpine, AMPT, alpha-methyl-DOPA, and neuroleptics does not appear to be very impressive. However, it is possible that this might be due in part to the use of insufficient doses, as judged by the similar infrequency of sedative effects following these treatments, and in part to the ability of the brain to withstand and compensate for pharmacological assaults. Moreover, reserpine, AMPT, alpha-methyl-DOPA, and most neuroleptics reduce the functional efficacy of NA systems in addition to that of DA. In a wide variety of behavioral situations, it has been found that the deleterious effects of reducing DA function in experimental animals were offset by a simultaneous reduction of NA function (Antelman & Caggiula, 1976).

Data from the primate separation model of depression (Section 7.2.4) may also be relevant. If group-housed monkeys are separated, a "despair" syndrome develops, of which the most prominent feature is huddling in a fetal position (Suomi et al., 1970). Using this model, Kraemer & McKinney (1979) found that huddling was increased by AMPT. (The selective NA synthesis inhibitor fusaric acid decreased huddling, indicating that AMPT-induced huddling was mediated by DA, rather than NA.) It was found, however, that the dose of AMPT required to increase huddling varied from 12.5 mg/kg to 100 mg/kg, depending on the animal's rearing conditions and previous experience of separation. Huddling could also be induced by AMPT in singly reared or unseparated animals, but in these cases, doses up to 500 mg/kg were required. One way of looking at these results is to say that the induction of a depression-like behavior by AMPT was potentiated either by a concurrent stress (separation) or by particular kinds of personal history (e.g., repeated separation). These results may be considered in relation to the small but significant effect of stressful "life events" either in the period leading up to the onset of depression or in the more distant past (Brown & Harris, 1978; Lloyd, 1980a,b; see Section 20.1). Although reducing DA function pharmacologically does not usually induce depression (subject to the qualifications expressed above), these considerations suggest that depression might well result from a combination of reduced DA function and the appropriate environmental conditions (see also Anisman & Zacharko, 1982). It is plausible that the occurrence of reserpine depression in patients with a prior history of depression, and depression associated with the stress of Parkinson's disease, could reflect a mechanism of this kind.

ten

ANTIDEPRESSANTS AND DOPAMINE

Traditionally, discussions of the mechanisms of action of antidepressant treatments have focused on NA and 5-HT systems rather than on DA (Schildkraut, 1978; Murphy et al., 1978a). The possibility that antidepressants might also increase the activity of brain DA systems was first suggested by the observation that Parkinson's disease, a known DA deficiency syndrome, may sometimes be successfully treated by tricyclic antidepressants (Randrup et al., 1975) or by ECS (Balldin et al., 1980b, 1981; Lebensohn & Jenkins, 1975). The possibility that antidepressants might increase DA function had been neglected primarily because in early studies, tricyclic antidepressants had been found to block the neuronal uptake of NA and 5-HT, but they were believed to be ineffective against DA uptake (Carlsson, 1970). It was subsequently demonstrated, however, that antidepressant drugs do in fact block DA uptake, and this effect is shared by some drugs, such as butriptyline and iprindole, which are relatively ineffective as NA and 5-HT uptake blockers (Friedman et al., 1977; Halaris et al., 1975; Hytell, 1978; Koide & Uyemura, 1980; Kowalik et al., 1984; Randrup & Braestrup, 1977). Although these actions are generally several orders of magnitude less potent than the effects on NA and 5-HT, it is possible that the necessary concentrations, in the micromolar range, might be reached in the brains of patients receiving antidepressant drug therapy (Dingell et al., 1964; Jori et al., 1971).

On the other hand, many tricyclic antidepressants also possess DA receptor blocking activity (Karobath, 1975). As a result, the effect of antidepressant treatment on postsynaptic cell firing depends on the net outcome of two opposing effects: the enhancement of synaptic transmission by uptake blockade and the reduction of transmission by receptor blockade. It might be anticipated that the combination of these two effects might have rather variable consequences for transmission across DA synapses, and this is indeed the case.

Under most circumstances, drugs such as apomorphine, which stimulate DA receptors, activate a striatonigral feedback pathway, which inhibits firing in nigral DA neurons. This change is accompanied by a decrease in DA synthesis. Dopamine receptor blocking drugs have the opposite effects (Carlsson, 1975b). Dopamine synthesis can therefore be used as a way of assessing the net effect of tricyclics on DA transmission. Carlsson and Lindqvist (1978a) found that DA synthesis was increased in a dose-dependent fashion by some tricyclic antidepressants and decreased by others; a third group produced no consistent change. This suggests that antidepressant drugs given acutely do not have a common effect on DA transmission. A further observation, which is in keeping with the conclusion that the effects of antidepressants on DA transmission are slight, is that pretreatment with DMI, imipramine, or nortriptyline did not affect the ability of rats to discriminate between saline and a low dose of amphetamine (Schechter 1980). The perception of the presence of amphetamine is known to be mediated by a central DA system (Ho & Huang, 1975; Schechter & Cook, 1975), so a significant change in DA transmission should be reflected in a change in performance on this task.

10.1. CHRONIC STUDIES: PRESYNAPTIC EFFECTS

10.1.1. Synthesis and Turnover

In view of the time course of antidepressant therapy—effects are usually seen after two- to three-week treatments—studies employing chronic antidepressant administration are probably of greater relevance than studies of the effects of acute pretreatment. However, the effects of chronic antidepressant treatment on DA synthesis and turnover appear to be minimal. Brain DA content was increased slightly by two weeks of treatment with mianserin (Leonard & Kafoe, 1976; Sugrue, 1980c) but unaffected by chronic DMI, imipramine, maprotiline, chlorimipramine, iprindole, or ECS (Evans et al., 1976; Leonard & Kafoe, 1976; Sugrue, 1980c). Dopamine synthesis in striatum and limbic forebrain, measured by the accumulation of DOPA after DOPA decarboxylase inhibition, was decreased slightly by chronic imipramine (Friedman et al., 1974), but unaffected by other tricyclics (DMI, protriptyline) or by ECS (Modigh, 1976; Neff & Costa, 1967).

Turnover of DA, estimated by levels of the DA metabolites DOPAC and HVA was unaffected by chronic DMI, imipramine, maprotiline, chlorimipramine, or ECS (Modigh, 1976; Sugrue, 1980c). It has been reported that DA turnover measured by a different method, the incorporation of tritiated tyrosine into DA (conversion index), was unaffected by chronic iprindole and mianserin, but reduced by DMI and imipramine (Leonard & Kafoe, 1976). However, these latter results appear to be an artifact of this particular method of measuring turnover, because they arose from an increase in the availability of tritiated tyrosine. All in all, the biochemical activity of DA neurons appears to be remarkably unaffected by chronic antidepressant treatment.

Deprivation of REM sleep is the only antidepressant treatment that has been reported to increase DA turnover (Wojcik & Radulovacki, 1981). However, this change appears to result from the stresses attendant on the REM deprivation procedure, rather than from sleep deprivation as such (Farber et al., 1983).

10.1.2. Autoreceptors

The activity of DA neurons is regulated in part by feedback pathways from the striatum and nucleus accumbens to the DA cell-body areas (Bunney & Aghajanian, 1976b; Wang, 1981) and in part by autoreceptors situated on the DA cell bodies (Skirboll et al., 1979) that are responsive to DA released from dendrites (Groves et al., 1975). In contrast to the lack of effect of antidepressants on biochemical measures of DA activity, a number of studies have claimed that chronic antidepressant treatments increase the activity of DA cells by decreasing the inhibitory effects of DA autoreceptor stimulation. However, the evidence is rather equivocal.

Small doses of the DA receptor agonist apomorphine reduce locomotor activity in rats, apparently by a selective activation of DA autoreceptors (Strombom, 1977). Serra and co-workers (1979) first demonstrated that the sedative effect of low doses of apomorphine was abolished by chronic (10 day), but not acute, treatment with the tricyclic antidepressants imipramine and amitriptyline, and the atypical antidepressant mianserin. This effect was subsequently confirmed using imipramine, amitriptyline, doxepin, and nomifensine (Zebrowska-Lupina & Kozyrska, 1980), and it was also seen following chronic, but not acute treatment with MAOIs (Serra et al., cited by Chiodo & Antelman, 1982), lithium (Harrison-Read, 1980), and ECS (Serra et al., 1981a). Repeated ECS treatment also abolished the synchronization of EEG activity which accompanies apomorphine-induced sedation (Mereu et al., 1982). Deprivation of REM sleep has been found to be an effective antidepressant (Gillin, 1983), and this treatment, too, reduced apomorphine-induced sedation, the effect being greater after three nights sleep deprivation than after one night (Serra et al., 1981b).

However, a number of studies have failed to confirm these effects. One study found no change in the sedative effect of apomorphine after a series of 10 daily ECS (Ehlers et al., 1983), and one published (Spyraki & Fibiger, 1981) and at least three unpublished studies (Chiodo, Liebman et al., personal communications; unpublished personal observations) were unable to demonstrate attenuation of apomorphine-induced sedation after chronic tricyclic treatment. Another study, which used the anorexic effects of apomorphine as a behavioral probe, did confirm the effect, but only marginally: chronic treatment with DMI was found to attenuate the apomorphine-induced reduction of eating time, but the effect was small and unreliable (Willner & Towell, 1982b).

Despite the lack of consensus shown in behavioral studies, autoreceptor desensitization has also been demonstrated electrophysiologically. Autoreceptor stimulation by low doses of apomorphine inhibits the firing of DA cells in the substantia nigra (Skirboll et al., 1979). This effect was reduced by repeated administration (10 days) of ECS, the tricyclics amitriptyline or imipramine, or the atypical antidepressant iprindole (Chiodo & Antelman, 1980a,b). Autoreceptor desensitization by the MAOI phenelzine has also been demonstrated, in this case using microiontophoretic application of DA in the substantia nigra, rather than systemic administration of apomorphine (Antelman et al., 1982).

In 25–50‰ of cells studied in animals treated with imipramine or amitriptyline for 10 days or more, the effect of apomorphine was actually reversed, and excitation rather than inhibition was seen (Chiodo & Antelman, 1980c). Perhaps as a consequence of this change in the properties of DA autoreceptors, it has also been reported that the number of active DA cells encountered in electrode tracks through the substantia nigra and A10 DA cell body regions was increased by chronic DMI treatment (Chiodo & Bunney, 1982). An additional finding, potentially of great significance, was that the development of autoreceptor subsensitivity depended simply on the passage of time: 10 days after 2 days imipramine treatment, the same degree of subsensitivity was seen as 2 days after 10 days treatment (substantially greater than 2 days after 2 days treatment); a similar effect was also obtained with ECS (Antelman et al., 1982; Chiodo & Antelman, 1980a,b).

As yet, however, other groups of workers have been unable to support these findings. Two studies found no change in apomorphine-induced inhibition of DA cell firing following chronic tricyclic treatment (MacNiell & Gower, 1982; Welch et al., 1982). A third study did find a reduced effect of apomorphine following repeated ECS administration, but the same effect was also seen after a single ECS, which is ineffective as an antidepressant (Tepper et al., 1982). An attempt to demonstrate a delayed effect of a single ECS using behavioral sedation to test for autoreceptor subsensitivity was also unsuccessful (Creese et al., 1982).

Biochemical evidence for autoreceptor desensitization is even more equivocal. Inhibition of DA synthesis (measured by the accumulation of the DA metabolite DOPAC) is another consequence of DA autoreceptor stimulation (Roth et al., 1976). Serra and co-workers (1979) reported that in addition to abolishing the sedative effect of apomorphine, chronic antidepressant drug treatment also blocked the apomorphine-induced inhibition of DA release. This effect has since been confirmed (Holcomb et al., 1982). However, ECS and REM sleep deprivation, which also blocked the sedative effect of apomorphine, had no effect on the apomorphine-induced inhibition of DA synthesis (Farber et al., 1983; Serra et al., 1981a,b). Indeed, one study reported an increase in apomorphine-induced inhibition of DA synthesis five days after the end of a course of ECS treatment (Reches et al., 1984).

Autoreceptors are also found on DA terminals (Starke et al., 1977); stimulation of these receptors inhibits the increase in DA synthesis which occurs following a blockade of DA impulse flow by the drug gamma-butyrolactone (Roth, 1979). Using this model, Holcomb and co-workers (1982) found no change in DA terminal autoreceptor sensitivity following chronic administration of imipramine or iprindole according to the same schedule as used by Serra and co-workers (1979). Lee and Tang (1982) have reported that three to four weeks of treatment with DMI or nomifensine did cause a reduction in the binding of DA by striatal membranes; this technique has been assumed to measure presynaptic (i.e., axon terminal) rather than postsynaptic receptors (Bannon et al., 1980; Nagy et al., 1978). However, as noted below, receptor binding studies are of doubtful functional significance. Furthermore, the supposed presynaptic localization of DA binding sites has recently been called into question (Creese et al., 1983).

Clearly, it is not possible at present to draw any definite conclusion as to the effect of chronic antidepressant administration on DA neurons. However, if, as claimed, these treatments do desensitize DA autoreceptors, the result should be an augmented response to activation of DA neurons. The firing rate of substantia nigra cells is increased by mild pressure applied to the tail, which also elicits DA-dependent behaviors (Chiodo et al., 1979, 1980). The increase in firing rate evoked by tail pressure was found to be enhanced by repeated treatment with amitriptyline, imipramine, iprindole, and ECS, though only the first two effects were statistically significant (Chiodo & Antelman, 1980a,b). These results suggest a way of resolving the discrepancy between the studies reporting increased DA activity, as a result of autoreceptor desensitization, and those reporting no change in DA turnover. An increase in turnover, consequent on an increase in cell firing, might well be observed if the animals were subjected to activating stimuli during the period in which turnover is measured.

10.2. CHRONIC STUDIES: POSTSYNAPTIC EFFECTS

10.2.1. Neuroendocrine Studies

Since, for all practical purposes, functional DA receptors are found only within the central nervous system, neuroendocrine methods at present provide the only way of studying DA receptor function in human subjects. As described in Section 9.1.4, DA has been implicated in the excitatory control of growth hormone (GH) release, and in the inhibitory control of prolactin release. A number of studies have attempted to use these neuroendocrine effects of DA to assay the effects of chronic antidepressant treatment on postsynaptic DA receptor function.

It is possible in animals to preclude any contamination of the results by changes in presynaptic DA activity by administering reserpine, and thereby abolishing monoaminergic neurotransmission. In reserpine-pretreated rats, it is found that apomorphine alone does not stimulate GH release, but apomorphine does enhance the stimulatory effect of the NA agonist clonidine. Repeated (7 day) ECS was found to enhance the stimulatory effect of apomorphine, whereas the response to clonidine alone was unaffected, suggesting an increase in the DA-receptor-mediated response (Balldin et al., 1980a; Eden & Modigh, 1977). However, clinical tests of GH release are equivocal. Costain and co-workers (1982) reported increased apomorphine-induced GH secretion in depressed patients following a course of ECS, but most workers have found that ECS did not change apomorphine-induced GH release in depressed or Parkinsonian patients (Balldin et al., 1982; Christie et al., 1982; Meco et al., 1981). Methamphetamine-induced GH release was similarly unaffected by ECS (Slade & Checkley, 1980). Furthermore, a reduction in apomorphine-stimulated GH release has been reported following chronic amitriptyline treatment in depressed patients (Costain et al., 1982) and after 24 hours sleep deprivation in normal volunteers (Lal et al., 1981). These findings would tend to suggest that the sensitivity of hypothalamic DA receptors is not altered in a consistent fashion by antidepressants. However, the validity of apomorphine-stimulated GH release as a model of DA function is not well established. The model may fail, for example, to detect the increase in DA receptor sensitivity, which is known to accompany withdrawal from chronic neuroleptic drug treatment (Brambilla et al., 1979; Tamminga et al., 1977). In consequence, it is difficult to have confidence in any conclusions drawn from these studies.

Inhibition of prolactin release is probably a more reliable model of DA function. Fuxe and co-workers (1982b) have reported that chronic anti-

depressant administration to rats decreased or did not change basal prolactin levels; studies of the effects of chronic ECS or antidepressant drug
treatment on basal prolactin levels in depressed patients have variously
reported a decrease (Coppen & Ghose, 1978), no change (Balldin et al.,
1982; Cooper et al., 1981; Meltzer et al., 1977; Widerlov et al., 1978), or
an increase (Asnis et al., 1980a; Cooper et al., 1981). Again, however, in
view of the complex nature of the feedback control of pituitary hormones
(Moore et al., 1980), measures of basal hormone levels are of doubtful
significance.

A better measure is given by the response to DA agonist challenges.
Four out of six studies have reported antidepressant-induced increases
in the inhibitory effects of DA agonist drugs on prolactin secretion. Clear
increases in apomorphine and DOPA-induced prolactin inhibition were
observed following repeated ECS in depressed and Parkinsonian patients
[in studies by Balldin and co-workers (1982) and Meco and co-workers
(1981), though not in a third study (Christie et al. 1982)]. A fourth study
reported an increase in the prolactin-inhibiting effect of another DA agonist, bromocryptine, following chronic amitriptyline treatment in depressed patients (Coppen & Ghose, 1978). In rats, Meltzer and co-workers
(1981b) saw no effect of chronic ECS on amphetamine-induced prolactin
inhibition, but Balldin (1981) did demonstrate a small increase in apomorphine-induced prolactin inhibition following repeated ECS. The balance of these findings suggests that DA receptor responsiveness was increased by chronic antidepressant treatments. Checkley and co-workers
(1984) have suggested that the use of a general anesthetic may delay the
emergence of ECS-induced neuroendocrine changes; this factor could explain why the results are somewhat inconsistent.

10.2.2. Behavioral Studies

Although the responsiveness of the DA receptors mediating neuroendocrine responses is of some interest, behavioral probes produce evidence
more directly relevant to the psychological involvement of DA systems.
As outlined in Chapter 8, DA agonist drugs, including the indirectly acting agonists amphetamine and DOPA, and the direct receptor agonist
apomorphine, produce a dose-dependent pattern of behavioral effects. At
moderate doses, locomotor hyperactivity is seen, whereas at higher doses,
this is superseded by a characteristic pattern of stereotyped behavior. It
is now generally accepted that the locomotor stimulant effect of moderate
doses is mediated by the mesolimbic DA system, whereas the stereotyped
behavior seen at high doses is mediated by the nigrostriatal system (see
Section 8.0).

An impressive body of evidence demonstrates that following chronic,
but not acute, antidepressant treatments, behaviors elicited by moderate
doses of DA receptor agonists are enhanced, indicating increased respon-

siveness in the mesolimbic DA system. Repeated ECS has been shown to enhance the locomotor stimulant effects of apomorphine (Green et al., 1980, 1983b; Green & Deakin, 1980; Modigh, 1975, 1979; Modigh, 1984; Wielosz, 1981—but not Lerer et al., 1982), amphetamine (Ehlers et al., 1983; Wielosz, 1981), methylamphetamine (Green et al., 1977a), and a cocktail of DOPA with the MAOI tranylcypromine (Atterwill, 1980; Evans et al., 1976; Cross et al., 1979). Repeated ECS also enhanced the discriminative-stimulus properties of apomorphine and amphetamine (White & Barrett, 1981). Similarly, chronic treatment with tricyclic antidepressant drugs and the atypical antidepressants mianserin and iprindole has been shown to enhance apomorphine and amphetamine-induced locomotor activity (Serra et al., 1979; Spyraki & Fibiger, 1981; Willner & Montgomery, 1981). Similar effects have been observed following REM sleep deprivation (Fergusen & Dement, 1969; Tufik et al., 1978).

It is possible that these results might not reflect an increase in postsynaptic responsiveness, but rather they could reflect the absence of the sedative component of stimulant drug action, as a result of the decrease in autoreceptor sensitivity described above. However, two further observations rule out this possibility, at least in the case of ECS. First, enhancement by repeated ECS of the stimulant effect of DA was seen when DA was injected directly into the nucleus accumbens (Heal & Green, 1978; Modigh, 1979); this effect was also seen with dibutyryl-cAMP (Heal & Green, 1978). The locomotor stimulant effect of dibutyryl-cAMP is mediated "beyond the DA receptor," because this effect is not blocked by DA receptor antagonists (Heal et al., 1978). Second, the locomotor stimulant effect of apomorphine was enhanced by repeated ECS following pretreatment with reserpine, at a dose which abolishes presynaptic DA activity (Modigh, 1975, 1984). Similarly, in the case of REM sleep deprivation, the enhanced responsiveness to DA agonist drugs was undiminished following the inhibition of DA synthesis (Tufik, 1981). These results point clearly to an increase in the sensitivity of structures postsynaptic to mesolimbic DA neurons.

The effects of repeated antidepressant treatments on the nigrostriatal system are less clear cut. One behavior that is mediated primarily by the nigrostriatal system, the circling induced by apomorphine in unilaterally nigrostriatal lesioned animals (Moore & Kelly, 1978), was enhanced by repeated ECS (Green et al., 1977a) but not by subchronic tricyclic antidepressant treatment (Delina-Stula & Vassout, 1979b). Most attempts to assess nigrostriatal activity have examined apomorphine- or amphetamine-induced stereotyped behavior. Some studies have shown increases in stereotyped behavior following chronic treatment with a variety of antidepressant drugs (Willner & Montgomery, 1981; Willner et al., 1984; Zebrowska-Lupina, 1980), but others failed to show this effect (Bhavsar et al., 1983; Delina-Stula & Vassout, 1979b; Maj et al., 1979a; Spyraki & Fibiger, 1981). Similarly, five studies have found an increase in apomorphine stereotypy after repeated ECS (Bhavsar et al., 1981, 1983; Globus et al., 1981; Modigh, 1979; Serra et al., 1981a), whereas a sixth did not (Wielosz, 1981). Increases in apomorphine stereotypy have been reported following REM sleep deprivation (Tufik et al., 1978; Zelger & Carlini, 1982).

It is possible that some of the negative reports reflect the vagaries of the rating scale used to measure stereotypy, which is highly nonlinear (Fray et al., 1980); enhancement of stereotypy might be observed more readily if a range of stereotypy-inducing drug doses was tested, rather than the customary single dose, or, alternatively, if stereotyped behavior was sampled repeatedly over a period of hours. This latter procedure was adopted in two of the studies that reported increases in stereotypy with antidepressant drugs (Willner & Montgomery, 1981; Willner et al., 1984). Had we confined the experiment to a single observation shortly after administration of the challenge, as in some studies (e.g., Bhavsar et al., 1983), we should not have seen any differences. Additionally, in two of the negative reports, testing was carried out only one hour after the final antidepressant injection, a considerably shorter period than is usually employed. Furthermore, in one of these studies, only seven days of treatment were used, which is probably too short to expect to observe an effect of antidepressant drugs. On balance, and taking these methodological observations into account, the results point to an increase in nigrostriatal responsiveness similar to that observed in the mesolimbic system, particularly when ECS is used.

The mechanism of these effects is obscure. The only clue at present is that the ECS-induced increase in stimulation of locomotor activity by apomorphine (and also by the 5-HT receptor agonist quipazine) was blocked by lesions of the noradrenergic locus coeruleus (Green & Deakin, 1980) and by catecholamine synthesis inhibition (Green et al., 1980). Exactly how the changes in DA responsiveness might be dependent on an intact NA system is at present a mystery. Electroconvulsive shock (ECS) is known to cause a surge of NA release (Baldessarini, 1975b). However, the enhanced effect of apomorphine was not prevented by pretreatment with the beta-blocker propranolol prior to each ECS (Green et al., 1980), indicating either that the effect is mediated by alpha-receptors or that the ECS-induced surge is NA release is irrelevant.

10.2.3. Receptor Binding Studies

In contrast to the equivocal results of neuroendocrine probes, the behavioral evidence demonstrates very clearly that chronic antidepressant treatment causes an increase in DA transmission. All that is needed to complete the picture is direct biochemical evidence of changes in postsynaptic DA receptors. Unfortunately, biochemical studies of DA receptors provide no support at all.

The ligand [³H]spiroperidol is assumed to bind specifically to postsynaptic DA receptors in the striatum (Howlett & Nahorski, 1980; Nagy et al., 1978). A number of studies have found no change in the specific binding of [³H]spiroperidol by striatal tissues following chronic ECS (Atterwill, 1980; Bergstrom et al., 1978; Bergstrom & Kellar, 1979a; Deakin et al., 1981; Globus et al., 1981; Lerer et al., 1982; Reches et al., 1984); neither did chronic ECS alter DA-stimulated adenyl cyclase activity (Green et al., 1977a). Similarly, there have been several reports that chronic treatment with antidepressant drugs does not change DA-receptor binding (Peroutka & Snyder, 1980a; Rehavi et al., 1980b; J. Rosenblatt et al., 1979; Tang & Seeman, 1980; Tang et al., 1981), and in one series of experiments, it was reported that [³H]spiroperidol binding to striatal membranes, which was unaffected by a single treatment with DMI or imipramine, was actually decreased by four weeks of treatment (Koide & Matsushita, 1981a,b). Dopamine receptor binding in striatum and frontal cortex was unaffected by four night's deprivation of REM sleep (Farber et al., 1983).

Although the effect of antidepressant treatments on postsynaptic DA receptor sensitivity has not yet been measured directly by electrophysiological recording methods, the weight of biochemical evidence points strongly to the conclusion that chronic antidepressant treatments do not increase the sensitivity of postsynaptic DA receptors. It seems likely, therefore, that the increases in behavioral responses to the activation of postsynaptic DA receptors are mediated by structures situated beyond the DA receptors—for example, "downstream" neurons. This conclusion is also suggested by the increased response to dibutyryl-cAMP reported by Heal & Green (1978), because this compound is thought to act beyond the receptor. It should be noted, however, that receptor binding studies do not measure physiological sensitivity. Reports of changes in physiological sensitivity without corresponding changes in binding are not uncommon. Typically, chronic antidepressant treatment is found to reduce binding measures of alpha-adrenergic and 5-HT receptors, whereas electrophysiological recording studies show an increased responsiveness to agonist drugs (Charney et al., 1981c; see Chapters 13 and 17). In view of these discrepancies, the failure to demonstrate antidepressant-induced changes in DA receptor binding is of questionable significance.

10.3. CONCLUSIONS: ANTIDEPRESSANTS AND DA

Despite the lack of biochemical confirmation, there is very strong evidence of increased responsiveness in structures postsynaptic to mesolimbic DA neurons following a wide variety of chronic antidepressant treatments. There is also good evidence indicating postsynaptic hyperreactivity in the nigrostriatal DA system and in the pituitary receptors mediating the inhibition of prolactin secretion. The latter result is particularly interesting in view of the observation that, pharmacologically, the receptors mediating prolactin inhibition resemble DA autoreceptors in their response to the isomers of the DA autoreceptor agonist 3-PPP (Hjorth et al., 1981, 1982) rather than postsynaptic receptors (E. Eriksson, personal communication). The antidepressant-induced increase in responsiveness therefore appears to be a function of postsynaptic location rather than receptor type.

Although the synthesis and turnover of DA are virtually unaffected by chronic antidepressant treatments, indicating that there are no gross changes in presynaptic activity, the evidence for subsensitivity of DA autoreceptors cannot be ignored, despite the difficulty that has been experienced in establishing the conditions under which the effect may be reliably replicated. Like an increase in postsynaptic responsiveness, a decrease in presynaptic responsiveness, if confirmed, would also have the effect of increasing the level of DA function.

The effects of MAOIs on DA function have not been examined, except in the controversial autoreceptor desensitization paradigm (Antelman et al., 1982). Considering that abnormalities of DA transmission are most readily apparent in endogenous depressions (see Chapter 9), where MAOIs are ineffective (see Section 1.1.4), it would not be surprising if MAOIs failed to potentiate DA-mediated behaviors. Another treatment which probably does not enhance DA transmission is lithium. Although useful primarily as an antimanic agent, lithium also exerts antidepressant effects (Ramsey & Mendels, 1981). However, in 10 out of 12 studies reviewed by Bunney and Garland (1983), lithium was found to block the development of behavioral supersensitivity to DA agonist drugs brought about by chronic understimulation of DA receptors. As the DA receptor blocker pimozide causes a decrease in manic symptomatology (Post et al., 1980b), this effect of lithium may well be relevant to its antimanic properties, but it seems likely that the key to its antidepressant effects must be sought elsewhere.

Although there is clear evidence that postsynaptic responsiveness in DA systems is increased by tricyclic and many "atypical" antidepressants, by ECT, and by REM sleep deprivation, these changes have not usually been reported to increase the basal level of DA-mediated functions [the studies of Modigh (1975) and Wielosz (1981) are exceptions]; the effects of antidepressants are usually manifest only when agonist drugs are used to increase receptor stimulation. However, an increase would be expected in the efficacy of stimuli that activate DA systems, and as discussed in Chapter 8, a number of behavioral effects of antidepressants may potentially be interpreted in these terms (Section 8.3.3). It is also possible that a number of the effects of antidepressant treatments in animal models of depression depend on an increase in DA function (Section 8.3.2). These indirect indications of increased DA responsiveness are supplemented by the observation that chronic administration of DMI, imipramine, or ami-triptyline to cats produced EEG changes similar to those induced by DA agonists (Neal & Bradley, 1979).

The evidence reviewed indicates that chronic tricyclic antidepressant and ECS treatments increase the excitability of systems that include a DA component. It is therefore of great interest that tricyclic antidepressants and ECT are most effective in depressions characterized by psychomotor retardation, and they may actually make agitated depressions worse (Bielski & Friedel, 1976; Nelson & Charney, 1981). As discussed in the previous chapter, retarded depressions are associated with a reduced level of DA function and a favorable response to treatment with DA agonist drugs (Section 9.4). Taken together, the evidence from animal models and from basic behavioral neuroscience (Chapter 8), the clinical evidence (Chapter 9), and the evidence that chronic antidepressant treatment increases DA function (this chapter) present a refreshingly coherent picture.

eleven

NORADRENALINE AND DEPRESSION: THEORETICAL PERSPECTIVES

In comparison to the analysis of DA systems undertaken in Chapters 8–10, almost every aspect of the contribution of NA systems to depression is more difficult to assess. This problem begins with anatomy of the NA systems, and it continues through their behavioral functions (this chapter), their status in depression (Chapter 12), and their pharmacology (Chapter 13).

Noradrenaline-containing cell bodies are situated almost exclusively in a group of nuclei in the pons and medulla first described in detail by Ungerstedt (1971). The largest and most compact of these nuclei, the locus coeruleus (nucleus A6), contains only about 1500 cells in the rat, but their axons have a remarkably wide terminal distribution. The major output pathway, the dorsal NA bundle, runs through the dorsal tegmentum of the midbrain, passes through the lateral hypothalamus in the medial forebrain bundle, and then fans out to innervate the whole of the neocortex, hippocampus, and amygdala; another branch of the same axons innervates the cerebellar cortex (Fig. 11.1.a). The nature of the neocortical NA innervation is as striking as its extent: the fibers enter the cortex

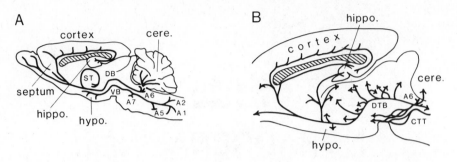

Fig. 11.1. The major NA pathways of the rat forebrain. (*a*) Redrawn from Ungerstedt (1971). DB, dorsal bundle; VB, ventral bundle; ST, stria terminalis. (*b*) Redrawn from Lindvall and Bjorklund (1974). CTT, central tegmental tract; DTB, dorsal tegmental bundle.

at the frontal pole and run caudally all the way to the occipital pole, giving off frequent laterally oriented branches (Morrison et al., 1980). As NA fibers release transmitter not just at nerve endings but also from varicosities along their length, the system resembles nothing so much as a sprinkler system, which when turned on applies NA to the cortex in a uniform spray.

The second pathway described by Ungerstedt (1971), the ventral NA bundle, was less well defined. The ventral bundle originates in a number of smaller nuclei (A1, A2, A3, A5, A7, and others); their ascending axons run together in the central tegmental tract to terminate mainly in the hypothalamus (Fig. 11.1a). Most of the descending NA innervation of the spinal cord also arises from these nuclei.

In 1974 Lindvall and Bjorklund developed the more sensitive glyoxylic acid technique, which allowed the visualization of a large number of additional details of the distribution of NA fibers. Application of this technique changed the picture in three important ways. First, the dorsal bundle, now known as the *dorsal tegmental bundle*, was seen to be even more complex in its terminal distribution than previously believed (Fig. 11.1b). In particular, some axons run ventrally into the central tegmental tract and terminate in the hypothalamus. Second, an additional system, the dorsal periventricular system, was described, which originates in nucleus A2, gains fibers from the locus coeruleus and from NA cell bodies scattered along its course, and runs medial to the dorsal tegmental bundle, terminating mainly in the tectum and thalamus. Third, with the development of a better understanding of the afferent and efferent projections of the individual NA nuclei, it became necessary to question the assumption that the ventral bundle contains a uniform functional system of fibers (Lindvall & Bjorklund, 1974, 1978).

Although these and numerous other small discoveries greatly complicate the picture, it remains true that the NA innervation of the forebrain derives largely from the locus coeruleus, via the dorsal bundle, whereas that of the hypothalamus arises mainly from more caudal cell groups, projecting through the central tegmental tract. In this discussion, the terms *dorsal bundle* and *ventral bundle* have been retained; they are used loosely to refer to the ascending projections of the locus coeruleus and of other brainstem NA-containing nuclei, respectively. Although this terminology is no longer appropriate to deal adequately with the anatomy of NA pathways, it does still provide a basis for discussing the behavioral literature, which for the most part has not yet caught up with the anatomical developments.

11.1. THE VENTRAL NA BUNDLE

Unlike the DA systems behavioral changes associated with the NA systems have been difficult to detect and even more difficult to characterize. It is convenient to deal first with the ventral bundle, because in comparison to the dorsal bundle, very little is known about its behavioral functions.

Nuclei A1 and A2, the two largest of the cells groups that contribute to the ventral bundle, are heavily interconnected. A2 is a part of the dorsal vagal complex, which contains the major sensory and motor nuclei of the autonomic nervous system. The major hypothalamic terminal areas of A1 and A2 are the paraventricular nucleus and the median eminence, which are the areas most intimately involved in the hypothalamic regulation of pituitary neuroendocrine function; these areas also send projections back to A1 and A2. These anatomical considerations strongly suggest a role for the ventral bundle in autonomic and neuroendocrine function (Sawchenko, 1982).

Noradrenaline systems are implicated in a variety of neuroendocrine effects (Ettigi & Brown, 1977; Risch et al., 1981d); the control of ACTH release is of particular interest, because a substantial proportion of depressed patients show evidence of hypothalamic–pituitary–adrenal (HPA) hyperactivity (see Section 3.3.2). Many studies have demonstrated that NA exerts a tonic inhibitory effect over the HPA axis (Ettigi & Brown, 1977; Risch et al., 1981d), and it seems likely that this influence is mediated by the ventral bundle. Cells containing corticotropin releasing factor (CRF), which stimulates pituitary ACTH secretion, are located in the parvovellular division of the paraventricular nucleus of the hypothalamus (PVN-PC) (Paull et al., 1982). The vast majority of NA cells, which project to the PVN-PC, are found in A1 and A2, and only 6% are in the locus coeruleus (Sawchenko, 1982). There is also an NA mechanism in the median eminence which inhibits the release of CRF from axon terminals (Ganong, 1977). This area of the hypothalamus receives an NA input from a number of brainstem NA cells groups, which exclude the locus coeruleus (Palkovits et al., 1980). These observations suggest that the noradrenergic inhibition of ACTH release is mediated by activity in the ventral bundle.

However, the functions of the ventral bundle are not exclusively neuroendocrine. 6-Hydroxydopamine lesions of the ventral bundle have been found to cause a modest increase in food intake and body weight (Ahlskog, 1974). The neuroanatomical specificity of these effects has been questioned (Lorden et al., 1976; Oltmans et al., 1977), but the results have recently been replicated, and pharmacological evidence suggests that the overeating does result from NA depletion (Hernandez & Hoebel, 1982). Investigations employing intrahypothalamic drug injection combined with small hypothalamic lesions have revealed that these effects are mediated by beta-receptors, and the crucial pathway is a projection from brainstem NA cell groups through the ventral bundle to the perifornical nucleus of the hypothalamus (Leibowitz, 1975; Leibowitz & Brown, 1980b; Leibowitz & Rossakis, 1978a). The ventral bundle therefore appears to mediate some aspect of satiety. Activation of the dorsal bundle, by contrast, stimulates feeding. This effect is mediated by alpha-receptors situated in the paraventricular hypothalamus and innervated from the locus coeruleus (Leibowitz, 1978, 1980; Leibowitz & Brown, 1980a).

Lesions of the ventral bundle have also been found to disinhibit responding for brain stimulation reward (Hoebel, 1979); this effect has also been observed following some pharmacological treatments that reduce NA function (Antelman & Caggiula, 1977; White et al., 1978) and following electrolytic lesions that probably damaged the ventral bundle (Corbett, 1980). Suppression of ICSS by ventral bundle activity might mean that the ventral bundle inhibits a "reward system" (see Section 7.2.6). A generalized effect of this kind is suggested by the observation that ventral bundle lesions also disinhibited sexual behavior (Hoebel, 1979). Alternatively, the inhibitory effect of the ventral bundle on ICSS might be related to its effect on feeding: it has been observed that ICSS is sometimes equivalent to a food reward, in the sense that ICSS rates at some electrodes are increased by food deprivation and decreased by prefeeding (Hoebel, 1976; Hoebel & Teitelbaum, 1962; Olds, 1958; Rolls, 1982; see also Section 7.2.6). Even so, the effect of ventral bundle lesions would still be of interest, since studies in people have shown that satiety decreases food intake by reducing the perceived pleasantness of food (Cabanac, 1971; Toates, 1981). On either interpretation, therefore, the ventral bundle may modulate some aspect of the pleasantness of rewards.

One potential locus for an inhibitory effect on reward mechanisms is the amygdala. This structure is a major terminal area of the ventral bundle, and it sends back reciprocal connections to A1 and A2 (Price & Amaral, 1981; Schwaber et al., 1982). The amygdala has long been assumed to be involved in the mediation of both positive and negative affective states, because in animals and also in people, damage to the amygdala results in placidity and a failure to respond to reward or punishment (Goddard, 1964; Narabashi, 1972), and stimulation can elicit a variety of positive and negative emotional states (Kaada, 1972; Mark & Ervin, 1970; Heath, 1964). In rats, single unit recording studies have found evidence of cells that responded primarily to visual stimuli associated with rewards such as food, whereas other cells were activated primarily by aversive stimuli (Rolls, 1982; Sanghera et al., 1979).

Electrical stimulation of the amygdala has been reported to disrupt the storage of memories about rewards and punishments (Kesner, 1981). The relevant neuropharmacological findings are that administration of beta-receptor blockers to the central nucleus of the amygdala disrupted the retention of aversive conditioning, in rabbits, whereas blockade of alpha receptors had the opposite effect (Gallagher et al., 1981). Two important questions relevant to the interpretation of these results have not yet been answered. They are whether positively motivated learning shows the opposite pharmacological specificity and whether the noradrenergic innervation of beta-receptors in central nucleus originates in the ventral bundle. However, it is tempting to speculate that the beta-receptor–mediated input, which amplifies aversive signals, arises from the ventral bundle, whereas the alpha-receptor–mediated input, which inhibits them, arises from the dorsal bundle; the central nucleus is known to receive inputs from both sources (Fallon et al., 1978). This situation would be parallel to that in the hypothalamus, where the beta-receptor–mediated input from the ventral bundle inhibits signals of food reward, whereas the alpha-receptor–mediated input from the dorsal bundle stimulates food intake. This line of argument suggests that in both of its major terminal regions (the hypothalamus and the amygdala) activation of the ventral bundle might amplify aversive events and reduce the impact of pleasant events—exactly the situation that obtains in depression (Chapter 4).

Like the ascending projections through the ventral bundle, descending NA pathways also modulate responses to aversive stimuli. Pain sensitivity is increased by alpha-adrenergic stimulation of the nucleus raphe magnus (Hammond et al., 1980a,b; see also Sections 15.2.2 and 18.1.1.1); the intrinsic NA innervation of this nucleus originates in nuclei A1, A5, A7, and A8 (Sagen & Proudfit, 1981). Again, the dorsal bundle appears to exert an opposite effect: electrical stimulation of the locus coeruleus reduces pain sensitivity (Sandberg & Segal, 1978).

The question of what stimuli activate the ventral bundle is difficult to answer, as the diffuse distribution of NA-containing cell bodies in nuclei other than the locus coeruleus makes electrophysiological recording almost impossible, and the extensive invasion of fibers originating in the locus coeruleus into the terminal areas of the ventral bundle makes it difficult to assess the effects of NA release from ventral bundle terminals specifically. However, there are a number of hypothalamic areas in which axons of locus coeruleus cells do not terminate, including the median eminence (Palkovits et al., 1980). It has recently been reported that exposure to stress (a loud noise) caused a rapid depletion of NA in the median eminence (Siegel et al., 1983).

A picture emerges of the ventral bundle as a system that is activated by stress and has the effect of increasing the relative prominence of aversive stimuli. Although these might be grounds for considering ventral bundle hyperactivity as a strong candidate to mediate the pathophysiology of depression, two important discrepancies must be noted. The first is that a high level of activity in the ventral bundle would not be compatible with the elevated serum cortisol levels seen in endogenous depression. And second, although severely depressed patients are hypersensitive to secondary aversive stimuli, they are relatively insensitive to physical pain (see Section 4.2.2). These considerations suggest that a hypothesis of ventral bundle hyperactivity might be tenable in the case of mild depressions, but to explain the pathophysiology of severe depressions we should probably look elsewhere.

11.2. THE DORSAL NA BUNDLE

The extraordinary anatomy of the dorsal NA bundle almost compels the conclusion that this system must fulfill a significant and essential role in brain function. However, the small number of cells involved and their very widespread terminal innervation severely constrain the specificity of the information that the pathway could transmit. Although there is evidence for some degree of localization within the locus coeruleus in relation to its anatomical projections (McNaughton & Mason, 1980), electrophysiological recording studies indicate that locus coeruleus cells tend to fire as a synchronous assembly (Aston-Jones & Bloom, 1981a,b). Hence whatever the functions of the dorsal bundle, they are likely to be of a general nature.

This is one of the few points on which there is a broad consensus of agreement. Indeed, the behavioral role of the dorsal bundle has been so elusive that some workers have suggested that its involvement in behavior might be incidental to some more basic task, such as the regulation of the brain's blood supply (Sharp & Schwartz, 1977; Harik et al., 1979). This particular hypothesis was based originally on the observation of NA terminals on cerebral blood vessels (Swanson et al., 1977). The NA projections to larger, superficial blood vessels arise outside the brain (Harper et al., 1972), but it does appear that the smaller intracortical vessels, including capillaries, are innervated from the locus coeruleus (Kasamatsu, 1983). Stimulation of the locus coeruleus has been variously reported to cause a reduction (Raichle et al., 1975), an increase (Kawamura et al., 1978), or no change (Delanqy et al., 1978) in cerebral blood flow, whereas lesions of the locus coeruleus have been reported to increase cerebral blood flow but to decrease responsiveness to changes in blood CO_2 content (Bates et al., 1977).

Clearly, the role of the dorsal bundle in cerebral blood flow is complex. Irrespective of the exact solution to this problem, if the exercise of a subtle control over blood supply were the only demonstrable function of the dorsal bundle, then a hypothesis that this pathway has important psychological functions would be difficult to maintain. However, the dorsal bundle does also have behaviorally relevant effects on neuronal activity in its terminal regions. Indeed, it has been suggested that dorsal bundle-related changes in cerebral blood flow may to some extent be secondary to changes in neuronal firing (Tsubokawa et al., 1980). This section will review briefly the ebb and flow of ideas about the behavioral functions of the dorsal bundle; more comprehensive reviews have recently been provided by McNaughton and Mason (1980), Mason (1981), and Gray (1982).

11.2.1. Learning and Memory

11.2.1.1. Reward

One of the earliest hypotheses of NA function equated NA release with a "reward" signal. Numerous studies have reported that performance for brain stimulation reward is depressed by alpha-adrenergic antagonists, or by clonidine, which at low doses selectively suppresses NA cell firing and NA release by stimulating NA autoreceptors (Starke et al., 1977). However, these drugs have sedative effects (see Section 13.3.2), and as with DA receptor blocking drugs, the problem arises of distinguishing an inhibition of reward mechanisms from nonspecific performance deficits. Some studies that have attempted to address this issue have concluded that clonidine does specifically inhibit brain stimulation reward (Hunt et al., 1978; Liebman et al., 1982b). However, other studies have reached the opposite conclusion (Sinden & Atrens, 1983). The effects of postsynaptic alpha-blockers are clearly nonspecific (Liebman et al., 1982b).

The NA hypothesis of reward was originally postulated by Stein (1968) on the basis of the observation that ICSS caused the release of NA. Initially, the hypothesis gained support from the finding that ICSS could be obtained from electrodes implanted anywhere along the course of the dorsal bundle, from the locus coeruleus to its terminal fields (Crow, 1972; Crow et al., 1972; German & Bowden, 1974; Phillips et al., 1977; Segal & Bloom, 1976a). However, it later became apparent that destruction of the dorsal bundle failed to reduce the rate of responding through those same electrodes (Clavier & Routtenberg, 1976; Clavier et al., 1976), and anatomical studies showed that the correspondence between self-stimulation sites and the trajectory of the dorsal bundle were not as close as had been previously assumed (Corbett & Wise, 1979). As a result of these observations, two influential reviews concluded that the dorsal bundle is not involved in mediating the rewarding effects of ICSS (Fibiger, 1979; Wise, 1978).

This issue, apparently closed, was reopened in a paper reporting that NA appeared to be a potent reinforcer of T-maze learning in rats, when injected into the perifornical region of the lateral hypothalamus (Cytawa et al., 1980). However, this effect, first observed by Olds as long ago as 1962, is probably an artifact resulting from changes in the disposition of calcium rather than the reflection of a physiological interaction with synaptic receptors (Bozarth, 1983).

There remains the possibility that dorsal bundle activation plays a role in mediating the effects of natural rewards, such as food and water. This was suggested by the observation of Anlezark and co-workers (1973) that electrolytic lesions of the locus coeruleus impaired running for a wet mash reward in an L-shaped alley; this finding has subsequently been confirmed (Koob et al., 1978b; Sessions et al., 1976). However, electrolytic lesions are nonspecific, and by their nature cannot be restricted to a single pathway. Studies using 6-OHDA to destroy NA neurons specifically are almost unanimous in finding no change in the performance of rewarded behavior, despite the fact that this procedure usually produces more severe depletions of forebrain NA than do electrolytic lesions. Gray (1982) reviewed 27 studies in which forebrain NA was depleted either by stereotactic injections of NA into the dorsal bundle or by neonatal 6-OHDA treatment. In 23 studies there was no effect on performance, and in two of the remaining four studies, performance actually improved. Given this evidence, the hypothesis of NA mediation of reward must be decisively rejected, attractive though it may have been.

11.2.1.2. Learning

Another early hypothesis of dorsal bundle function, closely related to the reward hypothesis but less obviously relevant to depression, postulated a role in learning. This hypothesis suggested that the dorsal bundle was responsible for "instructing" the cortex to make structural changes at active synapses in order to make a permanent record of the current pattern of activity (Crow & Arbuthnott, 1972; Kety, 1972). However, although some studies have found deficient runway learning after electrolytic lesions of the locus coeruleus, this is the exception rather than the rule; the same papers also reported normal acquisition of a wide variety of other learning tasks (Koob et al., 1978b; Sessions et al., 1976). Similarly, despite severe depletions of forebrain NA, by more than 95% in some cases, 6-OHDA lesions have not been found to impair learning in a large number of studies, using a diversity of learning tasks and motivational conditions (reviewed by Mason, 1981; Gray, 1982).

Despite this extensive literature, a role for NA in memory function has been postulated on other grounds. An apparent amnesia may be induced in experimental animals by a variety of treatments administered before or within a short time after training, and these include the NA synthesis inhibitor diethyldithiocarbamate (DDC) (Martinez et al., 1981). The relevance of this observation is questionable, however, because DDC-induced amnesia could be reversed by peripheral administration of NA or adrenaline (which do not cross the blood–brain barrier) (Meligeni et al., 1978; McGaugh et al., 1979). Moreover, other NA synthesis inhibitors, which may be more specific pharmacologically than DDC, did not produce amnesia (Haycock et al., 1977). Three potentially more revealing findings were that DDC-induced amnesia was reversed by intraventricular injections of NA (Stein et al., 1975a; Meligeni et al., 1978), that learning of a visual discrimination reversal task was improved by stimulation of the locus coeruleus (Segal and Edelson, 1978), and that a 6-OHDA–induced lesion of the dorsal bundle prevented the facilitatory effects of vasopressin on memory function (Kovacs et al., 1979). These results provide somewhat more direct support for a facilitatory role for NA in memory formation (though clearly not an essential role, given that learning proceeds normally in the absence of forebrain NA).

A fundamental problem in attempting to understand results of this kind is that they are almost invariably interpreted in terms of the "consolidation theory" of memory, which assumes that the physical changes underlying memory formation take time to "set," and during this vulnerable period, memory traces may be obliterated or strengthened by drugs or other treatments (McGaugh, 1966). However, there is now compelling evidence that this hypothesis is incorrect. Experimentally induced amnesias appear to be failures of memory retrieval rather than of memory storage, because a variety of "reminder" treatments can reinstate "forgotten" memories (Miller & Springer, 1973; Lewis, 1979). Whatever dorsal bundle activation is doing to memory, it is unlikely to facilitate "consolidation," because in the light of "reminder" and other similar experiments, there no longer remains any convincing reason to believe in the existence of such a process (see e.g., Misanin et al., 1968; Lewis, 1979).

There is strong empirical evidence that memory formation does involve a vulnerable period, but a better conceptualization may be at a psychological level: during this period, the recently acquired information is being processed to establish the cues necessary for its later retrieval (Lewis, 1979). The common feature of treatments that facilitate memory formation, or counteract experimentally induced amnesias, may be that they produce moderate increases in arousal (Gold & Sternberg, 1978; Martinez et al., 1981) and perhaps increase the efficiency of the information processing necessary for memory retrieval. This interpretation of the facilitatory effect of NA is consistent with other analyses of dorsal bundle function discussed below.

11.2.1.3. Synaptic Plasticity

Notwithstanding the inadequacies of memory consolidation theory and the apparently minimal involvement of NA in learning, there is evidence for an involvement of the dorsal bundle in plasticity at the synaptic level. This evidence derives primarily from studies of the responsiveness of cells in the visual cortex of kittens, by Kasamatsu, Pettigrew, and colleagues. In the normal animal, a high proportion of cells in the visual cortex may be driven through either eye, but following a period of monocular visual deprivation, the deprived eye loses this ability. In an elegant series of experiments, it was demonstrated that this functional reorganization was blocked by intracortical application of 6-OHDA and could be restored by NA infusions; the effects were confined to the area of cortex adjacent to the site of drug application and were apparently mediated by beta-receptors (Kasamatsu, 1983). 6-Hydroxydopamine has been found to reduce the plasticity of another property of visual cortical cells—their directional selectivity (Daw et al., 1981). Similarly, destruction of the dorsal bundle prevented the long-lasting potentiation of postsynaptic potentials, that follows electrical stimulation of the hippocampus (Goddard et al., 1980) and the recovery of normal behavioral function in infant rats subjected to frontal lobe lesions (Sutherland et al., 1981). The problem here is that plasticity in the kitten visual system disappears at 12–13 weeks of age [though plasticity could be restored in adult cats by infusion of very high doses of NA (Kasamatsu, 1983)]. Similarly, completed recovery of function after neocortical damage usually is seen only in juvenile animals. The relevance of these observations to adult animals is therefore unclear (and their relevance to depression even more so).

11.2.2. Attention and Arousal

11.2.2.1. The Dorsal Bundle Extinction Effect

In contrast to the minimal effects of dorsal bundle lesions on the acquisition of new behaviors, many studies have reported that "extinction" is impaired in dorsal bundle lesioned animals, that is, they continue to perform behaviors when a previously available reward has been withdrawn (reviewed by Mason, 1981; Mason & Iversen, 1979; Gray, 1982). The dorsal bundle extinction effect (DBEE) is not seen under all circumstances; in particular, it is absent from partial reinforcement paradigms, in which rewards are only available for some responses (Gray, 1982; Mason, 1981). The DBEE has proved rather resistant to behavioral analysis, though several of the hypotheses advanced to explain the effect have potential relevance for theories of depression.

One obvious hypothesis is that dorsal bundle lesioned animals are inflexible and are unable to change their habits. This hypothesis is clearly wrong, since a number of studies have found that lesioned animals are quite capable of changing their behavior when an alternative rewarded response is made available, as in reversal learning (Mason & Iversen, 1977a; Roberts et al., 1976). A second unsuccessful hypothesis is that dorsal bundle lesioned animals are unable to withhold a response. This hypothesis falls because there are a number of behavioral paradigms in which dorsal bundle lesioned animals do successfully withhold responses. Two examples are *differential reinforcement of low rate*, in which rewards are contingent on waiting for a predetermined period before making another response (Mason & Iversen, 1977b), and *passive avoidance behavior*, in which the animal avoids electric shock by not moving [no effect of the lesion in 7/10 studies reviewed by Gray (1982)].

A third possible explanation of the DBEE is that the dorsal bundle may inform other areas of the brain of the occurrence of nonreward, so that a lesioned animal would be less aware that it was no longer being rewarded. Since animals find nonreward ("frustration") aversive (Adelman & Maatsch, 1952; Gray, 1967), this effect could be quite relevant to depression. The hypothesis was advanced on the rather indirect evidence that dorsal bundle lesions raised the threshold at which electrical stimulation of the septal area evoked the "theta" rhythm in the hippocampal EEG; this change was restricted to frequencies of theta (around 7.7 Hz) which were known to be associated with nonreward (Gray et al., 1975). However, the same frequencies of theta also occur in relation to sniffing and exploratory activity in the absence of nonreward (Morris & Black, 1978). It has also been reported that dorsal bundle lesions failed to abolish the invigorating effect of frustration (Mason & Iversen, 1978).

A fourth hypothesis is that the dorsal bundle plays a central role in fear and anxiety. As there are very close similarities—behavioral, pharmacological, anatomical, and neurophysiological—between fear and frustration, this formulation is very close to the frustration hypothesis. The hypothesis is based on the observation that in monkeys, electrical stimulation of the locus coeruleus elicited behaviors characteristic of fear, whereas lesions induced placidity and a failure to respond to threatening stimuli, such as a rubber snake (Redmond et al., 1976). In rats, however, dorsal bundle lesions do not usually impair the performance of fear-motivated behaviors. As noted above, lesioned animals usually show normal passive avoidance performance (Gray, 1982). Similarly, active avoidance performance is either unaffected by dorsal bundle lesions (Mason & Fibiger, 1979a) or is actually improved (Mason & Fibiger, 1979b; Ogren & Fuxe, 1977), though this evidence is less telling, as antianxiety drugs may also improve active avoidance performance (Gray, 1982). The antianxiety effect in people of the beta-blocker propranolol (Tyrer & Lader, 1974) would be consistent with an involvement of the dorsal bundle in anxiety. However, this action of propranolol is probably mediated peripherally, because practotol, a beta-blocker which does not cross the blood–brain barrier, is also an effective antianxiety agent (Bonn et al., 1972).

11.2.2.2. Attention

Two recent hypotheses of dorsal bundle function and the DBEE, proposed by Mason (1981; Mason & Iversen, 1979) and Gray (1982), lead the field at present (which is hardly surprising, given that they were constructed in order to overcome the deficiencies of earlier efforts). Although hotly debated (see Gray, 1982), the two positions both ascribe attentional functions to the dorsal bundle and are to some extent convergent.

Mason hypothesizes that the primary function of the dorsal bundle is to suppress attention to irrelevant stimuli. As a consequence, lesioned animals are overattentive. In a learning task, they associate the reward with a wider range of environmental stimuli than do normal animals, and as a result they have more connections to "unlearn" when it comes to extinction, which gives rise to the DBEE (Mason & Iversen, 1979; Mason, 1981). This is a potentially powerful hypothesis, because it can explain a number of other behavioral changes, which may follow dorsal bundle lesions; two examples will be given. *Latent inhibition* occurs when a stimulus is presented repeatedly in the absence of reward; the animal learns to ignore it, and when it is subsequently associated with reward, the animal is slow to connect (Mellgren & Ost, 1971). *Blocking* occurs when a second, redundant stimulus is added to a stimulus that already reliably predicts reward; the animal fails to learn the association between the new stimulus and reward (Kamin, 1969). Dorsal bundle lesions have been reported to attenuate both of these effects (Mason & Fibiger, 1979c; Lorden et al., 1980), as predicted by Mason.

A problem in assessing Mason's hypothesis is that Fibiger, who was involved in its formulation, has reported an inability to replicate many of the detailed findings on which it was originally based (Pisa & Fibiger, 1980; Pisa et al., 1981). Indeed, the DBEE itself is a far from robust phenomenon; its demonstration often depends on choosing (arbitrarily) the right extinction criterion (Pisa et al., 1981; McCormick & Thompson, 1982; Tombaugh et al., 1982b), and even then it does not always appear (Tombaugh et al., 1982b). A hypothesis at this level of complexity does not, therefore, seem to be warranted by the evidence currently available.

Gray explains the DBEE by hypothesizing that the dorsal bundle transmits information relating to nonreward; the hypothesis is embedded in a far more wide-reaching theory of the neuropsychological basis of anxiety (Gray, 1982; Gray et al., 1982), which will not be discussed in detail. This hypothesis of dorsal bundle function closely resembles the frustration and anxiety hypotheses discussed earlier but differs in two important respects. First, anxiety is held to be a function not of the dorsal bundle but of the septohippocampal system; the involvement of the dorsal bundle in anxiety is limited by the fact that it is only one of several inputs. Second, it is assumed that the dorsal bundle transmits information about conditioned stimuli associated with unpleasant events (warning signals), rather than about the unpleasant events themselves (Gray, 1982).

At first sight, it may not be apparent why this is designated an "attentional" hypothesis; the reason lies in Gray's wider theory of anxiety. In the theory, the function of the septohippocampal system is to process information about the occurrence of conditioned stimuli and novel stimuli. The dorsal bundle serves to amplify signals in hippocampal circuits, the cognitive correlate of which is an enhancement of attention to those stimuli. In addition to stimuli warning of the imminence of an aversive event, the dorsal bundle also carries information predicting the occurrence of rewards. The processing of these signals by the hippocampus is also enhanced. However, dorsal bundle lesions do not disrupt rewarded behavior because although the hippocampus needs to know of the occurrence of these events, they have no control over hippocampal output (Gray, 1982).

It will be clear that unlike the earlier hypotheses of dorsal bundle function, which can be evaluated on their merits, Gray's hypothesis cannot easily be divorced from the larger theory of which it is a part. Space precludes an adequate discussion of the larger theory (see Gray et al., 1982), which would, in any case, involve too great a digression. Instead, it will be more appropriate to consider in its own right the electrophysiological evidence on which Gray's view of dorsal bundle function is based.

11.2.2.3. Arousal

In refreshing contrast to the controversial behavioral data, a much clearer portrait of dorsal bundle function can be drawn from electrophysiological studies. The two important questions are: Under what circumstances is the pathway activated? What are the consequences for information processing in its target areas? Both questions may be answered.

Early studies in anesthetized animals found that locus coeruleus cells fired in a slow tonic manner, and they responded reliably only to painful stimuli or to electrical stimulation of peripheral nerves (Bird & Kuhar, 1977; Cedarbaum and Aghajanian, 1976). Linked with the observation that tonic firing rate varied with the sleep–wake cycle, being highest in waking and lowest in paradoxical sleep (Hobson et al., 1975; Steriade & Hobson, 1976), these findings supported a role in the maintenance of wakefulness, which had earlier been suggested on pharmacological

grounds (Jouvet, 1972; Amaral & Sinnamon, 1977). However, it is clear
from more recent studies that this picture is inadequate. In unanesthetized rats and monkeys, locus coeruleus cells have been found to respond
to a variety of nonnoxious stimuli, including tone pips, light flashes, and
mild skin taps (Aston-Jones & Bloom, 1981a,b; Foote et al., 1980; Segal
& Bloom, 1976b); the most vigorous firing was seen in response to the
sight of a preferred food (Foote et al., 1980). Increases in locus coeruleus
firing were correlated with EEG arousal and behavioral orientation to
the source of stimulation and were also associated with episodes of spontaneous (nonevoked) EEG arousal. Repeated presentation of a stimulus
resulted in habituation of locus coeruleus responses and of behavioral
orienting responses (Foote et al., 1980). The response of locus coeruleus
cells to sensory stimulation was reduced not only during sleep but also
during grooming and consummatory activity (drinking). However, if a
stimulus succeeded in interrupting any of these activities, it also activated locus coeruleus cells (Aston-Jones & Bloom, 1981a,b).

It is clear from these studies that locus coeruleus neurons are activated
by stimuli that command attention. Two further pieces of evidence suggest a causal role for the dorsal bundle in arousal by a significant stimulus. First, it has been reported that the phasic arousal response to electrical stimulation of the medial reticular formation in cats was
substantially decreased by the monoamine-depleting drug reserpine. The
response was restored by DOPA, but manipulation of 5-HT had no effect,
implicating NA (or possibly DA) in phasic arousal (Friedman & Horvath,
1980). Second, infusions of NA into the hippocampus of rats increased
"diversive exploration" of a novel environment. Compared to normal animals, infused animals inspected (i.e., attended to) a larger number and
range of stimuli (Flicker & Geyer, 1982).

Studies of cells postsynaptic to dorsal bundle terminals have clarified
the physiological mechanism of NA-mediated phasic arousal responses.
In general, the effect of NA in a variety of terminal sites is to increase
signal-to-noise ratio; NA usually has inhibitory effects, but background
firing rate is suppressed far more than responses to other inputs. Iontophoretic application of NA has been found to enhance the responses of
cerebellar Purkinje cells to electrical stimulation of climbing fibers
(Freedman et al., 1977), of auditory cortex cells to sounds (Foote et al.,
1975), and of cells in somatosensory cortex to mechanical stimulation of
the skin (Waterhouse & Woodward, 1980; Waterhouse et al., 1981). Similarly, electrical stimulation of the locus coeruleus enhanced the response
of hippocampal cells to a tone stimulus associated with food reward; pharmacological studies confirmed that this effect was mediated by NA release
in the hippocampus (Segal & Bloom, 1976a,b).

From these studies it is apparent that the dorsal bundle carries a message to the forebrain, which says, in effect: "Something interesting has
just happened; pay attention!" The behavioral consequences depend on

the outcome of the subsequent information processing. More generally, "NA neurons increase the signal-to-noise ratio of the cells on which they impinge. . . . Their behavioral function then depends on the characteristics of the target organs which they innervate" (Gray, 1982, pp. 358–359).

11.2.2.4. Implications

Although it is very pleasing in scientific terms to have a clear answer to what has been an extremely perplexing problem, the potential relevance of this "alarm bell" hypothesis of dorsal bundle function to depression is not immediately apparent. However, if the the dorsal bundle mediates attention to a significant stimulus, a decreased level of dorsal bundle function should be reflected in a reduced ability to sustain attention, which should in turn be manifest as a difficult in maintaining ongoing behavior. As described in Chapter 4 (Section 4.1.2), difficulties in sustaining concentration and effort are characteristic of endogenously depressed patients. Vigilance experiments, although technically possible, are difficult to perform in animals, and the effects of manipulations of the dorsal bundle have not yet been tested. However, two other lines of evidence support this approach.

First, it has been observed that in a group of depressed patients, the retrieval of poorly processed material from memory was enhanced by amphetamine; this effect was probably mediated by effects at NA synapses, as there was a significant inverse relationship between memory enhancement and basal NA activity, as measured by CSF concentrations of the NA metabolite MHPG (Reus et al., 1979a). The amphetamine-induced memory enhancement probably reflects an arousal effect rather than a specific effect on memory, because in another study, memory impairments in depressed patients were almost perfectly correlated with their inability to sustain motor effort. Significantly, both of these quantities were also highly correlated with severity of depressed mood (Cohen et al., 1982c). Similar observations have been made in amnesic patients suffering from Korsakoff's disease. The severity of their amnesia was inversely related to central NA turnover (as estimated from CSF levels of NA metabolites), and NA receptor stimulation improved their memory performance (McEntee & Mair, 1978, 1980). Difficulties of concentration are apparent in Korsakoff's syndrome, and they may be etiologically related to the memory disorder (McEntee & Mair, 1980); current theories of amnesia emphasize that the problem arises from a failure to process information adequately (Stern, 1981).

The second line of evidence relating a decrease in NA function to an inability to sustain behavior comes from animal studies; feeding behavior is one clear example. An alpha-adrenergic system in the hypothalamus has long been known to stimulate feeding (Grossman, 1962). More recently, this system has been localized to the paraventricular nucleus (PVN) and was shown to originate in the locus coeruleus (Leibowitz, 1978, 1980; Leibowitz & Brown, 1980a) (as distinct from the ventral bundle "satiety system" described earlier). Studies in which the hypothalamic feeding system have been manipulated pharmacologically have demonstrated that increasing or decreasing dorsal bundle NA function has no effect on the initiation of eating or on the rate of food intake. The effect is rather on the length of meals, which is decreased by reducing NA function (Rossi et al., 1982) and is increased by NA infusions (Grinker et al., 1982; Ritter & Epstein, 1975). These results demonstrate that, in relation to feeding, dorsal bundle activity functions primarily to maintain the behavior.

11.3. NA AND STRESS

The experiments reviewed in the previous section suggest that the attentional functions of the dorsal bundle underlie the ability to maintain concentration and effort. The significance of this conclusion lies in the fact that NA function is disrupted by stress. Consequently, changes in NA function serve as a mechanism which mediates the debilitating effects of stress on performance.

11.3.1. Data

The learned helplessness model of depression, described in Chapters 4 and 7, provides the most direct link between NA function and depression, though as noted in earlier discussions, the paradigm is far from being the perfect model. NA neurons are activated by stress. However, uncontrollable electric shocks activate NA neurons substantially more than controllable shocks, as indicated by a greater release of NA (Weiss et al., 1976). As a result, uncontrollable, but not controllable, shocks cause a decrease in brain NA levels, as demand exceeds supply (Anisman et al., 1980a; Schutz et al., 1979; Swensson & Vogel, 1983; Weiss et al., 1970, 1976). The most dramatic effects of stress are usually seen in the hypothalamus (Siegel et al., 1983; Swensson & Vogel, 1983; J. Weiss et al., 1981, 1982). The depletions of hypothalamic NA seen after uncontrollable stress are modest, reaching a maximum of 35% (Schutz et al., 1979) but usually much smaller. However, even small depletions could severely compromise the functional capacity of NA terminals, because as much as 70–80% of synaptic NA may not be readily available for release (Glowinski, 1973).

   Although it makes good functional sense that in conditions of menace and impotence "alarm bells" should ring more intensely and/or more continuously, the manner in which the brain processes information about controllability and predictability has not yet been established, and the anatomical route by which this information impinges on NA systems is unknown. However, the consequences of stress-induced NA depletion are reasonably well understood.

As discussed in Chapter 7 (Section 7.2.1), uncontrollable shock produces a variety of behavioral deficits in experimental animals, the most intensively studied of which is the learning difficulty which Seligman and colleagues call *learned helplessness*. Before addressing the question of whether the effects of uncontrollable shock on NA transmission are responsible for the associated behavioral deficits, a brief digression is necessary, as some evidence indicates that uncontrollable shock may produce two distinct behavioral syndromes, depending on the intensity of the shock.

This possibility was first raised by Glazer and Weiss (1976a,b), who observed that prolonged exposure to moderate-intensity electric shocks (1 mA) produced long-lasting learning deficits, which could be observed as much as a week later, whereas brief exposure to severely painful shocks (4 mA) produced a transient deficit lasting less than an hour in these experiments, though in later studies using a more sensitive behavioral assay, effects were seen for up to two days (J. Weiss et al., 1981, 1982). The authors laid the groundwork for a great deal of spurious debate by proposing that the short-term deficit was mediated by NA depletion, which was observed 30 minutes after shock termination in the hypothalamus, brain-stem, and forebrain (Weiss et al., 1975, 1976), but the long-term deficit was mediated by learning rather than by neurochemical changes. This distinction has been likened to discussing whether "the stuff that comes out of the tap is water or H_2O" (Gray, 1982, p. 379). Arguments at this level are necessarily futile and almost certainly misleading (see Chapter 2). However, the question of whether uncontrollable shock has two distinct sets of physiological consequences is a real one.

Most of the evidence casts doubt on the need for a distinction between short- and long-term helplessness effects, because their similarities outweigh their differences. In the first place, both effects are seen only when shock is uncontrollable (Glazer & Weiss, 1976a,b). Second, as discussed below, the two effects respond similarly to pharmacological manipulations. Third, NA depletion has been observed not only after severe (4 mA) shocks (J. Weiss et al., 1976, 1981, 1982), but also after moderate (1.5 mA) and very mild (0.15 mA) shocks (Anisman & Sklar, 1979; Anisman et al., 1979a, 1980a; Schutz et al., 1979; Swensson & Vogel, 1983).

One of these studies provides a potential explanation of the time course of the long-term helplessness effect. Anisman and Sklar (1979) observed depletion of NA in the hypothalamus of mice following 60 mild but unavoidable shocks. Twenty-four hours later, no differences in NA level or in rate of synthesis were detectable. However, 10 shocks, which were without effect in control animals, produced significant depletion of NA in previously shocked animals. It therefore appears that the prolonged effect of moderate uncontrollable shock arises not because the stress produces prolonged changes in NA function but because those changes are rapidly reinstated on subsequent exposure to stress.

The reason that this effect is not seen in severely stressed animals is that the mechanism of recovery is different. Although exposure to very mild uncontrollable shocks reduced NA level in the hypothalamus, no change was seen in the hindbrain, where the NA cell bodies are situated (Anisman & Sklar, 1979). However, severe stress also depleted NA from the locus coeruleus (J. Weiss et al., 1982), and this different may be important. Extensive pharmacological depletion of NA causes a compensatory increase in NA synthesis by induction of the synthetic enzymes tyrosine hydroxylase and DBH. However, it seems likely that depletion of cell body NA may be essential to trigger this effect, because the increase in enzyme activity was observed first in the cell body, and it did not appear in terminal regions until two to three days later (Reis et al., 1974; Zigmond, 1979).

It is usually assumed that NA depletion in response to stress occurs because the rate of utilization of transmitter outstrips its rate of synthesis (see, e.g., Weiss et al., 1970, 1976). Preexposure to chronic stress protects an animal against stress-induced NA depletion and also protects it against the learned helplessness performance deficits (Platt & Stone, 1982; Weiss et al., 1975). The mechanism of these effects is the same as in the case of pharmacologically induced NA depletion: induction of tyrosine hydroxylase increases the synthesis of NA, which ensures an adequate supply of transmitter (Musacchio et al., 1969; Thoenen, 1970; Weiss et al., 1975). Consequently, chronic subjection to an intense stressor not only protects against a reduction in NA level but also causes an increase in NA turnover in response to an acute stress (Ritter & Ritter, 1977; Stone, 1975; Stone & McCarty, 1983; Thoenen, 1970; Weiss et al., 1975; Zigmond & Harvey, 1970). In other words, the reason that the sensitization to shock observed after mild stress (Anisman & Sklar, 1979) is not seen following severe stress is that if NA depletion is sufficiently extensive, there is a compensatory increase in NA synthesis.

It is not clear from the data described so far which NA system is involved in the performance deficits that follow from uncontrollable stress. However, a recent study of regional changes in NA following uncontrollable shock found a high correlation between motor activity in the subsequent helplessness test and NA levels in the hypothalamus and brain stem (Weiss et al., 1982). As in another experiment shock-induced changes in brainstem NA were confined to the locus coeruleus and were not seen in the A1 and A2 regions (J. Weiss et al., 1981, 1982), these findings implicate the projection from the locus coeruleus to the hypothalamus in the uncontrollable-shock-induced motor deficits. This conclusion is supported by the observation that exposure to cold or to severe electric shocks caused a depletion of NA in the hypothalamus, and, concommitantly, there was a decrease in the stimulation of feeding caused by a sudden drop in blood glucose (Ritter et al., 1978). The significance of this finding is that "glucoprivic feeding" is mediated by the PVN alpha-adrenergic feeding system (Leibowitz, 1980), which, as noted in Section 11.2.2.4, is innervated from the locus coeruleus.

It has been implicitly assumed in the foregoing discussion that NA depletion is causally related to the learned helplessness performance deficits rather than simply correlated to them, and the observation that chronic stress protects against both provides some support for this view. Direct support comes from pharmacological studies. Learned helplessness effects could be mimicked by the catecholamine depleting drugs tetrabenazine and reserpine or by the NA synthesis inhibitor FLA-63 (Anisman et al., 1979a,b; Weiss et al., 1975). As with the effects of uncontrollable shock, these pharmacological effects were ameliorated by prior experience with escapable shock (Anisman et al., 1979b). In a complementary fashion, the effects of inescapable shock could be ameliorated either by prior shock treatment (see above) or by daily administration of tetrabenazine (Glazer et al., 1975).

Conversely, administration of the alpha-receptor agonist clonidine prevented or reversed helplessness effects (Anisman et al., 1979a,b, 1980b). It is not immediately obvious that clonidine would increase the stimulation of postsynaptic receptors, because at low doses, clonidine preferentially stimulates presynaptic $alpha_2$-receptors, causing a reduction of endogenous NA release (Starke et al., 1975, 1977). However, the preference of clonidine for pre- over postsynaptic receptors is small (Starke et al., 1975), and at the doses used by Anisman and co-workers a substantial postsynaptic effect would be expected. Moreover, if, as hypothesized, NA release is low in the helpless animal owing to depletion of supplies of NA, then the presynaptic effects of clonidine would have minimal consequences. In a related procedure, moderate doses of clonidine have been shown to increase the frequency of jumping in response to intense foot shock, and it was demonstrated that this effect was blocked by the postsynaptic alpha-receptor antagonist phentolamine (Nishikawa et al., 1983).

The results of pharmacological studies in the "behavioral despair" model (Section 7.2.2) are similar to those described for learned helplessness. Although NA depletions have not been reported, forced swimming has been found to increase NA turnover (Miyauchi et al., 1981). Agonists and antagonists at beta-receptors were without effect in this test (Porsolt et al., 1979), but immobility was reduced by a variety of agents that enhance alpha-receptor activation, including high doses of clonidine, phenylephrine [an alpha-receptor agonist, which unlike clonidine is highly specific for postsynaptic receptors (Starke et al., 1975)], the catecholamine precursor tyrosine, and blockers of NA uptake (Gibson et al.,

1982; Porsolt, 1981). Yohimbine, which increase NA activity by a selective antagonism of presynaptic alpha$_2$-receptors, also antagonized immobility (Porsolt et al., 1979; Zebrowska-Lupina, 1980). Conversely, immobility was increased by the catecholamine synthesis inhibitor AMPT (Porsolt et al., 1979). The alpha-receptor antagonist phenoxybenzamine did not increase immobility (Porsolt et al., 1979) but did prevent the attenuation of immobility by antidepressants (Borsini et al., 1981; Miyauchi et al., 1981). Immobility was increased substantially in animals with 6-OHDA-induced depletion of forebrain NA (Willner & Thompson, unpublished observations).

These studies demonstrate that the debilitating effects of aversive events on later performance may be reversed by alpha-receptor agonists or mimicked by treatments that reduce adrenergic function. The most obvious conclusion is that the performance deficits are mediated by a decrease in the functional activity of locus coeruleus NA cells. However, this conclusion has recently been challenged. Weiss and co-workers (1982, 1984) found that immobility in the "behavioural despair" test was reversed by infusions of clonidine or NA directly over the locus coeruleus and was enhanced by similar infusions of alpha-receptor antagonists. Similarly, the immobility caused by uncontrollable electric shock could be prevented by infusion of an MAOI into the locus coeruleus (Weiss et al., 1984) or reversed by clonidine infusions (J. Weiss et al., 1982).

These effects of clonidine are similar to those seen on systemic administration, but may be subject to a very different interpretation. Because the effects were restricted to the region of the locus coeruleus and because clonidine suppresses the firing of NA cells, it was suggested that immobility results from an increase in forebrain NA release, rather than a decrease. This conclusion was supported by the observation that immobility was increased by infusions of the alpha-receptor agonist phenylephrine into the lateral ventricle (Weiss et al., 1984).

At first sight, the conclusion that clonidine reverses immobility by suppressing the release of NA in the forebrain appears compelling. However, this conclusion is not consistent with earlier results showing that the effects of uncontrollable shock could be mimicked by pharmacological treatments such as tetrabenazine or FLA-63, which produce a global decrease in NA function (Anisman et al., 1979a,b; Glazer et al., 1975; Weiss et al., 1975). There is an alternative explanation for Weiss's results. The locus coeruleus sends an inhibitory alpha-adrenergic input to a group of cholinergic cells in its immediate vicinity (Hobson et al., 1974a,b; Steriade & Hobson, 1976). In addition to inhibiting NA cell firing, these cholinergic cells would also be inhibited by clonidine infusions over the locus coeruleus and would be activated by alpha-adrenergic antagonists.

It is perfectly plausible that the effects of alpha-adrenergic agents on learned helplessness could be mediated by an interaction with this cholinergic system, as the learned helplessness performance deficits may be mimicked by cholinomimetic drugs and reversed by anticholinergics (see Section 14.1.1). In fact, this interaction may be of profound functional significance, and it will be discussed more fully in Part 4 (Sections 19.2.2, 19.3, 20.1).

11.3.2. Theory

It is worth reiterating and amplifying the main points of the foregoing discussion, as it provides a plausible basis for understanding the involvement of NA in depression. The first point is that stress activates the dorsal bundle and increases NA release. Prolonged activation leads to a depletion of NA in terminal regions, as the utilization of transmitter exceeds supply, leading to a "functional lesion," the consequences of which depend upon the particular terminal areas which suffer this fate. The inability to sustain responding that is shown by "helpless" animals in response to prolonged, if mild, electric shocks (Anisman & Sklar, 1979; Glazer, & Weiss, 1976a,b) or to water immersion (Porsolt et al., 1977a,b; J. Weiss et al., 1981, 1982) may be mediated at the hypothalamic level, because good correlations between biochemical and behavioral changes were observed in this area (Weiss et al., 1982). A similar effect at the level of the hippocampus and cortex would result in an inability to sustain attention, as discussed earlier. The difficulty which depressed patients have in sustaining attention and effort has been described in Section 4.1, and there is some evidence that this difficulty is correlated with the severity of depressed mood (Cohen et al., 1982c).

Second, stress sensitizes NA cells to respond more vigorously to a subsequent stress, leading to a more rapid "functional lesion" (Anisman & Sklar, 1979). A possible mechanism is provided by the discovery of cells in the midbrain which fire in response to a stimulus that has been paired with shock (Vertes & Miller, 1976). These cells were situated in the nucleus reticularis pontis caudalis, and they appear to be identical to the cholinergic cell group described above. This group of cells is reciprocally interconnected with the locus coeruleus; in addition to receiving an inhibitory input from the locus coeruleus (see above), they also send an excitatory projection back (Engberg & Svensson, 1980; Olpe et al., 1983; Steriade & Hobson, 1976). It therefore seems likely that the sensitization to shock observed in the NA system is mediated by an increase in cholinergic activity. The best-known characteristic of this cholinergic cell group is that the cells increase their activity at the onset of REM sleep (Hobson et al., 1974a,b; Steriade & Hobson, 1976). Consequently, in addition to mediating sensitization to the NA-depleting effect of stress, this same mechanism could account for the decreased latency to enter REM sleep shown by many depressed patients (see Section 3.3.2, and also Chapters 14, 19, 20).

Third, if stress is severe enough to deplete NA within the locus coeruleus, a recovery process is set into action. Production of the enzymes that synthesize NA is increased, and this results, after a delay of several days, in an increase in the synthetic capacity of NA terminals, which averts the threat of a "functional lesion" on reexposure to stress. Consequently, there is a paradoxical adaptation on repeated exposure to severe stressors, which is not seen with milder or controllable stress (Anisman & Sklar, 1979; Glazer & Weiss, 1976b).

In offering their experimental paradigm—the short-lived behavioral sequelae of intense electric shock—as an animal model of depression, Weiss and co-workers (1982, 1984) observe a number of similarities between helpless animals and the DSM-III criteria for a major depressive disorder (see Section 7.2.1). However, the effects of intense electric shock dissipate within at most three days (J. Weiss et al., 1981, 1982). In order to make a DSM-III diagnosis of major depressive disorder (Section 3.1.2), there is only one essential and nonnegotiable requirement: the disorder must have been present for a minimum of two weeks. The more persistent effects of mild shock may therefore provide a better model for major depressions. There is a potentially significant parallel in the clinical literature. The evidence for a relationship between major life stresses and depression is not very compelling (see Section 20.1), but some studies suggest that depression may be closely associated with a high level of chronic mild stress (Billings et al., 1983; Kanner et al., 1981). One implication is that the animal model developed recently by Katz and colleagues, which employs chronic unpredictable low-grade stressors (Section 7.2.3), may prove a valuable research tool.

Before concluding this discussion and moving on to the clinical literature, one further set of observations is worth noting. It has been pointed out that in people, the characteristics of depression and mania also serve as descriptions of individuals occupying high (alpha) and low (omega) status roles (Gardner, 1982). A theoretical approach based on these similarities conceptualizes mania and depression as responses to triumph and defeat; that is, as vestigial attributes of dominance hierarchies handed down from evolutionary history, which were appropriate to simple social groupings but are maladaptive in the modern world (Price, 1967). The analogy between affective disorders and social status roles is supported by the finding of Henry and co-workers that within a colony of mice, position in the dominance hierarchy determined the nature of the response to stress. Dominant mice responded to repeated immobilization by increases in blood pressure and adrenaline secretion, but subordinate mice responded with an increase in the secretion of corticosteroids (Henry et al., 1976; Henry & Stevens, 1977). As noted earlier (Sections 3.3.2), high corticosteroid secretion is a characteristic of many depressed people.

More recently it has been reported that in rat colonies, the position of an animal in the dominance hierarchy was highly correlated with tyrosine hydroxylase activity in the locus coeruleus, which strongly suggests a relationship between NA activity and social dominance (J. Weiss et al., 1982). It is uncertain which set of dorsal bundle terminals mediate this effect; modest correlations were also observed in the hypothalamus and olfactory tubercle (the presence of a higher correlation with cell body tyrosine hydroxylase activity than with terminal regions presumably reflects the presence in the latter of an additional, and heavy, innervation from the ventral bundle).

The implied link between NA activity, aggressive behavior, and affective disorders allows a further specification of the hypothesis developed in this section. A low level of NA synthesis in the locus coeruleus results in submissive behavior, which in turn is associated with high levels of corticosteroid secretion. These are both symptoms of endogenomorphic depression; in reactive depressions, however, an increase in aggression is equally likely and corticosteroid levels are normal. The implication is that a low level of NA function may be associated with endogenomorphic, rather than reactive, depressions. As discussed more fully in Part 4, the possibility that endogenous depressions might be associated with mild stress and low NA function, and that an increase in stress level could trigger neurochemical recovery, provides a basis for understanding both spontaneous recovery from endogenous depression and also the switch from depression to mania (see Section 20.3).

twelve

NORADRENALINE AND DEPRESSION: CLINICAL STUDIES

Chapter 11 described two mechanisms by which changes in NA systems might contribute to the pathophysiology of depression. Hyperactivity in the ventral bundle system (Section 11.1) has a number of interesting features but may be inconsistent with some of the clinical evidence. The more promising approach (Section 11.3) arises from the learned helplessness literature. Uncontrollable stress causes a "functional lesion" in the dorsal bundle system, resulting in an inability to sustain effort; an additional feature is that under the appropriate conditions the system would switch from underactivity to overactivity. This model may be seen as a theoretical basis for the original version of the catecholamine hypothesis of depression, which postulated a reduction of NA transmission in depression and an increase in mania (Schildkraut, 1965; see Section 1.1.1). In the present chapter, the catecholamine hypothesis of depression is tested against the clinical evidence.

12.1. NA FUNCTION IN DEPRESSION

The numerous studies of NA function in depression may be divided into two broad groups: those that deal with topics on which there is some measure of consensus and those that do not. Regrettably, most of the material to be covered in the next three sections falls into the latter category.

12.1.1. Peripheral NA Function

Peripheral NA function is of interest for two reasons: some peripheral processes may serve as useful models of central processes, and peripheral NA function may reflect central NA function through NA control of the autonomic nervous system. Studies of peripheral NA function in depression are utterly confusing on both counts. The situation is not improved by the fact that there are numerous indices of peripheral NA function, and the relationship between them is not at all clear.

Tyramine displaces NA from storage vesicles, resulting in the release of NA and an alpha-receptor–mediated increase in blood pressure. These are largely peripheral effects, as tyramine penetrates the CNS poorly (Ghose et al., 1975; Pickar et al., 1979). Some studies have reported an increase in sensitivity to tyramine in depressed patients (Coppen & Ghose, 1978; Friedman, 1978; Ghose et al., 1975) and a similar increase in sensitivity to the hypertensive effect of the directly acting NA agonist phenylephrine (Coppen & Ghose, 1978; Friedman, 1978). However, a reduced hypertensive response to tyramine has also been observed (Siever et al., 1981a). Another study reported an increase in the pressor response to NA following recovery, implying that the response may have been reduced during the depression, though no comparison with normal subjects was made (Prange et al., 1967).

The situation is further complicated by the fact that there is a strong negative correlation between tyramine sensitivity and baseline plasma NA concentration (Pickar et al., reported by Siever et al., 1981a). This finding implies that depressed patients who are hypersensitive to tyramine should have had low plasma NA levels. However, there are a number of reports that plasma NA levels were elevated in depression (Esler et al., 1982; Lake et al., 1982; Louis et al., 1975; Wyatt et al., 1971) and also in mania (Lake et al., 1982). Two studies reporting a decrease in the physiological sensitivity of leukocytic beta-receptors in depressed patients are consistent with these observations, as a decrease in receptor sensitivity can be understood as a homeostatic response to high NA levels (Extein et al., 1979b; Pandey et al., 1979a). On the other hand, it has also been reported that the number of beta-receptors on lymphocytes was higher in depression and mania than in recovered patients and normal controls (Sarai et al., 1982).

The studies that found increased peripheral alpha-receptor sensitivity in depression are supported by reports from two laboratories of an increase in the number of alpha$_2$-receptors in blood platelets of depressed patients (Kafka et al., 1980; Garcia-Sevilla et al., 1981; Siever et al.,

1983b; Smith et al., 1983). In another study, a higher number of alpha$_2$-receptors was observed during episodes of postpartum depression, compared with women who did not become depressed following childbirth (Metz et al., 1983). However, an increased number of alpha$_2$-receptors has been observed in schizophrenic patients (Kafka et al., 1980), implying that whatever the significance of this change, it is not restricted to depression.

Furthermore, the opposite result, a decrease in the number of platelet alpha-receptors in depressed patients, has been reported by one of the groups who found increases in physiological sensitivity to tyramine and phenylephrine (Wood & Coppen, 1982, 1983). Several studies using a different measuring technique have reported that the number and sensitivity of alpha$_2$-receptors were unchanged in depressed patients (Daiguji et al., 1981; Lenox et al., 1982; Pimoule et al., 1983). Moreover, the functional significance of changes in the number of platelet alpha-receptors is questionable in the light of two reports of their normal physiological responsiveness in depressed patients, as measured by the stimulation of cAMP synthesis by NA (Murphy et al., 1974c; Wang et al., 1974). These two studies also reported a normal inhibition by NA of prostaglandin-stimulated cAMP synthesis; a third study found that this effect of NA was reduced in platelets from depressed subjects (Siever et al., 1983b).

Two avenues are open to make sense of these contradictory data. The first, which would encompass many of the experimental findings, is to conclude that in depression NA levels are high and beta-receptors are desensitized homeostatically, but for some reason, alpha-receptors become supersensitive. However, this approach fails to account for a significant proportion of the findings, including reports of reduced numbers of alpha-receptors (Wood & Coppen, 1982, 1983) and increased numbers of beta-receptors (Sarai et al., 1982). Furthermore, the observation that tyramine sensitivity is inversely proportional to NA level in depressed patients (see above) suggests that their alpha-receptors can and do show normal homeostatic regulation. The second approach is to appeal to diagnostic heterogeneity. Variability of plasma NA concentration appears to be very high among unipolar depressed patients (who constitute the majority in most of the studies described) (Lake et al., 1982), and it may even be bimodal (Lake et al., 1981, cited by Siever et al., 1981a). It is possible, therefore, that there might be two distinguishable groups of patients—one with low plasma NA and high alpha- (and beta-) receptor sensitivity, and a second with high NA and low alpha- (and beta-) receptor sensitivity (Siever et al., 1981a).

Neither of these hypotheses is particularly appealing. However, studies of plasma dopamine-beta-hydroxylase (DBH), the enzyme which synthesizes NA from DA, tend to support the latter hypothesis. Dopamine-beta-hydroxylase may be a further marker of NA activity (Major et al.,

1981), because the enzyme is located within synaptic vesicles, and a fraction is released along with NA (Smith & Winkler, 1972; Viveros et al., 1968). The results of studies measuring plasma DBH in depressed patients are highly variable. The majority have reported no difference in plasma DBH activity between depressed patients and controls (Fahndrich et al., 1982; Honecker et al., 1981; Lamprecht et al., 1974; Mathew et al., 1981; Markianos et al., 1982; Nasr et al., 1980; Shopsin et al., 1972; Wetterberg et al., 1972). Several studies have reported lower DBH activity in depression, which would indicate a decreased release of NA (Daiguji et al., 1982, cited in Matuzas et al., 1982; Meltzer et al., 1976; Puzynski et al., 1983a; Strandman et al., 1978; Yu et al., 1980), and two studies have reported higher DBH activity, which would indicate the opposite (Friedman & Stolk, 1978; Matuzas et al., 1982). A flattening of the circadian rhythm of plasma DBH in depressed patients, with the elimination of the major afternoon peak, has been reported (van Cauter & Mendelwicz, 1978). However, another study observed flattening of the circadian rhythm in manic patients, but a normal rhythm in depression (Markianos & Lykouras, 1981).

In fact, if, for the sake of argument, all of the studies reviewed in this section are deemed to provide equivalent information, 13 of the findings suggest that peripheral NA activity is increased in depression, 14 suggest a decrease, and 16 suggest no change. If only studies of receptors are included, because these are the studies that might be modeling central NA function, the tally is nine for an increase, seven for a decrease, and seven for no change. It is remarkable that so much work has provided so little in the way of interpretable data.

12.1.2. NA Metabolism

This chaotic picture does not stop at peripheral NA function, but also extends to peripheral studies of the NA metabolizing enzymes monoamine oxidase (MAO) and catechol-O-methyltransferase (COMT). Different studies of red cell COMT activity in depressed patients have found an increase (Gershon & Jonas, 1975; Shulman et al., 1978), no change (Dunner et al., 1976b; Ebstein et al., 1976; Mattson et al., 1974; White et al., 1976), or a decrease (Briggs & Briggs, 1973; Cohn et al., 1970; Dunner et al., 1971; Puzynski et al., 1983b). When the results from depressed patients are compared with controls of the same sex, it has been variously reported that COMT was elevated in depressed men (Shulman et al., 1978), reduced in depressed men (Fahndrich et al., 1982), elevated in depressed women (Gershon & Jonas, 1975; Fahndrich et al., 1980, 1982), and reduced in depressed women (Briggs & Briggs, 1973; Cohn et al., 1970; Dunner et al., 1971; Puzynski et al., 1983b). Some studies have reported lower COMT in bipolar patients than in unipolars (Cohn et al., 1970; Dunner et al., 1971), whereas others found no difference (Gershon

& Jonas, 1975; Puzynski et al., 1983b). The great variety of these results suggests the possibility of an alteration in circadian rhythms, rather than a simple quantitative change. However, there seems little point at present in any further attempt to interpret these inconsistent data.

Studies of blood platelet MAO are a little less unsatisfactory. A number of studies have concurred in finding reduced MAO activity in bipolar patients (Gershon, 1978; Gershon et al., 1979; Landowski et al., 1975; Meltzer & Arora, 1980; Murphy & Weiss, 1972; Murphy et al., 1974b; Orsulak et al., 1978; Sullivan et al., 1977a,b), although not all studies have observed this difference (Edwards et al., 1978; Puzynski et al., 1983c; White et al., 1980), and the opposite result has also been reported (Belmaker et al., 1976; Fahndrich et al., 1982). Low platelet MAO activity has also (again inconsistently) been associated with chronic schizophrenia and alcoholism (Major et al., 1979a; Murphy & Wyatt, 1975; Wyatt & Murphy, 1975). In keeping with these observations, which suggest that low platelet MAO might be related to a variety of psychiatric disorders, a survey of a random sample from the normal population revealed that the group of people with the lowest MAO activity had a higher psychiatric morbidity than those with the highest MAO activity (Buchsbaum et al., 1976). In a two-year follow-up, a group of college students designated "at risk," on the basis of low platelet MAO, were found to have a poor occupational and educational performance and to report more mental health problems among their families (Coursey et al., 1982).

Other studies of predominantly unipolar depressions have reported increases in platelet MAO activity (Klaiber et al., 1972; Oreland et al., 1981; Nies et al., 1971, 1973, 1974), but here also there are negative reports (Edwards et al., 1978; Honecker et al., 1981; White et al., 1980). Perhaps more interesting are studies associating high platelet MAO with anxiety states. High MAO activity has been observed in anxiety disorders (Mathew et al., 1980), "psychogenic" depressions (White et al., 1980), depressions secondary to anxiety (Davidson et al., 1980), and anxious depressions (Landowski, 1977; Gudeman et al., 1982). It is precisely these mixed anxiety–depression conditions in which monoamine oxidase inhibiting antidepressants (MAOIs) are clinically effective (Paykel et al., 1979; Quitkin et al., 1979; Robinson et al., 1973; Ravaris et al., 1976; Tyrer, 1976).

If these observations are of etiological significance, however, one interesting implication is that the therapeutic actions of MAO inhibitors may well take place outside the brain. High platelet MAO activity is found in anxious depressions, but platelet MAO activity is not correlated with MAO activity in the brain (Wiberg et al., 1977a,b). Furthermore, what little evidence there is does not suggest any abnormality of MAO activity in the brain of depressed patients. In one postmortem study of the brains of people who had committed suicide, MAO and COMT activities were found to be normal (Grote et al., 1974). In a second study, MAO activity was reduced in the brains of suicides who were alcoholic, but was normal in suicides who were not also alcoholic (Gottfries et al., 1975).

12.1.3. NA Turnover: Central Studies

It is usually assumed that central NA systems are of greater interest than peripheral systems. As noted in Section 9.3, it is possible that central NA synthesis could be influenced by the availability of the precursor amino acid tyrosine. A number of studies have indicated that in depression there could be a deficiency of tyrosine (Benkert et al., 1971; Birkmayer & Linauer, 1970; Kishimoto & Hama, 1979) or of tyrosine transport into the brain (Bridges et al., 1976; Gaillard & Tissot, 1979; Goodnich et al., 1980). There are inconsistencies in the literature, however (e.g., De Myer et al., 1981), and there is little evidence that these changes are sufficient to compromise NA synthesis. Postmortem studies of suicide brains have not demonstrated changes in NA levels (Bourne et al., 1968; Beskow et al., 1976; Pare et al., 1969) or in the activity of the synthetic enzymes tyrosine hydroxylase or DBH (Grote et al., 1974). However, Birkmayer and Riederer (1975) did observe a reduction in NA (relative to unspecified controls) in the red nucleus of three depressed patients (minimum age 75) who died of natural causes, and this finding was subsequently confirmed in a comparison of nine depressed patients with 16 age-matched controls (Riederer et al., 1980). This study also reported that in 6 of the 14 brain areas studied there was a reduction in the level of MHPG, which is thought to be the major central metabolite of NA (Maas & Landis, 1968; Schanberg et al., 1968). Unfortunately, these results are almost impossible to interpret, owing to the fact that the patients were receiving antidepressant drugs until a few days before they died, and many antidepressant drugs reduce MHPG levels (see Section 13.2.2).

Studies of MHPG in CSF samples have given largely negative results. Post and co-workers did report a reduction of CSF MHPG, and also VMA, a minor central metabolite of NA, in both unipolar and bipolar depressed patients, as compared to manic patients and normal controls (Post et al., 1973a; Jimerson et al., 1975). However, a subsequent study by the same group failed to replicate this effect (Post & Goodwin, 1978). Subrahmanyam (1975) also reported reduced CSF MHPG in depressed patients, but seven other groups found no difference between depressed patients and normal controls (Agren, 1980a; Berger et al., 1980; Major et al., 1979b; Shaw et al., 1973; Traskman et al., 1981; Wilk et al., 1972) or manic patients (Ashcroft et al., 1971, cited by Schildkraut, 1973). It has been consistently reported that CSF MHPG values did not differ between unipolar and bipolar depressed patients (Agren, 1980a; Ashcroft et al., 1971, cited by Schildkraut, 1973; Post et al., 1973a).

Other CSF markers of NA turnover are equally unforthcoming. Studies that measured CSF levels of NA itself have not reported reductions in depression (Christensen et al., 1980; Post et al., 1978b), although a decrease in adrenaline has been observed in depressed patients, which returned to normal with clinical recovery (Christensen et al., 1980). One study reported an increase in CSF NA in depressed patients, which was associated with high levels of anxiety. However, while differing from healthy volunteers, depressed patients were not different from neurological controls (Post et al., 1981a,b). As noted above, DBH, the enzyme that synthesizes NA from DA, may be a further marker of NA activity, and it has been reported that in normal volunteers, CSF NA, DBH, and MHPG were significantly intercorrelated (Ballenger et al., 1981). In one study, there was no difference in CSF DBH activity between patients suffering from unipolar or bipolar depression, schizoaffective disorders, schizophrenia, alcoholism, or personality disorders, although a decrease was observed in bipolar patients in the manic phase (Lerner et al., 1978). A subsequent study by the same group reported that CSF DBH was elevated in depressed patients (and reduced in mania) relative to normal controls (Uhde et al., 1980).

It is possible that these discouraging findings might reflect the diagnostic heterogeneity of depression; a wide scatter of CSF MHPG values has been noted (Ashcroft et al., 1971, cited by Schildkraut, 1973; Wilk et al., 1972), and CSF MHPG has been reported to be both positively (Shaw et al., 1973) and negatively (Davis et al., 1981) correlated with severity of depression. Support for this position comes from a study in which increases in suicidal ideation and behavior were strongly associated with low CSF MHPG levels, but also appeared to be associated with high CSF MHPG levels (Agren, 1980a,b).

However, it may simply be that CSF measures of NA turnover give a very poor estimate of NA turnover in the brain. In general, CSF measures are thought to provide a better estimate of brain function than peripheral measures, but NA systems may be an exception to this rule. Levels of MHPG in urine and in lumbar CSF are usually found to be correlated (Agren, 1982; Shaw et al., 1973), but the size of the correlation is not impressive (Aberg-Wistedt et al., 1982; Beckman & Goodwin, 1980; Post et al., 1981a). MHPG in the brain correlates well with MHPG in cisternal CSF (Elsworth et al., 1982), but the concentration gradient for MHPG within the CSF is very shallow, (Bertillson et al., 1982b; Sjostrom et al., 1975; Ziegler et al., 1977), and unlike the DA and 5-HT metabolites HVA and 5-HIAA, there is no correlation between MHPG levels in early (lumbar) and late (cisternal) CSF samples (Bertilsson et al., 1982b).

These observations suggest that the spinal contribution to MHPG measured in the lumbar CSF may be substantial. Release of MHPG from the spinal cord has been demonstrated (Kessler et al., 1976a,b), and blockade of CSF flow does not appear to alter lumbar MHPG concentration (Post et al., 1973c). Additionally, probenecid, which blocks the transport of 5-HIAA and HVA out of the CSF and, by amplifying CSF concentrations, improves the quality of experimental findings (see Section 9.1.5), has only minimal effects on MHPG (Gordon et al., 1973; Korf et al., 1971). It is possible, in other words, that peripheral measures of NA turnover might reflect central NA function better than lumbar CSF measures. It should be noted in this context that the NA innervation of the forebrain originates largely in the locus coeruleus, whereas the spinal cord is innervated primarily by the more caudal A1 and A2 cell groups.

12.1.4. MHPG Excretion

A reduction of MHPG in the urine of depressed patients, compared to healthy controls, was first reported in 1968 by Maas and co-workers. The rationale for studying urinary MHPG as an index of central NA function rests on the observation that in the periphery, MHPG is a minor metabolite of NA, the major metabolite being vanillylmandelic acid (VMA) and, to a much lesser extent (5% approx), normetanephrine (NM) (Glowinski et al., 1965; Maas & Landis, 1968, 1971; Maas et al., 1972a). The actual proportion of urinary MHPG originating in the human central nervous system remains highly controversial; estimates vary between 20% (Blombery et al., 1980) and 80% (Ebert & Kopin, 1975). The most recent analysis of this problem indicates that MHPG in human urine exists largely in the form of equal concentrations of two further metabolites—MHPG sulfate and MHPG glucuronide—of which the former derives almost exclusively from the brain, whereas the latter largely reflects peripheral sympathetic function (Peyrin & Pequignot, 1983).

Irrespective of the relative contributions of CNS and periphery to urinary MHPG, the conclusion that the reduced MHPG excretion in depressed patients (Maas et al., 1968) reflects a change in the central component is supported by the finding of no concomitant decrease in the excretion of NA or of its peripheral metabolites VMA and NM (Campanini et al., 1970; Coper et al., 1972; Jones et al., 1975; Maas et al., 1971, 1973; Puzynski et al., 1980; Schildkraut et al., 1978). Furthermore, a clear relationship has been observed between urinary MHPG excretion and one measure of central NA function. Noradrenaline neurons of the locus coeruleus are at their least active during REM sleep (Hobson et al., 1975): in manic–depressives and in characterologically depressed patients, an inverse correlation was found between REM sleep time and MHPG excretion (Schildkraut et al., 1973).

Since the original report of Maas and co-workers, a large literature has developed associating abnormalities of urinary MHPG excretion with depression. This literature is rather unusual in that considerable attention has been paid to the diagnostic heterogeneity of depression. However, the precise nature of the abnormalities is difficult to define.

Overall, undifferentiated groups of depressed patients or patients diagnosed as suffering from endogenous depression or primary affective disorder have usually, but not always (Agren, 1982; Beckman & Goodwin, 1980), been found to have a reduced excretion of MHPG (Crow et al., 1984; Goodwin & Potter, 1979; Jones et al., 1975; Maas et al., 1968; McKnew & Cytryn, 1979; Puzynski et al., 1980; Sharpless, 1977; Taube et al., 1978). A return to normal MHPG levels in patients who recovered from depression, but not in those who did not recover, has also been reported (Pickar et al., 1978). A number of independent longitudinal studies of small numbers of bipolar patients have found that MHPG levels were lower in depression and higher in mania than in periods of normal mood (Bond et al., 1972; Greenspan et al., 1970; Jones et al., 1973; Post et al., 1977). Decreased MHPG therefore appears to be associated with the depressed state in some patients. Defining who those patients are is more problematic.

Bipolar patients are usually reported to excrete less MHPG than unipolars (Beckman & Goodwin, 1980; Garfinkel et al., 1977, 1979; Goodwin & Potter, 1979; Jones et al., 1975; Sacchetti et al., 1979; Schatzberg et al., 1982; Schildkraut et al., 1978), or characterological depressions (Schildkraut et al., 1973, 1978). Comparison of bipolar patients with controls is more equivocal: decreased MHPG excretion has usually been reported (Beckman & Goodwin, 1980; Garfinkel et al., 1977; Goodwin & Potter, 1979; Jones et al., 1975; Schatzberg et al., 1982), but there are exceptions (Agren, 1982; Garfinkel et al., 1979; Vestergaard et al., 1978). The reason for the discrepancy may be that the bipolar classification is itself heterogeneous: Beckman & Goodwin (1980) observed reduced MHPG excretion in patients diagnosed as Bipolar I (prior history of mania), but not in patients diagnosed as Bipolar II (prior history of hypomania). In one of the studies that failed to observe a difference between bipolar patients and controls 16 of the 19 bipolar patients were in the bipolar II group (Agren, 1982).

Excretion of MHPG in unipolar depressed patients, compared to normal controls, is more variable. There are reports that MHPG excretion was reduced (Jones et al., 1975; Pickar et al., 1978), unchanged (Agren, 1982; Schatzberg et al., 1982), and increased (Beckman & Goodwin, 1980; Garfinkel et al., 1979; Vestergaard et al., 1978). Again, the answer may lie in diagnostic heterogeneity. Schatzberg and co-workers (1982) suggest that there may be three subgroups, characterized by low, normal, and high levels of MHPG excretion. The existence of a low MHPG subgroup is supported by a substantial body of evidence (discussed below) showing that patients with low MHPG excretion show a better therapeutic response to imipramine and certain other drugs. Patients with abnormally high MHPG excretion also showed a significantly better response to these drugs than did patients in the intermediate range (though not responding as well as the low MHPG group); these patients were also characterized by abnormally high plasma cortisol levels (Schildkraut et al., 1981; Schatzberg et al., 1982).

To summarize, MHPG excretion appears to be reduced during depressive episodes in some, but not all, bipolar patients, and in some unipolar patients; there appears also to be a group of unipolars in whom MHPG excretion is abnormally high.

The relationship of changes in NA turnover to the clinical symptomatology of depression is rather elusive. One important question is whether MHPG excretion simply reflects changes in physical activity. Ebert and co-workers (1972) reported that MHPG excretion was increased when depressed patients increased their level of physical activity; this effect was later replicated by Beckman and co-workers (1976). However, negative results have also been reported (Sweeney et al., 1978a), and vigorous exercise by normal subjects has been found not to increase MHPG excretion (Goode et al., 1973; Hollister et al., 1978). Moreover, decreased MHPG excretion has been reported in agitated depression (Greenspan et al., 1970; Jones et al., 1975; Schildkraut, 1974), and agitated and retarded depressions have been found not to differ on this measure (Jones et al., 1975; Schildkraut, 1974; Goodwin & Post, 1975). A recent study noted a significant inverse relationship between MHPG level and the sum of agitation and retardation ratings (Agren, 1982), but since psychomotor change (in either direction) strongly differentiates endogenous from reactive depression (Nelson & Charney, 1981; see Section 3.3.1), this finding supports the association of low MHPG with endogenous depressions (Schildkraut et al., 1973, 1978), but adds little further insight. Finally, two out of three longitudinal studies of bipolar patients have noted that increases in MHPG excretion preceded the switch into mania by up to four days (Bond et al., 1972; Jones et al., 1973; but not Post et al., 1977). From these findings, it is clear that decreased MHPG excretion in depression is not just a reflection of decreased physical activity.

Within the depressed group, MHPG excretion has not usually been found to correlate with the severity of depression (Agren, 1982; Beckman & Goodwin, 1980; Jones et al., 1975; Schildkraut et al., 1973, 1978). However, two studies have reported correlations between MHPG excretion and anxiety (Beckman & Goodwin, 1980) or guilt (Cobbin et al., 1979). In addition, Maas and co-workers (1971) observed that in depressed patients an initially low MHPG excretion increased to normal levels during a (presumably stressful) intravenous infusion procedure. In this study, no change was seen in control subjects; in another study, however, the stress of an intravenous infusion did increase MHPG excretion in normal volunteers (Peyrin & Pequignot, 1983). Furthermore, naval aviators and radar operators were found to excrete more MHPG during (presumably highly stressful) landings of aircraft on aircraft carriers; these changes were not seen during simulations (which presumably were less stressful) (Rubin et al., 1970). An increase in MHPG excretion has also been observed in volunteer subjects exposed to painful electric shocks (Buchsbaum et al., 1981). Finally, Sweeney and co-workers (1978a) found that in depressed patients subjected to 8 hours of either enhanced or restricted activity, MHPG excretion showed no relation to activity level; however, those patients who responded to either procedure with an increase in anxiety increased their MHPG excretion, whereas those who responded with decreases in anxiety decreased their MHPG excretion.

Taken together, these findings suggest that low MHPG excretion may reflect a low level of anxiety, whereas normal or high MHPG levels may reflect a high level of anxiety. However, this conclusion is misleading. In the recent study of Peyrin and Pequignot (1983), stress did increase total MHPG excretion. However, the increase was confined to the glucuronide conjugate of MHPG, which reflects peripheral sympathetic activity (see above); stress had no effect on the central component of urinary MHPG (MHPG sulfate). These data appear to preclude a relationship in depressed patients between changes in central NA turnover and level of anxiety.

The psychological correlates of low MHPG excretion in depression remain elusive. However, the animal literature reviewed in Chapter 11 makes a clear prediction that central NA turnover should determine the ability to sustain effort or concentration. This question has not been addressed in depressed patients, but two studies in normal subjects would support such a relationship. In one, Bond and Howlett (1974) found that performing mental arithmetic was associated with an increased production of MHPG sulfate, which derives from the brain, with no change in the production of MHPG glucuronide. In the other study, Post and co-workers (1981a) examined the relationship between MHPG excretion and scores on the Minnesota Multiple Personality Inventory (MMPI); MHPG excretion was found to be inversely correlated with scores on two scales: depression and fatiguability.

12.1.5. Central NA Receptors

In addition to changes in NA turnover, depressed patients also show some evidence of altered NA receptor function. Beta-adrenergic receptors and alpha$_1$-receptors, which are by far the two most numerous adrenergic receptor types in the brain, have not been studied. No abnormality of presynaptic alpha$_2$-receptors is apparent. However, the responsiveness of postsynaptic alpha$_2$-receptors appears to be reduced.

Presynaptic alpha$_2$-receptors have been studied by means of the drug clonidine, which in people, has been found, to reduce plasma MHPG and blood pressure (Charney et al., 1981a,b; Leckman et al., 1980b). In animals, clonidine is known to depress the firing of locus coeruleus cells, by an action at presynaptic alpha$_2$-receptors (Cedarbaum & Aghajanian, 1977; Svensson & Usdin, 1978), resulting in a decrease in MHPG formation (Anden et al., 1976; Braestrup, 1974; Charney et al., 1981a,b). The hypotensive effect of clonidine also appears to be mediated by presynaptic receptors; this effect could be observed following the microinjection of clonidine in the vicinity of NA cell bodies (Rockhold & Caldwell, 1980), and it was abolished by 6-OHDA-induced destruction of NA neurons (Warnke & Hoefke, 1977). These responses to clonidine may therefore represent a measure of presynaptic alpha$_2$-receptor sensitivity. Clonidine has been found to depress plasma MHPG equally in depressed patients and controls (Charney et al., 1982b) and also to cause equal reductions in blood pressure (Charney et al., 1982b; Checkley et al., 1981). There is nothing in these findings to suggest any alteration in presynaptic alpha$_2$-receptor function in depressed patients.

Postsynaptic alpha$_2$-receptors have been studied using the neuroendocrine strategy; the major tool for this purpose is growth hormone (GH). Growth hormone is secreted episodically throughout the day and night; these surges are abolished by lesions of the ventromedial or arcuate nuclei of the hypothalamus (Martin et al., 1978), which have been shown to contain the recently identified growth hormone releasing factor (GHRF) (Bloch et al., 1983). Noradrenaline appears to be the major stimulus to GHRF release, since GH secretion is also blocked by reserpine, by the selective NA synthesis inhibitor FLA-63, and by alpha-receptor blockers (Eden & Modigh, 1977; Lovinger et al., 1976; Terry & Martin, 1981). The receptors involved are of the alpha$_2$-type: GH release is stimulated by the specific alpha$_2$ agonist clonidine (Terry & Martin, 1981) and is abolished by the specific alpha$_2$ antagonist yohimbine (Laakman et al., 1981). Alpha$_2$-receptors are located both presynaptically (autoreceptors) and postsynaptically (Starke et al., 1977). However, the alpha$_2$-receptors involved in GH release are clearly postsynaptic, because clonidine has been shown to stimulate GH release even after presynaptic NA activity was abolished by reserpine (Eden & Modigh, 1977) or FLA-63 (Terry & Martin, 1981). The NA stimulus to GH release probably arises primarily from the ventral NA bundle, because the major surge of GH release is at the onset of sleep (Martin et al., 1978), when the activity of locus coeruleus neurons is falling (Steriade & Hobson, 1976). A preferential involvement of the ventral bundle is also indicated on anatomical grounds, as one of the two GHRF-containing nuclei, the ventromedial nucleus does not receive any input from the locus coeruleus (Palkovits et al., 1980).

Five independent studies have recently demonstrated a blunted GH response to clonidine in endogenously depressed patients, compared to normal controls (Charney et al., 1982b; Checkley et al., 1981; Glass et al., 1982; Matussek et al., 1980; Siever et al., 1982b) or to patients with other psychiatric diagnoses (Matussek et al., 1980). A blunted GH response to clonidine is also observed in postmenopausal women (Matussek et al., 1980; Siever et al., 1982b). However, in all five studies the blunted GH response in depressed patients was still present when age and sex were controlled, and in one of the studies, a difference between depressed patients and controls could be discerned even among postmenopausal women (Siever et al., 1982b). A blunted response has also been noted in some control subjects who were heavy alcohol users (Matussek et al., 1980). It may be relevant that both alcohol users and postmenopausal women have an increased risk of developing depression (Goodwin & Erikson, 1979). The only other psychiatric condition in which a decreased GH response to clonidine has been reported is obsessive–compulsive disorder (Siever et al., 1983a); interestingly, obsessive–compulsive patients also respond favorably to the tricyclic antidepressant clorimipramine (Marks et al., 1980; Thoren et al., 1980).

Two other stimuli to GH release are DMI and insulin. In both cases, the response is blocked by phentolamine, an alpha-receptor antagonist, indicating that the effect is mediated by NA (Blackard & Heidingsfelder, 1968; Laakman, 1980). A large literature demonstrates blunting of the GH response to insulin in endogenously depressed patients (Carroll, 1972; Caspar et al., 1977; Endo et al., 1974; Gruen et al., 1975; Mueller et al., 1969; Sachar et al., 1971, 1973a, 1975). A blunted response to DMI has also been reported; the response was reduced in unipolar and bipolar endogenously depressed patients, but increased in neurotic depressions (Laakman, 1980; Sawa et al., 1980). Like the GH response to clonidine, responses to insulin and DMI are greatly reduced in postmenopausal women, but the blunted response in depression does not appear to be a result of this artifact.

Growth hormone release is also stimulated in people by amphetamine (Besser et al., 1969). It was originally reported that the GH response to amphetamine was reduced in endogenously depressed patients (Langer et al., 1976). In this case, however, controlling for the blunted responses of postmenopausal women (Halbreich et al., 1980) abolished the difference between depressed patients and controls (Checkley & Crammer, 1977; Checkley, 1979; Halbreich et al., 1982). Unlike the GH response to clonidine, DMI, and insulin, the response to amphetamine is probably mediated by DA rather than NA, because the effect was enhanced rather than suppressed, by alpha- and beta-blockers (Rees et al., 1970). As discussed in Section 9.1.3, neuroendocrine tests of DA receptor function in depression have not usually reported abnormalities.

In addition to GH, amphetamines also stimulate the release of ACTH (Besser et al., 1969). The ACTH response to amphetamine does appear to be mediated by alpha-adrenergic receptors, because it could be blocked by the alpha-receptor blocker thymoxamine (the beta-blocker propranolol enhanced the response) (Rees et al., 1970). A blunted ACTH response to methamphetamine has been observed in endogenously depressed patients, compared to normal controls, recovered depressed patients, neurotic depressions, and schizophrenics (Checkley, 1979; Checkley & Crammer, 1977; Sachar et al., 1980).

These studies concur with the GH responses to clonidine, DMI, and insulin in demonstrating that, in depressed patients, the responsiveness of postsynaptic alpha-receptors is reduced. The relationship to endogenous NA activity is uncertain, however. A positive correlation between MHPG excretion and GH response to insulin has been reported (Garver et al., 1975), but so has a negative correlation between MHPG excretion and the GH response to clonidine (Siever et al., 1982b).

12.2. TREATMENTS THAT DECREASE NA FUNCTION

The catecholamine hypothesis of depression makes the clear prediction that drugs which reduce the level of stimulation at postsynaptic NA receptors should induce depression. As in the case of the DA hypothesis (Section 9.2), however, the evidence from this quarter is extremely weak.

12.2.1. NA Depletion

A number of drugs that deplete the brain of DA have similar effects at NA synapses. These include reserpine, alpha-methyldopa, and alpha-methylparatyrosine (AMPT), which act, respectively, by blockade of storage, by displacement of NA from stores, and by synthesis inhibition. As previously discussed, there is no evidence that AMPT can induce depression, and the evidence for alpha-methyldopa- and reserpine-induced depression is weak (see Section 9.2).

It is possible to prevent NA synthesis independently of effects on DA neurons by inhibiting DBH, the enzyme which synthesizes NA from DA. The effects of two DBH inhibitors, fusaric acid and disulfiram, have been studied in people. These drugs are specific NA synthesis inhibitors in the sense that they do not affect DA synthesis; they do, however, have a variety of other effects unrelated to catecholamine systems. Of the two, fusaric acid has fewer unwanted effects. Goodwin & Sack (1974) gave fusaric acid to eight manic patients; the result was a slight worsening in the two most severely ill patients and a slight increase in psychosis ratings in the five with preexisting psychosis. Psychotic reactions have also been reported in a high proportion of alcoholics treated with disulfiram (Martensen-Larsen, 1951; Major et al., 1979a; Smilde, 1963). There was no evidence of a depressive effect in these studies; neither was depression commented on as a side effect of studies of fusaric acid administration to healthy volunteers (Hartman & Keller-Teschke, 1979; Hartman et al., 1983; Hidaka et al., 1973; Kato et al., 1980) or to patients with Parkinson's disease (Mena et al., 1971). However, a recent Polish study reported that depression can, in fact, be a frequent side-effect of disulfiram treatment (Jakimov-Venulet et al., 1981). Also, an intriguing study of depression associated with chronic scurvy has pointed out that vitamin C deficiency decreases DBH activity; like scurvy, the associated depression also responds rapidly to vitamin C treatment (Dixit, 1979).

12.2.2. Clonidine

As discussed above, clonidine is a relatively specific alpha-receptor agonist, which, at low doses, selectively stimulates alpha$_2$-receptors, most of which are located presynaptically. In animals, the consequence is a decrease in the activity of NA cells, rather than an increase (Cedarbaum & Aghajanian, 1977; Starke & Altman, 1973). A clonidine-induced decrease in plasma MHPG level (Leckman et al., 1980b; Charney et al., 1981a,b) indicates that clonidine also decreases NA activity in people. The fact that clonidine also decreases plasma NA, by decreasing central sympathetic activity (Matussek et al., 1980; Metz et al., 1978), suggests that these presynaptic effects outweigh any concurrent postsynaptic stimulation.

These observations explain why clonidine, although an alpha-receptor stimulant, has primarily sedative effects in people (Barnett & Cantor, 1968; Checkley et al., 1981; Davies et al., 1977; Kugler et al., 1980; Lal et al., 1975; McRaven et al., 1971). Clonidine has been reported to decrease anxiety in depressed patients (Uhde et al., 1980), which, as noted in Section 12.1.4, most probably reflects a decrease in peripheral sympathetic activity. Clonidine does not appear to induce depression, but antimanic effects have been reported (Giannini et al., 1983; Jouvent et al., 1980).

12.2.3. Receptor Blockers

The effects on mood of antagonists at postsynaptic alpha-receptors do not appear to have been studied. Depression has occasionally been reported as a side effect of the beta-blocker propranolol (Waal, 1967). However, the incidence of depression is low (Fitzgerald, 1967). In the most recent report, 3 out of 34 patients treated for hypertension with propranolol developed depression; the effects were severe and dose-dependent, and they remitted when the drug was discontinued (Petrie et al., 1982). However, one of these three patients had previously been clinically depressed, and a second had a family history of depression, suggesting that the precipitant effect of propranolol might have been rather nonspecific.

12.3. TREATMENTS THAT INCREASE NA FUNCTION

A variety of methods are available for increasing NA receptor stimulation. Unlike the largely negative results found in studies of treatments which decrease NA function, many treatments which enhance NA function do have antidepressant properties.

12.3.1. Salbutamol

Salbutamol, an agonist at beta$_2$-receptors, is the only directly acting NA receptor agonist to have been investigated for its effect on mood (other than clonidine, which decreases NA activity in the dose range at which it is administered to people). Simon and colleagues have reported, mainly on the basis of uncontrolled studies, that salbutamol is an effective antidepressant (Jouvent et al., 1977; Simon et al., 1978; Widlocher, 1978). In these studies, a very high response rate was observed, with improvement within three days, and sometimes within one day. Confirmation of a high response rate, but not of the rapidity of onset, was obtained in a further (independent) open study (Belmaker et al., 1982). Unlike the studies of Simon and co-workers, the latter trial used oral rather than intravenous salbutamol administration. These results are interesting insofar as salbutamol trials involved a high proportion of patients resistant to other forms of therapy. In a single controlled trial, salbutamol was found to be superior to chlorimipramine by the fifth day of treatment, and the difference was still present on the fifteenth day (Lecrubier et al., 1980).

12.3.2. Precursors

As noted in Section 9.3.1, the mood-elevating effects of the catecholamine precursor DOPA are not impressive. However, the effect of DOPA administration in people is primarily to increase DA synthesis and turnover; NA turnover, assessed by urinary MHPG excretion, is only increased at very high doses (Bunney et al., 1971; Goodwin et al., 1971). It is possible to bypass DA and to influence NA synthesis directly by using the artificial precursor dihydroxyphenylserine (DOPS). A single dose of DOPS has been reported to have "inconsistent activating and mood-elevating effects" in depression (D. Murphy, reported by Gelenberg et al., 1982). The size of the effect on NA turnover was not reported. It should also be noted that there is no way of knowing, in people, the proportion of NA synthesis from DOPS that actually takes place in DA neurons.

As previously discussed (Section 9.3.1), a double-blind controlled study of six patients (three/group) has demonstrated an antidepressant effect of tyrosine, which is the precursor to DOPA (Gelenberg et al., 1982). The effect of tyrosine administration on brain DA synthesis is uncertain, but it is known that in some circumstances tyrosine can increase brain NA turnover (Sved et al., 1979). An antidepressant response to tyrosine in two patients has also been reported by Goldberg (1980); there is a suggestion that this effect might have been mediated by NA, rather that DA, in the fact that both patients had previously responded to amphetamine. The significance of this observation lies in the relationship between amphetamine response and NA turnover, which is discussed in the following section.

12.3.3. Amphetamine

Although amphetamine does not appear to be of value in the sustained treatment of depression (Ban, 1969, Klerman, 1972), many depressed patients respond to amphetamine with a short-lasting brightening of mood. It has been found that patients in whom amphetamine has this effect are likely to respond well to treatment with those tricyclic antidepressants (imipramine, DMI, and nortriptyline) which act predominantly at NA synapses (Fawcett & Simonopoulos, 1971; Fawcett et al., 1972; Maas et al., 1972b; Van Kammen et al., 1977; van Kammen & Murphy, 1978). In normal volunteers the euphoric response to amphetamine appears to be mediated primarily by DA, because the response was blocked by the catecholamine synthesis inhibitor AMPT and by the DA-receptor blocker pimozide, but not by the NA-receptor blockers phentolamine or propranolol (Jonsson et al., 1971; Jonsson, 1972). However, in depressed patients, the situation may be different, since it has been observed consistently that depressed patients who respond to amphetamine with mood elevation have a low urinary excretion of MHPG (Beckman et al., 1976; Fawcett & Simonopoulos, 1971; Fawcett et al., 1972; Maas et al., 1972b). As described below, this relationship also obtains for those tricyclic antidepressants that act primarily at NA synapses.

12.3.4. MHPG Levels and Response to Tricyclics

The classic action of tricyclic antidepressants is blockade of the neuronal reuptake of NA and 5-HT, which has the effect of prolonging the synaptic action of the transmitter and consequently of enhancing its postsynaptic actions. Desmethylated (secondary) tricyclics such as DMI and nortryptiline have a substantially (1–3 orders of magnitude) greater effect on NA uptake than on 5-HT. Imipramine is less selective, but still some 5–10 times more potent as an inhibitor of NA uptake (Maitre et al., 1982; Randrup & Braestrup, 1977). As with the mood response to amphetamine, there appears to be an important relationship between the antidepressant response to "noradrenergic" tricyclics and the urinary excretion of MHPG prior to treatment.

In numerous studies, patients with a low urinary excretion of MHPG prior to treatment have been found to show a better antidepressant response to imipramine, DMI, and nortriptyline than patients with high MHPG excretion (Aberg-Wistedt et al., 1982; Beckman & Goodwin, 1975; Cazzulo et al., 1982; Cobbin et al., 1979; Hollister et al., 1980; Maas et al., 1972b, 1982; Martin et al., 1980; Rosenbaum et al., 1980; Schatzberg et al., 1980; Schildkraut et al., 1981; Steinbook et al., 1979). Only one study, which reported on a total of eight patients, failed to observed this relationship (Charney et al., 1981b). This literature has been criticized on the grounds that the criterion for deciding between "low" and "high" MHPG excretors varies between laboratories (Kelwala et al., 1983). However, the consensus is impressive, particularly considering that MHPG levels in depressed patients do not usually fall outside the normal range (Hollister, 1981).

The tetracyclic antidepressant maprotiline is a specific blocker of NA uptake, virtually without effect on 5-HT (Maitre et al., 1975; Waldmeier et al., 1976). Like the "noradrenergic" tricyclics, maprotiline also gives better results in patients with low pretreatment MHPG excretion (Rosenbaum et al., 1980; Schatzberg et al., 1981; Schildkraut et al., 1981). One study by Ridges and co-workers (1980) has reported that there was no relationship between pretreatment MHPG excretion and response to maprotiline. However, as noted in Section 12.1.4, a group of unipolar patients with abnormally high MHPG excretion also responded better to imipramine or maprotiline than patients with MHPG in the normal range (Schildkraut et al., 1981). Inspection of the data of Ridges' study reveals that the patient who responded best had an abnormally high MHPG level (Ridges et al., 1980, Table 6). Removal of this patient uncovers a significant negative correlation between clinical response and pretreatment MHPG in the remaining patients (Spearman rho $= 0.72, p < 0.05$). These results are therefore fully consistent with those described above.

As might be expected from the fact that CSF MHPG levels do not accurately reflect NA turnover in the brain (see Section 12.1.3), the relationship between low MHPG and response to "noradrenergic" tricyclics has not been confirmed in CSF studies (Aberg-Wistedt et al., 1982; Dahl et al., 1982; Roccatagliata et al., 1981). Indeed, in two of these reports a better response to imipramine (Roccatagliata et al., 1981) or DMI (Aberg-Wistedt et al., 1982) was found in patients with higher CSF MHPG concentrations. However, in one of these studies, interpretation of the result is confounded by the fact that the high MHPG group also had higher depression scores prior to treatment (Mann–Witney $U = 5.5, p < 0.05$, calculated from Roccatagliata et al., 1981, Table I). In the second study, the relationship between CSF MHPG level and depression scores was not reported; it is noteworthy, however, that this study also did report the usual inverse relationship between DMI response and urinary MHPG level (Aberg-Wistedt et al., 1982).

In contrast to the clear superiority of "noradrenergic" tricyclics in patients with low MHPG excretion, a high MHPG excretion has been reported to predict a therapeutic response to the "serotonergic" tricyclic chlorimipramine (Sacchetti et al., 1979). The rationale for this effect lies in the observation of a reciprocal relationship between urinary MHPG and CSF 5-HIAA in depressed patients (Goodwin et al., 1978). Normal (high) MHPG therefore implies low CSF 5-HIAA, and as discussed in

Section 16.3.4, low CSF 5-HIAA predicts a good response to "serotonergic" antidepressants.

A number of studies have reported that high pretreatment MHPG excretion predicts a good response to amitriptyline (Beckman & Goodwin, 1975; Cazzullo et al., 1982; Cobbin et al., 1979; Modai et al., 1979; Schildkraut, 1974). Equally often, however, response to amitriptyline is found to be unrelated to MHPG level (Coppen et al., 1979; Gaertner et al., 1980; Maas et al., 1982; Mendlewicz et al., 1982b; Sacchetti et al., 1979; Spiker et al., 1980). These discrepancies are not surprising, as, contrary to a commonly held belief, amitriptyline is not a selective 5-HT uptake inhibitor. Indeed, in many studies, amitriptyline is actually somewhat more potent as an inhibitor of NA uptake (e.g., Blackburn et al., 1978; see also Section 15.3.4).

12.3.5. Selective NA Uptake Inhibitors

In addition to maprotiline, the therapeutic efficacy of which is well established (Montgomery, 1980), a number of other selective NA uptake inhibitors have been investigated, including amoxapine, viloxazine, and nisoxetine. Preliminary results with nisoxetine were discouraging: only 2 out of 12 patients responded, and the nonresponders reported severe side effects, including restlessness, agitation, and anxiety (Shopsin et al., 1981). It is possible, however, that these effects might result from poor penetration to the brain, with a consequent amplification of the peripheral effects, since results with amoxapine and viloxazine were very different, despite their apparently similar pharmacology.

Fujimori (1981) analyzed the results of 16 double-blind controlled trials of amoxapine, which taken together showed amoxapine to be superior not only to placebo but also to imipramine and amitriptyline. This superiority was particularly apparent on early evaluations, including a significant effect at one week (Fujimori, 1981; Hekimian et al., 1978). In one study, significant antidepressant effects were reported after only four days of treatment (Hekimian et al., 1978). The rapid onset of amoxapine's antidepressant action, and its superiority to amitriptyline, were confirmed in a well-controlled recent study (McNair et al., 1984). Similarly, placebo-controlled studies of viloxazine have confirmed a clear antidepressant effect (Ekdawi, 1975; Pinder et al., 1977), and again there are reports that the onset is more rapid than with imipramine (Floru et al., 1976, cited by Shopsin et al., 1981; Melgar & Lazzari, 1975) or amitriptyline (Rentford et al., 1976).

12.4. PRELIMINARY CONCLUSIONS: NA AND DEPRESSION

The conclusions about NA function in depression which emerge from this review are similar in some ways to those about DA function drawn in

Chapter 9. In both cases, there is reasonable good evidence that catecholamine turnover is low in some depressed patients and that drugs
which cause appropriate increases in synaptic transmission are effective
antidepressants. However, there is little evidence that pharmacologically
induced decreases in function will cause depression of mood. Arguments
were advanced in Chapter 9 as to why the failure to confirm predictions
about the pharmacological induction of depression may not be as crucial
as they might appear (Section 9.4). There is little point in going over the
same ground again; suffice it to say that the depressions associated with
low NA function in chronic scurvy (Dixit, 1979) could prove to be more
significant than the failure to induce depression by means of an acute
challenge with an NA synthesis inhibitor.

Considering that urinary excretion of MHPG has been the major tool
for assessing central NA function, it is remarkable that any progress at
all has been made in establishing abnormalities of central NA function
in depression. The usefulness of peripheral MHPG levels is particularly
surprising when it is remembered that peripheral NA function appears
to undergo major upheavals in depressed patients, the nature of which
defies agreement (Sections 12.1.1 and 12.1.2). Nevertheless, it is clear
from MHPG excretion studies (Section 12.1.4) that a substantial proportion of severely depressed patients do show a reduction of central NA
turnover. MHPG reflects primarily the activity of the forebrain projections of the locus coeruleus, which, despite its small size, provides the
great majority of NA synapses in the brain (Section 11.2). It has been
observed, for example, that damage to the locus coeruleus results in a
proportional reduction in brain MHPG concentration (Crawley et al.,
1980; Korf et al., 1973a–c), and electrical stimulation of the locus coeruleus increases brain MHPG concentrations. So too does stress, provided
that the locus coeruleus is intact (Korf et al., 1973a–c; Stone, 1975).

The work reviewed in Chapter 11 suggests a relevant function of ascending projections of the locus coeruleus: the ability to maintain effort
or concentration (Section 11.2.2.4). The most pertinent clinical finding is
the inverse relationship observed (in nondepressed subjects) between
MHPG excretion and fatiguability (Post et al., 1981a). This relationship
suggests that in depressed people NA function may be relatively normal
for much of the time, but may fail when it is necessary to sustain effort.
As this is rarely a constant requirement, it is not surprising that 24-hour
urine samples usually show MHPG values which are low, but within the
normal range.

The other biochemical abnormality that is consistently observed in
depressed patients, the reduced sensitivity of the postsynaptic alpha$_2$-
receptors that stimulate the secretion of GH, is more difficult to interpret.
As discussed earlier, it is probable but by no means certain that these
receptors are innervated by the ventral NA bundle. Consequently, these
subsensitive receptors might provide a mechanism through which the

ventral bundle fails to inhibit ACTH secretion, resulting in nonsuppression on the dexamethasone suppression test (DST). One study has, in fact, reported an association between an abnormal GH response to insulin and nonsuppression on the DST (Berger et al., 1982a).

If an abnormal DST result does reflect a low level of central NA function, then DST nonsuppression should predict a therapeutic response to "noradrenergic" tricyclics. Two studies have reported that DST nonsuppressors did not respond better to imipramine than they did to amitriptyline (Greden et al., 1981; Peselow et al., 1983a). However, given that amitriptyline is a potent NA uptake inhibitor (see above), this is hardly surprising. Two other studies have reported that like low NA turnover, DST nonsuppression does, in fact, predict a favorable antidepressant response to imipramine and an unfavorable response to specific 5-HT uptake inhibitors (W. Brown et al., 1980; Fraser, 1983).

There is little evidence at present from which to deduce the origin of the reduction in postsynaptic alpha$_2$-receptor sensitivity. Receptor subsensitivity could represent a homeostatic response to high levels of activity in the ventral bundle; as noted in the previous chapter, ventral bundle hyperfunction would have relevant behavioral consequences (Section 11.1). The evidence of the DST, however, suggests that in the majority of severely depressed patients ventral bundle function is low. It is possible that high ventral bundle activity, resulting in a compensatory desensitization of hypothalamic alpha-receptors, might be found in those patients whose DST response is normal. If this were true, however, it would follow that abnormal DST responses and abnormal GH responses to alpha-receptor stimulation should not occur in the same patients, but apparently they do (Berger et al., 1982a).

The coexistence of these two abnormalities suggests an alternative hypothesis: subsensitivity of postsynaptic alpha-receptors could be a consequence of changes in ACTH and cortisol secretion. As far as I am aware, this possibility has not been investigated. However, it is known that alpha$_2$-receptors on blood platelets (Metz et al., 1983) and the GH response to alpha-receptor agonists (Section 12.1.5) are responsive to changes in estrogen level. Estrogen and ACTH exert similar effects on beta-adrenergic receptors (see Section 13.3.3.3), so an effect of ACTH on alpha-receptors is quite plausible. It has also been reported that ACTH administration increased MHPG excretion in people (Hauger-Klevene & Moyano, 1973), which suggests that hyperactivity in central NA systems, leading to a compensatory decrease in receptor sensitivity, could be secondary to changes in HPA activity in some patients. This would explain why, in one study, very high cortisol levels were associated with the highest levels of MHPG excretion (Schildkraut et al., 1981; see Section 12.1.4).

This account implies that reduced sensitivity of alpha-receptors in depressed patients might be secondary to an increase in HPA activity rather than the other way round. An explanation of abnormal HPA activity must then be sought elsewhere, and as described in Chapter 14, an increase in cholinergic activity provides a highly plausible alternative.

This discussion highlights the difficulty of assessing the functional significance of changes in parameters of neurotransmitter function. Up to this point it has been largely assumed that the results can be taken at face value: a low turnover of NA means a low level of synaptic transmission and a drug which enhances the level of stimulation of postsynaptic receptors increases transmission through the synapse. However, as discussed in Chapter 1 (Section 1.1.4), it is possible to construct a theory in which these same findings have exactly the opposite meaning (Segal et al., 1974). The clinical evidence alone is insufficient to resolve this dilemma, and the evidence from animal behavior, while favoring the original version of the catecholamine hypothesis, is far from conclusive. Fortunately, the effects of antidepressant drugs, which are considered in the following chapter, provide a means of arbitrating between the two opposing interpretations.

thirteen

ANTIDEPRESSANTS AND NORADRENALINE

If NA transmission is abnormal in depression, it should not be difficult to establish the direction of change by using the simple rule that the the effect of antidepressants is in the opposite direction. In practice, life is not so simple. The original catecholamine hypothesis of depression was based in part on the known NA-enhancing effects of antidepressant drugs (Schildkraut, 1965), but the reformulated catecholamine hypothesis was also derived from pharmacological evidence: in this case, the NA-reducing effects of chronic antidepressant treatment (Segal et al., 1974; Sulser et al., 1978).

During the course of chronic antidepressant administration, these two types of effect coexist, and remarkably little attention has been paid to the question of which of them predominates. This chapter describes some of the many varying effects of antidepressant treatments at NA synapses, and it assesses their net effect on NA transmission. In order to illustrate the complexity of the problem and the method of approach, I have begun with an outline of the effects of a single antidepressant treatment. The main discussion, however, concerns the status of NA transmission following a period of chronic antidepressant administration, typically one to four weeks.

13.1. ACUTE EFFECTS

Blockade of noradrenaline reuptake, which prolongs the action of NA at the synapse, is, of course, the best known action of tricyclic antidepressants. Secondary tricyclics, such as DMI, nortriptyline, and protriptyline, are somewhat more potent blockers of NA uptake than are tertiary tricyclics, such as amitriptyline, imipramine, and doxepin; this finding has been replicated many times (Carlsson et al., 1969a; Fuller, 1981; Maitre et al., 1982). The potentiation of adrenergic transmission which results from uptake blockade was one of the principal foundations of the catecholamine hypothesis of depression. One of the most curious phenomena in antidepressant drug research is that this effect is only rarely mentioned in contemporary discussions of the mechanism of action of antidepressants [for example, the recent *Typical and Atypical Antidepressants: Molecular Mechanisms* (Costa & Racagni, 1982a) mentions NA uptake on only 11 of its 390 pages]. Two reasons may be tentatively advanced for this fall from favor. One is that the various slowly developing effects of antidepressants, particularly changes in receptor function, are more in keeping with the modern view of the brain as an adaptive dynamic self-regulating system. The other is that around the time that this view began to emerge, the so-called atypical antidepressants were discovered. The introduction of antidepressants that are chemically dissimilar from the tricyclics and MAOIs threw into question the assumption that antidepressants work by potentiating adrenergic transmission, because some of these newer drugs appeared neither to inhibit MAO nor to block NA reuptake.

It has since transpired that most of the atypical antidepressants do actually potentiate adrenergic transmission, though the mechanisms vary. Mianserin, for example, which has little or no effect on NA uptake *in vivo* (Baumann & Maitre, 1977; Goodlet et al., 1977), is a potent antagonist at presynaptic alpha$_2$-receptors (Baumann & Maitre, 1977; J. Brown et al., 1980; Maggi et al., 1980), and it consequently increases NA turnover (Fludder & Leonard, 1979b; Leonard & Kafoe, 1976; Sugrue, 1980b). Trazodone, like mianserin, is also a potent antagonist at alpha$_2$-receptors (J. Brown et al., 1980; Maggi et al., 1980). Nomifensine, although considerably more potent as a DA uptake inhibitor than the tricyclics, does inhibit NA uptake, and it is more potent in this regard than many tricyclics (Algeri et al., 1982; Blackburn et al., 1978; Randrup & Braestrup, 1977). Even the selective 5-HT uptake inhibitor zimelidine, although several orders of magnitude more potent at 5-HT synapses, shows some slight antagonism of NA uptake at high doses (Carlsson & Lindqvist, 1978a; Fuller, 1981).

The most problematic atypical antidepressant, supposedly, is iprindole, which apparently is utterly devoid of effects on NA uptake or turnover (Gluckman & Baum, 1969; Lahti & Maickel, 1971; Rosloff & Davis, 1974).

Nonetheless, iprindole potentiates the electrophysiological effects of ion-tophoretically applied NA (Bevan et al., 1975), and it is comparable in potency to imipramine and DMI (Bradshaw et al., 1974). These results are rarely quoted in discussions of the status of iprindole, perhaps because the biochemical mechanism remains obscure. Indeed, if effective anti-depressants are being sought that fail to potentiate adrenergic trans-mission, the best candidates may be the MAOIs, rather than the atypical antidepressants: MAOIs elevate brain NA concentrations, but much of the increase appears to be in a cytoplasmic pool and is probably una-vailable for release (Finberg & Youdim, 1983).

The fact that tricyclic antidepressants increase synaptic concentrations of NA does not necessarily mean that they potentiate adrenergic trans-mission, since they also have a variety of other effects. One consequence of increasing intrasynaptic NA concentrations is the stimulation of in-hibitory presynaptic alpha$_2$-autoreceptors. As a result, there is a reduc-tion in the firing rate of locus coeruleus cells (McMillen et al., 1980; Nyback et al., 1975; Scuvee-Moreau & Dresse, 1979; Svensson & Usdin, 1978), which is accompanied by a fall in NA synthesis (Carlsson & Lindqv-ist, 1978a; Nielsen et al., 1975; Rosloff & Davis, 1978). The reduction in firing rate is directly proportional to, and commensurate with, the block-ade of NA uptake (Quinlaux et al., 1982).

Most studies have consistently reported that secondary tricyclics re-duce NA turnover, as would be expected given that these drugs increase autoreceptor stimulation and decrease the firing rate of locus coeruleus cells. However, tertiary tricyclics, which also block NA uptake, do not reduce NA turnover (Nielsen, 1975; Nielsen & Braestrup, 1977; Roffman et al., 1977; Schildkraut et al., 1976; Sugrue, 1980a; Tang et al., 1978). At low doses, the difference most probably reflects the fact that the ter-tiary tricyclics are relatively weak uptake blockers. At higher doses, an-other factor comes in to play: the tertiary tricyclics, amitriptyline in par-ticular, are potent antagonists at alpha$_2$-receptors (J. Brown et al., 1980; Maggi et al., 1980; Tang & Seeman, 1980), which results in the neu-tralization of their autoreceptor-stimulant effects.

What are the consequences for adrenergic transmission? The answer depends to some extent on the type of postsynaptic receptor involved. Secondary tricyclics, such as DMI, combine a decrease in turnover with a powerful blockade of NA uptake. At synapses where beta-receptors pre-dominate, the net result of acute DMI administration is an increase in adrenergic transmission. This has been demonstrated by electrophysiol-ogical recording from noradrenergically innervated cells in the cerebel-lum (Schultz et al., 1981), hippocampus (Huang, 1979b), and cortex (Brad-shaw et al., 1974; Bunney & Aghajanian, 1976c). Similar effects have also been observed, in cortex, with imipramine (Bradshaw et al., 1974) and viloxazine (Jones & Roberts, 1977). Although drugs such as ami-triptyline and chlorimipramine block NA uptake less strongly, it may be assumed that they too enhance beta-adrenergic transmission, since they do not reduce turnover; the appropriate single-unit recording studies have not yet been carried out.

These conclusions are relatively straightforward only because tricycl-ics show negligible affinity for beta-receptors (Peroutka & Snyder, 1981a). The situation with respect to alpha-adrenergic transmission is more com-plex, since in addition to the effects already described, tricyclics also act as antagonists at postsynaptic alpha-receptors (J. Brown et al., 1980). A high affinity for alpha-receptors is observed in receptor binding assays (Hall & Ogren, 1981; Tang & Seeman, 1980; U'Prichard et al., 1978), and the affinity appears to correlate with sedative effects in people. Tertiary tricyclics, which have a high affinity for alpha-receptors, have sedative properties, whereas secondary tricyclics, which have a low affinity for alpha-receptors, have activating properties (U'Prichard et al., 1978). (This finding is frequently overinterpreted to mean that tertiary tricyclics are clinically more efficacious in agitated depressions and that secondary tricyclics are better in retarded depressions; there is no evidence that such is the case.)

As a result of their dual effect—uptake blockade and receptor antag-onism—the net effects of tricyclics on alpha-adrenergic transmission are rather variable. DMI, which is a potent NA uptake blocker and a rela-tively weak alpha-receptor antagonist, has been found to enhance alpha-adrenergic transmission in the facial motor nucleus, the lateral geni-culate nucleus of the thalamus, and the spinal cord. Tertiary tricyclics, on the other hand, which are weaker uptake blockers and stronger re-ceptor antagonists, tend to enhance transmission at low doses and block transmission at high doses (Menkes & Aghajanian, 1981; Menkes et al., 1980; Sangdee & Frantz, 1979).

Two important conclusions may be drawn from this discussion. The first is that, given the multiple effects of antidepressants, it makes little sense to select a single aspect of neuronal function for study, in isolation from the system of which it is a part. The second is that the net effect of drugs on the integrated functioning of the system as a whole can be as-sessed only by techniques that measure postsynaptic function in response to physiological stimulation *in vivo*.

13.2 CHRONIC EFFECTS

13.2.1 Presynaptic Receptors

As discussed in earlier chapters, presynaptic alpha$_2$-receptors situated on the cell bodies inhibit the firing of NA cells in the locus coeruleus, and alpha$_2$-receptors on axon terminals play an important inhibitory role in regulating NA release (Langer, 1977; Starke et al., 1977; Westfall,

1977; see also Chapters 1, 11, 12). The effects of low doses of clonidine (0.1 mg/kg or less), which preferentially stimulate presynaptic alpha$_2$-receptors (Anden et al., 1976; Delina-Stula et al., 1979; Drew et al., 1979), have been used as an assay system in which to test the effects of anti-depressant treatment on NA autoreceptors. In addition to reducing NA cell firing rate and NA turnover, "presynaptic" doses of clonidine also cause hypothermia and a variety of sedative effects. The presumption that the sedative effects of clonidine result from autoreceptor-mediated inhibition of the locus coeruleus (Delina-Stula et al., 1979), has recently been questioned on the grounds that lesions of the dorsal bundle or locus coeruleus, which produced large depletions of forebrain NA, had little effect on clonidine-induced sedation (Nassif et al., 1983; Velley et al., 1982). However, the implications of these results are not as clear-cut as they at first appear. For the first week after the operation, lesioned an-imals were hypoactive compared to controls, and without knowing the mechanism of their subsequent recovery (see also Roberts et al., 1981), the possibility that receptors on surviving neurons became hypersensitive to clonidine cannot be excluded.

The effects of chronic antidepressant administration on some physio-logical and behavioral effects of low doses of clonidine are summarized in Tables 13.1 and 13.2. With only one exception (Bhavsar et al., 1983), a reduction in autoreceptor responsiveness has always been observed fol-lowing imipramine (13 studies) and DMI (eight studies). Because imi-pramine and DMI are potent inhibitors of NA uptake, this effect probably represents an adaptive change secondary to increased intrasynaptic lev-els of NA (see Section 13.1). Decreased sensitivity to clonidine was also seen following ECS (five studies), REM-sleep deprivation (two studies) and salbutamol (one study); in these cases, the neurochemical mechanism is less obvious. Again, different results were obtained by Bhavsar and co-workers (1981, 1983), who reported an increase in clonidine-induced sedation after ECS or imipramine. Conceivably, the discrepant results could reflect their use of a rating scale to measure sedation, which in addition to locomotor activity also includes assessment of a variety of other indices, including posture, righting reflexes, and yawning.

Not all antidepressants are able to desensitize alpha$_2$-receptors. With only two exceptions, no reduction in sensitivity to "presynaptic" doses of clonidine was seen with amitriptyline or clorimipramine, which are less selective as NA uptake blockers (five studies). Neither was alpha$_2$-re-ceptor desensitization seen with trazodone (three studies), which is in-effective as an NA uptake blocker (Silvestrini, 1982). In four studies, chronic treatment with mianserin, which on acute administration is a potent antagonist of alpha$_2$-receptors (see above), actually increased sen-sitivity to clonidine (Tables 13.1 and 13.2).

It will not have escaped attention that DMI and imipramine, which reliably reduce autoreceptor function, are the antidepressants for which

TABLE 13.1. EFFECTS OF CHRONIC ANTIDEPRESSANT TREATMENT ON SOME PHYSIOLOGICAL AND BIOCHEMICAL CHANGES ELICITED BY A LOW DOSE OF CLONIDINE

Model	Days of Treatment	Effect of clonidine			Reference
		Decreased	No Change	Increased	
Reduction of locus coeruleus firing rate	14	IMI[a]	CMI		Svensson, 1980
	11	IMI			Svensson & Usdin, 1978
	12	DMI[b]			McMillen et al., 1980
Reduction of NA release					
Whole brain	7	IMI			Von Voigtlander et al., 1978
Synaptosomes	21	CLORG			Cohen et al., 1980, 1982b
	14			MIA[c]	Cerrito & Raiteri, 1981; Raiteri et al., 1983b
Rat atria	14	DMI, NOR, IP[c]			Crews & Smith, 1978, 1980
Reduction of whole brain	12	DMI			McMillen et al., 1980
MHPG concentration	9	DMI		MIA	Sugrue, 1980b, 1981
	14	DMI, IMI, ECS	AMI, IP, NOR, NIS, PARG, SAL, TRAZ		Sugrue, 1982a,b
	14	IMI	AMI		Tang et al., 1978
	10	ECS	DMI, MIA		Heal et al., 1981
Hypothermia	4–7	AMI, CMI, IMI, IP, NOM, OP, PRO, TRI, VIL			Von Voigtlander et al., 1978
	7	IMI, ECS			Pilc & Vetulani, 1982
	11	IMI			Gorka & Zacny, 1981
Inhibition of electrically induced vas deferens contractions	22	DMI, CLORG, TRAN			Finberg & Youdim, 1982

AMI: amitriptyline; CLORG: clorgyline; CMI: chlorimipramine; DMI: desmethylimipramine; ECS: electro-convulsive shock; IMI: imipramine; IP: iprindole; MIA: mianserin; NIS: nisoxetine; NOM: nomifensine; NOR: nortriptyline; OP: opipramol; PARG: pargyline; PRO: protriptyline; SAL: salbutamol; TRAN: tranylcypromine; TRAZ: trazodone; TRI: trimipramine; VIL: viloxazine. [c] Response to NA challenge rather than clonidine.

[a] Response to DMI challenge rather than clonidine. [b] Response to DMI challenge rather than clonidine.

TABLE 13.2. EFFECTS OF CHRONIC ANTIDEPRESSANT TREATMENT ON CLONIDINE-INDUCED SEDATION

Model	Days of Treatment	Sedation			Reference
		Decreased	No Change	Increased	
Locomotor activity	21	IMI, ECS[a]	TRAZ		Passarelli & Scotti, 1982, 1983
	21	CLORG			Cohen et al., 1980
	10	ECS			Heal et al., 1981
	2	REM-D[b]			Mogilnicka & Pilc, 1981
	7	IMI[c]			Von Voigtlander et al., 1978
	4	AMI, DMI, IMI, CMI, MIA, NOM			Kostowski & Malatynska, 1983
	10	SAL			Mogilnicka, 1982
Acoustic startle	14	DMI	AMI, IP		Davis, 1982
Exploratory behavior	15	DMI			Spyraki & Fibiger, 1980
	4	CMI, DMI, IMI, MIA	AMI, NOM		Kostowski & Malatynska, 1983
	10	SAL			Mogilnicka, 1982
EEG synchronization	21	IMI, ECS	TRAZ		Passarelli & Scotti, 1982, 1983
Rating scale	10			ECS, IMI	Bhavsar et al., 1981, 1983

[a] Abbreviations as in Table 13.1.
[b] REM-D: REM-sleep deprivation, which unlike other antidepressant treatments is effective on acute administration (Gillin, 1983).
[c] Result reported as nonsignificant, but an interaction clearly apparent in the published data.

a good clinical response is associated with a low pretreatment NA turnover (Section 12.3.4). This suggests that autoreceptor desensitization could be an important mechanism by which these drugs increase NA activity in depressions characterized by low NA function.

Studies in depressed patients also provide evidence that some antidepressants can desensitize NA autoreceptors. As described in the previous chapter (Section 12.1.5), the hypotensive effect of clonidine and the reduction by clonidine of plasma MHPG have been used to assess presynaptic alpha$_2$-receptor function in people. Although there is no evidence that blood pressure and MHPG responses to clonidine are abnormal in depressed people (Section 12.1.5), a number of studies have reported that these responses, and also clonidine-induced sedation, were attenuated by chronic (two to four weeks) administration to depressed patients of DMI, amitriptyline, or the MAOI clorgyline (Charney et al., 1981b, 1983; Checkley et al., 1981; Glass et al., 1982; Mavroidis et al., 1984; Siever et al., 1981c).

The finding that amitriptyline desensitized alpha$_2$-receptors in depressed patients (Charney et al., 1983) is interesting in relation to the ineffectiveness of amitriptyline in most animal experiments; blockade of the presynaptic effects of clonidine by amitriptyline or chlorimipramine was observed in only two studies (Tables 13.1 and 13.2). However, both of these studies used doses of antidepressants (2 mg/kg) that were much lower than those usually employed (Kostowski & Malatynska, 1983; Von Voigtlander et al., 1978). As the lower dose is probably more comparable to the clinical situation, the possibility that a desensitizing effect of amitriptyline and chlorimipramine on alpha$_2$-autoreceptors may be masked at higher doses clearly merits further study. However, autoreceptor desensitization is not a general property of chronic antidepressant treatments in people: mianserin did not inhibit the effects of clonidine on blood pressure or plasma MHPG (Charney & Heninger, 1983).

Receptor binding studies using radio-labeled clonidine, which is presumed to bind specifically to alpha$_2$-receptors (Greenberg et al., 1976; U'Prichard et al., 1977), are summarized in Table 13.3. It is difficult to reconcile this picture with the behavioral and physiological results summarized above. For example, DMI, which clearly reduces the functional sensitivity of alpha$_2$-autoreceptors (Tables 13.1 and 13.2) either increased [^{3}H]clonidine binding (three studies) or had no effect (three studies). It is possible that these discrepancies reflect the fact that in many areas of the brain only a small proportion of alpha$_2$-receptors are located presynaptically. In rat cortex, the destruction of NA terminals caused only a minimal decrease (Morris et al., 1981), or even an increase (U'Prichard et al., 1979), in the number of [^{3}H]clonidine binding sites. From these results, it would seem that the majority of alpha$_2$-receptors are located postsynaptically, at least in the cortex.

TABLE 13.3. EFFECTS OF CHRONIC ANTIDEPRESSANT TREATMENT ON [³H]CLONIDINE BINDING

Site	Days of Treatment	[³H]Clonidine Binding Reduced	No Change	Increased	Reference
Brainstem	21	CLORG, PHEN[a]	PARG		Cohen et al., 1982a,b
	14	AMI			Smith et al., 1981
	21	IMI	CLORG		Campbell & McKernan, 1982
Limbic forebrain	4			DMI	Johnson et al., 1980
	7		CMI, DMI, IMI, NIA, NOR, MIA		Asakura et al., 1982
Hypothalamus	14	AMI			Smith et al., 1981
	10	ECS			Stanford & Nutt, 1982
	10			DMI	Stanford et al., 1983
Cortex	21	CLORG, PHEN	PARG		Cohen et al., 1982a
	3			IP	Reisine et al., 1980
	28	IMI			Vetulani et al., 1980
	21	IMI			Pilc & Vetulani, 1982
	14	PARG	AMI, DMI, ECS, IMI, IP, MIA, NIS, NOR		Sugrue, 1982b
	14		ECS		Bergstrom & Kellar, 1979a
	10		DMI		Stanford et al., 1983
	10	ECS			Stanford & Nutt, 1982
	7			CMI, DMI, IMI, NIA, NOR, MIA	Asakura et al., 1982
	21		AMI		Peroutka & Snyder, 1980b
	21	IMI, CLORG			Campbell & McKernan, 1982
	14		IMI		Mikuni et al., 1983
	2		REM-D		Mogilnicka & Pilc, 1981

[a] Abbreviations as in Table 13.1 and 13.2, plus NIA: nialamide; PHEN: phenelzine.

However, it is unclear whether the anatomical diversity of alpha$_2$-receptors is sufficient to explain the discrepant binding results. Although chronic DMI may increase [^{3}H]clonidine binding, there is no evidence that DMI increases postsynaptic alpha$_2$-receptor function (see below), and the results of two studies actually suggest a decrease (Eriksson et al., 1982; Glass et al., 1982). Moreover, it would be expected that presynaptic receptors might predominate in the locus coeruleus. [^{3}H]Clonidine binding to locus coeruleus receptors was indeed reduced by amitriptyline (Smith et al., 1981), yet in functional tests, amitriptyline is generally ineffective (Tables 13.1 and 13.2). An alternative explanation of the discrepancies may be that the data of receptor binding experiments are simply not very informative as guides to physiological responsiveness—an unpalatable conclusion that will, however, be reached repeatedly in the course of this book.

One series of experiments has reported that in depressed patients, imipramine, amitriptyline, or ECS caused a reduction of [^{3}H]clonidine binding to platelet alpha$_2$-receptors (Garcia-Sevilla et al., 1981; Smith et al., 1983). In these studies, platelet [^{3}H]clonidine binding was elevated in depressed patients prior to treatment. Imipramine has also been found to reduce [^{3}H]clonidine binding to blood platelets in rats (Campbell & McKernan, 1982). However, a study of platelet binding of [^{3}H]rauwolscine, which is a more specific antagonist at alpha$_2$-receptors, found no differences between depressed patients and controls, and no changes were seen during three weeks of treatment with chlorimipramine or amitriptyline (Pimoule et al., 1983). Similarly, clorgyline (Siever et al., 1983b), amoxapine (U'Prichard et al., 1982), and lithium (Wood & Coppen, 1983) have also been found not to affect platelet alpha-receptor binding. The simplest conclusion to draw from these results is perhaps that platelet binding is not a very useful model for studying central alpha-receptor function.

13.2.2 Synthesis and Turnover

During chronic treatment with imipramine and DMI, a gradual recovery is seen in the firing rate of locus coeruleus cells, which probably reflects the reduction of autoreceptor sensitivity. However, after one to two weeks of treatment, firing rates were still substantially reduced in comparison with untreated animals (Huang et al., 1980; McMillen et al., 1980; Svensson & Usdin, 1978). Similarly, a reduced synthesis of NA has usually been observed after one to three weeks of DMI treatment (Nielsen & Braestrup, 1977; Rosloff & Davis, 1978; Segal et al., 1974). Despite this reduced level of presynaptic activity, long-term administration of DMI is usually, though not always (Sugrue, 1982, a,b), found to enhance NA turnover, as measured by the production of MHPG (McMillen et al., 1980; Roffman et al., 1977; Sugrue, 1980c; Tang et al., 1978, 1979;). Because

NA synthesis is reduced, the increase in NA release leads to a decrease in brain NA level (Roffler-Tarlov et al., 1973; Schildkraut, 1975). The increase in NA turnover following chronic DMI treatment is in marked contrast to the reduction in turnover seen after acute administration.

Some years ago, specific binding sites for imipramine were described in the rat brain, which appear to be associated with the 5-HT uptake system (Raisman et al., 1979a,b; see Section 15.1.5.). More recently, specific DMI binding sites have also been described, which are associated with the NA uptake system (Langer & Raisman, 1983; Rehavi et al., 1982). Chronic administration of DMI and other antidepressants did not affect DMI binding (Racagni et al., 1983), which is consistent with the earlier observation that the blockade of NA uptake by DMI does not change during chronic treatment (Roffler-Tarlov et al., 1973; Schildkraut, 1975). As the effects of DMI on the NA uptake system remain constant during chronic treatment, it is usually assumed that the discrepancy between decreased presynaptic activity, and increased turnover may be explained by an increase in the amount of NA released per impulse. This effect is not unexpected, in that it probably reflects a desensitization of the axon terminal alpha$_2$-autoreceptors which inhibit NA release.

Another secondary tricyclic, protriptyline, has also been reported to increase NA turnover on chronic administration (Schildkraut, 1975; Schildkraut et al., 1971), and a return to control levels was observed with nortriptyline (Roffman et al., 1977). The picture for imipramine is less clear, with some studies reporting that NA turnover remained low following chronic administration, whereas others observed an increase. It is possible that the discrepancies simply reflect a difference in the length of treatment. In those studies that reported a decrease in turnover, imipramine was administered for only 10 or 11 days (Friedman et al., 1974; Mogilnicka & Klimek, 1979a; Nielsen & Braestrup, 1977), whereas increased turnover was seen in studies in which drug treatment lasted for more than two weeks (Roffman et al., 1977; Schildkraut, 1975; Schildkraut et al., 1971). In a related study, CSF levels of DBH, a marker for NA release (see Section 12.1.3), were reduced in rhesus monkeys after one week of imipramine treatment but returned to normal by two weeks (Lerner et al., 1980). These results suggest that imipramine increases NA turnover, provided that the period of administration is sufficiently prolonged.

Two other treatments that reliably increase NA turnover on chronic administration are ECS (Ebert et al., 1973; Ladisch et al., 1969; Modigh, 1976; Musacchio et al., 1969; Schildkraut, 1975) and mianserin (Fludder & Leonard, 1979a; Kafoe et al., 1976; Przegalinski et al., 1981; Sugrue, 1980c; Tang et al., 1979). The effect of ECS is probably related to the desensitization of alpha$_2$-autoreceptors (see above). The effect of mianserin is more difficult to explain, considering that after chronic mianserin treatment autoreceptors apparently become supersensitive (Cerrito &

Raiteri, 1981; Raiteri et al., 1983b; Sugrue, 1980b, 1981; see Table 13.1). It is possible that the effect depends on an interaction between NA and 5-HT systems (Racagni et al., 1983), which are also affected by mianserin (Chapter 16). A number of other atypical antidepressants have also been reported to enhance NA turnover on chronic treatment, by mechanisms that have not yet been determined; these drugs include trazodone, danitracen, and pizotifen (Przegalinski et al., 1981). Salbutamol also has this effect (Svensson et al., 1981). In consequence, after chronic administration, salbutamol is no longer a selective beta-receptor agonist, but also indirectly stimulates postsynaptic alpha-receptors.

As might be expected from their failure to affect NA turnover acutely (Section 13.1) and their failure to desensitize alpha$_2$-receptors chronically (Tables 13.1 and 13.2), amitriptyline and chlorimipramine do not alter NA turnover on chronic administration (Mogilnicka & Klimek, 1979a; Nielsen & Braestrup, 1977; Roffman et al., 1977; Sugrue, 1980c; Tang et al., 1978). Other drugs that fail to affect NA turnover on chronic administration are iprindole (Rosloff & Davis 1974, 1978) and maprotiline (Sugrue, 1980c). A variety of MAOIs have also been reported not to affect NA turnover, even though these drugs do substantially raise brain NA levels (Campbell et al., 1979, 1980).

To summarize the animal literature, chronic administration of antidepressant agents either increases NA turnover [DMI, protriptyline, imipramine (?), ECS, some atypical antidepressants], or it produces no significant change (amitriptyline, chlorimipramine, nortriptyline, MAOIs, some atypical antidepressants). Taking these results together with the acute NA-enhancing effects of antidepressants (Section 13.1), it is clear that, with the possible exception of MAOIs and zimelidine, antidepressants, in animals, increase the stimulation of postsynaptic adrenergic receptors on chronic administration. In order to establish the overall postsynaptic effects of antidepressants, changes in postsynaptic receptor function must also be taken into account; these will be discussed below.

Studies of NA turnover in depressed patients during antidepressant treatment have given more variable results. Chronic administration of DMI, imipramine, or nortriptyline has been reported to increase (Cobbin et al., 1979; Perry et al., 1978), not to change (Halaris & De Met, 1978; Maas et al., 1972b) and to decrease (Aberg-Wistedt et al., 1982; Beckman & Goodwin, 1975; Linnoila et al., 1982) MHPG excretion; a decrease in plasma MHPG has also been reported (Charney et al., 1981b). These findings are difficult to interpret for two main reasons. First, antidepressants may be presumed to affect peripheral NA metabolism. For example, DMI has been observed to decrease urinary excretion of the peripheral NA metabolite VMA (Linnoila et al., 1982). Although it is unclear exactly what proportion of urinary MHPG derives from the brain (see Section 12.1.4), it is possible that a decrease in NA turnover peripherally might mask an increase in central turnover. However, CSF studies, which are probably free of peripheral contamination, are also inconsistent, with reports of a decrease in MHPG level during DMI treatment (Potter et al., 1981), and no change during DMI (Dahl et al., 1982) or imipramine (Roccatagliata et al., 1981). The second problem is that changes in NA turnover during treatment are confounded with changes in clinical state and with the relationship between clinical improvement on these drugs and pretreatment MHPG level (see Section 12.3.4). Unfortunately, taking these factors into account does not greatly clarify the situation. Some studies have reported larger increases in NA turnover in clinical responders (Goodwin et al., 1975; Halaris & De Met, 1978; Maas et al., 1972b), but other studies have reported a decrease in NA turnover in responders (Beckman & Goodwin, 1975; Roccatagliata et al., 1981) or no relationship between MHPG changes and clinical change (Perry et al., 1978). However, in two of the studies in which MHPG excretion increased during treatment, this was associated with a low pretreatment NA level (Maas et al., 1972b; Cobbin et al., 1979). It is not clear whether this relationship holds more generally.

With one exception (Goodwin et al., 1975), amitriptyline has been found to decrease MHPG excretion (Beckman & Goodwin, 1975; Cobbin et al., 1979), plasma MHPG level (Charney et al., 1983), and CSF MHPG level (Mendlewicz et al., 1982b). Chlorimipramine has also been found to decrease CSF MHPG levels (Asberg et al., 1975; Siwers et al., 1977); this effect was proportional to the CSF concentration of the chlorimipramine metabolite desmethylchlorimipramine, which is a more potent inhibitor of NA uptake (Traskman et al., 1979; Traskman-Bendz et al., 1981). The specific 5-HT uptake inhibitors zimelidine and femoxetine are usually found not to alter urinary (Aberg-Wistedt et al., 1982) or CSF (Dahl et al., 1982; Potter et al., 1981) MHPG levels, but one study has reported a decrease with zimelidine (Linnoila et al., 1982). Studies of mianserin have been inconsistent, with reports of an increase in urinary MHPG (Perry et al., 1978) and a decrease in CSF MHPG (Mendlewicz et al., 1982b).

The MAOIs clorgyline and pargyline have been reported not to change CSF NA level, but to decrease MHPG and DBH; responders showed an increase, and nonresponders showed a decrease in NA level, but there was no significant relationship to MHPG changes (Major et al., 1979b). Finally, no change in urinary MHPG was observed during treatment with the MAOI phenelzine (Beckman & Murphy, 1977).

With the possible exception of the most potent NA uptake inhibitors, this evidence leans more toward the conclusion that the tricyclic antidepressants decrease, rather than increase, NA turnover in depressed people. The recent observation that an increase in plasma and urinary MHPG followed withdrawal from amitriptyline, DMI, or imipramine (Charney et al., 1982c) would tend to support this conclusion. However, given the fact that tricyclics enhance transmission through adrenergic synapses, a decrease in turnover does not imply a decrease in synaptic transmission. Indeed, there is nothing in the evidence, animal or human, to suggest that a decrease in turnover is anything other than an adaptive response to the NA-enhancing effects of antidepressants, as observed with acute administration of secondary tricyclics in animal experiments.

13.3 CHRONIC EFFECTS ON POSTSYNAPTIC RECEPTOR FUNCTION

13.3.1. Postsynaptic Alpha$_2$-Receptors

Chronic antidepressant treatment does not have marked effects on post-synaptic alpha$_2$-receptors, as assessed by neuroendocrine techniques. In rats pretreated with AMPT to suppress endogenous NA release, chronic ECS increased the inhibitory effect of clonidine on plasma corticosterone (Steiner & Grahame-Smith, 1980a). However, in rats pretreated with reserpine for the same purpose, the GH response to clonidine was unaffected by ECS (Balldin et al., 1980a), but reduced by imipramine (Eriksson et al., 1982). In baboons, the GH response was unaffected by either DMI (McWilliam et al., 1983) or ECS, though an increased response was observed seven days after withdrawal (McWilliam et al., 1981, 1982). In depressed patients, the GH response to clonidine was unchanged by three to six weeks of treatment with DMI, amitriptyline, clorgyline, or ECS (Charney et al., 1982a, 1983; Siever et al., 1982a; Slade & Checkley, 1980); in one study the response was increased after one week's treatment, but declined again over the following two weeks (Glass et al., 1982).

A second effect mediated by postsynaptic alpha$_2$-receptors is the inhibition of 5-HT release from synaptosomes. The receptors mediating this effect, which are presynaptic as far as the 5-HT system is concerned but postsynaptic to NA terminals, have been termed "presynaptic heterore-ceptors;" pharmacologically they are not identical to alpha$_2$-autoreceptors (Raiteri et al., 1983a). Two recent studies have reported that unlike alpha$_2$-autoreceptors, the alpha$_2$-heteroreceptors inhibiting 5-HT release were unaffected by chronic administration of mianserin (Raiteri et al., 1983b) or DMI (Schlicker et al., 1982).

13.3.2. Alpha$_1$-Receptors

By contrast, there is now considerable evidence that chronic antidepressant treatment increases the functional efficacy of the far more numerous postsynaptic alpha$_1$-receptors. Modigh (1975) reported that a course of seven daily ECS treatments enhanced the locomotor stimulant effect of clonidine in reserpinized mice; because reserpine pretreatment abolishes NA release, a presynaptic explanation of this result can be excluded.

Repeated ECS has also been found to enhance the locomotor stimulant effect of amphetamine. In this experiment the response to the DA agonist apomorphine was unaltered. Consequently, the results indicate an increase in adrenergic function (Ehlers et al., 1983).

Antidepressant drugs have similar effects. The locomotor stimulation induced by high doses of clonidine in mice was enhanced by chronic (10 day) treatment with imipramine, amitriptyline, mianserin, or danitracen (Maj et al., 1979a). Chronic, but not acute treatment with a variety of typical (imipramine, amitriptyline) or atypical (mianserin, iprindole, maprotiline, zimelidine) antidepressants also enhanced clonidine-induced aggression in mice (Maj et al., 1980; 1981); the selective NA uptake inhibitor nisoxetine was also effective, but the selective 5-HT uptake inhibitors citalopram and fluoxetine were not (Maj et al., 1982). Chronic, but not acute treatment with typical (imipramine, DMI, amitriptyline, chlorimipramine) and atypical (mianserin, iprindole, danitracen, maprotiline, zimelidine) antidepressants has also been found to potentiate apomorphine-induced aggression in mice (Maj et al., 1979b). Because both clonidine- and apomorphine-induced aggression could be blocked by the alpha$_1$-receptor antagonist phenoxybenzamine (Maj et al., 1979b, 1980), these results strongly suggest enhancement of central alpha$_1$-receptor function by antidepressants.

Two recent studies have also demonstrated enhancement of alpha$_1$-receptor function in the spinal cord. In one, an increase in the hind limb flexor reflex was observed in rats treated for 14 days with imipramine; alpha$_1$-receptors were implicated by the fact that the enhancement could be blocked by phenoxybenzamine (Maj et al., 1983). In the other study, three weeks of treatment with DMI, amitriptyline, or iprindole enhanced the excitatory effect of the selective alpha$_1$-receptor agonist phenylephrine (Starke et al., 1975) on the acoustic startle response (Davis, 1982).

Electrophysiological studies are fewer in number but demonstrate more directly an increase in alpha$_1$-receptor responsiveness following antidepressant treatment. Chronic administration of imipramine, DMI, amitriptyline, chlorimipramine, and iprindole has been reported to enhance postsynaptic responses to iontophoretically applied NA in the facial motor nucleus (Menkes et al., 1980), the lateral geniculate nucleus of the thalamus (Menkes & Aghajanian, 1981), and the amygdala (Wang & Aghajanian, 1980); fluoxetine was ineffective, as was chlorpromazine (Menkes et al., 1980; Wang & Aghajanian, 1980). Other studies have reported that antidepressant treatment did not change the response to NA of cells in the hippocampus (De Montigny & Aghajanian, 1978; Gallager & Bunney, 1979), and decreased the response to NA in cingulate cortex (Delina-Stula et al., 1982; Olpe & Schellenberg, 1980) and cerebellum (Schultz et al., 1981). In all of these cases, however, the responses were mediated by beta-receptors, as opposed to alpha-receptor mediation in the areas in which antidepressant-induced enhancements were seen.

In fact, the only studies that fail to demonstrate a clear antidepressant-induced enhancement of alpha$_1$-receptor–mediated functions have been those carried out in depressed patients! Three of these studies involved blood pressure measurements. Pickar and co-workers (1980b) reported an increase in tyramine sensitivity following three to four weeks of clorgyline treatment. This result is compatible with an increase in postsynaptic alpha-receptor sensitivity, but since tyramine acts indirectly, a decrease in presynaptic receptor sensitivity is an equally likely explanation. Coppen and Ghose (1978) found a decrease in tyramine sensitivity following two to six weeks on amitriptyline; they also observed an increased sensitivity to NA and a decreased sensitivity to phenylephrine. The last of these findings represents a decrease in alpha$_1$-receptor sensitivity, but the effect was highly correlated with a poor clinical outcome (Coppen & Ghose, 1978). In a subsequent study, ECS was not found to change pressor responses to tyramine or phenylephrine (Ghose, 1980). In a rather different test, the effects of phenylephrine (and also tyramine) on pupil size were reduced by DMI (Shur & Checkley, 1982) but unaffected by mianserin (Shur et al., 1983); the effect of DMI was present after only one week of treatment and probably reflects alpha$_1$-receptor blockade (Shur & Checkley, 1982). However, an increased pupillary response to phenylephrine has been reported following three to five weeks of treatment with tranylcypromine (Sitaram et al., 1983, cited by Janowsky & Risch, 1984b). With this one exception, these studies do not support the picture of increased alpha$_1$-receptor sensitivity that emerges clearly from the animal literature. However, because peripheral measures were used in all cases, they carry little weight.

Unlike the desensitizing effect of antidepressants on presynaptic alpha$_2$-receptors, which appears in most animal studies to be restricted to a narrow range of antidepressant agents (see above), the enhancement of postsynaptic alpha$_1$-receptor sensitivity may be a general property of antidepressants. An experiment by Davis and co-workers illustrates the difference between the two effects. In this study, the postsynaptic stimulatory effect of phenylephrine was enhanced by DMI, amitriptyline, and iprindole, but of these drugs, only DMI also reduced clonidine-induced sedation (Davis, 1982). However, although sensitization of alpha-receptors is caused by some surprising drugs, such as iprindole and zimelidine, two potential limitations on the generality of the effect should be noted. First, some drugs that specifically potentiate 5-HT transmission (citalopram and fluoxetine, though not zimelidine), while effective as antidepressants (see Section 16.3.4), did not enhance clonidine-induced aggression (Maj et al., 1982) and therefore may be devoid of alpha-receptor sensitizing properties. Second, information concerning the effects of chronic MAOI treatment on alpha$_1$-receptor function is restricted to two of the human studies, using peripheral measures.

As usual, receptor binding data are not in agreement with the functional studies. The ligands most commonly employed to study alpha-receptor binding are dihydroergocryptine (DHE) and WB4101. The majority of experiments using these ligands have reported that alpha-receptor binding was unaffected by chronic treatment with imipramine (Campbell & McKernan, 1982; Peroutka & Snyder, 1980a; J. Rosenblatt et al., 1979), DMI and chlorimipramine (Kellar & Bergstrom, 1983), iprindole (Reisine et al., 1980), mianserin (Leonard, 1982), clorgyline (Campbell & McKernan, 1982), or ECS (Bergstrom & Kellar, 1979a). In one study, amitriptyline was found to increase binding (Rehavi et al., 1980b), and two studies have reported decreased binding with imipramine (Vetulani et al., 1980) or clorgyline (R. Cohen et al., 1980).

Binding studies using prazosin, which is considered to be the most specific ligand for alpha$_1$-receptors currently available (Massingham et al., 1981; Miach et al., 1980), gives results that are a little more consistent with the functional data. Following chronic administration of DMI, amitriptyline, or iprindole, no changes in prazosin binding were observed in spinal cord, thalamus, or cortex (Davis, 1982; Menkes et al., 1983). However, imipramine has been found to increase prazosin binding in the spinal cord (Maj et al., 1983), and increased prazosin binding in cortex and brain stem has been observed after chronic administration of amitriptyline or clorgyline (Campbell & McKernan, 1982).

A recent experiment by Menkes and co-workers (1983) may shed some light on why binding studies often give results that do not accurately reflect the functional state of synapses. Although in this experiment prazosin binding was unchanged by antidepressant treatment, there was an increase in the ability of phenylephrine to displace prazosin from binding sites. In most binding sites, receptor antagonists are employed as ligands, because antagonists dissociate more slowly from the receptor; the speed of dissociation of agonist ligands makes agonist binding much more difficult to measure. In the study of Menkes and co-workers (1983), antidepressants did not change the binding characteristics of prazosin (antagonist), but the affinity of the receptor for phenylephrine (agonist) was apparently increased. This suggests that antidepressants may produce a conformational change in alpha$_1$-receptors, shifting them into a more agonist-preferring state. Such a change would not necessarily be reflected accurately if antagonist ligands are used in binding studies.

13.3.3. Beta-Receptors

13.3.3.1. Phenomena

The best known and best established postsynaptic effect of antidepressants is a decrease in the sensitivity of beta-adrenergic receptors, which requires at least five days of treatment, develops over one to three weeks, and persists for several days after withdrawal. In contrast to some other receptor systems, there is reasonable agreement between functional studies and those using receptor binding techniques—up to a point.

The model used to study beta-receptor function relies on the fact that beta-receptor stimulation activates the enzyme adenylate cyclase, which leads to the production within the postsynaptic cell of cyclic AMP (cAMP). Beyond the fact that cAMP serves as an intracellular hormone, or "second messenger" in many physiological systems, including the nervous system (Greengard, 1976), its physiological functions in relation to beta-receptors are poorly understood, though there is a growing understanding of the molecular events preceding and following cAMP synthesis (Limbird, 1981; Rodbell, 1980). Because the production of cAMP in response to an NA challenge may be blocked by beta-receptor but not alpha-receptor antagonists, it would appear that alpha-receptors are not generally linked to a cAMP generating system. Consequently, the cAMP response to NA serves as an assay system for the responsiveness of beta-adrenergic receptors.

Many studies have demonstrated that the sensitivity of the NA-stimulated cAMP generating system is increased by treatments that reduce the synaptic availability of NA, such as 6-OHDA lesions (Vetulani et al., 1976b), reserpine (Dismukes & Daly, 1974), or prolonged beta-receptor blockade (Wolfe et al., 1978). In 1975, Vetulani and Sulser first demonstrated that chronically increasing the synaptic availability of NA, by means of MAOIs or tricyclic antidepressants, led to a profound decrease in beta-receptor sensitivity (Vetulani & Sulser, 1975; Vetulani et al., 1976a). The discovery was timely, coming as it did in the wake of the failure to demonstrate the antidepressant efficacy of DOPA (Section 9.3.1), the observation that iprindole was apparently without effect on NA transmission (Gluckman & Baum, 1969), the realization that the chronic time course of clinical antidepressant treatment might be a matter of consequence, and the report of Segal and co-workers that chronic DMI treatment decreased NA synthesis (Segal et al., 1974).

In addition to tricyclic antidepressants and MAOIs, the desensitization of beta-receptors appears to be a property shared by virtually all antidepressants. Electroconvulsive shock (Vetulani et al., 1976a) and lithium (Belmaker et al., 1983) reduce NA-stimulated cAMP production on chronic treatment, and atypical antidepressants for which this effect has been demonstrated include iprindole (Wolfe et al., 1978; Vetulani et al., 1976a), mianserin (Mishra et al., 1980), buproprion (Gandolfi et al., 1983), salbutamol (Lerer et al., 1981), and the specific 5-HT uptake inhibitor zimelicline (Mishra et al., 1980). In fact, two other specific 5-HT uptake inhibitors, fluoxetine and citalopram (see Section 16.3.4), are the only antidepressants that have been found not to reduce the activity of the NA-stimulated cAMP generating system (Hyttel et al., 1984; Mishra et al., 1979).

The decrease in the functional sensitivity of beta-receptors is accompanied, in most cases, by a reduction in cortical beta-receptor binding, which is usually measured using the specific beta-receptor ligand dihydroalprenolol (DHA). This effect was first reported for DMI, doxepin, and iprindole in 1977 (Banerjee et al., 1977), and it has subsequently been widely confirmed and extended to many other typical and atypical antidepressants (Bergstrom & Kellar, 1979b; Clements-Jewery, 1978; Cohen et al., 1982a; Maggi et al., 1980; Pandey et al., 1979b; Peroutka & Snyder, 1980a,b; Sugrue, 1982b). The list of active agents includes trazodone (Clements-Jewery, 1978), for which cAMP data have not been reported, and ECS (Bergstrom & Kellar, 1979a; Gillespie et al., 1979; Pandey et al., 1979b; Stanford & Nutt, 1982). Some studies have reported a decrease in beta-receptor binding following chronic lithium treatment (J. Rosenblatt et al., 1979; Treiser & Kellar, 1979), but this effect is controversial (Kafka et al., 1982; Maggi & Enna, 1980). One study has also reported a decrease in DHA binding following three day REM sleep deprivation (Mogilnicka et al., 1980), although a subsequent study using seven days of REM sleep deprivation failed to confirm this observation (Radulovacki & Micovic, 1982); the corresponding experiment using cAMP stimulation does not appear to have been carried out. In every case other than the controversial REM sleep deprivation, the decrease in beta-receptor binding was brought about by a decrease in the number of binding sites (B_{max}), with no change in their affinity for the ligand (K_D) (see Section 1.2.1).

A reduction in beta-receptor function, as measured by the cAMP technique, is not invariably accompanied by decreased beta-receptor binding. Mianserin decreases cAMP stimulation, but it does not appear to affect beta-receptor binding (Asakura et al., 1982; Clements-Jewery, 1978; Sellinger-Barnette et al., 1980), and similar effects are also seen with zimelidine and nisoxetine (Mishra et al., 1979, 1980; Sugrue, 1982b). These findings, taken together with the observation that the magnitude of the changes in beta-receptor binding (maximum 30–40%) is much smaller than the corresponding changes in cAMP stimulation, suggests that the receptor desensitization may involve an "uncoupling" of the receptor from its effector mechanism (Homburger et al., 1980; Su et al., 1980), which may or may not be followed by the disappearance of receptors.

Reduction of beta-receptor sensitivity is a relatively specific effect of chronic antidepressant treatment, which is not shared by other agents. Nisoxetine, which has not demonstrated antidepressant properties (Section 12.3.5), can apparently reduce cAMP stimulation (Mishra et al., 1979). So too can chlorpromazine (Schultz, 1976), though as noted earlier chlorpromazine does have antidepressant properties in some patients (Section 9.2.4). However, a wide range of other nonantidepressants, including diazepam, atropine, phenobarbital, haloperidol, and cocaine, have been reported not to affect DHA binding (Sellinger-Barnette et al., 1980).

In view of the dissociations between binding and functional effects seen with mianserin, zimelidine, and nisoxetine, further studies of the effects of nonantidepressants on the cAMP response would seem warranted.

In the majority of experiments, beta-receptor sensitivity has been studied in brain samples taken from cortex or limbic forebrain. Although very clear and robust decreases are observed in these areas after chronic antidepressant administration, the effect is less well established in other brain areas. Chronic ECS has not been found to change beta-receptor binding in hypothalamus or cerebellum, though in the same studies, reductions were observed in cortex and hippocampus (Kellar & Bergstrom, 1983; Stanford & Nutt, 1982). Similarly, although DMI reduced binding in all areas, tranylcypromine was effective in cortex but not in hippocampus (Stanford et al., 1983). These regional differences, which clearly require further investigation, may be related to the observation that only the $beta_1$-receptor subtype is affected by antidepressants, but the $beta_2$-receptor subtype is not (Minneman et al., 1982).

The effects of antidepressants on beta-receptors in the human brain have not yet been investigated; there are no obvious beta-receptor–mediated psychological effects, and in contrast to alpha-adrenergic, DA and 5-HT systems, there is little evidence for beta-receptor–mediated neuroendocrine responses. In the baboon, the beta-antagonist ICI 118,551 has been observed to increase plasma growth hormone levels. In keeping with the evidence of cAMP studies, a decreased GH response to this agent has been observed following three weeks of DMI treatment or after repeated ECS (McWilliam et al., 1982, 1983). In rats, salbutamol has sedative effects, which are probably mediated by beta-receptor stimulation (Mogilnicka, 1982); a recent study reported that salbutamol-induced sedation was blocked by chronic, but not acute treatment with tricyclic antidepressants or by the 5-HT uptake inhibiting antidepressants (see Section 16.3.4) citalopram and fluvoxamine (Przegalinski et al., 1983). It is possible that salbutamol-induced sedation could be developed as a technique for studying central beta-receptor function in people.

13.3.3.2. Mechanisms

It is generally assumed that beta-receptor desensitization by antidepressants is a form of adaptive regulation to increased intrasynaptic levels of NA. This presumption is supported by a variety of observations. First, 6-OHDA-induced destruction of presynaptic terminals has been shown to abolish the effects of DMI on cAMP stimulation and on beta-receptor binding (Janowsky et al., 1982; Schweitzer et al., 1979; Wolfe et al., 1978). Beta-receptor blockade with propranolol had the same effect (Okada et al., 1982; Wolfe et al., 1978), confirming the importance of beta-receptor stimulation. Second, beta-receptor desensitization shows specificity to the isomers of oxaprotiline: the (+)-isomer, which inhibits NA uptake, also induces subsensitivity of beta-receptors, whereas the (-)-isomer has neither effect (Delina-Stula et al., 1982; Mishra et al., 1982). And third, a number of studies have demonstrated a more rapid induction of beta-receptor desensitization by combining the administration of an antidepressant with an alpha-receptor antagonist, which further increases postsynaptic NA concentrations by blocking inhibitory presynaptic autoreceptors (Crews et al., 1981; Johnson et al., 1980; Kendall et al., 1982a; Wiech & Ursillo, 1980).

However, a recent study reported that although the alpha$_2$-antagonist yohimbine accelerated the desensitization of beta-receptors by imipramine and DMI, no interaction was observed with seven other antidepressants (Kendall et al., 1982a). In view of this finding, it seems unlikely that the potentiation of beta-receptor desensitization by yohimbine does operate simply by increasing postsynaptic NA concentrations. Indeed, it is clear that increased intrasynaptic levels of NA cannot explain all cases of desensitization. Iprindole, in particular, presents a problem, since intrasynaptic levels of NA are not increased by this agent. However, the desensitizing effects of iprindole, like those of DMI, do require an intact presynaptic terminal: 6-OHDA-induced destruction of NA terminals abolished the effects of iprindole on beta-receptor binding (Wolfe et al., 1978) and on cAMP stimulation (Janowsky et al., 1982). Electroconvulsive shock (ECS) apparently operates through a different mechanism, because in this case, intact presynaptic terminals are not a requirement (Vetulani et al., 1976b).

In addition to secreting classical neurotransmitters, most—perhaps all—nerves also contain, and probably secrete, peptides (Costa, 1982; Hokfelt et al., 1980). Although the functions of neuropeptides are largely unknown, the thesis that they act as "co-modulators," regulating the sensitivity of neurotransmitter receptors (Kumakura et al., 1980), has recently become fashionable (see, e.g., Barbacchia et al., 1983; Sulser et al., 1983). As yet there is no evidence to support or refute the hypothesis that neuropeptides are involved in the desensitization of beta-receptors by antidepressants.

Recent evidence suggests that 5-HT systems may play a role in the effects of antidepressants on beta-adrenergic receptors. In animals subjected to 5,7-dihydroxytryptamine (5,7-DHT)-induced destruction of 5-HT terminals, chronic administration of DMI failed to reduce the density of cortical beta-receptors (Brunello et al., 1982; Sulser et al., 1983). However, 5-HT lesions had no effect on the functional desensitization of beta-receptors by DMI, as assessed by cAMP stimulation (Sulser et al., 1983). These results support the view that beta-receptor desensitization is a two-stage process, of which the first stage is the "uncoupling" of the receptor from mechanisms mediating postsynaptic physiological changes (Homburger et al., 1980; Su et al., 1980). Because the effect of 5-HT lesions are on the "uncoupled" receptor rather than on the cAMP generating system, it is unclear whether this particular NA–5-HT interaction is of functional significance. The interpretation of these results is further complicated by the observations that 5-HT lesions reduced the binding of a beta-receptor agonist to cortical membranes (Manier et al., 1983) and also reduced the electrophysiological responsiveness of cortical cells to NA (Ferron et al., 1982).

Whatever the nature of the interaction, the dissociation observed after 5-HT lesions between the effects of antidepressants on beta-receptor binding and their effects on cAMP further underscores the unreliability of receptor binding studies as indices of physiological function.

13.3.3.3. Significance?

The effects of antidepressants on beta-receptors are very firmly established, and, without question, investigations into their mechanism have led to important advances in our understanding of the processes of adaptive regulation in the nervous system. However, if this is the mechanism of clinical action of antidepressants, as many people assume, then a major paradox must be resolved. The reformulated version of the catecholamine hypothesis of depression (Segal et al., 1974; Sulser, 1978, 1982) proposes that tricyclic antidepressants are effective in depression not because they increase NA transmission, as originally proposed by Schildkraut (1965) and others, but rather the reverse: they act by decreasing NA transmission. In order for this hypothesis to work, it is insufficient that the changes at beta-receptors merely compensate for antidepressant-induced increases; they must actually overcompensate. If they do not, then the net result will still be an increase in NA transmission rather than a decrease (Fig. 13.1). As Svensson and co-workers observed, "Although the reduced sensitivity . . . of central beta-receptor sites following antidepressant therapy may be of clinical significance, it seems hard to believe that the adaptive change . . . should over-ride its cause, the increased synaptic availability of NA" (Svensson et al., 1981, p. 74). It is only recently that this paradox has been recognized (Maas, 1980; Waldmeier, 1981; Willner & Montgomery, 1980a), and there have been few attempts to resolve it. Studies that potentially address the issue of the net effect of antidepressants on beta-adrenergic transmission are summarized in Table 13.4.

Since the activation of beta-receptors stimulates cAMP production, it is possible that a change in beta-adrenergic function might be reflected in a parallel change in basal cAMP level. Chronic antidepressant administration has not been found to alter basal cAMP levels, suggesting that there is no net change in beta-adrenergic function (Frazer & Mendels, 1977; Gandolfi et al., 1983; Janowsky et al., 1982; Vetulani et al., 1976a). However, the value of this approach is limited by the fact that a proportion (unknown) of cortical cAMP is produced at sites other than

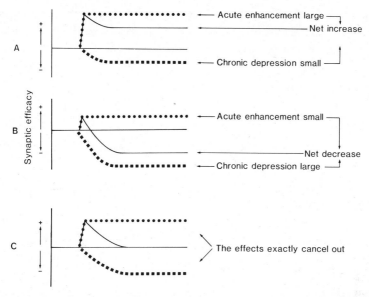

Fig. 13.1 Three models for the effects of tricyclic antidepressants on beta-adrenergic transmission. Model A corresponds to the original catecholamine hypothesis (Schildkraut, 1965), and Model B corresponds to the reformulated catecholamine hypothesis (Segal et al., 1974).

beta-receptors. A better technique would be to study the stimulation of cAMP production by beta-receptor activation under physiological conditions. One study has attempted to do this by examining the cAMP response in cortex, following electrical stimulation of the locus coeruleus. The response was reduced by DMI, but not by imipramine, iprindole, or nomifensine, even after prolonged treatment. Some suppression was seen with chlorimipramine and mianserin, but only at very high doses (Korf et al., 1979).

Another model that has been used to assess beta-adrenergic function *in vivo* is the pineal gland. Like cortical beta-receptors, pineal beta-receptors show a reduced cAMP response to the beta-receptor agonist isoprenaline after chronic administration of DMI or nialamide (Moyer et al., 1979, 1981). Pineal beta-receptors are innervated by fibers of the sympathetic nervous system arising in the superior cervical ganglion, and input through this system is increased by darkness (Brownstein & Axelrod, 1974). Accordingly, in one study, rats were maintained in constant light for a week, then switched briefly (one minute) into darkness. Acute DMI pretreatment caused a large increase in pineal cAMP formation, but chronic DMI treatment did not, thus demonstrating receptor subsensitivity (Heydorn et al., 1980). Unfortunately, the period of dark exposure was too brief to affect cAMP levels in control animals. Consequently, it is impossible to determine whether chronic DMI reduced syn-

TABLE 13.4. EFFECTS OF CHRONIC ANTIDEPRESSANT TREATMENT ON THE INTEGRATED FUNCTIONING OF BETA-ADRENERGIC SYNAPSES

Model	Agent[a]	Effect	Reference
Biochemical Studies			
cAMP in brain:			
Basal level	DMI	=	Frazer & Mendels, 1977
	BUP	=	Gandolfi et al., 1983
	DMI, IP	=	Janowsky et al., 1982
	CMI, IMI, IP, NOM	=	Korf et al., 1979
	DMI, ECS, IP	=	Vetulani et al., 1976a
Response to locus coeruleus	DMI	↓	Korf et al., 1979
stimulation	CMI, IMI, IP, MIA, NOM	=[b]	
cAMP in pineal:			
Basal level	DMI	↑	Heydorn et al., 1980
	DMI	↑	Moyer et al., 1979
	DMI	↑	B. Weiss et al., 1982
Response to dark exposure	DMI	?	Heydorn et al., 1980
Response to electrical stimulation	DMI	=	B. Weiss et al., 1982
Pineal melatonin:			
Response to dark exposure	DMI	=	Cowen et al., 1983
	DMI, NIA	↓	Heydorn et al., 1982
Response to antidepressant	CMI	↑	Wirz-Justice et al., 1980
Basal secretion	DMI	↑[c]	Thompson et al., 1983
Electrophysiological Studies			
Basal firing rate:			
Cerebellum	DMI	↓[d]	Schultz et al., 1981
Hippocampus	DMI	↑[d]	Huang, 1979a
Response to iontophoretic NA:			
Cerebellum	DMI	↓	Schultz et al., 1981
Cingulate cortex	OX	↓	Delina-Stula et al., 1982
	CMI, DMI, MAP, TRAN	↓	Olpe & Schellenberg, 1980
Hippocampus	ECS	=	De Montigny, 1980
	CMI, IMI	=	De Montigny & Aghajanian, 1978
	CMI, ZIM	=	De Montigny et al., 1981a
	AMI, CMI, DMI, IMI, IP	=	Gallager & Bunney, 1979
Response to locus coeruleus stimulation (hippocampus)	DMI	=	Huang, 1979a
Behavioral Studies			
Resistance to extinction			
Eyeblink conditioning (rabbits)	DMI	=	Montgomery & Willner, 1980
Lever pressing, runway	DMI	=	Willner et al., 1981a

TABLE 13.4. (Continued)

Model	Agent[a]	Effect	Reference
Amphetamine anorexia	DMI	=	Willner & Montgomery, 1980b, 1981
	DMI, IP	=	Willner et al., 1984
	MIA	↓	Willner et al., 1984
Thiopentone sleeping time	AMI, CMI, DIB, DMI, DOTH, DOX, FLU, IP, MIA, MAP, OP, VIL, ZIM	↑ [d,e]	Mason & Angel, 1983, 1984
	BUP, NOM, TOF, TRAZ	=	

[a] Abbreviations as in Table 13.1, plus BUP: buproprion; DIB: dibenzepin; DOTH: dothiepin; DOX: doxepin; FLU: fluoxetine; MAP: maprotiline; NIA: nialamide; OX: oxaprotiline; TOF: tofenacin; ZIM: zimelidine.

[b] Some suppression with CMI and MIA at high doses.

[c] This study was carried out in depressed patients; all other studies used rats, except Montgomery and Willner, 1980 (rabbits).

[d] NA has inhibitory effect, so an increase implies a decrease in adrenergic transmission, and vice versa.

[e] Forty-eight hour delay between final treatment and testing.

aptic function below control levels. A second experiment was more successful in this respect. Pineal cAMP formation was studied in response to electrical stimulation of the superior cervical ganglion; the response was greatly enhanced by acute DMI pretreatment, and repeated DMI treatment returned the response to the level seen in control animals (B. Weiss et al., 1982). This result suggests that receptor subsensitivity simply compensates for an antidepressant-induced enhancement of input, but does not overcompensate. In all of these studies, basal cAMP levels were increased by DMI on acute or chronic administration (Heydorn et al., 1980; Moyer et al., 1979; B. Weiss et al., 1982).

One consequence of cAMP formation in the pineal is the synthesis of melatonin, which results in a dose-dependent fashion from the stimulation of beta-receptors. Pineal melatonin synthesis has also been used to estimate beta-adrenergic function. One study reported that the nighttime rise in melatonin was reduced by administration of DMI twice a day for seven days (Heydorn et al., 1982). However, DMI once daily for 10 days did not produce this effect in a second study (Cowen et al., 1983). In a third study, it was observed that a variety of antidepressants, administered in the middle of the light phase, elevated melatonin levels; chronic treatment with chlorimipramine reduced the effect but did not abolish or reverse it (Wirz-Justice et al., 1980). A fourth study found that in depressed patients, melatonin secretion levels were elevated after one week of DMI administration, and no reduction was seen in two further weeks of treatment (Thompson et al., 1983).

Overall, there is very little in the biochemical data to suggest that beta-adrenergic function is altered markedly by chronic antidepressant treatment. Electrophysiological studies, though slightly more complex, lead to a similar conclusion. After chronic antidepressant administration, a decreased sensitivity to iontophoretically applied NA has been observed in cingulate cortex (Delina-Stula et al., 1982; Olpe & Schellenberg, 1980) and in cerebellar Purkinje cells (Schultz et al., 1981). However, the baseline firing rate of Purkinje cells was reduced by some 50–70% (Schultz et al., 1981). Since NA is inhibitory on Purkinje cells, this represents an increase in adrenergic function. Given this change, it is difficult to conclude that the reduced sensitivity to NA represents a decrease in synaptic transmission; the change in baseline firing makes it almost impossible to interpret the reduced effect of NA. No baseline data were reported in the cingulate cortex studies.

Chronic DMI treatment has been reported to increase the baseline firing rate of hippocampal cells (Huang, 1979a). This finding would appear to indicate a decrease in beta-adrenergic function were it not for the fact that four other studies have found that the response of hippocampal cells to iontophoretically applied NA was unchanged by chronic administration of DMI, various other tricyclics, iprindole, zimelidine, or ECS (De Montigny, 1980; De Montigny & Aghajanian, 1978; De Montigny et al., 1981a; Gallager & Bunney, 1979). This paradox was resolved by a subsequent experiment in which it was found that changes in the firing rate of hippocampal cells after administration of DMI for varying lengths of time were an exact reflection of changes in the firing rate of locus coeruleus cells (Huang et al., 1980). The implication is that, contrary to appearances, chronic antidepressant treatment did not change the functioning of hippocampal synapses, and, indeed, despite changes in basal firing rate, the proportional reduction of firing in response to stimulation of the locus coeruleus was unaltered by chronic DMI (Huang, 1979a).

There have been very few behavioral studies of antidepressant effects on beta-adrenergic synapses, primarily because there are no behavioral models that unequivocally reflect beta-receptor stimulation. One attempt to address this question utilized the fact that lesions of the dorsal NA bundle prolong resistance to extinction (the dorsal bundle extinction effect; see Section 11.2.2.1). Because this effect is probably mediated by the NA projection to the hippocampus, which involves mainly beta-receptors, a decrease in beta-adrenergic function should result in resistance to extinction. In three different behavioral paradigms, chronic administration of DMI did increase resistance to extinction. However, this effect was observed only if the tests were carried out following withdrawal from the drug; no changes were seen during the course of drug treatment (Montgomery & Willner, 1980; Willner et al., 1981a). Although there is some question as to whether these effects are actually mediated by the dorsal bundle (Willner & Towell, 1982a), the results suggest that the slow development of receptor sensitization during antidepressant treatment simply compensates for the acute NA-enhancing effects of the drug, and it is unmasked when the drug is withdrawn.

A second attempt to address this question behaviorally was based on the observation that manipulations of central beta-adrenergic transmission have an inverse effect on the duration of thiopentone anesthesia. With some exceptions, chronic administration of a variety of typical and atypical antidepressants (see Table 13.4) increased thiopentone anesthesia, indicating that functional transmission through beta-receptors was reduced (Mason & Angel, 1983, 1984). Unfortunately, in these studies behavioral testing was carried out 48 hours after the final antidepressant treatment, so it is unclear whether the results represent chronic effects of the drugs or withdrawal effects similar to those observed by Willner and co-workers (1981; Montgomery & Willner, 1980).

A third behavior that appears to be mediated by beta-receptors is the anorexic effect of low doses of amphetamine (Leibowitz, 1975; Leibowitz & Rossakis, 1978b; Samanin et al., 1977). Again, attenuation of this effect has been observed during withdrawal from DMI or iprindole, but not during the course of chronic treatment (Willner & Montgomery, 1980b, 1981; Willner et al., 1984). Interpretation of these results is complicated by the fact that DMI and iprindole inhibit the metabolism of amphetamine. Mianserin, which does not have this effect, did attenuate amphetamine anorexia during the course of chronic treatment (Willner et al., 1984), suggesting a decrease in beta-adrenergic function. However, since an alpha-adrenergic system stimulates feeding (Section 11.2.2.4), changes in amphetamine anorexia might equally well be caused by an increase in alpha-adrenergic function. This issue has not yet been resolved.

Taken together, the simplex conclusion to be drawn from the biochemical, electrophysiological, and behavioral studies of beta-adrenergic function during chronic antidepressant treatment is that changes in receptor function act simply to restore the status quo. There is no compelling evidence that desensitization of beta-receptors leads to a decrease in the integrated functioning of beta-adrenergic synapses.

It is possible to shed some further light on the relevance of beta-receptor desensitization to the clinical effects of antidepressants by examining the relative potencies of antidepressant drugs in the two situations, as described in Chapter 6 (Willner, 1984c). The approximate clinical doses for a variety of antidepressant drugs were given in Table 6.1. A recent review (Enna et al., 1981) summarized data on a variety of drugs, of which trazodone, which is one of the least potent drugs clinically, had the greatest effect on beta-receptor binding. Studies carried out under comparable conditions (three to four weeks treatment at 10 mg/kg; binding assayed in cortical samples) show the following order of potency: trazodone > DMI = doxepin > imipramine > amitriptyline > iprindole (data

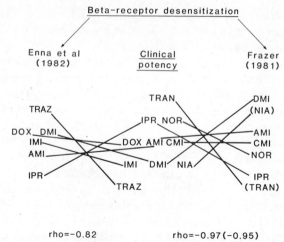

Fig. 13.2 The relative clinical potency of antidepressant drugs compared with their desensitizing effect on cortical beta-receptors (modified from Willner, 1984c). Clinical potencies are taken from Table 6.1. In the study of Frazer (1981), the drugs in parentheses were
administered at doses different from the other drugs. AMI, amitriptyline; CMI, chlorimipramine; DMI, desmethylimipramine; DOX, doxepin; IMI, imipramine; IPR, iprindole; NIA,
nialamide; NOR, nortriptyline; TRAN, tranylcypromine; TRAZ, trazodone.

from Clements-Jewery, 1978; Maggi et al., 1980; Peroutka & Snyder,
1980a). As shown in Fig. 13.2, comparison with the order of clinical potencies reveals a significant inverse relationship (rho $= -0.82, p < 0.05$).
Another study, using a shorter treatment time (16 days), reported the
following order of potency for the reduction of beta-receptor binding: DMI
> nialamide > amitriptyline > chlorimipramine > nortriptyline > iprin-
dole > tranylcypromine (Frazer, 1981; Sellinger-Barnette et al., 1980).
Again, there is a highly significant negative correlation with clinical
potency (rho $= -0.97$, $p < 0.01$); the relationship is hardly altered by
removing from this series nialamide and tranylcypromine, which were
administered at doses different from the other drugs (rho $= -0.95$).
   Clearly, the size of the effect on beta-receptors caused by a fixed dose
of different antidepressants is not the ideal quantity to compare with the
different dosages producing the same level of clinical effect; unfortunately, the information available in the literature is as yet insufficient
to support a more appropriate correlation. A second problem is that the
studies from which the above data were drawn measured beta-receptors
using the ligand [^{3}H]DHA, which labels both beta$_1$-receptors which are
desensitized by antidepressants, and beta$_2$-receptors, which apparently
are not (Minneman et al., 1982). Nevertheless, it is difficult to see how
taking either of these points fully into account could turn the negative
correlations shown in Fig. 13.2 into the positive correlations required by
the hypothesis that antidepressants exert their clinical actions by desensitizing beta-receptors.

In fact, there are a number of additional observations which suggest that far from alleviating depression, a decrease in beta-receptor function may actually be harmful. For example, physostigmine, a drug which amplifies the synaptic effects of ACh causes a rapid desensitization of cortical beta receptors (Groom et al., 1983). However, far from being an antidepressant, physostigmine has severe dysphoric effects (Janowsky et al., 1973a,b; see Chapter 14).

Recent studies of the effects of steroid hormones on beta-receptors also present a picture exactly opposite to that which would be predicted from the effects of antidepressants on beta-receptors. Depression is two to three times more frequent in women than in men (Weissman & Paykel, 1974), and symptoms of depression are experienced by 50% of women taking oral contraceptives (Parry & Rush, 1979). However, beta-receptor responsiveness is lower in females than in males (Sulser & Mishra, 1982; Wagner & Davies, 1980), is increased by ovariectomy (Wagner & Davies, 1980), and is decreased by estradiol (Biegon et al., 1982; Wagner et al., 1979). Similarly, depressive episodes are accompanied by abnormally elevated pituitary–adrenal activity (Carroll, 1982) and cortisol levels (Carroll et al., 1976), and there is an extremely high incidence of depression in Cushing's disease (Kelly et al., 1980). It is possible that high cortisol levels may even be of etiological significance in depression, because depressions associated with Cushing's syndrome were relieved by treatments that lowered cortisol levels (Kelly et al., 1983). However, it has been observed that NA-stimulated cAMP generation was decreased by cortisol (Mobley and Sulser, 1980a,b) and by ACTH (Kendall et al., 1982a), and was increased by adrenalectomy (Minneman et al., 1982; Mobley & Sulser, 1980a,b). Although ACTH did not alter the number of beta-receptors, ACTH was actually more effective than imipramine in reducing beta-receptor function, as assessed by NA-stimulated cAMP generation; no further reductions were produced by combining hormone and drug treatment (Kendall et al., 1982a). Indeed, when these effects of cortisol and ACTH are taken into account, it is even questionable whether antidepressants do in fact desensitize central beta-receptors in depressed people.

The results indicate that the more potently a drug desensitizes beta-receptors, the less potent it will be clinically. This finding, taken together with the discrepant effects of steroid hormones, strongly suggests that the desensitization of cortical beta-receptors by antidepressant drugs is not responsible for their therapeutic effects.

13.4 CONCLUSIONS: NA, DEPRESSION, AND ANTIDEPRESSANTS

With hindsight, the widespread belief that beta-receptor desensitization is responsible for the clinical effects of antidepressants can be seen to have arisen from two sources: from the robustness and generality of the effect and from its historical priority, by some three to five years, over other slowly developing effects of antidepressants which were described subsequently. However, the appeal of this hypothesis has been based entirely on a circular argument: desensitizing beta-receptors is something that antidepressants do, so that is what makes them antidepressants. In fact, when an attempt is made to consider how this effect is integrated with the various other effects of chronic antidepressant treatment to influence the overall level of transmission through the beta-adrenergic system, there is little evidence that changes in beta-receptors represent anything more than a homeostatic mechanism which counteracts the NA-enhancing effects of antidepressants.

The situation at alpha-receptors is rather different. The response of postsynaptic alpha$_1$-receptors increases during chronic treatment with a wide variety of antidepressants (Section 13.3.2). One particularly striking aspect of these results is that the effect is reliably seen with amitriptyline, which on acute treatment is an alpha-receptor blocker (Section 13.1.2). Taken together with the observation that in animal studies, NA turnover is either increased or unchanged (Section 13.2.2), the increase in alpha-receptor sensitivity means an overall increase in the integrated functioning of the alpha-adrenergic system.

This conclusion is fully consistent with the animal models reviewed in Chapter 11, and it allows a clear judgment to be made as to the relative merits of the two opposing catecholamine hypotheses of depression. As chronic treatment with antidepressants increases alpha-adrenergic function, the pharmacological evidence strongly supports the original version of the catecholamine hypothesis as proposed by Schildkraut (1965): that depression is associated with a reduction of transmission through NA (or more specifically, alpha-adrenergic) synapses.

As the desensitization of beta-receptors by antidepressants does not appear to be responsible for their clinical effects, the pharmacological evidence does not support the reformulated version of the catecholamine hypothesis (Segal et al., 1974).

fourteen

ACETYLCHOLINE AND DEPRESSION

Several years before attention was focused on the catecholamines and 5-HT, by the reports that depression could be induced by reserpine and by the discovery of antidepressant drugs, it was observed that the cholinergic agonist physostigmine induced a range of depressive symptoms, including fatigue, retardation, social withdrawal, and depressed mood (Rowntree et al., 1950). Conversely, the possible antidepressant properties of the cholinergic antagonist atropine were noted as early as 1932 (Hoch & Mauss, 1932).

A number of studies confirmed these observations, and in the early 1970s, Janowsky and co-workers developed a hypothesis that integrated this literature with the burgeoning work on noradrenergic mechanisms. The initial observation was that in rats, the stimulant effects of methylphenidate, which is presumed to act via catecholaminergic mechanisms, were blocked by physostigmine. It was also found that in psychiatric patients, physostigmine blocked the stimulant and euphoric effects of methylphenidate; conversely, the anergic and depressant effects of physostigmine were reversed by methylphenidate. It was therefore proposed that mood was regulated by the balance of activity in cholinergic and catecholaminergic systems, with depression resulting from a cholinergic predominance, and mania from an adrenergic predominance: the cholinergic–adrenergic balance hypothesis (Janowsky et al., 1972a,b, 1973b).

This chapter reviews recent work relating ACh to mood regulation: the role of ACh in animal models of depression and the functions of brain cholinergic systems, the status of cholinergic transmission in depression, the effects of cholinergic agonists and antagonists on mood, and the effects of antidepressants on cholinergic transmission. The relationship between ACh and other neurotransmitter systems is considered in more detail in Chapter 19.

14.1 ACETYLCHOLINE AND BEHAVIOR

14.1.1. Animal Models of Depression

As discussed below, studies of the behavioral functions of central cholinergic functions present an extremely confusing picture. Despite this disarray, which presumably reflects the anatomical complexity and functional diversity of cholinergic systems, a consistent picture emerges from studies of the role of cholinergic mechanisms in animal models of depression. In almost every case that has been studied, "depressive" phenomena in animal models are potentiated by acetylcholine and are reversed by antagonists at muscarinic cholinergic receptors.

An involvement of cholinergic mechanisms in "learned helplessness" phenomena (Section 7.2.1) is suggested by the observation that levels of ACh in various forebrain areas, and also ACh synthesis and release, were increased following exposure to inescapable stressors of various kinds (Aprison et al., 1975; Finkelstein et al., 1984; Karczmar et al., 1973; Romano & Shih, 1983). These changes were not seen, however, following escapable stress (Karczmar et al., 1973). The cholinomimetic agent physostigmine has been found to mimic the effect of inescapable shock on subsequent escape performance (Anisman et al., 1981), and, conversely, learned helplessness was reversed by the anticholinergic drug scopolamine (Anisman et al., 1979b, 1981). A similar reversal of "behavioral despair" (Section 7.2.2) by anticholinergics has also been reported (Browne, 1979). In animals exposed to chronic intermittent stress (Section 7.2.3), scopolamine did not restore to normal their deficient passive avoidance learning, but it did reverse the elevation of plasma corticosteroids (Katz & Hersh, 1981). In this study, scopolamine was administered chronically, which raises the possibility that neurochemical adaptation might be responsible for the failure to reverse the behavioral deficit.

As discussed in Chapter 7, exposure to uncontrollable stress in either the learned helplessness or the chronic intermittent stress paradigm produces deficits in rewarded behaviors. The effects of cholinergic agents have not been examined in the specific reward paradigms that have been advanced as animal models of depression (Section 7.2.6). However, in other paradigms, responding for brain-stimulation reward is suppressed by cholinomimetic agents (Stark & Boyd, 1963; Olds & Ho, 1973) and is enhanced by anticholinergics (Pradhan & Dutta, 1971).

Increased cholinergic activity also appears to play a role in muricidal behavior (Section 6.3.4). Increased levels of ACh have been found in the amygdala of muricidal rats (Ebel et al., 1973), and the acetylcholinesterase inhibitor physostigmine and other cholinomimetic agents are found to induce muricide in animals that do not already show this behavior or to potentiate muricide in those that do (Eichelman, 1979). Conversely, muricide was suppressed by anticholinergics (Horovitz et al., 1966; Smith et al., 1970). In a related model, systemic administration of the anticholinergic drug atropine did not affect the passive avoidance deficit induced by olfactory bulbectomy (Section 6.5.4), but application of atropine to the medial amygdala did block this effect (Lloyd et al., 1982). Conversely, infusions of the cholinomimetic agent carbachol into the medial amygdala of normal rats produced a passive avoidance deficit similar to that of olfactory bulbectomized animals, which could be reversed by atropine (Broekkamp et al., 1982).

It is striking that unlike either the catecholamines (Chapters 8 and 11) or 5-HT (Chapter 15), elevation of cholinergic activity is seen both in the models in which behavioral output is decreased and also in the bulbectomy and muricide models, in which behavioral output is increased. It might also be added that anticholinergic drugs are effective in a number of models that are not being considered in detail on account of their low validity, including potentiation of the stimulant effects of DOPA (Sigg & Hill, 1967; Section 6.3.1), potentiation of yohimbine toxicity (Malick, 1981; Section 6.3.2), and reserpine reversal (Lapin, 1967; Section 6.5.1). In addition, ACh appears to be involved in the control of circadian rhythms. Animal models based on abnormalities of circadian rhythms have not been extensively studied, and the role of ACh, or, indeed, of any other neurochemical systems, in adaptation to changes in the light–dark cycle (Section 6.5.7) has not been investigated specifically. However, these models involve a phase advance of diurnal rhythms (Goodwin et al., 1982b); in endogenous depression, phase advance of diurnal rhythms is associated with an early onset of REM sleep (Kupfer, 1976; see Section 3.3.2), which is known to be controlled by cholinergic cells in the lower brain stem (Hobson et al., 1975; McCarley, 1982; see also Section 19.2.2).

This commonality across the varying types of model raises the possibility that cholinergic changes might underlie the other neurochemical changes seen in animal models of depression. As a counterweight to this suggestion, it must be added that in most cases, the cholinergic involvement in animal models is rather less straightforward than one might wish. As noted above, scopolamine reversed the hormonal effects of chronic unpredictable stress, but failed to reverse the behavioral sequelae (Katz & Hersh, 1981). Anticholinergic drugs also appear to work differently from antidepressants in the "behavioral despair" model: whereas

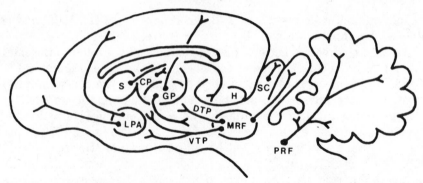

Fig. 14.1. The major cholinergic pathways of the rat forebrain. CP, caudate-putamen (striatum); DTP, dorsal tegmental pathway; GP, globus pallidus (pallidum); H, hippocampus; LPA, lateral preoptic area (substantia innominata); MRF, midbrain reticular formation; PRF, pontine reticular formation; S, septum; SC, superior colliculus; VTP, ventral tegmental pathway. From P. R. Lewis and C. C. D. Shute, Cholinergic pathways in the CNS. In L. L. Iversen, S. D. Iversen, and S. H. Snyder, eds. *Handbook of Psychopharmacology*, Vol. 9. Plenum Press, New York, 1978. Reprinted by permission of the authors and Plenum Press.

antidepressants delay the onset of immobility, anticholinergics reduce immobility by an indiscriminate stimulation of locomotor activity (Kitada et al., 1981; see Section 7.2.2). Anticholinergics increase responding for brain stimulation reward, but they have not been tested in the specific paradigms in which antidepressants have been shown to improve performance (Section 7.2.6). It is possible that the increased response rate simply reflects locomotor stimulation; techniques are available to investigate this issue (Liebman, 1983), but as yet the effect of anticholinergics in these paradigms has not been examined.

This analysis suggests that, in the case of the models in which motor output is diminished, the role of ACh could be explained in terms of locomotor stimulation. Models in which motor output increases are also problematic. In the muricide model, the suppressive effect of atropine was only seen at doses that also impaired motor coordination (Horovitz et al., 1966), though the potentiating effect of cholinergic agonists is not so easily explained away. Finally, as noted above, the effects of cholinergic agents on olfactory bulbectomized animals are only seen when the drugs are applied directly to the medial amygdala.

14.1.2. Cholinergic Pathways and Behavior

As may be seen in Fig. 14.1, the distribution of ACh pathways in the brain is rather complex. However, two major pathways may be delineated. The first of these is in many respects synonymous with the classical ascending reticular activating system. The cholinergic reticular system originates in the midbrain reticular formation (MRF). One branch, the dorsal tegmental pathway, innervates the tectum and thalamus; the other, the ventral tegmental pathway, innervates first the basal forebrain, and then the cerebral cortex, via a synapse in the lateral preoptic area (substantia innominata) or in the ventral part of the globus pallidus. The cell bodies of the ventral branch are located mainly in the midbrain dopaminergic nuclei. The second major cholinergic pathway, sometimes known as the cholinergic limbic system, originates in the nuclei of the medial septum and diagonal band, and innervates the hippocampus. In addition to these systems, there are also cholinergic cells in the pontine reticular formation (see also Section 11.3), a cholinergic pathway that descends from the globus pallidus to the thalamus, and an intrinsic cholinergic innervation of the striatum. To complicate matters further, there are also dense noncholinergic connections between many of the areas that receive a cholinergic input (Lewis & Shute, 1978).

It does seem likely, however, that in many instances, activation of the two major cholinergic pathways, at least, may be coordinated, possibly by means of a noncholinergic input from the lateral preoptic area to the medial septum. Electrical stimulation of the MRF leads to the release of ACh in the cerebral cortex (Szerb, 1967), accompanied by EEG desynchronization, the hallmark of cortisal arousal. The arousal response appears to be mediated by the cholinergic reticular system, since cholinergic agonists also produce cortical arousal, whereas antimuscarinic drugs such as atropine and scopolamine produced a long-lasting EEG synchronization (Marczynski & Burns, 1976; Vanderwolf et al., 1975). Electrical stimulation of the MRF also produces a characteristic pattern of synchronized activity in the hippocampus, known as the theta rhythm (Maynert et al., 1975). The generation of low frequency theta waves by electrical stimulation of the medial septal area may be blocked by atropine; hence it appears to depend on the activation of the cholinergic septohippocampal pathway. Higher frequencies of theta, however, are atropine insensitive (Vanderwolf et al., 1975, 1978). The lower frequencies of theta, which are atropine sensitive, are generated when an animal is in a state of alert immobility (Gray, 1982; O'Keefe & Nadel, 1978; Vanderwolf et al., 1975, 1978), such as when behavior has been interrupted by a stimulus signifying the imminent delivery of an electric shock (Whishaw, 1972; Graeff et al., 1980); higher frequencies of theta, which are atropine-insensitive, appear to be associated with active movement (O'Keefe & Nadel, 1978; Vanderwolf et al., 1975, 1978).

It would therefore appear that following the presentation of a novel, significant, or otherwise interesting event, both the cholinergic reticular system and the cholinergic limbic system may be activated to produce, respectively, low voltage, desynchronized activity in the cortical EEG, and low frequency hippocampal theta. At other times, activity in the two systems may be dissociated, as when an animal is awake (cortical arousal) and engaged in active movement (high frequency, atropine-resistant hippocampal theta). Both systems appear to be active during REM sleep, which is characterized, inter alia, by cortical arousal, hippocampal theta, and behavioral inhibition (O'Keefe & Nadel, 1978; Steriade & Hobson, 1976, Vanderwolf et al., 1975, 1978). The fact that cholinergic cells in the pontine reticular formation show their highest activity during alert waking and REM sleep, with very low activity during quiet waking and non-REM sleep (Steriade & Hobson, 1976; Vertes, 1977), combined with the demonstration that REM sleep may be induced by cholinergic stimulation of the pontine reticular formation (Jouvet, 1975; Karczmar & Dun, 1978), suggests strongly that the activity of pontine ACh cells may be linked with that of forebrain cholinergic systems, probably via ascending noncholinergic cells within the reticular formation.

In view of the extent and complexity of the cholinergic innervation, it is hardly surprising that it is extremely difficult to construct generalizations about the behavioral functions "the ACh system," and such generalizations tend to be hedged around with "ifs" and "buts" (see Anisman & Bignami, 1978; Bignami & Michaluk, 1978). There is a broad consensus, however, that the behavioral effects of cholinergic activation are primarily inhibitory. Behavior suppressed by a variety of contingencies, including nonreward, a conditioned fear stimulus, and the threat of punishment, is usually restored by centrally acting anticholinergics; these effects are not seen with anticholinergics that fail to cross the blood–brain barrier (Anisman, 1975; Bignami, 1976; Carlton & Markiewicz, 1971). As intimated above, however, the nature of the suppressed response and the signaling conditions used may greatly influence the drug effect (Frontali et al., 1976; Bignami & Michaluk, 1978). For example, scopolamine reinstates a habituated exploratory response, while having no effect on a habituated startle response (Williams et al., 1974). These ramifications will not be discussed in detail; the digression would not provide further clues relating ACh to depression.

The predominant behavior-inhibitory effects of cholinergic activation are consistent with the effects of cholinergic agents in the learned helplessness, "behavioral despair" and self-stimulation paradigms, as described in the previous section: behavior in each of these models is increased by anticholinergics. It is difficult to determine the locus of these effects, however, since motor behavior is arrested by the application of cholinergic agonists to a variety of forebrain sites. These include the septal area, caudate nucleus, and central gray; cholinergic stimulation of the caudate nucleus and globus pallidus may also produce catalepsy (Karczmar & Dun, 1978). All of these sites may be involved, since, as noted above, arousing events activate a variety of cholinergic pathways.

The suppression of hyperactivity in muricidal or olfactory bulbectomized rats by the application of anticholinergics to the medial amygdala may be explained by the observation that in contrast to other forebrain ACh pathways, cholinergic systems in the amygdala have excitatory behavioral effects. Cholinergic stimulation of the amygdala has been shown to restore behavior suppressed by a conditioned fear stimulus and to disrupt passive avoidance (Goddard, 1969), whereas anticholinergics applied to the amygdala failed to disinhibit punished responding (Margules, 1971). There are other similar observations. The effects of cholinergic agents in the amygdala are usually the opposite of those seen on systemic administration. The cholinergic input to the amygdala arises from the substantia innominata (Nagai et al., 1982), and it therefore is a part of the cholinergic reticular activating system. Since activation of this system is frequently accompanied by behavioral inhibition, it seems likely that the behavioral consequences of activating the cholinergic input to the amygdala are usually masked by the concurrent activation of other cholinergic pathways.

14.1.3 Acetylcholine and Stress

As noted in Section 14.1.1, forebrain cholinergic systems are activated by inescapable stressors. These effects resemble the NA depletion associated with inescapable shock (Anisman & Sklar, 1979; Cassens et al., 1980), in that increased ACh synthesis could be reinstated by the presentation of a stimulus which had previously been paired with shock (Hintgen et al., 1976). There are cells in the pontine reticular formation that are activated by a stimulus previously paired with shock, but not by a stimulus paired with food (Vertes & Miller, 1976). These cells are probably cholinergic (see Section 11.3.2) and so may be the point of entry from which a stimulus paired with shock activates the diffuse ascending cholinergic reticular system.

Activation of the cholinergic system by stress has a number of important consequences. One is the release of ACTH (see Section 14.2.1). In addition to stimulating the adrenal cortex, ACTH also acts on the brain, and a variety of behavioral effects have been described for analogues of ACTH which are devoid of adrenocorticotrophic activity. Lesions of the parafascicular nucleus of the thalamus, which receives a heavy cholinergic input, have been found to abolish some of the behavioral effects of ACTH and related peptides (Greidanus et al., 1974), which suggests that ACTH may function in a positive feedback role to facilitate cholinergic transmission. Corticosteroids also appear to enhance cholinergic function, particularly in the hippocampus (see Section 19.2.3). It is possible that these ACTH- and corticosteroid-mediated positive feedback effects could be implicated in the paradoxical finding that chronic stress increased the hippocampal release of ACh, while simultaneously increasing the number of cholinergic receptors (Finkelstein et al., 1984; Gilad et al., 1983).

Another consequence of stress-induced activation of the cholinergic reticular system, which is of particular interest, is a decrease in sensitivity to painful stimulation. A variety of stressors reduce pain sensitivity (see Sections 15.2.3 and 18.1.1.1), and some stress-induced analgesias may be antagonized by muscarinic receptor antagonists (Romano & King, 1980; Weinberg et al., 1981). Systemic or intraventricular administration of cholinergic agonists also reduces pain sensitivity. Analgesic effects are seen with local application to hindbrain, midbrain, or hypothalamic sites (but not to striatum or hippocampus), and are blocked by antimuscarinic drugs (Harris et al., 1969; Ireson, 1970; Karczmar & Dun, 1978; Metys et al., 1969; Pedigo et al., 1975).

The system that has received the greatest attention in relation to stress-induced analgesia is the endogenous opiate system, which is discussed in more detail in the Chapter 18. It has been suggested that cholinergic agonists might produce analgesia by stimulating the release of endogenous opiates (Pedigo & Dewey, 1981). However, opiate antagonists do not completely block the analgesic effect of cholinergic agonists, and in some cases there was no block at all (Katayama et al., 1982; Koehn et al., 1980; Pedigo et al., 1975; Romano & King, 1981). Furthermore, cholinergic analgesia was unaffected by the inactivation of serotonergic neurotransmission (Koehn & Karczmar, 1977), which appears to be crucial for opiate analgesia (see Section 15.2.2). Cholinergic analgesia is therefore not identical to opiate analgesia. On the other hand, under some circumstances, opiate analgesia does depend on a cholinergic link (MacLennan et al., 1983; Weinberg et al., 1981). As discussed below (Section 17.2.1), cholinergic stimulation causes the release of ACTH; suppression of ACTH release by dexamethasone has been found to attenuate both opioid (MacLennan et al., 1982, 1983) and cholinergic (Romano & King, 1982) analgesias.

As observed earlier (Section 14.1.1), if it is possible to escape from stress, the cholinergic system may not be activated (Karczmar et al., 1973), which suggests that failure to cope may be the factor responsible for switching on the system. In keeping with this conclusion, it has been reported that increases in ACh synthesis in the midbrain occurred at times when avoidance performance was declining (Aprison et al., 1968; Aprison & Hintgen, 1970). Curiously, activation of the cholinergic system may be delayed for a period of hours after the termination of the stress (Saito et al., 1976; Kajaczowska, 1975), rather than occurring during the period of exposure to the stressor, when, presumably, failure to cope would become apparent to the animal. Furthermore, these delayed increases in cholinergic activity are also apparent in animals which have coped successfully with the stress. Kamin (1957) first demonstrated, and many other workers subsequently confirmed, that the speed of relearning of an active avoidance response is a function of the time that intervenes between training and retraining. Specifically, performance is poor at intermediate retention intervals of 1 to 6 hours but good at shorter or longer intervals. The deterioration in performance at intermediate retention intervals is caused by an increase in freezing, which interferes with active avoidance behavior (Anisman & Waller, 1973a,b). A number of studies have shown that the "Kamin effect" may be prevented by centrally acting anticholinergic drugs (but not by anticholinergics which fail to cross the blood–brain barrier) (Anisman, 1973; Anisman & Kokkinidis, 1974; Carlton, 1969; Thompson & Nielson, 1972). Septal lesions have also been found to abolish the "Kamin effect" (Anisman & Kokkinidis, 1974), implicating the septohippocampal cholinergic pathway.

These results suggest that cholinergic activation is not related to failure to cope with stress specifically, but rather to the aftermath of attempting to cope. Since active coping attempts involve the participation of noradrenergic systems (Section 11.3), this "cholinergic rebound" (Manto, 1967; Carlton, 1969), fits very closely within the framework of Janowsky's adrenergic–cholinergic balance hypothesis (see Chapter 19).

14.2 CHOLINERGIC FUNCTION IN DEPRESSION

The evidence from animal models of depression, together with the evidence that cholinergic systems are activated by stress and in the aftermath of stress, provides good grounds for predicting an increase in cholinergic transmission in depression. The clinical evidence does, in fact, indicate that in endogenous depression there is an increase in the responsiveness of muscarinic cholinergic systems.

14.2.1. Biological Markers

As discussed in Section 3.3.2, the two major biological markers identified in endogenous depression are a decreased latency to enter REM sleep and an increase in pituitary–adrenal activity, which is reflected in a high level of circulating corticosteroids and an early escape from suppression of corticosteroid levels by dexamethasone. There is evidence to suggest that both of these phenomena might reflect cholinergic hyperactivity in depressed patients.

There is a substantial body of evidence (reviewed by Janowsky & Risch, 1984b) that ACh mediates the stress-induced release of ACTH and cortisol. In particular, hypothalamic implants of atropine have been found to prevent stress-induced ACTH release (Hedge & De Wied, 1971; Kaplanski & Smelik, 1973). Cholinergic mechanisms also seem to be involved in circadian variation of pituitary–adrenal activity. In animals (Krieger, 1973) and in people (Ferrari et al., 1977), the major peak of cortisol secretion, which occurs in the early hours of the morning, was blocked by atropine administration in the evening but not at other times of day.

In the dexamethasone suppression test (DST), evening administration of the synthetic corticosteroid analogue dexamethasone blocks the morning rise of serum ACTH and cortisol levels, but endogenously depressed patients either fail to suppress their cortisol levels or, more commonly, escape from suppression during the course of the day (Carroll, 1982; see Section 3.3.2). A number of studies have demonstrated that physostigmine, which increases cholinergic activity, blocks the suppressive effect of dexamethasone in nondepressed volunteers, mimicking the change seen in depression (Carroll et al., 1978, 1980; Doerr & Berger, 1983).

As discussed in Section 14.1.2, the induction of REM sleep depends on the activation of a group of cholinergic cells in the pontine reticular formation, the tegmental giant cell field. Application of the cholinergic agonist carbachol directly in this region of the pontine reticular formation, but not in neighboring brainstem areas, caused a reduction in REM latency and an increase in REM duration (Amatruda et al., 1975; Baghdoyan et al., 1982, cited by McCarley, 1982; Silberman et al., 1980). Activity in the pontine ACh cells is highest at the onset of REM sleep and falls toward the end of a REM period; the inverse pattern of activity is seen in the neighboring locus coeruleus (NA) and dorsal raphe nucleus (5-HT). This reciprocal relationship is the basis for a neuronal model of sleep control (Hobson et al., 1974a,b; McCarley, 1982; Steriade & Hobson, 1976), but it also has important consequences for the manner in which the brain responds to uncontrollable stress (Section 11.3; see also Section 19.2.2).

The sleep of depressed patients is characterized by a short REM latency and an increased REM density, particularly during the first REM period (Kupfer et al., 1978, 1983; Kupfer & Thase, 1983; see Section 3.3.2). In nondepressed volunteers, intravenous infusions of physostigmine or the muscarinic receptor agonist arecoline have been found to cause a reduction of REM latency comparable to that seen in endogenous depression. This effect was blocked by the centrally acting antimuscarinic drug scopolamine, but not by methscopolamine, which does not cross the blood–brain barrier. As with naturally occurring REM periods, subjects awakened from physostigmine or arecoline-induced REM sleep were very likely to report that they had been dreaming (Gillin et al., 1978; Sitaram et al., 1976, 1977, 1978a,b). Again, cholinergic stimulation mimics the changes seen in depression.

14.2.2. Muscarinic Receptor Responsiveness

The studies showing cholinergic induction of REM sleep and ACTH release are consistent with the hypothesis that cholinergic systems are hyperactive in depression, but they provide no information as to the possible mechanisms. However, it has also been observed that the ACTH and cortisol responses to physostigmine or arecoline were greater in depressed patients than in normals and in other groups of psychiatric patients. Furthermore, cholinergic agonists also release beta-endorphin and prolactin (Risch et al., 1982a,b, 1983), and relatively higher serum concentrations of these hormones were also observed in depressed patients, following a cholinergic challenge with physostigmine or arecoline (Janowsky et al., 1983; Risch et al., 1982a,b, 1983). These findings suggest that depressed patients have an enhanced response to stimulation of muscarinic receptors.

Evidence that muscarinic receptor responsiveness is enhanced in depressed patients has also been found in sleep studies: the induction of REM sleep by arecoline was significantly faster in depressed patients than in nondepressed controls (Sitaram et al., 1980), and depressed subjects were more likely to wake up after physostigmine infusions (Berger et al., cited by Janowsky & Risch, 1984a). The effect of arecoline on REM latency was also elevated in patients who had previously been depressed but were not at the time of testing, and in nondepressed subjects with a family history of depression (Sitaram et al., 1980, 1982). Although most of the sleep abnormalities of depressed patients normalize on recovery, it has been found that on some parameters the sleep of recovered unipolar depressive patients was still disturbed, compared to age- and sex-matched controls. They do not sleep as deeply, spend more time awake, and have a greater night to night variability (Hauri et al., 1974). Increased REM density during the first REM period is also seen following recovery from depression (Foster et al., 1976; Schultz & Trojan, 1979). It is of interest, therefore, that in one study the latency of REM sleep induction by arecoline was inversely correlated with REM density during the first REM period, in both patients and controls. This suggests that a persistent increase in cholinergic responsiveness may underly the residual sleep disorders seen in depressed patients following remission.

In addition to neuroendorine and sleep studies, depressed patients also show an enhanced pupillary constriction following instillation of the cholinergic agonist pilocarpine into the eye (Sitaram, 1983, cited by Janowsky & Risch, 1984a). Similarly, depressed patients are more likely to experience nausea and vomiting following physostigmine administration (Janowsky et al., 1983). The picture of cholinergic hypersensitivity in depressed patients is also supported by two recent studies of muscarinic receptor binding, using the ligand quinuclidinyl benzilate (QNB). Myerson and co-workers (1982) reported that QNB binding was increased in the frontal cortex of suicide victims, compared to murder victims, and similarly, Nadi and co-workers (1984) reported an increase in the number of QNB binding sites in fibroblasts taken from depressed patients and grown in culture.

However, there are also three contrary observations. First, depressed and nondepressed subjects did not differ in the extent to which arecoline lowered body temperature (Sitaram et al., 1980); this observation probably means that cholinergic hypersensitivity is specific to certain physiological systems. Second, in a neuroendocrine study no differences in physiological responsiveness to arecoline were detected in depressed patients following recovery (Nurnberger et al., 1982). In view of the persistence of a very limited set of the sleep abnormalities following recovery, it might be predicted that cholinergic abnormalities might be more difficult to detect in recovered patients, so this result is not particularly surprising. Finally, depressed patients do not appear to be more sensitive than controls to physostigmine reversal of dexamethasone suppression (Berger et al., 1982b). It should be noted, however, that those depressed patients with the highest muscarinic sensitivity would already be dexamethasone nonsuppressors and therefore would be excluded from this comparison.

14.2.3. Conclusions

The abnormalities of REM sleep and pituitary–adrenal function in endogenous depression strongly suggest that cholinergic transmission may be increased in depressed patients. Acetylcholine turnover in the brain of depressed people has not been studied, though high levels of choline have been reported in red blood cells of some depressed patients (Hanin, 1983). However, from the animal literature demonstrating increased ACh turnover in stressful conditions, it seems quite likely that increased turnover might be demonstrable in depression. Equally, the increased responsiveness to muscarinic agonists could represent a decrease in the functioning of antagonistic systems, such as NA or 5-HT (see Chapter 19).

It is possible that the observed increase in the number of muscarinic cholinergic receptors could provide a sufficient explanation for the apparent changes in cholinergic transmission. It is difficult, however, to explain why muscarinic receptors become more responsive, since these receptors, like others, appear to function homeostatically. It has been shown, for example, that muscarinic receptor sensitivity is increased by chronic administration of atropine (Raiteri et al., 1983b). One possibility is that in depressed patients receptor regulation is abnormal. Although hypotheses of abnormal receptor regulation are very much in vogue as explanations of receptor changes in psychiatric conditions, the enthusiasm with which these hypotheses are promulgated is not, as far as I am aware, matched by any supporting evidence. Until such time as it can be demonstrated that abnormal receptor regulation is more than a theoretical possibility, it seems better to seek an alternative explanation for the apparent paradox of high muscarinic receptor responsiveness in stressful conditions. Indeed, the observation that in animals both the release of ACh and the sensitivity of muscarinic receptors were increased by chronic stress (Finkelstein et al., 1984; Gilad et al., 1983) demonstrates that the coexistence of these two forms of cholinergic hyperactivity is normal, albeit paradoxical.

The observation that QNB binding was increased in fibroblasts which were removed from depressed patients and then grown in cultures (Nadi et al., 1984) cannot be explained by abnormal receptor regulation, because regulatory control by neurotransmitter and/or co-transmitter release are absent in cell cultures. Taken together with the evidence suggesting increased muscarinic responsiveness in depressed patients in remission, it seems likely that an increased muscarinic receptor responsiveness is a characteristic of some depressive people, irrespective of whether or not they are currently depressed. The consequence would be an exaggerated response when cholinergic mechanisms were activated by stress.

14.3. CHOLINERGIC AGENTS AND MOOD

14.3.1. Cholinergic Agonists

A cholinergic hypothesis of depression would predict that cholinergic agonist drugs should have depressive effects. As reviewed in Chapters 9, 12, and 16, it has proved to be very difficult to induce depressive symptoms by means of pharmacological challenges to DA, NA, and 5-HT systems. Increasing cholinergic activity does induce depression—but only in affect disorder patients. Cholinergic activity is enhanced by drugs that inhibit enzyme acetylcholinesterase and prevent the destruction of ACh. Intensification of depression by the anticholinesterase diisopropylfluorophosphate (DFP), together with psychomotor retardation and feelings of fatigue, was first reported by Rowntree and co-workers in 1950. Janowsky and co-workers later confirmed that physostigmine reliably produced a worsening of depressive symptoms, including depressed mood (Janowsky & Risch 1984a,b; Janowsky et al., 1973a,b, 1974, 1983; Risch et al., 1981c). The effects were centrally mediated by muscarinic receptors. They were not produced by neostigmine, a cholinesterase inhibitor that does not cross the blood–brain barrier, and they were blocked by anticholinergic agents that cross the blood–brain barrier, but not by methscopolamine, which does not (Janowsky et al., 1973a, 1974).

A number of recent studies have employed the muscarinic receptor agonist arecoline, rather than cholinesterase inhibitors, which stimulate both muscarinic and nicotinic receptors. Like centrally acting cholinesterase inhibitors, arecoline also intensifies depressed mood (Nurnberger et al., 1982; Risch et al., 1981a). Depression has also been reported as a side effect in some patients given precursors of ACh for the treatment of tardive dyskinesias (Casey, 1979; K. Davis et al., 1979; Tamminga et al., 1976) or Alzheimer's disease (Bajada, 1982; Smith et al., 1982); like the effect of physostigmine, these depressions were reversible by atropine (Casey, 1979).

In addition to the induction of depression, cholinergic agonists also have antimanic effects. Infusions of physostigmine (but not neostigmine, which does not cross the blood—brain barrier)cause an atropine-reversible reduction in motor activity, talkativeness, euphoria, and other symptoms in manic or hypomanic patients (Carroll et al., 1973; Davis, et al., 1978; Janowsky et al., 1974; Modestin et al., 1973a,b; Shopsin et al., 1975b). In these studies, the administration of anticholinesterases to manic patients also induced or intensified depressed mood (Davis et al., 1978; Gershon & Shaw, 1961; Janowsky & Risch, 1984a,b; Janowsky et al., 1973a,b, 1974; Modestin et al., 1973a,b; Risch et al., 1981c). Antimanic effects of the ACh precursor lecithin have also been reported (B. Cohen et al., 1980, 1982).

The studies reviewed above constitute strong evidence that cholinergic agonists have antimanic properties and intensify existing depressions. Furthermore, Oppenheimer and co-workers (1979) have reported that physostigmine induced a depressed mood in the majority of a group of stable bipolar patients maintained on lithium. As in the case of "reserpine depression," however (Section 9.2.1), it is questionable whether true depressions are induced by cholinergic agonists in people who are not and have never been depressed.

Severe depressive reactions have been reported in marijuana-intoxicated subjects who were given intravenous infusions of physostigmine; the effect was reversed by atropine, indicating that it was mediated by muscarinic receptors (El-Yousef et al., 1973; Davis et al., 1976). These patients were described as being "as depressed as any patient with clinical endogenous depression . . . that we have seen" (El-Yousef et al., 1973, p. 324). In nondrugged, nondepressed volunteers, however, the primary symptoms displayed during physostigmine infusions are lack of energy, psychomotor retardation, social withdrawal, and feelings of being drained (Janowsky & Risch, 1984a). These symptoms seem very similar to the reserpine-induced "pseudo-depression" described by Goodwin and co-workers (see Section 9.2.1). Mild to moderate depressed mood is sometimes present (Janowsky et al., 1973a, 1974, 1983; Risch et al., 1981a), but this does not appear to be at all comparable in severity to that experienced by the subjects who had first taken marijuana. Indeed, some studies have reported that complete absence of depressed mood in nondepressed subjects infused with physostigmine (Davis et al., 1976; Oppenheimer et al., 1979; Greden, 1982, cited by Janowsky & Risch, 1984a). Similarly, the depressive effect of the ACh precursor deanol in tardive dyskinesia patients was seen only in patients who were also depressed (Casey, 1979). The muscarinic agonist arecoline has been reported to induce a depressed mood in some normal volunteers, but anxiety, hostility, and confusion are equally common (Nurnburger et al., 1982; Risch et al., 1981a); these other negative affects are also frequently mentioned in studies with other cholinomimetic agents.

It is possible that the greater depressive effect of cholinergic agonists in affect-disorder patients than in other psychiatric patients or in normal controls simply reflects the enhanced sensitivity of affect disorder patients to cholinergic stimulation, as discussed in the previous section. However, this seems unlikely to be the whole explanation, since the great majority of psychiatric patients and normal volunteers feel fatigued and enervated following the administration of cholinergic agonists. Although there is some suggestion that the fatigue is more intense in affect-disorder patients (Janowsky & Risch, 1984a; Janowsky et al., 1983; Risch et al., 1981c), the difference is insufficient to explain the pronounced discrepancy in mood effects between affect-disorder patients and others.

It seems more likely that cholinergic agonists produce rather nonspecific unpleasant feelings, which transmute into sadness and depressed mood in people who are or have been depressed. As in the Schachter and Singer (1962) study of adrenaline-induced emotional states (see Section 9.4), different attributions of the nature of nonspecific unpleasant feelings could eventuate in depression, in other negative affective states, or, in subjects more fully briefed on the nature of the experient, in no emotional response at all. Longitudinal studies in normal subjects who later become depressed will be required to test between an attributional hypothesis of this kind and the hypothesis that depressed mood is a specific consequence of cholinergic stimulation in depressive people.

14.3.2. Anticholinergics

The possibility that atropine and related drugs might, at high doses, be effective antidepressant agents was first suggested by Hoch and Mauss in 1932; a number of subsequent studies have supported this claim (reviewed by Janowsky & Risch, 1984a,b). Recently, Jimerson and co-workers (1982, cited by Janowsky & Risch, 1984a) have reported some limited success in treating depression with the anticholinergic trihexylphendyl. Similar effects have also been found with biperiden. In this study, the drug was particularly effective in alleviating depressed mood and the endogenous symptoms of retardation and agitation; antidepressant effects were most pronounced in patients with abnormal results on the DST, which tends to support the supposition that dexamethasone nonsuppression reflects cholinergic hypersensitivity (Kasper et al., 1981). A switch from depression to mania caused by the anticholinergic procyclidine in a bipolar patient has also been reported (Coid & Strang, 1982). In the only well-controlled study of anticholinergic treatment in depression, Beckman and Moises (1982) found that severely depressed patients reported improvements of mood and other symptoms during intravenous infusions of biperden, but not during placebo infusions.

Anticholinergics have also been reported to elevate mood when used as antiparkinsonian agents, causing feelings of euphoria, associated with a feeling of well-being and increased sociability (Jellinek et al., 1981; Smith, 1980); similar effects have also been reported in healthy volunteers (Schneider et al., 1975). Conversely, neuroleptic-treated patients may develop depression after withdrawal of anticholinergics (administered to counteract parkinsonian side effects). These depressions could be reversed by reinstating their anticholinergic medication (Jellinek et al., 1981).

Studies evaluating the effectiveness of antidepressant drugs sometimes compare the drug to an "active placebo" treatment. Instead of using an inert placebo, the placebo contains atropine to control for the presence of anticholinergic "side effects." Reviewing evaluative studies of tricyclic antidepressants, Thomson (1982) found that tricyclics were superior to inert placebo in 43 studies out of 68 (63%), but the tricyclic was superior to the atropine placebo in only one study out of seven (14%). These observations may provide further support for the hypothesis that anticholinergics have antidepressant activity. It should also be noted that if further research does not confirm this hypothesis, there would be serious implications for the methodological adequacy of placebo-controlled studies of tricyclic antidepressants. Specifically, it would be necessary to consider the possibility that "placebo amplification" ("I can feel the drug, so it must be doing me good") plays a major role in the antidepressant action of tricyclics, rather than any specific antidepressant effect (Thomson, 1982). As this conclusion would vitiate virtually everything that has ever been written about the mechanisms of action of tricyclic antidepressants, it is to be hoped that the antidepressant potential of anticholinergic drugs will not prove to be a mirage.

14.4. ANTIDEPRESSANTS AND ACETYLCHOLINE

If we assume, for the sake of peace of mind, that there is some substance to the claims that anticholinergic drugs have antidepressant activity, it becomes necessary to consider whether this action might contribute significantly to the clinical action of antidepressants. Many tricyclic antidepressants include blockade of muscarinic cholinergic receptors among their other pharmacological actions, which causes drowsiness, dryness of the mouth, blurred vision, and a number of other side effects. However, this property is not shared either by monoamine oxidase inhibitors or by a number of atypical antidepressants, including mianserin, nomifensine, and zimelidine. The affinity of tricyclics for muscarinic receptors is two to three orders of magnitude weaker than that of conventional muscarinic antagonists, such as atropine or benztropine (Hall & Ogren, 1981; Peroutka & Snyder, 1981a; Richelson, 1981; Snyder & Yamamura, 1977). Among the tricyclics, the correlation between their anticholinergic properties and their clinical potency is weak and nonsignificant [Spearman rho = 0.2, calculated using data on muscarinic receptor binding in Richelson (1981) and clinical data from Table 6.1].

During antidepressant treatment, tolerance develops to the anticholinergic effects. As a result, after chronic administration, there is little evidence for cholinergic receptor blockade. In an electrophysiological study, Menkes and Aghajanian (1981) found that after chronic treatment with amitriptyline, DMI, imipramine, or iprindole, the responsiveness of cells in the lateral geniculate nucleus to NA or 5-HT was enhanced (see Sections 13.3.1 and 17.3.1), but responses to the cholinergic agonist carbachol were unchanged. A similar lack of change in cholinergic responsiveness in hippocampal cells has also been reported, after long-term administration of imipramine or chlorimipramine (Gallager & Bunney, 1979). Indeed, in one study, chronic administration of imipramine or viloxazine changed the effect of ACh on cortical cells from a predominantly excitatory response to a predominantly inhibitory response (Jones, 1980a). In depressed people, muscarinic sensitivity has been investigated by utilizing the fact that cholinergic agonists instilled into the eye cause constriction of the pupil. Chronic administration of DMI caused a slight but nonsignificant increase in this effect (Shur & Checkley, 1982), and no changes were seen with the MAOI tranylcypromine (Sitaram et al., 1983).

As usual, receptor binding studies are inconclusive. In one study, an increase in muscarinic receptor binding was reported after chronic amitriptyline treatment (Rehavi et al., 1980b). In general, however, changes in muscarinic receptors have not usually been found during chronic administration of antidepressant drugs (Koide & Matsushita, 1981b; Maggi et al., 1980; Peroutka & Snyder, 1980a), though enhanced binding has been observed a week after withdrawal from imipramine or DMI (Koide & Matsushita, 1981b).

Although acute treatment with tricyclic antidepressants decreases cholinergic transmission, ECS appears to have the opposite effect. An increase in ACh synthesis has been observed in a number of brain areas following a single ECS or drug-induced seizure. However, no changes in choline uptake, brain ACh content, or ACh synthesis were seen following repeated ECS administration (Atterwill, 1980, 1984; Longoni et al., 1976). Of four studies of muscarinic receptor binding following repeated ECS, two studies reported no significant change (Kellar et al., 1981b; Deakin et al., 1981), and two reported a decrease (Dashieff et al., 1982; Lerer et al., 1984). Two functional studies have given opposing results. In one, repeated ECS was found to increase the release of corticosterone by oxotremorine; this response is mediated centrally by muscarinic receptors (Steiner & Grahame-Smith, 1980a,b). In the second study, by the same group, repeated ECS was found to reduce the cataleptic responses to high doses of cholinomimetic drugs (Green et al., 1979).

Taken together, the lack of correlation between anticholinergic and clinical potencies of tricyclics, the lack of evidence that these effects are still present after chronic treatment, the discrepant ECS findings, and the general inconclusiveness of receptor binding studies make it appear extremely unlikely that a reduction of muscarinic cholinergic transmission contributes significantly to clinical antidepressant effects. A further consideration that tends to strengthen this conclusion is that antidepressant effects of atropine and related drugs are apparent only at high doses, though in comparison to tricyclic antidepressants these drugs are far more potent anticholinergics.

fifteen

SEROTONIN AND DEPRESSION: THEORETICAL PERSPECTIVES

In previous chapters it has been established that exposure to uncontrollable stress increases activity in cholinergic systems and reduces NA and DA activity; these changes are reflected in behavioral inhibition and motivational impairments. As the involvement of 5-HT in depression differs in a number of important respects, it may be useful to begin by summarizing the major clinical conclusions. As discussed in Chapter 16, depression is associated with a reduced level of 5-HT function. However, this change does not normalize on clinical recovery, it is not caused by stress, and it is associated with psychomotor agitation, rather than retardation.

In order to arrive at these conclusions, it is necessary to negotiate a series of obstacles. The first is that two neurobehavioral models of 5-HT function in depression are current, and they make opposite predictions. One approach begins with a number of animal models of depression in which abnormal behavior, typified by hyperreactivity to aversive events, is associated with a decrease in 5-HT transmission. In the second approach, the central observation is that rewarded behavior is suppressed

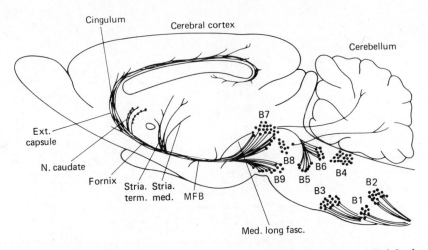

Fig. 15.1. The major serotonergic pathways of the rat forebrain. MFB, medial forebrain bundle. From J. R. Cooper, F. E. Bloom, and R. H. Roth, *The Biochemical Basis of Neuropharmacology*, 4th ed. Oxford University Press, New York, 1982. Reprinted by permission of the Oxford University Press.

by high 5-HT transmission. Both of these positions arise from the fact that the level of 5-HT function is inversely related to the level of behavioral reactivity. This chapter assesses which end of this dimension is more relevant for theories of depression.

The vast majority of 5-HT containing cells in the brain are located in a group of brainstem nuclei known as the raphe nuclei (Fig. 15.1). Although there are nine of these 5-HT containing cell groups, some 80% of forebrain 5-HT is provided by two of them, the dorsal raphe nucleus, B7, and the median raphe nucleus, B9 (Azmitia, 1978; Dahlstrom & Fuxe, 1965). Ascending fibers from both of these nuclei run in a number of different tracts, most of which join the medial forebrain bundle. The dorsal raphe nucleus innervates the striatum and thalamus (the mesostriatal pathway), and the median raphe nucleus innervates the hippocampus and septum (the mesolimbic pathway); both nuclei send fibers to the cortex and hypothalamus (Azmitia, 1978; Geyer et al., 1976a). The descending 5-HT innervation of the spinal cord is provided mainly be cell group B3, the nucleus raphe magnus.

High levels of 5-HT receptor stimulation have behavioral activating effects. An intense stimulation of 5-HT receptors may be achieved either by means of a direct receptor agonist, such as quipazine, or by a high dose of a 5-HT precursor, combined with an MAOI to prevent the breakdown of newly synthesized 5-HT. Either of these treatments produces a characteristic behavioral pattern of head weaving and "wet dog shakes," as well as postural changes such as hindlimb abduction and "Straub tail" (Green & Grahame-Smith, 1976; Jacobs & Klemfuss, 1975). These observations appear to be inconsistent with the generalization that high 5-HT activity suppresses behavior. However, these activating effects are mediated by 5-HT receptors in the spinal cord and lower brainstem (Jacobs & Klemfuss, 1975); the "5-HT syndrome" is a valuable tool for assessing drug effects on the functional responsiveness of 5-HT receptors (see Chapter 17) but is not a useful guide to the behavioral functions of forebrain 5-HT systems. This point is best illustrated by an experiment of M. Davis and co-workers (1980), in which it was observed that the startle response to a loud noise was increased by infusions of 5-HT into the spinal cord but suppressed by intraventricular infusions.

There is no standard way in which to address the "relevant" behavioral functions of different neurotransmitter systems. In the case of DA, there is a clear front-runner, the DA hypothesis of reward, which demands to be considered first. In the case of NA, a usable hypothesis emerges only after exploring a number of dead ends. In the case of 5-HT, the clearest line of approach is provided by a survey of animal models of depression.

15.1. 5-HT AND ANIMAL MODELS OF DEPRESSION

15.1.1. Learned Helplessness and Related Models

Unlike DA and NA, there is little evidence that 5-HT plays an important role in mediating the performance deficits that are seen in the aftermath of exposure to unpredictable and uncontrollable stress. Severe stress does increase the turnover of 5-HT; this effect is observed with stressors as diverse as heat, electric shock, food deprivation, and immobilization (Bliss et al., 1968; Curzon et al., 1972; Palkovitz et al., 1976; Ruther et al., 1966; Squires, 1974; Thierry et al., 1968). However, unlike the somewhat larger increases in NA turnover (Section 11.3.1), the effect on 5-HT turnover may be a consequence of stress per se, rather than uncontrollability; escapable and inescapable shock are usually found to produce similar changes (Weiss et al., 1981).

Some pharmacological studies do suggest a role for 5-HT in "learned helplessness" effects, but the results are inconsistent. The major pharmacological tools for studying 5-HT systems are the tryptophan and 5-HTP, the precursors of 5-HT, and the 5-HT synthesis inhibitor parachlorophenylalanine (PCPA). It has been reported that in mice, neither 5-HTP nor PCPA had any significant effect on the escape deficits that followed exposure to inescapable footshock (Anisman et al., 1979a). However, another study, using rats and a more intense electric shock, found that learning to escape electric shocks was disrupted by increasing 5-HT activity with 5-HTP or tryptophan. It was also observed that a low dose of 5-HTP or tryptophan potentiated the effect of a small number of shocks. Pretreatment with the 5-HT receptor antagonist methysergide blocked these effects and, also, counteracted the disruption of escape performance by inescapable shocks (Brown et al., 1982). These results suggest that if anything, learned helplessness involves an increase in 5-HT activity (as contrasted to the decrease in DA or NA activity described in previous chapters).

However, the opposite conclusion would be drawn from a study by Sherman & Petty (1980), in which the injection of 5-HT into the septum or frontal neocortex was found to reverse learned helplessness. This study differed from others in two potentially important respects: a very simple escape task was used (a single bar press), in which interference effects are usually not observed (Seligman & Beagley, 1975), and tests were carried out only 2 hours after helplessness induction, rather than the usual 24 hours. Consequently, the relationship of these experiments to others in the literature is not clear, a point underlined by the fact that injections of NA, which might be expected to reverse helplessness (Section 11.3), did not do so in this study (Sherman & Petty, 1980). However, DMI did reverse helplessness when injected into the frontal cortex, and at no other site—an interesting observation in view of the evidence implicating frontal cortex in depression (Chapter 7). It was also observed that in a number of brain areas—septum, hippocampal cortex, entorhinal cortex (Sherman & Petty, 1980) and frontal cortex (Petty & Sherman, 1983)—5-HT turnover was reduced following uncontrollable shock. In this study, controllable shock did not reduce 5-HT turnover (Sherman & Petty, 1980), and neither was the effect seen in animals that did not later demonstrate helplessness (Petty & Sherman, 1983).

Studies of "behavioral despair" (Section 7.2.2) are similarly inconsistent. Some results suggest that immobility is increased by 5-HT activity. Immobility was increased by tryptophan (Gibson et al., 1982) or 5-HTP (Gorka et al., 1979) and was decreased by the 5-HT antagonist cyproheptadine (Browne, 1979; Gorka & Wojtasik, 1980; Porsolt et al., 1979) and by a variety of antidepressants which include 5-HT receptor blockade as a prominent action (Porsolt, 1981). On the other hand, the 5-HT agonists quipazine and fenfluramine and the 5-HT uptake blockers femoxetine and fluoxetine have all been reported to decrease immobility (Porsolt et al., 1978a, 1979). Other studies have observed no effect with quipazine, fenfluramine, and femoxetine (Borsini et al., 1981; Gorka et al., 1979; Gorka & Wojtasik, 1980) or with the 5-HT receptor antagonists methiothepin and metergoline (Borsini et al., 1981; Porsolt et al., 1979).

The only obvious way of resolving these discrepancies would be by the demonstration of regional differences in 5-HT activity—perhaps a decrease in 5-HT turnover in frontal cortex and an increase elsewhere in the brain. At present, however, it is difficult to draw any conclusions as to how, if at all, 5-HT systems are involved in the phenomena of learned helplessness and "behavioral despair." In a related model, PCPA has not been found to induce "depressive" behaviors in monkeys or to alter the response to separation (Kraemer & McKinney, 1979; Redmond et al., 1971).

15.1.2. Models That Involve Hyperactivity

This discouraging picture does not extend to another group of models. Of the 12 animal models of depression judged to have some degree of validity (Section 7.3), three models—muricide (Section 6.3.4), social isolation (Section 6.5.5), and olfactory bulbectomy (Section 6.5.4)—involve behavioral hyperactivity. In every case, there is clear evidence for a reduction in 5-HT activity.

It has been consistently observed in a large number of studies that reducing 5-HT activity by blocking 5-HT synthesis or by chemical or electrical lesions to the raphe nuclei, will induce mouse killing in a high proportion of rats that do not show this behavior and potentiate muricide in those that already do (reviewed by Albert & Walsh, 1982; Eichelman, 1979). A complementary observation is that muricidal rats have a reduced central turnover of 5-HT (Valzelli et al., 1981) and a compensatory increase in the number of 5-HT receptors (Enna et al., 1981). A variety of other procedures that induce muricide may also work by reducing 5-HT activity. For example, intraventricular administration of 5-HT has been found to block the muricide induced by thiamine deficiency (Onodera et al., 1981). Conversely, raising 5-HT activity by systemic administration of 5-HT precursors, receptor agonists, or uptake blockers, or by intraventricular injections of 5-HT, suppresses muricide in spontaneous killer rats or in rats rendered muricidal by 5-HT depletion (Albert & Walsh, 1982; Eichelman, 1979). The blockade of muricide by tricyclic antidepressants (Section 6.3.4) appears to be mediated by 5-HT, as small depletions of 5-HT, which did not themselves induce muricide in nonkillers, block the antimuricidal effect of tricyclics (Eisenstein et al., 1982; Marks et al., 1978).

One procedure that reliably induces muricide in adult rats is social isolation (Sofia, 1969a; Valzelli & Bernasconi, 1971); as with other muricidal animals, social isolates are found to have reduced 5-HT turnover (Garattini et al., 1967; Valzelli & Bernasconi, 1979). Although rats reared in isolation from the time of weaning show hyperactivity rather than muricide (Garzon & Del Rio, 1981), these animals also have reduced 5-HT synthesis (Segal et al., 1973; Yanai & Sze, 1983) and a depletion of whole brain 5-HT (Segawa et al., 1982); preliminary evidence reported in one study suggested that there might also be a concomitant increase in the number of 5-HT receptors (Segawa et al., 1982).

It would be premature to infer that low 5-HT activity is responsible for the hyperactivity in socially isolated animals, since an increase in DA activity has also been detected. Isolated animals have an increase in DA turnover (Thoa et al., 1977) and more DA receptors (Guisado et al., 1980), which presumably explains why they are more sensitive to the stimulant effects of amphetamine (Einon & Sahakian, 1979). However, it may be inferred that the suppression of hyperactivity by antidepressants in isolated animals (Section 6.5.5) is mediated by 5-HT rather than DA, because although some antidepressants have DA-receptor blocking properties (Chapter 10), isolation reared animals are relatively insensitive to DA-receptor blockade (Sahakian & Robbins, 1977).

A reduction of 5-HT activity is clearly implicated in the olfactory bulbectomy model by the fact that the effects of olfactory bulbectomy—hyperactivity, defective passive avoidance learning, irritability, and elevation of plasma corticosteroids—could all be mimicked by injections of the 5-HT neurotoxin 5,6-dihydroxytryptamine (5,6-DHT) into the olfactory bulb; the catecholamine neurotoxin 6-OHDA was ineffective. Antidepressants, which normalize the effects of bulbectomy (Section 6.5.4), also reversed the effects of the 5-HT lesion (Cairncross et al., 1979). The changes caused by bulbectomy could also be reversed by 5-HT uptake blockers (fluoxetine, zimelidine) or 5-HT agonists (quipazine, fenfluramine) (Broekkamp et al., 1980; Lloyd et al., 1982). Conversely, the effects of antidepressant administration were blocked by the 5-HT receptor antagonist metergoline (Garrigou et al., 1981; Lloyd et al., 1982).

To complete the circle, olfactory bulbectomized animals also display muricide (Albert & Walsh, 1982). Although one study has reported results which suggest that bulbectomy-induced muricide might have a noradrenergic basis (Oishi & Ueki, 1980), others have found that, like other instances of muricide and like other effects of bulbectomy, muricide induced by lesions of the olfactory bulb was blocked by 5-HTP administration (DiChiara et al., 1971; Vergnes et al., 1974).

The results strongly suggest that the behavioral and endocrine consequences of damaging the olfactory bulb are caused by the destruction of a 5-HT pathway, which terminates in or passes through this area. The medial amygdala also participates in this group of behavioral effects. The deficit in passive avoidance learning shown by bulbectomized animals was reversed by injections of antidepressants or 5-HT (but not NA) at this site; both sets of effects were blocked by the 5-HT antagonist metergoline (Broekkamp et al., 1980; Garrigou et al., 1981; Lloyd et al., 1982). Similarly, imipramine has been found to suppress muricide when injected into the medial amygdala (Horowitz et al., 1966). A different region of the amygdala may be involved in mediating effects related to learned helplessness: DMI, NA, and 5-HT were all ineffective in reversing learned helplessness when injected into the medial amygdala (Sherman & Petty, 1980), but a lesion of the basolateral amygdala has been found to block the effect of imipramine in the "behavioral despair" procedure (Gorka et al., 1979). Manipulations of the basolateral amygdala have no effects on muricidal (Horovitz et al., 1966) or olfactory bulbectomized animals (Garrigou et al., 1981).

Although, individually, the olfactory bulbectomy, muricide, and social isolation models are of moderate to low validity (Section 7.3), their validity is enhanced by the convergent evidence they provide: all three models appear to represent manifestations of an underlying reduction in 5-HT activity. It therefore becomes important to ask whether any behavioral feature of these models provides a possible link with psychological theories of depression. There are two such links. The first is that social isolation might model certain etiological factors in depression, such as early parental loss or poor social support (Section 20.1). The analogy is so tenuous that it will not be pursued at this point, but it will be considered later in the light of the clinical evidence (Section 19.3). The second point of contact with the clinical literature is that the feature of olfactory bulbectomized animals that is reversed most specifically by antidepressants (Section 6.5.4), is a deficiency in passive avoidance learning. The animals are slow to learn not to do things that lead to trouble, and as a result they receive more punishments than a normal animal in the same situation.

15.2. 5-HT AND RESPONSIVENESS TO AVERSIVE STIMULI

15.2.1 Response Suppression

Deficient passive avoidance learning is in fact a characteristic of animals in which 5-HT transmission has been reduced by whatever means. In passive avoidance learning paradigms, an animal must refrain from making a response in order to avoid punishment. The response which the animal is required to withhold is either one that it has been trained to make, by, for example, the use of food rewards, or one that is a part of its natural behavioral repertoire. The former are also known as conflict procedures, for obvious reasons. The latter are typically exploratory responses. In the "step-down" paradigm, the animal is shocked if it steps down from a small platform; in the "step-through" paradigm, the animal must stay in one part of the apparatus.

As discussed below, in some behavioral tests, the method used to reduce 5-HT function greatly influences the results. In the case of passive avoidance procedures, however, performance is impaired by all of the procedures which have been used to reduce 5-HT function. As noted above, injections of the 5-HT neurotoxin 5,6-DHT into the olfactory bulb impaired "step-through" passive avoidance learning (Cairncross et al., 1979). Intraventricular injections of 5,6-DHT have also been found to reduce the suppressive effects of electric shock in animals pressing a lever for food reward (Stein et al., 1975b). 5,7-Dihydroxytryptamine (5,7-DHT) is another 5-HT neurotoxin. Injection of 5,7-DHT along the course of the ascending 5-HT fibers has been reported to reinstate bar pressing (Tye et al., 1977) and running (Fuxe et al., 1978b) suppressed by electric shock. Similar effects have also been observed following electrolytic lesions of the median raphe nucleus (Srebro & Lorens, 1975; Thornton & Goudie, 1978). Finally, pharmacological reduction of 5-HT function by receptor antagonists or by the 5-HT synthesis inhibitor PCPA also restores behavior suppressed by punishment, although occasionally this result has not been observed (Winokur & Bagchi, 1974); the effect of PCPA can be counteracted by increasing 5-HT availability with 5-HTP (Cook & Sepinwall, 1975; Geller & Blum, 1970; Geller et al., 1974; Graeff, 1974; Graeff & Schoenfeld, 1970; Robichaud & Sledge, 1969; Wise et al., 1973). In addition to restoring behavior suppressed by shock, PCPA has also been found to restore behavior suppressed by a conditioned stimulus associated with shock (Hartmann & Geller, 1971); the same effect has also been reported following injections of chlordiazepoxide or GABA into the dorsal raphe nucleus (Thiebot et al., 1980).

The fact that 5-HT depleted animals tend to be hyperactive could provide a trivial explanation for their inability to suppress behavior that leads to punishment. However, this does not appear to be the reason. For one thing, the increase in responding is relatively specific to punished behavior; in the majority of studies cited above, reducing 5-HT function did not increase responding in the absence of punishment. A second problem with this explanation is that hyperactivity is not a reliable consequence of 5-HT depletion. Electrolytic lesions of the raphe nuclei or, more specifically, of the median raphe nucleus do produce a state of hyperactivity (Geyer et al., 1976b; B. Jacobs et al., 1974; Lorens et al., 1976; Srebro & Lorens, 1975). However, PCPA-induced 5-HT depletion produces variable results (Brody, 1970; Fibiger & Campbell, 1971; Kohler & Lorens, 1978; Tenen, 1967; Williams et al., 1974), and no change in locomotor activity, or sometimes a decrease, has been reported following more selective 5,7-DHT-induced lesions (Deakin et al., 1979; Geyer et al., 1980; Hole et al., 1976; Lorens et al., 1976).

Are 5-HT depleted animals less afraid of being punished? This hypothesis would very readily explain why they are not deterred by punishment. Indeed, a classic action of antianxiety drugs is precisely that they restore responding suppressed by punishment, just as do anti-5-HT treatments (Gray, 1982; Geller & Seifter, 1960; Hill & Tedeschi, 1971). However, anti-5-HT treatments appear to enhance, rather than reduce, fear responses. 5,7-Dihydroxytryptamine lesions, for example, have been observed to increase urination and defecation in a novel environment, while reducing exploratory behavior (Deakin et al., 1979). Similarly, PCPA has also been found to increase freezing in a novel environment (Brody, 1970; Ellison & Bresler, 1974; Marsden & Curzon, 1976); PCPA is a relatively nonspecific treatment, but this effect does appear to be mediated by 5-HT, as it could be reversed by tryptophan (Marsden &

Curzon, 1976). These results indicate that if anything, 5-HT depleted animals are more, rather than less fearful.

Consistent with an increase in emotionality, it is found that following PCPA treatment or lesions of the raphe nuclei, animals are hyperresponsive to the first few presentations of sudden visual, tactile, and auditory stimuli (Dalhouse, 1976; Davis & Sheard, 1974; Geyer et al., 1976b; Vergnes & Penot, 1976b). Hyperreactivity in a startle test has also been demonstrated following ventricular infusions of 5,7-DHT (Geyer et al., 1980). Conversely, the retention of conditioned fear is impaired by a variety of treatments which enhance 5-HT function (Archer, 1982; Essman, 1973a,b), and intraventricular administration of 5-HT reduces startle responses (Geyer et al., 1975; M. Davis et al., 1980).

Another characteristic of 5-HT depleted animals, which may be a consequence of their hyperreactivity, is that they show an enhanced aggressive response to electric shock (Ellison & Bresler, 1974; Jacobs & Cohen, 1976; Sheard & Davis, 1976; Vergnes & Penot, 1976a). Conversely, aggression induced by social isolation is decreased by treatments that increase 5-HT transmission, such as the 5-HT uptake inhibitor zimelidine (Ogren et al., 1980). Because there is general agreement that shock-induced fighting and isolation-induced fighting are defensive in nature (Albert & Walsh, 1982), these findings strengthen the conclusion that 5-HT depletion increases, rather than decreases fear.

Perhaps the most significant finding is that, in two studies, PCPA-treated animals were hypoactive under conditions of dim illumination and quiet. However, when tested with noise and bright lights, they showed large increases in activity; control animals showed more intense freezing in these conditions (Brody, 1970; Ellison & Bresler, 1974). Taken together with the earlier observations, these results suggest the general hypothesis that the activation of 5-HT pathways functions to inhibit behavior under conditions of emotional arousal. In consequence, 5-HT depleted animals are unable to suppress their behavior appropriately when threatening environmental contingencies require it.

Two predictions follow from this hypothesis. The first is that 5-HT depleted animals should not be hyperactive under conditions of low emotional arousal. As noted above, electrolytic lesions of the raphe nuclei reliably induce hyperactivity, but even so, the effect is not usually observed in a familiar environment (Geyer et al., 1976b; Lorens et al., 1971). Also relevant are observations indicating that reduction of 5-HT activity has a far less powerful restorative effect on behavior suppressed by nonreward than on behavior suppressed by punishment (Beninger & Phillips, 1979; Davis, 1979, cited by Gray, 1982; Tye et al., 1977).

The second prediction is that performance on tests involving escape and active avoidance behaviors should be unaffected or facilitated by manipulations of 5-HT, because these situations do not require behavioral inhibition, and any freezing in response to an unfamiliar or frightening environment would interfere with active performance. PCPA and electrolytic lesions of the raphe nuclei have usually, though not always, been found to facilitate active avoidance performance (Brody, 1970; Ogren et al., 1981a; Srebro & Lorens, 1975; Tenen, 1967); facilitation of active avoidance has also been observed following intracisternal administration of the more specific treatment 5,7-DHT (Breese & Cooper, 1975). Injection of 5,7-DHT directly into the ascending 5-HT pathways does not appear to affect active avoidance performance (Hole et al., 1976; Fuxe et al., 1978b; Ogren et al., 1981a), and neither did another specific 5-HT neurotoxin p-chloroamphetamine (Ogren et al., 1981a). These studies stand in marked contrast to the impairment of passive avoidance performance, which has been consistently observed following treatments that reduce 5-HT function.

A number of studies indicate that the increased responsiveness and lack of behavioral inhibition that accompany a reduction in 5-HT function are mediated by the 5-HT projection from the median raphe nucleus to the hippocampus and septum. The descending 5-HT pathways are clearly excluded. Intraventricular injections of 5-HT decreased the magnitude of the acoustic startle response, but injections into the spinal cord had the opposite effect (M. Davis et al., 1980). Electrolytic lesions restricted to the dorsal raphe nucleus had no effect on activity in a novel environment, startle responses, or a variety of other behaviors. However, lesions restricted to the median raphe nucleus produced effects similar to those of total destruction of the raphe system (Geyer et al., 1976b; B. Jacobs et al., 1974; Srebro & Lorens, 1975).

The extent of the behavioral changes following median raphe lesions was correlated with the extent of destruction of 5-HT terminals in the hippocampus and septum (Geyer et al., 1976a,b; Williams & Azmitia, 1981), implicating the 5-HT projection from the median raphe nucleus to the hippocampus and septum in these effects. Destruction of the hippocampus (Jacobs et al., 1975) or septum (Vergnes & Penot, 1976b) blocks the effects of PCPA or median raphe lesions, from which it may be deduced that the 5-HT input exerts an inhibitory influence over septohippocampal functioning.

15.2.2. Pain

A further feature of 5-HT-depleted animals is that they appear to have an increased sensitivity to pain. For example, the threshold for jumping in response to an electric shock, a classic pain test (Evans, 1961), was reduced by 5,7-DHT infusions in the path of the ascending 5-HT fibers or into the cerebral ventricles; these effects were accompanied by large decreases in forebrain 5-HT content, but there was no change in NA or DA (Harvey & Simansky, 1981). Curiously, 5,7-DHT infusions directly into the raphe nuclei do not produce the same change in pain sensitivity

(Harvey & Simansky, 1981; Hole & Lorens, 1975). This discrepancy probably results from nonspecific damage caused by the infusion, because the raphe nuclei are located in the "central grey" region, which almost certainly contains other neural systems involved in the processing of nociceptive information.

An increased sensitivity to electric shock is also seen following other, less specific 5-HT-depleting procedures. Jump thresholds are decreased by PCPA and were restored by 5-HTP (Fibiger et al., 1972; Smith, 1979; Telner et al., 1979; Tenen, 1967). Tryptophan-free diets also cause hyperalgesia, which is reversible by tryptophan (Lytle et al., 1975; Messing et al., 1976). Conversely, fluoxetine, a specific 5-HT uptake inhibitor, has been found to increase jump thresholds (Harvey & Simansky, 1981) and to reverse the hyperalgesia induced by PCPA or by a tryptophan-free diet (Messing et al., 1975, 1976).

In addition, many studies have demonstrated an increase in jump thresholds following forebrain lesions, that reduced 5-HT levels (reviewed by Harvey & Simansky, 1981), but not following lesions that did not affect 5-HT (Lints & Harvey, 1969). Lesions placed in the raphe nuclei do not produce this effect (Harvey et al., 1974; Hole & Lorens, 1975), but then, as noted above, neither do 5,7-DHT lesions of this area. 5-HT is implicated in the increased sensitivity to pain following forebrain lesions by the observation that normal responsiveness could be restored by 5-HTP (Smith, 1979; Yunger & Harvey, 1976). The fact that reversal of hyperalgesia still occurred following pretreatment with an inhibitor of peripheral 5-HTP metabolism confirms that this effect is centrally mediated (Yunger & Harvey, 1976).

Clearly, central 5-HT systems modulate responsiveness to painful electric shocks, but do that affect pain? One alternative interpretation, a change in sensory thresholds, may be rule out. In none of the studies cited did manipulations of 5-HT alter the threshold for the detection of a shock, as assessed behaviorally by flinching rather than by jumping (Evans, 1961). However, a more serious problem is whether a decrease in jump threshold simply reflects the loss of behavioral inhibition described in the preceding section. One finding that makes this a very real possibility is that the effects of 5-HT manipulations appear to be test-specific. In contrast to the clear evidence implicating 5-HT in responses to electric shock in the flinch–jump test, 5,7-DHT lesions of forebrain 5-HT pathways failed to affect the paw-lick response to noxious heat in rats placed on a hot-plate (Hole et al., 1976). Similarly, the 5-HT uptake inhibitor fluoxetine also fails to produce analgesia on this test (Harvey & Simansky, 1981; Sugrue & McIndewar, 1976; Yaksh & Wilson, 1979). On the other hand, two other specific 5-HT uptake inhibitors, zimelidine and alaproclate, have been found to suppress paw licking (Ogren & Holm, 1980), as has the indirectly acting 5-HT receptor agonist fenfluramine

(Rochat et al., 1982), but the tail-flick response to heat, another pain test, was apparently unaffected by these drugs.

It appears from these findings that the involvement of 5-HT in responses to pain is limited, either by the nature of the test (jumping as opposed to paw lick or tail flick) or by the nature of the noxious stimulus (electric shock versus heat). Nevertheless, there are a number of lines of evidence which indicate that manipulations of 5-HT do modulate pain perception, and that the effects cannot be explained entirely by changes in behavioral inhibition. The most direct evidence comes from human studies. In a placebo-controlled study, the specific 5-HT uptake inhibitor zimelidine has been found to reduce self-ratings of pain in patients with chronic pain syndromes (Johansson & Von Knorring, 1979; Johansson et al., 1980), and in an uncontrolled study, zimelidine has been reported to reduce the pain of migraine headaches (Sylvalahti et al., 1979a).

There is also electrophysiological evidence that 5-HT modulates the perception of painful stimuli. In primates, nociceptive information is transmitted primarily by the spinothalamic tract; iontophoretic application of 5-HT to neurons of the spinothalamic tract in monkeys has been found to produce a selective suppression of responses to nociceptive cutaneous stimuli while enhancing responses to nonnoxious stimuli (Willis, 1981). A similar preferential blockade by 5-HT of responses to noxious stimulation has also been observed in dorsal horn neurons in cats (Belcher et al., 1978; Randic & Yu, 1976; Headley et al., 1978). Electrical stimulation of the nucleus raphe magnus (NRM) produces behavioral analgesia and the same selective blockade of nociceptive information in monkey spinothalamic (Willis, 1981) and cat dorsal horn (Besson et al., 1981) neurons as is seen with iontophoretic application of 5-HT. Although some doubt remains (Besson et al., 1981; Willis, 1981), it seems likely that these effects are mediated by the 5-HT pathway which descends from the NRM to the spinal cord, since the blockade of nociceptive transmission by NRM stimulation was itself blocked by prior PCPA-induced 5-HT depletion (Rivot et al., 1979).

There is also evidence implicating ascending 5-HT neurons in analgesic responses. Stimulation of the dorsal raphe nucleus suppresses responses to noxious stimuli of neurons in the parafascicular nucleus of the thalamus, another area traditionally implicated in pain perception; this effect could be mimicked by iontophoretic application of 5-HT and could be abolished by 5,7-DHT pretreatment (Andersen & Dafny, 1982).

There is extremely strong evidence that 5-HT systems also play an essential role in a variety of other analgesic phenomena. Analgesic effects are induced by electrical stimulation of a number of brainstem sites, most notably the central (or periaqueductal) grey (PAG) (Reynolds, 1969). These effects are observed most reliably from 5-HT-containing nuclei: within the PAG, the most potent site is the dorsal raphe nucleus, while the NRM, which lies outside the PAG, is even more potent (Besson et al.,

1981). With repeated stimulation, tolerance develops. However, a normal analgesic response to NRM stimulation in cats was restored by 5-HTP (Oliveras et al., 1978). It has also been demonstrated in human subjects that tolerance to the analgesic effect of PAG stimulation was attenuated by a tryptophan-rich diet (Hosobuchi, 1978).

It is now clear that the analgesic effects of brain stimulation depend largely on the activation of endogenous opiate systems (see also Section 18.1), because stimulation-produced analgesia can usually be blocked by opiate receptor antagonists (Akil et al., 1976b). Many studies have shown that morphine induces analgesia when injected into the PAG (Yaksh & Rudy, 1978) and the NRM (Dickenson et al., 1979); these effects could be blocked by 5-HT receptor antagonists (Dickenson et al., 1979; Yaksh et al., 1976). Similarly, the analgesic effects of systemic morphine administration are blocked by electrolytic lesions of the NRM (Proudfit & Anderson, 1975; Yaksh et al., 1977), by 5,6-DHT lesions of descending 5-HT pathways (Genovese et al., 1973; Vogt, 1974), or by PCPA (Tenen, 1968; Vogt, 1974). Furthermore, systemic injections of morphine (Deakin et al., 1977; Fields & Anderson, 1978; Oleson et al., 1978) or microinjections in the PAG (Fields & Anderson, 1978) have been found to activate NRM neurons. These findings add up to an overwhelming demonstration that the analgesic effects of opiates are mediated by a system of 5-HT fibers which descends from the nucleus raphe magnus.

15.2.3. Stress

As noted above, the turnover of 5-HT is increased by a diversity of severe stressors; this is matched by an increase in the activity of tryptophan hydroxylase, the enzyme that synthesizes 5-HT (Azmitia & McEwen, 1974). The evidence reviewed in the preceding section suggests that the function of this increased 5-HT activity might be to promote analgesia, as part of an adaptive response that increases the ability to cope with stress. This supposition is supported by the further observation that the corticosteroid response to stress, which serves just this purpose, also depends on the activation of 5-HT systems. Valine is a neutral amino acid that enters the brain on the same carrier mechanism as tryptophan. The increase in circulating corticosteroids which normally accompanies restraint stress was substantially reduced by preadministration of valine, but could be restored by tryptophan. Tyrosine, which also competes for the same carrier, did not reverse the effect of valine (Kennett & Joseph, 1981; Joseph & Kennett, 1983). These results imply that the pituitary–adrenal response to stress depends on an increase in 5-HT synthesis and release, which in turn requires an increase in tryptophan availability. Since the release of ACTH from the pituitary is accompanied by the release of the endogenous analgesic agent beta-endorphin (Rossier et al.,

1980; Risch et al., 1982a), 5-HT is implicated in the mediation of yet another analgesic effect.

Viewed as a whole, the results show that 5-HT plays a central role in the response to aversive events. Stressors of various kinds activate 5-HT cells; the consequences are a decrease in sensitivity to pain, an increase in circulating corticosterone, and suppression of behavior. An animal unable to respond to stress by activating the 5-HT system copes poorly. It is irritable, hyperresponsive to unpleasant events, and unable to suppress behaviors that lead to punishment. The evidence reviewed in Chapter 4 demonstrates that depression is characterized by an increase in the prominence of aversive events. Clearly, a decrease in 5-HT function is a strong candidate to mediate these changes, and, as will be seen in Section 16.4, depressed people who show evidence of low 5-HT turnover resemble 5-HT-depleted animals to a remarkable degree.

15.3   SEDATIVE EFFECTS

15.3.1.   "Behavioral Depression"

A theory of depression has been proposed by Aprison and colleagues which is based on a premise diametrically opposed to that outlined in the preceding paragraph. These workers have observed that rats or pigeons pressing a lever for intermittent food pellets or milk show a decrease in behavioral output when administered 5-HTP (Aprison & Ferster, 1961; Aprison & Hintgen, 1966). As described in Section 6.5.3, this behavioral change has been put forward as an animal model of depression, on the basis of the observation that normal behavior was restored by some antidepressant drugs (Aprison et al., 1982; Nagayama et al., 1980, 1981). The implications of the latter observation for the mechanisms of action of antidepressant drugs will be considered in Chapter 17. What concerns us here is the nature of the behavioral change induced by 5-HTP, and its physiological basis.

A particular problem in analyzing the role of 5-HT systems is that only a very small proportion (around 1%) of 5-HT is located in the central nervous system (Cooper et al., 1982). Consequently, there is a very high possibility that changes in peripheral 5-HT might be responsible for any behavioral effects observed following pharmacological manipulations. This problem has not arisen in earlier discussions, because the conclusions relied largely on the results of intracranial manipulations, such as the central application of 5-HT neurotoxins. However, in the case of a theory that is based on the action of a 5-HT precursor, which has both peripheral and central actions, the possibility of a peripheral locus of action must be seriously considered. Approximately 90% of 5-HT is in the gut, and it requires little imagination to see how gastrointestinal effects might reduce behavioral output, particularly when food rewards are being used.

The 5-HTP-induced behavioral depression observed by Aprison and co-workers was correlated in time with an increase in 5-HT concentrations in the forebrain (Aprison & Hintgen, 1966; Smith et al., 1976). Furthermore, unlike the *l*-isomer of 5-HTP, the *d*-isomer has only minimal effects on brain 5-HT levels, and it is only weakly active in the behavioral test (Penn et al., 1977). These results certainly suggest a central site of action. However, a variety of compounds are available which at low doses block the peripheral actions of 5-HTP but do not enter the brain. These include the 5-HT receptor antagonist xylamidine tosylate (Copp et al., 1967) and the drugs benserazide (Pletscher & Gey, 1963) and carbidopa (Warsh & Stancer, 1976), which block the decarboxylation of 5-HTP to 5-HT. All three of these agents have been found to abolish the depressant effect of 5-HTP on rewarded lever pressing (Carter & Appel, 1976; Carter et al., 1978; Willner & Rayner, unpublished observations). This finding strongly suggests that the effect is mediated peripherally.

The depression of rewarded behavior by treatments intended to increase 5-HT transmission has been observed in a variety of different paradigms, but in most cases it is difficult to infer that changes in brain 5-HT systems are responsible. The consumption of alcohol by rats is decreased by a variety of treatments which increase brain 5-HT function, including 5-HTP (Geller, 1973; Myers et al., 1972; Rockman et al., 1979a,b). However, a recent study found that, like the reduction of lever pressing, the effect of 5-HTP on ethanol consumption was also blocked by peripheral inhibition of 5-HT synthesis (Geller et al., 1981), using benserazide at a dose that has minimal central effects (Arendt et al., 1981; Pletscher & Gey, 1963). Similarly, 5-HTP and other 5-HT agonist treatments have been found to decrease the intake of sweet foods and fluids (Wurtman & Wurtman, 1979; Fuller & Owen, 1981). However, exactly the same effect is seen with subcutaneous administration of 5-HT, which does not cross the blood–brain barrier (Montgomery & Burton, 1983).

Aprison and co-workers (1982) assume that the behavioral mechanism of the 5-HTP induced "behavioral depression" is a decrease in the rewardingness of the reward for which the animal is working. This hypothesis is apparently contradicted by the finding that animals will work for brain-stimulation reward delivered through electrodes implanted in the median raphe nucleus. However, 5-HT does not appear to be involved in the rewarding effect at these electrodes, as a number of 5-HT antagonist procedures, including 5,7-DHT lesions of ascending 5-HT pathways failed to affect raphe self-stimulation (Deakin, 1980). Intracranial self-stimulation (ICSS) at most other electrode sites is usually found to be unchanged or facilitated by treatments that decrease 5-HT activity and is suppressed by 5-HT agonists (Poschel & Ninteman, 1971). These results are consistent with Aprison's hypothesis.

However, while a change in reward mechanisms is a possible explanation of "behavioral depression," it is by no means the only explanation. Nonspecific sedation is an equally obvious candidate. Many studies have reported decreases in locomotor activity following the administration of 5-HTP or tryptophan. As with 5-HTP-induced "behavioral depression," these appear to be peripheral effects, because they are blocked by peripherally acting inhibitors of 5-HT synthesis (Modigh, 1973, 1974; Tricklebank et al., 1980).

If 5-HT agonists did attenuate rewards, then animals might find the experience of 5-HT agonists unpleasant. Unfortunately, the appropriate experiments to assess this possibility have not yet been carried out. Animals do not choose to self-administer fenfluramine (Baxter et al., 1973; Woods & Tessell, 1974), which suggests that they do not find this drug particularly pleasant; however, in view of the preceding observations, it is quite possible that peripheral mechanisms make a major contribution to this state of affairs. A second procedure, which is widely used to examine the punishing properties of drugs, involves allowing animals to drink a novel tasting fluid or to eat an unusual food, and then to administer the drug. On reexposure to the novel taste, the animals may avoid it. Both fenfluramine and 5-HTP have been found to support "conditioned taste aversions" (Goudie & Thornton, 1975; Zabik & Roache, 1983), but again it is not possible to conclude from this that animals find the drugs unpleasant. In addition to the possibility that the "punishing" effects are mediated peripherally, the interpretation of "conditioned taste aversions" is fraught with difficulties. This problem is best illustrated by the fact that drugs such as amphetamine, which animals do avidly self-administer, also serve as "punishers" in "conditioned taste aversion" experiments (Goudie & Thornton, 1975). Indeed, the observation that amphetamine self-administration was increased by intraventricular injections of 5,7-DHT and by the 5-HT receptor antagonist metergoline (Lyness et al., 1980; Lyness & Moore, 1983) could be interpreted in exactly the opposite way, that is, as a decrease in reward resulting from a decrease in 5-HT. This conclusion follows from the fact that in the self-administration paradigm, animals carefully control their intake of stimulant drugs, increasing their response rate when the size of the reward is reduced, and decreasing their response rate when the size of the reward is increased (Schuster, 1975).

15.3.2. Satiety

Food consumption is the area in which the most extensive behavioral analysis of the "depressant" effect of 5-HT agonist treatments is available. Although systemic administration of the 5-HT synthesis inhibitor PCPA has very variable effects on food intake (Hoebel, 1978), it is well-established that food intake is reduced by a variety of 5-HT agonist treatments, including 5-HTP (Blundell & Latham, 1979; Blundell & Leshem, 1975), fluoxetine, a 5-HT uptake inhibitor (Goudie et al., 1976), and the 5-HT releasing agent fenfluramine (reviewed by Blundell, 1977; Hoebel, 1978). These effects appear to be mediated in part by central mechanisms, because feeding was also suppressed by intraventricular administration of 5-HTP or 5-HT (Leibowitz, 1980) and was increased by intraventricular administration of PCPA (Breisch & Hoebel, 1975; Breisch et al., 1976).

Examination of the fine structure of behavior reveals that 5-HTP and fenfluramine reduce food intake in two ways, by reducing the size of meals and by slowing the rate of eating (Blundell & Latham, 1979, 1980; Burton et al., 1981). Of these, the reduction of meal size is mediated peripherally, possibly by a reduction in the rate of gastric emptying (Davies et al., 1983). This effect of 5-HTP was blocked by a peripherally acting inhibitor of 5-HT synthesis (Blundell & Latham, 1979), and it may be mimicked by peripheral injection of 5-HT, which does not cross the blood–brain barrier (P. Fletcher, personal communication). However, the reduction in eating rate by 5-HTP is probably a central effect, since it was not blocked by peripheral synthesis inhibition (Blundell & Latham, 1979) and was not seen with peripheral 5-HT (P. Fletcher, personal communication).

A reduced eating rate is compatible with the notion that the food tastes less pleasant to the animal. However, it is well established, in animals and in people, that food tastes less pleasant toward the end of a meal (Cabanac, 1971; Rolls, 1982). Additional evidence suggests that the reduction of eating rate by 5-HT is not an isolated pharmacological effect on reward mechanisms, but rather an augmentation of the naturally occurring process of satiety. For example, the rate of eating decreases during the course of a meal (Blundell & Latham, 1980); in fenfluramine-treated animals, food intake was initially normal, but during the meal, they slowed down more than did controls (Blundell et al., 1976; Knoll, 1983).

The most significant observation is that after the end of a meal, the delay in settling down for a postprandial nap was much reduced in fenfluramine-treated animals (Blundell & McArthur, 1981). This perhaps unpromising observation actually affords a significant insight into the behavioral mechanism of fenfluramine's anorexic action and, by extension, the role of 5-HT. A characteristic "satiety sequence" has been described in rats and other animals, which begins at the termination of eating, and consists of a short period of grooming or exploratory activity, followed by sleep (Antin et al., 1975; Smith & Gibbs, 1979). There is a positive correlation between the size of a meal and the duration of the postprandial nap (Bernstein, 1975; Danguir et al., 1979). The satiety sequence does not occur simply because an animal stops eating. Rather, it is specifically related to satiety: animals implanted with a gastric fistula, which prevented food from reaching the stomach, did not show the sequence, and neither did animals eating food adulterated with quinine (Antin et al., 1975). However, fenfluramine-treated animals did show the full satiety sequence (Blundell & McArthur, 1981), which strongly supports the view that fenfluramine augments satiety responses rather than rendering the food unpalatable.

A group of responses known collectively as "relaxation behavior," which in some respects are similar to the "satiety sequence," has been described in cats. Relaxation is induced by pleasurable stimuli, such as milk drinking or petting, and is characterized by grooming and drowsiness, accompanied by EEG synchronization (Beyer et al., 1971; Buchwald et al., 1964; Roth et al., 1967). Both behavioral relaxation and EEG synchronization following milk drinking were abolished by PCPA, but could be restored by 5-HTP (Cervantes et al., 1983). Although these observations do not distinguish between central and peripheral 5-HT, a central mechanism is suggested by the observation that EEG synchronization may also be induced by low frequency electrical stimulation of the raphe nuclei; this effect is similarly abolished by pharmacological treatments that reduce 5-HT function (Kostowski, 1971; Kostowski et al., 1969).

These findings imply that activity in 5-HT systems mediates the transition from active instrumental and consummatory behaviors to relaxation and sleep. At some anterior hypothalamic sites, ICSS induces sleep (Angyan, 1974). Contrary to the usual findings (see above), in these areas responding for brain stimulation reward is increased by 5-HTP (Poschel & Ninteman, 1968) and reduced by PCPA (Gibson et al., 1970; Phillips et al., 1976b). These observations suggest that under the appropriate conditions, 5-HT activity can have rewarding effects.

15.4. CONCLUSIONS

A simple (but short-sighted) summary of all of the work reviewed in this chapter would be to say that activating 5-HT systems inhibits behavior. A more adequate account must ask under what physiological conditions this behavioral inhibition would be apparent.

On the basis of studies of the behavioral effects of electrical stimulation of the brainstem, Hess (1957) postulated a balance between two fundamental motivational systems, which he called "ergotrophic" and "tropotrophic"; the "ergotropic" mode, which involves activation of the sympathetic nervous system, mediates exploration, motor excitability, and aggression, whereas the "tropotrophic" mode, which involves activation of the parasympathetic system, underlies rest, sleep, and digestion. Brodie and Shore (1957) suggested, on the basis of minimal evidence, that the ergotrophic system was controlled by NA, and the tropotrophic system by 5-HT. Although, as we have seen in earlier chapters, the ergotrophic system is considerably more complex than this, recent studies of satiety and relaxation strongly support their conceptualization of 5-HT function. More recently, Ellison pointed out that ergotrophic mechanisms are dominant when animals are in strange or potentially threatening environments, whereas tropotrophic mechanisms are dominant in the animal's home environment. Activation of 5-HT systems, he suggests, can be considered as "placing the brain into a state of consciousness appropriate for an animal in its nest" (Ellison, 1975).

At first sight, the activation of 5-HT systems by intense and prolonged stress appears to be totally incompatible with this formulation. However, another classic theoretical structure is readily to hand, in the shape of Selye's general adaptation syndrome (Selye, 1952). On first exposure to stress, the sympathetic nervous system is activated, the adrenal medulla secretes adrenaline, and the organism prepares for "fight or flight" (Cannon, 1932). But if, in spite of these measures, the problem remains, the body settles down to a prolonged struggle. Control shifts to the parasympathetic system, corticosteroids are released into the circulation, and there is a decrease in pain sensitivity, which we now know to be mediated by the release of endorphins into the blood stream and within the central nervous system. As reviewed above, the crucial element in all of these responses is an intact and functioning 5-HT system.

Although two very different sets of behavioral circumstances are involved, therefore, the common function of 5-HT activation is to prepare the body for "rest and recuperation," in one case, at its ease, and in the other, under seige. Conditions of threat or mild stress also involve a degree of 5-HT activation, which is essential for the inhibition of ongoing behavior seen in these circumstances.

In summary, the 5-HT-depleted animal presents a very sorry spectacle. It is unable to summon up the resources that would mitigate the effects of prolonged stress. It is irritable and aggressive. It is less likely to refrain from doing things that lead to punishment, and when the punishment arrives, it is more sensitive to pain. In addition, it cannot relax, and it does not even have the satisfaction of sitting back to enjoy reflecting on a good meal. In Chapters 19 and 20, further consideration will be given to the circumstances which give rise to this state of affairs.

sixteen

SEROTONIN AND DEPRESSION: CLINICAL STUDIES

In the previous chapter, I argued that the model of depression based on the suppression of behavior by high levels of 5-HT transmission (Aprison et al., 1982) has probably been overinterpreted. This hypothesis would predict that high levels of 5-HT function should be detectable in depressed people, that drugs which enhance 5-HT function should induce depression, and that drugs which decrease 5-HT function should act as antidepressants. In fact, none of these hypotheses are supported by the clinical evidence reviewed in this chapter. The sorry state of the 5-HT-depleted animal provides a starting point for an alternative set of hypotheses, which form an expanded version of the original indoleamine hypothesis of depression (Section 1.1.3): that low levels of 5-HT function should be detectable in depressed people, particularly in association with psychomotor agitation; that drugs which decrease 5-HT function should induce depression; and that drugs which increase 5-HT function should act as antidepressants. The clinical literature supports the first and third of these hypotheses.

16.1.   5-HT FUNCTION IN DEPRESSION

Aspects of 5-HT function have been extensively studied in depressed people, with reasonably coherent results. There is little evidence that the metabolism of 5-HT or the functioning of 5-HT receptors show any significant alteration. However, there is considerable evidence that in a substantial proportion of severely depressed patients the turnover and uptake of 5-HT are abnormally low.

16.1.1.   Synthesis

A possible abnormality of 5-HT synthesis was the subject of one of the earliest biochemical hypotheses of depression, which was unusual in postulating not only a biochemical disorder, but also a mechanism to explain it. The hypothesis proposed that the high circulating levels of cortisol present in many depressed patients could activate the hepatic enzyme tryptophan pyrrolase, resulting in an increase in the utilization of tryptophan for the synthesis of kynurenine and consequently in a decrease in the amount of tryptophan available for 5-HT synthesis (Curzon, 1969; Lapin & Oxenkrug, 1969). In addition to diverting tryptophan away from the brain, increased kynurenine could also reduce 5-HT synthesis in another way, by inhibiting the transport of tryptophan across the blood–brain barrier (Green & Curzon, 1970). More recently, it has been suggested that the "kynurenine shunt" could also be responsible for the depressive side effects of oral contraceptives, since kynurenine synthesis is also activated by estrogens (Parry & Rush, 1979).

Intriguing though this hypothesis may be, the evidence tends not to support it. Activation of the kynurenine shunt has been demonstrated only in animal studies; in human studies, changes in blood cortisol have not been shown to affect blood tryptophan levels, which are normal even under the extremely high cortisol levels seen in Cushing's disease (Kelly et al., 1983). Indeed, there is some evidence that tryptophan may actually be removed from the blood more slowly in depressed patients, rather than more rapidly (Coppen et al., 1974; Shaw et al., 1976; Spano et al., 1975), and normal excretion of kynurenine has been observed in depressed patients, both under baseline conditions (Wood et al., 1978) and following a tryptophan load (Frazer et al., 1973).

Although the "kynurenine shunt" is probably not responsible, a number of studies have reported that levels of free plasma tryptophan (i.e. not bound to plasma proteins) were reduced in depression (Coppen et al., 1973; Nakaya, 1976; Stein et al., 1976). However, other studies failed to observe this difference (Garfinkel et al., 1976; Moller et al., 1976; Riley & Shaw, 1976; Wirz-Justice et al., 1975), and the opposite result, an increase in free plasma trypotophan, has also been reported (Niskanen et al., 1976). Similar anomalies are also present in studies of total tryptophan levels (reviewed by Burns & Mendels, 1979). These studies are subject to a variety of methodological problems, including the need to control for diet and the plasma concentrations of other amino acids. In a recent well-controlled study, De Myer and co-workers (1981) observed a decrease in plasma tryptophan concentration in depressed patients compared to normal controls; reduction of this difference was significantly correlated with clinical recovery during the course of the study.

Under normal conditions, tryprophan hydroxylase, the rate-limiting enzyme for 5-HT synthesis, is unsaturated. Consequently, in animals (Green & Grahame-Smith, 1976; Nielsen & Moore, 1982) and in people (Gillman et al., 1981; Young & Gautier, 1981a,b), the availability of tryptophan controls the rate of 5-HT synthesis and turnover. However, it is unclear whether abnormalities of peripheral tryptophan, if present in depression, would actually lead to changes in central 5-HT synthesis; the literature that demonstrates control of 5-HT synthesis by tryptophan availability has typically employed gross fluctuations in plasma tryptophan concentrations, brought about either by tryptophan loading or by a tryptophan-free diet.

In fact, despite the possibility of abnormal plasma tryptophan concentrations in depression, and some evidence that blood–brain transport of tryptophan might be impaired (Gaillard & Tissot, 1979), normal levels of tryptophan have been found in the ventricular CSF of depressed patients undergoing psychosurgery (Bridges et al., 1976; Curzon et al., 1980), and a report of reduced tryptophan in the lumbar CSF of depressed patients (Coppen et al., 1972a) was not confirmed (Ashcroft et al., 1973). Postmortem studies of the brains of suicide victims are equivocal. Three studies found reduced 5-HT levels (Lloyd et al., 1974; Pare et al., 1969; Shaw et al., 1967), confined, in one case, to the dorsal and inferior central raphe nuclei (Lloyd et al., 1974), but three other studies found no significant differences (Beskow et al., 1976; Bourne et al., 1968; Cochran et al., 1976). In one of the studies in which differences were observed, these disappeared when the age difference between the two samples was taken into account (Pare et al., 1969).

16.1.2. Turnover

In addition to measuring brain levels of 5-HT, some of the postmortem studies also measured levels of 5-HIAA, which is the only major metabolite of 5-HT; other things being equal, the rate of breakdown of 5-HT will provide a measure of the amount of 5-HT released. These results are also rather equivocal. Three studies of suicide victims found normal levels of 5-HIAA (Cochran et al., 1976; Lloyd et al., 1974; Pare et al., 1969), whereas a decrease in brain 5-HIAA was found in two other studies of suicides (Beskow et al., 1976; Bourne et al., 1968) and in a study of four depressed patients, one of them in remission, who died of natural causes

(Birkmayer & Riederer, 1975). However, in one of these studies, the difference disappeared when the results were reanalyzed, controlling for the time between death and dissection (Beskow et al., 1976; Gottfries, 1980); this observation casts some doubt on the reality of differences reported in other postmortem investigations.

There have been a number of rather futile attempts to assess brain 5-HT turnover by measuring urinary levels of 5-HIAA. Although there are some reports that urinary 5-HIAA was low in depression (Puzynski et al., 1979), more commonly, no change is reported (Martin et al., 1980; Markianos et al., 1982; Riederer et al., 1974). These studies are not particularly informative, since approximately 99% of 5-HIAA originates outside the central nervous system (Cooper et al., 1982), and there is no correlation between urinary and CSF 5-HIAA concentrations (Bertilsson et al., 1982a). Consequently, urinary 5-HIAA is not considered to be a reliable index of central 5-HT activity (see e.g. Nomra et al., 1977).

There is, however, a good correlation between 5-HIAA concentrations measured in lumbar and in cisternal CSF (Banki & Molnar, 1981; Bertilsson et al., 1982b). Measurement of 5-HIAA in lumbar CSF therefore provides a reasonable estimate of brain 5-HT turnover, despite contamination from spinal 5-HT. Two studies have measured brain 5-HIAA more directly during the course of psychosurgical operations. In the first, reduced ventricular 5-HIAA was reported in depressed patients, compared to anxious patients and neurological controls (Bridges et al., 1976), but this finding was not replicated (Curzon et al., 1980). The second study did, however, report a reduction in cisternal 5-HIAA in depressed patients (Curzon et al., 1980).

Ashcroft and Sharman first reported that lumbar 5-HIAA was reduced in depressed patients in 1960. Subsequent studies, in roughly equal numbers, have either supported this observation or found no difference between depressed patients and controls (Table 16.1). When the accumulation of 5-HIAA in CSF is studied following the administration of probenecid, which blocks the transport of 5-HIAA out of the CSF and should amplify any differences which are present (see Section 9.1.5), the discrepancies remain. It has usually been found that postprobenecid 5-HIAA accumulation was reduced in depression, particularly in bipolar patients (Bowers, 1974a; Van Praag et al., 1973), but still, no significant changes were reported in several studies (Table 16.1).

There have been a number of reports that CSF 5-HIAA levels were bimodally distributed in depressed subjects (Asberg et al., 1976a; Goodwin & Potter, 1978; Van Praag, 1982a), though not all studies have confirmed this observation (Berger et al., 1980; Maas et al., 1982), and it may simply reflect the fact that 5-HIAA levels are higher in women than in men (Asberg et al., 1973; Maas et al., 1982). Nonetheless, it is possible that the failure of CSF 5-HIAA studies to reach a consensus may arise from the fact that 5-HT turnover is indeed low, but only in a subgroup

TABLE 16.1. STUDIES OF CENTRAL 5-HT TURNOVER IN DEPRESSION

Reduced	No Change
Basal CSF 5-HIAA levels	
Agren, 1980b	Ashcroft et al, 1973
Asberg & Traskman, 1981	Banki & Arato, 1983
Ashcroft & Sharman, 1960	Bowers, 1972
Ashcroft et al, 1966	Bowers et al, 1969
Banki, 1977a,b	Fotherby et al, 1963
Coppen et al, 1972b	Goodwin & Post, 1972
Dencker et al, 1966	Goodwin et al, 1973a
McLeod & McLeod, 1972	Jori et al, 1975
Mendels et al, 1972	Papeschi & McClure, 1971
Traskman et al, 1981	Roos & Sjostrom, 1969
Van Praag & Korf, 1971a	Sjostrom & Roos, 1972
Van Praag et al, 1970	Subramanyam, 1975
	Van Praag et al, 1973
Post-Probenecid 5-HIAA accumulation	
Banki, 1977b	Berger et al, 1980
Bowers, 1974a	Bowers, 1972
Roos & Sjostrom, 1969	Goodwin et al, 1973a
Sjostrom, 1973	Jori et al, 1975
Sjostrom & Roos, 1972	
Vanderheyden et al, 1981	
Van Praag et al, 1970, 1973	

of depressed patients. This appears to be the case for both DA and NA turnover (Sections 9.1.5 and 12.1.4). A difference that is present only in certain patients would tend to be obscured when diagnostically hetero-geneous groups of patients are studied.

With one exception (Davis et al., 1981), low 5-HIAA levels have not correlated significantly with severity of depression (Ashcroft et al., 1966; Banki, 1977b; Banki & Arato, 1983; Goodwin et al., 1973a). Furthermore, although Post and co-workers (1973c) found that 5-HIAA levels were elevated when depressed patients were asked to simulate mania, it has not usually been found that 5-HIAA was related to psychomotor retar-dation (Goodwin et al., 1973a; Van Praag et al., 1973) or to level of phys-ical activity (Banki, 1977a; Papeschi & McClure, 1971; Van Praag & Korf, 1971a; Weiss et al., 1974).

However, there is one subgroup of depressed patients in whom 5-HT turnover is clearly reduced. Asberg and co-workers (1976b) were the first to observe that depressives with abnormally low CSF 5-HIAA levels were more likely to have attempted suicide. This finding has been widely corroborated (Agren, 1980b; Banki & Arato, 1983; Banki et al., 1981a,b; Montgomery & Montgomery, 1982; Traskman et al., 1981; Van Praag, 1982a). In one study, a follow-up revealed that all seven patients who subsequently succeeded in killing themselves had had 5-HIAA levels below the median when initially studied (Traskman et al., 1981).

The specificity of the association between low 5-HT turnover and affective disorders is at present uncertain. Normal 5-HT turnover has been observed in obsessive–compulsive patients (Thoren et al., 1980). However, low CSF 5-HIAA levels have been observed in personality disordered subjects (G. Brown et al., 1979, 1982), in patients with schizoaffective disorder (Traskman et al., 1981; Van Praag, 1982a), and in alcoholics (Ballenger et al., 1979; Rosenthal et al., 1980). The extent to which the people with low 5-HT turnover who succumb to these disorders are also depressed is not clear, though among schizoaffective patients, the relationship may be quite strong (Van Praag, 1982a). Low 5-HIAA is also found in apparently nondepressed suicide attempters (Asberg & Traskman, 1981; Traskman et al., 1981); estimates of the proportion of suicide attempters who are depressed at the time of their attempt vary between 23% (Krupinski et al., 1965) and 82% (Van Praag, 1982a).

A further observation—that low 5-HIAA was particularly associated with violent suicide attempts (Asberg et al., 1976b; Banki & Arato, 1983; Traskman et al., 1981)—has not always been confirmed (Van Praag, 1982a). However, low levels of 5-HIAA were associated with a high level of aggressive thinking (Asberg et al., 1980) and with a history of aggressive behavior in a prison population (Bioulac et al., 1978, 1980) and in personality-disordered military personnel (G. Brown et al., 1979, 1982). Rather than being associated with depression specifically, it appears that low 5-HT turnover may be related to an increase in violent behavior, which may be manifest either as aggression or as suicide. Indeed, in the military personnel referred to above, there was a strong association between histories of violence and suicide attempts (Brown et al., 1982). In addition, it has frequently been observed that low 5-HIAA in depressed patients is associated with high levels of anxiety and agitation (Asberg et al., 1980; Banki, 1977b; Banki et al., 1981b; Fujiwara & Otsuki, 1974; Leckman et al., 1980a).

There are a number of reasons for thinking that low 5-HT turnover is not a symptom that accompanies an episode of depression, but rather a state-independent marker, which confers a predisposition to become depressed. First, manic patients have also been shown to have low CSF 5-HIAA levels (Banki, 1977a; Coppen et al., 1972b; Dencker et al., 1966; Mendels et al., 1972) or a reduced accumulation of 5-HIAA following probenecid administration (Sjostrom & Roos, 1972). With only one exception (Ashcroft et al., 1966), studies that failed to find evidence of reduced 5-HT turnover in mania also found no changes in depression (Bowers et al., 1969; Goodwin & Post, 1972; Roos & Sjostrom, 1969). Second, when low 5-HIAA is observed in depressed patients, it is usually found to remain low during periods of remission (Dencker et al., 1966; Goodwin et al., 1973b; Mendels et al., 1972; Sjostrom & Roos, 1972; Van Praag & De Haan, 1979). Third, patients with abnormally low 5-HIAA levels are found to have a higher frequency of depressive episodes (van Praag & De Haan, 1979). They also have a higher incidence of depression among their first-degree relatives (van Praag & De Haan, 1979); similarly, low CSF 5-HIAA also predicts a family history of depression in healthy volunteers (Sedvall et al., 1980).

16.1.3. Catabolism

The interpretation of a reduction in CSF 5-HIAA depends to some extent on whether the metabolism of 5-HT proceeds normally. A decrease in turnover only implies a decrease in 5-HT release if there is no concomitant reduction in the breakdown of 5-HT. As previously discussed (Sections 9.1.2, 12.1.2), abnormalities of platelet MAO have been described in depressed patients, but it remains to be demonstrated that these have significant implications for central monoaminergic transmission. Additionally, platelet MAO has a low affinity for 5-HT (Murphy & Donnelly, 1974), and there is no evidence from postmortem studies that there are any abnormalities of brain MAO in suicide victims, unless they were also alcoholic (Grote et al., 1974; Gottfries et al., 1975).

One potentially interesting finding was that platelet MAO activity was inversely correlated with the severity of guilt feelings in neurotically depressed patients; this relationship was observed for MAO-A but not for MAO-B (Perris et al., 1980). The significance of this observation is that MAO-A is the form of MAO that metabolizes 5-HT (Finberg & Youdim, 1983). There is also some evidence that platelet MAO activity may be positively correlated with CSF 5-HIAA concentration (Oreland et al., 1981). It follows that guilt may be a part of the constellation of symptoms associated with low 5-HT turnover.

16.1.4. Receptors

As the decreased turnover of 5-HT seen in a high proportion of depressed patients cannot be explained by changes in MAO activity, it most probably represents a reduction in the release of 5-HT. It is usually assumed that a decrease in 5-HT release implies a decrease in 5-HT function. However, there is an alternative interpretation. The "hypersensitive serotonin receptor" theory of Aprison and colleagues (1982) suggest that when low 5-HT turnover occurs it is in response to an abnormally high level of 5-HT transmission brought about by supersensitive receptors. This theory exactly parallels the reformulated catecholamine hypothesis of Segal and co-workers (1974), which attributed low NA turnover to hypersensitive adrenergic receptors (Section 1.1.4). In principle, the neuroendocrine strategy provides a means of assessing the sensitivity of a limited set of 5-HT receptors. In practice, however, it has not yet proved very informative.

5-Hydroxytryptophan (5-HTP), the precursor of 5-HT, inhibits the release of TRH (Ettigi & Brown, 1977), but this response has not been studied in depressed patients. 5-Hydroxytryptophan has also been reported to stimulate growth hormone (GH) release (Imura et al., 1973; Wirz-Justice et al., 1976). However, some studies failed to observe this effect (Muller et al., 1974; Westenberg et al., 1982). Furthermore, there have been reports that GH release by 5-HTP was actually augmented by pretreatment with the 5-HT receptor blocker methysergide (Richards et al., 1980) and that GH release was suppressed by the 5-HT agonist fenfluramine (Willoughby et al., 1982). At the very least, these results imply that there are both stimulatory and inhibitory effects of 5-HT on GH secretion. A reduced GH response to 5-HTP has been reported in depressed patients (Takahashi et al., 1973); this finding has not been replicated (Meltzer et al., 1983b), and in any case, it is impossible to interpret.

As discussed in earlier chapters, one of the best established biological markers of endogenous depression is an increase in hypothalamic–pituitary–adrenal (HPA) activity, which is detectable either as an increase in circulating levels of cortisol or as an abnormally brief suppression of cortisol secretion by dexamethasone. Although 5-HTP stimulates ACTH release (Ettigi & Brown, 1977), there is no clear relationship between 5-HT function and HPA activity in depressed patients. In one study, a slight correlation between CSF cortisol and 5-HIAA levels was observed, but only because both were correlated with height (Traskman et al., 1980). Two other studies have reported an inverse relationship between CSF 5-HIAA levels and postdexamethasone cortisol levels, which is the opposite of what would be expected if 5-HT function determined the response on the DST (Banki & Arato, 1983; Carroll et al., 1981b). Furthermore, as noted above, low 5-HT turnover, when present, is state-independent, whereas HPA abnormalities are state-dependent. Unlike the 5-HT abnormalities, abnormal dexamethasone suppression is not normally seen in manic episodes or during remission (Carroll, 1982).

It has recently been reported that the cortisol response to a 5-HTP challenge was enhanced in depressed patients, indicating an increase in 5-HT receptor function. As this effect was significantly greater in suicidal patients, and was also present in mania, it might represent a compensatory change secondary to a decrease in 5-HT turnover (Meltzer et al., 1983b). However, studies of a different neuroendocrine response, the release of prolactin by 5-HT agonists (De La Fuente & Rosenbaum, 1981; Ettigi & Brown, 1977), do not support the conclusion that 5-HT receptors are hypersensitive in depression. In the study of Meltzer and co-workers (1983b) there were no alterations in the prolactin response to 5-HTP; in another recent study, the prolactin response to fenfluramine was reduced in depressed patients (Siever et al., 1984), suggesting if anything a decrease in 5-HT receptor function.

There is some evidence that prolactin release by opiates may depend on 5-HT activation (Koenig et al., 1979). Depressed patients have been reported to show a blunted prolactin response to morphine (Extein et al., 1980b) and methadone (Judd et al., 1982, 1983), which again might indicate reduced 5-HT receptor function, but obviously this observation is subject to a variety of alternative explanations. Studies of prolactin release by TRH in depression have reported an increase (Coppen et al., 1980a; Maeda et al., 1975; Winokur et al., 1982), an decrease (Asnis et al., 1981; Ehrensing et al., 1974; Linnoila, 1978), and no change (Coppen et al., 1980a).

Taken together, these observations do not provide strong or convincing evidence that 5-HT receptor function is abnormal in depression. This conclusion is supported by a postmortem study of depressed patients dying of natural causes, which found no abnormality in the number or sensitivity of 5-HT receptors (Blessed et al., 1982, cited by Perry et al., 1983). However, another recent postmortem study has reported an increase in the number of 5-HT$_2$ receptors in the brains of suicide victims (Stanley et al., 1983); in view of the association between suicide and low 5-HT turnover, this result can probably best be understood as being secondary to a chronically reduced level of receptor stimulation.

16.1.5. Uptake

The removal of 5-HT from the synaptic cleft is effected primarily by reuptake mechanisms, rather than by enzymatic degradation. A 5-HT uptake system in blood platelets has pharmacological properties that are similar to those of neuronal uptake (Sneddon, 1973; Stahl & Meltzer, 1978a). Platelet 5-HT uptake has been extensively studied as a model of 5-HT uptake by presynaptic nerve terminals. The heuristic value of this model is enhanced by the observation that blood platelets contain an enzyme, neuron-specific enolase, that was previously found only in nerve cells, which suggests a common embryological origin for the two cell types (Marangos et al., 1980). It is also possible that the activity of the platelet 5-HT uptake system may be under the control of the central nervous system. Physostigmine, a drug that can cause depression under some circumstances (Section 14.3), has been reported to reduce the uptake of 5-HT by platelets; this effect was not blocked by methylscopolamine, a drug that antagonizes some of the effects of physostigmine peripherally but does not cross the blood–brain barrier (Rausch et al., 1982).

With occasional exceptions (Oxenkrug, 1979), it has usually been found that 5-HT uptake was reduced in blood platelets from severely depressed patients, compared to normal controls (Born et al., 1980; Coppen et al.,

1978, 1980b; Ehsanullah, 1980; Ehsanulla et al., 1979; Giret et al., 1980; Hallstrom et al., 1976; Kaplan & Mann, 1982; Malmgren et al., 1981; Meltzer et al., 1981a; Mirkin & Coppen, 1981; Scott et al., 1979; Tuomisto & Tukainen, 1976; Tuomisto et al., 1979). In one study, reduced 5-HT uptake was also observed in neurotic depressives (Ehsanullah 1980; Ehsanullah et al., 1979), but more usually, neurotic depressives have not been found to differ from normal volunteers (Hallstrom et al., 1976; Malmgren et al., 1981; Mirkin & Coppen, 1980).

Like 5-HT turnover, platelet 5-HT uptake is a state-independent marker, as the decrease is also observed in depressed patients following recovery (Coppen et al., 1980b). Uptake is usually increased by lithium (Coppen et al., 1980b; Corona et al., 1982; Murphy et al., 1969), but tricyclic antidepressant treatment usually has no effect, or reduces uptake further, and in general, changes in 5-HT uptake do not correlate with clinical recovery (Coppen & Wood, 1979; Corona et al., 1982; Tuomisto et al., 1979; see also Section 17.2.2).

The significance of platelet uptake studies has been enhanced by the discovery of **high** affinity binding sites for [^{3}H]imipramine (Raisman et al., 1979a,b). Lesion studies have demonstrated that in the brain these sites are located primarily on presynaptic terminals of 5-HT neurons (Chuang et al., 1982; Gross et al., 1981b; Sette et al., 1981). They are closely associated with the 5-HT uptake site, though the two are not identical (Langer et al., 1982a; Raisman et al., 1982; Rehavi et al., 1983). [^{3}H]Imipramine binding sites are also found in blood platelets, and these appear to be pharmacologically identical to those in the brain (Langer et al., 1980; Rehavi et al., 1980a).

With two exceptions (Mellerup et al., 1982; Whitaker et al., 1984), a reduction in the number of [^{3}H]imipramine binding sites has usually been observed in blood platelets taken from depressed patients (Asarch et al., 1981; Briley et al., 1980, 1982b; Langer et al., 1981, 1982b; Paul et al., 1981; Raisman et al., 1982). One study of bipolar patients in remission failed to find any difference between patients and controls (Berrettini et al., 1982b). However, the patients had been treated with lithium, which increases platelet 5-HT uptake and [^{3}H]imipramine binding. Other investigations have reported that, like the abnormality of 5-HT uptake, the reduction in [^{3}H]imipramine binding persisted during treatment and following recovery (Langer et al., 1982b; Langer & Raisman, 1983).

One recent, apparently well-controlled study reported that imipramine binding was increased by 35%, rather than decreased, in the brains of suicide victims, as compared with a control group of homicide victims (Meyerson et al., 1982). However, two other postmortem studies of brain [^{3}H]imipramine binding are consistent with the platelet literature. In one, a decrease in imipramine binding was observed in frontal cortex of suicide brains compared with well-matched controls (Stanley et al., 1982, 1983); in the second, imipramine binding was reduced in the hippocampus and occipital cortex of depressed patients who died of natural causes, as compared with Alzheimer's disease patients and nonpsychiatric controls (Perry et al., 1983).

16.2. TREATMENTS THAT REDUCE 5-HT FUNCTION

On the basis of the animal literature reviewed in Chapter 15 and the decrease in 5-HT turnover observed in a substantial proportion of severely depressed patients, it might be expected that pharmacological treatments that reduce 5-HT transmission would cause depression. However, as was the case for DA and NA, there is no strong evidence to support this prediction.

16.2.1. Treatments Acting Presynaptically

Reserpine and related drugs reduce the release of 5-HT, as well as that of DA and NA, by preventing the storage of transmitter in presynaptic terminals (see Sec. 1.1.1). As discussed in earlier chapters, reserpine-induced depressions were frequently reported in the 1950s, but there is some doubt as to their reality (Goodwin et al., 1972). However, arguments have been advanced as to why the presence of absence of reserpine-induced depression is not crucial to the catecholamine hypotheses of depression, and these arguments apply equally well to 5-HT (Chapters 9 and 12).

The results of reducing 5-HT transmission by blocking 5-HT synthesis with PCPA have been reported in a total of six normal volunteers, 22 medical patients, and one opiate addict. Reduction of 5-HT function by 60–80% produced restlessness, tiredness, anxiety, agitation, and confusion, but no more than the occasional mild depression (Carpenter, 1970; Cremata & Koe, 1966; Engelman et al., 1967; Sicuteri et al., 1970). Note, however, that this pattern of symptoms may be a mild form of the pattern that is characteristically seen in depressed patients with low CSF 5-HIAA levels (see Section 16.1.2).

Despite the lack of any pronounced depressive effect, PCPA has been found to block the therapeutic response to antidepressant drugs. Shopsin and co-workers reported that in two patients successfully treated with imipramine, depression returned within two days of adding PCPA and lifted when PCPA was withdrawn. The catecholamine synthesis inhibitor AMPT did not have this effect (Shopsin et al., 1975a). In a subsequent study, a similar reversible blockade of antidepressant effects by PCPA was reported in five patients successfully treated with the MAOI tranylcypromine (Shopsin et al., 1976). Although these studies involved a very small number of patients, they implicate 5-HT in the mechanism of antidepressant action of imipramine and tranylcypromine, though the implications for the pathophysiology of depression are much weaker.

16.2.2. Receptor Blockers

The other way to reduce 5-HT transmission is by blockade of postsynaptic 5-HT receptors. A number of studies in the late 1960s reported that the 5-HT receptor blockers methysergide (Dewhurst, 1968; Haskovec, 1969) and cinanserin (Kane, 1970) exerted rapid therapeutic effects in mania; however, subsequent controlled studies could not confirm these claims (reviewed by Van Praag, 1978). Methysergide, which is used in the treatment of migraine, has not been reported to alter mood in normal subjects of in depressed patients.

    A number of antidepressant drugs, including some tricyclics (e.g., amitriptyline) and some newer atypical antidepressants (e.g., mianserin, trazodone) include potent 5-HT receptor blockade among their other pharmacological properties. This fact, which clearly is of some significance for evaluating the involvement of 5-HT in depression, will be discussed more fully in the following chapter. It is simply noted here that the "other pharmacological properties" include 5-HT stimulant effects, which may outweigh the receptor blockade. The classic action of amitriptyline, for example, is blockade of 5-HT uptake, and a 5-HT stimulant action of trazodone has also been noted at high doses (Maj et al., 1979c).

16.3. TREATMENTS THAT INCREASE 5-HT FUNCTION

In general, pharmacological treatments that increase 5-HT function have been found to have antidepressant properties, in contrast to the largely negative findings with treatments which reduce 5-HT function. There is also some evidence for antimanic effects, though the literature in this case is slight. The majority of studies have employed the 5-HT precursors tryptophan and 5-HTP. More recently, specific inhibitors of 5-HT uptake have been investigated, and there is also a small literature on the effects of 5-HT receptor agonists.

16.3.1. Tryptophan

Under normal circumstances, the enzyme tyrosine hydroxylase, which is the rate-limiting enzyme in the synthesis of catecholamines, is fully saturated. Consequently, it should not theoretically be possible to increase catecholamine synthesis by administration of tyrosine, and this accounts for the fact that there have been only two attempts to use tyrosine as an antidepressant (Section 12.3.2). However, tryptophan hydroxylase, the rate-limiting enzyme in the synthesis of 5-HT, is not normally saturated.

As a result, the antidepressant potential of tryptophan has been extensively investigated.

Clinical trials of tryptophan in depression have been the subject of numerous recent reviews, which concur in failing to reach a conclusion: there is considerable evidence to support the therapeutic efficacy of tryptophan, and an equally large body of negative findings (Burns & Mendels, 1979; Cole et al., 1980; Cooper, 1979; Van Praag, 1980, 1982b). The most recent investigation, which (unlike previous trials) studied out-patients rather than in-patients, reported that tryptophan was superior to placebo and was equivalent to amitriptyline (Thompson et al., 1982). In contrast to the equivocal antidepressant status of tryptophan alone, a number of double-blind studies, as well as some open trials, have established that the combination of tryptophan with an MAOI was superior to MAOI alone (Coppen, 1967; Coppen et al., 1963; Glassman & Platman, 1969; Gutierrez & Alino, 1971; Pare, 1963). This effects has not generally been observed with tricyclic antidepressants (Alino et al., 1973; Pare, 1963; Shaw et al., 1972, 1975). One study has reported a potentiation by tryptophan of the antidepressant effect of chlorimipramine, a 5-HT uptake inhibiting tricyclic (Walinder et al., 1976), but an attempt to replicate this effect using zimelidine, a more specific 5-HT uptake inhibitor, was unsuccessful (Walinder et al., 1981). The discrepancy between the successful potentiation of MAOIs by tryptophan and the lack of effect with tricyclics most probably arises from the "ceiling effect," inherent in the fact that tricyclics are more effective clinically than MAOIs.

Some of the negative findings with tryptophan may simply reflect methodological inadequacies; two possible sources of error are particularly worthy of note (Gelenburg et al., 1982; Van Praag, 1982b). First, an effect of tryptophan in a subgroup of patients might be obscured in a more heterogeneous group. It has been observed, for example, that the efficacy of tryptophan was positively correlated with increases in plasma tryptophan levels during treatment (Chouinard et al., 1979) and was inversely correlated with the initial pretreatment plasma tryptophan level (calculated in relation to the levels of other large neutral amino acids with which tryptophan competes for the same blood–brain transport mechanism) (Moller et al., 1980). Unfortunately, no studies have yet attempted to relate the therapeutic effects of tryptophan to pretreatment CSF 5-HIAA levels. Second, there may be a "therapeutic window" for tryptophan: blood levels of tryptophan have tended to be lower in studies reporting a successful outcome than in those reporting a negative outcome (Gelenburg et al., 1982; Young & Sourkes, 1977). A number of factors could contribute to an inhibiting effect of tryptophan at high doses. These include the formation of active compounds such as tryptamine, which could interfere with 5-HT function, and the reduction of catecholamine synthesis by successful competition with tyrosine for blood–brain transport (Gelenberg et al., 1982).

A further factor which might be relevant is that only a small proportion of tryptophan is actually converted to 5-HT, the major metabolic route being the formation of kynurenine in the liver. A number of studies have examined the effects of combining tryptophan with an inhibitor of hepatic tryptophan metabolism (allopurinol or nicotinamide). This combination appeared to be successful in some patients (Calandra et al., 1981; Chouinard et al., 1979; Shopsin, 1976), but it has not been convincingly demonstrated that the combination is better that tryptophan alone.

Two double-blind controlled trials have reported antimanic effects of tryptophan (Murphy et al., 1974a; Prange et al., 1974), though a third controlled study failed to demonstrate this effect (Chambers & Naylor, 1978). An antimanic effect of tryptophan, taken together with the probable antidepressant effect and some evidence suggesting a better antidepressant effect in bipolar patients (Farkas et al., 1976; Murphy et al., 1974a), support the picture of reduced 5-HT function in both depression and mania suggested by the biochemical findings (Section 16.1.2). However, it remains possible that the supposed antimanic effect simply reflects a sedative action (Burns & Mendels, 1979).

In normal volunteers, the most consistently observed effect of tryptophan is, in fact, mild sedation (Charney et al., 1982d; Greenwood et al., 1974, 1975). However, a recent study also reported that the majority of subjects also experienced a "high" and "mellow" feeling of tranquillity after intravenous tryptophan infusions (Charney et al., 1982d).

16.3.2. 5-HTP

Mood elevating effects in nondepressed subjects have also been observed with the other 5-HT precursor, 5-HTP. Trimble and co-workers (1975) administered high doses of 5-HTP intravenously to nondepressed volunteers after pretreatment with a peripheral decarboxylase inhibitor, to confine 5-HT formation to the brain. One of the eight subjects became depressed, but the other seven experienced a euphoric effect. In a similar study, 5-HTP, but not placebo infusions, induced elation in 34 of 35 infusions, in a total of 16 subjects (Graw et al., 1976; Puhringe et al., 1976). Elation was also seen in 10 out of 18 patients receiving 5-HTP in the treatment of myoclonus (Van Woert et al., 1977).

Studies of 5-HTP in depression are fewer in number than those of tryptophan. Early trials were unsuccessful (Pare & Sandler, 1959; Kline et al., 1964; Glassman, 1969). However, more recent studies, using larger doses of 5-HTP, have tended to report positive antidepressant effects. A review of open studies, with a total of 350 patients, found improvement in 191 patients (54%) (Van Praag, 1982b), including one study which reported a 50% recovery rate in "therapy-resistant" patients (Van Hiele, 1980). In double-blind trials, 5-HTP has been found to be superior to placebo (Bartlett & Paillard, 1974; Van Praag, 1982b, 1983; Van Praag et al., 1972), superior to the MAOI nialamide (Lopez-Ibor et al., 1976), and as effective as imipramine (Angst et al., 1977) or chlorimipramine (Van Praag, 1982b). Additionally, the combination of chlorimipramine and 5-HTP was found to be superior to either treatment alone (Van Praag et al., 1974; Van Praag, 1982b). In fact, only two controlled studies have failed to demonstrate therapeutic efficacy for 5-HTP. One involved brief (maximum 16 days) treatment of a small number of therapy-resistant patients (Brodie et al., 1973). In the second, the combination of 5-HTP and the MAOI clorgyline was found to be better than 5-HTP alone, and 5-HTP was better than placebo. The differences between 5-HTP and the other two groups were not statistically significant, but this may well be because the numbers in each group were small (Mendlewicz & Youdim, 1980).

Although the first placebo-controlled study of 5-HTP in depression had only five subjects in each group, the three patients who responded to 5-HTP all were found to have abnormally low pretreatment 5-HT turnover, as measured by the accumulation of 5-HIAA in the CSF following a probenecid challenge (Van Praag et al., 1972). This superior response to 5-HTP in patients with low 5-HT turnover was recently replicated in a larger study (Van Praag, 1982b). A similar finding of low urinary 5-HIAA in 5-HTP responders has also been reported (Fujiwara & Otsuki, 1974). These observations strengthen the presumption that 5-HTP exerts its antidepressant effect by enhancing central 5-HT transmission.

However, other possibilities must also be considered. Unlike tryptophan, 5-HTP is converted almost exclusively to 5-HT. In common with DOPA, however (Section 9.3.1), much of this conversion takes place outside the brain, unless 5-HTP is accompanied by a peripheral decarboxylase inhibitor. Also, because the enzyme responsible for 5-HTP decarboxylation is nonspecific (Yuwiler et al., 1959), much of the central conversion of 5-HTP to 5-HT takes place in catecholamine neurons, displacing DA and NA and reducing catecholamine function. However, the evidence of previous chapters suggests that a reduction of catecholamine function would be unlikely to account for any mood elevating effects of 5-HTP. In fact, recent evidence suggests that interference with catecholaminergic transmission might actually detract from the therapeutic effect of 5-HTP. The combination of the 5-HTP with the catecholamine precursor tyrosine produced better antidepressant effects than 5-HTP alone, in two double blind controlled studies of patients with low central 5-HT turnover (Van Praag, 1983).

In a potentially important recent development, 5-HTP was found to be prophylactically effective in reducing the relapse rate of both unipolar and bipolar patients, particularly those with persistently low CSF 5-HIAA. In a long-term study of 20 patients with recurrent depressions, 17 relapsed during a year on placebo, compared to only six during a year on 5-HTP; the frequency of relapses and intensity of depressions were also correspondingly smaller on 5-HTP. Five of seven patients with post-probenecid CSF 5-HIAA accumulation in the normal range (measured during remission) relapsed on 5-HTP, compared with only 1 of 13 patients with persistently low 5-HT turnover (Van Praag & De Haan, 1980). In a subsequent report, the prophylactic efficacy of 5-HTP was estimated to be equal to that of lithium in unipolar patients, but somewhat inferior in bipolars (Van Praag & De Haan, 1981).

16.3.3. Receptor Agonists

Unlike precursors of 5-HT, 5-HT receptor agonists have been studied only minimally in affective disorders. A number of open studies have reported antimanic effects of fenfluramine (Cookson & Silverstone, 1976; Murphy et al., 1978b; Pearce, 1973). However, in one study it was noted that the effect was primarily one of sedation, with little effect on manic ideation (Cookson & Silverstone, 1976). Fenfluramine has also been reported to have antidepressant effects, particularly in bipolar patients (Murphy et al., 1978b). Conversely, depressions have been reported after withdrawal from fenfluramine in obese patients who were using it as an appetite suppressant (Steel & Briggs, 1972).

16.3.4. Uptake Inhibitors

Potentiation of 5-HT transmission by blockade of the reuptake system has been recognized as a potential mechanism of antidepressant action since the discovery that tricyclic antidepressants have this effect (Section 1.1). Secondary tricyclics, such as nortriptyline and DMI, are considerably more potent as NA uptake inhibitors, but the difference is much smaller for the tertiary tricyclics such as amitriptyline and imipramine. The frequent assertion that amitriptyline is a "serotonergic" antidepressant, which is virtually without effect on NA uptake (Maas, 1975), is something of an overstatement. Where both systems have been studied under the same conditions, amitriptyline has been found to exert roughly equipotent effects on 5-HT and NA uptake, varying in different studies by not more than a factor of 2 in either direction. Only chlorimipramine, among the tricyclics, is clearly more potent as a 5-HT uptake inhibitor by a factor of 10 (Carlsson et al., 1969a,b; Maitre et al., 1982; Ross & Renyi, 1975).

Although one study reported that patients who responded to amitriptyline had lower pretreatment CSF levels of 5-HIAA (Goodwin et al., 1978), others have found no difference in 5-HIAA between responders and nonresponders (Maas et al., 1982; Mendlewicz et al., 1982b), and the opposite results, a higher pretreatment 5-HT turnover in amitriptyline responders, has also been reported (Goodwin & Post, 1975). Studies of chlorimipramine are similarly equivocal. One study reported lower pretreatment 5-HIAA in responders (Van Praag, 1977). However, other studies have not confirmed this relationship (Traskman et al., 1979; Trask-man-Bendz et al., 1981), and in one study, 5-HIAA was elevated in chlorimipramine responders (Van Scheyen et al., 1977).

In fact, it would be surprising if these studies had succeeded in showing low 5-HT turnover to predict clearly the patients who would respond to "serotonergic" tricyclics, because both amitriptyline and chlorimipramine are metabolized to active compounds—nortriptyline and desmethylch-lorimipramine—which act predominantly as blockers of NA uptake. Nor-triptyline may actually be ineffective in patients with low CSF 5-HIAA levels (Asberg et al., 1973). The search for a more specific 5-HT uptake inhibitor led to the development of zimelidine (Carlsson, 1981), which is approximately 25 times more potent against 5-HT uptake; the active me-tabolite norzimelidine is also 10 times more potent at 5-HT synapses (Ross & Renyi, 1975; Ross et al., 1976; Ross, 1979). 5-HT agonist properties of zimelidine have been demonstrated in people (Siwers et al., 1977; Aberg & Holmberg, 1979), though at the doses used clinically, an effect on NA is also apparent (Bertilsson et al., 1980).

Clinical studies of zimelidine have strongly supported its efficacy in depression. In addition to showing positive effects in preliminary open studies (reviewed by Heel et al., 1982), four controlled studies have found zimelidine to be superior to placebo (Astra, 1982, cited by Heel et al., 1982; Claghorn et al., 1983; Georgotas et al., 1982; Norman et al., 1983), and 11 studies have found zimelidine to be at least as effective as tricyclic antidepressants (Claghorn et al., 1983; Heel et al., 1982). In some trials it was reported that zimelidine had better effects on anxiety and mood than amitriptyline (Montgomery et al., 1981) or DMI (Aberg-Wistedt, 1982), or that it produced faster antidepressant effects (Aberg, 1981; Georgotas et al., 1980; Montgomery et al., 1981), but these effects have not generally been noted. As is found with 5-HTP, a low pretreatment CSF 5-HIAA level does appear to predict a better response to zimelidine (Aberg-Wistedt et al., 1981, 1982).

A number of other specific 5-HT uptake inhibitors are also under in-vestigation. Femoxetine (Buus Lassen et al., 1975) was originally re-ported to be less effective than amitriptyline (Ghose et al., 1977), but subsequent studies found that the two drugs were equally effective (Bojholm et al., 1979; Reebye et al., 1982) and that femoxetine was su-perior to placebo (Dahl et al., 1982). Response to femoxetine was not, however, related to 5-HT turnover (Dahl et al., 1982). In open studies, antidepressant effects have also been reported for the 5-HT uptake in-hibitors indalpine (Sechter et al., 1984), fluoxetine (Shopsin et al., 1981), fluvoxamine (Amin et al., 1984; Feldman & Denber, 1982; Saletu et al., 1977), and citalopram (Bjerkenstedt et al., 1984; Gastpar & Gastpar, 1982; Pedersen et al., 1982). A recent double-blind controlled study re-ported that fluvoxamine was as effective as chlorimipramine (Coleman & Bloch, 1982), but as yet, no double-blind comparisons with placebo have been reported. Similarly, in double-blind trials, citalopram appears to be as effective as chlorimipramine and nianserin (Kragh-Sorensen, 1983, cited by Hytell et al. 1984; Mertens, 1983, cited by Hytell et al. 1984; but not Bech, 1984) and indalpine appears to be as effective as imipramine, chlorimipramine, and maprotiline (reviewed by Sechter et al., 1984). Finally, although some early studies expressed reservations concerning the antidepressant status of fluoxetine, (Shopsin et al., 1981), more recent evidence from double-blind trials indicates that this drug too is as efficacious as tricyclic antidepressants and superior to placebo (Stark & Hardison, 1984).

16.4. CONCLUSIONS: 5-HT AND DEPRESSION

The results of antidepressant trials of agents that enhance 5-HT function are generally encouraging. Although rather equivocal results were obtained in early trials of tryptophan, these have now been superseded by the demonstration that 5-HTP and the selective 5-HT uptake inhibitors have clear antidepressant properties. As acute intravenous infusions of both tryptophan and 5-HTP have been shown to elevate mood, it seems likely that the antidepressant effect of "serotonergic antidepressants" does result from the fact that they enhance 5-HT function, rather than some other unknown effect that develops slowly during the course of chronic treatment.

The status of "serotonergic antidepressants" was called into question for a time by the failure of amitriptyline and chlorimipramine to show selective activity in patients with a low central turnover of 5-HT. However, as chlorimipramine is only marginally selective as a 5-HT uptake inhibitor, and amitriptyline not at all, this prediction should never have been made. 5-Hydroxytryptophan and zimelidine do appear to be more effective in patients with low CSF 5-HIAA levels prior to treatment. This would be expected from the similar relationships between transmitter turnover and antidepressant efficacy seen with drugs that enhance DA or NA transmission (Sections 9.4 and 12.3.4). However, the 5-HT system differs from the catecholamines in one very important respect: when present, low 5-HT turnover is a characteristic of the depressive person rather than the depressed state. There is no evidence that the switch from depression to mania in bipolar patients involves a change from low to high levels of 5-HT turnover. When low CSF 5-HIAA is present in depression, 5-HT turnover remains low in manic episodes and in periods of remission.

The other major abnormality of 5-HT in depressed patients has two manifestations: a decrease in [3H]imipramine binding and a decrease in 5-HT uptake. Remarkably, nobody, as far as I am aware, has investigated the relationship between these changes in depressed people and central

5-HT turnover. Indeed, it is not even possible to say whether low 5-HT uptake and low [³H]imipramine binding coexist. However, it does not seem unreasonable to assume that the various abnormalities of 5-HT function will be found in the same subgroup of depressed people. For one thing, like decreased 5-HT turnover, reduction of 5-HT uptake and [³H]imipramine binding are also independent of the depressed state. Most of the other major biological abnormalities associated with depression are state-dependent, and they return more-or-less to normal on clinical recovery; this is true of cholinergic activity (Section 14.2), which is known to affect platelet 5-HT uptake (Rausch et al., 1982). An animal study provides further evidence that low turnover and low uptake of 5-HT might coexist in depression: 5-HT function in the hypothalamus undergoes marked circadian changes, and in this model, uptake and turnover of 5-HT do co-vary (A. Wirz-Justice, personal communication).

In two of three postmortem studies, a decrease in [³H]imipramine binding has been observed in the brain of suicidal or depressed subjects, as well as in their blood platelets. Monoamine oxidase-A, the form of MAO that is responsible for the metabolism of 5-HT to 5-HIAA, is located within neurons (Finberg & Youdim, 1983). It is therefore theoretically possible that low 5-HIAA levels could simply be a result of low uptake, which protects 5-HT from exposure to MAO. In this case, low CSF levels of 5-HIAA could occur with no decrease, or perhaps even an increase, in the stimulation of postsynaptic 5-HT receptors.

However, there is a good indication that low 5-HT turnover does mean low 5-HT function, in the very close symptomatic correspondence between patients with low CSF 5-HIAA levels and animals depleted of forebrain 5-HT. As described in the previous chapter, 5-HT depletion in animals results in aggression, hyperemotionality, and hyperreactivity to pain or threat. In people, low 5-HT turnover is associated with anxiety, agitation, and aggression, which is manifest either as sociopathic behavior or as suicide attempts. In both cases, the syndrome may be summarized in one word—irritability. An important feature of the 5-HT depleted animal is that it is unable to suppress behavioral responses to aversive stimulation. It may be this characteristic of the depressed person who suffers from a chronically underactive 5-HT system that is responsible for the fact that low 5-HT turnover is more closely associated with the presence and severity of suicide attempts than with global depression scores or depressed mood.

Low 5-HT turnover is not specific for depression as such but is also associated with alcoholism and personality disorders. This cluster of disorders comes together in the group of chronic mild depressions known as "depression spectrum disorders" or "character spectrum disorders" (see Section 3.4.4). "Depression spectrum disorder" is seen mainly in women who have a high incidence of depression among their female relatives, while their male relatives tend to be alcoholic and sociopathic (Winokur et al., 1971). "Character spectrum disorder" first comes to attention as a character disorder such as sociopathy, which is associated with concomitant alcohol or drug abuse and depression (Akiskal et al., 1981). The status of 5-HT transmission in these "borderline personality disorders" has not been explicitly examined. However, there is clearly a strong prediction that these patients will be found to have low CSF levels of 5-HIAA and low platelet 5-HT uptake, in much the same way that "subaffective dysthymic disorder" patients have abnormal results on the DST and short REM sleep latencies (Section 3.3.3). If biological markers indicative of low 5-HT transmission can indeed be demonstrated in people with borderline personality disorders, their chronic irritability, and their inability to cope adequately with disappointment and stress could be understood in terms of the known functions of forebrain 5-HT systems.

seventeen

ANTIDEPRESSANTS AND SEROTONIN

Although the evidence reviewed in the previous chapter clearly demonstrates that the activity of 5-HT systems is reduced in a substantial proportion of depressed patients, the significance of these observations has been disputed. The obvious interpretation is that depression is associated with a reduction in 5-HT neurotransmission—this is the classical "indoleamine hypothesis of depression" (Lapin & Oxenkrug, 1969). An alternative interpretation has been proposed by Aprison and colleagues (see Sections 15.3.1 and 17.1.4). They suggest that as a consequence of a chronic low level of 5-HT function in depressive people, there develops a compensatory supersensitivity of postsynaptic receptors, which restores transmission through the synapse to normal. On exposure to stress, 5-HT neurons are activated, and the postsynaptic effects of 5-HT are amplified by the supersensitive receptors, precipitating a depressive episode. The putative increase in 5-HT transmission is held to underlie depression, rather than the decrease in transmission postulated by the classical hypothesis. (Aprison et al., 1978, 1982).

One obvious problem for this theory is that 5-HT precursors appear to be effective antidepressants, and indeed, appear to be most effective as antidepressants in the subgroup of patients to whom the theory applies—those with low 5-HT turnover (Section 15.3). The theory attempts to deal with this observation by postulating that 5-HT precursors work by inducing receptor subsensitivity (Aprison et al., 1978, 1982). Since, in these circumstances, subsensitivity to 5-HT would develop in order to counteract the effects of an increase in 5-HT release, it seems unlikely that the outcome would actually be a decrease in transmission through the synapse. However, it is not impossible.

Another problem is that the theory predicts that drugs which reduce 5-HT transmission should exert rapid antidepressant effects. They do not. Although it has been suggested that 5-HT receptor blockers might have some antimanic potential (Section 17.3.3), any antidepressant activity that they might possess remains unremarked. Similarly, reduction of 5-HT synthesis has been reported to block, rather than potentiate, the therapeutic effect of antidepressants (Section 17.2.1). Nonetheless, the theory has a certain currency, and it cannot be dismissed out of hand, particularly as there is considerable evidence, described below, that some antidepressant drugs can in fact decrease some aspects of 5-HT function.

The situation regarding 5-HT is therefore that two competing theories make opposite assumptions about the nature of 5-HT dysfunction in depression. Consequently, they make opposite predictions for the effects of antidepressants, and the effect of antidepressants on 5-HT transmission may be used to test between them. Exactly the same problem was encountered in Chapter 13 in relation to NA, and the analysis applied there is also appropriate here. The effects of acute antidepressant administration are first considered briefly, followed by a more extensive survey of the effects of chronic treatment. The object is to synthesize the effects of antidepressants on various aspects of 5-HT function in order to ascertain the net effect on the integrated functioning of 5-HT synapses.

17.1. ACUTE EFFECTS

17.1.1. Presynaptic Effects

The "hypersensitive 5-HT receptor" theory is, of course, at odds with the best known action of antidepressants on 5-HT systems, the blockade of transmitter uptake. In general, tertiary tricyclics, such as amitriptyline and imipramine, are rather more potent as 5-HT uptake blockers than secondary tricyclics, and as discussed in Section 16.3.4, imipramine and amitriptyline are roughly equipotent (Carlsson et al., 1969a; Maitre et al., 1982; Randrup & Braestrup, 1977). The specific 5-HT uptake inhibitor zimelidine is an effective antidepressant, as are fluoxetine, indalpine, and citalopram (Section 16.3.4). ECS activates 5-HT neurons, causing an increase in 5-HT release (Ebert et al., 1973; Engel et al., 1971; Evans et al., 1976; Shields, 1972); Interestingly, a decrease in 5-HT uptake has been observed 24 hours following a single ECS administration (Minchin et al., 1983). The MAO inhibitor clorgyline has also been found to exert a relatively specific inhibition of 5-HT uptake (Lai et al., 1980); clorgyline is a specific inhibitor of the A- form of MAO, which breaks down 5-HT (Finberg & Youdim, 1983), and in common with other MAO-A inhibitors, it is an effective antidepressant (Murphy et al., 1981).

Not all antidepressants are 5-HT uptake inhibitors, however. Maprotiline and viloxazine, which are potent inhibitors of NA uptake, are extremely weak blockers of 5-HT uptake, as are several other atypical antidepressants, including iprindole and mianserin, and some secondary tricyclics, DMI in particular (Blackburn et al., 1978; Maitre et al., 1982; Randrup & Braestrup, 1977; Zis & Goodwin, 1980). It should be remembered in this context that the relatively specific NA uptake inhibitor nortriptyline was ineffective in depressed patients with low 5-HT turnover (Asberg et al., 1973; see Section 15.3.3).

In addition to their effects on 5-HT uptake, acute treatment with tricyclics or zimelidine also affect the activity of 5-HT neurons. The firing rate of 5-HT containing cells in the raphe nuclei is reduced by these drugs (Scuvee-Moreau & Dresse, 1979; De Montigny et al., 1981a), as is the rate of synthesis of 5-HT (Carlsson & Lindqvist, 1978a). These are presumably negative feedback effects mediated by 5-HT autoreceptors, as the changes in firing rate and synthesis are proportional to the blockade of 5-HT uptake (Carlsson & Lindqvist, 1978a; Quinaux et al., 1982). The decrease in firing rate is reflected in a decrease in 5-HT turnover. Potent 5-HT uptake inhibitors, such as zimelidine or chlorimipramine, reliably reduce turnover, imipramine and amitriptyline give variable results, and no changes in turnover are seen with DMI, iprindole, or mianserin (Corrodi & Fuxe, 1969; Leonard & Kafoe, 1976; Marko & Meek, 1979; Ross et al., 1981; Van Wijk et al., 1977).

17.1.2. Postsynaptic Effects

Although antidepressants which block 5-HT uptake also reduce presynaptic 5-HT function, as reflected in measures of firing rate, synthesis, and turnover, the net outcome is an increase in the bombardment of postsynaptic receptors. This is best illustrated by considering the specific 5-HT uptake inhibitor zimelidine. Zimelidine is also highly potent in reducing presynaptic 5-HT activity (Carlsson & Lindqvist, 1978a). Nonetheless, measures of postsynaptic 5-HT function are increased. Zimelidine has been found to increase the frequency of head twitches induced by low doses of the 5-HT precursor 5-HTP (Ogren et al., 1979, 1982) and to enhance the stimulant effect of 5-HTP on locomotor activity (Buus Lassen, 1978), and on the secretion of prolactin (Meltzer et al., 1981b) and corticosteroids (Lahti & Barsuhn, 1980).

This analysis of the effects of zimelidine is relatively straightforward only because zimelidine interacts extremely weakly with postsynaptic 5-HT receptors. This is not the case, however, for the majority of antidepressant drugs. Two distinct 5-HT receptor binding sites are recognized, the 5-HT_1 site, labeled in binding experiments by radioactive 5-HT, and the 5-HT_2 site, labeled by radioactive spiroperidol (Peroutka & Snyder, 1981b, 1982; see also Section 17.3.4). While most antidepressants have only a weak affinity for 5-HT_1 sites, many tricyclic and atypical antidepressants have a marked affinity for 5-HT_2 receptors. Mianserin, amitriptyline, and nortriptyline show this effect most strongly, imipramine, DMI, and chlorimipramine rather weakly, and iprindole and zimelidine hardly at all (Leysen et al., 1982; Ogren et al., 1979; Peroutka et al., 1981; Tang & Seeman, 1980).

The brain also contains sites that bind mianserin with high affinity (Dumbrille-Ross et al., 1980, 1981). Unlike the imipramine and DMI binding sites that are associated with 5-HT and NA uptake mechanisms (Sections 16.1.5 and 13.2.2), mianserin binding sites are closely associated with postsynaptic 5-HT_2 receptors (Barbacchia et al., 1983). On acute administration, mianserin has no significant 5-HT potentiating actions. However, mianserin has been reported to antagonize a wide range of responses to direct 5-HT receptor agonists or to 5-HTP. These include behavioral activation (R. Gold et al., 1980; Maj et al., 1978; Ogren et al., 1979; Sakai & Deguchi, 1980), behavioral depression (Jones, 1980b; Nagayama et al., 1981), and neuroendocrine effects (Lahti & Barsuhn, 1980; Meltzer et al., 1981b).

In considering the net effect of antidepressants on 5-HT transmission, therefore, blockade of postsynaptic receptors must be set against the increase in receptor bombardment brought about by uptake blockade. The considerable degree of variability in which of these two opposing effects predominates may be illustrated by considering three tricyclic antidepressants. In the case of chlorimipramine, powerful blockade of uptake is combined with weak blockade of receptors, and the outcome is a potentiation of 5-HT transmission, as indicated by potentiation of various effects of 5-HTP, including head twitches (Ogren et al., 1979), effects on spinal reflexes (Sangdee & Franz, 1979), and neuroendocrine responses (Lahti & Barsuhn, 1980; Meltzer et al., 1981b). In the case of amitriptyline, moderate blockade of uptake is combined with powerful blockade of receptors. There are occasional reports of potentiation of 5-HT transmission by amitriptyline (Sangdee & Franz, 1979) or of no effect (Hwang & Van Woert, 1980), but more usually the outcome is a reduction in 5-HT transmission. Acute amitriptyline administration has been reported to reduce electrophysiological (Menkes et al., 1980) and behavioral (Jones, 1980b) responses to 5-HT, and to reduce 5-HTP-induced head twitches (Ogren et al., 1979), behavioral depression (Nagayama et al., 1980, 1981), and prolactin secretion (Meltzer et al., 1981b). Imipramine, which combines uptake blockade comparable to that of amitriptyline with receptor antagonism comparable to that of chlorimipramine, gives rather variable results (Bradshaw et al., 1974; Ogren et al., 1979).

The fact that many antidepressant drugs show some degree of blockade of 5-HT receptors, which may predominate over their 5-HT enhancing effects, has been advanced as support for the hypothesis that some depressions may be a reflection of hyperactive 5-HT mechanisms (Aprison et al., 1982). This does not appear at all likely. In addition to the arguments already advanced, it is clearly not a general property of antidepressant drugs that they antagonize 5-HT receptors to an extent sufficient to predominate over the 5-HT enhancing effect of blockade of the 5-HT uptake system. Furthermore, many nonantidepressants have an affinity for 5-HT_2 receptors, which is considerably greater than that of antidepressants; these include traditional 5-HT receptor blockers and neuroleptics (Leysen et al., 1982; Peroutka & Snyder, 1982). One of the drugs that has the highest affinity for 5-HT_2 receptors is the neuroleptic spiroperidol; although antidepressant effects have been claimed for some other neuroleptics (Section 9.3.3), there is no evidence that spiroperidol shares this property.

There is also another problem. Reviewing the effects of antidepressants on NA transmission, it became clear that some antidepressants block alpha-adrenergic receptors on acute administration, but chronic treatment reverses this effect (Chapter 13). It is now necessary to consider whether the antidepressants that block 5-HT transmission on acute administration still do so following a period of chronic treatment.

17.2. CHRONIC STUDIES: PRESYNAPTIC EFFECTS

17.2.1. Autoreceptors

In contrast to the extensive literature concerning antidepressant effects on NA autoreceptors (Section 13.3.1), there have been very few studies of presynaptic 5-HT function during chronic antidepressant administration. In one study, the firing rate of dorsal raphe cells was unaltered by two-week administration of DMI, imipramine, iprindole, or femoxetine (Blier & DeMontigny, 1980), and neither these drugs nor chlorimipramine altered the response of raphe cells to 5-HT (Blier & De Montigny, 1980; Svensson, 1980) or to LSD, which at low doses is a selective 5-HT autoreceptor agonist (Haigler & Aghajanian, 1974). These results suggest that unlike NA autoreceptors, 5-HT autoreceptors are not desensitized by chronic antidepressant treatment.

If autoreceptors were to become desensitized, the most powerful 5-HT uptake blockers would presumably be the drugs most likely to induce this effect. The reduction of 5-HT turnover by zimelidine was apparently unaltered by chronic treatment (Ogren et al., 1981b). However, in a single-unit recording study, which measures autoreceptor sensitivity more directly, it was found that during two-week treatment with zimelidine (at a dose slightly higher than that used by Ogren and co-workers), the number of normally active raphe cells gradually returned to control levels; this change was associated with a decrease in autoreceptor sensitivity to LSD (Blier & De Montigny, 1983). Similar results have recently been reported with the MAOIs phenelzine and clorgyline (Blier & De Montigny, 1984a). These studies suggest that under some circumstances chronic antidepressant treatment may induce 5-HT autoreceptor subsensitivity.

17.2.2. Uptake

5-HT uptake mechanisms have been studied either directly by measuring the uptake of radiolabeled 5-HT into synaptosomes or blood platelets, or indirectly by measuring the binding of radiolabeled imipramine to sites that are closely associated with the machinery for 5-HT uptake (Langer et al., 1980; see Section 16.1.5). Other things being equal, a decrease in 5-HT uptake would presumably result in an increased intrasynaptic 5-HT concentration and enhancement of 5-HT transmission.

Uptake studies in animals have given variable results. A further decrease in 5-HT uptake has been reported in the rat brain following chronic ECS (Minchin et al., 1983). The selective 5-HT uptake blockers zimelidine and citalopram continued to block 5-HT uptake on chronic treatment (Hyttel et al., 1984; Ogren et al., 1981b). Mianserin, nomifensine, or iprindole, which had no effect on acute administration, also had no effect chronically (Segawa et al., 1982). Chronic imipramine treatment, on the other hand, has been reported to increase 5-HT uptake, but the significance of this observation is unclear, since the effect was present in brain slices but absent in synaptosomes (Barbaccia et al., 1983).

Imipramine binding studies in animals show more of a consensus. There are a number of reports that [3H]imipramine binding to brain and/ or to blood platelets was decreased by chronic treatment with imipramine or DMI (Barbaccia et al., 1983; Briley et al., 1982a; Kinnier et al., 1980; Langer et al., 1980; Racagni et al., 1983), by repeated ECS (Langer et al., 1981), and by 3 nights REM sleep deprivation (Mogilnicka et al., 1980); again, mianserin and iprindole were ineffective (Barbaccia et al., 1983; Kinnier et al., 1980). Chronic treatment with lithium, which in addition to its well-established antimanic effect (Gerbino et al., 1978) also has antidepressant properties (Ramsey & Mendels, 1981), also decreased [3H]imipramine binding (Plenge & Mellerup, 1982). In every case, in which decreases in [3H]imipramine binding were observed, the changes were brought about by a change in the number of binding sites rather than in their affinity for imipramine. Chronic treatment with a high dose of zimelidine increased the number of [3H]-imipramine binding sites but also decreased their affinity for [3H]-imipramine; the net effect of these two changes on total [^{3}H]-imipramine binding was not reported (Fuxe et al., 1983).

It is not obvious that antidepressants should be expected to reduce [^{3}H]imipramine binding or 5-HT uptake in human studies, since it is usually reported that 5-HT uptake and imipramine binding are already low in blood platelets taken from depressed patients (Section 16.1.5). In contrast to the decrease seen in animal studies, a clinical study recently reported that treatment of depression with tricyclic antidepressants failed to affect [^{3}H]imipramine binding, while maprotiline and ECT produced a small, nonsignificant increase (Langer & Raisman, 1983).

There have been a number of clinical studies of 5-HT uptake. Although a tendency to "normalization" of low 5-HT uptake by antidepressants has sometimes been noted (Giret et al., 1980; Meltzer et al., 1984), it has usually been found that there was a further decrease in platelet 5-HT uptake during therapy with imipramine, DMI, amitriptyline, nortriptyline, chlorimipramine, and zimelidine (Coppen & Wood, 1980; Coppen et al., 1981; Meltzer et al., 1981a; Tuomisto et al., 1979; Ross et al., 1980). A decrease in platelet 5-HT uptake has also been observed following two to three weeks of treatment of bipolar manic or depressed patients with lithium (Meltzer et al., 1983a); however, other studies have reported the opposite effect (Born et al., 1980; Coppen et al., 1980b) or no change in 5-HT uptake (Scott et al., 1979).

17.2.3. Turnover

In clinical studies of depressed patients, reduction of 5-HT turnover (assessed by CSF levels of 5-HIAA) has been observed after treatment with specific 5-HT uptake inhibitors, such as chlorimipramine, zimelidine and femoxetine (Asberg et al., 1975; Bertillsson et al., 1976; Dahl et al., 1982; Siwers et al., 1977; Traskman et al., 1979), and also following less specific treatments, such as imipramine and amitriptyline (Bowers, 1974b; Mendlewicz et al., 1982b; Papeschi & McClure, 1971; Post & Goodwin, 1974). Decreased 5-HT turnover has also been reported following treatment with the very weak 5-HT uptake inhibitors DMI (Dahl et al., 1982) and nortriptyline (Asberg et al., 1973), though the latter effect was not confirmed in a later study (Bertilsson et al., 1976). Mianserin, however, did not appear to affect 5-HT turnover (Mendlewicz et al., 1982b). Ethical considerations in clinical studies require that the number of lumbar punctures be minimized. Consequently, there are no data on the effects of acute treatment with which to compare these results.

Comparisons between acute and chronic treatment have been made in animal studies; in most cases, 5-HT turnover appears to change little during the course of chronic antidepressant treatment. Drugs such as DMI and mianserin, which do not affect turnover acutely, have no effect chronically; zimelidine and chlorimipramine, which decrease turnover acutely, produce a similar change after chronic treatment; and both increases and decreases in turnover have been reported following chronic imipramine treatment (Alpers & Himwich, 1972; Leonard & Kafoe, 1976; Marko & Meek, 1979; Meek & Werdinius, 1970; Ross et al., 1981; Sherman, 1979; Sugrue, 1980c, 1983; Svensson, 1978; Van Wijk et al., 1977). As the effects of chronic treatment appear to be broadly similar to the effects of acute treatment, there is no reason to suppose that decreases in 5-HT turnover, when present, represent anything other than a partial compensation for the enhancing effects of 5-HT uptake blockade.

The effects of chronic administration of MAOIs on 5-HT turnover are unclear. MAOIs inhibit the catabolism of 5-HT, resulting in increased levels of 5-HT and a concomitant decrease in 5-HIAA. In one study, after chronic treatment with the MAO-A inhibitor clorgyline, a compensatory reduction in 5-HT synthesis was observed (Waldmeier et al., 1981). However, in other experiments 5-HIAA levels returned to normal after chronic treatment with a variety of MAOIs (Campbell & Marshall, 1974; Campbell et al., 1979). It should be noted that although MAOIs raise brain 5-HT levels, most of the increase is in a cytoplasmic pool and is probably unavailable for release. In one study, functional changes in 5-HT transmission were observed only after almost total inhibition of both the A- and B- forms of MAO (Green et al., 1977b).

There does appear to be some adaptation to the effect of ECS on 5-HT turnover. There have been many such studies in animals; most are agreed that a single ECS increases 5-HT turnover, but both decreases and increases are seen following repeated treatment and usually, changes in either direction are small (Charney et al., 1981c). A similar lack of agreement as to whether ECS increases or decreases 5-HT turnover is also apparent in clinical studies (Abrams et al., 1976; Ashcroft et al., 1966; Bowers et al., 1969; Nordin et al., 1971).

The effects of chronic antidepressant administration on presynaptic 5-HT function may be summarized as follows. Some treatments, including mianserin, maprotiline, and possibly the MAOIs, do not affect the functioning of 5-HT neurons to any significant extent after chronic treatment. However, most treatments, including ECS, enhance presynaptic 5-HT function by reducing 5-HT uptake, though this effect tends to be compensated to some extent by a reduction in 5-HT turnover.

17.3. CHRONIC STUDIES: POSTSYNAPTIC EFFECTS

17.3.1. Electrophysiological Studies

The results of single unit recording studies of antidepressant effects on postsynaptic responses to 5-HT are summarized in Table 17.1. In all brain

TABLE 17.1. EFFECTS OF CHRONIC ANTIDEPRESSANT TREATMENT ON ELECTROPHYSIOLOGICAL RESPONSIVENESS TO 5-HT RECEPTOR STIMULATION

Site	Agent[a]	Response to[b] 5-HT	5-MeO-DMT	Raphe stimulation	Reference
Hippocampus	ZIM	=		↑	Blier & de Montigny, 1983
	ECS	↑			De Montigny, 1981
	CMI	↑			De Montigny et al., 1981a
	ZIM	=			
	AMI,CMI,DMI,IMI,IP	↑			De Montigny & Aghajanian, 1978
	CMI,IMI	↑			Gallager & Bunney, 1979
		=			Blier & De Montigny 1984b
	MIA,IMI, IND	=			
Amygdala	DMI,IMI,IP	↑	↑	↑	Wang & Aghajanian, 1980
	FLU	=	=	=	
Ventral LGN	AMI,CMI,DMI,IMI,IP	↑			De Montigny & Aghajanian, 1978
Dorsal LGN	DMI,IMI,IP,(CMI)[c]	↑	↑		Menkes & Aghajanian, 1981
Facial motor nucleus	AMI,IMI,DMI,IP	↑	=		Menkes et al., 1980
	FLU	=			
Cortex	CMI,DMI	=			Olpe, 1981
	CLORG	↓			Olpe & Schellenberg, 1981

[a] AMI: amitriptyline; CMI: chlorimipramine; CLORG: clorgyline; DMI: desmethylimipramine; ECS: electroconvulsive shock; FLU: fluoxetine; IMI: imipramine; IND: indalpine; IP: iprindole; ZIM: zimelidine.
[b] ↑: response enhanced by chronic antidepressant treatment; =: no change; ↓: response attenuated by chronic antidepressant treatment.
[c] Effect of CMI not significant.

areas studied other than the cerebral cortex, the postsynaptic response to iontophoretically applied 5-HT was enhanced by chronic (two to three weeks) administration of tricyclic antidepressants (seven studies), iprindole (five studies), mianserin (one study), and ECS (one study). Enhancement of 5-HT responsiveness is not confined to the inhibitory responses observed in most systems, but also extends to the excitatory response to 5-HT seen in the facial motor nucleus (Menkes et al., 1980). Antidepressant-induced supersensitivity has also been observed in response to intravenous or iontophoretic application of the receptor agonist 5-methoxydimethyltryptamine (5-MeO-DMT) (Menkes et al., 1980; Wang & Aghajanian, 1980). Unlike 5-HT itself, this agent is not a substrate for the 5-HT uptake system (Ross & Renyi, 1969), so interpretation of the effects of 5-MeO-DMT is not confounded by drug-induced blockade of 5-HT uptake. Responsiveness to 5-HT and 5-MeO-DMT was not altered by chronic administration of chlorpromazine or fluoxetine (De Montigny & Aghajanian, 1978; Menkes & Aghajanian, 1981; Menkes et al., 1980; Wang & Aghajanian, 1980).

In addition to enhancing the postsynaptic effects of 5-HT applied iontophoretically, imipramine, amitriptyline, and iprindole were also found to enhance the response of cells in the amygdala to electrical stimulation of ascending 5-HT pathways (Wang & Aghajanian, 1980). Like fluoxetine, but unlike other antidepressants, zimelidine has been reported not to change the responsiveness of postsynaptic 5-HT receptors to iontophoretically applied 5-HT (Blier & De Montigny, 1983; De Montigny et al., 1981a). Another specific 5-HT uptake inhibitor, indalpine, was similarly inactive at postsynaptic 5-HT receptors (Blier & De Montigny, 1984b). However, like other treatments, zimelidine did enhance the response to electrical stimulation of ascending 5-HT pathways (Blier & De Montigny, 1983). A presynaptic effect of zimelidine is likely to be responsible for this discrepancy. As previously discussed, there is some evidence that chronic zimelidine treatment can desensitize presynaptic 5-HT autoreceptors (Section 17.2.1), and one consequence of such an effect would be an increase in the amount of 5-HT released per impulse.

The observation that chronic antidepressant treatments enhance 5-HT receptor function is consistent with the classical 5-HT hypothesis of reduced 5-HT functioning in depression, but not with the newer reformulations which posit an increase in 5-HT transmission. A further observation which would be consistent with the earlier hypothesis was that the responsiveness of hippocampal cells to 5-HT shows a diurnal variation, being highest in the evening (De Montigny, 1981). Typically, endogenous depressions show a similar pattern, with evening improvements in the clinical picture.

In contrast to the enhanced responsiveness of noncortical areas, responses to 5-HT in cingulate and rostral cortex were unchanged by DMI, chlorimipramine, or the nonantidepressant MAOI deprenyl and were decreased by the antidepressant MAOI clorgyline (Olpe, 1981; Olpe & Schellenberg, 1981). The implication that cortical 5-HT receptors might respond to antidepressants differently from those in subcortical areas is supported by a study of visual evoked potentials (VEP) in occipital cortex. The application of 5-HT to the surface of the cortex in rabbits was found to reduce the amplitude of the later components of the VEP, but chronic treatment with amitriptyline or zimelidine attenuated this effect (Pawloski et al., 1982). Given the possibility of regional variations in the effect of antidepressants on 5-HT receptors, it should be noted that the occipital cortex is unlikely to be an important site of antidepressant action (Chapter 5).

17.3.2. Neuroendocrine Studies

The results of neuroendocrine studies are less straightforward than the electrophysiological findings. Although 5-HT mechanisms are involved in a number of neuroendocrine responses, including stimulation of prolactin, ACTH, and growth hormone, and inhibition of TRH (see Section 16.1.4), there have been few studies of the effects of antidepressants on these systems, and the results are somewhat contradictory.

The effects of chronic antidepressant administration on basal serum prolactin levels in rats are extremely variable. Prolactin level was hardly affected by imipramine, amitriptyline, fluoxetine, or clorgyline, and it was increased by mianserin and amoxapine (Cooper et al., 1981; Fuxe et al., 1982b,c). Zimelidine and DMI have been reported to decrease prolactin level, but the effect of DMI, at least, was probably not mediated by 5-HT, since the effect was unchanged by lesioning 5-HT pathways (Fuxe et al., 1982b,c). It has been suggested that the reduction of serum prolactin by zimelidine represents a decrease in 5-HT function (Fuxe et al., 1982b,c). However, this inference appears unwarranted, given that prolactin levels were unaffected by the destruction of 5-HT pathways (Fuxe et al., 1982b,c). In any case, the effect was observed only at low doses of zimelidine, (Fuxe et al., 1982b), and although the doses used may be clinically relevant, no change in prolactin levels was seen in depressed patients treated with zimelidine for three to seven weeks (Syvalahti et al., 1979b).

Interpretation of the effects of zimelidine is made even more difficult by the fact that although serum prolactin levels were reduced 24 hours after the final treatment (Fuxe et al., 1982b,c), if the tests were carried out after only two hours a large increase in prolactin was observed (Fuxe et al., 1983). Furthermore, even though 5-HT stimulates the release of both prolactin and cortisol, zimelidine had exactly the opposite pattern of effects on serum cortisol levels. Cortisol levels were reduced by approximately 40% 2 hours after the final zimelidine treatment but were increased by approximately 100% after 24 hours (Fuxe et al., 1983). As discussed below, it is unclear whether 2 hours or 24 hours is a more relevant time for clinical comparisons. Whatever the answer to this question, it is difficult to see how the pattern of results obtained by Fuxe and co-workers may be explained coherently. Perhaps the most important conclusion to draw is that the multiple neurotransmitter controls of neuroendocrine function (Ettigi & Brown, 1977) mean that basal hormone levels are poor tools for assessing neurotransmitter function.

Challenges to 5-HT receptor systems are potentially more informative than studies of basal hormone levels. In rats, the prolactin response to 5-HTP was increased by 3 weeks administration of imipramine, DMI, or lithium but was decreased by amitriptyline and iprindole; imipramine was also found to enhance the response to the direct receptor agonist quipazine (Meltzer et al., 1981b). However, in depressed patients an increase in the prolactin response to tryptophan (Charney et al., 1982d) was observed with both imipramine and amitriptyline (Charney & Heninger, 1983). The effect of zimelidine and other specific 5-HT uptake inhibitors on the prolactin response to 5-HT agonists has not yet been examined.

Electroconvulsive shock (ECS) has been the subject of several studies. Balldin and co-workers (1980a) reported that repeated ECS reduced the growth hormone response to a 5-HTP challenge in reserpine-pretreated rats. However, it is difficult to interpret this result as a decrease in 5-HT receptor function, as 5-HT appears to play a minor role in the control of growth hormone, and it is not clear that the stimulatory effect of 5-HTP, when present, is in fact mediated by 5-HT (see Section 16.1.4). The stimulation of prolactin secretion by 5-HTP is more clearly mediated by 5-HT (Ettigi & Brown, 1977; Section 16.1.4). This response was not affected in rats by repeated ECS (Meltzer et al., 1981b). However, the same treatment did increase 5-HTP-induced cortisol secretion (Steiner & Grahame-Smith, 1980a). Similarly, in depressed patients, ECS enhanced the prolactin response to TRH, which is probably mediated by 5-HT (Coppen et al., 1980a).

The neuroendocrine studies concur with the single-unit studies in finding that chronic treatment with imipramine, DMI, and (probably) ECS increases 5-HT receptor function. They differ over amitriptyline and iprindole, which enhanced responses to 5-HT in single-unit studies, but may reduce 5-HT responsiveness in the neuroendocrine model. As yet, however, the latter effect has only been seen in a single animal study, and in human subjects, neuroendocrine responsiveness was increased by amitriptyline.

17.3.3. Behavioral Studies

Behavioral probes of 5-HT receptors also provide evidence that their responsiveness is increased by chronic antidepressant treatments. The evidence is clearest in the case of ECS. Chronic (seven to ten days), but not acute, ECS has consistently been observed to increase responses to a variety of 5-HT agonists. The effect was first observed by Green and coworkers, who showed that ECS enhanced the hyperactivity produced by the 5-HT precursor tryptophan (administered in combination with the MAOI tranylcypromine, in order to prevent the destruction of newly synthesized 5-HT). Since the synthesis and accumulation of 5-HT following tryptophan administration were unchanged by ECS, a postsynaptic change was indicated; this was confirmed by the observation that ECS also enhanced the hyperactivity induced by the direct receptor agonists 5-MeO-DMT and quipazine (Evans et al., 1976; Green et al., 1977a; Costain et al., 1979). Other 5-HT-mediated effects enhanced by chronic ECS include the induction of head twitches by 5-HTP (Green et al., 1983a,b; Lebrecht & Nowak, 1980) and by lithium (Bhavsar et al., 1981, 1983), which apparently works through a 5-HT mechanism (Wielosz & Kleinrok, 1979), and also 5-HT-mediated hyperthermic responses (Vetulani et al., 1981). Enhanced 5-HT responses were present for up to six days following the final shock (Green et al., 1977a). Convulsions induced chemically by bicuculline have also been found to enhance 5-HT responsiveness, but neither subconvulsive doses of bicuculline nor subconvulsive shocks had this effect (Green et al., 1977a; Nutt et al., 1980a). Subconvulsive shocks are also ineffective clinically.

The enhancement of 5-HT-mediated responses by ECS depends on intact 5-HT transmission. Blockade of 5-HT synthesis with PCPA, or administration of 5-HT receptor blockers prior to each ECS, did not affect responses to 5-HT agonists in control animals but did prevent their enhancement by ECS (Green et al., 1980). More surprisingly, the effect also requires intact NA systems. The hyperactivity induced by quipazine was unaffected by blockade of NA synthesis with AMPT or by 6-OHDA induced lesions of the dorsal NA bundle, but like 5-HT depletion, these treatments did prevent their enhancement by ECS (Green & Deakin, 1980; Green et al., 1980). It is not known why an intact NA system is required for ECS to cause changes in 5-HT transmission. The interdependence of monoaminergic systems clearly merits further study. The enhancement of DA transmission by ECS also appears to depend on an intact dorsal NA bundle (Section 10.2.2), and an intact 5-HT system is required for antidepressants to reduce the number of beta-receptors (though not their functional capacity) (Section 13.3.3.2).

In contrast to the clear consensus that 5-HT receptor function is enhanced by ECS, the picture derived from behavioral studies of antidepressant drugs is much more confusing (Table 17.2). In general, studies that have tested the behavioral responsiveness of 5-HT systems very soon (up to two hours) after the final antidepressant treatment have reported no effect or a decrease in 5-HT mediated behaviors. The results of tests carried out at longer intervals (12–72 hours) vary greatly. In order to

TABLE 17.2. 5-HT RECEPTOR FUNCTION AFTER CHRONIC TREATMENT WITH ANTIDEPRESSANT DRUGS: BEHAVIORAL STUDIES

Behavior	Agonist Probe[a]	Antidepressant[b]	≤2	12–24	≤48	Reference
Head twitch	5-MeO-DMT (high dose)	ZIM		→		Fuxe et al., 1981
	5-HTP + TC	ZIM	←	→		
5-HT syndrome	5-HTP	ZIM	→	→	=	Ogren et al., 1982
	5-MeO-DMT	CMI,FLU		→	→	Stolz et al., 1983
	5-MeO-DMT	CMI		=		Lucki & Frazer, 1982
	TRY + TC	FLU, ZIM	=			Hwang & van Woert, 1980
Impairment of avoidance learning	5-MeO-DMT	ZIM		→		Fuxe et al., 1982c
Analgesia	5-MeO-DMT	ZIM		←		Fuxe et al., 1983
Head twitch	5-MeO-DMT	AMI	→		←	Friedman & Dallob, 1979
		IMI	=		←	
	5-MeO-DMT	MIA			→	Blackshear & Sanders-Bush, 1982

Delay of Testing (hours) spans the ≤2, 12–24, and ≤48 columns.

		Drugs[b]			Reference
	5-MeO-DMT (high dose)	DMI,IMI	→	→	Fuxe et al., 1982a, 1983
	5-MeO-DMT (low dose)	DMI,IMI	←	←	Ogren et al., 1982
	5-HTP	DMI,IMI	=	=	Green et al., 1983b
	5-HTP	DMI	←	←	Bhavsar et al., 1983
	Li	IMI	←	←	Stolz & Marsden, 1982
5-HT syndrome	5-MeO-DMT	AMI	→	←	Stolz et al., 1983
	5-MeO-DMT	IMI	→	←	
		IP	=	=	
	5-MeO-DMT	AMI,DMI,IP	=	=	Lucki & Frazer, 1982
	TRY + TC	AMI,TRAZ	=		Hwang & van Woert, 1980
	TRY + TC	IMI	←		De Montigny et al., 1981b
	5-HTP	AMI		←	Rowland et al., 1982
	5-HTP	AMI		←	Mogilnicka & Klimek, 1979b
		DAN,MIA	=	=	
Sleep	5-HT[c]	AMI,DMI,IMI,MIA	←	←	Jones, 1980b
5-HT syndrome	5-MeO-DMT	NIA,PARG,PHEN	→	→	Lucki & Frazer, 1982
	5-MeO-DMT	CLORG,PHEN	=	=	Renyi 1984

[a] 5-MeO-DMT: 5-Methoxy-dimethyl-tryptamine; 5-HTP: 5-hydroxy-tryptophan; TC: tranylcypromine; Li: Lithium; TRY: tryptophan.
[b] Antidepressants are arranged in three groups: first: CMI, FLU and ZIM; middle: others. Abbreviations as in Table 14, plus DAN: danitracen; FLU: fluoxetine; NIA: nialamide; PARG: pargyline; PHEN: phenelzine; TRAZ: trazodone.
[c] This experiment was carried out in young chicks, in which 5-HT crosses the blood–brain barrier.

discuss these findings, it is convenient to consider separately three groups of drugs: those which powerfully inhibit 5-HT uptake [zimelidine, fluoxetine, and chlorimipramine (Ogren et al., 1979)], other tricyclic and atypical antidepressants, and the MAOIs.

Although there is one report of an increased response (analgesia) to the 5-HT receptor agonist 5-MeO-DMT following chronic administration of zimelidine (Fuxe et al., 1983), the powerful 5-HT uptake inhibitors (zimelidine, fluoxetine, chlorimipramine) have usually been reported to decrease responses to 5-MeO-DMT or to a high dose of 5-HTP plus an MAOI. These results suggest a decrease in the responsiveness of post-synaptic receptors. However, in order to assess synaptic functioning, the consequences of uptake blockade must be set against those of a decrease in receptor sensitivity. The combination of a high dose of 5-HTP with an MAOI produces a high and sustained intrasynaptic 5-HT concentration, and therefore minimizes any contribution of 5-HT uptake blockade to receptor stimulation. Similarly, 5-MeO-DMT is a direct receptor agonist and is unaffected by the uptake system. However, the response to a lower dose of 5-HTP, when administered alone, was enhanced by chronic zimelidine treatment (Fuxe et al., 1982c), suggesting that at moderate levels of receptor stimulation, zimelidine-induced uptake blockade outweighs any decrease in receptor sensitivity.

Drugs in the second group have usually been reported to enhance 5-HT receptor function (Table 17.2). The exception is the observation that DMI, imipramine, and mianserin reduced the number of head twitches produced by a high dose of 5-MeO-DMT or by 5-HTP plus an MAOI (Blackshear & Sanders-Bush, 1982; Fuxe et al., 1982a, 1983). However, the same treatment with DMI or imipramine hardly affected the response to 5-HTP alone (Ogren et al., 1982), and it significantly enhanced the response to a low dose of 5-MeO-DMT (Fuxe et al., 1983). Enhancement by DMI of the response to a range of doses of 5-HTP (without an accompanying MAOI) has also been reported (Green et al., 1983b). It is possible that head twitches are a behavioral manifestation of a low level of 5-HT receptor stimulation, which at higher levels of stimulation is superseded by the "5-HT syndrome" (Drust et al., 1979), in much the same way that locomotor stimulation evoked by DA agonists is suppressed at high doses by the emergence of stereotyped behavior (Kelly et al., 1975: see Chapter 8). In this case, the reduction of head twitches observed by Fuxe and co-workers at high doses of 5-MeO-DMT might indicate an increased level of 5-HT receptor stimulation, rather than a decrease. Alternatively, the results could mean an increase in receptor responsiveness with a decrease in the maximal response. Because maximal receptor stimulation is unlikely to occur physiologically, the enhanced response to a low dose of the receptor agonist is probably the more meaningful result.

In one study of MAOIs, the 5-HT syndrome induced by 5-MeO-DMT or LSD was greatly attenuated (Lucki & Frazer, 1982), suggesting a decrease in 5-HT receptor responsiveness; such an effect has also been observed electrophysiologically (Olpe & Schellenberg, 1981; Section 16.3.1). However, in another study MAOIs did not alter the 5-HT syndrome (Renyi, 1984).

With the possible exception of MAOIs, therefore, behavioral studies indicate that the chronic administration of antidepressant drugs enhances transmission across the 5-HT synapse, either by blocking 5-HT uptake (group 1) or by increasing receptor responsiveness to agonists (group 2)—provided that testing is delayed for several hours following the final drug treatment. Similar results have also been reported for ECS. Lebrecht and Nowak (1980) observed an enhancement of tryptophan-induced head twitches 24 hours after the final ECS treatment, but no effect was seen after only 1 hour. The implications of this time dependence are discussed below.

5-HT dependent behaviors are also enhanced by three other treatments, for which antidepressant efficacy is less well established. Salbutamol and other beta-receptor agonists have been found to increase the hyperactivity induced by 5-HT agonists, the 5-HT syndrome, and 5-HTP-induced head twitches (Cowen et al., 1982; Nimgaonkar et al., 1983; Ortman et al., 1981). Unlike the effects of other agents described above, enhancement of 5-HT responses was present after a single pretreatment, and the response was not increased further by chronic administration; it may be relevant that a rapid onset of antidepressant effects has been claimed for salbutamol (Section 12.3.1). The 5-HT enhancing effect of beta-receptor agonists, unlike those of ECS, were not abolished by lesions of the dorsal NA bundle, presumably because beta-receptor agonists act postsynaptically (Nimgaonkar et al., 1983; Ortman et al., 1981). Second, chronic treatment with lithium, which has antidepressant properties in addition to its antimanic effect (Ramsey & Mendels, 1981) enhanced the development of 5-HT receptor sensitivity induced by reserpine (Friedman et al., 1979), and when added to tricyclics or ECS enhanced the 5-HT syndrome (De Montigny et al., 1981b). Chronic lithium has also been reported to enhance the depressant effect of 5-HTP on spinal reflex pathways (Sangdee & Frantz, 1980). Finally, deprivation of REM sleep (Gillin, 1983; Vogel, 1983) has been reported to enhance quipazine-induced head shakes (Mogilnicka, 1981). In another study, REM deprivation did not appear to affect the induction of the 5-HT syndrome by quipazine or 5-MeO-DMT, but it did enhance responses to tryptophan and 5-HTP (Santos & Carlini, 1983).

The fact that 5-HT receptor function is usually unchanged or reduced for the first few hours after the final antidepressant treatment but increases thereafter makes the clinical implications of the results a little difficult to assess, and the precise timing of the change from suppression to enhancement assumes a central importance. If the period of reduced activity is sufficiently brief, it could, for example, be confined to the patient's sleeping hours (in the case of a treatment administered once daily in the evening). Conversely, if the period of reduced activity lasts for 24 hours or more, than the later increase in 5-HT receptor function is probably a withdrawal effect, which would not normally be seen until the termination of treatment. Unfortunately, there are few data from which to resolve this issue. If studies of 5-MeO-DMT- and 5-HTP-induced head twitches are excluded (because, as described above, this measure could give misleading results), only five studies have examined the behavioral effects of the drugs in group 2 at the 12–24 hour time interval. Of these, three reported increases in 5-HT function and two found no change (Table 17.2). One study of 5-HTP-induced head-twitches should be added to this list. Green and co-workers (1983b) observed an increase in 5-HTP-induced head twitches following DMI, and since this study reported a full dose-response curve for 5-HTP, the results are not open to misinterpretation.

Despite the equivocal nature of the evidence, these data can probably be taken as indicating that the primary effect of antidepressants is an increase, rather than a decrease, in 5-HT function, at clinically relevant time intervals. The agonist challenge techniques used to assay 5-HT receptor function behaviorally involves gross changes in behavior, resulting, presumably, from an extremely high level of receptor stimulation; this applies particularly to the 5-HT syndrome. Under these conditions, further enhancement of function becomes increasingly difficult to demonstrate. Consequently, it follows that the technique is likely to underestimate increases in 5-HT function, and overestimate decreases. A further implication is that at physiological levels of receptor stimulation, the switch from a net reduction in receptor function to a net increase is likely to occur earlier that would be apparent in studies of the kind reviewed in Table 17.2.

17.3.4. Receptor Binding Studies

In light of evidence discussed in earlier chapters, it will come as no surprise to learn that the results of receptor binding studies are generally inconsistent with those obtained by electrophysiological and behavioral methods.

There are two types of binding site for 5-HT (Peroutka & Snyder, 1981b,1982). The 5-HT$_1$ binding site has a high affinity for radiolabeled 5-HT. Destruction of 5-HT neurons by lesions of the raphe nuclei does not reduce the number of [^{3}H]5-HT-binding sites (Bennett & Snyder, 1976), showing that the 5-HT$_1$ site is probably localized postsynaptically. However, the presynaptic 5-HT autoreceptors that modulate 5-HT release have pharmacological characteristics similar to those of the 5-HT$_1$ site (Martin & Sanders-Bush, 1982). The 5-HT$_2$ receptor has a lower affinity for 5-HT, but a high affinity for [^{3}H]spiroperidol (Leysen et al., 1978). Pharmacologically, this site is clearly associated with 5-HT and is easily distinguishable from the DA receptor sites located in the striatum and nucleus accumbens, which may also be labeled with spiroperidol (Leysen et al., 1978; List & Seeman, 1981). 5-HT$_2$ binding sites are also labeled very specifically by [^{3}H]ketanserin (Leysen et al., 1981,1982). Like the 5-HT$_1$ sites, the 5-HT$_2$ sites appear to be postsynaptic, since [^{3}H]spiroperidol and [^{3}H]ketanserin binding are unaffected by raphe lesions (Dumbrille-Ross et al., 1982; Leysen et al., 1983). LSD, the ligand used in early studies of 5-HT receptor binding (Bennett & Aghajanian, 1974), appears to label both 5-HT$_1$ and 5-HT$_2$ receptors equally (Peroutka & Snyder, 1982).

The 5-HT$_1$ receptor is known to be linked to a cyclic AMP (cAMP) generating system (Fillion et al., 1979; Peroutka et al., 1981), which has been studied mainly in hippocampal tissues, though differences in the regional distribution and many other characteristics of 5-HT$_1$ binding sites and those of the 5-HT-stimulated cAMP system would argue that these two measures are independent (Nelson et al., 1980a,b; Leysen, 1984). As yet, neither of these mechanisms has been shown to mediate any of the behavioral effects of 5-HT (Leysen, 1984). On the basis of pharmacological studies, it has been suggested that the 5-HT$_1$ and 5-HT$_2$ receptors might mediate, respectively, the inhibitory and excitatory synaptic actions of 5-HT (Peroutka & Snyder, 1982). Irrespective of the merits of this hypothesis (see Leysen, 1984), the 5-HT$_2$ receptor does appear to mediate the 5-HT syndrome: the ability of a range of drugs to block 5-HTP- or LSD-induced head twitches is highly correlated with their affinity for [^{3}H]LSD or [^{3}H]spiroperidol binding sites. These effects are totally uncorrelated with the affinity of the drugs for [^{3}H]5-HT-binding sites, indicating that 5-HT$_1$ sites are not involved (Leysen, 1984; Ogren et al., 1979; Peroutka & Snyder, 1982).

Fuxe and colleagues, in a series of publications, have reported that antidepressant drugs, in particular, zimelidine, alter the characteristics of 5-HT$_1$ binding sites in a complex fashion (Fuxe et al., 1979, 1981, 1982a–c, 1983). The results of binding experiments generally are analyzed using a graphical technique known as a Scatchard plot. If a single receptor type is present, this plot consists of a straight line, the slope and intercept of which define, respectively, the affinity of the ligand for its receptor, and the number of receptor sites. In the studies of Fuxe and colleagues, antidepressants produce a curved Scatchard plot for [^{3}H]5-HT binding, which is interpreted to mean that two binding sites are now present—a small number of high affinity sites and a large number of low affinity sites. It is further hypothesized that "the appearance of a high and a low affinity component in [^{3}H]5-HT binding sites ... represents a selective downregulation of 5-HT$_1$ receptors leading to a stabilization of 5-HT synaptic transmission" (Fuxe et al., 1983, p. 390). It is unclear why, exactly, these consequences would follow from the appearance of two binding sites. More fundamentally, it does not necessarily follow from the results that antidepressant-treated animals do have two 5-HT binding sites (there are other mechanisms which could produce a curved Scatchard plot). If two sites are present, it is also unclear whether they would have the characteristics imputed to them, as these depend on the arbitrary fitting of two straight lines to what in some cases is not obviously a curve (see Fuxe et al., 1981, Fig. 1B; 1982a, Fig. 2B).

The complex change in 5-HT_1 binding sites reported by Fuxe and colleagues have not been observed by any other authors. Studies of the effects of chronic antidepressant treatment on binding to 5-HT_1 and 5-HT_2 receptors are summarized in Tables 17.3 and 17.4. The overwhelming impression from other laboratories is that antidepressant treatments do not, in general, change 5-HT_1 receptor binding (17 studies). Monoamine oxidase inhibitors may be an exception to this rule, since four studies (three from the same laboratory) have reported a decrease in $[^3\text{H}]5\text{-HT}$ binding following chronic MAOI treatment. Imipramine may be another exception: four independent studies have reported a decrease in $[^3\text{H}]5\text{-HT}$ binding, though three others did not. As this effect is not seen with any other tricyclic, it is unlikely to be significant (Table 17.3).

There are some reports that chronic antidepressant treatment can reduce the activity of the hippocampal 5-HT stimulated cAMP generating system, which may be linked to the 5-HT_1 receptor (Fillion et al., 1981; Fuxe et al., 1983), though this effect has not always been observed (Barbacchia et al., 1983). However, in the hippocampus, antidepressants do not appear to change binding to 5-HT_1 sites (Fuxe et al., 1983). Chronic lithium treatment, on the other hand, has been found to reduce $[^3\text{H}]5\text{-HT}$ binding in the hippocampus, but in this case, no changes were seen in the cortex (Maggi & Enna, 1980; Treiser & Kellar, 1980). All in all, there is little reason to believe that antidepressants markedly affect the functioning of 5-HT_1 binding sites.

In contrast to the relative insensitivity of 5-HT_1 sites, there are now a large number of reports that chronic treatment with antidepressant drugs reduced the binding of $[^3\text{H}]$spiroperidol to 5-HT_2 receptors (Table 17.4). The effect may show some regional specificity. In a recent study Fuxe and co-workers (1983) reported that zimelidine and DMI decreased 5-HT_2 receptor binding in frontal cortex, but in dorsal cortex, DMI had no effect and zimelidine increased binding slightly. In other publications, however, the same authors have also reported that both drugs decreased 5-HT_2 receptor binding in both locations (Fuxe et al., 1982a,b). It is unclear at present to what extent the effects of antidepressants on 5-HT_2 receptors depend upon an intact presynaptic 5-HT innervation. In one study the same reductions in binding were observed after destruction of the raphe nuclei (Dumbrille-Ross et al., 1982), but in another the effects of antidepressants were counteracted by pretreatment with the 5-HT neu-

TABLE 17.3. EFFECTS OF CHRONIC ANTIDEPRESSANT TREATMENTS ON 5-HT$_1$ SITES LABELED WITH [^{3}H]5-HT

Agent	Effect on Binding	References
ECS	=	Atterwill, 1980; Bergstrom & Kellar, 1979a
Tricyclics		
Amitriptyline	=	Lucki & Frazer, 1982; Peroutka & Snyder, 1980a; Savage et al., 1980; Stolz et al., 1983
Chlorimipramine	=	Lucki & Frazer, 1982; Kellar & Bergstrom, 1983; Savage et al., 1979, 1980; Stolz et al., 1983; Takahashi et al., 1982; Wirz-Justice et al., 1978
DMI	=	Bergstrom & Kellar, 1979b; Koide & Matsushita, 1981a; Lucki & Frazer, 1982; Peroutka & Snyder, 1980a
	↓	Maggi et al., 1980
Imipramine	=	Koide & Matsushita, 1981a; Lucki & Frazer, 1982; Stolz et al., 1983
	↓	Fuxe et al., 1982a,b; Maggi et al., 1980; Peroutka & Snyder, 1980a; Segawa et al., 1979
Atypical Antidepressants		
Iprindole	=	Lucki & Frazer, 1982; Peroutka & Snyder, 1980a; Segawa et al., 1982; Stolz et al., 1983
Mianserin	=	Leonard, 1982; Blackshear & Sanders-Bush, 1982
	↓	Segawa et al., 1982
Nomifensine	=	Segawa et al., 1982
Nisoxetine	=	Maggi et al., 1980
Fluoxetine	=	Maggi et al., 1980; Peroutka & Snyder, 1980a; Savage et al., 1979; Stolz et al., 1983
Zimelidine	↓	Fuxe et al., 1979, 1981, 1982a,b
MAOIs		
Clorgyline	↓	Savage et al., 1979, 1980
Pargyline	=	Savage et al., 1980
	↓	Lucki & Frazer, 1982; Peroutka & Snyder, 1980a
Phenelzine	↓	Lucki & Frazer, 1982
Nialamide	↓	Lucki & Frazer, 1982; Savage et al., 1980

rotoxin p-chloroamphetamine (Fuxe et al., 1982c). It has recently been reported that chronic treatment with the selective and potent 5-HT uptake inhibitor citalopram did not affect the number of 5-HT$_2$ binding sites despite continued blockade of 5-HT uptake (Hyttel et al., 1984). These results suggest that the effect of antidepressants on 5-HT$_2$ receptors is probably not related to enhanced receptor stimulation by 5-HT.

TABLE 17.4. EFFECTS OF CHRONIC ANTIDEPRESSANT TREATMENTS ON 5-HT$_2$ SITES LABELED WITH [^{3}H]SPIROPERIDOL

Agent	Effect on Binding	References
ECS	↑	Green et al., 1983a,b; Kellar et al., 1981a; Vetulani et al., 1981
Tricyclics		
Amitriptyline	=	Stolz et al., 1983
	↓	Dumbrille-Ross et al., 1982; Kellar et al., 1981a; Peroutka & Snyder, 1980a,b; Tang et al., 1981
Chlorimipramine	↓	Stolz et al., 1983
DMI	↓	Dumbrille-Ross et al., 1982; Fuxe et al., 1982a,b, 1983; Hall et al., 1982; Peroutka & Snyder, 1980a; Tang et al., 1981
	↑	Green et al., 1983a,b
Imipramine	=	Briley et al., 1982a; Stolz et al., 1983
	↓	Fuxe et al., 1982a,b; Kendall et al., 1982b; Peroutka & Snyder, 1980a
Atypical Antidepressants		
Iprindole	↓	Kellar et al., 1981a; Kendall et al., 1982b; Peroutka & Snyder, 1980a; Stolz et al., 1983
Mianserin	↓	Barbacchia et al., 1983; Blackshear & Sanders-Bush, 1982; Kendall et al., 1982b
Trazodone	↓	Kendall et al., 1982b; D. Taylor et al., 1981
Fluoxetine	=	Peroutka & Snyder, 1980a
	↓	Stolz et al., 1983
Zimelidine	↓	Hall et al., 1982; Fuxe et al., 1982a,b, 1983
Citalopram	=	Hyttel et al., 1984
Amphetamine	↓	Nielsen et al., 1980
MAOIs		
Pargyline	↓	Kendall et al., 1982b; Peroutka & Snyder, 1980a
Tranylcypromine	↓	Kellar et al., 1981a

It is also unclear whether these changes are of functional significance. The ability of antidepressant drugs to reduce the number of 5-HT$_2$ receptors is not shared by a number of nonantidepressants, including the 5-HT receptor blockers methysergide and metergoline, and the neuroleptics chlorpromazine and haloperidol (Maggi et al., 1980; Peroutka & Snyder, 1980a; Stolz et al., 1983). However, amphetamine does reduce 5-HT$_2$ receptor binding (Nielsen et al., 1980), and while acute administration of amphetamine may have beneficial effects on mood, chronic treatment apparently does not (see Section 9.3.2). A more serious discrepancy, which makes it extremely unlikely that changes in 5-HT$_2$ receptor binding mediate the clinical effects of antidepressants, is that repeated ECS has the opposite effect. Three independent studies have reported that the number of $5\text{-}HT_2$ receptors was increased by repeated ECS, rather than decreased (Green et al., 1983a,b; Kellar et al., 1981a; Vetulani et al., 1981).

Effects of antidepressant drugs on $5\text{-}HT_2$ receptor binding are particularly perplexing. As noted above, the $5\text{-}HT_2$ receptor appears to be responsible for at least some of the behavioral effects of 5-HT agonist drugs. Consequently, the enhancement of receptor binding by ECS provides a potential mechanism for the enhancement of 5-HT mediated behavioral effects by repeated ECS. However, it then becomes extremely difficult to explain why antidepressant drugs, which have behavioral effects similar to ECS, have the opposite effects on receptor binding. It is not possible to explain the discrepancy by pointing to the observation that at short intervals after the final antidepressant treatment, behavioral measures suggest a decrease in 5-HT transmission. The standard interval for binding studies is 24 hours, and decreases in $5\text{-}HT_2$ receptors have also been observed after delays of 48 (Barbacchia et al., 1983) and 72 hours (Stolz et al., 1983). At these times there seems little question that the behavioral effects are generally enhanced (Table 17.2). In one recent study, an increase in $5\text{-}HT_2$ receptor binding, commensurate with that seen with ECS, was also observed following chronic DMI treatment (Green et al., 1983b). Conceivably, the decrease in binding reported by the majority of studies may result from methodological inadequacies.

17.4. CONCLUSIONS: ANTIDEPRESSANTS AND 5-HT

Until such time as it becomes clearer what the relationship is between binding measures and postsynaptic functioning, the simplest way to handle the discrepant data on the effects of antidepressant drugs on $5\text{-}HT_2$ receptor binding is to ignore them and to concentrate on functional measures. In fact, there are many examples in the literature in which changes in receptor binding do not in any simple way reflect concomitant changes in functional responsiveness (see Chapters 10 and 13).

Electrophysiological, neuroendocrine, and behavioral measures present a reasonably coherent picture of enhanced 5-HT receptor function following a variety of antidepressant treatments, including, inter alia, tricyclic antidepressants and ECS. Taken together with a potentiation of presynaptic 5-HT function by most antidepressants, which persists during chronic treatment, the overall picture is one of enhanced transmission at 5-HT synapses. This conclusion is consistent with the original "indoleamine hypothesis of depression," but not with the "hypersensitive serotonin receptor" theory.

It must be added that with the exception of ECS, the evidence is less compelling than the comparable evidence for enhancement of alpha-adrenergic function (Chapter 13). As discussed above, this uncertainty reflects in part the paucity of evidence concerning the time, following the cessation of chronic treatment, at which the increase in receptor function emerges. More important, there is a shortage of studies that allow an assessment to be made of the overall net effect of pre- and postsynaptic changes. The majority of behavioral studies summarized in Table 17.2 involve techniques that minimize the importance of presynaptic effects, either by the nature of the pharmacological probe (5-MeO-DMT, or 5-HTP plus an MAOI) or by the nature of the behavioral test (the 5-HT syndrome).

These problems do not apply to the electrophysiological studies summarized in Table 17.1, because modestly sized responses to 5-HT itself were studied. Seven out of eight studies reported that chronic administration of tricyclic antidepressants enhanced responsiveness to 5-HT. A significant feature of these results is that responsiveness was enhanced not only by chlorimipramine, which enhances 5-HT function on acute administration, and by DMI and iprindole, which have no effect on acute administration, but also by amitriptyline, which on acute administration is a powerful receptor antagonist. Similarly, in the only behavioral study to test responsiveness to 5-HT (using young chicks, in which 5-HT crosses the blood–brain barrier), an increase was seen not only with DMI and imipramine but also with amitriptyline and mianserin (Jones, 1980b; Table 17.2).

Another approach, which potentially will give the clearest perspective on integrated synaptic functioning, is to study the effects of antidepressants on 5-HT dependent functions, dispensing with the need for an agonist probe. Two examples may be cited. One is the olfactory bulbectomy model. As previously described (Section 15.1.2.), there is strong evidence that the various effects of bulbectomy result from destruction of a 5-HT pathway terminating in the medial amygdala. Chronic treatment with a variety of antidepressants, including mianserin and amitriptyline, reversed the effects, irrespective of whether they were induced by bulbectomy or by 5-HT depletion (Cairncross et al., 1979). This would be fairly conclusive evidence that antidepressants increase 5-HT transmission, were it not for a problem noted earlier (Section 6.5.4): there is some question as to whether the effects of antidepressants in this model are seen during chronic treatment or only during withdrawal (Noreika et al., 1981).

A second example is the observation that zimelidine pretreatment in rats reduced the consumption of morphine and alcohol (Rockman et al., 1979a,b, 1980). These effects presumably reflect an increase in 5-HT transmission, given that acute zimelidine pretreatment clearly does potentiate 5-HT (Section 17.1.2), that at low doses zimelidine acts specifically on 5-HT systems (Heel et al., 1982), and that alcohol consumption is also reduced by 5-HTP or by intraventricular administration of 5-HT (Geller, 1973; Hill, 1974; Myers et al., 1972). If chronic zimelidine treatment were to reduce 5-HT function, as suggested by Aprison and by Fuxe (Aprison et al., 1982; Fuxe et al., 1983), this would imply a reversal of the acute effects. However, during treatment with zimelidine over a period of five days, far from increasing, the alcohol and morphine consumption fell even lower (Rockman et al., 1979a,b, 1980). These results are not unexpected, given the observation that chronic zimelidine increased the postsynaptic response to electrical stimulation of the raphe system (Blier & De Montigny, 1983), and they support the conclusion that antidepressant drugs given chronically increase 5-HT transmission.

The exceptions are the MAOIs, which in two studies out of three (Olpe, 1981; Lucki & Frazer, 1982; but not Renyi, 1984), were found to reduce 5-HT receptor function. As these drugs do not appear to increase 5-HT turnover after chronic administration, it seems possible that synaptic transmission may also be reduced. The olfactory bulbectomy model provides a further indication that MAOIs do not enhance 5-HT transmission. Normal behavior in this model (Section 6.5.4) was restored by chronic treatment with a variety of tricyclic and atypical antidepressants, but not by the MAOI tranylcypromine (Cairncross et al., 1978, 1979; Noreika et al., 1981). While more studies of MAOIs are clearly needed, it is difficult to refrain from speculating that the failure to potentiate 5-HT transmission may be one reason that MAOIs are clinically ineffective in severe depressions.

eighteen

OTHER NEUROTRANSMITTER SYSTEMS

In addition to the "big four" (NA, 5-HT, DA, and ACh), the cast of characters studied in relation to depression or antidepressants also includes a number of other neurotransmitter systems, which have been examined in a much more exploratory and less systematic fashion. This chapter reviews the relevant literature on endogenous opiates (endorphins), non-opioid peptides, gamma-aminobutyric acid (GABA), and histamine. In view of the fragmentary nature of this literature, it seems important to attempt wherever possible to discuss the involvement of these minor characters in relation to the known exploits of the leading actors.

18.1 GAMMA-AMINOBUTYRIC ACID

The inhibitory neurotransmitter gamma-aminobutyric acid (GABA) is found throughout the brain and is probably active at more synapses than any other neurotransmitter. Cells using GABA-ergic transmission include short-axoned local interneurons in most brain areas, as well as a number of longer pathways. Antagonism of GABA-ergic transmission produces convulsions, and, conversely, GABA agonists are anticonvulsants (Mandel & De Feudis, 1979). In the psychiatric context, GABA mechanisms have usually been discussed in relation to anxiety, primarily because antianxiety drugs increase GABA-ergic neurotransmission (Gray, 1982; Mandel & De Feudis, 1979), and there is a very close anatomical relationship between GABA receptors and benzodiazepine receptors (the "GABA-benzodiazepine receptor complex") (Braestrup & Nielsen, 1980; Guidotti et al., 1979). More recently, clinical studies have implicated GABA in the affective disorders; some supporting evidence is also available from animal models of depression. In both cases, it is possible to integrate the evidence for GABA-ergic mechanisms in affective disorders with the literature on 5-HT.

18.1.1. Animal Models of Depression

The olfactory bulbectomy and muricide models, which are closely related (Section 15.1.2), provide the clearest evidence for GABA-ergic involvement in animal models of depression. In both cases, there is evidence for a deficiency of GABA-ergic transmission.

Systemic administration of the GABA-mimetic drugs progabide and muscimol has been found to reverse the passive avoidance deficit shown by olfactory bulbectomized rats; the GABA receptor antagonist bicuculline blocked this effect (Lloyd et al., 1983). The medial amygdala is a major site at which fibers leaving the olfactory bulbs terminate (Cairncross et al., 1979), and this projection includes GABA-ergic fibers (Mack & Mandel, 1976). However, GABA did not inhibit muricide when applied to the medial amygdala, and, similarly, application of bicuculline to the amygdala did not block the effect of systemic progabide (Lloyd et al., 1982). Unlike other agents active in the olfactory bulbectomy model, therefore, GABA-ergic drugs do not act directly within the medial amygdala. The site of action may be in the immediate vicinity of the olfactory bulbs, since in spontaneously muricidal rats, the level of GABA in the region of the olfactory bulbs was reduced by approximately 30%, and injections of GABA into the olfactory bulbs suppressed muricide (Mack et al., 1975; Mandel et al., 1978). As the behavioral changes seen in both the olfactory bulbectomy and muricide models appear to result primarily from a reduction of 5-HT activity (Section 15.1.2), an interaction between 5-HT and GABA-ergic neurons in the region of the olfactory bulb seems likely.

Progabide has also been found to reverse learned helplessness (Lloyd et al., 1983). The mechanism of this effect is more obscure but may involve the hippocampus. In this area, GABA injections prevented or reversed helplessness, and bicuculline blocked the reversal of helplessness by DMI applied to the frontal cortex (Sherman & Petty, 1980; Petty & Sherman, 1981). Finally, progabide has also been found to suppress sleep, and at low doses the effect is selective for REM periods, with no effect on non-

REM sleep (Lloyd et al., 1983). In all of these models, therefore, the data would predict an antidepressant effect of GABA agonists.

18.1.2. Clinical Studies

A number of recent studies have reported data that indicate reduced GABA turnover in depression. With one exception (Post et al., 1980a) low levels of GABA have been reported in the CSF of medication-free depressed patients, compared to neurological patients (B. Gold et al., 1980), normal volunteers (Gerner & Hare, 1981), and hospitalized medical patients (Kasa et al., 1982). Low plasma GABA levels have also been reported in unipolar primary depressions, but not in bipolar depressions or in secondary depressions (which were mainly secondary to schizophrenia) (Petty & Schlesser, 1981). In manic patients, plasma GABA levels were elevated (Petty & Schlesser, 1981). However, as patients were not medication-free in this study, it is possible that the elevation of GABA level in manic patients was an artifact of neuroleptic drug treatment (Mao & Costa, 1978). Low plasma GABA has also been reported in bipolar patients who were not ill at the time the samples were taken. The significance of these observations is unclear, however, since in this study, patients did not differ from controls in CSF GABA levels (Berrettini et al., 1982a).

The enzyme glutamic acid decarboxylase (GAD), which synthesizes GABA from glutamic acid, is released from nerve terminals along with GABA and therefore serves as another marker of GABA turnover (Mao & Costa, 1978). Low GAD activity has been reported in a number of brain areas of unipolar depressed patients studied postmortem (Perry et al., 1977). It has also been found that depressed patients had a reduced plasma GAD activity, compared to schizophrenic patients, patients with organic brain damage, and normal volunteers (Kaiya et al., 1982). In this study, low GAD activity was also found in neurotic patients (Kaiya et al., 1982), which suggests that low GABA turnover may be associated with anxiety rather than depression. The lack of change in plasma GABA in bipolar depressed patients (Petty & Schlesser, 1981) would be consistent with this speculation.

Two recent studies, one open, and the other a double-blind comparison with imipramine, have reported antidepressant effects of the GABA agonist drug progabide (Morselli et al., 1980, 1981). Mood elevating effects have also been observed with another GABA agonist, THIP (Krogsgaard-Larsen, reported by Lloyd et al., 1983), and antidepressant effects have been reported with the anticonvulsant drug carbamazepine (Ballenger & Post, 1980; Post & Uhde, 1982), which may indirectly activate GABA-ergic mechanisms (Bernasconi & Martin, 1979), among its other biochemical effects (Post et al., 1982, 1983).

There is rather more evidence that anticonvulsants, which are likely to be GABA agonists, have antimanic effects. The anticonvulsants valproate (Emrich et al., 1980, 1982, 1983a), carbamazepine (Ballenger & Post, 1980; Okuma et al., 1973; Post & Uhde, 1982), keto-carbamazepine (Emrich et al., 1982), and dipropylacetamide (Lambert et al., 1975) have all been shown to exert antimanic and prophylactic effects in bipolar patients. The beta-blocker propranolol also exerts antimanic effects at high doses. This effect cannot be attributed to blockade of beta-receptors because it is shared by both isomers of propranolol. Only one of them is a beta-blocker (Emrich et al., 1979a; Rackensperger et al., 1976), but at high doses, both isomers of propranolol have GABA-ergic activity (Bernasconi, 1982).

The effectiveness of GABA-ergic agents in both mania and depression strengthens the suspicion arising out of animal models that disorders of GABA in the affective disorders are linked to disorders of 5-HT, since low 5-HT activity also predisposes to both conditions (Section 16.1.2). There is also a symptomatic resemblance between low 5-HT depressions and low GABA depressions. Low 5-HT is found in a variety of conditions characterized primarily by irritability and low tolerance for frustration (Section 16.1.2); as noted above, reduced plasma GAD activity was found both in depressed and in neurotic patients (Kaiya et al., 1982). It remains to be seen whether, like low 5-HT activity (Section 16.1.2), low GABA activity is also a characteristic of suicide victims.

18.1.3. Antidepressants and GABA

Although GABA-ergic agents may have antidepressant effects, there is little evidence that conventional antidepressants work through GABA-ergic mechanisms.

Two studies have reported that GABA receptor binding was unchanged by repeated ECS (Atterwill, 1984; Cross et al., 1979), and three studies of benzodiazepine receptors, which are closely associated with GABA receptors (Guidotti et al., 1979), also reported that repeated ECS did not cause any changes (Bowdler et al., 1983; Cross et al., 1979; Deakin et al., 1981). Two other studies found a small increase in benzodiazepine receptor binding after repeated ECS (McNamara et al., 1980; Paul & Skolnick, 1978). However, functional studies of GABA receptors following chronic ECS or antidepressant drug treatment are unanimous in finding no alterations. A number of studies have reported no change in electrophysiological responsiveness to the iontophoretic application of GABA, in a variety of brain areas; agents tested include tricyclics, MAOIs, atypical antidepressants, and ECS (De Montigny, 1980; De Montigny & Aghajanian, 1978; De Montigny et al., 1981a; Olpe & Schellenberg, 1980, 1981; Schultz et al., 1981). Similarly, repeated ECS administration did not alter the threshold at which GABA antagonist drugs evoked epileptic seizures (Cowen et al., 1980; Nutt et al., 1980b).

At high doses, acute administration of some antidepressants has been reported to alter GABA uptake and release (Snodgrass et al., 1973), but the effects of chronic antidepressant drug treatment on the functioning of GABA-ergic neurons has not been studied. Repeated ECS has been found to increase striatal GABA synthesis (Atterwill, 1984). However, it has also been found that repeated ECS increased GABA concentration and decreased GABA turnover in the nucleus accumbens and striatum; taken together, these two changes suggest that the release of GABA was reduced in these two brain areas. (Bowdler et al., 1983; A. Green et al., 1978, 1982). The increase in striatal GABA concentration was not confirmed in another study (Deakin et al., 1981) possibly because appropriate precautions were not taken to prevent further changes from occurring postmortem (Bowdler et al., 1983).

If ECS does reduce GABA release this would be at variance with the reported antidepressant effects of GABA agonist drugs. It is quite possible, however, that different GABA mechanisms are involved in the two cases. The reversal by GABA of passive avoidance learning deficits in the olfactory bulbectomized rat has been localized to the olfactory bulb, and appears to be linked to deficiencies of 5-HT (see above). However, the reduction of GABA release by ECS is specific to the intrinsic GABA-ergic interneurons of the nucleus accumbens and striatum. GABA concentrations were unaffected by ECS in the substantia nigra, cortex or hippocampus (though an increased GABA concentration in the latter two structures was observed following chemically induced convulsions) (Bowdler et al., 1983; A. Green et al., 1978, 1982). In view of this regional specificity, it is unlikely that changes in GABA release constitute the primary action of ECS.

It will be recalled that the enhancement of DA mediated behaviors observed following repeated ECS and, less consistently, chronic antidepressant drug administration, depend on changes "beyond the DA receptor" (see Section 10.2.2). Because the time course of ECS-induced changes in GABA release parallels that of ECS-induced changes in DA mediated behaviors, and the nucleus accumbens and striatum are the areas in which the two major DA pathways terminate (Chapter 8), Green and coworkers (1978, 1982; Bowdler et al., 1983) have suggested that a decrease in GABA-ergic activity in the nucleus accumbens and striatum could be responsible for the "dopaminergic" behavioral changes. Since the enhancement of DA mediated behaviors requires an intact NA system (see Section 10.2.2), it seems likely that changes in GABA release might also be secondary to changes in NA transmission. This speculation receives support from the observation that in human subjects, levels of GABA in the CSF were positively correlated with NA and MHPG concentrations (Post et al., 1980a).

18.2. ENDOGENOUS OPIATES

It is often forgotten that up until the introduction of modern antide-pressants in the late 1950s, the drug most frequently used in the treat-ment of depression was opium, which was recommended by Kraepelin (1901), particularly for agitated depression. A resurgence of interest in opiates followed the demonstration in the early 1970s that the brain con-tains opiate receptors (Pert & Snyder, 1973; Terenius, 1973). This dis-covery was rapidly followed by the isolation and identification of two closely related families of endogenous peptides, with analgesic actions and a high affinity for opiate receptors. The enkephalins (Hughes et al., 1975), which are made up of five amino acids, are widely distributed within the brain, the highest concentrations being found in the midbrain central grey, amygdala, ventral tegmental area, and locus coeruleus (Si-mantov, 1981). Beta-endorphin (Li & Chung, 1976) is a much longer pep-tide (31 amino acids), which has the same terminal sequence as the en-kephalins; originally discovered in pituitary extracts, beta-endorphin has also been identified in the hypothalamus and certain other brain areas (Simantov, 1981). Collectively, the enkephalins, beta-endorphin, and a variety of other peptides of related structure, are known as endorphins (i.e., endogenous morphines).

The proliferation of endorphin neurotransmitters has been paralleled by the realization that there also exist multiple subtypes of opiate re-ceptor, which are differentially distributed within the central nervous system (Chang et al., 1979; Smith & Simon, 1980; Terenius, 1980). The different receptor subtypes appear to be differentially implicated in a variety of behavioral and physiological actions, and since opiate agonists vary in their affinity for different receptors, their spectra of activity also differ (Lord et al., 1977). As there are as yet no relevant clinical impli-cations, the problems arising from the existence of multiple opiate re-ceptors will not be discussed further.

The endorphins are synthesized by the breakdown of substantially larger peptides (Bradbury et al., 1976; Huang et al., 1979; Kimura et al., 1977), and there is no reuptake mechanism or other machinery that would allow recycling. This means that for every peptide molecule released, a new precursor molecule must be synthesized in the cell body and trans-ported down the axon to the nerve ending (Hokfelt et al., 1980). In terms of their energy requirements, therefore, peptide transmitters are ex-tremely expensive, compared to classical neurotransmitters. In view of the inefficiency associated with their use, it seems likely that peptides (opioid and nonopioid) modulate activity in the nervous system over a relatively long time scale rather than participating in the moment to moment transfer of information. Some workers have speculated that this is a property which might well be expected of the systems that regulate mood, but the evidence is as yet insufficient to assess this idea.

18.2.1. Opiates and Behavior

Opiate drugs such as morphine and heroin have two striking properties. On the one hand, they are powerful analgesic agents, while on the other, they are highly addictive recreational drugs. It is now known that the analgesic and rewarding properties of opiates both arise from the stimulation of receptors for endogenous opiates.

18.2.1.1. *Stress and Analgesia*

As described in Section 15.2.3, analgesia may be induced in animals (Reynolds, 1969) or in people (Hosobuchi et al., 1977) by electrical stimulation of a number of sites in the midbrain or brainstem. Effective stimulation-produced analgesia (SPA) sites correspond closely to the sites at which microinjection of exogenous opiates or of endorphins produce analgesia (Bloom et al., 1976; Sherman & Liebeskind, 1980), and lesions of these sites, or the destruction of descending 5-HT pathways, block the analgesic action of systemically administered opiates (Proudfit & Anderson, 1975; Yaksh et al., 1977; see also Section 15.2). Furthermore, cross-tolerance is seen between SPA and morphine (Mayer & Hayes, 1975) or endorphins (Wei & Loh, 1976). These findings indicate that SPA and opiate analgesia are similarly mediated. The sites that support SPA and opiate analgesia are rich in enkephalin-containing terminals (Simantov, 1981), which implies that SPA might operate by releasing enkephalin at these sites. This supposition is confirmed by the observations that medial brainstem stimulation, in human subjects, does release endorphins into the CSF (Akil et al., 1978) and that SPA is reduced by the opiate antagonist naloxone (Adams, 1976; Akil et al., 1976b; Oliveras et al., 1977).

Analgesia may also be produced by exposure to a variety of stressors, including footshock (Akil et al., 1976a), cold water immersion (Bodnar et al., 1978a), immobilization (Amir & Amit, 1978), and rotation (Hayes et al., 1978a). Like SPA, these effects are also mediated in part by activation of the endogenous opiate system, because exposure to electric shock elevates brain endorphin levels (Madden et al., 1977), and stress-induced analgesias may be partially reversed by naloxone (Amir & Amit, 1978; Satoh et al., 1979). Exposure to a previously neutral stimulus that has been paired with stress also produces analgesia (Chance et al., 1978; Fanselow & Bolles, 1979; MacLennan et al., 1980), which is completely blocked by opiate antagonists (Maier et al., 1980) and is cross-tolerant with morphine (Drugan et al., 1981). Exposure to a conditioned fear stimulus has also been found to reduce enkephalin receptor binding, suggesting increased occupancy of receptor sites by endogenous enkephalin (Chance et al., 1978).

Not all analgesias are mediated by endorphins. Naloxone only partially reverses SPA (Akil et al., 1976b), and stress-induced analgesias are also only partially reversed by naloxone, or sometimes not at all (Akil et al., 1976a; Bodnar et al., 1978b; Chance & Rosencrans, 1980a; Hayes et al., 1978a). Similarly, cross-tolerance between morphine analgesia and SPA (Chesner & Chan, 1978) or stress-induced analgesia (Bodnar et al., 1978d; Chance & Rosencrans, 1980b) is only partial. Furthermore, lesions to the dorsal column of the spinal cord, which eliminate morphine-produced analgesia, have been reported not to affect footshock-induced analgesia (Hayes et al., 1978b).

It therefore appears that there are two forms of stress-induced analgesia, of which one involves activation of the endorphin system (i.e., it can be blocked by naloxone, and it is cross-tolerant with morphine), whereas the other does not. The length of exposure to stress is a major determinant of which type is exhibited. Initial exposure to stress produces an analgesia that is not naloxone-reversible, but following prolonged exposure this is superseded by a naloxone-reversible analgesia, which is presumed to be endorphin-mediated (Grau et al., 1981; Lewis et al., 1980). The crucial factor in engaging the endogenous opiate system is not the length of stress exposure per se, but rather that with longer exposure the animal comes to learn that it is unable to control the stress. Animals were found to be analgesic immediately following exposure to identical regimes of escapable or inescapable electric shock, but only the analgesia induced by inescapable shock was reversed by the opiate antagonist naltrexone (Jackson et al., 1979; Maier et al., 1980).

There are a number of resemblances between the analgesic response to uncontrollable stress and the performance deficit (learned helplessness), which develops concurrently. Both phenomena are prevented by prior experience with escapable shock ("immunization"), and both may be reversed by prolonged exposure to escapable shock ("therapy") (Moye et al., 1981; Williams & Maier, 1977). They also have a similar time course (Maier et al., 1979). Like the changes in NA transmission underlying learned helplessness (Section 11.3), the analgesic reaction which follows inescapable shock could also be reinstated the following day by a brief reexposure to electric shock (Jackson et al., 1979). Furthermore, both the analgesia (MacLennan et al., 1983) and the learning deficit (Anisman et al., 1979b, 1981) could be reversed by the anticholinergic drug scopolamine. However, the two phenomena may be dissociated. Both pituitary removal and dexamethasone administration abolished the analgesia produced by inescapable shock (MacLennan et al., 1982, 1983), but the deficiency in escape learning was unaffected by either procedure (MacLennan et al., 1983).

The fact that stress-induced analgesia requires an intact and functioning pituitary implies that ultimately the analgesia is mediated by the release of beta-endorphin into the circulation. As cholinergic agonists cause beta-endorphin release (Risch et al., 1982a), the likely sequence of events is as follows. Uncontrollable stress causes a functional lesion in NA terminals, which releases ACh systems from inhibition (Section 13.3), leading to the cholinergic stimulation of beta-endorphin secretion, either by a direct action in the hypothalamus or via the stimulation of midbrain endorphin systems.

As stress-induced analgesia is attenuated by hypophysectomy, but learned helplessness is not, analgesia is ruled out as an explanation of the performance deficit. It remains possible however, that some other actions of endorphins could be involved in this phenomenon. In fact, deficient shuttle-box escape performance following inescapable shock was reversed by blockade of opiate receptors with naltrexone (Maier et al., 1983). As noted in earlier chapters, learned helplessness may also be reversed by DA and alpha-adrenergic agonists (Sections 8.3.2 and 11.3.1). Opiate receptors are known to be located presynaptically on terminals of a variety of neuronal systems, including NA and DA, and stimulation of these receptor inhibits the release of transmitter (Arbilla & Langer, 1978; Llorens et al., 1978; Pollard et al., 1979). In view of these observations, it is likely that naltrexone reverses the learned helplessness performance deficit by enhancing the release of NA and/or DA. If this conclusion is correct, a possible implication could be that the activation of endorphins by uncontrollable stress takes place not only in the midbrain regions that mediate opiate analgesia, but throughout the brain.

18.2.1.2. Opiates and Reward

The rewarding effects of opiates are anatomically distinct from their analgesic effects. Whereas the sites that mediate opiate analgesia are localized in the region of the midbrain central grey, the most effective site for eliciting opiate self-administration in rats is the ventral tegmental area (VTA). The doses of morphine or heroin required to support behaviors rewarded by drug administration to the VTA are very much lower than in any other brain area (Bozarth, 1983; Bozarth & Wise, 1981a,b; Phillips & LePiane, 1980), and rewarding effects of enkephalin have also been reported at this site (Hoebel et al., 1981; Phillips et al., 1982). Furthermore, microinjection of an opiate antagonist into the VTA has been found to block the intravenous self-administration of heroin, whereas injections at other sites were ineffective (Britt & Wise, 1981).

The VTA is, of course, the area of origin of the DA cells of the mesolimbic system (see Chapter 8). Stimulation of opiate receptors in the VTA excites DA cells, and a number of studies have found that the rewarding effects of opiates are blocked by DA receptor antagonists or by 6-OHDA-induced destruction of DA terminals in the nucleus accumbens (see Section 8.1.1). It seems likely therefore that the rewarding effect of exogenously applied opiates depends on the activation of the mesolimbic DA system. What is not known is whether opiates excite DA cells directly or act indirectly by inhibiting the release of transmitter from axons that inhibit DA cells. This distinction could have important consequences for the interpretation of opiate reward mechanisms (see below).

Like the mesolimbic DA system (see Section 8.2.1), endogenous opiate systems also play a role in the effects of natural rewards. Systemic or intracranial administration of opiate agonists increases food and water intake, and antagonists have the opposite effect (Belluzi & Stein, 1978; Grandison & Guidotti, 1977; Hoebel et al., 1981; Margules et al., 1978; Morley & Levine, 1982; Siviy et al., 1982b; Yim et al., 1982). These effects on food and water intake appear to be mediated via a change in the taste, since the intake of palatable diets or sweet solutions is suppressed far more by opiate antagonists than that of plain lab chow or water (Apfelbaum & Mandenoff, 1981; King et al., 1979; Le Magnen et al., 1980; Ostrowski et al., 1980; Sclafani et al., 1982).

Although, at first sight, the rewarding effects of opiates appear to have little in common with their analgesic effects, an impression supported by the differential anatomical localization of these two phenomena, further behavioral analysis suggests that there could be an important behavioral commonality. As noted in Section 15.3.2, stimuli that are rewarding in some circumstances may be aversive in others; food, for example, tastes pleasant if hungry but unpleasant if satiated (Blass & Hall, 1976; Cabanac, 1971; Rolls, 1982; Toates, 1981). Naloxone does not usually affect food consumption during the first minutes of a feeding session, but it does bring the meal to an early conclusion (Jalowiec et al., 1981; Siviy et al., 1982a). Perhaps naloxone enhances the aversive component of food intake. This conclusion is suggested by studies showing that naloxone administration to rats abolished their preference for a sweet solution, and it even caused them to reject sweet solutions for which they normally had a strong preference (Le Magnen et al., 1980; Siviy et al., 1982b).

The suggestion that opiates might act to suppress the aversive concomitants of rewarding events is supported by studies of brain-stimulation reward. Morphine and enkephalin facilitate ICSS (Esposito & Kornetsky, 1978; Reid & Bozarth, 1978), and as with opiate self-administration (see above), these actions are most potent when opiates are applied directly to the VTA (Broekkamp et al., 1976, 1979). Conversely, opiate antagonists have been reported to suppress ICSS (Franklin & Robertson, 1982; Schaefer & Michael, 1981; Stapleton et al., 1979; Stein & Belluzi, 1978; West et al., 1983). However, rewarding brain stimulation also has clear aversive effects. Animals show approach–avoidance conflict behavior (Miller, 1951) in relation to the lever which delivers brain stimulation (Clark, 1982; Olds & Olds, 1963; Neeley & Stellar, 1983), and if stimulation is prolonged, animals will switch it off if given the opportunity to do so (Hoebel, 1976; Olds & Olds, 1963; Shizgal & Matthews, 1977). The intensity of these aversive effects varies greatly between electrode implantation sites. In the lateral hypothalamus, stimulation is primarily rewarding, with mixed appetite-aversive effects being observed only in the border region between the lateral and medial hypothalamus (Hoebel, 1976; Olds & Olds, 1963). Significantly, in many studies the suppressive effect of opiate antagonists on ICSS is small or nonexistent (Esposito et al., 1980; Holzman, 1974; Kornetsky et al., 1979; Lorens & Sainati, 1978; Potter et al., 1982; Stilwell et al., 1980; Van der Kooy et al., 1977; Wauquier et al., 1974). The most reliable suppressive effects of naloxone are found when ICSS electrodes are implanted in the midbrain central grey region (Schaefer & Michael, 1981; Stein & Belluzi, 1978). It is unlikely to be coincidental that, of all the sites which support ICSS, the central grey is the site that produces the most powerful aversive reactions (Chi & Flynn, 1971; Ellison & Flynn, 1968; Hutchinson & Renfrew, 1978; Stein, 1968).

This discussion raises the possibility that opiates enhance rewards indirectly by suppressing the transmission of information about punishment carried in fibers that would normally inhibit the firing of DA cells in the VTA. This formulation amounts to a unified hypothesis of endorphin function (Le Magnen et al., 1980): endorphins act to suppress the consequences of aversive events. There is, in fact, one set of observations that links opiate reward and analgesia directly. Food deprivation, which increases the incentive value of food rewards (Toates, 1981), releases endorphins (Gambert et al., 1980) and induces analgesia (Bodnar et al., 1978c). However, other stressors that induce opiate analgesia, such as uncontrollable shock, reduce rather than increase, the incentive value of rewards (Section 7.2.1). In particular, uncontrollable stress has been found to decrease ICSS through electrodes implanted in the VTA (Zacharko et al., 1982, 1983). It therefore seems rather unlikely that opiate mechanisms in the VTA are activated by uncontrollable stress.

What, then, is the functional significance of opiate reward mechanisms, if they are not activated either by stress or by natural rewards? Panksepp and co-workers (1978, 1980) have reviewed the evidence that specific brain systems have evolved to provide a substrate for social cohesion and that the release of endorphins underlies the rewarding effects of contact with other animals. It was found, for example, that distress vocalizations, in infants from a variety of species subjected to maternal separation, were increased by naloxone and were reduced by morphine. The contribution of endogenous opiate systems was confirmed by demonstrating that like morphine, electrical stimulation of the midbrain central grey also caused a naloxone-reversible reduction in distress vocalizations, elicited in this case, in adult animals, by electrical stimulation of various forebrain areas (Herman & Panksepp, 1981). The implications of the hypothesis that social reinforcement is the natural stimulus which activates opiate-reward mechanisms will be explored further in Section 19.3.

18.2.2. Opiates and Depression

As activity in central opioid systems reduces the psychological impact of aversive events and may mediate the impact of social rewards, there are good grounds for predicting that opiate agonists might act as antide-pressants. Endorphins are released in response to stress, and high levels of stress are associated with depression; consequently, an elevation of circulating endorphin levels in depressed patients would also be expected. The implications for central opioid function are less clear. A high level of stress would tend to increase activity in some opioid circuits, but a low level of social reinforcement would tend to decrease activity in others. As both of these factors are implicated in the etiology of depression (Section 20.1), the consequences for central opioid function in depression are rather indeterminate.

18.2.2.1. Endorphin Function in Affective Disorders

A number of studies have attempted to measure CSF opioid levels in affective disorder patients; as expected, the results are inconclusive. Ter-enius and co-workers (1976; Lindstrom et al., 1978) reported increased CSF opioid levels in manic and depressed patients compared to normal controls, with a tendency for manic patients to have somewhat higher values. The same group of workers recently reported lower opioid levels in bipolar depressed patients than in unipolar depressions (Agren et al., 1982). However, two other groups did not find any difference among de-pressed, manic, and normal subjects (Davis et al., 1982; Pickar et al., 1982a), though one of them did find lower concentrations in the depressed phase than in the manic phase, in the small number of patients for whom both sets of data were available (Pickar et al., 1980a, 1982a).

Similar discrepancies exist in studies which have measured beta-en-dorphin levels, using specific radioimmunoassay procedures. Risch (1982) and Brambilla and co-workers (1982; Genazzani et al., 1982) found ele-vated plasma levels of beta-endorphin in depressed patients, compared to normal controls. This difference is to be expected, considering that many depressed patients have elevated pituitary–adrenal activity (see Section 3.3.2), and beta-endorphin is co-released with ACTH (Risch et al., 1982a; Rossier et al., 1980). Nevertheless, in another study, Emrich and co-workers (1979b) found no differences in plasma beta-endorphin levels between depressed and nondepressed subjects, and Pickar and co-workers (1983) found no differences in CSF samples.

The major problem is that high endorphin levels are not at all specific to affective disorders. In the original reports of high CSF endorphin levels in affective disorder patients, even higher levels were found in schizo-phrenics (Terenius et al., 1976; Lindstrom et al., 1978). However, later studies did not confirm this general relationship (Emrich et al., 1979b;

Pickar et al., 1982a). It now appears that acute schizophrenic conditions are associated with elevated endorphin levels, whereas levels may be reduced in chronic schizophrenics (Domshke et al., 1979; Rimon et al., 1980). Tucker (1981) has suggested that acute schizophrenia is associated with very high levels of anxiety, and this may be the common factor; in two studies, it has been observed that endorphin levels in depressed patients were positively correlated with anxiety level (Pickar et al., 1982a; Agren et al., 1982). The implication that high CSF endorphin levels are associated with anxiety rather than depression, is supported by the further observation of abnormally high endorphin levels in anorexia nervosa, another condition with high levels of associated anxiety (Pickar et al., 1982a).

More generally, high endorphin levels may be an indicator of high levels of stress but may not discriminate between affective disorders and other stressful psychiatric and nonpsychiatric conditions. Increases in plasma beta-endorphin have been observed as a concomitant of surgical stress (Pickar et al., 1982a), and depressed patients with high CSF opioid levels reported greater somatic distress, such as headaches or stomach aches (Davis et al., 1982). The involvement of endogenous opiate systems in the response to stress was discussed in greater detail earlier in this chapter (Section 18.2.1.1).

In addition to an association with high levels of anxiety, it has also been observed that CSF endorphin levels were higher in depressed patients who had attempted suicide than in those who had not (Agren et al., 1982). This pattern of symptoms is very reminiscent of that of patients with low 5-HT turnover (see Section 16.1.2). As opiate analgesia depends crucially upon the activation of ascending and descending 5-HT pathways (Section 15.2.2), elevation of endorphin levels should be associated with an increase in 5-HT turnover. It is therefore important to emphasize the paradox inherent in the association of both high endorphin levels and low 5-HT turnover with the same syndrome of anxiety and irritability. Perhaps the fundamental problem in people with chronically low 5-HT turnover is that their 5-HT system is insufficiently responsive to activation by stress-induced endorphin release. Alternatively, it may simply be that CSF endorphin levels do not adequately reflect the activity of endorphin pathways in the brain.

Although a variety of hormonal responses are influenced by opiate agonists and anatagonists, there have as yet been very few attempts to utilize these to assess opiate receptor function in depression. As noted in Section 16.1.4, three studies have reported a decrease in the prolactin response to morphine (Extein et al., 1980b) or methadone (Judd et al., 1982, 1983). It is possible that these results represent a reduction in opiate receptor sensitivity, perhaps in response to elevated endorphin levels (see below). However, since prolactin secretion in response to opiate agonists may involve 5-HT (see Section 16.1.4), an abnormality of 5-HT function is an equally plausible explanation. No evidence for opiate receptor changes in depressed patients was found in a fourth neuroendocrine study, which examined cortisol secretion in response to naloxone challenge (Extein et al., 1982b).

18.2.2.2. Opiate Challenges and Mood

There is little evidence that opiate antagonists have marked effects on mood. Only low doses of naloxone have been administered to depressed patients, and no mood changes were reported (G. Davis et al., 1977; Emrich et al., 1979a; Terenius et al., 1977). The administration of a high dose of naloxone was reported to cause a substantial reduction in manic symptoms, but subsequent attempts to replicate this finding were relatively unsuccessful, antimanic effects being noted in only a small proportion of subjects (Janowsky et al., 1978, 1979; Judd et al., 1980). No antimanic effects were observed by another group of workers (G. Davis et al., 1980). In normal volunteers, Grevert and Goldstein (1978) did not observe any depressive effect of a high dose of naloxone (10 mg). Even higher doses do produce a range of dysphoric feelings in normal subjects, including depressed mood, but with irritability and anxiety predominating (Jones & Herning, 1979; Pickar et al., 1982a). These changes are reminiscent of those associated with low 5-HT turnover (Section 16.1.2). A depression-like syndrome has been reported following chronic administration of another antagonist, naltrexone, to normal volunteers, but the implications of this finding are unclear, since no effect was observed with acute naltrexone (Hollister et al., 1981). The observation that opiate addicts are at high risk for depression following withdrawal from methadone maintenance treatment (M. Gold et al., 1979) is also susceptible to a variety of interpretations.

Studies of opiate agonists as potential antidepressant agents are a little more encouraging. Although, as noted above, the "opium cure" (Kraepelin, 1901) was in use for half a century, its discontinuation preceded the advent of controlled clinical trials. Some recent studies have suggested antidepressant effects of opiates during or following acute intravenous infusions of beta-endorphin (Angst et al., 1979; Gerner et al., 1980; Kline et al., 1977), but negative results have also been reported with beta-endorphin (Pickar et al., 1981) and methadone (Extein et al., 1981). Moreover, in one study (Kline et al., 1977), though not in another (Gerner et al., 1980), beta-endorphin produced equal improvements in schizophrenic and other nondepressed psychiatric patients. There have been very few studies of chronic opiate administration, owing to the risk of addiction. Antidepressant effects have been reported in trials of methadone (Pickar et al., 1982b) and of the mixed agonist–antagonist drugs cyclazocine (Fink et al., 1970) and buprenorphine (Emrich et al., 1982, 1983b); mood elevating effects of buprenorphine have also been noted during its use as an analgesic in postoperative patients (Harcus et al., 1980).

18.2.3. Antidepressants and Opiate Mechanisms

There have been few studies of endogenous opiates in relation to the mechanism of action of antidepressant treatments; most of those concern ECS. A single ECS has been found, in human subjects, to increase plasma beta-endorphin levels (Emrich et al., 1979b; Inturissi et al., 1982), and in animals, naloxone pretreatment antagonized many of the physiological effects of ECS, such as respiratory depression and EEG slowing (Holaday & Belenky, 1980). A single ECS did not, however, alter brain levels of met-enkephalin (A. Green et al., 1978; Hong et al., 1979). Synergism between morphine and some tricyclic antidepressants has been reported (Lee & Spencer, 1977), but the mechanism of this effect is unknown. It has also been reported that in the rat "behavioral despair" test (Section 7.2.2), the actions of DMI and chlorimipramine were antagonized by naloxone, but naloxone did not influence the effects of mianserin, nomifensine, or MAOIs (DeVoize et al., 1982, 1983).

Chronic ECS increased met-enkephalin, but not beta-endorphin, levels in some brain areas, which could indicate a reduction in met-enkephalin release (A. Green et al., 1978; Hong et al., 1979). Equally, however, an increased brain level of enkephalin might represent an increase in synthesis and an increase in release. This interpretation is suggested by the observations that chronic lithium administration increased brain enkephalin levels and also decreased pain sensitivity (Bloom et al., 1983). Recently, repeated ECS has been reported to enhance opiate-receptor binding (Holaday et al., 1983), whereas the opposite result has been reported for chronic DMI (Reisine & Soubrie, 1982). Repeated ECS has been found in one functional study to enhance responses to a morphine challenge (Belenky & Holaday, 1981), while in a second, a reduced response to morphine was observed (Katz & Schmaltz, 1980). Because of these many discrepancies, it would be premature to attempt to draw any conclusions as to how, if at all, endogenous opiate systems might be involved in the actions of antidepressant agents.

18.3. HISTAMINE

It has not yet been convincingly demonstrated that histamine is a neurotransmitter, though evidence to this effect is accumulating. The anatomical localization of histaminergic pathways, if they exist, is poorly defined, and so, too, are their functions (J. Green et al., 1978; J. Schwartz et al., 1979; Richelson, 1981). Intraventricular administration of histamine in cats has been observed to suppress eating (Clineschmidt & Lotti,

1973) but to stimulate drinking (Gerald & Maickel, 1972), to reduce body temperature (Brezenoff & Lomax, 1970), and to produce a number of neuroendocrine and cardiovascular effects (J. Green et al., 1978; Richelson, 1981); all of these changes may be blocked by antihistamines. Intraventricular or systemic administration of histamine also produces arousal (Monnier et al., 1970); conversely, the commonest side effect of antihistamines is sedation (Beavan, 1976; Douglas, 1975).

Although antihistamines are active in some animal models of depression (see Chapters 6 and 7), there is insufficient evidence either from animal models or from basic brain research to speculate on a potential involvement of histamine in affective disorders. Neither is there any clinical evidence to suggest that affective disorders are associated with abnormalities of peripheral or central histamine function, though peripheral histamine responses may be attenuated in schizophrenia (J. Green et al., 1978). The only reason at present for discussing histamine in relation to depression is that tricyclic antidepressants are powerful antagonists at histamine receptors. This is hardly surprising, given that imipramine was originally developed as a potential antihistamine (Kuhn, 1958).

18.3.1. Antidepressants and Histamine Receptors

Two types of peripheral histamine receptor, known as H_1 and H_2, are distinguished by their differential sensitivity to agonist and antagonist drugs; both types are found within the central nervous system (Black et al., 1972; J. Schwartz et al., 1979). The histamine H_2-receptor is linked to a system that generates cyclic adenosine monophosphate (cAMP) (Kanof & Greengard, 1978), whereas the histamine H_1-receptor is linked to a system that generates cyclic guanosine monophosphate (Richelson, 1981). H_1-receptor stimulation also generates cAMP, but the contribution of H_1-receptors to histamine stimulated cAMP formation *in vivo* is small (Maayani et al., 1982). It has been noted that the physiological effects of stimulating peripheral H_1-receptors are similar to those of simulating muscarinic cholinergic receptors, and there are also some similarities in the regional distribution of these two receptor types within the brain (Richelson, 1981).

Receptor binding studies have shown that some tricyclic antidepressants have a very high affinity for H_1-receptors. Amitriptyline and doxepin, in particular, have a higher affinity than do the classical antihistamines; indeed, tricyclics are more potent at H_1-receptors than they are at blocking NA and 5-HT uptake (Coupet & Szuchs-Myers, 1981; Diffley et al., 1980; Figge et al., 1979; Hall & Ogren, 1981; Peroutka & Snyder, 1981a; Richelson, 1981; Tran et al., 1978). However, H_1-receptor blockade is not a specific effect of antidepressants, since in addition to antihistamines some neuroleptic drugs are also extremely potent at H_1-receptors

(Coupet & Szuchs-Myers, 1981; Richelson, 1981). Furthermore, there is considerable variability between tricyclics, which does not correlate with their clinical potencies [Spearman rho = 0.2, calculated using Table 6.1 and data in Richelson (1981)]. Atypical antidepressants also vary greatly in their affinity for H_1-receptors. Mianserin has an affinity comparable to that of amitriptyline, whereas iprindole has a rather weak affinity, and the affinity of nomifensine and zimelidine is very low (Hall & Ogren, 1981; Richelson, 1981).

Most workers have assumed that the action of antidepressants at H_1-receptors may contribute to their sedative effects. Nobody, as far as I am aware, has suggested that this action may be relevant to the antidepressant effect.

Tricyclics, and the atypical antidepressants mianserin and iprindole, have also been found to block histamine-stimulated cAMP formation, which is the functional measure of H_2-receptor activation (Green & Maayani, 1977; Kanof & Greengard, 1978; Maayani et al., 1982; Olianas et al., 1982; Pandey et al., 1982; Psychoyos, 1981). Amitriptyline has also been reported to block the H_2-receptor-mediated depression of cortical cell firing by iontophoretically applied histamine (Haas, 1979), though in hippocampal slices, potentiation of electrophysiological effects of histamine by tricyclics has been observed (Olianas et al., 1982).

There have been relatively few studies of the effects of chronic antidepressant treatment on H_2-receptors (and none at all of H_1-receptors). One study has reported that the blockade of histamine-stimulated cAMP production by antidepressants was still present following chronic administration of amitriptyline or DMI. Receptor subsensitivity was also seen after chronic, but not acute treatment with the MAOI phenelzine (Pandey et al., 1982). Similarly, the hypothermic effect of the H_2-receptor agonist impromidine was reduced after acute or chronic treatment with mianserin (Nowak et al., 1979), and also after chronic, but not acute ECS (Pilc & Rokosz-Pelc, 1983; Vetulani, 1984). However, in another functional study it was found that animals chronically treated with imipramine or mianserin did not differ from controls in histamine-stimulated cAMP production and were hypersensitive to the electrophysiological effects of histamine (Olianas et al., 1982). It is possible that these results may represent withdrawal effects, since the experiments were carried out 48 hours after the final drug treatment.

It has been suggested that H_2-receptor blockade could constitute the mechanism of clinical action of antidepressants (Green & Maayani, 1977; Kanof & Greengard, 1978). Although in the current state of relative ignorance of the role of histamine in brain function it would be unwise to rule out this possibility, it seems unlikely. There is no correlation between blockade of histamine-stimulated cAMP formation and the clinical potency of antidepressants (Spearman rho = -0.07, calculated using data compiled by Maayani et al., 1982), and neuroleptics and antihistamines are as potent as antidepressants at H_2-receptors (Coupet & Szuchs-Myers, 1981). One uncontrolled study has reported antidepressant effects in the majority of a group of depressed patients treated with the antihistamine diphenhydramine (Hankoff et al., 1964), but since most antihistamines are nonspecific and share many of the actions of tricyclic antidepressants (Richelson, 1981), the significance of this observation is questionable.

18.4. NONOPIOID PEPTIDES

The recent proliferation of putative peptide transmitters is largely a result of the development of immunohistochemical and radioimmunoassay methods for detecting them. More than 20 pharmacologically active nonopioid neuropeptides have now been identified in the brain. Although originally identified in the hypothalamus as factors controlling the release of pituitary hormones (Guillemin, 1978), neuropeptides are found throughout the brain, with the highest concentrations, in most cases, being found in limbic structures (Hokfelt et al., 1980). Most of the peptides found in the CNS are also found in peripheral tissues, particularly the gut (Pearse, 1977). Most—perhaps all—neuropeptides coexist in neurons alongside classical neurotransmitters, the two being co-released (Hokfelt et al., 1980). As the electrophysiological actions of neuropeptides are very slow, of the order of minutes, rather than milliseconds, it seems likely that they act as long-term modulators of neuronal function rather than as classical neurotransmitters.

Nemeroff and Prange have proposed the bold hypothesis that similar functions are served by the same peptide within and outside the central nervous system. Central administration of angiotensin, for example, elicits drinking in nondeprived animals, whereas peripherally, angiotensin controls water loss by the kidney; luteinizing hormone releasing hormone (LHRH), which releases pituitary sex hormones, also elicits mounting behavior (Nemeroff & Prange, 1978). However, this principle cannot in most cases be used to predict behavioral effects of neuropeptides, and the task of unraveling their behavioral functions has hardly begun. The analysis is complicated by the fact that

> many of the peptides have overlapping molecular structures, which permit interaction at receptors primarily intended for other peptides. Such effects, in addition to the ubiquity of peptide function in the periphery and central nervous system, often lead to the induction of a multitude of behaviours when peptides are administered at pharmacological doses. These multiple points of interaction, together with the exceedingly short half lives and the great difficulty with which peptides pass through the

blood–brain barrier make any specific physiological interpretation of peripherally administered peptide-induced behaviour nearly impossible. (Cohen & Cohen, 1981, p. 216).

There are some fragmentary data on the possible involvement of nonopioid peptides in animal models of depression. In one study, for example, alpha-melanocyte–stimulating hormone (MSH) and somatostatin were found to reduce immobility in the rat "behavioral despair" procedure (Kastin et al., 1978). In another, learned helplessness was reversed by intraventricular administration of antivasopressin serum (Leshner et al., 1978). However, in view of our relative ignorance of the behavioral effects of nonopioid neuropeptides, there seems little point at present in reviewing this literature with a view to making clinical predictions.

18.4.1. Thyrotropin-Releasing Hormone

Following the initial reports of Prange and co-workers (1972) and Kastin and co-workers (1972), a number of studies have reported that thyroid stimulating hormone releasing factor (TRH) has antidepressant effects. However, the therapeutic effect does not appear to be at all specific for depression: TRH has mild euphoric effects in normal volunteers, but alcoholics and schizophrenics improved as much as depressed patients in a clinical trial (Loosen & Prange, 1979). Claims for the effectiveness of TRH in depression vary greatly between studies, but it appears in general to be somewhat inferior to tricyclic antidepressants (Cohen & Cohen, 1981; Hollister et al., 1977).

The majority of TRH studies have been concerned with neuroendocrine rather than antidepressant effects. It is well established that the thyroid stimulating hormone (TSH) response to TRH is blunted in approximately 30–40% of depressed patients, and it tends to normalize with patient recovery (Extein et al., 1982a; Hollister et al., 1977; Kastin et al., 1972; Kirkegaard et al., 1978; Langer et al., 1983; Loosen et al., 1979; Loosen & Prange, 1980; Prange et al., 1972; Sternbach et al., 1982). Diminished responsiveness to TRH does not appear to be secondary to an increase in TRH secretion. On the contrary, there is some evidence that depressed people have a slightly reduced level of thyroid function (Prange et al., 1976).

Other abnormal hormonal responses to TRH have also been reported in depressed patients, but these vary in their replicability. As noted in an earlier chapter, stimulation of prolactin release by TRH has been reported as increased, decreased, or unchanged in depressed patients (see Section 16.1.4). Diminished growth hormone responses to TRH may be present in a small proportion of depressed patients, but this result also is rather elusive (Brambilla et al., 1978; Linkowski et al., 1980a; Loosen & Prange, 1980; Prange, 1977; Schlienger et al., 1980).

The blunted TSH response to TRH appears to be specific to primary, as against secondary, depression (Asnis et al., 1980b; Extein et al., 1980a; M. Gold et al., 1980), though another claim, that the abnormality is specific to unipolar, as against bipolar, depression (Extein et al., 1980a; M. Gold et al., 1980) has not been supported (Amsterdam et al., 1979; Bjorum & Kierkegaard, 1979; Kirkegaard et al., 1978; Mendelwicz et al., 1979). However, a blunted TSH response to TRH is not specific to depression as against other conditions. Though most frequent in depression, it is also seen in manic patients, parkinsonian patients, alcoholics, patients with anorexia nervosa, and schizophrenics (Loosen & Prange, 1982). In one study, normalization of the TSH response in schizophrenics was found to accompany successful neuroleptic therapy (Langer et al., 1983).

Furthermore, blunted TSH responses to TRH are also produced by hyperthyroidism, elevated glucocorticoids, a variety of drugs including alcohol, and advancing age (Martin et al., 1977). Elevated glucocorticoids present a particular problem, since, as mentioned frequently in earlier chapters, adrenocortical hyperactivity is seen in many depressed patients. It is unlikely, however, that this factor alone can explain the blunted TSH response in depression, since the abnormal TSH response appears to be independent of an abnormal response on the DST; the majority of depressed patients show abnormal responses on one or other of these tests, but only a minority are abnormal on both (Asnis et al., 1981; Extein et al., 1982a; Targum et al., 1982; Winokur et al., 1982). However, one study did report an inverse correlation between serum cortisol levels in depressed patients and TSH response to TRH (Loosen et al., 1978), which would support the view that TSH blunting could be an artifact of elevated serum cortisol.

It is at present unclear what, if any, is the specific neurotransmitter abnormality that underlies the abnormal TSH response to TRH. Two studies have reported an inverse correlation between CSF 5-HIAA and peak TSH response to TRH, suggesting that the blunted response might be a product of high 5-HT activity (Banki & Arato, 1983; P. Gold et al., 1977). A possible mediation by low NA activity has also been suggested (Extein et al., 1982a), on the basis of the observation that NA depletion can result in reduction of TRH, and possibly TSH, levels (Reichlin, 1975). One study found a correlation in men, but not in women, between TSH response and urinary MHPG, which could be consistent with an NA hypothesis (Sternbach et al., 1983), but this relationship was not found in a second study (Davis et al., 1981). Either of these mechanisms—high 5-HT or low NA—would also be consistent with TSH blunting being an artifact of high cortisol levels. However, no alterations in TSH response to TRH were induced by acute pharmacological manipulation of either 5-HT or NA systems (Kierkegaard et al., 1977).

The mechanism of antidepressant action of TRH is also an open question. It seem possible that stimulation of thyroid function is an important component of the effect, as antidepressant effects of triiodothyronine (T3) are well documented. Although T3 by itself is ineffective, a large number of uncontrolled studies (reviewed by Prange et al., 1976, Goodwin et al., 1982a) and one recent double-blind controlled trial (Goodwin et al., 1982a) have shown that T3 potentiates the antidepressant effect of tricyclic antidepressants and induces a response to tricyclics in patients previously refractory to treatment. Triiodothyronine causes numerous physiological changes, but two in particular stand out as potential explanations of how T3 enhances the action of antidepressant drugs. First, there is behavioral (Strombom et al., 1977) and receptor-binding (Gross et al., 1981a) evidence that T3 increases alpha$_1$-receptor function, an effect shared by antidepressant drugs and ECS (see Section 13.3.2). Second, T3 has been found to increase the number of cardiac beta-receptors (Williams et al., 1977); conversely, hypothyroid rats have fewer cortical beta-adrenergic receptors (Gross et al., 1980), and their electrophysiological responsiveness is also reduced (Marwaha & Prasad, 1981). As the reduction of beta-receptor binding by antidepressant drugs is inversely related to their clinical effectiveness (see Section 13.3.3.3), it is quite possible that T3 potentiates antidepressant drug action by preventing the desensitization of beta-receptors.

18.4.2. Other Peptides

Nonopioid peptides other than TRH have been very little studied. In one study, 6 of 12 endogenously depressed patients improved on LHRH, but three also improved on placebo, and the difference was not significant (Benkert et al., 1974). In normal volunteers, LHRH produced a mild alerting effect but no mood change (McAdoo et al., 1978), and antidepressant effects have not been noted in impotent patients treated with LHRH (Cohen & Cohen, 1981). Abnormal hormonal responses to LHRH have sometimes been observed, but these are variable and inconsistent across studies (Brambilla et al., 1978; Ettigi et al., 1979; Linnoila et al., 1979).

Antidepressant effects have been reported in two studies of melanocyte stimulating hormone (MSH) inhibiting factor (MIF), but only at low doses; at higher doses, MIF caused a worsening of symptoms (Ehrensing & Kastin, 1974, 1978). If MIF does have antidepressant potential, an anticholinergic effect is the most probable mechanism. There is some evidence that MIF relieves and MSH aggravates Parkinson's disease (Marx, 1975). This suggests that MSH may facilitate cholinergic transmission; ACTH, which is structurally very similar (Lazarus et al., 1976), probably has a similar effect (see Section 14.1.3).

Finally, improvements in learning and memory have been reported in depressed patients administered DDAVP, a synthetic analogue of arginine vasopressin, but the same improvements were also seen in nonde-pressed controls. Of two patients whose depression improved on DDAVP, one relapsed while still receiving the drug (P. Gold et al., 1979).

Future research with nonopioid peptides will undoubtedly demonstrate that some peptides have antidepressant properties and will clarify the nature of abnormal responses to peptide challenges. However, the evi-dence that is currently available does not give grounds for confidence that this route will provide major new insights or solve any otherwise intractable problems.

nineteen

NEUROTRANSMITTER INTERACTIONS

Earlier chapters have considered the involvement in depression of individual neurotransmitter systems, making only passing reference to interactions between different systems. Although some of the empirical issues are not conclusively resolved, the variety of different research approaches provides convergent evidence, from which reasonably clear conclusions may be drawn. The major changes in neurotransmission associated with severe depressions are (1) a reduced level of DA function, related to psychomotor retardation, and reflecting a reduced level of incentive motivation; (2) a reduced level of 5-HT function, related to psychomotor agitation, and reflecting an inability to relax; (3) a reduced level of NA function, related to endogenous symptoms, and reflecting an inability to maintain effort; and (4) cholinergic hyperactivity, also related to endogenous symptoms, and reflecting a high level of stress. Antidepressants reverse these changes, primarily by actions on NA and 5-HT neurons.

It remains, in these final chapters, to piece together an overview of the psychobiology of depression. As a basis for the theory of depression which is outlined in Chapter 20, this chapter first reviews the relationships between some of the neurotransmitter systems discussed earlier. A picture of the relevant neurotransmitter interactions is beginning to emerge, even though their complexity and variety make it impossible at present to give a complete account. This chapter considers first the interactions among the monoamine transmitters and next the interactions between the monoamines and ACh; from a functional point of view, the ACh–NA interactions described in Section 19.2.2 are probably the most interesting. In the final section, two sets of interactions are outlined. One involves NA, DA, and ACh, and the second involves 5-HT, endorphins, and GABA. Together they provide a basis for understanding much of the phenomenology of depression.

19.1. MONOAMINE–MONOAMINE INTERACTIONS

19.1.1. NA–DA

Perhaps surprisingly, the monoamine–monoamine interactions that are least adequately understood are those between NA and DA. From a review of the literature, Antelman and Caggiula (1977) concluded that treatments that reduce NA functioning enhanced DA function, provided that testing was carried out under conditions of behavioral activation. However, the obvious explanation, that NA systems exert a tonic inhibition over DA systems, is probably incorrect. In fact, the situation appears to be the opposite. Direct measurements of DA turnover show that treatments that increase the activity of locus coeruleus NA cells facilitate DA activity, whereas treatments that reduce dorsal bundle function also reduce DA activity (Anden & Grabowska, 1976; Donaldson et al., 1976). This paradox is explained by the hypothesis that under conditions of low NA and DA activity there is a build-up of DA in nerve terminals, which may then be released by an activating stimulus (Antelman & Caggiula, 1977). When NA activity is low over a prolonged period, the concomitant low release of DA leads to a compensatory increase in DA receptor sensitivity (Kostowski et al., 1978), which also contributes to the apparent enhancement of DA function.

The synergism between dorsal bundle activity and DA activity is not mediated by direct monosynaptic connections, because the DA cell body areas are among the few forebrain sites where NA axons do not terminate (Lindvall & Bjorklund, 1974). One possible route by which NA activity might influence DA neurons is via pathways descending from the cerebral cortex to the striatum, which could then influence DA cell firing via the striatonigral feedback pathway (Antelman & Caggiula, 1977). As NA facilitates cortical information processing (Section 11.2.2), and DA mediates the arousing effects of environmental stimuli on behavior (Section 8.3), this transcortical route could be considered as a substrate for the facilitation of motor arousal (DA) by sensory arousal (NA).

19.1.2. NA–5-HT

Antelman and Caggiula (1977) suggested an alternative route by which locus coeruleus cells might excite DA cells, via inhibition of 5-HT cells in the dorsal raphe nucleus, which have inhibitory connections with DA cells (see below). However, this route seems less likely. 5-HT cells in the dorsal raphe are heavily innervated by NA terminals (Baraban & Aghajanian, 1981), but pharmacological studies show that these connections are excitatory rather than inhibitory (Svensson et al., 1975). In anesthetized animals, dorsal raphe cells are excited by alpha-adrenergic agonists and are completely silenced by infusion of alpha-adrenergic antagonists (Baraban & Aghajanian, 1980). The origin of the NA input to the dorsal raphe is uncertain (Pradhan & Bose, 1978), but the locus coeruleus seems a likely candidate, given the observation that during REM sleep electrical silence is seen not only in the locus coeruleus (Aston-Jones & Bloom, 1981a; Hobson et al., 1975) but also in the dorsal raphe (McGinty & Harper, 1976; Trulson & Jacobs, 1979b).

By contrast, cells in the median raphe nucleus, and perhaps also the nucleus raphe magnus, have a reciprocal inhibitory relationship with locus coeruleus NA cells, which is illustrated by the fact that these cells displayed their highest rates of firing during REM sleep (Sheu et al., 1974). Microinjections of alpha-receptor agonists into the median raphe nucleus reduce 5-HT activity and produce a variety of behavioral and physiological effects similar to those of median raphe lesions (see Chapter 15), while alpha-antagonists have the opposite effects (Kostowski & Gomulka, 1974; Plaznik et al., 1983). Disinhibition of median raphe activity appears to be the route by which clonidine causes sedation, as this effect of clonidine was blocked by median raphe lesions (Kostowski et al., 1981).

Although, as noted above, alpha adrenergic activation facilitates dorsal raphe activity in anesthetized animals, the effects are less dramatic in unanesthetized animals (Heym et al., 1981). As a result, the inhibition of median raphe activity by locus coeruleus activity is a rather more prominent effect, and lesions of the locus coeruleus produce robust increases in forebrain 5-HT turnover (Kostowski, 1975, 1980). The two-way nature of these inhibitory effects is shown by the complementary observation that destruction of the median raphe nucleus increases NA synthesis in the locus coeruleus (MacRae-Deguerce et al., 1982) and increases forebrain NA turnover (Kostowski et al., 1974).

In addition to these inhibitory interactions between the cells of the locus coeruleus and the median raphe, the forebrain projection systems of these two nuclei overlap to a great extent, and mutual inhibition of the release of transmitter from terminals in the cerebral cortex has also been demonstrated (Frankhuyzen & Mulder, 1982; Schlicker et al., 1982).

19.1.3. 5-HT–DA

Inhibitory effects of 5-HT on DA are also well documented. The DA terminal areas, the nucleus accumbens and striatum, both receive a 5-HT input from the dorsal raphe nucleus (Azmitia, 1978; Costall et al., 1976; Geyer et al., 1976b). Amphetamine- or DA-induced hyperactivity were suppressed by administration of 5-HT to the nucleus accumbens (Costall et al., 1979; Jones et al., 1981) or by intraventricular injections of 5-HT (Warbritton et al., 1978). Conversely, local depletion of 5-HT within the nucleus accumbens was found to potentiate amphetamine-induced hyperactivity (Lyness & Moore, 1981). In both cases, there is evidence that the influence of 5-HT is exercised "downstream" from the DA synapses (Jones et al., 1981; Lyness & Moore, 1981).

Similarly, most studies have found an inverse relationship between amphetamine-induced stereotyped behavior, which is mediated by the nigrostriatal DA system, and 5-HT receptor stimulation (Dickinson & Curzon, 1983; Weiner et al., 1973). At intense levels of stereotypy, the results are less straightforward but the doses of DA agonists required to produce these behaviors are no longer pharmacologically specific (Carter & Pyrock, 1981; Costall & Naylor, 1974). Enhancement of stereotypy was seen with local 5-HT depletion of the striatum (Carter & Pycock, 1981).

In addition to this postsynaptic interaction, a 5-HT pathway originating in the dorsal raphe nucleus also inhibits the activity of DA cells in the substantia nigra (Bunney & Aghajanian, 1976a; Dray et al., 1976). Animals subjected to prolonged social isolation have both a reduction of 5-HT activity and an increase in DA activity (Section 15.1.2). In view of the inhibitory effect of 5-HT neurons on DA neurons, it seems more than likely that the former effect is responsible for the latter. Furthermore, the inhibition of DA systems by 5-HT may contribute to the hyperactivity of 5-HT depleted animals, given that their hyperactivity is blocked by inhibition of catecholamine synthesis (Kostowski, 1975).

19.1.4. Implications

There is now a problem. The reciprocal interactions between the NA cells of the locus coeruleus and the 5-HT cells of the median raphe imply that if NA activity is low, then 5-HT activity is high, and vice versa. Similarly, the inhibitory effect of 5-HT cells in the dorsal raphe on DA cells and on the output from DA cells implies that if 5-HT activity is low, then DA activity should be high. How, then, is it possible for depression to be associated with low activity in all three neurotransmitter systems?

The solution to this paradox is in three parts. First, the three systems contribute to different symptoms of depression: retardation (DA), agitation (5-HT), and inability to concentrate (NA). However, this observation is of only limited value in resolving the paradox, since all of these symptoms may coexist in the same patient.

The second part of the solution is less obvious. Under most circumstances, the exigencies of the moment require the activation either of catecholaminergic systems or of 5-HT systems, but not of both. Consider a hungry carnivore searching for food. It hears a noise, orients to it, and processes the information that there is a potential prey. This information activates appropriate behaviors: stalking, chasing, fighting, killing, and eating. Satiated, it grooms itself then searches for a safe place and sleeps. Successful execution of the first stages of this sequence require NA and DA; the final stages require 5-HT. The sequence as a whole involves an orderly transition in which each transmitter system is activated in turn; behavior will be disrupted if any of the systems fail.

19.2. MONOAMINE–ACETYLCHOLINE INTERACTIONS

The third factor of importance in understanding how depression could be associated both with low catecholamine activity and with low 5-HT is that these three transmitters do not operate within a closed system, and other influences may override the NA–5-HT and 5-HT–DA interactions. ACh is the most significant example.

19.2.1. ACh–DA

As noted in Chapter 14, the original impetus for the adrenergic–cholinergic balance hypothesis of depression was the observation of Janowsky and co-workers (1972b) that cholinergic stimulation blocked methylphenidate-induced stereotypy, which is elicited primarily by stimulation of DA receptors in the caudate nucleus. Conversely, amphetamine stereotypy, which is similarly mediated, was enhanced by anticholinergics (Costall & Naylor, 1972). This antagonism between DA and ACh in the caudate nucleus is also seen in animals with unilateral lesions of the nigrostriatal DA system; both amphetamine and anticholinergics cause these animals to walk in circles, turning away from the lesioned side (Corrodi et al., 1972).

These interactions arise from the fact that nigrostriatal DA neurons terminate on (Groves, 1983) and inhibit (Bartholini et al., 1973; Trabucchi et al., 1975) the intrinsic striatal cholinergic cells. This is usually assumed to be the mechanism by which anticholinergic drugs exert therapeutic effects in Parkinson's disease (Pradhan & Bose, 1978). However, it is unclear whether the striatal ACh cells are linked functionally with the major ascending cholinergic systems (see Section 14.1.2). A low level of DA activity, as is found in retarded depressions, would increase ACh turnover, but there is no reason to suppose that this effect would result in "cholinergic" manifestations of depression, such as an increase in ACTH secretion (Section 14.2.1). Furthermore, a primary increase in striatal ACh function would cause psychomotor retardation, but this would be associated with a compensatory increase in DA activity, mediated by the striatonigral feedback pathway (Pradhan & Bose, 1978), rather than the decrease in DA activity which is actually found. Consequently, despite its interesting pharmacological properties, there is reason to doubt whether the striatal DA–ACh interaction is of direct relevance to depression.

The observation that cholinergic stimulation suppresses intracranial self-stimulation (Section 14.1.1) is of rather more interest. As discussed earlier, ICSS at medial forebrain bundle sites depends on the indirect activation of the mesolimbic DA system (Section 8.2.1). Similarly, the self-administration of cocaine, which is also mediated by the mesolimbic DA system (Section 8.2.1), was facilitated by atropine (anticholinergic) and suppressed by physostigmine (cholinomimetic) (Wilson & Schuster, 1973). The anatomical basis for these interactions is uncertain. Unlike the situation in the striatum, DA activity does not affect ACh turnover in the nucleus accumbens (Bartholini et al., 1973). However, the nucleus accumbens does contain a high density of cholinergic terminals, which could modulate the output of the DA system (Jones et al., 1981). If, like other forebrain ACh systems, activity in these cholinergic neurons is increased by stress, this could be the mechanism by which stress reduces the performance of appetitively motivated behaviors. The possibility of another, related, ACh–DA interaction will be discussed below (Section 19.3.1).

19.2.2. ACh–NA

The concept of an inverse relationship between ACh and catecholaminergic mechanisms is supported by a number of clinical studies. Janowsky and co-workers (1982, cited by Janowsky & Risch, 1984a) observed that in a mixed group of psychiatric patients, those subjects who had intense negative responses to a cholinergic challenge (physostigmine) had lower elevations of mood in response to methylphenidate and, also, had smaller methylphenidate-induced improvements in psychomotor and cognitive performance. Similarly, Nurnberger and co-workers (1982, cited by Janowsky & Risch, 1984a) observed an inverse relationship between the behavioral excitation following amphetamine and the reduction of REM sleep latency by the cholinomimetic agent arecoline. It is uncertain whether these results are more relevant to NA or DA, because amphetamine and methylphenidate release both catecholamines. However, the fact that in depressed patients the mood-elevating effect of amphetamine is a function of NA turnover (Section 12.3.3) suggests that an ACh-NA interaction might be responsible. An inverse relationship between cholinergic function and NA function is also suggested by the finding of Siever and co-workers (1981b) that the patients with the most dramatic negative responses to cholinergic challenges also had a blunted growth hormone response to the NA agonist clonidine (Section 12.1.5).

The antagonism between ACh and NA is illustrated by the observation that if a cell in the cortex could be inhibited by NA, it could also be excited by ACh (Reader et al., 1979). The interaction between NA and ACh is not, however, one of mutual inhibition. Locus coeruleus NA cells do inhibit the cortical release of ACh (Visi, 1980), and the activity of cholinergic cells in the pontine reticular formation (Vivaldi et al., 1980). However, pontine ACh cells have excitatory connections with the locus coeruleus (Engberg & Svensson, 1980; Olpe et al., 1983), and in human volunteers the cholinomimetic drug physostigmine increased CSF MHPG concentration (K. Davis et al., 1977).

The interaction between pontine ACh cells and the locus coeruleus is most immediately apparent in studies of their electrical activity during sleep. As noted above, cells in the locus coeruleus exhibit their lowest firing rates during REM sleep. Pontine cholinergic cells, however, are at their most active during REM sleep, as are forebrain cholinergic systems (Section 14.1.2). These observations, combined with the effects on REM sleep of pharmacological probes localized to the pontine reticular formation indicate that the cycle of alternating periods of REM and non-REM sleep is controlled by the oscillation of activity between these two groups of cells (McCarley, 1982; Steriade & Hobson, 1976). A formal model of REM sleep control supposes that cholinergic pontine neurons excite one another and also excite locus coeruleus cells. As activity in the locus coeruleus builds up, cholinergic cells are inhibited and the REM period comes to an end. However, as cholinergic activity falls, the excitatory drive to NA cells decreases; in addition, NA cells inhibit one another. Activity in the locus coeruleus therefore falls, cholinergic cells are disinhibited, and another REM period begins. A mathematical model of these processes confirms that the system would in fact behave as described (Steriade & Hobson, 1976). The mathematical simulation also shows that a reduction in the strength of the inhibitory component of the model (NA) causes a phase advance in the cycle resulting in an earlier onset of REM sleep, as observed in depression (Vogel, 1975; McCarley, 1982).

19.2.2.1. *On the Functional Significance of REM Sleep*

The cyclical activation of pontine NA and ACh cell groups during sleep represents the free running of the system in the absence of other inputs. During waking, however, the activity of both nuclei is also influenced by activity in other parts of the brain, and their mutual interaction may be manifest in a variety of psychological phenomena. It is possible, for example, that the build-up of self-inhibition within the locus coeruleus may contribute to the sequence of orienting to a novel stimulus, which involves the activation of locus coeruleus projections to the cortex and hippocampus (Section 11.2.2.3), followed by habituation, which is a cholinergic phenomenon (Carlton & Markiewicz, 1971).

From the studies reviewed in Sections 11.3 and 14.1.3, it seems likely that a shift of activity from the locus coeruleus to cholinergic systems may play a central role in the biphasic response to prolonged stress. Cholinergic cells are excited by stress and threat (Section 14.1.3.). This excitatory drive, superimposed on the NA–ACh reciprocal interaction model, would tend to counteract the inhibition arising from a build-up of activity in the locus coeruleus. Consequently, under stressful conditions, locus coeruleus cells would be subjected to a constant and unremitting activation. The eventual result is a depletion of transmitter stores, which is manifest as a "functional lesion." This occurs first in the hypothalamus, and with severe stress it is also seen in the region of the locus coeruleus. When that happens, production of the NA-synthesizing enzyme tyrosine hydroxylase starts to increase, resulting, several days later, in a restoration of synaptic transmission and recovery from behavioral depression (Section 11.3).

This analysis has rather important consequences, inter alia, for theories of dreaming. Over the years, numerous theories have attempted to explain the function of dreaming; their common feature is that none has achieved even a moderate degree of acceptance (see Crick & Mitchison, 1983; Drucker-Colin et al., 1979; E. Hartman, 1973). The discovery that dreaming occurs during periods of REM sleep increased the variety of theories but did not solve the central riddle. It may be, however, that there is a simple answer: REM sleep has no function. The psychological phenomena of dreaming are exactly what might be expected given that the brain is effectively in a waking state, but sensory input is minimized, motor output is absent, and so is conscious control of ideation. During sleep, the brain is periodically precipitated into this aroused condition by the interaction between pontine ACh and NA cell groups. In the waking animal, this interaction serves the supremely important role of controlling the switch from an active to a passive mode of stress control. However, in the sleeping animal, the alternate activation of the two nuclei follows directly from the nature of the connections between them, and further functional speculations are unnecessary. If, as suggested, the occurrence of REM sleep is an accidental by-product of stress control mechanisms, then this would go some way to explaining the striking pharmacological parallels between REM sleep control and depression (McCarley, 1982), and other interactions between sleep and mood which will be discussed further in the next chapter.

19.2.3. ACh–5-HT

The main evidence for an interaction between ACh and 5-HT also comes from sleep studies. As noted above, during REM sleep, when pontine ACh cells are at their most active, so too are cells in the median raphe nucleus (Sheu et al., 1974), while cells in the dorsal raphe, like locus coeruleus cells, are silent (McGinty & Harper, 1976; Trulson & Jacobs, 1979b). These relationships are most probably mediated via the interactions of ACh and 5-HT nuclei with the locus coeruleus, as described above. The simultaneous activation of cholinergic systems and the mesolimbic (median raphe) 5-HT system is consistent with the notion that both ACh and 5-HT are part of the central control mechanisms of the parasympathetic nervous system, with the observation that both systems stimulate ACTH release, and with the fact that both systems exercise primarily suppressive effects over behavior.

However, as intimated above, there are also mechanisms through which ACh and 5-HT exert opposing effects. Three such will be described. First, it has recently been reported that 5,7-DHT lesions of either the dorsal or the median raphe nuclei caused an increase in cortical ACh turnover, implying that 5-HT inhibits ACh release (Robinson, 1983). A second, similar, interaction has already been discussed at some length, so will only be recalled briefly here: in the amygdala, the effects of ACh in several animal models of depression may be counteracted by 5-HT, or, conversely, the effects of low 5-HT are counteracted by anticholinergics (Sections 14.1.1 and 15.1.2).

The third synergistic effect between high ACh and low 5-HT is rather indirect but potentially important; it arises from the fact that ACh stimulates the pituitary adrenal system, causing an elevation of plasma corticosterone (Section 14.2.1). Studies of patients with Cushing's disease suggest that high levels of circulating corticosterone might be of causal significance in depression (Section 13.3.3.3). In animal studies, corticosteroids have been found to reduce locomotor activity (Katz & Carroll, 1978; Bohus & De Kloet, 1981) and to increase submissive behavior (Leshner & Potitch, 1979; Leshner et al., 1980). These effects are mediated by corticosterone receptors in the hippocampus (Gerlach & McEwen, 1972; McEwen et al., 1969). Hippocampal administration of corticosterone reduces locomotor activity (Micco et al., 1979) and produces changes in the hippocampal EEG which suggest an increase in fearfulness (Valero et al., 1977). Furthermore, there is an inverse relationship between hippocampal corticosterone binding and social dominance (Valery et al., 1978, cited in Laborit, 1982). These findings imply that in addition to direct suppressive effects in the hippocampus, ACh also suppresses behavior via hippocampal effects of corticosterone. The interaction with 5-HT arises from the observation that destruction of the serotonergic input to the hippocampus increased the binding of glucocorticoids in hippocampal tissues (Angelucci et al., 1982). If there is a concomitant increase in the functional effects of corticosterone, the result would be an amplification of the behavioral suppressant effects of ACh.

19.3. NEUROTRANSMITTERS AND DEPRESSION

The neurotransmitter interactions outlined, taken together with the literature reviewed in previous chapters, provide a basis for sketching out two sets of alterations in the balance of neurotransmitter function which might be of considerable importance in understanding the physiological basis of depressive disorders.

19.3.1. NA–ACh–DA

The first interaction, outlined in Section 19.2.2 is based on the interaction between ACh and NA; it describes some of the processes that might occur during exposure to stress. Stress potently activates most—perhaps all—systems of cholinergic neurons (Section 14.1.3). Pontine cholinergic cells, in turn, activate NA cells of the locus coeruleus. The inhibitory effects of locus coeruleus activation on cholinergic function damp down the behavioral suppressant effects of ACh and permit active attempts to cope with the stress. However, if the stress is prolonged, severe, or uncontrollable, the balance of activity in ACh and NA systems changes. Self-inhibition reduces the activity of NA cells relative to that of their cholinergic input, and eventually, overstimulation causes a "functional lesion" of NA terminals, particularly in the hypothalamus and hindbrain (Section 11.3). This results, inter alia, in an inability of NA cells to maintain their inhibitory control over cholinergic function. The ensuing cholinergic predominance causes a suppression of active behavior; a disinhibition of median raphe 5-HT function as locus coeruleus activity falls might also contribute to this effect (Section 15.3.1). Cholinergic predominance may be associated with either an elevation or a reduction in NA turnover, depending on whether a "functional lesion" of NA terminals occurs (see Sections 11.3 and 12.1.4).

The ascendency of cholinergic systems stimulates the release of endorphins and ACTH, resulting in analgesia and the secretion of adrenal corticosteroids; the body switches from an active coping mode dominated by the sympathetic nervous system to a passive, parasympathetically dominated state of "conservation-withdrawal" (Schmale, 1973). On subsequent reexposure to stress, the changes in ACh (Hintgen et al., 1976), NA (Anisman & Sklar, 1979; Cassens et al., 1980), and endorphin (Jackson et al., 1979) systems are rapidly reinstated; consequently, exposure to chronic intermittent stress results in a semipermanent state of cholinergic dominance. Eventually, the cumulative effects are sufficiently intense to trigger an increase in NA synthesis, and recovery ensues (Section 11.3).

Although these effects provide a basis for understanding the mechanism by which prolonged stress causes first an increase and then a decrease in active coping behavior, a more fundamental problem remains unexplained. As described in earlier chapters, an increase in the ratio of cholinergic to adrenergic transmission is associated with biological markers characteristic of endogenous depression. Endogenous depression is defined by an inability to experience pleasurable events as pleasant. Much of the discussion in this book has concerned the motivational aspects of depression, but little attention has been paid to the neuronal circuitry that might mediate this fundamental symptom.

In an earlier discusion, I drew attention to the findings of Gallistel and colleagues (1981) concerning the anatomical basis of intracranial self-stimulation through electrodes in the classic ICSS site, the medial forebrain bundle. The substrate for ICSS appears to be a system of fibers that originates in the lateral hypothalamus and substantia innominata, and terminates on DA cells in the VTA (Section 8.2.1). Significantly, it has been demonstrated recently that uncontrollable shock specifically suppressed ICSS from electrodes implanted in the VTA, without affecting ICSS from electrodes implanted in the substantia nigra (Zacharko et al., 1982, 1983). Cells in the lateral hypothalamus and substantia innominata, which probably are the cells of origin of this "reward pathway," have electrophysiological characteristics which suggest that they signal the pleasantness of rewards, in that the ability of food and related stimuli to activate these neurons decreases as an animal approaches satiety (Rolls, 1982); subjectively, the perceived pleasantness of food in people is similarly affected by satiation (Cabanac, 1971).

It may be significant that the substantia innominata receives a heavy cholinergic input from the midbrain (Lewis & Shute, 1978; see Section 17.1.2). The pharmacology of the substantia innominata cells which subserve ICSS has not been investigated, but there is a strong prediction that they will be inhibited by ACh. Such an interaction, if confirmed, could explain the inhibitory effect of aversive stimulation on the ability to experience pleasure (Section 4.2), and by extension, to explain the failure to experience pleasure, which is the central symptom of endogenous depression. A further consequence of cholinergic inhibition of substantia innominata ICSS cells would be a reduced stimulation of DA cells in the VTA, causing the decrease in DA turnover which is characteristic of retarded depressions (Chapter 9).

19.3.2. Endorphins–5-HT–GABA

A second set of interactions addresses the significance of low 5-HT function in depression. Thus far, little has been said about the conditions that cause a reduction in 5-HT function. However, in one of the three animal models of depression in which 5-HT transmission is reduced, this change was brought about behaviorally by subjecting the animals to prolonged social isolation (Section 6.5.5). The psychological aspects of social isolation have largely been ignored up to this point. However, there is clinical evidence that social reinforcement, or rather the lack of it, may be of some importance in the etiology of depression (Section 20.1.2).

The studies of Panksepp and co-workers (1978, 1980) suggest that social reinforcment is mediated by the release of endorphins (Section 18.2.1.2). As reviewed in Section 15.2.2, the analgesic effects of endorphins are brought about by the activation of ascending and descending 5-HT systems. It therefore seems likely that the reduction of 5-HT function in socially isolated animals is also brought about by a decrease in endorphin release, and it reflects a reduction in social reinforcement.

There have been very few studies of the involvement of 5-HT in opiate-reward processes (Davis & Smith, 1983), but a case can be made for such an interaction. It has been reported that the self-administration of morphine was increased by median raphe lesions (Glick & Ross, 1983) and decreased by zimelidine pretreatment (Rockman et al., 1980). In most circumstances, these observations would be interpreted to mean that 5-HT antagonized the rewarding effect of morphine. However, as noted earlier (Section 15.3.1), animals "titrate" their drug rewards and increase their responding when the size of the reward is reduced. In fact, the increase in responding for morphine after median raphe lesions was shown to be associated with a decrease in sensitivity to morphine (Glick & Ross, 1983). A further indication that opiate reward processes are associated with activation of 5-HT systems is the observation that 5-HT turnover was reduced in the nucleus accumbens of morphine-dependent rats during a period of acute drug withdrawal. Interestingly, the reduction of 5-HT turnover was associated specifically with the absence of morphine reinforcement, as it was observed in animals trained to self-administer morphine, but not in yoked controls (Smith & Lane, 1983).

The involvement of other neurotransmitters in the opiate–5-HT system has not been studied extensively. However, there is evidence that some of the behavioral effects of a reduction of forebrain 5-HT function are mediated by a decrease in the activity of GABA neurons in or near the olfactory bulb (Section 18.1.1). It should also be noted that the opiate-reward system exerts an excitatory influence over mesolimbic DA activity.

19.3.3. Summary

To summarize, there appear to be two sets of neurotransmitter interactions which, from the evidence reviewed, may be of considerable importance for understanding the pathophysiology of depression. The first, which involves ACh, NA, and DA, mediates the effects of prolonged stress, while the second, which involves 5-HT, endorphins, and GABA, mediates the level of social reinforcement. The involvement of these two sets of brain systems in the symptomatology of depression will be explored further in the next chapter.

The reciprocal inhibitory interaction between the locus coeruleus (NA) and the median raphe nucleus (5-HT) suggests that there should be an antagonism between the first of these models (high ACh, low NA, low DA) and the second (low endorphins, low 5-HT, low GABA). However, other factors could override this relationship, and there are a number of ways in which the two models could function synergistically. As noted above, low 5-HT function (model 2) may in some circumstances potentiate ACh (model 1); conversely, as noted by Lewinsohn and others (Sec. 4.2.1), a decrease in motivation (model 1) results in a decrease in social reinforcement (model 2). In fact, it has been reported that the lowest turnover of both DA (model 1) and 5-HT (model 2) was found in the patients who were the most severely depressed (Goodwin & Sack, 1974).

As demonstrated in the next chapter, these two models provide a basis for integrating most of what we currently know about the etiology, phenomenology, and treatment of depression.

4

Synthesis

twenty

ELEMENTS OF A
THEORY OF DEPRESSION

When I began writing this book, it was not my intention to produce a theory of depression; the aim was simply to compile the available evidence. In so doing, however, the elements of a theory have emerged unbidden, needing only to be drawn together. In order to understand the psychobiology of depression, we need to understand the nature of the abnormalities, how they come into being, and how they are reversed by successful therapies. This chapter summarizes our current understanding of the answers to these questions and examines the extent to which the interactions between neurotransmitter systems outlined in the previous chapter can supply an account of their physiological basis.

20.1 THE ETIOLOGY OF DEPRESSION

Factors leading to depression may conveniently be divided into those that predispose to depression over a long period and those that are immediate precipitants. This is not a categorical separation, because there are times when it is not clear into which class a particular effect falls, and little is gained by attempting to maintain a hard and fast distinction. It is, however, a fairly useful way of organizing the literature. The current position on the etiology of depression has recently been summarized by Akiskal

(1979; 1984; Akiskal & Tashjian, 1983), whose reviews provide much of the empirical basis for the following discussion.

20.1.1. Stress and Strain

Most studies are agreed that the likelihood of entering an episode of depression is increased five or sixfold in the six months following the occurrence of stressful "life events" (Lloyd, 1980b). The stressors most commonly associated with depression are "exit" events, particularly sep- aration, and "undesirable" events, such as marital arguments (Fava et al., 1981; Lloyd, 1980b; Paykel et al., 1969). Arieti and Bemporad (1980) have emphasized that the important aspect of stress is not the occurrence of stressful events but their significance for the person to whom they occur. In other words, stress is in the experience of the stressed person, rather than being an intrinsic property of the stressor. Contrary to earlier beliefs, the presence or absence of stressful life events does not differ between endogenous and nonendogenous depressions (Section 3.2.3).

The study of stressful life events is fraught with pitfalls arising from a variety of sources, including problems in the contruction of the meas- uring instruments (Tennant et al., 1981) and the possibility that vul- nerable people court trouble by their life style, alienating others and causing the breakdown of relationships (Briscoe & Smith, 1975). As all studies of life events and depression have been carried out retrospectively, the methodological difficulties have been increased even further by the distortions of recall found in depressed people (Section 4.2.2). However, a number of studies, such as that of Brown and Harris (1978), have suc- ceeded in circumventing these problems (Tennant et al., 1981). Further- more, there is one stressor to which none of the methodological difficulties apply—bereavement. In every study which has examined this issue, a recent bereavement has been found to increase the incidence of depression (Lloyd, 1980b).

Although reliable, the relationship between life events and depression is not particularly strong. The incidence of depression following bereave- ment is only about 5% (Clayton, 1979; Parkes, 1972), and 50% of depres- sions occur in the absence of stressful life events of any kind (Lloyd, 1980b). In fact, life events appear to account for at most 10% of the var- iance in the incidence of depression (Lloyd, 1980b). However, evidence is accumulating to support the commonsense notion that chronic low grade stress, or "strain", may be a powerful predisposing factor. The major strains identified by Brown and Harris (1978) among working class women in inner London were having three or more young children living at home and being unemployed. Prolonged unemployment, which in ad- dition to its adverse effects on self-esteem also generates financial and other difficulties, carries a high risk of depression (Jahoda, 1979), the severity of which is significantly correlated with the number of unsuccessful job applications made (Feather & Barber, 1983). In another study, almost 40% of subjects reporting a high level of marital, financial, or work-related strain were clinically depressed (Aneshensel & Stone, 1982).

20.1.2. Other Predisposing Factors

In addition to a high level of strain, a number of other factors have been identified which put a person "at risk" for depression, including, for example, social class, sex, early parental loss, and heredity. These factors interact with precipitating events in bringing about the psychological changes that constitute the onset of an episode of depression. A rather obvious point, which is frequently overlooked, is that in order for this interaction to arise, the predisposing factors, if they are no longer themselves present, must give rise to long-lasting consequences which do still exist at the onset of a depressive episode. It is insufficient therefore to point to parental loss, say, as a risk factor, without explaining how the effect is transmitted down through time to increase the risk for depression many years later. Logically, predisposing effects can only be transmitted in the psychological make-up of the to-be-depressed person or in the environment to which the person is exposed.

A number of environmental factors have been described which place a person at risk for depression. The most prominent of these is a high level of stress and/or strain (see above). A second is the absence of social support. Brown and Harris (1978) reported that among women suffering a high level of stress, the incidence of depression was increased fourfold by the absence of an intimate, confiding relationship, and numerous other studies have demonstrated that a supportive environment protects against a wide variety of stressors (Caplan, 1981; Cobb, 1976). These findings may be readily integrated with the observations demonstrating a reciprocal relationship between pleasant and unpleasant events, such that a change in the frequency of one causes an inverse change in the intensity of the other (Section 4.2).

There is also clear evidence that the absence of social support predisposes to depression in its own right, even under conditions of low stress (Aneshensel & Stone, 1982; Williams et al., 1981). The implication is that social reinforcement contributes to psychological well-being. It is not clear whether the inability to obtain social reinforcement owing to a inadequate grasp of social skills (Section 4.2.1) consititutes a further risk factor, over and above the resulting dilution of social support. It is possible that the personality of depression-prone people (see below) alienates people who might otherwise provide social support; this has been suggested as an explanation of the higher rates of depression among separated or divorced women (Briscoe et al., 1973).

Although a characteristic "depressive style" of thinking, consisting of a tendency to accentuate the negative aspects of life and suppress the positive, has been extensively documented both in mild experimentally induced depressions and in severe clinical depressions, prospective studies have been rather unsuccessful in identifying a "depressive cognitive style" in people who were later to become depressed (Section 4.3). However, introversion does appear to be a personality characteristic of to-be-depressed people; introversion has been characterized as a tendency to overreact to punishment and underreact to rewards. At the very least, therefore, introversion must provide fertile ground on which depressive thinking might grow (Section 4.4.1).

It is likely that some cognitive precursors of depression have been overlooked as a result of ignoring the diagnostic heterogeneity of depression. At a phenomenological level, clinical descriptions of the gloomy "dysthymic temperament" (Akiskal, 1983; Akiskal et al, 1983) appear strikingly similar to Beck's (1967) "negative cognitive set." Dysthymic people are introverted and show biological signs associated with endogenous depression, such as shortened REM latency (Section 3.3.3); they are also at high risk to develop severe endogenous depression (Akiskal, 1983, 1984). Similarly, there appears to be a continuum of severity and risk rising from normal fluctuations of mood, through cyclothymic temperamental disorders to bipolar illness (Section 3.3.3).

A confounding factor in personality studies is that most of them have been restrospective, and they fail to distinguish personality traits that predispose to depression from those that are a result of having been depressed. It is possible that a number of traits reliably identified in previously depressed people, such as dependency, pessimism, and low self-confidence (Altman & Wittenborn, 1980; Blatt et al., 1976, 1982; Cofer & Wittenborn, 1980), may be residues rather than predispositions (Cassano et al. 1983). However, the fact that the experience of being depressed leaves a scar of this kind heightens the risk for a subsequent episode and so contributes to an explanation of the recurrent nature of depression.

The status of childhood loss as a factor predisposing to depression has been controversial, and some reviews have concluded that the case was not proven (Akiskal & McKinney, 1975). However, a more recent review, which considered specifically the effects of childhood bereavement, concluded that parental, particularly maternal, loss in childhood was associated with a two to threefold increase in the likelihood of adult depression; this was a consistent finding in the majority of studies reviewed (Lloyd, 1980a). Furthermore, in most studies there was also a strong relationship between childhood loss and severity of depression (Lloyd, 1980a). A number of factors have been identified that protect against the effects of losing a parent, including the quality of support available and an avoidance of excessive dependency on the surviving parent (Hilgard et al., 1960). Brown and Harris (1978) suggest that major loss events in childhood predispose to depression by adversely affecting the child's self-esteem and sense of control. A sense of helplessness has not been reliab[ly] identified as an antecedent of depression (Section 4.3.3), but this may [be] because the studies did not focus on the appropriate subgroup of depres- sives.

Parental loss is a predisposing factor in approximately a third of all adult depressives but is particularly prominent in the "character spectrum disorder" (Section 3.4) subgroup of characterological depressions (Rosenthal et al., 1981). It has also been consistently reported by numerous studies that childhood separation events, particularly bereavement, were related to subsequent suicide attempts (Levi et al., 1966; Lloyd, 1980a); this effect is dissociable from the effect of childhood loss on severity of depression (Birtchnell, 1970). The effects of childhood loss are not specific to depression. Separation predisposes to other forms of psychiatric morbidity, such as anxiety (Tennant et al., 1982), schizophrenia (Oltman et al., 1952), or drug dependence (Hartnoll et al., 1981). These findings have led Akiskal (1984) and Bowlby (1977) to suggest that childhood parental loss leads to "unstable" personality characteristics such as insecurity and social incompetence, which predispose toward depressive symptoms in a variety of psychiatric contexts and to suicidal gestures, but not to severe endogenous depression.

Women generally, and working class women in particular, are at higher risk for both major and minor depressions than men, by a factor of two to three (Boyd & Weissman, 1981; Hirschfeld & Cross, 1982). The reasons for this difference are not yet entirely clear. Rates of stressful life events (see above) do not differ between men and women, but the possibility that women suffer a higher level of strain has not been systematically examined. It is difficult to see how the oppressed position of the majority of women could fail to cause severe strain, as well as producing depression-prone personality traits. Although hormonal factors may also contribute (see below), these would hardly differentiate between women of differing social class. It therefore seems a reasonable assumption that higher levels of strain do make a significant contribution to the higher incidence of depression in women.

Heredity provides a final set of predisposing circumstances. There is some evidence for genetic transmission of unipolar depressions (Section 3.2.1), but little evidence as to what is transmitted. It is quite possible that this factor might be explained in its entirety by the genetic contribution to introversion (Eysenck, 1977). Bipolar disorders appear to be under stronger genetic control (Section 3.2.1). They also show epidemiological differences from unipolar depressions: bipolar disorders are more common among higher social classes and do not show sex differences (Boyd & Weissman, 1981; Hirshfeld & Cross, 1982). Again, the nature of the genetic contribution has not been investigated; a tendency to experience wider than normal mood fluctuations is an obvious possibility.

20.1.3. A Multifactorial Model

Excluding factors such as heredity which predispose to depression by as yet undetermined mechanisms, the major etiological influences described so far are a "depressive" introverted personality, an unstable personality structure resulting from early object loss, a high level of stress and/or strain, and the absence of social support. Studies which have examined the contribution of several factors suggest that although individually no one factor makes an overwhelming contribution, together they explain almost all of the variance. For example, in a large community sample, Aneshensel and Stone (1982) found a 2% incidence of depression in subjects with good social support, no recent loss events, and a low level of strain, compared with a 50% incidence with two or more loss events, a high level of strain, and poor support; this study did not include personality variables. Brown and Harris (1978) found a 1% incidence in women with no risk factors, and a 100% incidence in women suffering a high level of strain who had no intimate confiding relationship and had suffered early maternal loss.

There is not yet a mathematical model for the way in which the risk factors combine (see Aneshensel & Stone, 1982; Tennant et al., 1981), but these results encourage confidence in the belief that for the most part, depression results from an accumulation of the personality and environmental factors described above. In the case of depressions precipitated by stress, the critical level of risk is reached abruptly. However, the lack of any obvious discontinuity between mild and severe depressions (Sections 3.3.3) suggests that in depressions with no obvious precipitants, worsening of mood reflects a gradual rise in strain or deterioration of support. The discontinuity in these cases is in the decision to seek help, rather than in the onset of the depressive episode.

20.1.4. Brain Mechanisms

For all of the risk factors that have been discussed, it is possible to describe or deduce their physiological mechanisms. The clearest case is that of stress and strain, the physiological effects of which have been examined at length in earlier chapters. Exposure to prolonged or severe stress results in an increase in cholinergic activity, relative to that of DA and the dorsal NA system; the mechanism of this effect, in the interaction between pontine ACh cells and the NA cells of the locus coeruleus was described in Section 19.2.2. These changes, established in animal studies, are also seen in endogenously depressed people, as indicated by their failure to suppress serum cortisol in the DST and by their decreased latencies to enter REM sleep (Sections 3.3.2, 12.4, 14.2.1).

The sequelae of stress are related in part to habitual modes of coping. In addition to precipitating depression, life events are also found to precede the onset of other psychiatric and nonpsychiatric medical disorders, such as schizophrenia (S. Jacobs et al., 1974) and coronary thrombosis (Parkes, 1972), though with a lesser frequency (Lloyd, 1980b). Individual differences in the response to stress are also observable in animals. Dominant mice responded to repeated immobilization stress by increases in adrenaline secretion; whereas nondominant mice responded to the same stress by secreting cortisol (Henry, 1976; Henry & Stephens, 1977; Sections 11.3.2). The influence of social dominance on the response to stress in animals appears to be mediated by the level of NA activity in the locus coeruleus (J. Weiss et al., 1982), which determines the ease with which stress-induced cholinergic activity dominates the ACh–NA interaction (Sections 19.3.1). It is reasonable to assume that the level of NA function in people could similarly determine whether stressful life events precipitate depression (cholinergic dominance) or some other disorder that might reflect an adrenergic dominance, such as hypertensive disorders (see Janowsky & Risch, 1984b).

Exposure to a mild stress has been found to sensitize the brain to a subsequent presentation of the stressor (Anisman & Zacharko, 1982; Section 19.3.1). It would therefore be expected that, other things being equal, mood would deteriorate with prolonged exposure to a constant strain. This may account for the fact that the presence of a mild depression is itself a major risk factor in the development of a subsequent severe depression: 40% of mildly depressed patients were found to have developed severe endogenous depressions in a three- to four-year follow-up (Akiskal et al., 1978).

The ACh–NA interaction, which underlies the response to stress, also describes the "depressive personality," judging by the presence in dysthymic individuals of negative DST results and short REM latencies (Section 3.3.3). In dysthymic people, the nervous system is behaving as though already under stress. The source of the individual differences in cholinergic and/or catecholaminergic activity implied by this observation has not been determined. The regulation of noradrenergic activity by social status (see above) argues strongly for a role of developmental factors in setting the level of cholinergic–catecholaminergic balance. Equally, however, this could be one of the media through which genetic effects are expressed.

In a similar fashion, it seems likely that the unstable personality molded by an early parental loss, and the effects of poor social support, may also share a common physiological basis. In both cases, the contribution to depression is a low level of social reinforcement, and from the animal literature, there are grounds for predicting that these factors should be associated with a reduction in endorphin and 5-HT function (Section 19.3.2). Low 5-HT function is indeed found to be a predisposing factor in depression, rather than a precipitant. However, no studies have attempted to relate markers of 5-HT dysfunction either to early parental loss or to the quality of social support. Indeed, the three markers of 5-HT dysfunction, CSF 5-HIAA, platelet 5-HT uptake, and platelet [³H]imipramine binding, have not even been related to one another (Chapter 16). However, both low 5-HT function and early parental loss are associated not only with depression, but also with suicide and with a range of other problems such as alcoholism, drug dependence, and an unstable personality (see above, and Chapter 16). Given also that low 5-HT function mediates the behavioral disorders exhibited by the socially isolated animal, the prediction that low 5-HT function will be found to be associated with early parental loss and with poor social support can be made with some confidence. We shall see.

Finally, it should be noted that "loss events" might exert their precipitant effect via either or both of the mechanisms described. An event such as bereavement is stressful over and above the resulting decrease in social reinforcement; this may be appreciated by considering the difference between bereavement and a temporary separation, which reduces social reinforcement to the same extent but is far less stressful.

20.1.5. "Biological" Precipitants and Their Implications

In addition to the psychosocial determinants of depression described above, a number of pharmacological and physiological conditions have also been implicated as precipitants of depression; with only one major exception, they can be readily integrated within the framework described above. In numerical terms, these factors probably play a rather minor role in determining the prevalence of depression, but they are of theoretical interest, and where present, there are also important clinical implications.

The most familiar "pharmacological depressions" are those induced by reserpine and other catecholamine-depleting drugs or by cholinergic agonists. In both cases it is clear that these drugs exacerbate existing depressions. However, in nondepressed subjects the primary effect is one of apathy and sedation, but usually without depressed mood. Depressed mood is seen in nondepressed subjects only if they are predisposed to depression by virtue of having previously been depressed (Sections 9.1, 12.2, and 14.3.2).

There are two possible interpretations of these findings, and both of them may be correct. One is that depression of mood may require the presence of a stress, in addition to the drug-induced chemical imbalance, as has been observed in the primate separation model (Section 9.4). The drug then acts to shift the starting point of the physiological stress response in a fashion simlar to that suggested above for the "depressive personality." This conceptualization may apply to the apparently genuine depressions which occur in the context of some physical illnesses, such as Parkinson's disease (Section 9.2.3) or chronic scurvy (Section 12.1), or following withdrawal from amphetamine (Schick et al., 1973; Watson et al., 1972) or fenfluramine (Steel & Briggs, 1972). A second interpretation is that depression of mood may depend on a cognitive appraisal of the significance of psychomotor retardation, only occurring if physical activity is an important component of self-esteem (Mendels & Frazer, 1974). In this context it is worth noting that depression of mood is not a necessary component of even severe clinical depressions, and that pharmacologically induced "depressions" and "masked depressions" may not be all that dissimilar.

A variety of hormonal conditions also precipitate depression. The conditions that have received the most attention are hypothyroidism and adrenocortical hyperactivity. Hypothyroidism carries a risk of depression, whereas hyperthyroidism protects against depression (Whybrow et al., 1969), and thyroxine has some antidepressant activity (Section 18.4.1.). Hypothyroidism is associated with decreased beta-adrenergic function, whereas thyroxine has been found to increase both alpha- and beta-adrenergic function (Section 18.4.1.). The influence of thyroid function on mood may thus be understood in terms of the effects of thyroxine on adrenergic functioning. A high incidence of depression is also seen in Cushing's syndrome and other conditions in which adrenocortical activity is elevated. Again, there is evidence for a reduction of beta-adrenergic function (Section 13.3.3.3); the effects of cortisol on alpha-adrenergic activity have not been examined, but cortisol may also potentiate some actions of ACh (Section 19.2.3).

Similar effects have also been described for estrogen (Section 13.3.3.3), and oral contraceptives that contain estrogen and progesterone have mild depressive side effects. In addition to their effects on beta-receptors, there are a number of other ways in which estrogens might reduce catecholamine and 5-HT function, including inhibition of pyridoxal phosphate, a derivative of vitamin B6, which is required for the synthesis of NA and 5-HT; a number of studies have demonstrated antidepressant effects of pyridoxine in women taking oral contraceptives (Parry & Rush, 1979; see also Section 16.1.1). Effects of steroid hormones on NA function could be responsible for premenstrual accentuation of depression, though it is not yet clear whether premenstrual tension is specifically related to depression or whether it should be considered as a nonspecific stressor.

The clinical implication of these observations is that depressions associated with hormonal or pharmacological precipitants may respond to treatments that remove the pharmacological precipitant or restore normal endocrine function. This has been clearly demonstrated for oral contraceptives (Parry & Rush, 1979), cortisol-secreting tumors (Kelly et al., 1983), and thyroid hypofunction (Loosen et al., 1979). The theoretical significance is that all of these pharmacological and endocrine factors are consistent with a decrease in NA function, and they could be considered as functionally equivalent to low-grade stressors.

Another biological factor is sunlight. There is some evidence that in a subgroup of bipolar patients, winter episodes of mania may be precipitated by insufficient exposure to sunlight (Hawkins, 1980); conversely, overexposure can cause the disease lupus erythematosus, which carries a high risk for depression (Akiskal, 1982). Exposure to sunlight releases melanocyte-stimulating hormone (MSH) from the pituitary, and there is some evidence that inhibition of MSH release may have antidepressant effects (Ehrensing & Kastin, 1974, 1978; Section 18.4.2). As MSH is contained within the same pituitary cells that release ACTH (Lazarus et al., 1976), it seems reasonable to suppose that these effects might be explained by a sunlight-induced activation of the pituitary–adrenal axis.

The one precipitant of depression which cannot yet be easily assimilated to the present model is jet lag. Travel across two or more time zones can precipitate depression if the travel is from west to east and mania if the travel is from east to west (Weller, 1981). Given the pharmacological similarities between mood and sleep control (Section 19.2.2), it would not be surprising to find that the effects of jet lag were mediated by shifts in the balance of adrenergic and cholinergic activation. At present, however, further speculation is limited by the lack of information about the effects of circadian phase shifts on physiological function.

In discussing the joint action of physiological and psychosocial factors in causing depression, it is important to clarify once more the nature of the interaction (see Chapter 2). It only makes sense to talk in terms of the joint action of, for example, DA depletion and a cognitive appraisal (see above), if this form of words is being used as a shorthand to describe two independent models. In the psychological model, DA depletion is represented by a concept such as apathy, which is subjected to a cognitive appraisal. In the physiological model, DA depletion affects the outcome of the physiological processes that are activated in the course of making a cognitive appraisal. The fact that at present we have only the haziest notions about the nature of those processes is a source of confusion but does not change the logic.

20.2. THE SYMPTOMS OF DEPRESSION

The fact that several relatively independent factors contribute to the etiology of depression provides an obvious basis for understanding the varieties of depressive symptomatology. At one extreme, we might expect an endogenous depression to develop in a person with an introverted "depressive" personality, who was subjected to a high level of strain, and a stressful life event of a nonsocial kind, such as losing a job. At the other extreme, a person who has suffered early parental loss and in consequence has developed a histrionic personality, who now suffers a social loss and has poor social support, should develop a reactive depression. Any other combination of risk factors should produce an intermediate outcome.

These relationships have not been the subject of explicit empirical examination. However, they are implicit in the above discussion of the brain systems that mediate the effects of the various risk factors; this point will be amplified below. Before doing so, however, it will be useful to consider how the present position relates to some previous theoretical perspectives on depression.

20.2.1. Brain Mechanisms, Reward, and Satisfaction

It is a remarkable how few previous attempts there have been to produce a unified psychobiological account of depression. The one major exception is a series of publications by Akiskal and colleagues, which promulgate the view that melancholia results from a derangement of the neurochemical substrate of reinforcement. The mechanisms by which this change is brought about are not specified in detail, but it is suggested that changes in the hypothalamic reward system represent a "final common pathway" on which the various psychological and biological factors contributing to the etiology of depression converge (Akiskal, 1979; Akiskal & McKinney, 1973, 1975; Akiskal & Tashjian, 1983).

Central to Akiskal's position is the assumption that endogenous and nonendogenous depressions differ only in severity. This view has venerable antecedents (Lewis, 1934) but is contradicted by the empirical evidence that endogenous depressions need not be severe, and severe depressions need not be endogenomorphic (Section 3.4). Curiously, Akiskal and colleagues have undermined their own theoretical position by themselves contributing much of this evidence.

A second model (Klein, 1974) recognizes the distinction between endogenomorphic and neurotic depressions, and attributes the former to a dysfunctional reward mechanism and the latter to an increased responsiveness to aversive events. This model provides a useful means of addressing the variable symptomatology of depression (Section 3.4). However, both in people (Section 4.2) and in animals (Section 7.2); it has been demonstrated that reward and punishment systems do not function independently; reward mechanisms are suppressed by the occurrence of aversive events. These findings invalidate the distinction between underactive reward mechanisms and overactive punishment mechanisms as a basis for differentiating the two syndromes.

Perhaps the problem lies in the concept of a unitary "reward mechanism." The concept of reward is far from straightforward. For many years, the question of what it is about rewards that makes them rewarding was one of the major issues within psychology. Indeed, the roots of the controversy can be traced back to the differing opinions of Plato and Aristotle (Panksepp, 1981). In the first half of this century, Thorndike, Hull, Miller, and others took the view that the essential feature of a reward is that it reduces a drive. This principle makes sound biological sense, because it means that animals will like the things that do them good. However, it is incorrect. In the 1950s and 1960s it became clear that the hedonic value of rewards can be divorced from their biological consequences, and resides in the sensory properties of the reward (Sheffield & Roby, 1950; Sheffield et al., 1951; Pfaffman, 1960) or simply in being allowed to perform preferred behaviors (Premack, 1959). One finding will serve as an illustration. Water-deprived rats will lick vigorously at a stream of warm air, which—far from satisfying their thirst—actually causes a state of severe dehydration owing to water loss from the tongue (Oatley & Dickinson, 1970).

As a result of these and related observations, it is now generally accepted that rewards function primarily as incentives rather than as satisfiers. Indeed, because incentives activate behavior, rewards are usually associated with increases in drive, rather than decreases. Signals that inform a motivated animal that it is approaching a goal are also invested with incentive functions (Bindra, 1978). It follows that when an animal is performing a sequence of instrumental behaviors leading to the attainment and consumption of a goal object, much of the reward devolves on the anticipation of the eventual goal. In human terms, there is as much pleasure in traveling hopefully as in arriving.

However, it cannot be assumed that rewards constitute the sole source of psychological well-being. There is now little evidence that drive reduction is rewarding, in the sense that animals will work simply in order to reduce drives. However, a moment's introspection informs us that there is something very pleasant about the feelings of satisfaction that are experienced, for example, in the aftermath of a good meal. This positive hedonic tone that accompanies satisfaction is difficult to demonstrate experimentally in animals because it is associated with a decrease in the perceived pleasantness of the rewards that produced it (Section 15.3.2.). However, there is a strong presumption that when, for example, a cat purrs, asks to be stroked, and stretches contentedly after drinking a bowl of milk and before going to sleep, it does so under the influence of a positive hedonic tone. Certainly, these elements form no part of its behavior when under threat.

This analysis lends itself to an evolutionary rationale: it may be that a "good mood" flows from behaving in a way that maximizes the likelihood of survival. This involves acceding to two biological imperatives, which operate sequentially: it is necessary first to take active measures to ensure an adequate nutritional supply and then, having done so, to find a safe place and stay there to avoid predators (cf. Meddis, 1977). Conversely, the inability to act when action is called for or the inability to relax when no action is needed may form the behavioral substrata of "bad moods."

Irrespective of the merits of this rationale, it does seem that a sense of psychological well-being arises from two sources: the anticipation of future rewards, which is a function of actively striving to attain them, and the satisfaction of fulfillment, which is accompanied by behavioral quiescence. Further, the evidence suggests that the two forms of depression are associated, respectively, with the absence of these two sources of happiness.

20.2.2. Endogenomorphic Depressions

The predominant feature of endogenomorphic depressions is their autonomous course: not only is the melancholic unresponsive to attempts at reassurance, but also no improvement results from alleviating the conditions that precipitated the episode. As noted above, endogenomorphic depressions are usually considered to reflect a dysfunction of brain reward systems. On the basis of the evidence reviewed, it is possible to attempt an answer to the two pertinent questions: How does this state of affairs come into being, and how is it maintained?

As outlined in the previous section, current accounts of how instrumental behavior is generated rely heavily on the notion that reward and motivation are interdependent. It is clear from animal experiments that the performance of rewarded behaviors is reduced by exposure to uncontrollable stress (Section 7.2). What is usually observed in these experiments is a lack of motivation: animals work less to attain rewards. However, one study has reported a stress-induced decrease in the consumption of saccharine (Katz, 1982; see Section 7.2.3); this finding implies a reward deficit rather than simply a lack of motivation, since performance requirements in this case are minimal. In people, similar effects are also apparent. Exposure to uncontrollable aversive events, for example, in learned helplessness induction experiments, causes a motivational deficit (Section 4.3.2). It is also clear that an increase in the frequency of aversive events reduces the perceived pleasantness of pleasant events (Section 4.2). It seems, therefore, that in short-term studies in both animal and human subjects, both the sensitivity to rewards and the motivation to attain them are reduced by exposure to prolonged or uncontrollable stress.

Direct clinical confirmation of a specific relationship between high levels of stress and endogenomorphic depressions is lacking, because studies of the etiology of depression have made very little attempt to relate specific precipitants to patterns of depressive symptomatology. However, such a relationship may be deduced from the pattern of neurochemical changes that underlie endogenomorphic depressions. The two neurochemical effects which have been most consistently reported as sequelae of uncontrollable stress in animals are an increase in ACh turnover and a decrease in NA turnover. In depressed people, ACh turnover has not been measured, and although NA turnover does appear to be reduced in some depressed people, the methodological difficulties of measuring central NA turnover in people are formidable (Section 12.1.4). What is quite clear, however, is that in endogenomorphic depressions there is a change in the relative activity of these two systems. A shift in the balance of activity in ACh and NA systems is reflected by a reduced latency to enter REM sleep and by high levels of adrenocortical activity (Sections 12.4 and 14.2.1); these biological markers are absent from nonendogenomorphic depressions (Section 3.3.2).

Another effect of stress, which probably follows from stress-induced changes in ACh and NA systems, is a decrease in the ability of pleasurable stimuli to activate the mesolimbic DA system, reflected in a loss of incentive motivation (Sections 8.2.2 and 19.3.1). A reduced DA turnover is specific to retarded depressions (Section 9.1.5), which are almost invariably endogenomorphic (Section 3.3.1). It is possible that a reduction in DA turnover is partly responsible for the asymmetries of hemispheric functioning which are associated with changes in mood state. Specifically, changes in DA function may be responsible for changes in the level of left frontal activity, which may be confined to endogenomorphic depressions (Section 5.1.6).

It must be noted that in contrast to many of the phenomena of depression, little is known about the physiological basis of qualitative shifts in the accessibility of positively and negatively loaded information. Indeed, the only clear physiological observation is that the mood-related bias in information processing is associated with a shift in hemispheric dominance (Section 5.1). As memory access is controlled to some extent by level of motivation, it may be that the decreased accessibility of positive material results directly from the motivational and hedonic deficits that form the core of endogenomorphic depressions. As noted above, the motivational changes may reflect changes in DA function. A prediction that follows is that neuroleptic drugs, which are DA receptor antagonists, might mimic some of the changes seen in depression and decrease the accessibility of happy memories.

A loss of motivation, mediated by changes in forebrain DA systems, provides one approach to understanding the lack of reactivity of endogenomorphic depressions. As Beck (1983; see Section 4.4.2) has observed, in people who derive a high proportion of their pleasure from meeting self-imposed goals and only a low proportion from interactions with other people, a sense of apathy and worthlessness resulting from a failure to meet those goals cannot easily be replaced by attention and reassurance. The functional autonomy of endogenomorphic depressions is also assured by positive feedback mechanisms operating in both the psychological and the physiological spheres. At the psychological level, a variety of processes have been described that would tend to maintain the existence of a depressed mood. The most striking of these is the mutual amplification of depressed mood by negative information, and vice versa (Section 4.4.1). As previously noted, the physiological mechanisms of this vicious circle are not fully understood. At the physiological level, the intensity of endogenomorphic depressions is increased by the hypersecretion of cortisol, which has itself been implicated as a causative factor (Section 20.1.5). The quantitative contribution of high plasma cortisol levels to the autonomy of endogenomorphic depressions has not been investigated. It has been observed, however, that in endogenomorphic depressions the presence of depressive thinking is insufficient to explain variations in the severity of the depression (Giles & Rush, 1982; see Section 4.4.2).

Finally, it is possible to make a well-informed guess as to the evolutionary significance of endogenomorphic depressions. A number of authors have speculated that depression may be one aspect of an adaptive coping process, which conserves resources by passively submitting to a prolonged or uncontrollable stress (Engel, 1962; Klinger, 1975; Schmale, 1973). This appears to be an accurate description of endogenomorphic depressions. They are precipitated by prolonged or uncontrollable stress and are accompanied by an increased secretion of hormones that are known to serve precisely that function: cortisol, which increases the ability to withstand stress, and beta-endorphin, which reduces pain. These mechanisms were of undoubted value when an adverse physical environment formed the major source of stress. With the development of social organizations, the same mechanisms also formed a basis for the maintenance of stable hierarchies of social dominance, the purpose of which is to reduce the risk of physical damage by preventing fighting within the group (Section 11.3.2). It is far less obvious that passive acceptance is an appropriate way of coping with the modern world, where, with certain notable exceptions, uncontrollable stressors do not usually carry the threat of physical destruction.

20.2.3. Nonendogenomorphic Depressions

Nonendogenomorphic depressions are "reactive" in the sense of responding to attention and reassurance. Typically, though not invariably, they are of lesser severity, and usually the depression is accompanied by anxiety and/or hostility. Reactive depressions appear to form part of a spectrum of pathological conditions including alcoholism, drug dependence, and personality disorders, which to some extent represent alternative outcomes of a common underlying pathology (Section 3.3.4). Reactive depressions are particularly likely in people who derive enjoyment primarily from their role in social relationships (Beck, 1983; see Section 4.4.2). It does not seem unreasonable to suggest that the substantially higher incidence of reactive depressions among women (Weissman & Paykel, 1974) derives in large measure from the way in which society forces women into roles that deny them other sources of gratification (Scarf, 1980).

The central feature of endogenomorphic depressions is an insensitivity to rewards, leading to a loss of incentive. In neurotic depressions the problem is rather the absence of rewards, or, more specifically, social rewards, leading to a loss of satisfaction. As outlined in Section 19.3.2, it seems likely that an inadequate level of social reinforcement is reflected in a reduced activity of forebrain endorphin, 5-HT, and GABA systems. Behaviorally, the central feature of animals or people who show evidence of reduced 5-HT function is irritability (Sections 15.2 and 16.4); subjectively, the core of the problem may be experienced as a sense of insecurity.

Clinically, depressions that show evidence of low 5-HT function are characterized by high levels of agitation and anxiety, as well as serious suicide attempts (see below). This cluster of symptoms is strongly associated with psychotic features (Section 3.3.1), such as delusions of sinfulness, disproportionate guilt, or depressive hallucinations (Blatt et al., 1982; Nelson & Charney, 1981). These relationships imply that nonendogenomorphic depressions vary along a continuum of severity from neurotic to psychotic. The association of psychotic thinking with low 5-HT function may be related to disinhibition of the nigrostriatal DA system (Section 19.1.3), as high levels of DA activity are hypothesized to play an important role in the pathogenesis of schizophrenia.

The neuropsychological literature provides a second clue as to the physiological basis for a neurotic–psychotic dimension. The behavioral consequences of low 5-HT function in animal models of depression appear to be mediated by the amygdala, which is situated in the temporal lobe (Section 15.1.2). This localization is consistent with the finding that neurotic depressions are associated with damage to the temporal lobe of the nondominant cerebral hemisphere (Section 5.1.5). There is also considerable evidence that dysfunction of the dominant temporal lobe is associated with schizophrenia and related psychoses (Flor-Henry, 1979; Tucker, 1981). It is beyond the scope of this book to analyze the nature of this latter relationship. However, it seems reasonable to suggest that the progression from neurotic to psychotic depression might continue on through schizoaffective disorders to schizophrenia, with the relative preponderance of psychotic symptoms depending upon the extent to which 5-HT function is reduced in the dominant temporal lobe relative to the nondominant side.

As shown above, there are useful insights to be gained from a consideration of the evolutionary significance of endogenomorphic depressions. What of neurotic depressions? Here the ground is much less firm, but there is scope for speculation. 5-HT systems have widespread inhibitory effects on behavior (Chapter 15). Although it is reasonably clear why satiation with food should be accompanied by the suppression of active behavior (Section 15.3.2), it is much less immediately apparent why social reinforcement should be accompanied by behavioral suppression. However, one possibility is that social cohesion requires the suppression of intraspecies aggression, particularly the aggressive tendencies of parents toward their young.

Whatever the merits of this particular hypothesis, it is clear that a reduction in the level of 5-HT activity does release aggressive behavior in animals (Section 15.1.2) and in people (Section 16.4). Aggression in people may be directed either toward others or inwardly, in which case it might result in a suicide attempt; low 5-HT is predictive of both violence and suicide (Section 16.1.3). It is probably the intensity of depressive thinking, a central part of which is a negative view of the self (Section 4.3.1), that determines whether or not aggression will be interiorized. This formulation of the determinants of suicidal behavior is, of course, a restatement of Freud's (1917) concept of "anger turned inwards."

20.2.4. Mixed Syndromes

Although for the sake of clarity endogenomorphic and reactive depressions have been discussed separately, there is no reason to suppose that the two syndromes are mutually exclusive. On the contrary, as the various risk factors are largely independent, it is to be expected that mixed syndromes would frequently occur. Furthermore, the existence of one type of depression predisposes to the other. The endogenous depressive behaves in ways which make it likely that others will withdraw support; conversely, the reactive depressive's failure to find affection acts as a source of stress.

As the neural systems underlying depression exert their influence over widespread areas of the brain and are involved in the control of a multiplicity of behaviors, it is not surprising that the associated symptoms show a considerable degree of variability. Eating is a clear example. Eating is suppressed by reducing activity in the dorsal NA system (Section 11.2.2.4); consequently, endogenomorphic depressions usually involve loss of appetite and weight (Mathew et al., 1979). However, low 5-HT activity stimulates feeding (Section 15.3.2), so the effect on appetite of combining these two dysfunctions is indeterminate. In fact, loss of appetite is rather low on the list of the symptoms of endogenous depression (Nelson & Charney, 1981), and increased food intake with weight gain is not uncommon (Mathew et al., 1979).

The admixture of these two sets of changes also accounts for a serious discrepancy which will not have escaped the alert reader. I suggested in Section 20.2.2. that endogenomorphic depressions involve a stress-induced shift in the balance of activity in ACh and NA systems. The problem with this account is that the dexamethasone suppression test, which detects just this imbalance, is abnormal in only some 40–50% of endogenous depressions (Section 3.3.2). However, 5-HT stimulates ACTH secretion, and it is an essential link in the ACTH response to stress (Section 15.2.3). It transpires that the endogenous depressives who show normal dexamethasone suppression are those who have low central 5-HT turnover (Section 16.1.4). This means that reduced 5-HT activity effectively recalibrates the DST, such that it no longer provides an accurate measure of central ACh–NA balance. It is perfectly possible, in other words, that the ACh–NA balance is abnormal even when DST results are not. It is also possible that low 5-HT may potentiate some of the psychotropic effects of cortisol (Section 19.2.3), so achieving the depressive effects of cortisol even without an elevation of plasma levels.

The analysis of DA activity in depression is also subject to a similar limitation in the accuracy of the analytical tools currently available. In retarded depressions, central DA turnover is clearly reduced; equally clearly, in agitated depressions, central DA turnover is normal or even elevated (Section 9.1.5). As these are both subtypes of endogenous depression, activity in the mesolimbic DA system should be low in both cases. This remains perfectly possible. In agitated depressions, 5-HT function is low, and as a result, nigrostriatal DA activity is disinhibited (Section 19.1.3). As the nigrostriatal contribution heavily biases the assessment of DA turnover from CSF samples, a reduction in mesolimbic DA turnover could easily be masked.

More generally, it is possible that some reduction of mesolimbic DA activity could be a feature of all depressions. The mechanisms by which activity in the mesolimbic system is reduced in endogenomorphic depressions has been discussed at length. In reactive depressions, a reduction in the level of activity in the opiate reward system would also decrease mesolimbic DA activity (Section 18.2.1.2). This might be the reason that feelings of fatigue are prominent in both types of depression.

20.2.5. Animal Models of Depression: A Reappraisal

The foregoing account of the physiological basis of depressive symptomatology owes a considerable debt to insights derived from animal models of depression. It therefore seems appropriate to conclude this discussion by returning briefly to animal models, and noting that their status changes as a result of the development of a theory of depression.

First, it is clear that despite its faults (Section 7.2.1), investigations based on the learned helplessness model have been extremely productive in developing a model of the physiological basis of endogenomorphic depressions. How can this be reconciled with the reservations expressed earlier about the validity of the model? One problem is that helplessness induction procedures are associated with high levels of anxiety, which is not a prominent feature of endogenous depression. It is likely that this discrepancy simply reflects the acute time course of helplessness induction experiments. When stress is prolonged, symptoms of anxiety are much less prominent (see Section 7.2.3; Gray, 1982). A more serious reservation concerns the significance of feelings of helplessness as a core symptom in depression (Section 4.3). Parallel to this controversy was the question of whether animals are capable of learning that they are help-less. Alternative explanations of "helplessness" effects in animals attrib-uted the effects to inactivity. This issue was resolved when it became clear that both types of effect occur (Section 7.2.1). However, the physi-ological evidence derived from the model concerns the physiological basis of inactivity rather than "helplessness" (Sections 8.3.2, 11.3, 14.1.1, and 18.2.1.1). In effect, therefore, physiological studies have finessed the ques-tion of the centrality of feelings of helplessness. They have addressed a different aspect of the model—psychomotor retardation.

A second group of models—social isolation, olfactory bulbectomy, and muricide—appeared on first presentation to be based entirely on empir-ical observations and to have no theoretical rationale (Chapter 6). The finding that low 5-HT activity is responsible for the behavioral abnor-malities in these models (Section 15.1.2) was an important source of ev-idence in deciding whether depression is associated with "too much" 5-HT transmission or "too little." In the light of a theoretical account of reactive depressions, it now appears that there may after all be a theo-retical basis for these models. Social isolation may model a low level of social reinforcement (parental deprivation and poor social support), whereas muricide may model the aggression which forms part of the basis for suicidal behavior. Taken out of context, these relationships are totally lacking in plausibility, which highlights the fact that an animal model forms only one among a variety of sources of clinical and experimental evidence.

A third point of reappraisal concerns the pharmacological specificty of animal models. In assessing the available models (Chapters 6 and 7), responses to anticholinergics and stimulants were considered to be "false positives." From the theoretical position developed in this chapter, there would be nothing false about a response to these two classes of drugs in a model of endogenomorphic depression. However, they ought not to occur in a model of reactive depression. Sure enough, these agents are effective in reversing learned helplessness and "behavioral despair" (Sections 7.2.1 and 7.2.2), but are ineffective in the olfactory bulbectomy model (Sections 6.5.4). Conversely, the olfactory bulbecomy model responds to seroto-nergic drugs such as fluoxetine or zimelidine, but serotonergic agents appear to be ineffective in the "behavioral despair" procedure. Chlori-mipramine reversed "behavioral despair" in the mouse (in which it is metabolized to a potent NA uptake inhibitor), but not in the rat (where this transformation does not occur) (Section 7.2.1).

We may conclude that there is a two-way traffic between the validation of animal models and the process of theory construction. Models that have only a modest degree of validity can make important contributions to the development of a theory. The theory, in turn, can clarify the status of the model and explain its shortcomings.

20.3. RECOVERY FROM DEPRESSION

There is a bitter irony in the clinical observation that endogenomorphic depressions, which by definition are unresponsive to psychosocial interventions, are quite likely to recover even when left untreated, whereas reactive depressions, which respond to reassurance and attention, have a generally poor prognosis with a high likelihood of relapse (Akiskal et al., 1978; Klerman, 1978).

20.3.1. Reactive Depressions

It was proposed earlier in this chapter that reactive (i.e., nonendogenomorphic) depressions result from a group of factors which lead to a low level of social reinforcement. In the short term, this deficiency may be corrected by care and attention. In the long term, however, the patient will return to an environment in which the quantity and/or the quality of social relationships are insufficient to sustain a satisfying social existence; a relapse in such circumstances is almost inevitable. The enduring nature of the problem is reflected in the fact that when present, reduced levels of activity in central 5-HT and GABA systems (Section 19.3.2) are enduring traits of depressive people which do not change with clinical improvement (Sections 16.4 and 18.2.2).

What is to be done to lower the risk of relapse in reactive depressions? Tricyclic antidepressants and lithium, both of which enhance 5-HT function (Section 17.3), as well as the 5-HT precursor 5-HTP, have all been found to be of prophylactic value in preventing the recurrence of depression (Klerman, 1978; Section 16.3). However, this solution is far from ideal: the cost of preventing depression is the induction of drug dependence. Only if the depression were judged to carry a serious suicide risk could it be said that long term drug maintenance was definitely the lesser of these two evils. There are some conditions, such as diabetes or epilepsy, where drugs offer the only form of long term treatment, but reactive depression is not among them. If, as hypothesized, treatments that increase 5-HT function mimic the receipt of social reinforcement, then procedures that improve the quality of the patient's social environment should remove any need for long-term maintenance drug prescribing. Lonely people need friends more than drugs.

Now that the extended family is a thing of the past, the most obvious way of providing the long-term social support that reactive depressives need is by means of neighborhood support groups. It is a sorry reflection on our social and scientific priorities that at a time when spending on pharmaceuticals consumes an appreciable proportion of gross national product, organizations which offer friendship and counselling are hard pressed to obtain even minimal levels of financial support (see Ernst & Goodison, 1981). As far as I am aware, support has not even been available to perform an explicit evaluation of such organizations in the prophylaxis of depression, though the ability of good social support to protect against depression is well-established in other contexts (Aneshensel & Stone, 1982).

In addition to the progressive deterioration of traditional social structures, the level of social support available to many depressives is further reduced by their poor command of social skills (Section 4.2.1). A number of recent studies have demonstrated that training regimes designed to improve deficient social skills in depressed outpatients are at least as effective as tricyclic antidepressants in alleviating depressive symptoms (Bellack et al., 1983; Hersen et al., 1980; McLean & Hakstian, 1979; Zeiss et al., 1979). There is also evidence that social skills training may be superior to a course of amitriptyline in preventing subsequent relapse (Bellack et al., 1981). It goes without saying that there have as yet been no studies of the neurochemical correlates of poor social skill (? low 5-HT) or of the neurochemical consequences of social skills training.

It was noted earlier in this chapter that a low level of social reinforcement, which is assumed to reflect low 5-HT function, is associated not only with depression but also with a range of other conditions, including alcoholism and opiate dependence. Opiates activate brain 5-HT systems (Sections 17.2.2 and 19.3.2), and chronic alcohol consumption may also increase brain 5-HT activity (Ahtee & Eriksson, 1972, 1973), though the evidence here is more controversial (Ellingboe, 1978). There is a strong presumption that these behaviors represent a form of self-medication, which, like antidepressants, fills a need that the social environment is failing to provide.

20.3.2. Endogenous Depressions

In endogenomorphic depressions, exposure to a high level of uncontrollable stress causes reduction in the ability to respond to pleasant events, rendering the sufferer "nonreactive." However, unlike reactive depressions, which in the absence of medication can be overcome only by a restructuring of the relationships between depressed people and their environment, endogenomorphic depressions are self-limiting. This spontaneous recovery reflects a process of adaptation to stress: the stress-induced decrease in NA function is gradually overcome by an increase in the synthetic capacity of NA neurons (Section 11.3). The likelihood of triggering this recovery process increases in inverse proportion to the degree of noradrenergic dysfunction (Section 11.3). Two consequences of this mode of operation are that the more severe an endogenomorphic depression, the closer it is to recovering, and that mild depressions could continue indefinitely if left untreated.

In principle, it should be possible to devise therapeutic procedures to hasten adaptation to stress, but in practice this has proven rather difficult, and attempts to construct a therapy from ideas derived from the learned helplessness model have met with little success (Section 7.4.2). The present account would predict that the deliberate intensification of stress should hasten the process of recovery. Ethical considerations make it improbable that this prediction will ever be tested adequately in people. However, some mildly stressful procedures such as sleep deprivation (Gillin, 1983; Vogel, 1983) and jogging (Glasser, 1976; Greist et al., 1979) appear to be effective antidepressants, and studies in animals have shown that adaptation to stress does produce a positive response in the learned helplessness and "behavioral despair" models (Weiss et al., 1975; Platt & Stone, 1982; see Section 11.3).

Stone (1979) has suggested that antidepressant drugs work precisely because they mimic the process of adaptation to stress. The hypothesis was based on the observation that adaptation to stress and antidepressants both reduce the sensitivity of beta-adrenergic receptors. It now appears likely that beta-receptor desensitization is a negative feedback effect, which if anything retards the therapeutic action of antidepressants (Section 13.3.3.3). However, Stone's functional hypothesis still holds, in that, like adaptation to stress (Section 11.3), antidepressants also increase transmission through alpha-adrenergic synapses, though by a different mechanism (Section 13.4). The rather elusive desensitization of DA autoreceptors by antidepressants (Section 10.1.2) represents a second parallel between antidepressants and stress: it has recently been reported that immobilization stress also desensitizes DA autoreceptors (Antelman & Chiodo, 1984).

It would not, however, be correct to say that the simulation of adaptation to stress is the only relevant action of antidepressants. In addition to their effects on alpha-adrenergic transmission and (possibly) on DA autoreceptors, chronic administration of ECS and most antidepressant drugs also enhances DA and 5-HT transmission (Chapters 10 and 17). The effect on DA is allied to the alpha-adrenergic effect, in that a reduction of DA transmission is one of the sequelae of uncontrollable stress. The consequent motivational deficits may also be reversed by DA agonist drugs; the fact that these drugs are effective antidepressants (Section 9.3) reflects the intimate relationship between level of motivation and the ability to experience pleasure (Section 20.2.1). By contrast, as discussed in the previous section, the enhancement of 5-HT function by antidepressants is experienced as a decrease in irritability (Section 15.4) and does not form part of the process of adaptation to stress.

Paradoxically, it emerges from the present investigation that the MAOIs, which were the original antidepressants, are the group of antidepressant drugs of which the mechanisms of action are the least well understood. However, the limited usefulness of MAOIs has a bearing on another hypothesis of antidepressant drug action: that antidepressants work by suppressing REM sleep (Vogel, 1983). To some extent this hypothesis must be correct, because antidepressants do suppress REM sleep, and REM sleep deprivation has been shown to have antidepressant properties. However, the fact that MAOIs are very effective suppressors of REM sleep (Vogel, 1975), but clinically are only useful in mild depressions (Section 3.3.4) makes it most unlikely that REM sleep deprivation is the primary action of antidepressants. The present account would place a rather different emphasis on the relationship between antidepressant efficacy and suppression of REM sleep. Rather than seeing suppression of REM sleep as the primary effect of antidepressants, the very existence of REM sleep is assumed to be a by-product of the machinery for dealing with uncontrollable stress (Section 19.2.2).

20.3.3. The Switch to Mania

Clinically, bipolar depressions form a subgroup of endogenomorphic depressions (Chapter 3), and there seems little reason to suppose that the mechanisms of bipolar depression should be different from those described above. I have not attempted in this book to present a comprehensive analysis of the phenomenology of mania. However, it is necessary to consider briefly how the switch from depression to mania fits into the present picture.

In bipolar patients, episodes of mania or hypomania are frequently precipitated by tricyclic antidepressants (Section 3.2.1). Although tricyclics increase functional activity in both catecholaminergic (Chapters 10 and 13) and serotonergic (Section 16) systems, there are three good reasons not to attribute the switch process to the increase in 5-HT function. First, there is clinical evidence that NA function increases at the onset of manic episodes (Section 12.1.3), whereas 5-HT function is low in both phases of bipolar illness (Section 16.1.3). Second, specific "serotonergic" antidepressants are not usually found to precipitate manic or hypomanic episodes. Zimelidine, for example, did not precipitate switches into mania in a patient who did switch when given the "noradrenergic" agent DMI (Extein et al., 1979a). Manic episodes have been observed with the relatively selective 5-HT uptake inhibitor chlorimipramine, but only after several months of treatment (Van Scheyen, 1975). Given that mood switches precipitated by imipramine occur within days of the onset of treatment (Bunney, 1978), the induction of manic episodes by chlorimipramine most probably reflects the fact that the active metabolite of chlorimipramine has noradrenergic effects (Section 16.3.4).

The third reason for prefering a noradrenergic explanation of bipolar mood switches is that it is difficult to give a theoretical account of how 5-HT might be responsible for spontaneous, nonpharmacological manic episodes. However, a noradrenergic hypothesis is readily at hand. As noted above, the process of adaptation to stress involves an increase in enzyme synthesis in NA neurons, and it is several days before this is reflected in an increased synthesis of NA in nerve terminals. In all controlled systems that involve a time delay between registering a perturbation of the system and correcting it, there is an inherent tendency to overshoot the target (Bayliss, 1966). It therefore seems likely that the switch from depression to mania simply reflects the operation in NA neurons of this general tendency to overcompensate. What, then distinguishes bipolar from unipolar patients? The major difference appears to be that bipolars have more extreme "normal" mood swings (Section 3.3.3). The physiological mechanisms underlying volatility of mood have not been determined. However, it seems reasonable to assume that the irritability that results from a low level of 5-HT function might make a contribution.

20.3.4. On the Limited Specificity of Antidepressants

In general, it has been found that pharmacological treatments designed to affect NA, DA, or 5-HT transmission specifically are somewhat more effective in depressions that show evidence of a dysfunction in the target system (Sections 9.3, 12.3, and 16.3). However, there is little evidence that a depression defined by a particular biochemical abnormality will respond only to treatments designed to restore normal functioning. The relative nonspecificty of supposedly specific treatments has been a matter of some concern (see, e.g., Montgomery, 1982). It should not be. The two sets of factors implicated in the causation of depression act relatively independently to increase or decrease the sense of psychological well-being. Consequently, the untoward effects of one risk factor may be offset by the absence of others; it is clear, for example, that good social support confers resistance to stress (Section 20.1.2). When translated into the language of neurochemistry, this observation suggests that a treatment that specifically enhances 5-HT transmission should be of some value in endogenomorphic depressions even when there is no evidence of abnormal 5-HT function.

If this analysis is correct, it implies that there are inherent limitations on the specificity of antidepressant drug action. The important consequence is that future pharmacological developments are unlikely to uncover an antidepressant drug that is much more specific for diagnostic subgroups of depression than those that are already available. It is clear that antidepressant effects may be obtained by pharmacological actions on systems other than those activated by conventional antidepressant drugs: anticholinergic (Section 14.3.2), opiate (Section 18.2.2.2), and GABA-mimetic (Section 18.1.2) drugs all have antidepressant properties. These effects may be readily understood in relation to those already described (Section 19.3), and on that basis, it may be predicted that anticholinergics should be most effective in "low NA" depressions and opiates and GABA-mimetic drugs in "low 5-HT" depressions. However, there is no reason to expect that the specificity for chemically defined subgroups achieved with these novel antidepressant agents will exceed that of drugs that act specifically on NA or 5-HT systems.

With these reservations, the differential involvement of specific neurochemical systems in the overall symptomatology of depression has implications for the pharmacological management of an acute depressive episode. Endogenous depressions call for noradrenergic antidepressants (e.g., imipramine) and if psychomotor retardation is marked, a DA agonist (e.g., nomifensine) may be useful. However, if psychomotor agitation or psychotic thinking is marked, a serotonergic antidepressant (e.g., chlorimipramine) may be preferable, and in the latter case, the addition of a low dose of a neuroleptic may be helpful; neuroleptics should be avoided if retardation is also present. There is also a strong prediction that serotonergic antidepressants (which include lithium) will avoid the risk of precipitating manic episodes in bipolar patients, though if psychomotor retardation is pronounced, serotonergic agents will not reverse it.

I should have liked to end with some firmer recommendations for a rational prescribing policy, but this did not prove possible. The relative pharmacological nonspecificity of antidepressant drugs appears to arise because a "good mood" can be arrived at in various ways, rather than from any lack of ingenuity in drug design. There will be some advantage in treating depressions according to the presumed biochemical dysfunctions, but, sadly, it will not be dramatic.

twenty-one

STATUS AND PROSPECTS

I have tried in this book to present a parallel development of psychological and biological theory as applied to a common problem. The overriding assumption has been that the attempt to provide biological answers to psychological answers is fundamentally misconceived; both of these approaches are essential for an understanding of the psychobiology of depression, and neither has a logical or aesthetic priority. A recent review observed that "One may wonder how psychosocial stressors can trigger a disorder such as depression, which is reflected in brain dysfunction" (Akiskal & Tashjian, 1983). If the reader still finds this a source of wonder, then this book has failed in its main objective.

On the whole, the conclusions reached in this investigation of the psychobiology of depression have not required the rejection of previous theories. I have drawn attention to the limited ability of purely biochemical theories of depression to explain the phenomena they address. However, at a purely descriptive level, there is support for most of the theories summarized in Table 1.1. The weight of the evidence supports the position that the functional activity of NA systems (Schildkraut, 1965) and DA systems (Randrup et al., 1975) may be reduced in depression; that low 5-HT function predisposes to both depression and mania (Mendels et al., 1972); that low NA and low 5-HT function may coexist in depression (Prange et al., 1974) or may occur in separate groups of patients (Maas, 1975); and that ACh–NA balance is a crucial variable (Janowsky et al., 1972a). In fact, the only major theories to have been rejected are those

417

that attribute the therapeutic actions of antidepressant agents to a decrease in adrenergic (Segal et al., 1974; Sulser, 1978) or serotonergic (Aprison et al., 1978; Fuxe et al., 1983) transmission.

21.1. THE PSYCHOBIOLOGY OF DEPRESSION: A SUMMARY

The theory outlined in the preceding two chapters differs from the biochemical hypotheses which formed our point of departure in presenting a unified psychobiological perspective on depression. The major conclusions of the present investigation may be summarized as follows:

1. Depressions of clinical severity differ from normal mood swings quantitatively rather than qualitatively.

2. There are two forms of depression, endogenomorphic and reactive, which differ in their causation, pattern of symptoms, and prognosis.

3. Endogenomorphic depressions (melancholia) are characterized by a failure to respond to psychological reassurance, a lack of motivation, and an autonomous course; reactive depressions respond to psychosocial interventions and are associated with high levels of anxiety and hostility, and with psychotic thinking. Because the factors that give rise to the two forms are not mutually exclusive, the majority of depressions show a mixed pattern of symptoms, and the "pure" syndromes are correspondingly uncommon.

4. Endogenomorphic depressions are precipitated by high levels of uncontrollable stress or strain, which alter the balance of cholinergic and noradrenergic activity. The resulting cholinergic predominance is a semipermanent feature of the brains of people who suffer chronically from mild endogenomorphic depressions.

5. Endogenomorphic depressions may also be precipitated by a range of physicochemical agents that mimic these neurochemical effects, but only in people equipped to recognize the effects as "depression" by virtue of having previously been depressed.

6. The predominance of hypothalamic and forebrain cholinergic activity results in behavioral suppression, a reduced sensitivity to rewards, and an inability to sustain effort. As a result, the motivation to generate active behavior, which is mediated by the level of activity in the mesolimbic DA system, is also reduced.

7. The reduction of active coping behavior in the face of uncontrollable stress is a product of evolution that no longer serves an adaptive function.

8. The stress-induced increase in the ratio of cholinergic to noradrenergic activity causes an increase in the secretion of ACTH and beta-endorphin and a reduction in the latency to enter REM sleep. The endocrine effects are part of the machinery for coping with stress, but the sleep change is a nonfunctional by-product.

9. An eventual increase in the synthetic capacity of NA neurons brings about an adaptation to stress and spontaneous recovery from endogenomorphic depressions. Too great an increase precipitates a switch into mania or hypomania.

10. Reactive depressions are caused by an insufficiency of social reinforcement, which may result in part from the breakdown of traditional social structures and in part from a poor command of social skills. Early parental loss predisposes to depression by adversely affecting the ability to form close attachments.

11. Other things being equal, reactive depressions are more likely in people whose sense of psychological well-being depends primarily on social reinforcement.

12. The mechanism of reactive depression is a reduced activity of central endorphin, 5-HT, and GABA systems.

13. The major consequence of low 5-HT activity is an increased irritability, which may eventuate in a variety of psychiatric disorders, including violence, alcoholism, and drug dependence. To some extent, these latter may be considered to be attempts at self-medication.

14. A depressed mood creates a tendency to interpret information in the worst possible light, which further worsens mood.

15. The physiological mechanisms of this vicious circle are not fully understood, but they involve changes in left frontal and right parieto-temporal activity, which may reflect changes in DA and 5-HT function, respectively.

16. In people with a strong conscience, the negative information processing bias produces delusions of guilt. If 5-HT function is also low, the combination of violence and guilt may precipitate a suicide attempt.

17. Unless steps are taken to improve the quality of the available social support, reactive depressions have a high likelihood of relapse. The ability to form supportive relationships may be improved by training in social skills.

18. Tricyclic antidepressants, ECS, and a variety of other treatments simulate the processes of adaptation to stress and improvement of social support by increasing functional activity in alpha-adrenergic, DA, and

5-HT systems. These changes are brought about largely by increases in postsynaptic receptor responsiveness which develop during the course of chronic treatment.

19. Antidepressant-induced decreases in beta-adrenergic and 5-HT$_2$ receptor binding represent compensatory feedback effects which do not form part of the spectrum of therapeutic activity.

20. Anticholinergic, opiate, and GABA-mimetic drugs also show antidepressant activity (see 4 and 12), as do agents that act specifically to increase NA, DA, or 5-HT function.

21. There is some advantage in directing pharmacotherapeutic efforts toward identified neurochemical dysfunctions. However, the heterogeneous nature of depression limits the usefulness of this approach.

21.2. FUTURE DIRECTIONS

Having labored to produce a work of this length, I feel entitled to end with two brief homilies on the way in which future work should be carried out; one of these concerns the practice of research and the other the interpretation of results.

The development of any area of science begins by a period of more-or-less random fact gathering, and then matures into a set of generalizations linked by a theoretical framework. Subsequent research is then concerned largely with testing hypotheses derived from the theory, and as a result, modifying the theory and, if necessary, replacing it. Research in the psychobiology of depression has not followed this pattern. Beginning with the catecholamine hypothesis, a number of empirical generalizations have been proposed, but with the notable exception of two papers by Akiskal and McKinney (1973, 1975), there has been almost no attempt to discuss changes in neurotransmitter or neuroendocrine status in relation to the functioning of the brain. As a result, instead of moving forward into a period of theory testing, research has reverted to what in many cases amounts to little more than a random trawling through the body or brain in the hope of netting anything that will be statistically significant at a level sufficient to satisfy a journal referee. (If this seems an unduly harsh assessment, it should be qualified by adding that this impression is gained from reading reports of research, which may not always reflect the thinking behind them.) My first appeal, then, is for future clinically oriented research to be more systematic and much more closely related to theoretical issues.

My second plea is that the discussion of findings should extend beyond the immediate observations and recognize that the brain is a set of complex and interlinked functional systems acting together to produce behavior and subjective experiences. There is something almost endearing about the youthful exuberance that can elevate any chance observation into a "new theory of depression," but perhaps it is time to recognize the immaturity of this approach. There are two areas where this is particularly important. First, there is nothing in the literature to support the notion that some freak of nature is at work in depressed people, throwing up spontaneous biochemical abnormalities. If a biological abnormality is identified, there is almost certainly a reason; if the abnormality is a change in receptor function, then the most likely cause, in the drug-free patient at least, is an inverse change in transmitter release; the most likely reason for a change in transmitter release is a change in neuronal activity, which in turn probably reflects a change in environmental stimulation. Second, since antidepressants have a multiplicity of actions, the important questions concern their effects on neurotransmission, rather than on isolated aspects of synaptic functioning. It is quite clear, for example, that in many cases, the effects of antidepressants on the number of synaptic receptors are at best uninformative as indices of synaptic transmission, and they may be frankly misleading.

Finally, it should be recognized that we now possess the elements of a psychobiological theory of depression. We understand something of the factors that predispose to and precipitate depressive episodes, the way in which those factors act on the brain to produce psychological changes and the varieties of depressive symptomatology, the relationships between some of the brain systems involved, and the restoration of normal brain function by antidepressants. Future progress will depend on building a more comprehensive picture in each piece of this jigsaw, and the eventual solution will be complex, because a theory that spans several levels of psychological and biological explanation will almost certainly leave loose ends. There is no longer a place for the seductive idea that there must be a simple answer, if only we could find it. No deus ex machina (in the shape, perhaps, of a new synaptic transmitter) is going to appear suddenly on the stage, casting light where there was darkness and conferring instant understanding.

The object of this book has been to provide a current and reasonably comprehensive review of the psychobiology of depression. However, I would not wish the success or failure of the book to be judged by whether it becomes required reading for researchers in this field, or even by how long the conclusions survive; the pace of research is too fast to have more than modest expectations on either score. For me, the book will serve its purpose if it stimulates other workers to abandon the meaningless rivalry between psychological and biological explanations of depressive disorders and, instead, to carry forward the attempt to construct a psychobiological synthesis.

REFERENCES

The numbers in brackets at the end of each reference show the pages on which it is cited.

Aberg, A. (1981) Controlled cross-over study of a 5-HT uptake inhibiting and an NA uptake inhibiting antidepressant. *Acta Psychiatr. Scand.* **63** (Suppl. 290) 244–245. [323]

Aberg, A. and Holmberg, G. (1979) Preliminary clinical test of zimelidine (H 102/09), a new 5-HT uptake inhibitor. *Acta Psychiatr. Scand.* **59**, 45–58. [323]

Aberg-Wistedt, A. (1982) A double-blind study of zimelidine, a serotonin uptake inhibitor, and desipramine, a noradrenaline uptake inhibitor, in endogenous depression. I. Clinical findings. *Acta Psychiatr. Scand.* **66**, 50–65. [323]

Aberg-Wistedt, A., Jostell, K.-G., Ross, S.B., and Westerlund, D. (1981) Effects of zimelidine and desipramine on serotonin and noradrenaline uptake mechanisms in relation to plasma concentrations and to therapeutic effects during treatment of depression. *Psychopharmacology* **74**, 297–305. [323]

Aberg-Wistedt, A., Ross, S.B., Jostell, K.G., and Sjoquist, B. (1982) A double-blind study of zimelidine, a serotonin uptake inhibitor, and desipramine, a noradrenaline uptake inhibitor in endogenous depression. II. Biochemical findings. *Acta Psychiatr. Scand.* **66**, 66–82. [223, 233, 234, 250, 251, 323]

Abrams, R. and Taylor, M.A. (1974) Unipolar and bipolar depressive illness: Phenomenology and response to electroconvulsive therapy. *Arch. Gen. Psychiatr.* **30**, 320–322. [45]

Abrams, R., Essman, W.B., Taylor, M.A., and Fink, F. (1976) Concentration of 5-hydroxyindoleacetic acid, homovanillic acid and tryptophan in the cerebrospinal fluid of depressed patients before and after ECT. *Biol. Psychiatr.* **11**, 85–90. [339]

Abramson, L.Y. and Sackheim, H.A. (1977) A paradox in depression: Uncontrollability and self-blame. *Psychol. Bull.* **84**, 838–851. [62, 76]

Abramson, L.Y. and Seligman, M.E.P. (1977) Modelling psychopathology in the laboratory: History and rationale. In J.D. Maser and M.E.P. Seligman (Eds.), *Psychopathology: Animal Models.* Freeman, San Francisco, pp. 1–26. [101, 109]

Abramson, L.Y., Garber, J., Edwards, N.B., and Seligman, M.E.P. (1978a) Expectancy changes in depression and schizophrenia. *J. Abnorm. Psychol.* **87**, 102–109. [76]

Abramson, L.Y., Seligman, M.E.P., and Teasdale, J.D. (1978b) Learned helplessness in humans: Critique and reformulation. *J. Abnorm. Psychol.* **87**, 49–74. [77, 79, 126]

Abramson, L.Y., Garber, J., and Seligman, M.E.P. (1980) Learned helplessness in humans: An attributional analysis. In J. Garber and M.E.P. Seligman (Eds.), *Human Helplessness: Theory and Applications.* Academic, New York, pp. 3–34. [75]

Adams, J.E. (1976) Naloxone reversal of analgesia produced by brain stimulation in the human. *Pain* **2**, 161–166. [359]

Adelman, H.M. and Maatsch, J.L. (1952) Learning and extinction based upon frustration, food reward and exploratory tendency. *J. Exp. Psychol.* **52**, 311–315. [203]

Aderman, D. (1972) Elation, depression and helping behaviors. *J. Pers. Soc. Psychol.* **24**, 91–101. [68]

Agnoli, A., Ruggieri, S., Cerone, G., Aloisi, P., Baldessare, M., and Stramentolini, G. (1978) The dopamine hypothesis of depression: Results of treatment with dopaminergic drugs. In S. Garattini (Ed.), *Depressive Disorders.* F.K. Schattauer Verlag, Stuttgart, pp. 447–458. [174]

Agren, H. (1980a) Symptom patterns in unipolar and bipolar depression correlating with monoamine metabolites in the cerebrospinal fluid. I. General patterns. *Psychiatr. Res.* **3**, 211–223. [222, 223]

Agren, H. (1980b) Symptom patterns in unipolar and bipolar depression correlating with monoamine metabolites in the cerebrospinal fluid: II. Suicide. *Psychiatr. Res.* **3**, 225–236. [223, 311, 312]

Agren, H. (1982) Depressive symptom patterns and urinary MHPG excretion. *Psychiatr. Res.* **6**, 185–196. [223, 225, 226]

Agren, H., Terenius, L., and Wahlstrom, A. (1982) Depressive phenomenology and levels of cerebrospinal fluid endorphins. *Ann. N.Y. Acad. Sci.* **398**, 388–398. [364, 365]

Ahern, G.L. and Schwartz, G.E. (1979) Differential lateralization for positive versus negative emotion. *Neuropsychology* **17**, 693–698. [89]

Ahlqvist, R.P. (1948) Study of adrenotropic receptors. *Am. J. Physiol.* **153**, 586–600. [13]

Ahlskog, J.E. (1974) Food intake and amphetamine anorexia after selective forebrain norepinephrine loss. *Brain Res.* **82**, 211–240. [196]

Ahtee, L. and Eriksson, K. (1972) 5-hydroxytryptamine and 5-hydroxyindoleacetic acid content in brain of rat strains selected for their alcohol intake. *Physiol. Behav.* **8**, 123–126. [411]

Ahtee, L. and Eriksson, K. (1973) Regional distribution of brain 5-hydroxytryptamine in rat strains selected for their alcohol intake. *Ann. N.Y. Acad. Sci.* **215**, 126–134. [411]

Ainsworth, M.D.S. (1976) Discussion of papers by Suomi and Bowlby. In G. Serban and A. Kling (Eds.), *Animal Models in Human Psychobiology*. Plenum, New York, pp. 37–47. [133, 141]

Akil, H., Madden, J., Patrick, R.L., and Barchas, J.D. (1976a) Stress-induced increase in endogenous opiate peptides: Concurrent analgesia and its partial reversal by naloxone. In H. Kosterlitz (Ed.), *Opiates and Endogenous Opiate Peptides*. Elsevier/North Holland, Amsterdam, pp. 63–70. [359, 360]

Akil, H., Mayer, D.J., and Liebeskind, J.C. (1976b) Antagonism of stimulation-produced analgesia by naloxone, a narcotic antagonist. *Science* **191**, 961–963. [299, 359, 360]

Akil, H., Richardson, J., Hughes, J., and Barchas, J.D. (1978) Enkephalin-like material elevated in ventricular cerebrospinal fluid of pain patients after analgetic focal stimulation. *Science* **201**, 463–465. [359]

Akiskal, H.S. (1979) A biobehavioural approach to depression. In R.A. Depue (Ed.), *The Psychobiology of the Depressive Disorders: Implications for the Effects of Stress*. Academic, New York, pp. 409–437. [139, 141, 391, 401]

Akiskal, H.S. (1980) External validating criteria for psychiatric diagnosis: Their application in affective disorders. *J. Clin. Psychiatr.* **41**(12) (Sec. 2), 6–15. [54, 116]

Akisal, H.S. (1982) Affective disorders. In R. Berkow (Ed.), *Merck Manual of Diagnosis and Therapy*, 14th ed. Merck, Sharp & Dohme, Rahway, N.J., pp. 1448–1462. [400]

Akiskal, H.S. (1983) Dysthymic disorder: Psychopathology of proposed chronic depressive subtypes. *Am. J. Psychiatr.* **140**, 11–20. [57, 58, 394]

Akiskal, H.S. (1984) An integrative view on the etiology and treatment of depression. In J. Korf and L. Pepplinkhuizen (Eds.), *Depression: Molecular and Psychologically Based Therapies*. TGO Foundation, Drachten, pp. 98–111. [391, 394, 395]

Akiskal, H.S. and McKinney, W.T. (1973) Depressive disorders: Toward a unified hypothesis. *Science* **182**, 20–29. [139, 401, 420]

Akiskal, H.S. and McKinney, W.T. (1975) Overview of recent research in depression: Integration of ten conceptual models into a comprehensive clinical frame. *Arch. Gen. Psychiatr.* **32**, 285–305. [139, 394, 401, 420]

Akiskal, H.S. and Tashjian, R. (1983) Affective disorders. II. Recent advances in laboratory and pathogenetic approaches. *Hosp. Commun. Psychiatr.* **34**, 822–830. [392, 401, 417]

Akiskal, H.S., Djenderedjian, A.H., Rosenthal, R.H., and Khani, M.K. (1977) Cyclothymic disorder: Validating criteria for inclusion in the bipolar affective group. *Am. J. Psychiatr.* **134**, 1227–1233. [56]

Akiskal, H.S., Bitar, A.H., Puzantian, V.R., Rosenthal, T.L., and Walker, P.W. (1978) The nosological status of neurotic depression: A prospective three- to four-year follow-up examination in light of the primary-secondary and unipolar-bipolar dichotomies. *Arch. Gen. Psychiatr.* **35**, 756–766. [48, 57, 397, 410]

Akiskal, H.S., Rosenthal, R.H., Rosenthal, T.L., Kashgarian, M., Khani, M.K., and Puzantian, V.H. (1979) Differentiation of primary affective illness from situational, symptomatic and secondary depressions. *Arch. Gen. Psychiatr.* **36**, 635–643. [46–48, 81]

Akiskal, H.S., King, D., Rosenthal, T.L., Robinson, D., and Scott-Strauss, A. (1981) Chronic depressions, Part I. *J. Affect. Disord.* **3**, 297–315. [56, 58, 326]

Akiskal, H.S., Lemmi, H., Yerevanian, B., King, D., and Belluomini, J. (1982) The utility of the REM latency test in psychiatric diagnosis: A study of 81 depressed outpatients. *Psychiatr. Res.* **7**, 101–110. [55]

Akiskal, H.S., Hirschfeld, R.M.A., and Yerevanian, B.I. (1983) The relationship of personality to affective disorders: A critical review. *Arch. Gen. Psychiatr.* **40**, 801–810. [80, 394]

Albert, D.J. and Walsh, M.L. (1982) The inhibitory modulation of agonistic behaviour in the rat brain: A review. *Neurosci. Biobehav. Rev.* **6**, 125–143. [291, 292, 295]

Algeri, S., Ponzio, F., Achilli, G., and Perego, C. (1982) Biochemical effects of nomifensine on catecholaminergic systems: In vivo studies. In E. Costa and G. Racagni (Eds.), *Typical and Atypical Antidepressants: Molecular Mechanisms.* Raven, New York, pp. 219–228. [240]

Alino, J.J.L.-I., Gutierrez, J.L.A., and Iglesias, M.L.M. (1973) Trytophan and amitriptyline in the treatment of depression. A double-blind study. *Int. Pharmacopsychiatr.* **8**, 145–151. [319]

Allen, M.G. (1976) Twin studies of affective illness. *Arch. Gen. Psychiatr.* **33**, 1476–1478. [45]

Alloy, L.B. and Seligman, M.E.P. (1979) On the cognitive component of learned helplessness and depression. In G. Bower (Ed.), *The Psychology of Learning and Motivation,* Vol. 13. Academic, New York, pp. 219–276. [126]

Alpers, H.S. and Himwich, H.E. (1972) The effects of chronic imipramine administration on rat brain levels of serotonin, 5-hydroxyindoleacetic acid, norepinephrine and dopamine. *J. Pharmacol. Exp. Ther.* **180**, 531–538. [334]

Altenor, A., Kay, E., and Richter, M. (1977) The generality of learned helplessness in the rat. *Learn. Motiv.* **8**, 54–61. [122, 129]

Altman, J.H. and Wittenborn, J.R. (1980) Depression-prone personality in women. *J. Abnorm. Psychol.* **89**, 303–308. [74, 399]

Alvarez, A. (1971) *The Savage God: A Study of Suicide.* Weidenfeld & Nicolson, London. [35]

Amaral, D. and Sinnamon, H. (1977) The locus coeruleus: Neurobiology of a central noradrenergic nucleus. *Prog. Neurobiol.* **9**, 147–196. [206]

Amatruda, T., Black, D., KcKenna, T., McCarley, R.W., and Hobson, J.A. (1975) The effects of carbachol injections at brain stem sites. *Brain Res.* **98**, 501–515. [278]

American Psychiatric Association (1980) *DSM III—Diagnostic and Statistical Manual of Psychiatric Disorders,* 3rd ed. American Psychiatric Association, Washington, D.C. [36, 41, 42, 66, 130, 135]

Amin, M.M., Ananth, J.V., Coleman, B.S., Darcourt, G., Farkas, T., Goldstein, B., Lapierre, Y.D., Paykel, E., and Wakelin, J.S. (1984) Fluvoxamine: Antidepressant effects confirmed in a placebo-controlled study. *Clin. Neuropharmacol.* **7**, Suppl. 1, 580–581. [323]

Amir, S. and Amit, Z. (1978) Endogenous opioid ligands may mediate stress-induced changes in the affective properties of pain related behaviour in rats. *Life Sci.* **23**, 1143–1152. [359]

Amsel, A. and Roussel, J. (1952) Motivating properties of frustration. I. Effect on a running response of adding frustration to the motivational complex. *J. Exp. Psychol.* **43**, 363–368. [153]

References

Amsterdam, J.D., Winokur, A., Mendels, J., and Snyder, P. (1979) Distinguishing depression subtypes by thyrotropin response to TRH testing. *Lancet* **2**, 904. [372]

Amsterdam, J.D., Winokur, A., Caroff, S.N., and Conn, J. (1982a) The dexamethasone suppression test in outpatients with primary affective disorder and healthy control subjects. *Am. J. Psychiatr.* **139**, 287–291. [54]

Amsterdam, J.D., Winokur, A., Lucki, I., Snyder, P., Harris, R.I., Caroff, S., and Rickels, K. (1982b) Growth hormone, prolactin and thyrotropin responses to gonadotropin releasing hormone in depressed patients and healthy volunteers. *Psychoneuroendocrinology* **7**, 177–184. [166]

Anand, B.K. and Brobeck, J.R. (1951) Localization of a feeding center in the hypothalamus of the rat. *Proc. Soc. Exp. Biol. Med.* **77**, 323–324 [151]

Anden, N.-E. and Grabowska, M. (1976) Pharmacological evidence for a stimulation of dopamine neurons by noradrenaline neurons in the brain. *Eur. J. Pharmacol.* **39**, 275–282. [376]

Anden, N.-E., Strombom, U., and Svensson, T.H. (1973) Dopamine and noradrenaline receptor stimulation: Reversal of reserpine-induced suppression of motor activity. *Psychopharmacology* **29**, 289–298. [9]

Anden, N.-E., Grabowska, M., and Strombom, U. (1976) Different alpha-adrenoreceptors in the central nervous system mediating biochemical and functional effects of clonidine and receptor blocking agents. Naunyn Schmiedebergs Arch. Pharmacol. **292**, 43–52. [227, 243]

Andersen, E. and Dafny, D. (1982) An ascending serotonergic pathway modulates noxious input to the thalamus. In B.T. Ho, J.C. Schoolar, and E. Usdin (Eds.), *Serotonin in Biological Psychiatry*. Raven, New York, pp. 313–314. [298]

Anderson, D.C., Cole, J., and McVaugh, W. (1968) Variations in unsignalled inescapable preshock as determinants of responses to punishment. *J. Comp. Physiol. Psychol.* **65**, (Monog. Suppl.), 1–17. [123]

Anderson, P.W. (1972) More is different: Broken symmetry and the nature of the hierarchical structure of science. *Science* **177**, 393–396. [25, 26]

Andreasen, N.C. and Grove, W.M. (1982) The classification of depression: Traditional versus mathematical approaches. *Am. J. Psychiatr.* **139**, 45–52. [51, 52, 57]

Aneshensel, C.S. and Stone, J.D. (1982) Stress and depression: A test of the buffering model of social support. *Arch. Gen. Psychiatr.* **39**, 1392–1396. [393, 396, 411]

Angelucci, L., Pattocchioli, F.R., Bohus, B., and De Kloet, R. (1982) Serotonergic innervation and glucocorticoid binding in the hippocampus: Relevance to depression. In E. Costa and G. Racagni (Eds.), *Typical and Atypical Antidepressants: Molecular Mechanisms*. Raven, New York, pp. 365–370. [384]

Angst, J. (1966) *Zur Aetiologie und Nosologie endogener depressiver Psychosen* (Monographien aus dem Gesamtgebiete der Neurologie und Psychiatrie, No. 112). Springer, Heidelberg. [45]

Angst, J., Koukkou, M., Bleuler-Herzog, M., and Martens, H. (1974) Ergebnisse eines offenen und einen Doppelblindversuches von Nomifensin im Vergleich zu Imipramin. *Arch. Psychiatr. Nervenkr.* **219**, 265–276. [173]

Angst, J., Woggon, B., and Schoepf, J. (1977) The treatment of depression with 1-5-hydroxytryptophan versus imipramine. *Arch. Psychiatr. Nervenkr.* **224**, 175–186. [321]

Angst, J., Autenrieth, V., Brem, F., Koukkou, M., Meyer, H., Stassen, H.H., and Storck, U. (1979) Preliminary results of treatment with beta-endorphin in depression. In E. Usdin and W.E. Bunney (Eds.), *Endorphins in Mental Health Research*. Oxford University Press, New York, pp. 518–528. [366]

Angyan, L. (1974) Sleep induced by hypothalamic self-stimulation in cat. *Physiol. Behav.* **12**, 697–701. [304]

Anisman, H. (1973) Cholinergic mechanisms and alterations in behavioral suppression as factors producing time dependent changes in avoidance performance. *J. Comp. Physiol. Psychol.* **83,** 465–477. [277]

Anisman, H. (1975) Time-dependent variations in aversively motivated behaviors: Non-associative effects of cholinergic and catecholaminergic activity. *Psychol. Rev.* **82,** 359–385. [274]

Anisman, H. and Bignami, G. (1978) A comparative neurochemical, pharmacological, and functional analysis of aversively motivated behaviors. In H. Anisman and G. Bignami (Eds.), *Psychopharmacology of Aversively Motivated Behaviours.* Plenum, New York, pp. 487–512. [274]

Anisman, H. and Kokkinidis, L. (1974) Effects of central and peripheral adrenergic and cholinergic modification on time-dependent processes in avoidance performance. *Behav. Biol.* **10,** 161–171. [277]

Anisman, H. and Sklar, L.S. (1979) Catecholamine depletion in mice upon reexposure to stress: Mediation of the escape deficits produced by uncontrollable shock. *J. Comp. Physiol. Psychol.* **93,** 610–625. [141, 209, 210, 213, 214, 275, 384]

Anisman, H. and Waller, T.G. (1973a) Footshock produced excitation and inhibition of activity in rats. *Anim. Learn. Behav.* **1,** 93–95. [277]

Anisman, H. and Waller, T.G. (1973b) Effects of inescapable shock on subsequent avoidance learning: Role of response repertoire changes. *Behav. Biol.* **9,** 331–355. [277]

Anisman, H. and Zacharko, R.M. (1982) Depression: The predisposing influence of stress. *Behav. Brain Sci.* **5,** 89–137. [101, 131, 179, 397]

Anisman, H., Irwin, J., and Sklar, L.S. (1979a) Deficits of escape performance following catecholamine depletion: Implications for behavioural deficits induced by uncontrollable stress. *Psychopharmacology* **64,** 163–170. [125, 129, 157, 209, 211, 212, 289]

Anisman, H., Remington, G., and Sklar, L.S. (1979b) Effects of inescapable shock on subsequent escape performance. Catecholaminergic and cholinergic mediation of response initiation and maintenance. *Psychopharmacology* **61,** 107–124. [122, 125, 129, 157, 211, 212, 290, 360]

Anisman, H., Pizzino, A., and Sklar, L.S. (1980a) Coping with stress, norepinephrine depletion and escape performance. *Brain Res.* **191,** 583–588. [208, 209]

Anisman, H., Suissa, A., and Sklar, L.S. (1980b) Escape deficits induced by uncontrollable stress: Antagonism by dopamine and noradrenaline agonists. *Behav. Neural Biol.* **28,** 34–47. [157, 211]

Anisman, H., Glazier, S.J., and Sklar, L.S. (1981) Cholinergic influences on escape deficits produced by uncontrollable stress. *Psychopharmacology* **74,** 81–87. [270, 360]

Anlezark, G.M., Crow, T.J., and Greenaway, A.P. (1973) Impaired learning and decreased cortical norepinephrine after bilateral locus coeruleus lesions. *Science* **181,** 682–684. [200]

Ansel, R.D. and Markham, C.H. (1970) Effects of l-dopa in normal humans. In A. Barbeau and F.H. McDowell (Eds.), *L-Dopa and Parkinsonism.* F.A. Davis, Philadelphia, pp. 69–71. [172]

Antelman, S.M. and Caggiula, A.R. (1976) Norepinephrine-dopamine interactions and behavior. *Science* **195,** 646–653. [178, 196, 376, 377]

Antelman, S.M. and Chiodo, L.A. (1984) Stress-induced sensitization: A framework for viewing the effects of ECS and other antidepressants. In B. Lerer, R.D. Weiner, and R.H. Belmaker (Eds.), *ECT: Basic Mechanisms.* John Libbey, London, pp. 28–32. [412]

Antelman, S.M., Chiodo, L.A., and DeGiovanni, L.A. (1982) Antidepressants and dopamine autoreceptors: Implications for both a novel means of treating depression and understanding bipolar illness. In E. Costa and G. Racagni (Eds.), *Typical and Atypical Antidepressants: Molecular Mechanisms.* Raven, New York, pp. 121–132. [184, 191]

Antin, J., Gibbs, G., Holt, J., Young, R.C., and Smith, G.P. (1975) Cholecystokinin elicits the complete behavioural sequence of satiety in rats. *J. Comp. Physiol. Psychol.* **89**, 784–790. [303, 304]

Apfelbaum, M. and Mandenoff, A. (1981) Naltrexone suppresses hyperphagia induced in the rat by a highly palatable diet. *Pharmacol. Biochem. Behav.* **15**, 89–91. [362]

Aprison, M.H. and Ferster, C.B. (1961) Neurochemical correlates of behavior. I. Quantitative measurements of the behavioral effects of the serotonin precursor, 5-hydroxytryptophan. *J. Pharmacol. Exp. Ther.* **131**, 100–107. [300]

Aprison, M.H. and Hintgen, J.N. (1966) Neurochemical correlates of behavior. V. Differential effects of drugs on approach and avoidance behavior in rats with related changes in brain serotonin and noradrenaline. *Rec. Adv. Biol. Psychiatr.* **8**, 87–100. [300, 301]

Aprison, M.H. and Hintgen, J.N. (1970) Evidence of a central cholinergic mechanism functioning during drug-induced excitation in avoidance behavior. In E. Heilbron and A. Winter (Eds.), *Drugs and Cholinergic Mechanisms in the CNS.* Forsvarets Forskning-Sansalt, Stockholm, pp. 543–560. [276]

Aprison, M.H., Kariya, T., Hintgen, J., and Toru, M. (1968) Changes in acetylcholine, norepinephrine and 5-hydroxytryptamine concentrations in several discrete brain areas of the rat during behavioral excitation. *Neurochemistry* **15**, 1131–1139. [276]

Aprison, M.H., Hintgen, J.A., and McBride, W.J. (1975) Serotonergic and cholinergic mechanisms during disruption of approach and avoidance behavior. *Fed. Proc.* **24**, 1813–1822. [270]

Aprison, M.H., Takahashi, R., and Tachiki, K. (1978) Hypersensitive serotonergic receptors involved in clinical depression—A theory. In B. Haber and M.H. Aprison (Eds.), *Neuropharmacology and Behavior,* Plenum, New York, pp. 23–53. [17, 327, 328, 418]

Aprison, M.H., Hintgen, J.N., and Nagayama, H. (1982) Testing a new theory of depression with an animal model: Neurochemical-behavioral evidence for postsynaptic serotonergic receptor involvement. In S.Z. Langer, R. Takahashi, T. Segawa, and M. Briley (Eds.), *New Vistas in Depression.* Pergamon, New York, pp. 171–178. [111, 300, 301, 307, 313, 327, 328, 331, 351]

Arana, G., Boyd, A.E., Reichlin, S., and Lipsitt, D. (1977) Prolactin levels in mild depression. *Psychosom. Med.* **39**, 193–197. [166]

Arbilla, S. and Langer, S.Z. (1978) Morphine and beta-endorphin inhibit release of noradrenaline from cerebral cortex but not of dopamine from rat striatum. *Nature* **271**, 559–560. [361]

Archer, T. (1982) Serotonin and fear retention in the rat. *J. Comp. Physiol. Psychol.* **96**, 491–516. [295]

Arendt, J., Ho, A.K., Laud, C., Marston, A., Nohria, V., Smith, J.A., and Symons, A.M. (1981) Differential effect of benserazide (Ro4-4602) on the concentration of indoleamines in rat pineal and hypothalamus. *Br. J. Pharmacol.* **72**, 257–262. [301]

Arieti, S. and Bemporad, J.R. (1980) The psychological organization of depression. *Am. J. Psychiatr.* **137**, 1360–1365. [73, 124, 392]

Asakura, M., Tsukamoto, T., and Hasegawa, K. (1982) Modulation of rat brain alpha$_2$- and beta-adrenergic receptor sensitivity following long-term treatment with antidepressants. *Brain Res.* **235**, 192–197. [247, 257]

Asarch, K.B., Shih, J.C., and Kubesar, A. (1981) Decreased ^{3}H-imipramine binding in depressed males and females. *Commun. Psychopharmacol.* **4**, 425–432. [316]

Asberg, M. and Traskman, L. (1981) Studies of CSF 5-HIAA in depression and suicidal behavior. *Adv. Exp. Med. Biol.* **133**, 739–752. [311, 312]

Asberg, M., Bertilsson, L., Tuck, D., Cronholm, B., and Sjoqvist, F. (1973) Indoleamine metabolites in the cerebrospinal fluid of depressed patients before and during treatment with nortriptyline. *Clin. Pharmacol. Ther.* **14**, 277–286. [310, 323, 329, 333]

Asberg, M., Ringberger, V.A., Sjoqvist, F., Thoren, P., Traskman, L., and Tuck, R.J. (1975) Monoamine metabolites in cerebrospinal fluid and serotonin uptake inhibition during treatment with chlorimipramine. *Clin. Pharmacol. Ther.* **21**, 201–207. [251, 333]

Asberg, M., Thoren, P., Traskman, L., Bertilsson, L., and Ringberger, V. (1976a) 'Serotonin depression': A biochemical subgroup within the affective disorders? *Science* **191**, 478–480. [310]

Asberg, M., Traskman, L., and Thoren, P. (1976b) 5-HIAA in the cerebrospinal fluid: A biochemical suicide predictor? *Arch. Gen. Psychiatr.* **33**, 1193–1197. [311, 312]

Asberg, M., Bertilsson, L., Rydin, E., Schalling, D., Thoren, P., and Traskman-Bendz, L. (1980) Monoamine metabolites in cerebrospinal fluid in relation to depressive illness, suicidal behavior and personality. In B. Angrist, G.D. Burrows, M. Lader, O. Lingjaerde, G. Sedvall, and D. Wheatley (Eds.), *Recent Advances in Neuropsychopharmacology*. Pergamon, New York, pp. 257–271. [312]

Ashcroft, G.W. and Sharman, D.F. (1960) 5-hydroxyindoles in human cerebrospinal fluid. *Nature* **186**, 1050–1051. [10, 309, 311]

Ashcroft, G.W., Crawford, T.B.B., Eccleston, D., Sharman, D.F., McDougall, E.J., Stanton, J.B., and Binns, J.K. (1966) 5-hydroxyindole compounds in the cerebrospinal fluid of patients with psychiatric or neurological disease. *Lancet* **2**, 1049–1052. [10, 311, 312, 334]

Ashcroft, G.W., Blackburn, I.M., Eccleston, D., Glen, A.I.M., Hartley, W., Kinloch, N.E., Lonergan, M., Murray, L.G., and Pullar, I.A. (1973) Changes on recovery in the concentrations of tryptophan and the biogenic amine metabolites in the cerebrospinal fluid of patients with affective illness. *Psychol. Med.* **3**, 319–325. [309, 311]

Askew, B.M. (1963) A simple screening procedure for imipramine-like anti-depressant drugs. *Life Sci.* **2**, 725–730. [110]

Asnis, G. (1977) Parkinson's disease, depression and ECT: A review and case study. *Am. J. Psychiatr.* **134**, 191–195. [170]

Asnis, G.M., Nathan, R.S., Halbreich, U., Halpern, F.S. and Sachar, E.J. (1980a) Prolactin changes in major depressive disorders. *Am. J. Psychiatr.* **137**, 1117–1118. [187]

Asnis, G.M., Nathan, R.S., Halbreich, U., Halpern, F.S., and Sachar, E.J. (1980b) TRH tests in depression. *Lancet* **1**, 424–425. [372]

Asnis, G.M., Sachar, E.J., Halbreich, U., Nathan, R.S., Ostrow, L., Soloman, M., and Halpern, F.S. (1981) Endocrine responses to thyrotropin-releasing hormone in major depressive disorder. *Psychiatr. Res.* **5**, 205–215. [315, 372]

Asnis, G.M., Halbreich, U., Sachar, E.J., Nathan, R.S., Ostrow, L.C., Novacenko, H., Davis, M., Endicott, J., and Puig-Antoch, J. (1983) Plasma cortisol secretion and REM period latency in adult endogenous depression. *Am. J. Psychiatr.* **140**, 750–753. [55]

Aston-Jones, G. and Bloom, F.E. (1981a) Activity of norepinephrine-containing locus coeruleus neurons in behaving rats anticipates fluctuations in the sleep-waking cycle. *J. Neurosci.* **1**, 876–886. [198, 206, 377]

Aston-Jones, G. and Bloom, F.E. (1981b) Norepinephrine-containing locus coeruleus neurons in behaving rats exhibit pronounced responses to non-noxious environmental stimuli. *J. Neurosci.* **1**, 887–900. [198, 206]

Atrens, D.M., Ljundberg, T., and Ungerstedt, U. (1976) Modulation of reward and aversion processes in the rat diencephalon by neuroleptics: Differential effects of clozapine and haloperidol. *Psychopharmacology* **49**, 97–100. [150]

Atterwill, C.K. (1980) Lack of effect of repeated electroconvulsive shock on ³H-spiroperidol and ³H-5HT binding and cholinergic parameters in rat brain. *J. Neurochem.* **35**, 729–734. [188, 190, 285, 347, 356, 357]

Atterwill, C.K. (1984) The effects of electroconvulsive shock on central cholinergic and inter-related neurotransmitter systems. In B. Lerer, R.D. Weiner, and R.H. Belmaker (Eds.), *ECT: Basic Mechanisms*. John Libbey, London, pp. 79–88. [285]

Avery, D.H., Wilson, L.G., and Dunner, D.L. (1983) Diagnostic subtypes of depression as predictors of therapeutic response. In P.J. Clayton and J.E. Barrett (Eds.), *Treatment of Depression: Old Controversies and New Approaches*. Raven, New York, pp. 193–205. [46, 57]

Ayd, F.J. and Blackwell, B., eds. (1970) *Discoveries in Biological Psychiatry*. Lippincott, Philadelphia. [3]

Azmitia, E.C. (1978) The serotonin-producing neurons of the midbrain median and dorsal Raphe nuclei. In L.L. Iversen, S.D. Iversen, and S.H. Snyder (Eds.), *Handbook of Psychopharmacology*, Vol. 9, Plenum, New York, pp. 233–314. [288, 378]

Azmitia, E.C. and McEwen, B.S. (1974) Adrenalcortical influence on rat brain tryptophan hydroxylase activity. *Brain Res.* **78**, 291–302. [299]

Babington, R.G. (1975) Antidepressives and the kindling effect. In S. Fielding and H. Lal (Eds.), *Antidepressants*. Futura, Mount Kisco, N.Y., pp. 113–124. [108]

Babington, R.G. (1981) Neurophysiologic techniques and antidepressive activity. In S.J. Enna, J.B. Malick, and E. Richelson (Eds.), *Antidepressants: Neurochemical, Behavioral and Clinical Perspectives*. Raven, New York, pp. 157–173. [108]

Babington, R.G., and Wedeking, P.W. (1973) The pharmacology of seizures induced by sensitization with low intensity brain stimulation. *Pharm. Biochem. Behav.* **1**, 461–467. [108]

Bainbridge, P.L. (1973) Learning in the rat: Effect of early experience with an unsolvable problem. *J. Comp. Physiol. Psychol.* **82**, 301–307. [122]

Bajada, S. (1982) A trial of choline chloride and physostigmine in Alzheimer's dementia. In S. Corkin, K. Davis, J. Growden, E. Usdin, and R. Wurtman (Eds.), *Alzheimer's Disease: A Report of Progress*. Raven, New York, pp. 427–432. [281]

Baker, A.G. (1976) Learned irrelevance and learned helplessness: rats learn that stimuli, reinforcers and responses are uncorrelated. *J. Exp. Psychol.: Anim. Behav. Proc.* **2**, 130–142. [125, 158]

Baldessarini, R.J. (1975a) An overview of the basis for amine hypotheses in affective illness. In J. Mendels (Ed.), *The Psychobiology of Depression*. Spectrum, Hampton, Va., pp. 69–83. [10]

Baldessarini, R.J. (1975b) Release of catecholamines. In L.L. Iversen, S.D. Iversen, and S.H. Snyder (Eds.), *Handbook of Psychopharmacology*, Vol. 3. Plenum, New York, pp. 37–137. [189]

Balldin, J. (1981) Experimental and clinical studies on neuroendocrine and behavioral effects of electroconvulsive therapy. Reports from the Departments of Psychiatry and Neurochemistry, St Jorgens Hospital, University of Goteborg, Sweden. [187]

Balldin, J., Bolles, P., Eden, S., Eriksson, E., and Modigh, K. (1980a) Effects of electroconvulsive treatment on growth hormone secretion induced by monoamine receptor agonists in reserpine-pretreated rats. *Psychoneuroendocrinology* **5**, 329–337. [165, 186, 252, 338]

Balldin, J., Eden, S., Granerus, A.-K., Modigh, K., Svanborg, A., Walinder, J., and Wallin, L. (1980) Electroconvulsive therapy in Parkinson's disease with 'on-off' phenomena. *J. Neural Trans.* **47**, 11–21. [181]

Balldin, J., Granerus, A.-K., Lindstedt, G., Modigh, K., and Walinder, J. (1981) Predictors for improvement after electroconvulsive therapy in Parkinsonian patients with on-off symptoms. *J. Neural Trans.* **52**, 199–211. [181]

Balldin, J., Granerus, A.-K., Lindstedt, G., Modigh, K., and Walinder, J. (1982) Neuro-endocrine evidence for increased responsiveness of dopamine receptors in humans following electroconvulsive therapy. *Psychopharmacology* **76**, 371–376. [186, 187]

Ballenger, J.C. and Post, R.M. (1980) Carbamazepine in manic-depressive illness: A new treatment. *Am. J. Psychiatr.* **137**, 782–790. [355, 356]

Ballenger, J.C., Goodwin, F.K., Major, L.F., and Brown, G.C. (1979) Alcohol and central serotonin metabolism in man. *Arch. Gen. Psychiatr.* **36**, 224–227. [312]

Ballenger, J.C., Post, R.M., and Goodwin, F.K. (1981) Neurochemistry of cerebrospinal fluid in normal individuals: Relationship between biological and psychological variables. In J.H. Wood (Ed.), *The Neurobiology of Cerebrospinal Fluid,* Vol. 2. Plenum, New York, pp. 143–155. [223]

Baltzer, V. and Weiskrantz, L. (1973) Antidepressant agents and reversal of diurnal activity cycles in the rat. *Biol. Psychiatr.* **10**, 199–209. [115]

Ban, T.A. (1969) The use of amphetamines in adult psychiatry. *Semin. Psychiatr.* **1**, 129–143. [11, 173, 233]

Banerjee, S.P., Kung, L.S., Riggi, S.J., and Chanda, S.K. (1977) Development of beta-adrenergic subsensitivity by antidepressants. *Nature* **268**, 455–456. [15, 257]

Banki, C.M. (1977a) Correlation between cerebrospinal fluid amine metabolites and psychomotor activity in affective disorders. *J. Neurochem.* **28**, 255–257. [167, 168, 311, 312]

Banki, C.M. (1977b) Correlation of anxiety and related symptoms with cerebrospinal fluid 5-hydroxyindoleacetic acid in depressed women. *J. Neural Trans.* **41**, 135–143. [311, 312]

Banki, C.M. and Arato, M. (1983) Amine metabolites and neuroendocrine responses related to depression and suicide. *J. Affect. Disord.* **5**, 223–232. [311, 312, 314, 372]

Banki, C.M. and Molnar, G. (1981) Cerebrospinal fluid 5-hydroxyindoleacetic acid as an index of central serotonergic processes. *Psychiatr. Res.* **5**, 23–32. [310]

Banki, C.M., Vojnik, M., and Molnar, G. (1981a) Cerebrospinal fluid amine metabolites, tryptophan and clinical parameters in depression. I. Background variables. *J. Affect. Disord.* **3**, 81–89. [168, 312]

Banki, C.M., Molnar, G., and Vojnik, M. (1981b) Cerebrospinal fluid amine metabolites, tryptophan and clinical parameters in depression. II. Psychopathological symptoms. *J. Affect. Disord.* **3**, 91–99. [168, 312]

Bannister, D. and Mair, J.M.M. (1968) *The Evaluation of Personal Constructs.* Academic, New York. [27]

Bannon, M.J., Bunney, S.D., Zigun, J.R., Skirboll, L.R., and Roth, R.H. (1980) Presynaptic dopamine receptors: Insensitivity to kainic acid and the development of supersensitivity following chronic haloperidol. *Naunyn Schmiedebergs Arch. Pharmacol.* **312**, 161–165. [185]

Baraban, J.M. and Aghajanian, G.K. (1980) Suppression of firing activity of 5-HT neurons in the dorsal raphe by alpha-adrenoceptor antagonists. *Neuropharmacology* **19**, 355–363. [377]

Baraban, J.M. and Aghajanian, G.K. (1981) Noradrenergic innervation of serotonergic neurons in the dorsal raphe: Demonstration by electron microscopic autoradiography. *Brain Res.* **204**, 1–11. [377]

Barbaccia, M.L., Brunello, N., Chuang, D.M., and Costa, E. (1983) On the mode of action of imipramine: Relationship between serotonergic axon terminal function and down-regulation of beta-adrenergic receptors. *Neuropharmacology* **22**, 373–383. [259, 330, 332, 346, 348, 349]

Barnett, A. and Taber, R.I. (1971) Antidepressant agents. In R.A. Turner and P. Hebborn (Eds.), *Screening Methods in Pharmacology.* Academic, New York, pp. 209–226. [110]

Barnett, A., Taber, R.I., and Roth, R.E. (1969) Activity of antihistamines in laboratory antidepressant tests. *Int. J. Pharmacol.* **8**, 73–79. [107]

Barnett, M.J. and Cantor, S. (1968) Observation on the hypotensive action of catapres (St155) in man. *Med. J. Aust.* **55**, 87–91. [231]

Barr, H.L., Langs, R.J., Holt, R.R., Goldberger, L., and Klein, G.S. (1972) *LSD: Personality and Experience.* Wiley-Interscience, New York. [21]

Barrett, R.J. and White, D.K. (1980) Reward system depression following chronic amphetamine: Antagonism by haloperidol. *Pharmacol. Biochem. Behav.* **13**, 555–559. [134, 135, 150]

Barry, H. and Miller, N.E. (1965) Comparison of drug effects on approach, avoidance, and escape motivation. *J. Comp. Physiol. Psychol.* **59**, 18–24. [156]

Bartholini, G., Stadler, H., and Lloyd, K.G. (1973) Cholinergic-dopaminergic relation in different brain structures. In E. Usdin and S.H. Snyder (Eds.), *Frontiers in Catecholamine Research.* Pergamon, New York, pp. 741–745. [379]

Bartlett, P. and Paillard, P. (1974) Étude clinique du 5-hydroxytryptophane dans les états depressifs du troisième age. *Cah. Med. Lyonnais* **50**, 1895–1901. [320]

Bates, D., Weinshilboum, R.M., Campbell, R.J., and Sundt, T.M. (1977) The effects of lesions in the locus coeruleus on the physiological responses of the cerebral blood vessels in cats. *Brain Res.* **136**, 431–443. [199]

Baumann, P.A. and Maitre, L. (1977) Blockade of presynaptic alpha-receptors and of amine uptake in the rat brain by the antidepressant mianserin. *Naunyn Schmiedebergs Arch. Pharmacol.* **300**, 31–37. [240]

Baxter, B.L., Gluckman, M.I., and Scerni, R. (1973) Differential self-injection behavior produced by fenfluramine versus other appetite inhibiting drugs. *Fed. Proc.* **32**, 754. [302]

Bayliss, L.E. (1966) *Living Control Systems.* English Universities Press, London. [414]

Bear, D.M. and Fedio, P. (1977) Quantitative analysis of interictal behaviour in temporal lobe epilepsy. *Arch. Neurol.* **34**, 454–467. [92]

Beavan, M.A. (1976) Histamine (Parts 1 and 2). *New Engl. J. Med.* **294**, 30–36, 320–330. [368]

Bech, P. (1981) Rating scales for affective disorders: Their validity and consistency. *Acta Psychiatr. Scand.* **65**, Suppl. 295. [51]

Bech, P. (1984) Citalopram versus clomipramine: A controlled clinical study. *Clin. Neuropharmacol.* **7**, Suppl. 1, 876–877. [324]

Beck, A.T. (1967) *Depression: Clinical, Experimental and Theoretical Aspects.* Harper & Row, New York. [71, 72, 76, 79, 394]

Beck, A.T. (1974) The development of depression: A cognitive model. In R.J. Friedman and M.M. Katz (Eds.), *The Psychology of Depression: Contemporary Theory and Research.* Wiley, New York, pp. 3–20. [71, 72, 79]

Beck, A.T. (1983) Cognitive therapy of depression: New perspectives. In P.J. Clayton and J.E. Barrett (Eds.), *Treatment of Depression: Old Controversies and New Approaches.* Raven, New York, pp. 265–290. [81, 82, 124, 404, 405]

Beck, A.T. and Harrison, R.P. (1982) Stress, neurochemical substrates and depression: Concomitants are not necessarily causes. *Behav. Brain Sci.* **5**, 101–102. [131]

Becker, A.L. (1971) A new adjunct to the treatment and management of depression: Intravenous infusion of chlorimipramine (Anafranil). *S. Afr. Med. J.* **45**, 168–170. [12]

Becker, H.S. (1953) Becoming a marihuana user. *Am. J. Sociol.* **59**, 235–242. [28]

Becker, J. (1979) Vulnerable self-esteem as a predisposing factor in depressive disorders. In R.A. Depue (Ed.), *The Psychobiology of the Depressive Disorders: Implications for the Effects of Stress.* Academic, New York, pp. 317–334. [72, 73]

Beckman, H. and Goodwin, F.K. (1975) Antidepressant response to tricyclics and urinary MHPG in unipolar patients: Clinical response to imipramine or amitriptyline. *Arch. Gen. Psychiatr.* **32**, 17–21. [233, 235, 250, 251]

Beckman, H. and Goodwin, F.K. (1980) Urinary MHPG in subgroups of depressed patients and normal controls. *Neuropsychobiology* **6**, 91–100. [223, 225, 226]

Beckman, H. and Moise, H.-W. (1982) The cholinolytic biperiden in depression: An acute placebo-controlled study. *Arch. Psychiatr. Nervenkr.* **231**, 213–220. [283]

Beckman, H. and Murphy, D.L. (1977) Phenelzine in depressed patients: Effects on urinary MHPG excretion in relation to clinical response. *Neuropsychobiology* **3**, 49–55. [251]

Beckman, H., Van Kammen, D.P., Goodwin, F.K., and Murphy, D.L. (1976) Urinary excretion of 3-methoxy-4-hydroxyphenylglycol in depressed patients: Modifications by amphetamine and lithium. *Biol. Psychiatr.* **11**, 377–387. [226, 233]

Beer, B. and Lenard, L.G. (1975) Differential effects of intraventricular administration of 6-hydroxydopamine on behavior of rats in approach and avoidance procedures: Reversal of avoidance decrements by diazepam. *Pharmacol. Biochem. Behav.* **3**, 879–886. [156]

Beigel, A. and Murphy, D.L. (1971) Unipolar and bipolar affective illness: Differences in clinical characteristics accompanying depression. *Arch. Gen. Psychiatr.* **24**, 215–220. [46, 168, 177]

Bein, H.J. (1982) Rauwolfia and biological psychiatry. *Trends Neurosci.* **4**, 37–39. [3, 168]

Belcher, G., Ryall, R.W., and Schaffner, R. (1978) The differential effects of 5-hydroxytryptamine, noradrenaline and raphe stimulation on nociceptive and non-nociceptive dorsal horn interneurones in the cat. *Brain Res.* **151**, 307–321. [298]

Belenky, G.L. and Holaday, J.W. (1980) Repeated electroconvulsive shock (ECS) and morphine tolerance: Demonstration of cross-sensitivity in the rat. *Life Sci.* **29**, 553–563. [367]

Bellack, A.S., Hersen, M., and Himmelhoch, J.M. (1981) Social skills training, pharmacotherapy and psychotherapy for unipolar depression. *Am. J. Psychiatr.* **138**, 1562–1567. [411]

Bellack, A.S., Hersen, M., and Himmelhoch, J.M. (1983) A comparison of social skills training, pharmacotherapy and psychotherapy for depression. *Behav. Res. Ther.* **21**, 101–107. [411]

Belluzi, J.D. and Stein, L. (1978) Do enkephalin systems mediate drive reduction? *Soc. Neurosci. Abstr.* **4**, 405. [362]

Belmaker, R.H., Ebbesen, K., Ebstein, R., and Rimon, R. (1976) Platelet monoamine oxidase in schizophrenia and manic-depressive illness. *Br. J. Psychiatr.* **129**, 227–232. [221]

Belmaker, R.H., Lerer, B., and Zohar, J. (1982) Salbutamol treatment of depression. In E. Costa and G. Racagni (Eds.), *Typical and Atypical Antidepressants: Clinical Practice,* Raven, New York, pp. 181–193. [232]

Belmaker, R.H., Lerer, B., Klein, E., Newman, M., and Dick, E. (1983) Clinical implications of research on the mechanism of action of lithium. *Prog. Neuropsychopharmacol.* **7**, 287–296. [256]

Beninger, R.J. (1983) The role of dopamine in locomotor activity and learning. *Brain Res. Rev.* **6**, 173–196. [153, 154, 156, 158]

Beninger, R.J. and Phillips, A.G. (1979) Possible involvement of serotonin in extinction. *Pharmacol. Biochem. Behav.* **10**, 37–42. [295]

Beninger, R.J. and Phillips, A.G. (1980) The effect of pimozide on the establishment of conditioned reinforcement. *Psychopharmacol.* **68**, 147–153. [153]

Beninger, R.J. and Phillips, A.G. (1981) The effect of pimozide during pairing on the transfer of classical conditioning to an operant discrimination. *Pharmacol. Biochem. Behav.* **14**, 101–105. [153, 154]

Beninger, R.J., MacLennan, A.J., and Pinel, J.P.J. (1980a) The use of conditioned defensive burying to test the effects of pimozide on associative learning. *Pharmacol. Biochem. Behav.* **12**, 445–448. [156]

Beninger, R.J., Mason, S.T., Phillips, A.G., and Fibiger, H.C. (1980b) The use of conditioned suppression to evaluate the nature of neuroleptic-induced avoidance deficits. *J. Pharm. Exp. Ther.* **213**, 623–627. [156]

Beninger, R.J., Mason, S.T., Phillips, A.G., and Fibiger, H.C. (1980c) The use of extinction to investigate the nature of neuroleptic-induced avoidance deficits. *Psychopharmacology* **69**, 11–18. [156]

Beninger, R.J., Phillips, A.G., and Fibiger, H.C. (1983) Prior training and intermittent retraining attenuate pimozide-induced avoidance deficits. *Pharmacol. Biochem. Behav.* **18**, 619–624. [156]

Benkert, O., Renz, A., Marano, C., and Matussek, N. (1971) Altered tyrosine daytime plasma levels in endogenous depression. *Arch. Gen. Psychiatr.* **25**, 359–363. [164, 222]

Benkert, O., Gordon, A., and Martschke, D. (1974) The comparison of thyrotropin releasing hormone, luteinizing hormone releasing hormone and placebo in depressive patients using a double-blind crossover technique. *Psychopharmacology* **40**, 191–198. [373]

Bennett, J.P. and Aghajanian, G.K. (1974) d-LSD binding to brain homogenates: Possible relationship to serotonin receptors. *Life Sci.* **15**, 1935–1944. [345]

Bennett, J.P. and Snyder, S.H. (1976) Serotonin and lysergic acid diethylamide binding in rat brain membranes: relationship to postsynaptic serotonin receptors. *Mol. Pharmacol.* **12**, 373–389. [344]

Berger, M., Doerr, P., Lund, R., Bronisch, T., and von Zerssen, D. (1982a) Neuroendocrinological and neurophysiological studies in major depressive disorders: Are there biological markers for the endogenous subtype? *Biol. Psychiatr.* **17**, 1217–1242. [53–55, 237]

Berger, M., Lund, R., Raonisch, T., and von Zerssen, D. (1982b) Der Einfluss eines Cholinergikums auf den REM-Schlaf gesunder Probanden und depressiver Patienten. In H. Beckman (Ed.), *Fortschritte Psychiatrischer Forschung*. Huber, Bern, pp. 323–327. [280]

Berger, P.A., Faull, K.F., Kilkowski, J., Anderson, P.J., Kraemer, H., Davis, K.L., and Barchas, J.D. (1980) CSF monoamine metabolites in depression and schizophrenia. *Am. J. Psychiatr.* **137**, 174–180. [167, 222, 310, 311]

Bergstrom, D.A. and Kellar, K.J. (1979a) Effect of electroconvulsive shock on monoaminergic receptor binding sites in rat brain. *Nature* **278**, 464–466. [190, 247, 255, 257, 347]

Bergstrom, D.A. and Kellar, K.J. (1979b) Adrenergic and serotonergic receptor binding in rat brain after chronic desmethylimipramine treatment. *J. Pharmacol. Exp. Ther.* **209**, 256–261. [257, 347]

Bergstrom, D.A., Treiser, S., and Kellar, K.J. (1978) Electroconvulsive shock and reserpine: Effects on monoaminergic receptor binding in rat brain. In E. Usdin and I.J. Kopin (Eds.), *Catecholamines: Basic and Clinical Frontiers*. Pergamon, New York, pp. 1786–1788. [190]

Bernasconi, R. (1982) The GABA hypothesis of affective illness: Influence of clinically effective anti-manic drugs on GABA turnover. In H.M. Emrich, J.B. Aldenhoff, and H.D. Lux (Eds.), *Basic Mechanisms in the Action of Lithium*. Excerpta Medica, Amsterdam, pp. 183–192. [356]

Bernasconi, R. and Martin, P. (1979) Effects of antiepileptic drugs on the GABA turnover rate. *Arch. Pharmacol.* **307**, 251. [355]

Bernstein, I.L. (1975) Relationship between activity, rest, and free feeding in rats. *J. Comp. Physiol. Psychol.* **89**, 253–257. [303]

Berrettini, W.H., Nurnberger, J.I., Hare, T., Gershon, E.S., and Post, R.M. (1982a) Plasma and CSF GABA in affective illness. *Brit. J. Psychiatr.* **141**, 483–487. [355]

Berrettini, W., Nurnberger, J., Post, R., and Gershon, E.S. (1982b) Platelet ^{3}H-imipramine binding in euthymic bipolar patients. *Psychiatr. Res.* **7**, 215–219. [316]

Bertilsson, L., Asberg, M., and Thoren, P. (1976) Differential effect of chlorimipramine and nortriptyline on cerebrospinal fluid metabolites of serotonin and noradrenaline in depression. *Eur. J. Clin. Pharmacol.* **21**, 194–200. [333]

Bertilsson, L., Tuck, J.R., and Siwers, B. (1980) Biochemical effects of zimelidine in man. *Eur. J. Clin. Pharmacol.* **18**, 483–487. [323]

Bertilsson, L., Tybring, G., Braithwaite, R., Traskman-Bendz, L., and Asberg, M. (1982a) Urinary excretion of 5-hydroxyindoleacetic acid—No relationship to the level in cerebrospinal fluid. *Acta Psychiatr. Scand.* **66**, 190–198. [309]

Bertilsson, L., Asberg, M., Lantto, O., Scalia-Tomba, G.-P., Traskman-Bendz, L., and Tybring, G. (1982b) Gradients of monoamine metabolites and cortisol in cerebrospinal fluid of psychiatric patients and healthy controls. *Psychiatr. Res.* **6**, 77–83. [223, 309]

Beskow, J., Gottfries, C.G., Roos, B.-E., and Winblad, B. (1976) Determination of monoamines and monoamine metabolites in the human brain. *Acta Psychiatr. Scand.* **53**, 7–20. [164, 222, 309, 310]

Besser, G.M., Butler, P.W.P., Landon, J. and Rees, L. (1969) Influence of amphetamines on plasma corticosteroid and growth hormone levels in man. *Br. Med. J.* **4**, 528–530. [229]

Besson, J.M., Oliveras, J.L., Chaouch, A., and Rivot, J.P. (1981) Role of the raphe nuclei in stimulation produced analgesia. In B. Haber, S. Gabay, M.R. Issidorides, and G.M. Alivisatos (Eds.), *Serotonin: Current Aspects on Neurochemistry and Function,* Plenum, New York, pp. 153–176. [298]

Betin, C., DeFeudis, F.V., Blavet, N., and Clostre, F. (1982) Further characterization of the behavioral despair test in mice: Positive effects of convulsants. *Physiol. Behav.* **28**, 307–311. [128]

Bevan, P., Bradshaw, C.M., and Szabadi, E. (1975) Effects of iprindole on responses of single cortical and caudate neurones to monoamines and acetylcholine. *Br. J. Pharmacol.* **55**, 17–25. [241]

Beyer, C., Almanza, J., De La Torre, L., and Guzman-Flores, C. (1971) Brain stem multiunit activity during "relaxation" behavior in the female cat. *Brain Res.* **29**, 213–222. [304]

Bhavsar, V.H., Dhumal, V.R., and Kelkar, V.V. (1981) The effect of some anti-epilepsy drugs on enhancement of the monoamine-mediated behavioral responses following the administration of electroconvulsive shocks to rats. *Eur. J. Pharmacol.* **74**, 243–247. [189, 243, 245, 339]

Bhavsar, V.H., Dhumal, V.R., and Kelkar, V.V. (1983) The effect of estradiol on the alterations in monoamine-mediated behavioral responses induced by administration of electroconvulsive shocks or imipramine to female rats. *Neuropharmacology* **22**, 751–756. [188, 189, 243, 245, 339, 341]

Biegon, A., Snyder, L., and McEwen, B.S. (1982) Effect of chronic treatment with ovarian steroids on neurotransmitter receptors in the rat brain. *Soc. Neurosci. Abstr.* **8**, 648. [267]

Bielski, R.J. and Friedel, R.O. (1976) Prediction of tricyclic antidepressant response: A critical review. *Arch. Gen. Psychiatr.* **33**, 1479–1489. [192]

Bignami, G. (1976) Nonassociative explanations of behavioral changes induced by central cholinergic drugs. *Acta Neurobiol. Exp.* **36**, 5–90. [274]

Bignami, G. (1978) Effects of neuroleptics, ethanol, hypnotic-sedatives, tranquillizers, narcotics and minor stimulants in aversive paradigms. In H. Anisman and G. Bignami

(Eds.), *Psychopharmacology of Aversively Motivated Behaviour*. Raven, New York, pp. 385–402. [155, 156]

Bignami, G. and Michaluk, H. (1978) Cholinergic mechanisms and aversively motivated behaviors. In H. Anisman and G. Bignami (Eds.), *Psychopharmacology of Aversively Motivated Behaviors*. Raven, New York, pp. 173–255. [279]

Billings, A.G., Cronkite, R.C., and Moos, R.H. (1983) Social-environmental factors in unipolar depression: Comparisons of depressed patients and non-depressed controls. *J. Abnorm. Psychol.* **92**, 119–133. [67, 83, 214]

Bindra, D.A. (1978) How adaptive behaviour is produced: A perceptual-motivational alternative to response-reinforcement. *Behav. Brain Sci.* **1**, 41–92. [154, 160, 402]

Bindra, D.A., ed. (1980) *The Brain's Mind: A Neuroscience Perspective on the Mind-Body Problem*. Gardner, New York. [28]

Bingley, T. (1958) Mental symptoms in temporal lobe epilepsy and temporal lobe gliomas. *Acta Psychiatr. Neurol.*, Suppl. 120, pp. 136–142. [92]

Binks, S.M. (1979) A reward reduction model of depression using self-stimulating rats: An appraisal. *Pharmacol. Biochem. Behav.* **10**, 441–443. [135]

Bioulac, B., Benezech, M., Renaud, B., Roche, D., and Noel, B. (1978) Biogenic amines in the 47,XYY syndrome. *Neuropsychobiology*, **4**, 366–370. [312]

Bioulac, B., Benezech, M., Renaud, B., Noel, B., and Roche, G. (1980) Serotonergic dysfunction in the 47,XYY syndrome. *Biol. Psychiatr.* **15**, 917–923. [312]

Bird, S. and Kuhar, M (1977) Iontophoretic application of opiates to the locus coeruleus. *Brain Res.* **122**, 523–533. [205]

Birkmayer, W. and Linauer, W (1970) Tryptophan-metabolismus bei Depressionpatients. *Arch. Psychiatr. Nervenkr.* **213**, 377–387. [164, 222]

Birkmayer, W. and Riederer, P (1975) Biochemical post-mortem findings in depressed patients. *J. Neural Trans.* **37**, 95–109. [164, 222, 310]

Birtchnell, J. (1970) The possible consequences of early parental death. *Br. J. Psychiatr.* **116**, 307–313. [295]

Bjerkenstedt, L., Edman, G., Flyckt, L., Sedvall, G., and Wiesel, F. (1984) Clinical and biochemical effects of citalopram in depressed patients. *Clin. Neuropharmacol.* **7**, Suppl. 1, 874–875. [323]

Bjorum, W. and Kirkegaard, C. (1979) Thyrotropin-releasing hormone test in unipolar and bipolar depression. *Lancet* **2**, 694. [372]

Black, J.W., Duncan, W.A.M., Durant, C.J., Ganellin, C.R., and Parsons, E.M. (1972) Definition and antagonism of histamine H_2-receptors. *Nature* **236**, 385–390. [368]

Black, R.S. and Robinson, R.G. (1982) Unilateral neurotoxic lesions of cortical dopaminergic, but not serotonergic pathways induce an asymmetrical behavioral response in the rat. *Soc. Neurosci. Abstr.* **8**, 894. [98]

Blackard, W.G. and Heidingsfelder, S.A. (1968) Adrenergic receptor control mechanism for growth hormone secretion. *J. Clin. Invest.* **47**, 1407–1414. [229]

Blackburn, T.P., Foster, G.A., Greenwood, D.T., and Howe, R. (1978) Effects of viloxazine, its optical isomers and its major metabolites on biogenic amine uptake mechanisms in vitro and in vivo. *Eur. J. Pharmacol.* **52**, 367–374. [235, 240, 329]

Blackshear, M.A. and Sanders-Bush, E. (1982) Serotonin receptor sensitivity after acute and chronic treatment with mianserin. *J. Pharmacol. Exp. Ther.* **221**, 303–308. [340, 342, 347, 348]

Blanc, G., Herve, D., Simon, H., Lisoprawski, A., Glowinski, J., and Tassin, J.P. (1980) Response to stress of mesocortical frontal dopaminergic neurons in rats after long-term isolation. *Nature* **284**, 265–276. [157]

Blaney, P.H. (1977) Contemporary theories of depression: Critique and comparison. *J. Abnorm. Psychol.* **86,** 203–223. [76, 79, 124, 127, 136]

Blashfield, R.K. and Morey, L.C. (1979) The classification of depression through cluster analysis. *Compr. Psychiatr.* **20,** 516–527. [57]

Blass, E.M. and Hall, W.G. (1976) Drinking termination: Interactions among hydrational, orogastric, and behavioral controls in rats. *Psychol. Rev.* **83,** 356–374. [362]

Blatt, S.J., D'Affliti, J.P., and Quinlan, D.M. (1976) Experiences of depression in normal young adults. *J. Abnorm. Psychol.* **85,** 383–389. [76, 124, 394]

Blatt, S.J., Quinlan, D.M., Chevron, E.S., and McDonald, C. (1982) Dependency and self-criticism: Psychological dimensions of depression. *J. Consult. Clin. Psychol.* **50,** 113–124. [76, 124, 394, 406]

Blier, P. and De Montigny, C. (1980) Effect of chronic tricyclic antidepressant treatment on the serotonergic autoreceptor: A microiontophoretic study in the rat. *Naunyn Schmiedebergs Arch. Pharmacol.* **314,** 123–128. [331]

Blier, P. and De Montigny, C. (1983) Electrophysiological investigations on the effects of repeated zimelidine administration on serotonergic neurotransmission. *J. Neurosci.* **3,** 1270–1278. [332, 335, 336, 351]

Blier, P. and De Montigny, C. (1984a) The effect of repeated administration of monoamine oxidase inhibitors on the firing of serotonergic and noradrenergic neurons. *Abstr. 14th CINP,* Florence, p. 38. [332]

Blier, P. and De Montigny, C. (1984b) Enhancement of serotonergic neurotransmission by non-tricyclic antidepressant drugs: Single cell studies in the rat. *Abstr. 14th CINP,* Florence, p. 829. [335, 336]

Bliss, E.L., Ailion, J., and Zwanziger, J. (1968) Metabolism of norepinephrine, serotonin and dopamine in rat brain with stress. *J. Pharmacol. Exp. Ther.* **164,** 122–134. [289]

Bloch, B., Brazeau, P., Ling, N., Bohlen, P., Esch, F., Wehrenberg, W.B., Bloom, F., and Guillemin, R. (1983) Immunohistochemical detection of growth hormone-releasing factor in brain. *Nature* **301,** 607–608. [228]

Blombery, P.A., Kopin, I.J., Gordon, E.K., Markey, S.P., and Ebert, M.H. (1980) Conversison of MHPG to vanillylmandelic acid: Implications for the importance of urinary MHPG. *Arch. Gen. Psychiatr.* **37,** 1095–1098. [224]

Bloom, F., Segal, D., Ling, N., and Guillemin, R. (1976) Endorphins: Profound behavioral effects in rats suggest new etiological factors in mental illness. *Science* **194,** 630–632. [359]

Bloom, F.E., Rogers, J., Schulman, J.A., Schultz, J., and Siggins, G.R. (1981) Receptor plasticity: Inferential changes after chronic treatment with lithium, desmethylimipramine or ethanol detected by electrophysiological correlates. In E. Usdin, W.E. Bunney, and J.M. Davis (Eds.), *Neuroreceptors: Basic and Clinical Aspects.* Wiley, New York, pp. 37–53. [14]

Bloom, F.E., Baetge, G., Deyo, S., Ettenberg, A., Koda, L., Magistretti, P.J., Shoemaker, W.J., and Staunton, D.A. (1983) Chemical and physiological aspects of the actions of lithium and antidepressant drugs. *Neuropharmacology,* **22,** 359–365. [367]

Blundell, J.E. (1977) Is there a role for serotonin (5-hydroxytryptamine) in feeding? *Int. J. Obesity* **1,** 15–42. [303]

Blundell, J.E. and Latham, C.J. (1979) Serotonergic influences on food intake: Effect of 5-hydroxtryptophan on parameters of feeding behavior in deprived and free-feeding rats. *Pharmacol. Biochem. Behav.* **11,** 431–437. [303]

Blundell, J.E. and Latham, C.J. (1980) Characterization of the behavioral changes underlying the effects of amphetamine and fenfluramine on food consumption, and the antagonism by pimozide and methergoline. *Pharmacol. Biochem. Behav.* **12,** 717–722. [303]

Blundell, J.E. and Leshem, M.B. (1975) The effect of 5-hydroxytryptophan on food intake and on the anorexic action of amphetamine and fenfluramine. *J. Pharm. Pharmacol.* **27**, 31–37. [303]

Blundell, J.E. and McArthur, R.A. (1981) Behavioral flux and feeding: Continuous monitoring of food intake and food selection, and the video-recording of appetitive and satiety sequences for the analysis of drug action. In S. Garattini and R. Samanin (Eds.), *Anorectic Agents: Mechanisms of Action and Tolerance.* Raven, New York, pp. 19–43. [303, 304]

Blundell, J.E., Latham, C.J., and Leshem, M.B. (1976) Differences between the anorexic action of amphetamine and fenfluramine: Possible effects on hunger and satiety. *J. Pharm. Pharmacol.* **28**, 471–477. [303]

Bodnar, R.J., Kelly, D.D., and Glusman, M. (1978a) Stress-induced analgesia: Time course of pain reflex alterations following cold water swim. *Bull. Psychonom. Soc.* **11**, 333–336. [359]

Bodnar, R.J., Kelly, D.D., Spiaggia, A., Ehrenberg, C., and Glusman, M. (1978b) Dose-dependent reductions by naloxone of analgesia induced by cold-water stress. *Pharmacol. Biochem. Behav.* **8**, 667–672. [360]

Bodnar, R.J., Kelly, D.D., Spiaggia, A., and Glusman, M. (1978c) Biphasic alterations of nociceptive thresholds induced by food deprivation. *Physiol. Psychol.* **6**, 391–395. [363]

Bodnar, R.J., Kelly, D.D., Steiner, S. and Glusman, M. (1978d) Stress-produced analgesia and morphine-produced analgesia: Lack of cross-tolerance. *Pharmacol. Biochem. Behav.* **8**, 661–666. [360]

Bohus, B., and De Kloet, E.R. (1981) Adrenal steroids and extinction behaviour: Antagonism by progesterone, deoxycorticosterone and dexamethasone of a specific effect of corticosterone. *Life Sci.* **28**, 433–440. [383]

Bojholm, S., Borup, C., Kvist, J., Petersen, I.-M., and Honore, P. Le F. (1979) A double-blind study of femoxetine and amitriptyline in patients with endogenous depression. *Nord. Psychiatr. Tidsskr.* **33**, 455–460. [323]

Bolles, R.C. (1972) The avoidance learning problem. In G. Bower (Ed.), *The Psychology of Learning and Motivation,* Vol. 6. Academic, New York, pp. 97–145. [95, 154]

Bond, P.A. and Howlett, D.R. (1974) Measurement of the two conjugates of 3-methoxy-4-hydroxyphenylglycol in urine. *Biochem. Med.* **10**, 219–228. [227]

Bond, P.A., Jenner, F.A., and Sampson, G. (1972) Daily variations of the urine content of 3-methoxy-4-hydroxyphenylglycol in two manic depressive patients. *Psychol. Med.* **12**, 81–85. [225, 226]

Bonn, J.A., Turner, P., and Hocks, D.C. (1972) Beta-adrenergic-receptor blockade with practolol in treatment of anxiety. *Lancet* **1**, 814–815. [204]

Born, G.V.R., Grignani, G., and Martin, K. (1980) Long-term effect of lithium on the uptake of 5-hydroxytryptamine by human platelets. *Br. J. Clin. Pharmacol.* **9**, 321–325. [315, 333]

Borod, J.C. and Caron, H.S. (1980) Facedness and emotion related to lateral dominance, sex and expression type. *Neuropsychology* **18**, 237–241. [86]

Borod, J.C., Caron, H.S., and Koff, E. (1981) Asymmetry of facial expression related to handedness, footedness and eyedness: A quantitative study. *Cortex* **17**, 381–390. [86]

Borsini, F., Bendotti, C., Velkov, V., Rech, R., and Samanin, R. (1981) Immobility test: Effects of 5-hydroxytryptaminergic drugs and role of catecholamines in the activity of some antidepressants. *J. Pharm. Pharmacol.* **33**, 33–37. [212, 290]

Bourne, H.R., Bunney, W.E., Colburn, R.W., Davis, J.M., Davis, J.N., Shaw, D.M., and Coppen, A.J. (1968) Noradrenaline, 5-hydroxytryptamine, and 5-hydroxyindoleacetic acid in hindbrains of suicidal patients. *Lancet* **2**, 805–808. [222, 309]

Bowden, D.M. and McKinney, W.T. (1972) Behavioral effects of peer separation, isolation and reunion on adolescent male rhesus monkeys. *Dev. Psychobiol.* **5**, 353–362. [132]

Bowdler, J.M., Green, A.R., Minchin, M.C.W., and Nutt, D.J. (1983) Regional GABA concentration and [^{3}H]-diazepam binding in rat brain following repeated electroconvulsive shock. *J. Neural Trans.* **56**, 3–12. [356, 357]

Bower, G.H. (1981) Mood and memory. *Am. Psychol.* **36**, 129–148. [71, 72]

Bowers, M.B. (1972) CSF 5-HIAA and HVA following probenecid in unipolar depressives treated with amitriptyline. *Psychopharmacol.* **23**, 26–30. [167, 168, 311]

Bowers, M.B. (1974a) Lumbar CSF 5-hydroxyindoleacetic acid and homovanillic acid in affective syndromes. *J. Nerv. Ment. Disord.* **158**, 325–330. [168, 310, 311]

Bowers, M.B. (1974b) Amitriptyline in man: decreased formation of central 5-hydroxyindoleacetic acid. *Clin. Pharmacol. Ther.* **15**, 167–170. [333]

Bowers, M.B., Heninger, G.R., and Gerbode, F. (1969) Cerebrospinal fluid 5-hydroxyindoleacetic acid and homovanillic acid in psychiatric patients. *Int. J. Neuropharmacol.* **8**, 255–262. [167, 311, 312, 334]

Bowlby, J. (1976) Human personality development in an ethological light. In G. Serban and A. Kling (Eds.), *Animal Models in Human Psychobiology.* Plenum, New York, pp. 27–36. [133, 141]

Bowlby, J. (1977) The making and breaking of affectional bonds. II. Aetiology and psychopathology in the light of attachment theory. *Br. J. Psychiatr.* **130**, 201–210. [395]

Boyd, J.H. and Weissman, M. (1981) Epidemiology of affective disorders. A reexamination and future directions. *Arch. Gen. Psychiatr.* **38**, 1039–1046. [47, 395]

Bozarth, M.A. (1983) Opiate reward mechanisms mapped by intracranial self-administration. In J.E. Smith and J.D. Lane (Eds.), *The Neurobiology of Opiate Reward Processes.* Elsevier, New York, pp. 331–359. [151, 200, 361]

Bozarth, M.A. and Wise, R.A. (1981a) Intracranial self-administration of morphine into the ventral tegmental area in rats. *Life Sci.* **28**, 551–555. [151, 361]

Bozarth, M.A. and Wise, R.A. (1981b) Localization of the reward-relevant opiate receptors. In L.S. Harris (Ed.), *Problems of Drug Dependence.* National Institute on Drug Dependence, Washington, D.C., pp. 158–164. [151, 361]

Bozarth, M.A. and Wise, R.A. (1981c) Heroin reward is dependent on a dopaminergic substrate. *Life Sci.* **29**, 1881–1886. [151]

Bracewell, R.J. and Black, A.H. (1974) The effects of restraint and noncontingent pre-shock on subsequent escape learning in the rat. *Learn. Motiv.* **5**, 53–69. [125]

Bradbury, A.F., Smyth, D.G., and Snell, C.R. (1976) Lipotropin: Precursor to two biologically active peptides. *Biochem. Biophys. Res. Commun.* **69**, 950–956. [358]

Bradshaw, C.M., Roberts, M.H.T., and Szabadi, E. (1974) Effects of imipramine and desipramine on responses of single cortical neurones to noradrenaline and 5-hydroxytryptamine. *Br. J. Pharmacol.* **52**, 349–358. [241, 330]

Braestrup, C. (1974) Effects of phenoxybenzamine, acaperone and clonidine on the level of 3-methoxy-4-hydroxyphenylglycol (MHPG) in rat brain. *J. Pharm. Pharmacol.* **26**, 139–141. [227]

Braestrup, C. and Nielsen, M. (1980) Benzodiazepine receptors. *Arzneim. Forsch.* **30**, 852–857. [20, 354]

Brambilla, F., Smeraldi, E., Sacchetti, E., Negri, F., Cocchi, D., and Muller, E. (1978) Deranged anterior pituitary responsiveness to hypothalamic hormones in depressed patients. *Arch. Gen. Psychiatr.* **35**, 1231–1236. [372, 373]

Brambilla, F., Bellodi, L., Negri, F., Smeraldi, E., and Malagoli, G. (1979) Dopamine receptor sensitivity in the hypothalamus of chronic schizophrenics after haloperidol therapy:

Growth hormone and prolactin response to stimuli. *Psychoneuroendocrinology* **4**, 329–339. [186]

Brambilla, F., Smeraldi, E., Sacchetti, E., Bellodi, L., Gennazzani, A.R., Facchinetti, F., and Muller, E.E. (1982) Neuroendocrine abnormalities in depressive illness. In E. Costa and G. Racagni (Eds.), *Typical and Atypical Antidepressants: Clinical Practice*, Raven, New York, pp. 329–340. [364]

Breese, G.R. and Cooper, B.R. (1975) Behavioral and biochemical interactions of 5,7-dihydroxytryptamine with various drugs when administered intracisternally to adult and developing rats. *Brain Res.* **98**, 517–527. [296]

Breisch, S.T. and Hoebel, B.G. (1975) Hyperphagia and transient obesity following intraventricular parachlorophenylalanine. *Fed. Proc.* **34**, 296. [303]

Breisch, S.T., Zemlan, F.P., and Hoebel, B.G. (1976) Hyperphagia and obesity following serotonin depletion with intraventricular parachlorophenylalanine. *Science* **192**, 382–385. [303]

Breslow, R., Kocis, J., and Belkin, B. (1981) Contributions of the depressive perspective to memory function in depression. *Am. J. Psychiatr.* **138**, 227–230. [70]

Brezenoff, H.E. and Lomax, P. (1970) Temperature changes following microinjection of histamine into the thermoregulatory centers of the rat. *Experientia* **25**, 51–52. [368]

Bridges, P.K., Bartlett, J.R., Sepping, P., Kantamaneni, B.D., and Curzon, G. (1976) Precursors and metabolites of 5-hydroxytryptamine and dopamine in the ventricular cerebrospinal fluid of psychiatric patients. *Psychol. Med.* **6**, 399–405. [164, 222, 309, 310]

Briggs, H.M. and Briggs, M. (1973) Hormonal influences on erythrocyte catechol-O-methyltransferase activity in humans. *Experientia* **29**, 279–280. [220]

Briley, M.S., Langer, S.Z., Raisman, R., Sechter, D., and Zarifian, E. (1980) Tritiated imipramine binding sites are decreased in platelets of untreated depressed patients. *Science* **209**, 303–305. [316]

Briley, M.S., Raisman, R., Arbilla, S., Casadamont, M., and Langer, S.Z. (1982a) Concomitant decrease in [^{3}H]imipramine binding in cat brain and platelets after chronic treatment with imipramine. *Eur. J. Pharmacol.* **81**, 309–314. [332, 348]

Briley, M.S., Raisman, R., Sechter, D., Langer, S.Z., and Zarifian, E. (1982b) ^{3}H-imipramine binding: A biochemical marker in depression. In S.Z. Langer, R. Takahashi, T. Segawa, and M. Briley (Eds.), *New Vistas in Depression*. Pergamon, New York, pp. 115–124. [316]

Briscoe, C.W. and Smith, J.B. (1975) Depression in bereavement and divorce. *Arch. Gen. Psychiatr.* **32**, 439–443. [134, 141, 392]

Briscoe, C.W., Smith, J.B., Robins, E., Marten, S., and Gaskin, F. (1973) Divorce and psychiatric disease. *Arch. Gen. Psychiatr.* **29**, 119–125. [393]

Britt, M.D. and Wise, R.A. (1981) Attenuation of intravenous heroin reward by ventral tegmental opiate receptor blockade. *Soc. Neurosci. Abstr.* **7**, 607. [361]

Brodie, B.B. and Shore, P.H. (1957) A concept for a role of serotonin and norepinephrine as chemical mediators in the brain. *Ann. N.Y. Acad. Sci.* **66**, 631–642. [304]

Brodie, B.B., Bickel, M.H., and Sulser, F. (1961) Desmethylimipramine, a new type of antidepressant drug *Med. Exp.* **5**, 454–458. [110]

Brodie, H.K.H., Sack, R. and Siever, L. (1973) Clinical studies of l-5-hydroxytryptophan in depression. In J. Barchas and E. Usdin (Eds.), *Serotonin and Behaviour*. Academic, New York, pp. 549–559. [167, 321]

Brody, B.A. and Pribram, K.H. (1978) The role of frontal and parietal cortex in cognitive processing: Tests of spatial and sequence functions. *Brain* **101**, 607–633. [94]

Brody, J.F. (1970) Behavioral effects of serotonin depletion and of p-chlorophenylalanine (a serotonin depletor) in rats. *Psychopharmacology* **17**, 14–33. [294–296]

Broekkamp, C.L., Van den Boggard, J.H., Hiejnen, H.J., Rops, R.H., Cools, A.R., and Van Rossum, J.M. (1976) Separation of inhibiting and stimulating effects of morphine on self-stimulation behavior by intracerebral injections. *Eur. J. Pharmacol.* **36**, 443–446. [362]

Broekkamp, C.L., Phillips, A.G., and Cools, A.R. (1979) Facilitation of self-stimulation behavior following intracerebral microinjections of opioids into the ventral tegmental area. *Pharmacol. Biochem. Behav.* **11**, 289–295. [362]

Broekkamp, C.L., Garrigou, D., and Lloyd, K.G. (1980) Serotonin-mimetic and antidepressant drugs on passive avoidance learning by olfactory bulbectomized rats. *Pharmacol. Biochem. Behav.* **13**, 643–646. [112, 292]

Broekkamp, C.L., Garrigou, D., and Lloyd, K.G. (1982) The importance of the amygdala in the effect of antidepressants on olfactory bulbectomised rats. In E. Costa and G. Racagni (Eds.), *Typical and Atypical Antidepressants: Molecular Mechanisms.* Raven, New York, pp. 371–375. [271]

Brown, G.L., Goodwin, F.K., Ballenger, J.C., Goyer, P.F., and Major, L.F. (1979) Aggression in humans correlates with cerebrospinal fluid amine metabolites. *Psychiatr. Res.* **1**, 131–139. [312]

Brown, G.L., Goodwin, F.K., and Bunney, W.E. (1982) Human aggression and suicide: Their relationship to neuropsychiatric diagnoses and serotonin metabolism. In B.T. Ho, J.C. Schoolar, and E. Usdin (Eds.), *Serotonin in Biological Psychiatry.* Raven, New York, pp. 287–307. [312]

Brown, G.W. and Harris, T. (1978) *Social Origins of Depression.* Tavistock, London. [50, 71, 79, 81, 101, 131, 178, 392–394, 396]

Brown, G.W., Sklair, F., Harris, T.O., and Birley, J.L.T. (1973) Life events and psychiatric disorders. I. Some methodological issues. *Psychol. Med.* **3**, 74–87. [133, 139]

Brown, J., Doxey, J.C., and Handley, S. (1980) Effects of alpha-adrenoceptor agonists and antagonists and of antidepressant drugs on pre- and postsynaptic alpha-adrenoceptors. *Eur. J. Pharmacol.* **67**, 33–40. [240–242]

Brown, L., Rosellini, R.A., Samuels, O.B., and Riley, E.P. (1982) Evidence for a serotonergic mechanism of the learned helplessness phenomenon. *Pharmacol. Biochem. Behav.* **17**, 877–883. [290]

Brown, W.A. and Shuey, I. (1980) Response to dexamethasone and subtype of depression. *Arch. Gen. Psychiatr.* **37**, 747–751. [54]

Brown, W.A., Johnston, R., and Mayfield, D. (1979) The 24-hour dexamethasone suppression test in a clinical setting: Relationship to diagnosis, symptoms and response to treatment. *Am. J. Psychiatr.* **136**, 543–547. [54]

Brown, W.A., Haier, R.J., and Qualls, C.B. (1980) Dexamethasone suppression test identifies subtypes of depression which respond to different antidepressants. *Lancet* **1**, 928–929. [237]

Browne, R.G. (1979) Effects of antidepressants and anticholinergics in a mouse "behavioral despair" test. *Eur. J. Pharmacol.* **58**, 331–334. [127, 128, 270, 290]

Brownstein, M. and Axelrod, J. (1974) Pineal gland: 24-hour rhythm in norepinephrine turnover. *Science* **184**, 163–165. [261]

Bruder, G.E. and Yozawitz, A. (1979) Central auditory processing and laterality in psychiatric patients. In J. Gruzelier and P. Flor-Henry (Eds.), *Hemispheric Asymmetries of Function and Psychopathology.* Elsevier, Amsterdam, pp. 561–580. [90]

Brunello, N., Chuang, D.M., and Costa, E. (1982) Use of specific brain lesions to study the site of action of antidepressants. In S.Z. Langer, R. Takahashi, T. Segawa, and M. Briley (Eds.), *New Vistas in Depression,* Pergamon, New York, pp. 141–145. [259]

Bryer, J.B., Borrelli, D.J., Matthews, E.J., and Kornetsky, C. (1983) The psychological correlates of the DST in depressed patients. *Psychopharmacol. Bull.* **19**, 633–637. [83]

Buchsbaum, M.S., Coursey, R.D., and Murphy, D.L. (1976) The biochemical high-risk paradigm: behavioral and familial correlates of low platelet monoamine oxidase activity. *Science* **194**, 339–341. [221]

Buchsbaum, M.S., Muscettola, G., and Goodwin, F.K. (1981) Urinary MHPG, stress response, personality factors and somatosensory evoked potentials in normal subjects and patients with major affective disorders. *Neuropsychobiol.* **7**, 212–224. [226]

Buchwald, A.M., Coyne, J.C., and Cole, C.S. (1978) A critical evaluation of the learned helplessness model of depression. *J. Abnorm. Psychol.* **87**, 180–193. [75, 76, 78, 79, 126, 127]

Buchwald, A.M., Strack, S., and Coyne, J.C. (1981) Demand characteristics and the Velten mood induction procedure. *J. Consult. Clin. Psychol.* **49**, 478–479. [72]

Buchwald, N.A., Horvath, F.E., Myers, E.J., and Wakefield, C. (1964) Electroencephalogram rhythms correlated with milk reinforcement in cats. *Nature* **201**, 830–831. [303]

Bunney, B.S. and Aghajanian, G.K. (1976a) The precise localization of nigral afferents in the rat as determined by a retrograde tracing technique. *Brain Res.* **117**, 423–435. [378]

Bunney, B.S. and Aghajanian, G.K. (1976b) D-Amphetamine induced inhibition of central dopaminergic neurons: Mediation by a striato-nigral feedback pathway. *Science* **192**, 391–393. [156, 183]

Bunney, B.S. and Aghajanian, G.K. (1976c) Dopamine and norepinephrine innervated cells in the rat prefrontal cortex: Pharmacological differentiation using microiontophoretic techniques. *Life Sci.* **19**, 1783–1792. [241]

Bunney, W.E. (1978) Psychopharmacology of the switch process in affective illness. In M.A. Lipton, A. DiMaschio, and K.F. Killam (Eds.), *Psychopharmacology: A Generation of Progress*. Raven, New York, pp. 1249–1259. [46, 413]

Bunney, W.E. and Davis, J.M. (1965) Norepinephrine in depressive reactions. *Arch. Gen. Psychiatr.* **13**, 483–494. [6, 17]

Bunney, W.E. and Garland, B.L. (1983) Possible receptor effects of chronic lithium administration. *Neuropharmacology* **22**, 367–373. [191]

Bunney, W.E., Murphy, D.L., and Goodwin, F.K. (1970) The switch process from depression to mania: Relationship to drugs which alter brain amines. *Lancet* **2**, 1022–1027. [46]

Bunney, W.E., Brodie, H.K.H., Murphy, D.L. and Goodwin, F.K. (1971) Studies of alpha-methyl-para-tyrosine, L-dopa and L-tryptophan in depression and mania. *Am. J. Psychiatr.* **127**, 872–881. [232]

Burchfield, S.R. (1979) The stress response: A new perspective. *Psychosom. Med.* **41**, 661–672. [130, 131, 139, 141]

Burns, D.B. and Mendels, J. (1979) Serotonin and affective disorders. In W.B. Essman and L. Valzelli (Eds.), *Current Developments in Psychopharmacology*, Vol. 5. Spectrum, New York, pp. 293–359. [309, 319, 320]

Burton, M.J., Cooper, S.J., and Popplewell, D.A. (1981) The effect of fenfluramine on the microstructure of feeding and drinking in the rat. *Br. J. Pharmacol.* **72**, 621–633. [303]

Butters, N., Soeldner, C., and Fedio, P. (1972) Comparison of parietal and frontal lobe spatial deficits in man: Extrapersonal vs. personal (egocentric) space. *Percept. Mot. Skills* **34**, 27–34. [94, 95]

Buus Lassen, J. (1978) Potent and long-lasting potentiation of two 5-hydroxytryptophan-induced effects in mice by three selective 5-HT uptake inhibitors. *Eur. J. Pharmacol.* **47**, 351–358. [329]

Buus Lassen, J., Squires, R.F., Christensen, J.A., and Molander, L. (1975) Neurochemical and pharmacological studies on a new 5-HT uptake inhibitor, FG 4963, with potential antidepressant properties. *Psychopharmacology* **42**, 21–26. [323]

Cabanac, W. (1971) Physiological role of pleasure. *Science* **173**, 1103–1107. [196, 303, 362, 385]

Cairncross, K.D., Wren, A.F., Cox, B., and Schnieden, H. (1977) Effects of olfactory bulbectomy and domicile on stress induced corticosterone release in the rat. *Physiol. Behav.* **19**, 485–487. [112]

Cairncross, K.D., Cox, B., Forster, C., and Wren, A.F. (1978) A new model for the detection of antidepressant drugs: Olfactory bulbectomy in the rat compared with existing models. *J. Pharmacol. Methods* **1**, 131–143. [112, 351]

Cairncross, K.D., Cox, B., Forster, C., and Wren, A.F. (1979) Olfactory projection systems, drugs and behaviour: A review. *Psychoneuroendocrinology* **4**, 253–272. [112, 292, 293, 350, 351, 354]

Calandra, C., Zappala, E., Bonomo, V., and Rapisarda, V. (1981) 5-OH-tryptophan in association with allopurinol in depressions. *Minerva Psychiatr. (Italy)* **22**, 131–135. [320]

Camp, D.M., Becker, J.B., and Robinson, T.E. (1982) Sex differences in the effects of early handling on brain and behavioral asymmetries. *Soc. Neurosci. Abstr.* **8**, 895. [98]

Campanini, T., Catlano, A., de Risio, C., and Mardighian, G. (1970) Vanillmandelicaciduria in the different clinical phases of manic-depressive psychosis. *Br. J. Psychiatr.* **116**, 435–436. [224]

Campbell, I.C. and Marshall, E.F. (1974) Effects of chronic regimens of phenelzine, tranylcypromine, and imipramine on rat brain norepinephrine and serotonin. *J. Pharmacol.* **5** (Suppl. 2), 14. [334]

Campbell, I.C. and McKernan, R.M. (1982) Central and peripheral changes in alpha-adrenoceptors in the rat in response to chronic antidepressant drug administration. In S.Z. Langer, R. Takahahi, T. Segawa, and M. Briley (Eds.), *New Vistas in Depression*, Pergamon, New York, pp. 153–160. [247, 248, 255]

Campbell, I.C., Robinson, D.S., Lovenberg, W., and Murphy, D.L. (1979) The effects of chronic regimens of clorgyline and pargyline on monoamine metabolism in the rat brain. *J. Neurochem.* **32**, 49–55. [250, 334]

Campbell, I.C., Murphy, D.L. Gallager, D.W., Tallman, J.F., and Marshall, E.F. (1980) Neurotransmitter-related adaptation in the central nervous system following chronic monoamine oxidase inhibition. In T.P. Singer, R.W. Von Korf, and D.L. Murphy (Eds.), *Monoamine Oxidase: Structure, Function and Altered Functions.* Academic, New York, pp. 517–530. [250]

Campbell, R. (1978) Asymmetries in interpreting and expressing a posed facial expression. *Cortex* **14**, 327–342. [86]

Cannon, W.B. (1932) *The Wisdom of the Body.* Norton, New York. [305]

Caplan, G. (1981) Mastery of stress: Psychosocial aspects. *Am. J. Psychiatr.* **138**, 413–420. [393]

Carey, R.J. (1982) Unilateral 6-hydroxydopamine lesions of dopamine neurons produce bilateral self-stimulation deficits. *Behav. Brain Res.* **6**, 101–104. [150]

Carlsson, A. (1961) Brain monoamines and psychotropic drugs. *Neuropsychopharmacol.* **2**, 417–421. [7, 9]

Carlsson, A. (1970) Effects of drugs on amine storage mechanisms. In H.J. Schumann and G. Kroneberg (Eds.), *New Aspects of Storage and Release Mechanisms of Catecholamines.* Springer, Heidelberg, pp. 223–233. [9, 181]

Carlsson, A. (1975a) Monoamine depleting drugs. *Pharmacol. Ther. B* **1**, 393–400. [168]

Carlsson, A. (1975b) Receptor mediated control of dopamine metabolism. In E. Usdin and W.E. Bunney (Eds.), *Pre- and Postsynaptic Receptors.* Dekker, New York, pp. 49–55. [182]

Carlsson, A. (1981) Some current problems related to the mode of action of antidepressant drugs. *Acta Psychiatr. Scand.* **63** (Suppl. 290), 63–66. [323]

Carlsson, A. and Lindqvist, M. (1978a) Effects of antidepressant agents on the synthesis of brain monoamines. *J. Neural Trans.* **43**, 73–91. [182, 240, 241, 329]

Carlsson, A. and Lindqvist, M. (1978b) Dependence of 5-HT and catecholamine synthesis on concentrations of precursor amino acids in rat brain. *Naunyn Schmiedebergs Arch. Pharmacol.* **303**, 157–164. [172]

Carlsson, A., Lindqvist, M., and Magnusson, T. (1957) 3,4-Dihydroxyphenylalanine and 5-hydroxytryptophan as reserpine antagonists. *Nature* **180**, 1200. [9, 10, 110]

Carlsson, A., Corrodi, H., Fuxe, K., and Hokfelt, T. (1969a) Effect of antidepressant drugs on the depletion of intraneuronal brain 5-hydroxytryptamine stores caused by 4-methyl-alpha-ethyl-meta-tyramine. *Eur. J. Pharmacol.* **5**, 357–366. [10, 240, 322, 328]

Carlsson, A., Corrodi, H., Fuxe, K., and Hokfelt, T. (1969b) Effects of some antidepressant drugs on the depletion of intraneuronal brain catecholamine stores cause by 4,alpha-dimethyl-meta-tyramine. *Eur. J. Pharmacol.* **5**, 367–373. [10, 322]

Carlton, P.L. (1961) Potentiation of the behavioral effects of amphetamine by imipramine. *Psychopharmacology* **2**, 364–376. [111]

Carlton, P.L. (1969) Brain acetylcholine and inhibition. In J. Tapp (Ed.), *Reinforcement and Behavior.* Academic, New York, pp. 286–327. [277]

Carlton, P.L. and Markiewicz, B. (1971) Behavioral effects of atropine and scopolamine. In E. Furchgott (Ed.), *Pharmacological and Biophysical Agents and Behavior.* Academic, New York, pp. 345–373. [274, 382]

Carmon, A. and Nachson, I. (1973) Ear asymmetry in perception of emotional nonverbal stimuli. *Acta Psychol.* **37**, 351–357. [86]

Carpenter, W.T. (1970) Serotonin now: Clinical implications of inhibiting its synthesis with para-chlorophenylalanine. *Ann. Intern. Med.* **73**, 607–629. [317]

Carroll, B.J. (1972) Studies with hypothalamic-pituitary-adrenal tests in depression. In B. Davis, B.J. Carroll, and R.M. Mowbray (Eds.), *Depressive Illness: Some Research Studies.* Charles C Thomas, Springfield, Ill., pp. 149–201. [229]

Carroll, B.J. (1977) The hypothalamus-pituitary-adrenal axis in depression. In G. Burrows (Ed.), *Handbook on Depression.* Excerpta Medica, Amsterdam, pp. 325–341. [53]

Carroll, B.J. (1978) Neuroendocrine function in psychiatric disorders. In M.A. Lipton, A. DiMaschio, and K.F. Killam (Eds.), *Psychopharmacology: A Generation of Progress.* Raven, New York, pp. 487–497. [53, 113, 166]

Carroll, B.J. (1982) The dexamethasone suppression test for melancholia. *Br. J. Psychiatr.* **140**, 292–304. [52, 54, 133, 266, 278, 314]

Carroll, B.J. and Mendels, J. (1976) Neuroendocrine regulation in affective disorders. In E.J. Sachar (Ed.), *Hormones, Behavior and Psychopathology.* Raven, New York, pp. 193–224. [53]

Carroll, B.J., Frazer, A., Schless, A., and Mendels, J. (1973) Cholinergic reversal of manic symptoms. *Lancet* **1**, 427–428. [282]

Carroll, B.J., Curtis, G.C., and Mendels, J. (1976) Cerebrospinal fluid and plasma free cortisol levels in depression. *Psychol. Med.* **6**, 235–244. [53, 113, 130, 266]

Carroll, B.J., Greden, J.F., Rubin, R.T., Haskett, R., Feinberg, M., and Schteingart, D. (1978) Neurotransmitter mechanisms of neuroendocrine disturbances in depression. *Acta Endocrinol.,* Suppl. 220, 14. [278]

Carroll, B.J., Greden, J.F., Haskett, R., Feinberg, M., Albala, A.A., Martin, F.I.R., Rubin, R.T., Heath, B., Sharp, P.T., McLeod, W.L., and McLeod, M.F. (1980) Transmitter studies of neuroendocrine pathology in depression. *Acta Psychiatr. Scand.* **61** (Suppl. 280), 183–199. [278]

Carroll, B.J., Feinberg, M., Greden, J.F., Tarika, J., Albala, A.A., Haskett, R.F., James, N.M., Kronfol, Z., Lohr, N., Steiner, M., De Vigne, J.P., and Young, E. (1981a) A specific laboratory test for the diagnosis of melancholia. Standardization, validation and clinical utility. *Arch. Gen. Psychiatr.* **38,** 15–22. [54]

Carroll, B.J., Greden, J.F., and Feinberg, M. (1981b) Suicide, neuroendocrine dysfunction and CSF-5HIAA concentrations in depression. In B. Angrist, G.D. Burrows, M. Lader, O. Lingjaerde, G. Sedvall, and D. Wheatley (Eds.), *Recent Advances in Neuropsychopharmacology.* Pergamon, New York, pp. 307–313. [314]

Carroll, B.J., Greden, J.F., Feinberg, M., Lohr, N., James, N.M., Steiner, M., Haskett, R.F., Albala, A.A., De Vigne, J.P., and Tarika, J. (1981c) Neuroendocrine evaluation of depression in borderline patients. *Psychiatr. Clin. North Am.* **4,** 89–99. [56]

Carson, T.C. and Adams, H.E. (1980) Activity valence as a function of mood change. *J. Abnorm. Psychol.* **89,** 368–377. [68, 81]

Carter, C.J. and Pycock, C.J. (1981) The role of 5-hydroxytryptamine in dopamine-dependent stereotyped behaviour. *Neuropharmacology* **20,** 261–265. [378]

Carter, R.B. and Appel, J.B. (1976) Blockade of the behavioral effects of 5-HTP by the decarboxylase inhibitor Ro4-4602. *Pharmacol. Biochem. Behav.* **4,** 407–409. [300]

Carter, R.B., Dykstra, L.A., Leander, J.D., and Appel, J.B. (1978) Role of peripheral mechanisms in the behavioral effects of 5-hydroxytryptophan. *Pharmacol. Biochem. Behav.* **9,** 249–253. [300]

Casey, D.E. (1979) Mood alterations during deanol therapy. *Psychopharmacology* **62,** 187–191. [281]

Caspar, R.C., Davis, J.M., Pandey, G.N., Garver, D.L., and Dekirmenjian, H. (1977) Neuroendocrine and amine studies in affective illness. *Psychoneuroendocrinology* **2,** 105–113. [165, 229]

Cassano, G.B., Maggini, C., and Akiskal, H.S. (1983) Short-term, subchronic and chronic sequelae of affective disorders. *Psychiatr. Clin. North Am.* **6,** 55–67. [394]

Cassens, G., Roffman, M., Kurue, A., Orsulak, P.J., and Schildkraut, J.J. (1980) Alterations in brain norepinephrine metabolism induced by environmental stimuli previously paired with inescapable shock. *Science* **209,** 1138–1140. [141, 275, 384]

Cazzullo, C.L., Sacchetti, E., Allaria, E., Motta, A., Conte, G., Gasperini, M., and Smeraldi, E. (1982) Is urinary MHPG a real predictor of drug response in primary depression? In E. Costa and G. Racagni (Eds.), *Typical and Atypical Antidepressants: Clinical Practice.* Raven, New York, pp. 237–247. [233, 235]

Cedarbaum, J.M. and Aghajanian, G.K. (1976) Noradrenergic neurons of the locus coeruleus: Inhibition by epinephrine and activation by the alpha-antagonist piperoxane. *Brain Res.* **112,** 413–419. [205]

Cedarbaum, J.M. and Aghajanian, G.K. (1977) Catecholamine receptors on locus coeruleus neurons: Pharmacological characterization. *Eur. J. Pharmacol.* **44,** 375–385. [227, 231]

Celesia, C.G. and Wanamaker, W.M. (1972) Psychiatric disturbances in Parkinson's disease. *Dis. Nerv. Syst.* **33,** 577–583. [170]

Cerrito, F. and Raiteri, M. (1981) Supersensitivity of central noradrenergic presynaptic autoreceptors following chronic treatment with the antidepressant mianserin. *Eur. J. Pharmacol.* **70,** 425–426. [244, 249]

Cervantes, M., Ruelas, R., and Beyer, C. (1983) Serotonergic influences on EEG synchronization induced by milk drinking in the cat. *Pharmacol. Biochem. Behav.* **18,** 851–855. [304]

Chambers, C.A. and Naylor, G.J. (1978) A controlled trial of L-tryptophan in mania. *Br. J. Psychiatr.* **132,** 555–559. [320]

Chance, W.T. and Rosencrans, J.A. (1980a) Lack of cross-tolerance between morphine and autoanalgesia. *Pharmacol. Biochem. Behav.* **11,** 639–642. [360]

Chance, W.T. and Rosencrans, J.A. (1980b) Lack of effect of naloxone on autoanalgesia. *Pharmacol. Biochem. Behav.* **11**, 643–646. [360]

Chance, W.T., White, A.C., Krynock, G.M., and Rosencrans, J.A. (1978) Conditional fear-induced decrease in the binding of [^{3}H]N-Leu-enkephalin to rat brain. *Brain Res.* **141**, 371–374. [359]

Chang, K.J., Cooper, B.R., Hazum, E., and Cuatrescasas, P. (1979) Multiple opiate receptors: Different regional distribution in the brain and differential binding of opiates and opioid peptides. *Mol. Pharmacol.* **16**, 91–104. [358]

Charatan, F.B. and Fisk, A. (1978) The mental and emotional results of strokes. *N.Y. State J. Med.* **78**, 1403–1405. [91]

Charney, D.S. and Heninger, G.R. (1983) Monoamine receptor sensitivity and depression: Clinical studies of antidepressant effects on serotonin and noradrenergic function. *Psychopharmacol. Bull.* **19**, 490–495. [246, 338]

Charney, D.S. and Nelson, J.C. (1981) Delusional and nondelusional unipolar depression: Further evidence for distinct subtypes. *Am. J. Psychiatr.* **138**, 328–333. [52, 172]

Charney, D.S., Heninger, G.R., Sternberg, D.E., Redmond, E.E., Leckman, J.F., Maas, J.W., and Roth, R.H. (1981a) Presynaptic adrenergic receptor sensitivity in depression. *Arch. Gen. Psychiatr.* **38**, 1334–1340. [227, 231]

Charney, D.S., Heninger, G.R., Sternberg, D.E., and Roth, R.H. (1981b) Plasma MHPG in depression: Effects of acute and chronic desipramine treatment. *Psychiatr. Res.* **5**, 217–229. [227, 231, 234, 246, 250]

Charney, D.S., Menkes, D.B., and Heninger, G.R. (1981c) Receptor sensitivity and the mechanism of action of antidepressant treatment: Implications for the etiology and therapy of depression. *Arch. Gen. Psychiatr.* **38**, 1160–1180. [334]

Charney, D.S., Heninger, G.R., and Sternberg, D.E. (1982a) Failure of chronic antidepressant treatment to alter growth hormone response to clonidine. *Psychiatr. Res.* **7**, 135–138. [252]

Charney, D.S., Heninger, G.R., Sternberg, D.E., Hafstad, K.M., Giddings, S., and Landis, D.H. (1982b) Adrenergic receptor sensitivity in depression: Effects of clonidine in depressed patients and healthy subjects. *Arch. Gen. Psychiatr.* **39**, 290–294. [228]

Charney, D.S., Heninger, G.R., Sternberg, D.E., and Landis, H. (1982c) Abrupt discontinuation of tricyclic antidepressant drugs: Evidence for noradrenergic hyperactivity. *Br. J. Psychiatr.* **141**, 377–386. [251]

Charney, D.S., Heninger, G.R., Reinhard, J.F., Sternberg, D., and Hafstad, K. (1982d) The effect of intravenous L-tryptophan on prolactin and growth hormone and mood in healthy subjects. *Psychopharmacology* **78**, 217–222. [320, 338]

Charney, D.S., Heninger, G.R., and Sternberg, D.E. (1983) Alpha-2 adrenergic receptor sensitivity and the mechanism of action of antidepressant therapy: The effect of long-term amitriptyline treatment. *Br. J. Psychiatr.* **142**, 265–275. [246, 251, 252]

Chaurasia, B.D. and Goswami, H.K. (1975) Functional asymmetry in the face. *Acta Anat.* **91**, 154–160. [86]

Checkley, S.A. (1978) A new distinction between the euphoric and antidepressant effects of methamphetamine. *Br. J. Psychiatr.* **133**, 416–423. [176]

Checkley, S.A. (1979) Corticosteroid and growth hormone responses to methylamphetamine in depressive illness. *Psychol. Med.* **9**, 107–115. [229]

Checkley, S.A. and Crammer, J.L. (1977) Hormone responses to methylamphetamine in depression: A new approach to the noradrenaline depletion hypothesis. *Br. J. Psychiatr.* **131**, 582–586. [229]

Checkley, S.A., Slade, A.P., and Shur, E. (1981) Growth hormone and other responses to clonidine in patients with endogenous depression. *Br. J. Psychiatr.* **138**, 51–55. [228, 231, 246]

Checkley, S.A., Meldrum, B.S., and McWilliam, J. (1984) Neuroendocrine studies of the mechanism of action of ECT. In B. Lerer, R.D. Weiner, and R.H. Belmaker (Eds.), *ECT: Basic Mechanisms*. John Libbey, London, pp. 101–106. [187]

Cherek, D.R., Lane, J.D., Freeman, M.E., and Smith, J.E. (1980) Receptor changes following shock avoidance. *Soc. Neurosci. Abstr.* **6**, 543. [157]

Chesner, G.B. and Chan, B. (1977) Footshock induced analgesia in mice: Its reversal by naloxone and cross-tolerance with morphine. *Life Sci.* **21**, 1569–1574. [360]

Chi, C.C. and Flynn, J.P. (1971) Neural pathways associated with hypothalamically elicited attack behaviour in cats. *Science* **171**, 203–205. [363]

Chiodo, L.A. and Antelman, S.M. (1980a) Electroconvulsive shock: Progressive dopamine autoreceptor subsensitivity independent of daily drug treatment. *Science* **210**, 799–801. [184, 185]

Chiodo, L.A. and Antelman, S.M. (1980b) Repeated tricyclics induce a progressive dopamine autoreceptor subsensitivity independent of daily drug treatment. *Nature* **287**, 451–454. [184, 185]

Chiodo, L.A. and Antelman, S.M. (1980c) Repeated tricyclic antidepressants induce a progressive "switch" in the electrophysiological response of dopamine neurons to autoreceptor stimulation. *Eur. J. Pharmacol.* **66**, 255–256. [184]

Chiodo, L.A. and Antelman, S.M. (1982) Do antidepressants induce dopamine autoreceptor subsensitivity? *Nature* **298**, 302–303.

Chiodo, L.A. and Bunney, B.S. (1982) Effects of chronic neuroleptic treatment on nigral dopamine cell activity. *Soc. Neurosci. Abstr.* **8**, 482. [183]

Chiodo, L.A., Caggiula, A.R., Antelman, S.M., and Lineberry, C.G. (1979) Reciprocal influences of activating and immobilizing stimuli on the activity of nigrostriatal dopamine neurons. *Brain Res.* **176**, 385–390. [159, 185]

Chiodo, L.A., Antelman, S.M., Caggiula, A.R., and Lineberry, C.G. (1980) Sensory stimuli alter the discharge rate of dopamine (DA) neurons: Evidence for two functional types of DA cells in the substantia nigra. *Brain Res.* **189**, 544–549. [159, 185]

Chouinard, G., Young, S.N., Annable, L., and Sourkes, T.L. (1979) Tryptophan, nicotinamide, amitriptyline and their combination in depression. *Acta Psychiatr. Scand.* **59**, 395–414. [319–320]

Christensen, N.J., Vestergaard, P., Sorensen, T., and Rafaelsen, O.J. (1980) Cerebrospinal fluid adrenaline and noradrenaline in depressed patients. *Acta Psychiatr. Scand.* **61**, 178–182. [223]

Christie, J.E., Whalley, L.J., Brown, N.S., and Dick, H. (1982) Effect of ECT on the neuroendocrine response to apomorphine in severely depressed patients. *Br. J. Psychiatr.* **140**, 268–273. [186, 187]

Chuang, D.M., Brunello, N., Kinnier, W.J., and Costa, E. (1982) Regulation of the high affinity binding sites for typical and atypical antidepressants in rat brain. In S.Z. Langer, R. Takahashi, T. Segawa, and M. Briley (Eds.), *New Vistas in Depression*. Pergamon, New York, pp. 133–139. [316]

Claasen, V. and Davies, J.E. (1969) Potentiation by tricyclic antidepressants of weight loss caused by amphetamine in rats. *Acta Physiol. Pharmacol. Ned.* **15**, 37–40. [111]

Claghorn, J., Gershon, S., Goldstein, B.J., Behrnetz, S., Bush, D.F., and Huitfeldt, B. (1983) A double-blind evaluation of zimelidine in comparison to placebo and amitriptyline in patients with major depressive disorder. *Prog. Neuropsychopharmacol.* **7**, 367–382. [323]

Clark, A. (1980) *Psychological Models and Neural Mechanisms*. Clarendon, Oxford.

Clark, D. (1982) A psychopharmacological analysis of intracranial self-stimulation. Unpublished Ph.D. thesis, University of Reading, England. [24]

Clark, D.M. and Teasdale, J.D. (1982) Diurnal variation in clinical depression and accessibility of memories of positive and negative experiences. *J. Abnorm. Psychol.* **91**, 87–95. [362]

Clavier, R.M. and Routtenberg, A. (1976) Brainstem self-stimulation attenuated by lesions of medial forebrain bundle but not by lesions of forebrain norepinephrine systems. *Brain Res.* **101**, 251–271. [199]

Clavier, R.M., Fibiger, H.C., and Phillips, A.G. (1976) Evidence that self-stimulation of the region of the locus coeruleus in rats does not depend upon noradrenergic projections to the telencephalon. *Brain Res.* **113**, 71–81. [199]

Clayton, P., Desmarais, L., and Winokur, G. (1968) A study of normal bereavement. *Am. J. Psychiatr.* **125**, 64–74. [66]

Clayton, P.J. (1979) The sequelae and non-sequelae of conjugal bereavement. *Am. J. Psychiatr.* **136**, 1530–1534. [392]

Clements-Jewery, S. (1978) The development of cortical beta-adrenoceptor subsensitivity in the rat by chronic treatment with trazodone, doxepin and mianserin. *Neuropharmacology* **17**, 779–781. [257, 266]

Clineschmidt, B.V. and Lotti, V.J. (1973) Histamine: Intraventricular injection suppresses ingestive behaviour of the cat. *Arch. Int. Pharmacodyn. Ther.* **206**, 288–298. [367]

Cobb, S. (1976) Social support as a moderator of life stress. *Psychosom. Med.* **38**, 300–314. [393]

Cobbin, D.M., Requin-Blow, B., Williams, L.R., and Williams, W.O. (1979) Urinary MHPG levels and tricyclic antidepressant drug selection. *Arch. Gen. Psychiatr.* **36**, 1111–1115. [226, 233, 235, 250, 251]

Cochran, E., Robins, E., and Grote, S. (1976) Regional serotonin levels in brain: A comparison of depressive suicides and alcoholic suicides with controls. *Biol. Psychiatr.* **11**, 283–294. [309]

Cofer, D.H. and Wittenborn, J.R. (1980) Personality characteristics of formerly depressed women. *J. Abnorm. Psychol.* **89**, 309–314. [74, 394]

Cohen, B.D., Penick, S.B., and Tartar, R.E. (1974) Antidepressant effects of unilateral electroconvulsive shock therapy. *Arch. Gen. Psychiatr.* **31**, 673–675. [89]

Cohen, B.M., Miller, A.L., Lipinsky, J.F., and Pope, H.G. (1980) Lecithin in mania: A preliminary report. *Am. J. Psychiatr.* **137**, 242–243. [282]

Cohen, B.M., Lipinsky, J.F., and Altesmar, R.F. (1982) Lecithin in the treatment of mania. *Am. J. Psychiatr.* **138**, 1162–1164. [282]

Cohen, D.B. (1979) Dysphoric affect and REM sleep. *J. Abnorm. Psychol.* **88**, 73–77. [54]

Cohen, R.M. and Cohen, M.R. (1981) Peptide challenges in affective illness. *J. Clin. Psychopharmacol.* **1**, 214–222. [371, 373]

Cohen, R.M., Campbell, I.C., Cohen, M.R., Torda, T., Pickar, D., Siever, L.J., and Murphy, D.L. (1980) Presynaptic noradrenergic regulation during depression and antidepressant drug treatment. *Psychiatr. Res.* **3**, 93–105. [17, 244, 245, 255]

Cohen, R.M., Campbell, I.C., Dauphin, M., Tallman, J.F., and Murphy, D.L. (1982a) Changes in alpha- and beta-receptor densities in rat brain as a result of treatment with monamine oxidase inhibiting antidepressants. *Neuropharmacology* **21**, 293–298. [247, 257]

Cohen, R.M., Ebstein, R.P., Daly, J.W., and Murphy, D.L. (1982b) Chronic effects of a monoamine oxidase inhibiting antidepressant: decreases in functional alpha-adrenergic autoreceptors precede the decrease in norepinephrine-stimulated cyclic adenosine $3':5'$-monophosphate systems in rat brain. *J. Neurosci.* **2**, 1588–1595. [244, 247]

Cohen, R.M., Weingartner, H., Smallberg, S.A., Pickar, D., and Murphy, D.L. (1982c) Effort and cognition in depression. *Arch. Gen. Psychiatr.* **39**, 593–597. [64–66, 207, 213]

Cohen, S. (1970) *Drugs of Hallucination.* Paladin, London. [21]

Cohn, C.K., Dunner, D.L., and Axelrod, J. (1970) Reduced catechol-O-methyltransferase activity in red blood cells of women with primary affective disorders. *Science* **170**, 1323–1324. [164–220]

Coid, B. and Strang, M. (1982) Mania secondary to procyclidine ("Kemadrin") abuse. *Br. J. Psychiatr.* **141**, 81–84. [283]

Colbert, J. and Harrow, M. (1968) Psychomotor retardation in depressive syndromes. *J. Nerv. Ment. Disord.* **145**, 405–419. [64]

Cole, C.S. and Coyne, J.C. (1977) Situational specificity of laboratory-induced learned helplessness. *J. Abnorm. Psychol.* **86**, 615–623. [75, 126]

Cole, E.N., Groom, G.V., Link, J., O'Flanagan, P.M., and Seldrup, J. (1976) Plasma prolactin concentrations in patients on clomipramine. *Postgrad. Med. J.* **52** (Suppl. 3), 93–100. [166]

Cole, J.O., Hartmann, E., and Brigham, P. (1980) L-tryptophan: Clinical studies. *McLean Hosp. J.* **5**, 37–71. [319]

Coleman, B.S. and Block, B.A. (1982) Fluvoxamine maleate, a serotonergic antidepressant: A comparison with chlorimipramine. *Prog. Neuropsychopharmacol. Biol. Psychiatr.* **6**, 475–478. [323]

Coleman, R.E. (1975) Manipulation of self-esteem as a determinant of mood of elated and depressed women. *J. Abnorm. Psychol.* **84**, 693–700. [68]

Colonna, L., Petit, M., and Lepine, J.P. (1979) Bromocryptine in depressive disorders. *J. Affect. Disord.* **1**, 173–177. [174]

Colpaert, F.C., Lenaerts, F.M., Niemegeers, C.J.E., and Janssen, P.A.J. (1975) A critical study on Ro-4-1284 antagonism in mice. *Arch. Int. Pharmacodyn.* **215**, 40–90. [110]

Colpaert, F.C., Niemegeers, C.J.E., and Janssen, P.A. (1978a) Neuroleptic interference with the cocaine cue: Internal stimulus control of behaviour and psychosis. *Psychopharmacology* **58**, 247–255. [152]

Colpaert, F.C., Niemegeers, C.J.E., and Janssen, P.A. (1978b) Discriminative stimulus properties of cocaine and D-amphetamine, and antagonism by haloperidol: A comparative study. *Neuropharmacology* **17**, 937–942. [152]

Cook, L. and Sepinwall, J. (1975) Behavioral analysis of the effects and mechanisms of action of benzodiazepines. In E. Costa and P. Greengard (Eds.), *Mechanisms of Action of Benzodiazepines*. Raven, New York, pp. 1–28. [294]

Cookson, J. and Silverstone, T. (1976) 5-hydroxytryptamine and dopamine pathways in mania: A pilot study of fenfluramine and pimozide. *Br. J. Clin. Pharmacol.* **3**, 942–943. [322]

Cooper, A.J. (1979) Tryptophan antidepressant: Physiological sedative, fact or fancy. *Psychopharmacology* **61**, 97–102. [319]

Cooper, D.S., Gelenberg, A.J., Wojcik, J.C., Saxe, V.C., Ridgeway, E.C., and Maloof, F. (1981) The effect of amoxapine and imipramine on serum prolactin levels. *Arch. Int. Med.* **141**, 1023–1025. [187, 337]

Cooper, J.R., Bloom, F.E., and Roth, R.H. (1982) *The Biochemical Basis of Neuropharmacology*, 4th ed. Oxford University Press, New York. [148, 149, 288, 300, 310]

Coper, H., Deyhle, G., Fahndrich, C., Fahndrich, E., Rosenberg, L., and Strauss, S. (1972) Excretion of vanillylmandelic acid, homovanillic acid, N-methylnicotinamide, and N-methyl-2-pyriodone-5-carboxamide in urine of voluntary test persons and psychiatric patients before and after administration of methionine. *Pharmakopsychiatria* **5**, 177–187. [224]

Copp, F.C., Green, A.F., Hodson, H.F., Randall, A.W., and Sim, M.F. (1967) New peripheral antagonists of 5-hydroxytryptamine. *Nature* **214**, 200–201. [300]

Coppen, A. (1967) The biochemistry of affective disorders. *Br. J. Psychiatr.* **113**, 1237–1264. [319]

Coppen, A. and Ghose, K. (1978) Peripheral alpha-adrenoceptor and central dopamine receptor activity in depressive patients. *Psychopharmacology* **59**, 171–177. [165, 166, 187, 218, 254]

Coppen, A. and Wood, K. (1979) Adrenergic and serotonergic mechanisms in depression and their response to amitriptyline. *Ciba Found. Symp.* **74**, 157–166. [316]

Coppen, A. and Wood, K.M. (1980) Peripheral serotonergic and adrenergic responses in depression. *Acta Psychiatr. Scand.* **61** (Suppl. 280), 21–28. [333]

Coppen, A., Shaw, D.M., and Farrell, J.P. (1963) Potentiation of the antidepressive effect of a monoamine-oxidase inhibitor by tryptophan. *Lancet* **1**, 90–91. [10, 319]

Coppen, A., Brooksbank, B.W.L., and Peet, M. (1972a) Tryptophan concentration in the cerebrospinal fluid of depressive patients. *Lancet* **1**, 1393. [309]

Coppen, A., Prange, A.J., Whybrow, P.C., and Noguera, R. (1972b) Abnormalities of indoleamines in affective disorders. *Arch. Gen. Psychiatr.* **26**, 474–478. [311, 312]

Coppen, A., Eccleston, E.G., and Peet, M. (1973) Total and free tryptophan concentration in the plasma of depressive patients. *Lancet* **2**, 60–63. [308]

Coppen, A., Brooksbank, B.W.L., Eccleston, E., Peet, M., and White, S.G. (1974) Tryptophan metabolism in depressive illness. *Psychol. Med.* **45**, 164–173. [308]

Coppen, A., Swade, C., and Wood, K. (1978) Platelet 5-hydroxytrytamine accumulation in depressive illness. *Clin. Chim. Acta* **87**, 165–168. [315]

Coppen, A., Rao, V.A.R., Ruthven, C.R., Goodwin, B.L., and Sandler, M. (1979) Urinary 3-hydroxy-4-methoxyphenylglycol is not a predictor for clinical response to amitriptyline in depressive illness. *Psychopharmacology* **64**, 95–97. [235]

Coppen, A., Rao, V.A.R., Bishop, M. Abou-Sahe, M.T., and Wood, K. (1980a) Neuroendocrine studies in affective disorders. I. Plasma prolactin response to thyrotropin-releasing hormone in affective disorders: Effect of ECT. *J. Affect. Disord.* **2**, 311–315. [315, 338]

Coppen, A., Swade, C., and Wood, K. (1980b) Lithium restores abnormal platelet 5-HT transport in patients with affective disorders. *Br. J. Psychiatr.* **136**, 235–238. [315, 316, 333]

Coppen, A., Swade, C., and Wood, K. (1981) The action of antidepressant drugs on 5-hydroxytryptamine uptake by platelets—Relationship to therapeutic effect. *Acta Psychiatr. Scand.* **63** (Suppl. 290), 236–243. [333]

Corbett, D. (1980) Long term potentiation of lateral hypothalamic self-stimulation following parabrachial lesions in the rat. *Brain Res. Bull.* **5**, 637–642. [196]

Corbett, D. and Wise, R.A. (1979) Intracranial self-stimulation in relation to the ascending noradrenegic fibre systems of the pontine tegmentum and caudal midbrain: A moveable electrode mapping study. *Brain Res.* **177**, 423–436. [200]

Cornfeldt, M., Fisher, B., and Fielding, S. (1982) Rat internal capsule lesion: A new test for detecting antidepressants. *Fed. Proc.* **41**, 1066. [135]

Corona, G.L., Cucchi, M.L., Santagostino, G., Frattini, P., Zerbi, F., Fenoglio, L., and Savoldi, F. (1982) Blood noradrenaline and 5-HT levels in depressed women during amitriptyline or lithium treatment. *Psychopharmacology* **77**, 236–241. [316]

Corrodi, H. and Fuxe, K. (1969) Decreased turnover in central 5-HT nerve terminals induced by antidepressant drugs of the imipramine type. *Eur. J. Pharmacol.* **7**, 56–59. [329]

Corrodi, H., Fuxe, K., and Lidbrink, P. (1972) Interaction between cholinergic and catecholaminergic neurons in rat brain. *Brain Res.* **43**, 397–416. [379]

Coryell, W., Gaffney, G., and Burkhardt, P.E. (1982) DSM-III melancholia and the primary-secondary distinction: A comparison of concurrent validity by means of the dexamethasone suppression test. *Am. J. Psychiatr.* **139**, 120–122. [54]

Costa, E. (1982) Perspectives in the molecular mechanisms of antidepressant action. In E. Costa and G. Racagni (Eds.), *Typical and Atypical Antidepressants: Molecular Mechanisms.* Raven, New York, pp. 21–26. [259]

Costa, E. and Racagni, G., eds., (1982a) *Typical and Atypical Antidepressants: Molecular Mechanisms,* Raven, New York. [240]

Costa, E. and Racagni, G., eds., (1982b) *Typical and Atypical Antidepressants: Clinical Practice.* Raven, New York. [105]

Costa, E., Garattini, S., and Valzelli, L. (1960) Interactions between reserpine, chlorpromazine and imipramine. *Experientia* **16**, 461–463. [109, 110]

Costain, D.W., Green, A.R., and Grahame-Smith, D.G. (1979) Enhanced 5-hydroxytryptamine-mediated behavioral responses in rats following repeated electroconvulsive shock: Relevance to the mechanism of the antidepressive effect of electroconvulsive therapy. *Psychopharmacology* **61**, 167–170. [339]

Costain, D.W., Cowen, P.J., Gelder, M.G., and Grahame-Smith, D.G. (1982) Electroconvulsive therapy and the brain: Evidence for increased dopamine-mediated responses. *Lancet* **2**, 400–404. [186]

Costall, B. and Naylor, R.J. (1972) Modification of amphetamine effects by intracerebrally administered anticholinergic agents. *Life Sci.* **11**, 239–253. [379]

Costall, B. and Naylor, R.J. (1974) Stereotyped and circling behaviour induced by dopaminergic agonists after lesions of the midbrain raphe nuclei. *Eur. J. Pharmacol.* **29**, 206–222. [378]

Costall, B. and Naylor, R.J. (1976) A comparison of the abilities of typical neuroleptic agents and of thioridazine, clozapine, sulpiride and metaclopramide to antagonize the hyperactivity induced by dopamine applied intracerebrally to areas of the extrapyramidal and mesolimbic systems. *Eur. J. Pharmacol.* **40**, 9–19. [149]

Costall, B. and Naylor, R.J. (1979) Behavioural aspects of dopamine agonists and antagonists. In A.S. Horn, J. Korf, and B.H.C. Westerink (Eds.), *The Neurobiology of Dopamine.* Academic, New York, pp. 555–576. [149]

Costall, B., Naylor, R.J., Marsden, C.B., and Pycock, C.J. (1976) Serotonergic modulation of the dopamine response from the nucleus accumbens. *J. Pharm. Pharmacol.* **28**, 523–526. [378]

Costall, B., Hui, S.-C.G., and Naylor, R.J. (1979) The importance of serotonergic mechanisms for the induction of hyperactivity by amphetamine and its antagonism by intra-accumbens (3,4-dihydroxyl-phenylamino)-2-imidazoline (DPI). *Neuropharmacology* **18**, 605–609. [378]

Costello, C.G. (1972) Depression: Loss of reinforcement or loss of reinforcer effectiveness? *Behav. Ther.* **3**, 240–247. [68, 136]

Costello, C.G. (1978) A critical review of Seligman's laboratory experiments on learned helplessness and depression in humans. *J. Abnorm. Psychol.* **87**, 21–31. [75, 76]

Coupet, J. and Szuchs-Myers, V.A. (1981) Brain histamine H_1 and H_2-receptors and histamine-sensitive adenylate cyclase: Effects of antipsychotics and antidepressants. *Eur. J. Pharmacol.* **74**, 149–155. [368–370]

Coursey, R.D., Buchsbaum, M.S., and Murphy, D.L. (1982) 2-year follow-up of subjects and their families defined as at risk for psychopathology on the basis of platelet MAO activities. *Neuropsychobiology* **8**, 51–56. [221]

Cowen, P.J., Nutt, D.J., and Green, A.R. (1980) Repeated electroconvulsive shock does not increase the susceptibility of rats to a cage convulsant (isopropylbicyclophosphate). *Neuropharmacology* **19**, 1025–1026. [357]

Cowen, P.J., Grahame-Smith, D.G., Green, A.R., and Heal, D.J. (1982) Beta-adrenoceptor agonists enhance 5-hydroxytryptamine-mediated behavioural responses. *Br. J. Pharmacol.* **76**, 265–270. [343]

Cowen, P.J., Fraser, S., Grahame-Smith, D.G., Green, A.R., and Stanford, C. (1983) The effect of chronic antidepressant administration on beta-adrenoceptor function of the rat pineal. *Br. J. Pharmacol.* **78**, 89–96. [262, 263]

Coyne, J.C., Aldwin, C., and Lazarus, R.S. (1980a) Depression and coping in stressful episodes. *J. Abnorm. Psychol.* **90**, 439–447. [78]

Coyne, J.C., Metalsky, G.I., and Lavelle, T.L. (1980b) Learned helplessness as experimenter-induced failure and its alleviation with attentional redeployment. *J. Abnorm. Psychol.* **89**, 350–357. [75, 77, 79]

Crane, G.E. (1957) Iproniazid (Marsilid) phosphate, a therapeutic agent for mental disorders and debilitating diseases. *Psychiatr. Res. Rep. Am. Psychiatr. Assoc.* **8**, 142–152. [3]

Crawley, J.N., Maas, J.W., and Roth, R.H. (1980) Biochemical evidence for simultaneous activation of multiple locus coeruleus efferents. *Life Sci.* **26**, 1373–1378. [235]

Creese, I. (1974) Behavioral evidence of dopamine receptor stimulation by piribedil (ET-495) and its metabolite S584. *Eur. J. Pharmacol.* **28**, 55–58. [174]

Creese, I. and Snyder, S.H. (1978) Behavioral and biochemical properties of the dopamine receptor. In M.A. Lipton, A. DiMaschio, and K.F. Killam (Eds.), *Psychopharmacology: A Generation of Progress.* Raven, New York, pp. 377–388. [104, 170]

Creese, I., Kuczenski, R. and Segal, D. (1982) Lack of behavioral evidence for dopamine autoreceptor subsensitivity after acute electroconvulsive shock. *Pharmacol. Biochem. Behav.* **17**, 375–376. [185]

Creese, I., Sibley, D.R., Hamblin, M.W., and Leff, S.E. (1983) Dopamine receptors in the central nervous system. In T. Segawa, H.I. Yamamura, and K. Kuriyama (Eds.), *Molecular Pharmacology of Neurotransmitter Receptors.* Raven, New York, pp. 125–133. [185]

Cremata, V.Y. and Koe, B.K. (1966) Clinical-pharmacological evaluation of p-chlorophenylalanine: A new serotonin-depleting agent. *Clin. Pharmacol. Ther.* **7**, 768–776. [317]

Crews, F.T. and Smith, C.B. (1978) Presynaptic alpha-receptor subsensitivity after long-term antidepressant treatment. *Science* **202**, 322–324. [244]

Crews, F.T. and Smith, C.B. (1980) Potentiation of responses to adrenergic nerve stimulation in isolated rat atria during chronic tricyclic antidepressant administration. *J. Pharmacol. Exp. Ther.* **215**, 143–149. [244]

Crews, F.T., Paul, S.M., and Goodwin, F.K. (1981) Acceleration of beta-receptor desensitization in combined administration of antidepressants and phenoxybenzamine. *Nature* **290**, 787–789. [259]

Crick, F. and Mitchison, G. (1983) The function of dream sleep. *Nature* **304**, 111–114. [382]

Crick, F., Barnett, L., Brenner, S., and Watts-Tobin, R. (1961) General nature of the genetic code for proteins. *Nature* **192**, 1227–1232. [25]

Cronin, D., Bodley, P., and Potts, L. (1970) Unilateral and bilateral ECT: A study of memory disturbance and relief from depression. *J. Neurol. Neurosurg. Psychiatr.* **33**, 705–713. [89]

Crosby, E.C., Humphrey, T., and Lauer, E.W. (1962) *Correlative Anatomy of the Nervous System.* Macmillan, New York. [89]

Cross, A.J., Deakin, J.F.W., Lofthouse, R., Longden, A., Owen, F., and Poulter, M. (1979) On the mechanism of action of electroconvulsive therapy: Some behavioral and biochemical consequences of repeated electrically induced seizures in rats. *Br. J. Pharmacol.* **66**, 111P. [188, 356]

Crow, T.J. (1972) Catecholamine-containing neurons and electrical self-stimulation. I. A review of some data. *Psychol. Med.* **2**, 414–421. [199]

Crow, T.J. and Arbuthnott, G.W. (1972) Function of catecholamine-containing neurones in mammalian central nervous system. *Nature* **238**, 245–246. [200]

Crow, T.J., Spear, P.J., and Arbuthnott, G.W. (1972) Intracranial self-stimulation with electrodes in the region of the locus coeruleus. *Brain Res.* **36**, 275–287. [199]

Crow, T.J., Deakin, J.F.W., Johnstone, E.C., Joseph, M.H., and Lawler, P.D. (1984) Mechanism of action of ECT—relevance of clinical evidence: Is noradrenergic failure associated with the development of depressive delusions. In B. Lerer, R.D. Weiner, and R.H. Belmaker (Eds.), *ECT: Basic Mechanisms*. John Libbey, London, pp. 148–155. [225]

Curtis, G.C., Cameron, O.G., and Nesse, R.M. (1982) The dexamethasone suppression test in panic disorder and agoraphobia. *Am. J. Psychiatr.* **139**, 1043–1046. [53]

Curzon, G. (1969) Tryptophan pyrrolase—A biochemical factor in depressive illness? *Br. J. Psychiatr.* **115**, 1367–1374. [308]

Curzon, G., Joseph, M.H., and Knott, P.J. (1972) Effects of immobilization and food deprivation on rat brain tryptophan metabolism. *J. Neurochem.* **19**, 1967–1974. [289]

Curzon, G., Kantamaneni, B.D., Van Boxel, P., Gillman, P.K., Bartlett, J.F., and Bridges, P.K. (1980) Substances related to 5-hydroxytryptamine in plasma and in lumbar and ventricular fluids of psychiatric patients. *Acta Psychiatr. Scand.* **61** (Suppl. 280), 3–20. [309, 310]

Cytawa, J., Jurkowlaniec, E., and Bialowas, J. (1980) Positive reinforcement produced by noradrenergic stimulation of the hypothalamus in rats. *Physiol. Behav.* **25**, 615–619. [200]

D'Elia, G. and Perris, C. (1973) Cerebral functional dominance and depression: An analysis of EEG amplitude in depressed patients. *Acta Psychiatr. Scand.* **49**, 191–197. [88]

D'Elia, G. and Perris, C. (1974) Cerebral functional dominance and memory function: An analysis of EEG integrated amplitude in depressed psychotics. *Acta Psychiatr. Scand.* **255**, 143–157. [89]

D'Elia, G. and Raotma, H. (1975) Is unilateral ECT less effective than bilateral ECT? *Br. J. Psychiatr.* **126**, 83–89. [89]

Da Prada, M., Saver, A., Burkard, W.P., Bartholini, G., and Pletscher, A. (1975) Lysergic and diethylamide: Evidence for stimulation of central DA receptors. *Brain Res.* **94**, 167–175. [21]

Dahl, L.-E., Lundin, L., Honore, P. Le F., and Dencker, S.J. (1982) Antidepressant effect of femoxetine and desipramine and relationship to the concentration of amine metabolites in cerebrospinal fluid: A double-blind evaluation. *Acta Psychiatr. Scand.* **66**, 9–17. [234, 255, 323, 333]

Dahlstrom, A. and Fuxe, K. (1965) Evidence for the existence of monamine neurons in the central nervous system. II. Experimentally induced changes in the amine levels of bulbospinal neuron systems. *Acta Physiol. Scand.* **64** (Suppl. 247), 1–36. [288]

Daiguji, M., Meltzer, H.Y., Tong, C., U'Pritchard, D.C., Young, M., and Kravitz, B. (1981) Alpha-2-adrenergic receptors in platelet membranes of depressed patients: No change in number or ^{3}H-yohimbine affinity. *Life Sci.* **29**, 2059–2064. [219]

Dalen, P., Ljundberg, T., and Ungerstedt, U. (1973) The modified amine hypothesis. *Lancet* **1**, 1196–1197. [169]

Dalhouse, A.D. (1976) Social cohesiveness, hypersexuality and irritability induced by p-CPA in the rat. *Physiol. Behav.* **17**, 679–686. [295]

Danguir, J., Nicolaidis, S., and Gerard, H. (1979) Relations between feeding and sleep patterns in the rat. *J. Comp. Physiol. Psychol.* **93**, 820–830. [303]

Dashieff, R.M., Savage, D.D., and McNamara, J.O. (1982) Seizures down-regulate muscarinic cholinergic receptors in hippocampal formation. *Brain Res.* **235**, 327–334. [285]

Davidson, R.J. and Fox, N.A. (1982) Asymmetrical brain activity discriminates between positive and negative affective stimuli in human infants. *Science* **218**, 1235–1237. [87]

Davidson, R.J., Schwartz, G.E., Bennett, J., and Goleman, D.J. (1979) Frontal versus parietal EEG asymmetry during positive and negative affect. *Psychophysiology* **16**, 202–203. [87]

Davidson, R.T., McLeod, M.N., Turnbull, C.D., White, H.L., and Feuer, E.J. (1980) Platelet monoamine oxidase activity and the classification of depression. *Arch. Gen. Psychiatr.* **37**, 771–773. [221]

Davies, D.S., Wing, L.M.H., Reid, J.L., Neil, E., Tippett, P., and Dollery, C.T. (1977) Pharmacokinetics and concentration-effect relationships of intravenous and oral clonidine. *Clin. Pharmacol. Ther.* **21**, 593–601. [231]

Davies, R.J., Rossi, J., Panksepp, J., and Zolovick, A.J. (1983) Fenfluramine anorexia: A peripheral locus of action. *Physiol. Behav.* **30**, 723–730. [303]

Davis, G.C., Bunney, W.E., Defraites, E.G., Kleinman, J.E., Kammen, D.P., Post, R.M., and Wyatt, R.J. (1977) Intravenous naloxone administration in schizophrenia and affective illness. *Science* **197**, 74–77. [366]

Davis, G.C., Buchsbaum, M.S., and Bunney, W.E. (1979) Analgesia to painful stimuli in affective illness. *Am. J. Psychiatr.* **136**, 1148–1151. [69]

Davis, G.C., Extein, I., Reus, V.I., Hamilton, W., Post, R.M., Goodwin, F.K., and Bunney, W.E. (1980) Failure of naloxone to reduce manic symptoms. *Am. J. Psychiatr.* **137**, 583–585. [366]

Davis, G.C., Buchsbaum, M.S., Naber, D., Pickar, D., Post, R., Van Kammen, D., and Bunney, W.E. (1982) Altered pain perception and cerebrospinal endorphins in psychiatric illness. *Ann. N.Y. Acad. Sci.* **398**, 366–374. [364, 365]

Davis, H. and Unruh, W.R. (1981) The development of the self-schema in adult depression. *J. Abnorm. Psychol.* **90**, 125–133. [74]

Davis, K.L., Hollister, L.E., and Overall, J. (1976) Physostigmine effects on cognition and affect in normal subjects. *Psychopharmacology,* **51**, 23–27. [282]

Davis, K.L., Hollister, L.E., Goodwin, F.K., and Gordon, E.K. (1977) Neurotransmitter metabolites in cerebrospinal fluid of man following physostigmine. *Life Sci.* **21**, 933–936. [381]

Davis, K.L., Berger, P.A., Hollister, L.E., and Defraites, E. (1978) Physostigmine in man. *Arch. Gen. Psychiatr.* **35**, 119–122. [282]

Davis, K.L., Hollister, L.E., and Berger, P.A. (1979) Choline chloride in schizophrenia. *Am. J. Psychiatr.* **136**, 1581–1584. [281]

Davis, K.L., Hollister, L.E., Mathe, A.A., Davis, B.M., Rothpearl, A.B., Faull, K.Y., Hsieh, J.Y.K., Barchas, J.D., and Berger, P.A. (1981) Neuroendocrine and neurochemical measurements in depression. *Am. J. Psychiatr.* **138**, 1555–1562. [223, 311, 372]

Davis, M. (1982) Agonist-induced changes in behaviour as a measure of functional changes in receptor sensitivity following chronic antidepressant treatment. *Psychopharmacol. Bull.* **18**, 137–147. [14, 103, 245, 253–255]

Davis, M. and Sheard, M.H. (1974) Habituation and sensitization of the rat startle response: Effect of raphe lesions. *Physiol. Behav.* **12**, 425–431. [295]

Davis, M., Astrachan, D.I., and Kass, E. (1980) Excitatory and inhibitory effects of serotonin on sensorimotor reactivity measured with acoustic startle. *Science* **209**, 521–523. [289, 295, 296]

Davis, W.D. and Smith, S.G. (1983) Effects of pharmacological lesions upon opiate reinforcement. In J.E. Smith and J.D. Lane (Eds.), *The Neurobiology of Opiate Reward Processes.* Elsevier, New York, pp. 281–307. [386]

Davitz, J. (1969) *The Language of Emotion.* Academic, New York. [36–40]

Daw, N.W., Rader, R.K., Robertson, T.W., and Ariel, M. (1982) Effects of 6-hydroxydopamine on visual deprivation in the kitten visual cortex. *J. Neurosci.* **3**, 907–914. [202]

Day, M.D. and Rand, M.J. (1963) Awakening from reserpine sedation by alpha-methyl dopa. *J. Pharm. Pharmacol.* **15**, 631–632. [110]

De Johnge, F.E.R.E.R. and Van der Helm, H.J. (1970) Plasma concentrations of thioridazine in patients with depression. *Acta Psychiatr. Scand.* **46**, 360–364. [171]

De La Fuente, J.-R. and Rosenbaum, A.H. (1981) Prolactin in psychiatry. *Am. J. Psychiatr.* **138**, 1154–1160. [314]

De Monbreun, B.G. and Craighead, W.E. (1977) Distortion of perception and recall of positive and neutral feedback in depression. *Cogn. Ther. Res.* **1**, 311–329. [70]

De Montigny, C. (1980) Electroconvulsive shock treatment increases responsiveness of forebrain neurons to serotonin: A microiontophoretic study in the rat. *Soc. Neurosci. Abstr.* **6**, 453. [262, 264, 356]

De Montigny, C. (1981) Enhancement of the 5-HT neurotransmission by antidepressant treatments. *J. Physiol. (Paris)* **77**, 455–461. [335, 336]

De Montigny, C. and Aghajanian, G.K. (1978) Tricyclic antidepressants: Long-term treatment increases responsivity of rat forebrain neurons to serotonin. *Science* **202**, 1303–1306. [253, 262, 264, 335, 336, 356]

De Montigny, C., Blier, P., Caille, G., and Kouassi, E. (1981a) Pre- and postsynaptic effects of zimelidine and norzimelidine on the serotonergic system: Single cell studies in the rat. *Acta Psychiatr. Scand.* **63** (Suppl. 290), 79–90. [262, 264, 329, 335, 336, 356]

De Montigny, C., Tan, A.-T., and Caille, G. (1981b) Short-term lithium enhances 5HT neurotransmission in rats administered chronic antidepressant treatments. *Soc. Neurosci. Abstr.* **7**, 646. [341, 343]

De Myer, M.K., Shea, P.A., Hendrie, H.C., and Yoshimura, N.N. (1981) Plasma tryptophan and five other amino acids in depressed and normal subjects. *Arch. Gen. Psychiatr.* **38**, 642–646. [164, 222, 309]

Deakin, J.F.W. (1980) On the neurochemical basis of self-stimulation with midbrain raphe electrode placements. *Pharmacol. Biochem. Behav.* **13**, 525–530. [301]

Deakin, J.F.W., Dickenson, A.H., and Dostrowsky, J.O. (1977) Morphine effects on rat raphe magnus neurons. *J. Physiol. (London)* **267**, 43P. [299]

Deakin, J.F.W., File, S.E., Hyde, J.R.G., and Macleod, N.K. (1979) Ascending 5-HT pathways and behavioral habituation. *Pharmacol. Biochem. Behav.* **10**, 687–694. [294]

Deakin, J.F.W., Owen, F., Cross, A.J., and Dashwood, M.J. (1981) Studies on possible mechanisms of action of electroconvulsive therapy: Effects of repeated seizures on rat brain receptors for monoamines and other neurotransmitters. *Psychopharmacology* **73**, 345–349. [190, 285, 356, 357]

Dean, A. and Lin, N. (1977) The stress-buffering role of social support. *J. Nerv. Ment. Disord.* **165**, 403–417. [142]

Delacour, J., Echevarria, M.J., Senault, B., and Houcine, O. (1977) Specificity of avoidance deficits produced by 6-hydroxydopamine lesions of the nigrostriatal system of the rat. *J. Comp. Physiol. Psychol.* **91**, 875–885. [156]

Delanqy, R.L., Wickliff, C.A., Zornetzer, S.F., and Dunn, A.J. (1978) Effects of locus coeruleus stimulation on regional blood flow in mice. *Soc. Neurosci. Abstr.* **4**, 271. [198]

Delina-Stula, A. and Vassout, A. (1979a) Differential effects of psychoactive drugs on aggressive responses in rats and mice. In M. Sandler (Ed.), *Psychopharmacology of Aggression*. Raven, New York, pp. 41–60. [107]

Delina-Stula, A. and Vassout, A. (1979b) Modulation of dopamine-mediated behavioral responses by antidepressants: Effects of single and repeated treatment. *Eur. J. Pharmacol.* **58**, 443–451. [188]

Delina-Stula, A., Baumann, P., and Buch, O. (1979) Depression of exploratory activity by clonidine in rats as a model for the detection of pre- and postsynaptic central noradrenergic receptor selectivity of alpha-adrenolytic drugs. *Naunyn Schmiedebergs Arch. Pharmacol.* **307**, 115–122. [243]

Delina-Stula, A., Hauser, K., Baumann, P., Olpe, H.-R., Waldmeier, P., and Storni, A. (1982) Stereospecificity of behavioral and biochemical responses to oxaprotiline—A new antidepressant. In E. Costa and G. Racagni (Eds.), *Typical and Atypical Antidepressants: Molecular Mechanisms.* Raven, New York, pp. 265–275. [252, 259, 262, 264]

DeMuth, G.W. and Ackerman, S.H. (1983) Alpha-methyldopa and depression: A clinical study and review of the literature. *Am. J. Psychiatr.* **140**, 534–538. [170]

Dencker, S.J., Malm, V., Roos, B.-E., and Werdinius, B. (1966) Acid monoamine metabolites of cerebrospinal fluid in mental depression and mania. *J. Neurochem.* **13**, 1545–1548. [311–313]

Dennenberg, V.H., Garbanati, J., Sherman, G., Yutzey, D.A., and Kaplan, R. (1978) Infantile stimulation induces brain lateralization in rats. *Science* **201**, 1150–1152. [97]

Dennenberg, V.H., Hofmann, M., Garbanati, J.A., Sherman, G.F., Rosen, G.D., and Yutzey, D.A. (1980) Handling in infancy, taste aversion, and brain laterality in rats. *Brain Res.* **200**, 123–133. [97]

Depue, R.A. (Ed.) (1979) *The Psychobiology of the Depressive Disorders: Implications for the Effects of Stress.* Academic, New York. [131]

Depue, R.A. and Monroe, S.M. (1978) Learned helplessness in the perspective of the depressive disorders: Conceptual and definitional issues. *J. Abnorm. Psychol.* **87**, 3–20. [45, 76, 79, 123, 124]

Depue, R.A. and Monroe, S.M. (1979) The unipolar-bipolar distinction in the depressive disorders: Implications for stress-onset interactions. In R.A. Depue (Ed.), *The Psychobiology of the Depressive Disorders: Implications for the Effects of Stress.* Academic, New York, pp. 23–53. [45, 124, 131.]

Depue, R.A., Slater, J.F., Wolfstetter-Kausch, H., Klein, D., Goplerud, E., and Farr, D. (1981) A behavioral paradigm for identifying persons at risk for bipolar depressive disorder: A conceptual framework and five validation studies. *J. Abnorm. Psychol. Monogr.* **90**, 381–437. [56]

Derry, P.A. and Kuiper, N.A. (1981) Schematic processing and self-reference in clinical depression. *J. Abnorm. Psychol.* **90**, 286–297. [70, 74]

Detre, T.P., Himmelhoch, J., Swartzburg, M., Anderson, B.M., Byck, R., and Kupfer, D.J. (1972) Hypersomnia and manic-depressive disease. *Am. J. Psychiatr.* **128**, 1303–1305. [46]

DeVoize, J.L., Rigal, F., Eschalier, A., and Trolese, J.F. (1982) Naloxone inhibits clomipramine in mouse forced swimming test. *Eur. J. Pharmacol.* **74**, 1–7. [367]

DeVoize, J.L., Rigal, F., Eschalier, A., Trolese, J.F., and Renoux, M. (1983) Influence of naloxone on antidepressant drugs in forced swimming test in mice. *Psychopharmacology* (in press). [367]

Dewhurst, W.G. (1968) Methysergide in mania. *Nature* **219**, 506–507. [318]

DiChiara, G., Camba, R., and Spano, P.F. (1971) Evidence for inhibition by brain serotonin of mouse killing behaviour in rats. *Nature* **233**, 272–273. [292]

Dickenson, A.H., Oliveras, J.L., and Besson, J.M. (1979) Role of the nucleus raphe magnus in opiate analgesia as studied by the microinjection technique in the rat. *Brain Res.* **170**, 95–111. [299]

Dickinson, S.L. and Curzon, G. (1983) Roles of dopamine and 5-hydroxytryptamine in stereotyped and non-stereotyped behaviour. *Neuropharmacology* **22**, 805–812. [378]

Diener, C. and Dweck, C. (1978) An analysis of learned helplessness: Continuous changes in performance, strategy, and achievement cognitions following failure. *J. Pers. Soc. Psychol.* **36**, 451–462. [78]

Diffley, D., Tran, V.H., and Snyder, S.H. (1980) Histamine H_1-receptors labelled in vivo: Antidepressant and antihistamine interactions. *Eur. J. Pharmacol.* **64**, 177–181. [368]

Dimond, S.J. and Farrington, L. (1977) Emotional response to films shown to the right or left hemisphere of the brain measured by heart rate. *Acta Psychol.* **41**, 255–260. [87]

Dimond, S.J., Farrington, L., and Johnson, P. (1976) Differing emotional response from right and left hemispheres. *Nature* **261**, 690–692. [87]

Dingell, J.V., Sulser, F., and Gillette, J.R. (1964) Species differences in the metabolism of imipramine and desmethylimipramine (DMI). *J. Pharmacol. Exp. Ther.* **143**, 14–22. [181]

Dismukes, R.J. and Daly, J.W. (1974) Norepinephrine-sensitive systems generating adenosine 3′,5′ monophosphate: Increased responses in cerebral cortical slices from reserpine-treated rats. *Mol. Pharmacol.* **10**, 933–940. [256]

Dixit, V.M. (1979) Cause of depression in chronic scurvy. *Lancet* **2**, 1077–1078. [230, 236]

Doerr, P. and Berger, M. (1983) Physostigmine-induced escape from dexamethasone suppression in normal adults. *Biol. Psychiatr.* **18**, 261–268. [278]

Doerr, P., Fichter, M., Pirke, K.M., and Lund, R. (1980) Relationship between weight gain and hypothalamic pituitary adrenal function in patients with anorexia nervosa. *J. Steroid Biochem.* **13**, 529–537. [53]

Domshke, W., Dickshas, A., and Mitznegg, P. (1979) CSF beta-endorphin in schizophrenia. *Lancet* **2**, 1024 [365]

Donaldson, I.M., Dolphin, A., Jenner, P., Marsden, D.C., and Pycock, C. (1976) The roles of noradrenaline and dopamine in contraversive circling behavior seen after unilateral electrolytic lesions of the locus coeruleus. *Eur. J. Pharmacol.* **39**, 179–191. [376]

Donnelly, E.F. and Murphy, D.L. (1973) Primary affective disorder: MMPI differences between unipolar and bipolar depressed subjects. *J. Clin. Psychol.* **29**, 303–306. [131, 168, 174]

Donnelly, E.F., Goodwin, F.K., Waldman, I.N., and Murphy, D.L. (1978) Prediction of antidepressant responses to lithium. *Am. J. Psychiatr.* **135**, 552–556. [46]

Donnelly, E.F., Waldman, I.N., Murphy, D.L., Wyatt, R.J., and Goodwin, F.K. (1980) Primary affective disorder: Thought disorder in depression. *J. Abnorm. Psychol.* **89**, 315–319. [90]

Donnelly, E.F., Murphy, D.L., Goodwin, F.K., and Waldman, I.N. (1982) Intellectual function in primary affective disorder. *Br. J. Psychiatr.* **140**, 633–636. [64]

Dorworth, T.R., and Overmeier, J.B. (1977) On "learned helplessness": The therapeutic effects of electroconvulsive shock. *Physiol. Behav.* **4**, 355–358. [122]

Douglas, W.W. (1975) Histamine antagonists. In L.S. Goodman and A. Gilman (Eds.), *The Pharmacological Basis of Therapeutics*. Raven, New York, pp. 603–611. [368]

Dray, A., Gonye, T.J., Oakley, N.R., and Tanner, T. (1976) Evidence for the existence of a raphe projection to the substantia nigra in rat. *Brain Res.* **113**, 45–57. [378]

Drew, G.M., Gower, A.J., and Marriott, A.S., (1979) Alpha$_2$-adrenoceptors mediate clonidine-induced sedation in the rat. *Br. J. Pharmacol.* **67**, 133–141. [243]

Drucker-Colin, R., Shkurovich, M., and Sterman, M.B. (Eds.) (1979) *The Functions of Sleep*. Academic, New York. [382]

Drugan, R.C., Grau, J.W., Maier, S.F., Madden, J., and Barchas, J.D. (1981) Cross-tolerance between morphine and long-term analgesic reaction to inescapable shock. *Pharmacol. Biochem. Behav.* **14**, 677–682. [359]

Drust, E.G., Sloviter, R.S., and Connor, J.D. (1979) Effect of morphine on "wet-dog" shakes caused by cerebroventricular injections of serotonin. *Pharmacol.* **18**, 299–305. [342]

Dubinsky, B. and Goldberg, M.E. (1971) The effect of imipramine and selected drugs on attack elicited by hypothalamic stimulation in the cat. *Neuropharmacology* **10**, 537–545. [108]

Dubinsky, B., Karpowicz, K. and Goldberg, M. (1973) Effects of tricyclic antidepressants on attack elicited by hypothalamic stimulation: Relation to brain biogenic amines. *J. Pharmacol. Exp. Ther.* **18**, 550–552. [108]

Dumbrille-Ross, A., Tang, S.A., and Seeman, P. (1980) High-affinity binding of [³H]mianserin to rat cerebral cortex. *Eur. J. Pharmacol.* **68**, 395–396. [330]

Dumbrille-Ross, A., Tang, S.A., and Coscina, D.V. (1981) Differential binding of ³H-imipramine and ³H-mianserin in rat cerebral cortex. *Life Sci.* **29**, 2049–2058. [330]

Dumbrille-Ross, A., Tang, S.W., and Coscina, D.V. (1982) Lack of effect of Raphe lesions on serotonin S₂ receptor changes induced by amitriptyline and desmethylimipramine. *Psychiatr. Res.* **7**, 145–151. [345, 346, 348]

Duncan, W.C., Pettigrew, K.D., and Gillin, J.C. (1979) REM architecture changes in bipolar and unipolar depression. *Am. J. Psychiatr.* **136**, 1424–1427. [54, 55]

Dunner, D.L. and Fieve, R.R. (1975) Affective disorders: Studies with amine precursors. *Am. J. Psychiatr.* **132**, 180–183. [178]

Dunner, D.L. and Fieve, R.R. (1978) The effect of lithium in depressive subtypes. In P. Deniker, C. Radouco-Thomas, and A. Villeneuve (Eds.), *Neuropsychopharmacology*. Pergamon, New York, pp. 1109–1115. [46]

Dunner, D.L., Cohn, C.K., Gershon, E.S., and Goodwin, E.S. (1971) Differential catechol-O-methyltransferase activity in unipolar and bipolar illness. *Arch. Gen. Psychiatr.* **25**, 348–353. [164, 220]

Dunner, D.L., Gershon, E.S., and Goodwin, F.K. (1976a) Hereditable factors in the severity of affective illness. *Biol. Psychiatr.* **11**, 31–42. [45]

Dunner, D.L., Levitt, M., Kumbaraci, T., and Fieve, R. (1976b) Erythrocyte catechol-O-methyltransferase activity in primary affective disorder. *Biol. Psychiatr.* **12**, 237–245. [220]

Dunner, D.L., Stallone, F., and Fieve, R.R. (1976c) Lithium carbonate and affective disorders. V. A double-blind study of prophylaxis in bipolar illness. *Arch. Gen. Psychiatr.* **33**, 117–120. [47]

Duvoisin, R.C. and Marsden, C.D. (1974) Reversal of reserpine-induced bradykinesia by alpha-methyldopa: New light on its modus operandi. *Brain Res.* **71**, 178–182. [110]

Eastman, C. (1976) Behavioral formulations of depression. *Psychol. Rev.* **83**, 277–291. [66]

Ebel, A., Mack, G., Stefanovic, V., and Mandel, P. (1973) Activity of choline acetyl transferase in the amygdala of spontaneous killer rats and in rats after olfactory lobe removal. *Brain Res.* **57**, 248–251. [271]

Ebert, M. and Kopin, I.J. (1975) Origins of urinary catecholamine metabolites. Differential labeling by dopamine ¹⁴C. *Trans. Assoc. Am. Physicians* **28**, 256–262. [224]

Ebert, M.A., Post, R.M., and Goodwin, F.K. (1972) Effect of physical activity on urinary MHPG excretion by depressed patients. *Lancet* **2**, 766. [226]

Ebert, M.H., Baldessarini, R.J., Lipinski, L.F., and Berv, K. (1973) Effects of electroconvulsive seizures on amine metabolism in the rat brain. *Arch. Gen. Psychiatr.* **29**, 397–401. [249, 328]

Ebstein, R., Belmaker, R.H., Benbenisty, D., and Rimon, R. (1976) Electrophoretic pattern of red blood cell catechol-O-methyltransferase in schizophrenia and manic-depressive illness. *Biol. Psychiatr.* **11**, 613–623. [220]

Echevarria-Mage, M.T., Senault, B., and Delacour, J. (1972) Effets de microinjections de 6-hydroxydopamine dans le système nigro-strié sur un apprentissage chez le rat blanc. *C.R. Acad. Sci.* **275**, 1155–1158. [156]

Edelstein, C.E., Roy-Byrne, P., Fawzy, F.I., and Dornfeld, L. (1983) Effects of weight loss on the dexamethasone suppression test. *Am. J. Psychiatr.* **140**, 338–341. [53, 54]

Eden, S. and Modigh, K. (1977) Effects of apomorphine and clonidine on rat plasma growth hormone after pretreatment with reserpine and electroconvulsive shocks. *Brain Res.* **129**, 379–384. [186, 228]

Edwards, D.J., Spiker, D.G., Kupfer, D.J., Foster, G., Neil, J.F., and Abrams, L. (1978) Platelet monoamine oxidase in affective disorders. *Arch Gen. Psychiatr.* **35**, 1443–1446. [221]

Ehlers, C., Indik, J.H., Koob, G.F., and Bloom, F.E. (1983) The effect of single and repeated electroconvulsive shock (ECS) on locomotor activity in rats. *Prog. Neuropsychopharmacol.* **7**, 217–222. [184, 188, 253]

Ehrensing, A.J. and Kastin, A.J. (1974) Melanocyte-stimulating hormone releasing inhibiting hormone as an antidepressant. *Arch. Gen. Psychiatr.* **30**, 63–65. [373, 400]

Ehrensing, R.H. and Kastin, A.J. (1978) Dose-related biphasic effect of prolyl-leucyl-glycinamide (MIF-I) in depression. *Am. J. Psychiatr.* **135**, 562–566. [373, 400]

Ehrensing, R.H., Kastin, A.J., Schalch, D.S., Friesen, H.G., Vargas, J.R., and Schally, A.V. (1974) Affective states and thyrotropin and prolactin responses after repeated injections of thyrotropin-releasing hormone in depressed patients. *Am. J. Psychiatr.* **131**, 714–718. [166, 315]

Ehsanullah, R.S.B. (1980) Uptake of 5-hydroxytryptamine and dopamine into platelets from depressed patients and normal subjects—influence of clomipramine, desmethylclomipramine and maprotiline. *Postgrad. Med. J.* **56** (Suppl. 1), 31–35. [316]

Ehsanullah, R.S.B., Mulgirigama, D.L., and Turner, P. (1979) Decreased uptake of 5-hydroxytryptamine and dopamine into blood platelets from depressed patients. *Br. J. Clin. Pharmacol.* **7**, 434P–435P. [316]

Eichelman, B. (1979) Role of biogenic amines in aggressive behaviour. In M. Sandler (Ed.), *Psychopharmacology of Aggression*. Raven, New York, pp. 61–93. [271, 291]

Eichelman, B. and Barchas, J. (1975) Facilitated shock-induced aggression following antidepressive medication in the rat. *Pharmacol. Biochem. Behav.* **3**, 601–604. [159]

Einon, D.F. and Sahakian, B.J. (1979) Environmentally-induced differences in susceptibility of rats to CNS stimulants and depressants: Evidence against a unitary explanation. *Psychopharmacology* **61**, 299–307. [292]

Einon, D.F., Morgan, M.J., and Sahakian, B.J. (1975) The development of intersession habituation and emergence in socially reared and isolated rats. *Dev. Psychobiol.* **8**, 553–559. [114]

Eisenstein, N., Iorio, L.C., and Clody, D.E. (1982) Role of serotonin in the blockade of muricidal behaviour by tricyclic antidepressants. *Pharmacol. Biochem. Behav.* **17**, 847–849. [291]

Ekdawi, M.Y. (1975) Viloxazine (Vivalan) comparison with imipramine. *J. Int. Med. Res.* **3** (Suppl. 3), 75–79. [235]

Ekman, P., Hager, J.C., and Friesen, W.V. (1981) The symmetry of emotional and deliberate facial actions. *Psychophysiology* **18**, 101–106. [86]

El-Yousef, M., Janowsky, D.S., Davis, J.M., and Rosenblatt, J.E. (1973) Induction of severe depression by physostigmine in marijuana intoxicated individuals. *Br. J. Addict.* **68**, 321–325. [282]

Ellingboe, J. (1978) Effects of alcohol on neurochemical processes. In M.A. Lipton, A. DiMascio, and K.F. Killam (Eds), *Psychopharmacology: A Generation of Progress*. Raven, New York, pp. 1653–1664. [411]

Ellison, G.D. (1975) Behavior and the balance between norepinephrine and serotonin. *Acta Neurobiol. Exp.* **35**, 499–515. [305]

Ellison, G.D. and Bresler, D.E. (1974) Tests of emotional behavior in rats following depletion of norepinephrine, of serotonin, or of both. *Psychopharmacology*, **34**, 275–288. [294, 295]

Ellison, G.D. and Flynn, J.P. (1968) Organized aggressive behaviour in cats after surgical isolation of the hypothalamus. *Arch. Ital. Biol.* **106**, 1–20. [363]

Elsworth, J.D., Redmond, D.E., and Roth, R.H. (1982) Plasma and cerebrospinal fluid 3-methoxy-4-hydroxyphenylethylene glycol (MHPG) as indices of brain norepinephrine metabolism in primates. *Brain Res.* **235**, 115–124. [223]

Emrich, H.M. (1982) A possible role of opioid actions in endogenous depression. In S.Z. Langer, R. Takahashi, T. Segawa, and M. Briley (Eds)., *New Vistas in Depression*. Pergamon, New York, pp. 233–237. [135]

Emrich, H.M, Cording, C., Piree, S., Kolling, A., Moller, H.-J., Van Zerssen, D., and Herz, A. (1979a) Action of naloxone in different types of psychosis. In E. Usdin, W.E. Bunney, and N.S. Kline (Eds.), *Endorphins in Mental Health Research*. Oxford University Press, New York, pp. 452–460. [356, 366]

Emrich, H.M., Hollt, V., Kissling, W., Fishler, M., Laspe, H., Heinemann, H., Van Zerssen, D., and Herz, A. (1979b) Beta-endorphin-like immunoreactivity in cerebrospinal fluid and plasma of patients with schizophrenia and other neuropsychiatric disorders. *Pharmakopsychiatr. Neuropsychopharmacol.* **12**, 267–276. [364, 367]

Emrich, H.M., Van Zerssen, D., Kissling, W., Moller, H.-J., and Windorfer, A. (1980) Effect of sodium valproate on mania: The GABA-hypothesis of affective disorders. *Arch. Psychiatr. Nervernkr.* **229**, 1–16. [356]

Emrich, H.M., Altmann, H., and Van Zerssen, D. (1982) Prophylactic action of sodium-valproate in manic depression: The GABA hypothesis of affective disorders. In S.Z. Langer, R. Takahashi, T. Segawa, and M. Briley (Eds.), *New Vistas in Depression*. Pergamon, New York, pp. 81–85. [356, 366]

Emrich, H.M., Gunther, R., and Dose, M. (1983a) Current perspectives in the pharmaco-psychiatry of depression and mania. *Neuropharmacology* **22**, 385–388. [356]

Emrich, H.M., Vogt, P., and Herz, A. (1983b) Possible antidepressant effects of opioids: Action of buprenorphine. *Ann. N.Y. Acad. Sci*, **398**, 108–112. [366]

Emson, P.C. and Lindvall, O. (1979) Distribution of putative transmitters in the cortex. *Neuroscience* **4**, 1–30. [99]

Endo, M., Endo, J., Nishikubo, M., and Hatotani, N. (1974) Endocrine studies in depression. In N. Hatotani and S. Karger (Eds.), *Psychoneuroendocrinology: Workshop Conference of the International Society for Psychoneuroendocrinology*. S. Karger, Basel, pp. 22–31. [229]

Engberg, G. and Svensson, T.H. (1980) Pharmacological analysis of a cholinergic receptor mediated regulation of brain norepinephrine neurons. *J. Neural Trans.* **49**, 137–150. [213, 381]

Engel, G.L. (1962) Anxiety and depression withdrawal: The primary effects of unpleasure. *Int. J. Psychoanal.* **43**, 89–97. [139, 405]

Engel, J., Hanson, L.C.F., and Roos, B.-E. (1971) Effect of electroshock on 5-HT metabolism in rat brain. *Psychopharmacology* **20**, 197–200. [328]

Engelman, K., Lovenberg, W., and Sjoerdsma, A. (1967) Inhibition of serotonin synthesis by p-chlorophenylalanine in carcinoid syndrome. *New Engl. J. Med.* **277**, 1103–1108. [10, 317]

Engelman, K., Horowitz, D., Jequier, E., and Sjoerdsma, A. (1968) Biochemical and pharmacologic effects of alpha-methylparatyrosine in man. *J. Clin. Invest.* **47**, 577–594. [10, 169]

Enna, S.J., Mann, E., Kendall, D., and Stancer, G.M. (1981) Effect of chronic antidepressant administration on brain neurotransmitter receptor binding. In S.J. Enna, J.B. Malick, and R. Richelson (Eds.), *Antidepressants: Neurochemical, Behavioral and Clinical Perspectives.* Raven, New York, pp. 91–105. [107, 265, 291]

Eriksson, E., Eden, S. and Modigh, K. (1982) Up- and down-regulation of central postsynaptic alpha$_2$ receptors reflected in the growth hormone response to clonidine in reserpine-pretreated rats. *Psychopharmacology,* **77,** 327–331. [248, 252]

Ernst, E. and Goodison, L. (1981) *In Our Own Hands: A Book of Self-Help Therapy.* Women's Press, London. [410]

Esler, M., Turbott, J., Schwartz, R., Leonard, P., Bobik, A., Skews, H., and Jackman, G. (1982) The peripheral kinetics of norepinephrine in depressed illness. *Arch. Gen Psychiatr.* **39,** 295–300. [218]

Esposito, R.U. and Kornetsky, C. (1978) Opioids and rewarding brain stimulation. *Neurosci. Biobehav. Rev.* **2,** 115–122. [362]

Esposito, R.U., Perry W., and Kornetsky, C. (1980) Effects of d-amphetamine and naloxone on brain self-stimulation. *Psychopharmacology* **69,** 187–191. [363]

Essman, W.B. (1973a) Age-dependent effects of 5-hydroxytryptamine upon memory consolidation and protein synthesis. *Pharmacol. Biochem. Behav.* **1,** 7–14. [295]

Essman, W.B. (1973b) Neuromolecular modulation of experimentally induced retrograde amnesia. *Confin. Neurol.* **35,** 1–22. [295]

Ettenberg, A., Pettit, H.O., Bloom, F.E., and Koob, G. (1982) Heroin and cocaine self-administration in rats: Mediation by separate neural systems. *Psychopharmacology* **78,** 204–209. [151, 153]

Ettigi, P.G. and Brown, G.M. (1977) Psychoneuroendocrinology of affective disorder: An overview. *Am. J. Psychiatr.* **134,** 493–501. [165, 166, 195, 314, 338]

Ettigi, P., Brown, G., and Seggi, J.A. (1979) TSH and LH responses in subtypes of depression. *Psychosom. Med.* **41,** 203–208. [373]

Evans, J.P.M., Grahame-Smith, D.G., Green, A.R., and Tordoff, A.F.C. (1976) Electroconvulsive shock increases the behavioral responses of rats to brain 5-hydroxytryptamine accumulation and central nervous system stimulant drugs. *Br. J. Pharmacol.* **56,** 193–199. [182, 188, 328, 339]

Evans, W.O. (1961) A new technique for the investigation of some analgesic drugs on a reflexive behavior in the rat. *Psychopharmacology* **2,** 318–325. [296, 297]

Everett, G.M. (1967) The DOPA response potentiation test and its use in screening for antidepressant drugs. In S. Garattini and M.N.G. Dukes (Eds.), *Antidepressant Drugs.* Excerpta Medica, Amsterdam, pp. 164–167. [106]

Everett, G.M. and Tolman, J.E.P. (1959) Mode of action of Rauwolfia alkaloids and motor sensitivity. In J. Masserman (Ed.), *Biological Psychiatry.* Grune & Stratton, New York, pp. 75–81. [6]

Everitt, B.J. and Keverne, E.B. (1979) Models of depression based on behavioral observations of experimental animals. In E.S. Paykel and A. Coppen (Eds.), *Psychopharmacology of Affective Disorders.* Oxford University Press, Oxford, pp. 41–59. [102, 109, 132]

Extein, I., Potter, W.Z., Wehr, T.A., and Goodwin, F.K. (1979a) Rapid mood cycles after a noradrenergic but not a serotonergic antidepressant. *Am. J. Psychiatr.* **136,** 1602–1603. [413]

Extein, I., Tallman, J., Smith, C.C., and Goodwin, F.K. (1979b) Changes in lymphocyte beta-adrenergic receptors in depression and mania. *Psychiatr. Res.* **1,** 191–197. [218]

Extein, I., Pottash, A.L.C., and Gold, M.S. (1980a) TRH test in depression. *New Engl. J. Med.* **302,** 923–924. [372]

Extein, I., Pottash, A.L.C., Gold, M.S., Sweeney, D.R., Martin, D.M., and Goodwin, F.K. (1980b) Deficient prolactin response to morphine in depressed patients. *Am. J. Psychiatr.* **137,** 845–846. [315, 365]

Extein, I., Pickar, D., Gold, M.S., Gold, P.W., Pottash, A.L.C., Sweeney, D.R., Ross, R.J., Rebard, R., Martin, D., and Goodwin, F.K. (1981) Methadone and morphine in depression. *Psychopharmacol. Bull.* **17**, 29–32. [366]

Extein, I., Pottash, A.L.C., and Gold, M.S. (1982a) Neuroendocrine abnormalities in affective disorders. *L'Encéphale* **8**, 203–211. [371, 372]

Extein, I., Pottash, A.L.C., and Gold, M.S. (1982b) A possible opioid receptor dysfunction in some depressive disorders. *Ann. N.Y. Acad. Sci.* **398**, 113–119. [366]

Eysenck, H.J. (1977) *Biological Basis of Personality.* Charles C. Thomas, Springfield, Ill. [395]

Fahndrich, E., Coper, H., Christ, W,. Helmchen, H., Muller-Oerlinghausen, B., and Pietzcker, A. (1980) Erythrocyte COMT activity in patients with affective disorders. *Acta Psychiatr. Scand.* **61**, 427–437. [220]

Fahndrich, E., Muller-Oerlinghausen, B., and Coper, H. (1982) Longitudinal assessment of MAO-, COMT-, and DBH-activity in patients with bipolar depression. *Int. Pharmacopsychiatr.* **17**, 8–17. [220, 221]

Falck, B., Hillarp, N.-A., Thieme, G., and Torp, A. (1962) Fluorescence of catecholamines and related compounds condensed with formaldehyde. *J. Histochem. Cytochem.* **10**, 348–354. [9]

Fallon, J.H., Koziell, D.A., and Moore, R.Y. (1978a) Catecholamine innervation of the basal forebrain, II. Amygdala, suprarhinal cortex and entorhinal cortex. *J. Comp. Neurol.* **180**, 509–523. [197]

Fallon, J.H., Riley, J.N., and Moore, R.Y. (1978b) Substantia nigra dopamine neurons: Separate populations project to neostriatum and allocortex. *Neurosci. Lett.* **7**, 157–162. [148]

Fanselow, M.S. and Bolles, R.C. (1979) Triggering of the endorphin analgesic reaction by a stimulus previously associated with shock: Reversal by naloxone. *Bull. Psychonom. Soc.* **14**, 88–90. [359]

Farber, J., Miller, J.D., Crawford, K.A., and McMillen, B.A. (1983) Dopamine metabolism and receptor sensitivity in rat brain after REM sleep deprivation. *Pharmacol. Biochem. Behav.* **18**, 509–513. [183, 185, 190]

Farkas, T., Dunner, D.L., and Fieve, R.R. (1976) L-tryptophan in depression. *Biol. Psychiatr.* **11**, 295–302. [320]

Fava, G.A., Munari, F., Pavan, L., and Kellner, R. (1981) Life events and depression: A replication. *J. Affect. Disord.* **3**, 159–165. [392]

Fawcett, J. and Simonopoulos, V. (1971) Dextroamphetamine response as a possible predictor of improvement with tricyclic therapy in depression. *Arch. Gen. Psychiatr.* **25**, 247–255. [233]

Fawcett, J., Maas, J.W., and Dekirmenjian, H. (1972) Depression and MHPG excretion. *Arch. Gen. Psychiatr.* **26**, 252–262. [173, 233]

Feather, N.T. and Barber, J.G. (1983) Depressive reactions and unemployment. *J. Abnorm. Psychol.* **92**, 185–195. [78, 393]

Feeney, D.M. and Wier, C.S. (1979) Sensory neglect after lesions of substantia nigra or lateral hypothalamus: Differential severity and recovery of function. *Brain Res.* **178**, 329–346. [158]

Feighner, J.P., Robins, E., Guze, S.B., Woodruff, R.A, Winokur, G., and Munoz, R. (1972) Diagnostic criteria for use in psychiatric research. *Arch. Gen. Psychiatr.* **26**, 57–63. [41, 47]

Feinberg, M. and Carroll, B.J. (1982) Separation of subtypes of depression using discriminant analysis. I. Separation of unipolar endogenous depression from non-endogenous depression. *Br. J. Psychiatr.* **140**, 384–391. [51]

Feinberg, M., Gillin, J.C., Carroll, B.J., Greden, J.F., and Zis, A.P. (1982) EEG studies of sleep in the diagnosis of depression. *Biol. Psychiatr.* **17**, 305–316. [54, 55]

Feldmann, H.S. and Denber, H.C.B. (1982) Long-term study of fluvoxamine: A new rapid-acting antidepressant. *Int. Pharmacopsychiatr.* **17**, 114–122. [323]

Fergusen, J. and Dement, W. (1969) The behavioral effects of amphetamine in REM deprived rats. *J. Psychiatr. Res.* **7**, 111–118. [188]

Ferrari, E., Bossolo, P.A., Vailati, A., Martinelli, I., Rea, A., and Nosari, I. (1977) Variations circadiennes des effets d'une substance vagolytique sur le système ACTH-secrétant chez l'homme. *Ann. Endocrinol. (Paris)* **38**, 203–213. [277]

Ferris, R.M., Maxwell, R.A., Cooper, B.R., and Soroko, F.E. (1982) Neurochemical and neuropharmacological investigations into the mechanisms of action of bupropion-HC1—A new atypical antidepressant agent. In E. Costa and G. Racagni (Eds.), *Typical and Atypical Antidepressants: Molecular Mechanisms.* Raven, New York, pp. 277–286. [127]

Ferron, A., Descarries, L., and Reader, T.A. (1982) Altered neuronal responsiveness to biogenic amines in rat cerebral cortex after serotonin denervation or depletion. *Brain Res.* **231**, 93–108. [260]

Ferster, C.B. (1965) Classification of behavioral pathology. In L. Krasner and L.P. Ullman (Eds.), *Research in Behavior Modification.* Holt, Rinehart & Winston, New York, pp. 6–26. [66]

Ferster, C.B. (1973) A functional analysis of depression. *Am. Psychol.* **28**, 857–870. [66, 136]

Fibiger, H.C. (1979) Drugs and reinforcement mechanisms: A critical review of the catecholamine theory. *Ann. Rev. Pharm. Toxicol.* **18**, 37–56. [150, 200]

Fibiger, H.C. and Campbell, B.A. (1971) The effects of parachlorophenylalanine on spontaneous locomotor activity in the rat. *Neuropharmacology* **10**, 25–32. [294]

Fibiger, H.C. and Phillips, A.G. (1981) Increased intracranial self-stimulation in rats after long-term administration of desipramine. *Science* **214**, 683–685. [135]

Fibiger, H.C., Mertz, P.H., and Campbell, B.A. (1972) The effect of para-chlorophenylalanine on aversive thresholds and reactivity to footshock. *Physiol. Behav.* **8**, 259–263. [297]

Fibiger, H.C., Zis, A.P., and McGeer, E.G. (1973) Feeding and drinking deficits after 6-hydroxydopamine administration in the rat: Similarities to the lateral hypothalamic syndrome. *Brain Res.* **55**, 135–148. [151]

Fibiger, H.C., Phillips, A.G., and Zis, A.P. (1974) Deficits in instrumental responding after 6-hydroxydopamine lesion of the nigro-neostriatal dopaminergic projection. *Pharmacol. Biochem. Behav.* **2**, 87–96. [156]

Fibiger, H.C., Zis, A.P., and Phillips, A.G. (1975) Haloperidol-induced disruption of conditioned avoidance responding: Attenuation by prior training or by anticholinergic drugs. *Eur. J. Pharmacol.* **30**, 309–314. [156]

Fields, H.L. and Anderson, S.D. (1978) Evidence that raphe-spinal neurons mediate opiate and midbrain stimulation-produced analgesia. *Pain* **5**, 333–349. [299]

Figge, J., Leonard, P., and Richelson, E. (1979) Tricyclic antidepressants: Potent blockade of histamine H_1 receptors of guinea pig ileum. *Eur. J. Pharmacol.* **58**, 479–483. [368]

Fillion, G., Beaudoin, D., Rouselle, J.C., Deniau, J.C., Fillion, M.P., Dray, F., and Jacob, J. (1979) Decrease of [^{3}H]5-HT high affinity binding and 5-HT adenylate cyclase activation after kainic acid lesions in rat brain striatum. *J. Neurochem.* **33**, 567–570. [345]

Fillion, G., Fillion, M.P., and Rouselle, J.C. (1981) Augmentation de l'affinité du recepteur 5-HT et diminution de l'activité adenylate cyclase sensible à la 5-HT par exposition prolongée à la 5-HT. *J. Physiol. (Paris)* **77**, 363–368. [346]

Finberg, J.P.M. and Youdim, M.B.H. (1983) Selective MAO A and B inhibitors: Their mechanism of action and pharmacology. *Neuropharmacology* **22**, 441–446. [241, 244, 313, 325, 329]

Finch, S.M. (1960) *Fundamentals of Child Psychiatry*. Norton, New York. [133]

Fink, M., Simeon, J., Itil, T.M., and Freedman, A.M. (1970) Clinical antidepressant activity of cyclazocine—A narcotic antagonist. *Clin. Pharmacol. Ther.* **11**, 41–48. [366]

Finkelstein, Y., Koffler, B., Rabey, J.M., and Gilad, G.M. (1984) Adaptive changes of the septo-hippocampal cholinergic system to prolonged stress. *Abstr. 14th CINP*, Florence, p. 290. [270, 275, 280]

Finnerty, E.P. and Chan, S.H.H. (1981) The participation of substantia nigra zona compacta and zona reticulata neurons in morphine suppression of caudate spontaneous neuronal activities in the rat. *Neuropharmacology*, **20**, 241–246. [151]

Fitzgerald, J.D. (1967) Propranolol-induced depression. *Br. Med. J.* **11**, 327–373. [231]

Flicker, C. and Geyer, M.A. (1982) Behavior during hippocampal microinfusions. I. Norepinephrine and diversive exploration. *Brain Res. Rev.* **4**, 79–104. [206]

Flor-Henry, P. (1974) Psychosis, neurosis and epilepsy. *Br. J. Psychiatr.* **124**, 144–150. [92]

Flor-Henry, P. (1976) Lateralized temporal-limbic dysfunction and psychopathology. *Ann. N.Y. Acad. Sci.* **280**, 777–797. [86, 88, 90]

Flor-Henry, P. (1979) On certain aspects of the localization of the cerebral systems regulating and determining emotion. *Biol. Psychiatr.* **14**, 677–698. [86, 88, 92, 406]

Flor-Henry, P. and Koles, Z.J. (1981) Studies in right/left hemispheric energy oscillations in schizophrenia, mania, depression, and normals. In C. Perris, D. Kemali, and L. Vacca (Eds.), *Advances in Biological Psychiatry*, Vol. 6. Karger, New York, pp. 60–67. [99]

Flor-Henry, P. and Yeudall, L.T. (1973) Lateralized cerebral dysfunction in depression and in aggressive criminal psychopathy: Further observations. *I.R.C.S. Med. Sci.* **73–7**, 5-0-4. [90]

Fludder, J.M. and Leonard, B.E. (1979a) Chronic effects of mianserin on noradrenaline metabolism in the rat brain: Evidence for a presynaptic alpha-adrenolytic action in vivo. *Psychopharmacology* **64**, 329–332. [240]

Fludder, J.M. and Leonard, B.E. (1979b) The effects of amitriptyline, mianserin, phenoxybenzamine and propranolol on the release of noradrenaline in the rat brain in vivo. *Biochem. Pharmacol.* **28**, 2333–2336. [249]

Fog, R. and Pakkenburg, H. (1971) Behavioral effect of dopamine and p-hydroxyamphetamine injected into corpus striatum of rats. *Exp. Neurol.* **31**, 75–86. [149]

Fogarty, S.J. and Hemsley, D.R. (1983) Depression and the accessibility of memories: A longitudinal study. *Br. J. Psychiatr.* **142**, 232–237. [70]

Folstein, M.F., Maiberger, R., and McHugh, P.R. (1977) Mood disorder as a specific complication of stroke. *J. Neurol. Neurosurg. Psychiatr.* **40**, 1018–1020. [91, 92]

Foote, S.L., Freedman, R., and Oliver, A.P. (1975) Effects of putative neurotransmitters on neuronal activity in monkey auditory cortex. *Brain Res.* **86**, 229–242. [206]

Foote, S.L., Aston-Jones, G., and Bloom, F.E. (1980) Impulse activity of locus coeruleus neurons in awake rats and monkeys is a function of sensory stimulation and arousal. *Proc. Natl. Acad. Sci. USA* **77**, 3033–3037. [206]

Foster, F.G., Kupfer, D.J. and Coble, P. (1976) Rapid eye movement density, an objective indicator in severe medical-depressive syndromes. *Arch. Gen. Psychiatr.* **33**, 1119–1123. [279]

Fotherby, K., Ashcroft, G.W., Affleck, J.W., and Forrest, A.D. (1963) Studies on sodium transfer and 5-hydroxyindoles in depressive illness. *J. Neurol. Neurosurg. Psychiatr.* **26**, 71–73. [311]

Foulds, G.A. (1975) The relationship between the depressive illnesses. *Br. J. Psychiatr.* **123**, 531–533. [57]

Fouriezos, G. and Wise, R.A. (1976) Pimozide-induced extinction of intracranial self-stimulation: Response patterns rule out motor performance deficits. *Brain Res.* **103**, 377–380. [151]

Fouriezos, G., Hansson, P., and Wise, R.A. (1978) Neuroleptic-induced attenuation of brain stimulation reward. *J. Comp. Physiol. Psychol.* **92**, 659–669. [151]

Fowles, D.C. and Gersh, F. (1979) Neurotic depression: The endogenous-neurotic distinction. In R.A. Depue (Ed.), *The Psychobiology of the Depressive Disorders: Implications for the Effects of Stress.* Academic, New York, pp. 55–80. [49]

Frances, A., Brown, R., Koskis, J., and Mann, J. (1981) Psychotic depression: A separate entity? *Am. J. Psychiatr.* **183**, 829–833. [52]

Francis, A.F., Williams, P., Williams, R., Link, J., Cole, E.N., and Hughes, D. (1976) The effect of clomipramine on prolactin levels. *Postgrad. Med. J.* **52** (Suppl. 3), 87–91. [166]

Frangos, E., Athanassenas, G., Tsitourides, S., Psilolignos, P., and Katsanou, N. (1983) Psychotic depressive disorder: A separate entity? *J. Affect. Disord.* **5**, 259–265. [52]

Frankhuysen, A.L. and Mulder, A.H. (1980) Noradrenaline inhibits depolarization-induced [^{3}H]serotonin release from slics of rat hippocampus. *Eur. J. Pharmacol.* **63**, 179–182. [377]

Franklin, K.B.J. and Robertson, A. (1982) Effects and interactions of naloxone and amphetamine on self-stimulation of the prefrontal cortex and dorsal tegmentum. *Pharmacol. Biochem. Behav.* **16**, 433–436. [362]

Fraser, A.R. (1983) Choice of antidepressant based on the dexamethasone suppression test. *Am. J. Psychiatr.* **140**, 786–787. [237]

Fray, P.J., Sahakian, B.J., Robbins, T.W., Koob, G.F., and Iversen, S.D. (1980) An observational method for quantifying the behavioural effects of dopamine agonists: Contrasting effects of D-amphetamine and apomorphine. *Psychopharmacology* **69**, 253–259. [189]

Frazer, A. (1975) Adrenergic responses in depression: Implications for a receptor deficit. In J. Wortis (Ed.), *Biological Psychiatry.* Wiley, New York, pp. 7–26. [165]

Frazer, A. (1981) Antidepressant drugs: Effect on adrenergic responsiveness and monoamine receptors. In E. Usdin, W.E. Bunney, and J.N. Davis (Eds.), *Neuroreceptors: Basic and Clinical Aspects.* Wiley, New York. pp. 85–98. [266]

Frazer, A. and Mendels, J. (1977) Do tricyclic antidepressants enhance adrenergic transmission? *Am. J. Psychiatr.* **134**, 1040–1042. [260, 262]

Frazer, A., Pandey, G.N., and Mendels, J. (1973) Metabolism of tryptophan in depressive disease. *Arch. Gen. Psychiatr.* **29**, 528–535. [308]

Freda, J.S. and Klein, S.B. (1976) Generality of the failure to escape (helplessness) phenomena in rats. *Anim. Learn. Behav.* **4**, 401–406. [122]

Freedman, D.X. and Halaris, A.E. (1978) Monoamines and the biochemical mode of action of LSD at synapses. In M.A. Lipton, A. DiMaschio, and K.F. Killam (Eds.), *Psychopharmacology: A Generation of Progress.* Raven, New York, pp. 347–359. [21]

Freedman, R., Hoffer, B.J., Woodward, D.J., and Puro, D. (1977) Interaction of norepinephrine with cerebellar activity evoked by mossy and climbing fibres. *Exp. Neurol.* **55**, 269–288. [206]

Freeman, A. and Melges, F. (1977) Depersonalization and temporal disintegration in acute mental illness. *Am. J. Psychiatr.* **134**, 679–681. [74, 95]

Freeman, A. and Melges, F. (1978) Temporal disorganization, depersonalization, and persecutory ideation in acute mental illness. *Am. J. Psychiatr.* **135**, 123–126. [74, 95]

Freud, S. (1917) Mourning and Melancholia. In J. Strachey (Ed.), *Collected Works of Sigmund Freud: The Standard Edition*, Vol. 14. Hogarth, London, 1957, pp. 237–258. [407]

Friedman, A.S. (1964) Minimal effects of severe depression on cognitive functioning. *J. Abnorm. Soc. Psychol.* **69**, 237–243. [63, 64]

Friedman, A.S., Granick, S., Cotten, H.W., and Cowitz, B. (1966) Imipramine (tofranil) vs. placebo in hospitalized psychotic depressives. *J. Psychiatr. Res.* **4**, 13–36. [159]

Friedman, D.P. and Horvath, F.E. (1980) Catecholaminergic involvement in phasic versus tonic electrocortical arousal. *Brain Res.* **194**, 572–577. [206]

Friedman, E. and Dallob, A. (1979) Enhanced serotonin receptor activity after chronic treatment with imipramine or amitriptyline. *Commun. Psychopharmacol.* **3**, 89–92. [340]

Friedman, E., Shopsin, B., Goldstein, M., and Gershon, S. (1974) Interactions of imipramine and synthesis inhibitors on biogenic amines. *J. Pharm. Pharmacol.* **26**, 995–997. [182, 249]

Friedman, E., Fung, F., and Gershon, S. (1977) Antidepressant drugs and dopamine uptake in different brain regions. *Eur. J. Pharmacol.* **42**, 47–51. [181]

Friedman, E., Dallob, A. and Levine, G. (1979) The effect of long-term lithium treatment on reserpine-induced supersensitivity in dopaminergic and serotonergic transmission. *Life Sci.* **25**, 1263–1266. [343]

Friedman, M. (1978) Does receptor supersensitivity accompany depressive illness? *Am. J. Psychiatr.* **135**, 107–109. [218]

Friedman, M.J. and Stolk, J.M. (1978) Depression, hypertension and serum dopamine-beta-hydroxylase activity. *Psychosom. Med.* **40**, 107–115. [220]

Fries, E.D. (1954) Mental depression in hypertensive patients treated for long periods with large doses of reserpine. *New Engl. J. Med.* **251**, 1006–1008. [3]

Frontali, M., Amorico, L., De Acetis, L., and Bignami, G. (1973) A pharmacological analysis of processes underlying differential responding: A review and further experiments with scopolamine, amphetamine, lysergic acid diethylamide (LSD), chlordiazepoxide, physostigmine and chlorpromazine. *Behav. Biol.* **18**, 1–74. [274]

Fujimori, M. (1981) Amoxapine, a new antidepressant: Overview. In S.Z. Langer, R. Takahashi, T. Segawa, and M. Briley (Eds.), *New Vistas in Depression*. Pergamon, New York, pp. 287–294. [235]

Fujiwara, J. and Otsuki, S. (1974) Subtype of affective psychoses classified by response on amine precursors and monoamine metabolism. *Folia Psychiatr. Neurol. Jpn.* **28**, 93–99. [312, 321]

Fuller, R.W. (1981) Enhancement of monoaminergic transmission by antidepressant drugs. In S.J. Enna, J.B. Malick, and E. Richelson (Eds.), *Antidepressants: Neurochemical, Behavioral and Clinical Perspectives*. Raven, New York, pp. 1–12. [240]

Fuller, R.W. and Owen, J.E. (1981) Suppression of milk drinking by the combination of fluoxetine and L-5-hydroxytryptophan in rats. *Res. Commun. Chem. Pathol. Pharmacol.* **34**, 137–140. [301]

Furneaux, W.D. (1956) *The Nufferno Manual of Speed Tests*. Institute of Psychiatry, London. [64]

Fuxe, K., Fredholm, B.B., Ogren, S.-O., Agnati, L.F., Hokfelt, B., and Gustafsson, J.A. (1978a) Pharmacological and biochemical evidence for the dopamine agonistic effect of bromocryptine. *Acta Endocrinol.* **88** (Suppl. 216), 27–46. [174]

Fuxe, K., Ogren, S.-O., Agnati, L.F., Jonsson, G., and Gustafsson, J.-A. (1978b) 5,7-Dihydroxytryptamine as a tool to study the functional role of central 5-hydroxytryptamine neurons. *Ann. N.Y. Acad. Sci.* **305**, 346–369. [294, 296]

Fuxe, K., Ogren, S.-O., and Agnati, L.F. (1979) The effects of chronic treatment with the 5-hydroxytryptamine uptake blocker zimelidine on central 5-hydroxytryptamine mechanisms. Evidence for the induction of a low affinity binding site for 5-hydroxytryptamine. *Neurosci. Lett.* **14,** 307–312. [345, 347]

Fuxe, K., Ogren, S.-O., Agnati, L.F., Eneroth, P., Holm, A.C., and Andersson, K. (1981) Long-term treatment with zimelidine leads to a reduction in 5-hydroxytryptamine neurotransmission within the central nervous system of the mouse and rat. *Neurosci. Lett.* **21,** 57–62. [340, 345–347]

Fuxe, K., Ogren, S.-O., Agnati, L.F., Andersson, K., and Eneroth, P. (1982a) Effects of subchronic antidepressant drug treatment on central serotonergic mechanisms in the malé rat. In E. Costa and G. Racagni (Eds.), *Typical and Atypical Antidepressants: Molecular Mechanisms.* Raven, New York, pp. 91–107. [341, 342, 345–348]

Fuxe, K., Ogren, S.-O., Andersson, K. Eneroth, P., and Agnati, L.F. (1982b) The effects of subchronic antidepressant drug treatment on the secretion of adrenohypophyseal hormones and of corticosterone in the male rat. In E. Costa and G. Racagni (Eds.), *Typical and Atypical Antidepressants: Molecular Mechanisms.* Raven, New York, pp. 109–120. [187, 337, 345–348]

Fuxe, K., Ogren, S.-O., Agnati, L.F., Andersson, K., and Eneroth, P. (1982c) On the mechanism of action of antidepressant drugs: Indications of reductions in 5-HT neurotransmission in some brain regions upon subchronic treatment. In S.Z. Langer, R. Takahashi, T. Segawa, and M. Briley (Eds.), *New Vistas in Depression.* Pergamon, New York, pp. 49–63. [337, 340, 342, 345, 347]

Fuxe, K., Ogren, S.-O., Agnati, L.F., Benfenati, F., Fredholm, B., Andersson, K., Zini, I., and Eneroth, P. (1983) Chronic antidepressant treatment and central 5-HT synapses. *Neuropharmacology* **22,** 389–400. [333, 337, 340–342, 345, 346, 348, 351, 418]

Gaertner, H.J., Kreuter, F., Scharek, G., Brinkschulte, M., and Breyer-Pfaff, U. (1980) Do urinary MHPG and plasma drug levels correlate with response to amitriptyline therapy. *L'Encéphale* **8,** 167–176. [235]

Gaillard, J.-M. and Tissot, R. (1979) Blood-brain movements of tryptophan and tyrosine in manic-depressive illness and schizophrenia. *J. Neural Trans.* (Suppl. 15), 189–196. [164, 222, 309]

Gainotti, G. (1972) Emotional behavior and hemispheric side of the lesion. *Cortex* **8,** 41–55. [91]

Galin, D. (1974) Implications for psychiatry of left and right cerebral specialization. *Arch. Gen. Psychiatr.* **31,** 572–583. [85]

Gallager, D.W. and Bunney, W.E. (1979) Failure of chronic lithium treatment to block tricyclic antidepressant-induced 5-HT supersensitivity. *Naunyn Schmiedebergs Arch. Pharmacol.* **307,** 129–133. [253, 262, 264, 285, 335]

Gallagher, M., Kapp, B.S., Pascoe, J.P., and Rapp, P.R. (1981) A neuropharmacology of amygdala systems which contribute to learning and memory. In Y. Ben-Ari (Ed.), *The Amygdaloid Complex.* Elsevier, New York, pp. 343–354. [197]

Gallistel, C.R. (1981) Precis of Gallistel's "The Organization of Action: A New Synthesis." *Behav. Brain Sci.* **4,** 609–650. [26]

Gallistel, C.R. and Beagley, G. (1971) Specificity of brain stimulation reward in the rat. *J. Comp. Physiol. Psychol.* **76,** 199–205. [135]

Gallistel, C.R., Shizgal, P., and Yeomans, J.S. (1981) A portrait of the substrate for self-stimulation. *Psychol. Rev.* **88,** 229–273. [151, 385]

Gambert, S.R., Garthwaite, T.L., Pontzer, C.H., and Hagen, T.C. (1980) Fasting associated with decrease in hypothalamic beta-endorphin. *Science* **210,** 1271–1272. [363]

Gandolfi, O., Barbaccia,M.L., Chuang, D.M., and Costa, E. (1983) Daily buproprion injections for 3 weeks attenuate the NE-stimulation of adenylate cyclase and the number of beta-adrenergic recognition sites in rat frontal cortex. *Neuropharmacology* **22,** 927–929. [256, 260, 262]

Ganong, W.F. (1977) Neurotransmitters involved in ACTH secretion: Catecholamines. *Ann. N.Y. Acad. Sci.* **297**, 509–517. [195]

Garattini, S., Giacalone, E., and Valzelli, L. (1967) Isolation, aggressiveness and brain 5-hydroxytryptamine turnover. *J. Pharm. Pharmacol.* **19**, 338–339. [291]

Garber, J. and Seligman, M.E.P., eds. (1980) *Human Helplessness: Theory and Applications.* Academic, New York. [74, 78, 122, 126]

Garber, J., Miller, W.R., and Seaman, S.F. (1979) Learned helplessness, stress and the depressive disorders. In R.A. Depue (Ed.), *The Psychobiology of the Depressive Disorders: Implications for the Effects of Stress.* Academic, New York, pp. 335–363. [75, 121, 122, 126]

Garcia-Sevilla, J.A., Zis, A.P., Hollingsworth, P.J., Greden, J.F., and Smith, C.B., (1981) Platelet alpha-2-adrenergic receptors in major depressive disorder. *Arch. Gen. Psychiatr.* **38**, 1327–1333. [218, 248]

Gardner, R. (1982) Mechanisms in manic-depressive disorder: An evolutionary model. *Arch. Gen. Psychiatr.* **39**, 1436–1441. [214]

Garfinkel, P.E., Warsh, J.J., Stancer, H.C., and Sibony, D. (1976) Total and free plasma tryptophan levels in patients with affective disorders. Effects of a peripheral decarboxylase inhibitor. *Arch. Gen. Psychiatr.* **33**, 1462–1466. [308]

Garfinkel, P.E., Warsh, J.J., Stancer, H.C., and Godse, D.D. (1977) CNS monoamine metabolism in bipolar affective disorder: Evaluation using a peripheral decarboxylase inhibitor. *Arch. Gen. Psychiatr.* **34**, 735–739. [225]

Garfinkel, P.E., Warsh, J.J., and Stancer, H.C. (1979) Depression: New evidence in support of biological differentiation. *Am. J. Psychiatr.* **136**, 535–539. [225]

Garrigou, D., Broekkamp, C.L.E., and Lloyd, K.G. (1981) Involvement of the amygdala in the effects of antidepressants on the passive avoidance deficit in bulbectomized rats. *Psychopharmacology* **74**, 66–70. [292]

Garver, D.L., Pandey, G.N., Dekirmenjian, H., and Jones, F.D. (1975) Growth hormone and catecholamines in affective disease. *Am. J. Psychiatr.* **132**, 1149–1154. [229]

Garzon, J. and Del Rio, J. (1981) Hyperactivity induced in rats by long-term isolation: Further studies on a new animal model for the detection of antidepressants. *Eur. J. Pharmacol.* **74**, 287–294. [114, 115, 291]

Garzon, J., Fuentes, J.A., and Del Rio, J. (1979) Antidepressants selectively antagonize the hyperactivity induced in rats by long-term isolation. *Eur. J. Pharmacol.* **59**, 293–296. [114]

Gastpar, M. and Gastpar, G. (1982) Preliminary studies with citalopram (Lu 10–171), a specific 5-HT reuptake inhibitor, as antidepressant. *Prog. Neuropsychopharmacol.* **6**, 319–325. [323]

Gatchel, R.J., Paulus, P.B., and Maples, C.W. (1975) Learned helplessness and self-reported affect. *J. Abnorm. Psychol.* **84**, 589–620. [124]

Gelenberg, A.J., Wojcik, J.D., Growden, J.H., Sved, A.F., and Wurtman, R.J. (1980) Tyrosine for the treatment of depression. *Am. J. Psychiatr.* **137**, 622–623. [172]

Gelenberg, A.J., Gibson, C.J., and Wojcik, J.D. (1982) Neurotransmitter precursors for the treatment of depression. *Psychopharmacol. Bull.* **18**, 7–18. [172, 232, 319]

Geller, I. (1973) Effects of para-chlorophenylalanine and 5-hydroxytryptophan on alcohol intake in the rat. *Pharmacol. Biochem. Behav.* **1**, 361–365. [301, 351]

Geller, I. and Blum, K. (1970) The effects of 5-HTP on para-chlorophenylalanine (p-CPA) attenuation of "conflict" behaviour. *Eur. J. Pharmacol.* **9**, 319–324. [294]

Geller, I. and Seifter, J. (1960) The effects of meprobamate, barbiturates, D-amphetamine and promazine on experimentally induced conflict in the rat. *Psychopharmacology* **1**, 482–492. [294]

Geller, I., Hartman, R.J., Croy, D.J., and Haber, B. (1974) Attenuation of conflict behavior with cinanserin, a serotonin antagonist: Reversal of the effect with 5-hydroxytryptophan and 2-methyltryptamine. *Res. Comm. Chem. Pathol. Pharmacol.* **1**, 165–174. [294]

Geller, I., Hartmann, R.J., and Messiha, F.S. (1981) Blockade of 5-HTP reduction of ethanol drinking with the decarboxylase inhibitor, Ro 4-4602. *Pharmacol. Biochem. Behav.* **15**, 871–874. [301]

Gennazzani, A.R., Facchinetti, F., Brambilla, F., Parrini, D., Petraglia, F., Scarone, S., and Facchini, V. (1982) Menopause, depression, and plasma opioids. In E. Costa and G. Racagni (Eds.), *Typical and Atypical Antidepressants: Clinical Practice.* Raven, New York, pp. 341–345. [364]

Genovese, E., Zonta, N., and Mantegazza, P. (1973) Decreased antinociceptive activity of morphine in rats pretreated intraventricularly with 5,6-dihydroxytryptamine, a long-lasting selective depletor of brain serotonin. *Psychopharmacology,* **32**, 359–364. [299]

Georgotas, A., Mann, J., Bush, D., and Gershon, S. (1980) A clinical trial of zimelidine in depression. *Commun. Psychopharmacol.* **4**, 71–77. [323]

Georgotas, A., Krakowski, M., and Gershon, S. (1982) Controlled trial of zimelidine, a 5-HT reuptake inhibitor, for treatment of depression. *Am. J. Psychiatr.* **139**, 1057–1058. [323]

Gerald, M.C. and Maickel, R.P. (1972) Studies on the possible role of brain histamine in behavior. *Br. J. Pharmacol.* **44**, 462–471. [368]

Gerbino, L., Olesahnsky, M., and Gershon, S. (1978) Clinical use and mode of action of lithium. In M.A. Lipton, A. DiMaschio, and K.F. Killam (Eds.), *Psychopharmacology: A Generation of Progress.* Raven, New York, pp. 1261–1275. [332]

Gerlach, J.L. and McEwen, B.S. (1972) Rat brain binds adrenal steroid hormone: Radioautography of hippocampus with corticosterone. *Science* **175**, 1133–1136. [383]

German, D.C. and Bowden, D.M. (1974) Catecholamine systems as the neuronal substrate for intracranial self-stimulation. *Brain Res.* **73**, 381–419. [199]

Gerner, R.H. and Gwirtsman, H.E. (1981) Abnormalities of dexamethasone suppression test and urinary MHPG in anorexia nervosa. *Am. J. Psychiatr.* **138**, 650–653. [53]

Gerner, R.H. and Hare, T.A. (1981) CSF GABA in normal subjects and patients with depression, schizophrenia, mania and anorexia nervosa. *Am. J. Psychiatr.* **138**, 1098–1101. [355]

Gerner, R.H., Post, R.M., and Bunney, W.E. (1976) A dopaminergic mechanism in mania. *Am. J. Psychiatr.* **133**, 1177–1180. [174]

Gerner, R.H., Post, R.M., Gillin, J.C., and Bunney, W.E. (1979) Biological and behavioral effects of one night's sleep deprivation in depressed patients and normals. *J. Psychiatr. Res.* **15**, 21–40. [177]

Gerner, R.H., Catlin, D.H., Gorelick, D.A., Hui, K., and Li, C.H. (1980) Beta endorphin: Intravenous infusion causes behavioral change. *Arch. Gen. Psychiatr.* **37**, 642–647. [366]

Gersh, F.S. and Fowles, D.C. (1979) Neurotic depression: The concept of anxious depression. In R.A. Depue (Ed.), *The Psychobiology of the Depressive Disorders: Implications for the Effects of Stress.* Academic, New York, pp. 81–104. [57, 113, 124]

Gershon, E.S. (1978) The search for genetic markers in affective disorders. In M.A. Lipton, A. DiMaschio, and K.F. Killam (Eds.), *Psychopharmacology: A Generation of Progress.* Raven, New York, p. 1197–1212. [221]

Gershon, E.S. and Jonas, W.Z. (1975) Erythrocyte soluble catechol-O-methyltransferase activity in primary affective disorder. *Arch. Gen. Psychiatr.* **32**, 1351–1356. [220]

Gershon, E.S., Mark, A., Cohen, N., Belizon, M., Baron, M., and Knocke, K.E. (1975) Transmitted factors in morbid risk of affective disorders—A controlled study. *J. Psychiatr. Res.* **12**, 283–299. [45]

Gershon, E.S., Targum, S.D., and Leckman, J.F. (1979) Platelet monoamine oxidase (MAO) activity and genetic vulnerability to bipolar (BP) affective illness. *Psychopharmacol. Bull.* **15**, 27–30. [221]

Gershon, S. and Shaw, F.H. (1961) Psychiatric sequelae of chronic exposure to organophosphorus insecticides. *Lancet* **1**, 1371–1374. [282]

Geyer, M.A., Warbritton, J.D., Menkes, D.B., Zook, J.A., and Mandell, A.J. (1975) Opposite effects of intraventricular serotonin and bufotenin on rat startle responses. *Pharmacol. Biochem. Behav.* **3**, 687–691. [295]

Geyer, M.A., Puerto, A., Dawsey, W.J., Knapp, S., Bullard, W.P., and Mandell, A.J. (1976a) Histologic and enzymatic studies of the mesolimbic and mesostriatal serotonergic pathways. *Brain Res.* **106**, 241–256. [288, 296]

Geyer, M.A., Puerto, A., Menkes, D.B., Segal, D.S., and Mandell, A.J. (1976b) Behavioral studies following lesions of the mesolimbic and mesostriatal serotonergic pathways. *Brain Res.* **106**, 257–270. [294–296, 378]

Geyer, M.A., Petersen, L.R., and Rose, G.J. (1980) Effects of serotonergic lesions on investigatory responding by rats in a holeboard. *Behav. Neural Biol.* **30**, 160–177. [294, 295]

Ghose, K. (1980) Assessment of peripheral adrenergic activity and its interactions with drugs in man. *Eur. J. Clin. Pharmacol.* **17**, 233–238. [254]

Ghose, K., Turner, P., and Coppen, A. (1975) Intravenous tyramine pressor response in depression. *Lancet* **1**, 1317–1318. [218]

Ghose, K., Gupta, R., Coppen, A., and Lund, J. (1977) Antidepressant evaluation and the pharmacological actions of FG 4963 in depressive patients. *Eur. J. Clin. Pharmacol.* **42**, 31–37. [323]

Giannini, A.J., Extein, I., Gold, M.S., Pottash, A.L.C., and Castellani, S. (1983) Clonidine in mania. *Drug Dev. Res.* **3**, 101–103. [231]

Gibson, C.J., Deikel, S.M., Young, S.N., and Binik, Y.M. (1982) Behavioral and biochemical effects of tryptophan, tyrosine and phenylalanine in mice. *Psychopharmacology* **76**, 118–121. [290]

Gibson, S., McGeer, E.G., and McGeer, P.L. (1970) Effect of selective inhibitors of tyrosine and tryptophan hydroxylases on self-stimulation in the rat. *Exp. Neurol.* **27**, 283–290. [304]

Gilad, G., Rabey, J.M., and Shenkman, L. (1983) Strain-dependent and stress-induced changes in rat hippocampal cholinergic system. *Brain Res.* **267**, 171–174 [275, 280]

Giles, D.E. and Rush, A.J. (1982) Relationship of dysfunctional attitudes and dexamethasone response in endogenous and nonendogenous depression. *Biol. Psychiatr.* **17**, 1303–1314. [81, 405]

Gillespie, D.D., Manier, D.H., and Sulser, F. (1979) Electroconvulsive treatment: Rapid subsensitivity of the norepinephrine receptor coupled adenylate cyclase system in brain linked to down-regulation of beta-adrenergic receptors. *Commun. Psychopharmacol.* **3**, 191–195. [257]

Gillespie, R.D. (1929) The clinical differentiation of types of depression. *Guy's Hosp. Rep.* **9**, 306–344. [58]

Gillin, J.C. (1983) The sleep therapies of depression. *Prog. Neuropsychopharmacol.* **7**, 351–364. [116, 183, 343, 412]

Gillin, J.C., Sitaram, N., Mendelson, W.B., and Wyatt, R.J. (1978) Physostigmine alters onset but not duration of REM sleep in man. *Psychopharmacology* **58**, 111–114. [278]

Gillman, P.K., Bartlett, J.R., Bridges, P.K., Hunt, A., Patel, A.J., Kantamaneni, B.D., and Curzon, G. (1981) Indolic substances in plasma, cerebrospinal fluid, and frontal cortex of human subjects infused with saline or tryptophan. *J. Neurochem.* **37**, 410–417. [309]

Giret, M., Launay, J.M., Dreux, C., Zarifian, E., Benyacoub, K., and Loo, H. (1980) Modifications of biochemical parameters in blood platelets of schizophrenic and depressive patients. *Neuropsychobiology* **6**, 290–296. [316, 333]

Glass, I.B., Checkley, S.A., Shur, E,. and Dawling, S. (1982) The effect of desipramine upon central adrenergic function in depressed patients. *Br. J. Pharmacol.* **141**, 372–376. [228, 246, 248, 252]

Glasser, W. (1976) *Positive Addiction.* Harper & Row, New York. [412]

Glassman, A.H. (1969) Indoleamines and affective disorders. *Psychosom. Med.* **2**, 107–114. [320]

Glassman, A.H. and Platman, S.R. (1969) Potentiation of monamine oxidase inhibitor by tryptophan. *J. Psychiatr. Res.* **7**, 83–88. [319]

Glassman, A.H. and Roose, S.P. (1981) Delusional depression. A distinct clinical entity? *Arch. Gen. Psychiatr.* **38**, 424–427. [52]

Glazer, H.I. and Weiss, J.M. (1976a) Long-term and transitory interference effects. *J. Exp. Psychol.: Anim. Behav. Proc.* **2**, 191–201. [209, 213]

Glazer, H.I. and Weiss, J.M. (1976b) Long-term interference effect: An alternative to "learned helplessness." *J. Exp. Psychol.: Anim. Behav. Proc.* **2**, 202–213. [125, 209, 213, 214]

Glazer, H.I., Weiss, J.M., Pohorecky, L.A., and Miller, N.E. (1975) Monoamines as mediators of avoidance-escape behaviour. *Psychosom. Med.* **37**, 535–543. [211, 212]

Glick, S.D. and Cox, R.D. (1978) Nocturnal rotation in normal rats: Correlation with amphetamine-induced rotation and effects of nigro-striatal lesions. *Brain Res.* **150**, 149–161. [96, 99]

Glick, S.D. and Jerussi, T.P. (1974) Spatial and paw preference in rats: Their relationship to rate-dependent effects of D-amphetamine. *J. Pharmacol. Exp. Ther.* **188**, 714–725. [96]

Glick, S.D. and Ross, D.A. (1983) Neuroanatomical substrates of opiate reinforcement—Lateralized effects. In J.E. Smith and J.D. Lane (Eds.), *The Neurobiology of Opiate Reward Processes.* Elsevier, New York, pp. 309–330. [386]

Glick, S.D., Jerussi, J.P., Waters, D.H., and Green, J.P. (1974) Amphetamine-induced changes in striatal dopamine and acetylcholine levels and relationship to rotation (circling behaviour) in rats. *Biochem. Pharmacol.* **23**, 3223–3225. [99]

Glick, S.D., Meibach, R.C., Cox, R.D., and Maayani, S. (1979) Multiple and interrelated asymmetries in rat brain. *Life Sci.* **25**, 395–400. [97]

Glick, S.D., Ross, D.A., and Hough, L.B. (1982) Lateral asymmetry of neurotransmitters in human brain. *Brain Res.* **234**, 53–63. [99]

Globus, M., Lerer, B., Hamburger, R., and Belmaker, R.H. (1981) Chronic electroconvulsive shock and chronic haloperidol administration are not additive in effects on dopamine receptors. *Neuropharmacology* **20**, 1125–1128. [189, 190]

Glowinski, J. (1973) Some characteristics of the "functional" and "main storage" compartments in central catecholamine neurons. *Brain Res.* **62**, 489–493. [5, 208]

Glowinski, J. and Axelrod, J. (1964) Inhibition of uptake of tritiated noradrenalin in the intact rat brain by imipramine and structurally related compounds. *Nature* **204**, 1318–1319. [8]

Glowinski, J., Kopin, I.J., and Axelrod, J. (1965) Metabolism of (^{3}H)norepinephrine in the rat brain. *J. Neurochem.* **12**, 25–30. [224]

Gluckman, M.I. and Baum, T. (1969) The pharmacology of iprindole, a new antidepressant. *Psychopharmacology* **15**, 169–185. [11, 240, 256]

Goddard, G.V. (1964) Functions of the amygdala. *Psychol. Bull.* **62**, 89–109. [197]

Goddard, G.V. (1969) Analysis of avoidance conditioning following cholinergic stimulation of amygdala in rats. *J. Comp. Physiol. Psychol. Monogr.* **68** 2 (Part 2), 1–18. [275]

Goddard, G.V., McIntyre, D.C., and Leech, C.K. (1969) A permanent change in brain function resulting from daily electrical stimulation. *Exp. Neurol.* **25**, 295–330. [108]

Goddard, G.V., Bliss, T.V.P., Robertson, H.A., and Sutherland, R.S. (1980) Noradrenaline levels affect long-term potentiation in the hippocampus. *Soc. Neurosci. Abstr.* **6**, 89. [202]

Gold, B.J., Bowers, M.B., Roth, R.H., and Sweeney, D.R. (1980) GABA levels in CSF of patients with psychiatric disorders. *Am. J. Psychiatr.* **137**, 362–364. [355]

Gold, M.S., Pottash, A.L.C., Sweeney, D.R., Kleber, H.D., and Redmond, D.E. (1979) Rapid opiate detoxification: Clinical evidence of antidepressant and antimanic effects of opiates. *Am. J. Psychiatr.* **136**, 982–983. [366]

Gold, M.S., Pottash, A.L.C., Ryan, M., Sweeney, D.R., Davies, R.K., and Martin, D.M. (1980) TRH-induced TSH response in unipolar, bipolar, and secondary depressions: Possible utility in clinical assessment and differential diagnosis. *Psychoneuroendocrinology* **5**, 147–155. [372]

Gold, P.E. and Sternberg, D.B. (1978) Retrograde amnesia produced by different treatments: Evidence for a common neurobiological mechanism. *Science* **201**, 367–369. [201]

Gold, P.W., Goodwin, F.K., Wehr, T., Rebar, R., and Sack, R. (1976) Growth hormone and prolactin response to levodopa in affective illness. *Lancet* **2**, 1308–1309. [165, 166]

Gold, P.W., Goodwin, F.K., Wehr, T., and Rebar, R. (1977) Pituitary thyrotropin releasing hormone in affective illness: Relationship to spinal fluid amine metabolites. *Am. J. Psychiatr.* **134**, 1028–1031. [372]

Gold, P.W., Weingartner, H., Ballenger, J.C., Goodwin, F.K., and Post R.M. (1979) Effects of 1-desamino-8-D-arginine vasopressin on behavior and cognition in primary affective disorder. *Lancet* **2**, 992–994. [374]

Gold, R., Morgenstern, R., and Fink, H. (1980) Effects of atypical antidepressants on LSD potentiated apomorphine hypermotility in rats. *Acta Biol. Med. Ger.* **39**, 917–921. [330]

Goldberg, I.K. (1980) L-tyrosine in depression. *Lancet* **2**, 364. [172, 232]

Goldstein, L. (1979) Some relationships between quantified hemispheric EEG and behavioral states in man. In J.H. Gruzelier and P. Flor-Henry (Eds.), *Hemispheric Asymmetries of Function and Psychopathology.* Elsevier, Amsterdam, pp. 237–254. [88]

Goldstein, S.G., Filskov, S.B., Weaver, L.A., and Ives, J.O. (1977) Neuropsychological effects of electroconvulsive therapy. *J. Clin. Psychol.* **33**, 798–806. [90]

Golin, S., Sweeney, P.D., and Shaeffer, D.E. (1981) The causality of causal attributions in depression: A cross-lagged panel correlational analysis. *J. Abnorm. Psychol.* **90**, 14–22. [78]

Goode, D., Dekirmenjian, H., Meltzer, H., and Maas, J.W. (1973) Relation of exercise to MHPG excretion in normal subjects. *Arch. Gen. Psychiatr.* **29**, 391–396. [226]

Goodlet, I., Mireylees, S.E., and Sugrue, M.F. (1977) Effects of mianserin, a new antidepressant, on the in vitro and in vivo uptake of monoamines. *Br. J. Pharmacol.* **61**, 307–313. [240]

Goodnich, P.J., Evans, H.E., Dunner, D.L., and Fieve, R.R. (1980) Amino acid concentrations in cerebrospinal fluid: Effects of aging, depression and probenecid. *Biol. Psychiatr.* **15**, 557–563. [164, 222]

Goodwin, A.M. and Williams, J.M.G. (1983) Mood-induction research: Its implications for clinical depression. *Behav. Res. Ther.* **20**, 373–382. [73, 76]

Goodwin, D.W. and Erickson, D.K., eds. (1979) *Alcoholism and Affective Disorders: Clinical Genetic and Biochemical Studies.* Spectrum, New York. [229]

Goodwin, F.K. (1972) Behavioral effects of L-dopa in man. In R.I. Shader (Ed.), *Psychiatric Complications of Medical Drugs*. Raven, New York, pp. 149–174. [173]

Goodwin, F.K. and Post, R.M. (1972) The use of probenecid in high doses for the estimation of central serotonin turnover in patients with affective illness. In J. Barchas and E. Usdin (Eds)., *Serotonin and Behavior*. Academic, New York, pp. 469–480. [311, 312]

Goodwin, F.K. and Post, R.M. (1975) Studies of amine metabolites in affective illness and in schizophrenia: A comparative analysis. In D.X. Freedman (Ed.), *Biology of the Major Psychoses*. Raven, New York, pp. 299–332. [226, 322]

Goodwin, F.K. and Potter, W.Z. (1978) The biology of affective illness: Amine neurotransmitters and drug response. In J.O. Cole, A.F. Schatzberg, and S.H. Frazier (Eds.), *Depression: Biology, Psychodynamics and Treatment*, Plenum, New York, pp. 41–73. [310]

Goodwin, F.K. and Potter, W.Z. (1979) Norepinephrine metabolite studies in affective illness. In E. Usdin, I.J. Kopin, and J. Barchas (Eds.), *Catecholamines: Basic and Clinical Frontiers*, Vol. 2. Pergamon, New York, pp. 1863–1865. [225]

Goodwin, F.K. and Sack. R.L. (1974) Central dopamine function in affective illness: Evidence from precursors, enzyme inhibitors, and studies of central dopamine turnover. In E. Usdin (Ed.), *Neuropsychopharmacology of Monoamines and Their Regulatory Enzymes*. Raven, New York, pp. 261–279. [172, 230, 387]

Goodwin, F.K., Murphy, D.L., Brodie, H.K.H., and Bunney, W.E. (1970) L-dopa, catecholamines and behavior: A clinical and biochemical study in depressed patients. *Biol. Psychiatr.* **2**, 341–366. [11, 172, 177]

Goodwin, F.K., Murphy, D.L., Brodie, H.K.H., and Bunney, W.E. (1971) Levo-DOPA: Alterations in behavior. *Clin. Pharmacol. Ther.* **13**, 383–396. [232]

Goodwin, F.K., Ebert, M.H., and Bunney, W.E. (1972) Mental effects of reserpine in man: A review. In R.I. Shader (Ed.), *Psychiatric Complications of Medical Drugs*. Raven, New York, pp. 73–101. [10, 28, 110, 169, 317]

Goodwin, F.K., Post, R.M, Dunner, D.L., and Gordon, E.K. (1973a) Cerebrospinal fluid amine metabolites in affective illness: The probenecid technique. *Am. J. Psychiatr.* **130**, 73–79. [9, 167, 168, 311]

Goodwin, F.K., Post, R.M., and Murphy, D.L. (1973b) Cerebrospinal fluid amine metabolites and therapies for depression. *Sci. Proc. Am. Psychiatr. Assoc.* **126**, 24–25. [313]

Goodwin, F.K., Post, R.M., and Sack, R.L. (1975) Clinical evidence for neurochemical adaptation to psychotropic drugs. In A.J. Mandell (Ed.), *Neurobiological Mechanisms of Adaptation and Behaviour*. Raven, New York, pp. 33–46. [251]

Goodwin, F.K., Cowdry, R.W., and Webster, M.H. (1978)Predictors of drug response in the affective disorders: Toward an integrated approach. In M.A. Lipton, A.DiMaschio, and K.F. Killam (Eds.), *Psychopharmacology: A Generation of Progress*. Raven, New York, pp. 1277–1288. [234, 322]

Goodwin, F.K., Prange, A.J., Post, R.M., Muscettola, G., and Lipton, M.A. (1982a) Potentiation of antidepressant effects by L-triiodothyronine in tricyclic nonresponders. *Am. J. Psychiatr.* **139**, 34–38. [373]

Goodwin, F.K., Wirz-Justice, A., and Wehr, T.A. (1982b) Evidence that pathophysiology of depression and the mechanism of action of antidepressant drugs both involve alterations in circadian rhythms. In E. Costa and G. Racagni (Eds.), *Typical and Atypical Antidepressants: Clinical Practice*. Raven, New York, pp. 1–11. [115, 116, 271]

Gordon, E.K., Oliver, J., Goodwin, F.K., Chase, T.N., and Post, R.M. (1973) Effect of probenecid on free 3-methoxy-4-hydroxyphenylethylene glycol (MHPG) and its sulfate in human cerebrospinal fluid. *Neuropharmacology* **12**, 391–396. [224]

Gorka, Z. and Wojtasik, E. (1980) The effect of antidepressants on behavioral despair in rats. *Pol. J. Pharmacol. Pharm.* **32**, 463–468. [127, 128, 290]

Gorka, Z. and Zacny, E. (1981) The effect of single and chronic administration of imipramine on clonidine-induced hypothermia in the rat. *Life Sci.* **28,** 2847–2854. [244]

Gorka, Z., Wojtasik, E., Kwiatek, H., and Maj., J. (1979) Action of serotoninmimetics in the behavioral despair test in rats. *Commun. Psychopharmacol.* **3,** 133–136. [127, 290, 292]

Gotlib, I.H. (1981) Self-reinforcement and recall: Differential deficits in depressed and non-depressed psychiatric inpatients. *J. Abnorm. Psychol.* **90,** 521–530. [70]

Gottfries, C.G. (1980) Human brain levels of monamines and their metabolites. Postmortem investigations. *Acta Psychiatr. Scand.* **61** (Suppl. 280), 49–61. [310]

Gottfries, C.G., Perris, C., and Roos, B.E. (1974) Visual averaged evoked responses and monoamine metabolites in cerebrospinal fluid. *Acta Psychiatr. Scand.* (Suppl. 255), 135–142. [98, 99]

Gottfries, C.G., Oreland, L., Wiberg, A., and Winblad, B. (1975) Lowered monamine oxidase activity in brains from alcoholic suicides. *J. Neurochem.* **25,** 667–673. [222, 313]

Goudie, A.J. and Thornton, E.W. (1975) Effects of drug experience on drug induced conditioned taste aversions: Studies with amphetamine and fenfluramine. *Psychopharmacology* **44,** 77–82. [302]

Goudie, A.J., Thornton, E.W., and Wheeler, T.J. (1976) Effects of Lilly 110140, a specific inhibitor of 5-hydroxytryptamine uptake, on food uptake and on 5-hydroxytryptophan-induced anorexia. Evidence for serotonergic inhibition of feeding. *J. Pharm. Pharmacol.* **28,** 218–320. [303]

Grabowska, M., Antkiewicz, L., and Mechaluk, J. (1974) The influence of LSD on locomotor activity in reserpinized mice. *Pol. J. Pharmacol. Pharm.* **26,** 499–504. [110]

Graeff, F.G. (1974) Tryptamine antagonists and punished behaviour. *J. Pharmacol. Exp. Ther.* **189,** 344–350. [294]

Graeff, F.G. and Schoenfeld, R.I. (1970) Tryptaminergic mechanisms in punished and non-punished behaviour. *J. Pharmacol. Exp. Ther.* **173,** 277–283. [294]

Graeff, F.G., Quintero, S., and Gray, J.A. (1980) Median raphe stimulation, hippocampal theta rhythm and threat-induced behavioral inhibition. *Physiol. Behav.* **25,** 253–261. [273]

Graham, P.M., Booth, J., Boranga, G., Galhenage, S., Myers, C.M., Teoh, C.L., and Cox, L.S. (1982) The dexamethasone suppression test in mania. *J. Affect. Disord.* **4,** 201–211. [54]

Grandison, L. and Guidotti, A. (1977) Stimulation of food intake by muscimol and beta-endorphin. *Neuropharmacology* **16,** 533–536. [362]

Grau, J., Hyson, R.L., Maier, S.F., Madden, J., and Barchas, J.D. (1981) Long-term stress-induced analgesia and activation of the opiate system. *Science* **213,** 1409–1411. [360]

Graw, P., Puhringe,, W., Lacoste, V., Wirz-Justice, A., and Gastpar, M. (1976) Intravenous L-5-hydroxytryptophan in normal subjects: An interdisciplinary precursor preloading study. II. Profile of psychotropic effects derived from protocols and psychometric investigations. *Pharmakopsychiatrie* **9,** 269–276. [320]

Gray, J.A. (1967) Disappointment and drugs in the rat. *Adv. Sci.* **23,** 595–605. [203]

Gray, J.A. (1970) The psychophysiological basis of introversion-extraversion. *Behav. Res. Ther.* **8,** 249–266. [80]

Gray, J.A. (1981) A critique of Eysenck's theory of personality. In H.J. Eysenck (Ed.), *A Model for Personality.* Springer, New York, pp. 246–276. [80]

Gray, J.A. (1982) *The Neuropsychology of Anxiety: An Enquiry into the Functions of the Septo-Hippocampal System.* Oxford University Press, New York. [20, 26, 199, 200, 202–205, 207, 209, 273, 294, 295, 354, 408]

Gray, J.A., and 27 other authors (1982) Précis and multiple book review of "The Neuropsychology of Anxiety: An Enquiry into the Functions of the Septo-Hippocampal System." *Behav. Brain Sci.* **5**, 469–534. [20, 204, 205]

Gray, J.A., James, D.T.D., and Kelly, P.H. (1975) Effect of minor tranquillizers on hippocampal theta rhythm mimicked by depletion of forebrain noradrenaline. *Nature* **258**, 424–425. [203]

Gray, T. and Wise, R.A. (1980) Effects of pimozide on lever pressing behavior maintained on an intermittent reinforcement schedule. *Pharmacol. Biochem. Behav.* **12**, 931–935. [152]

Greden, J.F. and Carroll, B.J. (1980) Decrease in speech pause times with treatment of endogenous depression. *Biol. Psychiatr.* **15**, 575–587. [64]

Greden, J.F. and Carroll, B.J. (1981) Psychomotor function in affective disorders: An overview of new monitoring techniques. *Am. J. Psychiatr.* **138**, 1441–1448. [64]

Greden, J.F., Albala, A.A., Haskett, R.F., Norman, M.J., Goodman, L., Steiner, M., and Carroll, B.J. (1980) Normalization of dexamethasone suppression test: A laboratory index of recovery from endogenous depression. *Biol. Psychiatr.* **15**, 449–458. [53]

Greden, J.F., Albala, A.A., Smokler, I.A., Gardner, R., and Carroll, B.J. (1981a) Speech pause time: A marker of psychomotor retardation among endogenous depressives. *Biol. Psychiatr.* **16**, 851–859. [65]

Greden, J.F., Kronfol, Z., Gardner, R., Feinberg, M., Mukhopadhyav, S., Albala, A.A., and Carroll, B.J. (1981) Dexamethasone suppression test and selection of antidepressant medications. *J. Affect. Disord.* **3**, 389–396. [237]

Green, A.R. and Costain, D.W. (1979) The biochemistry of depression. In E.S. Paykel and A. Coppen (Eds.), *Psychopharmacology of Affective Disorders*, Oxford University Press, Oxford, pp. 14–40. [6, 7]

Green, A.R. and Curzon, G. (1970) The effect of tryptophan metabolites on brain 5-hydroxytryptamine metabolism. *Biochem. Pharmacol.* **19**, 2061–2068. [308]

Green, A.R. and Deakin, J.F.W. (1980) Brain noradrenaline depletion prevents ECS-induced enhancement of serotonin- and dopamine-mediated behaviour. *Nature* **285**, 232–233. [188, 189, 339]

Green, A.R. and Grahame-Smith, D.G. (1976) Effects of drugs on the processes regulating the functional activity of brain 5-hydroxytryptamine. *Nature* **260**, 487–491. [288, 309]

Green, A.R., Heal, D.J., and Grahame-Smith, D.G. (1977a) Further observations on the effect of repeated electroconvulsive shock on the behavioural responses of rats produced by increases in the functional activity of 5-hydroxytryptamine and dopamine. *Psychopharmacology* **52**, 195–200. [188, 190, 339]

Green, A.R., Mitchell, B.D., Tordoff, A.F.C., and Youdim, M.B.H. (1977b) Evidence for dopamine deamination by both type A and type B monoamine oxidase in rat brain in vivo and for the degree of inhibition of enzyme necessary for increased functional activity of dopamine and 5-hydroxytryptamine. *Br. J. Pharmacol.* **60**, 343–349. [165, 334]

Green, A.R., Peralta, E., Hong, J.-S., Mao, C.C., Atterwill, C.K., and Costa, E. (1978) Alterations in GABA and met-enkephalin concentration in rat brain following repeated electroconvulsive shock. *J. Neurochem.* **31**, 607–611. [357, 367]

Green, A.R., Bloomfield, M.R., Atterwill, C.K., and Costain, D.W. (1979) Electroconvulsive shock reduces the cataleptogenic effect of both haloperidol and arecoline in rats. *Neuropharmacology* **18**, 447–451. [285]

Green, A.R., Costain, D.W., and Deakin, J.W.F. (1980) Enhanced 5-hydroxytryptamine and dopamine-mediated behavioural responses following convulsions. III. The effects of monoamine antagonists and synthesis inhibitors on the ability of electroconvulsive shock to enhance responses. *Neuropharmacology* **19**, 907–914. [188, 189, 339]

Green, A.R., Sant, K., Bowdler, J.M., and Cowen, P.J. (1982) Further evidence for a relationship between changes in GABA concentrations in rat brain and enhanced monoamine-mediated behaviors following repeated electroconvulsive shock. *Neuropharmacology* **21**, 981–984. [357]

Green, A.R., Johnson, P., and Nimgaonkar, V.L. (1983a) Increased 5-HT$_2$ receptor number in brain as a probable explanation for the enhanced 5-hydroxytryptamine-mediated behaviour following repeated electroconvulsive shock administration to rats. *Br. J. Pharmacol.* **80**, 173–177. [339, 348, 349]

Green, A.R., Heal, D.J., Johnson, P., Laurence, B.E., and Nimgaonkar, V.L. (1983b) Antidepressant treatments: effects in rodents on dose-response curves of 5-hydroxytryptamine- and dopamine-mediated behaviours and 5-HT$_2$ receptor number in frontal cortex. *Br. J. Pharmacol.* **80**, 377–385. [189, 339, 341, 342, 344, 348, 349]

Green, J.P. and Maayani, S. (1977) Tricyclic antidepressant drugs block histamine H$_2$ receptor in brain. *Nature* **269**, 163–165. [369]

Green, J.P., Johnson, C.L., and Weinstein, H. (1978) Histamine as a neurotransmitter. In M.A. Lipton, A. DiMaschio, and K.F. Killam (Eds.), *Psychopharmacology: A Generation of Progress*. Raven, New York, pp. 319–332. [367, 368]

Greenberg, D.A., U'Prichard, D.C., and Snyder, S.H. (1976) Alpha-noradrenergic receptor binding in mammalian brain: Differential labelling of agonist and antagonist states. *Life Sci.* **19**, 69–76. [246]

Greengard, P.A. (1976) Possible role for cyclic nucleotides and phosphorylated membrane proteins in postsynaptic actions of neurotransmitters. *Nature* **260**, 101–108. [14, 256]

Greenspan, K., Schildkraut, J.J., Gordon, E.K., Baer, L., Aronoff, M.S., and Durrell, J. (1970) Catecholamine metabolites in affective disorders. III. 3-methoxy-4-hydroxyphenylglycol and other catecholamine metabolites in patients treated with lithium carbonate. *J. Psychiatr. Res.* **7**, 171–183. [225, 226]

Greenwood, M.H., Friedel, J., Bond, A.J., Curzon, G., and Lader, M.H. (1974) The acute effects of intravenous infusion of L-tryptophan in normal subjects. *Clin. Pharmacol. Ther.* **16**, 455–464. [320]

Greenwood, M.H., Lader, M.H., Kantameneni, B.D., and Curzon, G. (1975) The acute effects of oral tryptophan in human subjects. *Br. J. Clin. Pharmacol.* **2**, 165–172. [320]

Gregoire, F., Brauman, H., De Buck, R., and Corvilain, J. (1977) Hormone release in depressed patients before and after recovery. *Psychoneuroendocrinology* **2**, 303–312. [165]

Greidanus, T.B. van W., Bohus, B., and De Wied, D. (1974) Differential localization of the influence of lysine vasopressin and of ACTH 4-10 on avoidance behaviour: A study in rats bearing lesions in the parafascicular nuclei. *Neuroendocrinology* **14**, 280–288. [275]

Greist, J.H., Klein, M.H., Eischens, R.R., Faris, J., Gurman, A.S., and Morgan, W.P. (1979) Running as treatment for depression. *Comp. Psychiatr.* **20**, 41–54. [412]

Grevert, P. and Goldstein, A. (1978) Endorphins: Naloxone fails to alter experimental pain or mood in humans. *Science* **199**, 1093–1095. [366]

Griffith, J.D., Cavanaugh, J., Held, N.N., and Oates, J.A. (1972) Dextroamphetamine: Evaluation of psychotomimetic properties in man. *Arch. Gen. Psychiatr.* **26**, 97–100. [27, 176]

Grinker, J., Marinescu, C., and Leibowitz, S.F. (1982) Effects of central injections of neurotransmitters on freely-feeding rats. *Soc. Neurosci. Abstr.* **8**, 604. [208]

Groom, G., Janowsky, D., and Risch, S.C. (1983) Physostigmine down-regulation of beta adrenergic receptors. *Psychopharm. Bull.* **19**, 670–675. [267]

Gross, G., Brodde, O.-E., and Schumann, H.-J. (1980) Decreased number of beta-adrenoceptors in cerebral cortex of hypothyroid rats. *Eur. J. Pharmacol.* **61**, 191–194. [373]

Gross, G., Brodde, O.-E., and Schumann, H.-J. (1981a) Regulation of alpha$_1$-receptors in the cerebral cortex of the rat by thyroid hormones. *Naunyn Schmiedebergs Arch. Pharmacol.* **316**, 45–50. [373]

Gross, G., Gothert, M., Ender, H.P., and Schumann, H.-J. (1981b) ^{3}H-imipramine binding sites in the rat brain. Selective localization on serotonergic terminals. *Naunyn Schmiedebergs Arch. Pharmacol.* **317**, 310–314. [316]

Grosscup, S.J. and Lewinsohn, P.M. (1980) Unpleasant and pleasant events and mood. *J. Clin. Consult. Psychol.* **36**, 252–259. [67–69, 81]

Grossman, S.P. (1962) Direct adrenergic and cholinergic stimulation of hypothalamic mechanisms. *Am. J. Physiol.* **202**, 875–882. [207]

Grote, S.S., Moses, S.G,. Robins, E., Hudgens, R.W., and Croninger, A.B. (1974) A study of selected catecholamine metabolizing enzymes: A comparison of depressive suicides and alcoholic suicides with controls. *J. Neurochem.* **23**, 791–802. [165, 221, 223, 313]

Groves, P.M. (1983) A theory of the functional organization of the neostriatum and the neostriatal control of voluntary movement. *Brain Res. Rev.* **5**, 109–132. [379]

Groves, P.M., Wilson, C.J., Young, S.J., and Rebec, G.V. (1975) Self-inhibition by dopaminergic neurons. *Science* **190**, 522–529. [183]

Gruen, P.H., Sachar, E.J., Altman, N., and Sassin, J. (1975) Growth hormone responses to hypoglycemia in postmenopausal depressed women. *Arch. Gen. Psychiatr.* **32**, 31–33. [165, 229]

Gruzelier, G. and Venables, P. (1974) Bimodality and lateral asymmetry of skin conductance orienting activity in schizophrenics: Replication and evidence of lateral asymmetry in patients with depression and disorders of personality. *Biol. Psychiatr.* **8**, 55–73. [90]

Gudeman, J.E., Schatzberg, A.F., Samson, J.A., Orsulak, P.J., Cole, J.O., and Schildkraut, J.J. (1982) Towards a biochemical classification of depressive disorders. VI. Platelet MAO activity and clinical symptoms in depressed patients. *Am. J. Psychiatr.* **139**, 630–633. [165, 221]

Guidotti, A., Baraldi, M., Schwartz, J.P., and Costa, E. (1979) Molecular mechanisms regulating the interactions between the benzodiazepines and GABA receptors in the central nervous system. *Pharmacol. Biochem. Behav.* **10**, 803–807. [354, 356]

Guillemin, R. (1978) Peptides in the brain: The new endocrinology of the neuron. *Science* **202**, 390–402. [370]

Guisado, E., Fernandez-Tome, P., Garzon, J., and Del Rio, J. (1980) Increased dopamine receptor binding in the striatum of rats after long-term isolation. *Eur. J. Pharmacol.* **65**, 463–464. [291]

Gur, R.E. (1978) Left hemisphere dysfunction and left hemisphere overactivation in schizophrenia. *J. Abnorm. Psychol.* **87**, 226–238. [89]

Gutierrez, J.L.A. and Alino, J.J.L.-I. (1971) Tryptophan and an MAOI (Nialamide) in the treatment of depression. *Int. Pharmacopsychiatr.* **6**, 92–97. [319]

Guze, S.B., Woodruff, R.A., and Clayton, P.J. (1971) Preliminary communication–secondary affective disorder: A study of 95 cases. *Psychol. Med.* **1**, 426–428. [47]

Gysling, R. and Wang, R. (1982) Morphine facilitates the activity of dopaminergic neurons in the rat ventral tegmental area. *Soc. Neurosci. Abstr.* **8**, 777. [151]

Haas, H.L. (1979) Histamine and noradrenaline are blocked by amitriptyline on cortical neurons. *Agents Actions* **9**, 83–84. [369]

Haggard, M.P. and Parkinson, A.M. (1971) Stimulus and task factors as determinants of ear advantages. *Q. J. Exp. Psychol.* **23**, 168–177. [86]

Haggendahl, J. and Lindqvist, M. (1964) Disclosure of labile monoamine fractions in brain and their correlation to behaviour. *Acta Physiol. Scand.* **60**, 351–357. [169]

Haigler, H.J. and Aghajanian, G.K. (1974) Lysergic acid diethylamide and serotonin: A comparison of effects on serotonin neurons and neurons receiving a serotonergic input. *J. Pharmacol. Exp. Ther.* **188,** 688–699. [331]

Halaris, A. and De Met, E.M. (1978) Studies of norepinephrine metabolism in manic and depressive states. In E. Usdin, I.J. Kopin, and J. Barchas (Eds.), *Catecholamines: Basic and Clinical Frontiers.* Pergamon, New York, pp. 1866–1888. [250, 251]

Halaris, A., Belendiuk, K., and Freedman, D.X. (1975) Antidepressant drugs affect dopamine reuptake. *Biochem. Pharmacol.* **24,** 1896–1898. [181]

Halbreich, U., Grunhaus, L., and Ben-David, M. (1979) Twenty four hour rhythm of prolactin in depressive patients. *Arch. Gen. Psychiatr.* **36,** 1183–1186. [166]

Halbreich, U., Asnis, G.M., Halpern, F.S., Tabrizi, M.A., and Sachar, E.J. (1980) Diurnal growth hormone response to dextroamphetamine in normal young men and postmenopausal women. *Psychoneuroendocrinology* **5,** 339–344. [229]

Halbreich, U., Sachar, E.J., Asnis, G.M., Quitkin, F., Nathan, R.S., Halpern, F.S., and Klein, D.F. (1982) Growth hormone response to dextroamphetamine in depressed patients and normal subjects. *Arch. Gen. Psychiatr.* **39,** 189–192. [165, 229]

Hall, H. and Ogren, S.-O. (1981) Effects of antidepressant drugs on different receptors in the brain. *Eur. J. Pharmacol.* **70,** 393–407. [242, 284, 368, 369]

Hall, H., Ross, S.B., and Ogren, S.-O. (1982) Effects of zimelidine on various transmitter systems in the brain. In E. Costa and G. Racagni (Eds.), *Typical and Atypical Antidepressants: Molecular Mechanisms,* Raven, New York, pp. 321–325. [348]

Hall, K.R.L. and Stride, E. (1954) The varying response to pain in psychiatric disorders; A study in abnormal psychology. *Br. J. Med. Psychol.* **27,** 48–60. [69]

Halliday, A.M., Davison, K., Browne, M.W., and Kreeger, L.C. (1968) A comparison of the effects on depression and memory of bilateral ECT and unilateral ECT to the non-dominant hemisphere. *Br. J. Psychiatr.* **114,** 997–1012. [89]

Halliwell, G., Quinton, R.M., and Williams, F.E. (1964) A comparison of imipramine, chlorpromazine and related drugs in various tests involving autonomic functions and antagonism of reserpine. *Br. J. Pharmacol.* **23,** 330–350. [111]

Hallstrom, C.O.S., Rees, W.L., Pare, C.M.B., Trenchard, A., and Turner, P. (1976) Platelet uptake of 5-hydroxytryptamine and dopamine in depression. *Postgrad. Med. J.* **52** (Suppl. 3), 40–44. [164, 316]

Hamilton, M. (1967) Development of a rating scale for primary depressive illness. *Br. J. Soc. Clin. Psychol.* **6,** 278–296. [57]

Hamilton, W.H. and Abramson, L.Y. (1983) Cognitive patterns and major depressive disorder: A longitudinal study in a hospital setting. *J. Abnorm. Psychol.* **92,** 173–184. [73]

Hammen, C.L. and Cochran, S.D. (1981) Cognitive correlates of life stress and depression in college students. *J. Abnorm. Psychol.* **90,** 23–27. [69, 78]

Hammen, C. and De Mayo, R. (1982) Cognitive correlates of teacher stress and depressive symptoms: Implications for attributional models of depression. *J. Abnorm. Psychol.* **91,** 96–101. [77, 78, 127]

Hammen, C.L. and Glass, D.R. (1975) Depression, activity and evaluation of reinforcement. *J. Abnorm. Psychol.* **84,** 718–721. [67]

Hammond, D.L., Levy, R.A., and Proudfit, H.K. (1980a) Hypoalgesia induced by microinjection of a norepinephrine antagonist in the raphe magnus: Reversal by intrathecal injection of a serotonin antagonist. *Brain Res.* **201,** 475–479. [197]

Hammond, D.L., Levy, R.A., and Proudfit, H.K. (1980b) Hypoalgesia following microinjection of noradrenergic antagonists in the nucleus raphe magnus. *Pain* **9,** 85–101. [197]

Hanin, I. (1983) RBC choline as a potential marker in psychiatric and neurological disease. In E. Usdin and I. Hanin (Eds.), *Biological Markers in Psychiatry and Neurology*. Pergamon, Oxford, pp. 187–189. [280]

Hankoff, L.D., Grundlach, R.H., Paley, H.M., and Rudorfer, L. (1964) Diphenhydramine as an antidepressant. *Dis. Nerv. Syst.* **25**, 547–553. [370]

Hannum, R.D., Rosellini, R.A., and Seligman, M.E.P. (1976) Retention and immunization of learned helplessness from weaning to adulthood. *Dev. Psychol.* **12**, 449–454. [122]

Hansom, H.M. and Climini-Venema, C.A. (1972) Effects of haloperidol on self-administration of morphine in rats. *Fed. Proc.* **31**, 503. [151]

Harcus, A.H., Ward, A.E., and Smith, D.W. (1980) Buprenorphine in post-operative pain: Results in 7500 patients. *Anesthesia* **35**, 382–386. [367]

Harik, S.I., Lamanna, J.C., Light, A.I., and Rosenthal, M. (1979) Cerebral norepinephrine: Influence on cortical oxidative metabolism in situ. *Science* **206**, 69–71. [198]

Harman, D.W. and Ray, W.J. (1977) Hemispheric activity during affective verbal stimuli: An EEG study. *Neuropsychology* **15**, 457–460. [88]

Harmon, T.M., Nelson, R.O., and Hayes, S.C. (1980) Self-monitoring of mood versus activity by depressed clients. *J. Consult. Clin. Psychol.* **48**, 30–38. [67]

Harnad, S., Doty, R.W., Goldstein, L., Jaynes, J., and Krauthamer, G., eds. (1977) *Lateralization in the Nervous System*. Academic, New York. [85]

Harness, B., Bental, E., and Carmon, A. (1977) Comparison of cognition and performance in patients with organic brain damage and psychiatric patients. *Acta Psychiatr. Belg.* **73**, 339–347. [65]

Harper, A.M., Deshmukh, V.D., Rowan, J.O., and Jennett, W.B. (1972) The influence of sympathetic nervous activity on cerebral blood flow. *Arch. Neurol.* **27**, 1–6. [198]

Harris, L.S., Dewey, W.L., Howes, J.F., Kennedy, J.S., and Pars, H. (1969) Narcotic-antagonist analgesics: Interactions with cholinergic systems. *J. Pharmacol. Exp. Ther.* **169**, 17–22. [276]

Harrison-Read, P.E. (1980) Behavioral evidence for increased dopaminergic activity after long-term lithium pretreatment in rats. *IRCS Med. Sci.* **8**, 313. [183]

Hartman, B.R. (1973) Immunofluorescence of dopamine-beta-hydroxylase: Application of improved methodology to the localization of the peripheral and central noradrenergic nervous tissue. *J. Histochem. Cytochem.* **21**, 312–332. [9]

Hartman, E. (1973) *The Functions of Sleep*. Yale University Press, New Haven, Conn. [382]

Hartman, E. (1968) Longitudinal studies of sleep and dream patterns in manic-depressive patients. *Arch. Gen. Psychiatr.* **19**, 312–329. [46]

Hartman, E. and Keller-Teschke, M. (1979) The psychological effects of dopamine beta-hydroxylase inhibition in normal subjects. *Biol. Psychiatr.* **14**, 455–462. [230]

Hartman, E., Oldfield, M., Adelman, S., and Edelberg, R. (1983) Psychological effects of dopamine beta-hydroxylase inhibition: A failure to replicate. *Psychopharmacology* **79**, 352–356. [230]

Hartman, R.J. and Geller, I. (1971) *p*-Chlorophenylalanine effects on a conditioned emotional response in rats. *Life Sci.* **10**, 927–933. [294]

Hartnoll, R.L., Mitchison, M.C., Battersby, A., Brown, G., Ellis, M., Fleming, P., and Headley, N. (1980) Evaluation of heroin maintenance in a controlled trial. *Arch. Gen. Psychiatr.* **37**, 877–884. [395]

Harvey, D.M. (1981) Depression and attributional style: Interpretations of important personal events. *J. Abnorm. Psychol.* **90**, 134–142. [78]

Harvey, J.A. and Simansky, K.J. (1981) The role of serotonin in modulation of nociceptive reflexes. In B. Haber, S. Gabay, M.R. Issidorides, and G.A. Alivisatos (Eds.), *Serotonin:*

Current Aspects on Neurochemistry and Function. Plenum, New York, pp. 681–705. [296, 297]

Harvey, J.A., Schlosberg, A.J., and Yunger, L.M. (1974) Effect of p-chlorophenylalanine and brain lesions on pain sensitivity and morphine analgesia in the rat. *Adv. Biochem. Psychopharmacol.* **10**, 233–245. [297]

Hasher, L. and Zacks, R.T. (1979) Automatic and effortful processes in memory. *J. Exp. Psychol. Gen.* **108**, 356–388. [65]

Haskovec, L. (1969) Methysergide in mania. *Lancet* **2**, 902. [318]

Hatotani, N., Nomura, J., and Kitayama, I. (1982) Changes of brain monoamines in the animal model for depression. In S.Z. Langer, R. Takahashi, T. Segawa, and M. Briley (Eds.), *New Vistas in Depression.* Pergamon, New York, pp. 65–72. [115]

Hauger-Klevene, J.H. and Moyano, M. (1973) ACTH-induced alterations in catecholamine metabolism in man. *J. Clin. Endocrinol. Metab.* **36**, 679–683. [237]

Hauri, P., Chernik, D., Hawkins, D., and Mendels, J. (1974) Sleep of depressed patients in remission. *Arch. Gen. Psychiatr.* **31**, 386–391. [279]

Hawkins, D. (1980) Sleep and circadian rhythm disturbances in depression. In J. Mendels and J.D. Amsterdam (Eds.), *The Psychobiology of Affective Disorders.* Karger, Basel, pp. 147–173. [400]

Haycock, J.W., Van Buskirk, R., and McGaugh, J.L. (1977) Effects of catecholaminergic drugs upon memory storage processes in mice. *Behav. Biol.* **20**, 281–310. [201]

Hayes, R.L., Bennett, G.J., Newlon, P.G., and Mayer, D.J. (1978a) Behavioral and physiological studies of non-narcotic analgesia in the rat elicited by certain environmental stimuli. *Brain Res.* **155**, 69–90. [360]

Hayes, R.L., Price, D.D., Bennett, G.J., Wilcox, G.L., and Mayer, D.J. (1978b) Differential effects of spinal cord lesions on narcotic and non-narcotic suppression of nociceptive reflexes: Further evidence for the physiologic multiplicity of pain modulation. *Brain Res.* **155**, 91–101. [360]

Headley, P.M., Duggan, A.W., and Griersmith, B.T. (1978) Selective reduction by noradrenaline and 5-hydroxytryptamine of nociceptive responses of cat dorsal horn neurons. *Brain Res.* **145**, 185–189. [298]

Heal, D.J. and Green, A.R. (1978) Repeated electroconvulsive shock increases the behavioural responses of rats to injection of both dopamine and dibutyryl cyclic AMP into the nucleus accumbens. *Neuropharmacology*, **17**, 1085–1087. [188, 190]

Heal, D.J., Phillips, A.G., and Green, A.R. (1978) Studies on the locomotor activity produced by injections of dibutyryl cyclic 3'5'-AMP into the nucleus accumbens of rats. *Neuropharmacology* **17**, 265–267. [188]

Heal, D.J., Akagi, H., Bowdler, J.M., and Green, A.R., (1981) Repeated electroconvulsive shock attenuates clonidine-induced hypoactivity in rodents. *Eur. J. Pharmacol.* **75**, 321–327. [244, 245]

Heath, R.G. (1963) Electrical self-stimulation of the brain in man. *Am. J. Psychiatr.* **120**, 571–577. [136]

Heath, R.G. (1964) Pleasure response of human subjects to direct stimulation of the brain: Physiologic and psychodynamic considerations. In R.G. Heath (Ed.), *The Role of Pleasure in Behavior.* Harper & Row, New York, pp. 219–243. [197]

Heath, R.G., John, S.B., and Fontana, C.J. (1968) The pleasure response: Studies by stereotaxic techniques in patients. In N.S. Kline and E. Laska (Eds.), *Computer and Electronic Devices in Psychiatry.* Grune & Stratton, New York, pp. 178–189. [136]

Hecaen, H. and Ajuriaguerra, J. (1964) *Lefthandedness.* Grune & Stratton, New York. [91]

Hedge, G.A. and De Wied, D. (1971) Corticotropin and vasopressin secretion after hypothalamic implantation of atropine. *Endocrinology* **88**, 1257–1259. [277]

Heel, R.C., Morley, P.A., Brogden, R.N., Carmine, A.A., Speight, T.M., and Avery, G.S. (1982) Zimelidine: A review of its pharmacological properties and therapeutic efficacy in depressive illness. *Drugs* **24**, 169–206. [323, 351]

Heilman, K.M., Scholes, R., and Watson, R.T. (1975) Auditory affective agnosia: Disturbed comprehension of affective speech. *J. Neurol Neurosurg. Psychiatr.* **38**, 69–72. [86]

Heilman, K.M., Schwartz, H.D., and Watson, R.T. (1978) Hypoarousal in patients with the neglect syndrome and emotional indifference. *Neurology* **28**, 229–232. [91]

Hekimian, L.J., Friedhoff, A.J., and Deever, E. (1981) A comparison of the onset of action and therapeutic efficacy of amoxapine and amitriptyline. *J. Clin. Psychiatr.* **39**, 633–637. [235]

Heltzer, J.E., Robins, L.N., Taibelson, M., Woodruff, R.A., and Wish, E.D. (1977) Reliability of psychiatric diagnosis. *Arch. Gen. Psychiatr.* **34**, 129–133. [41]

Hemphill, R.E., Hall, K.R.L., and Crookes, T.G. (1952) A preliminary report on fatigue and pain tolerance in depressive and psychoneurotic patients. *J. Ment. Sci.* **98**, 433–440. [69]

Heninger, G., DiMaschio, A., and Klerman, G.L. (1965) Personality factors in variability of response to phenothiazines. *Am. J. Psychiatr.* **121**, 1091–1094. [171]

Henry, G.M., Weingartner, H., and Murphy, D.L. (1973) Influence of affective states and psychoactive drugs on verbal learning and memory. *Am. J. Psychiatr.* **130**, 966–971. [65]

Henry, J.P. and Stephens, P.M. (1977) The social environment and essential hypertension in mice: Possible role of the innervation of the adrenal cortex. In W. DeLong, A. P. Provoost, and A. P. Shapiro (Eds.), *Hypertension and Brain Mechanisms*. Elsevier, New York, pp. 263–276. [214, 397]

Henry, J.P., Kross, M.E., Stephens, P.M., and Watson, F.M.C. (1976) Evidence that differing psychosocial stimuli lead to adrenal cortex stimulation by autonomic or endocrine pathways. In E. Usdin, R. Kvetansky, and I.J. Kopin (Eds.), *Catecholamines and Stress*. Pergamon, New York, pp. 457–468. [214, 397]

Herman, B.H. and Panksepp, J. (1981) Ascending endorphin inhibition of distress vocalization. *Science* **211**, 1060–1062. [363]

Hernandez, L. and Hoebel, B.G. (1982) Overeating after midbrain 6-hydroxydopamine: Prevention by central injection of selective catecholamine reuptake blockers. *Brain Res.* **245**, 333–343. [196]

Hersen, M., Bellack, A.S., and Himmelhoch, J.M. (1980) Treatment of unipolar depression with social skills training. *Behav. Modif.* **4**, 547–556. [411]

Hertting, G., Axelrod, J., and Whitby, L.G. (1961) Effect of drugs on the uptake and metabolism of ^{3}H-norepinephrine. *J. Pharmacol. Exp. Ther.* **134**, 146–153. [8]

Hess, W.R. (1957) *The Functional Organization of the Diencephalon.* Grune & Stratton, New York. [304]

Heydorn, W., Frazer, A., and Mendels, J. (1980) Do tricyclic antidepressants enhance adrenergic transmission? An update. *Am. J. Psychiatr.* **137**, 113–114. [261–263]

Heydorn, W.E., Caroff, S., and Frazer, A. (1982) Catecholamine-stimulated production of melatonin after administration of antidepressants. *Psychopharmacol. Bull.* **18**, 135–137. [262, 263]

Heym, J., Trulson, M.E., and Jacobs, B.L. (1981) Effects of adrenergic drugs on raphe activity in freely moving cats. *Eur. J. Pharmacol.* **74**, 117–125. [377]

Hidaka, H., Nagasaka, A., and Takeda, A. (1973) Fusaric (5-butylpicolinic) acid: Its effect on plasma growth hormone. *J. Clin. Endocrinol. Metab.* **37**, 145–147. [230]

Higley, J.D., Suomi, S.J., Scanlon, J.M., and McKinney, W.T. (1982) Plasma cortisol as a predictor of individual depressive behavior in rhesus monkeys (Macaca mulatta). *Soc. Neurosci. Abstr.* **8**, 461. [133]

Hilgard, J.R., Newman, M.F., and Fisk, F. (1960) Strength of adult ego following childhood bereavement. *Am. J. Orthopsychiatr.* **30**, 788–798. [394]

Hill, J. (1982) Reasons and causes: The nature of explanations in psychology and psychiatry. *Psychol. Med.* **12**, 501–514. [25, 29]

Hill, R.T. and Tedeschi, D.H. (1971) Animal testing and screening procedures in evaluation of psychotropic drugs. In R.H. Rech and K.E. Moore (Eds.), *An Introduction to Psychopharmacology.* Raven, New York, pp. 237–288. [110, 294]

Hill, S.Y. (1974) Intraventricular injection of 5-hydroxytryptamine and alcohol consumption in rats. *Biol. Psychiatr.* **8**, 151–158. [351]

Hinchcliffe, M.K., Lancashire, M., and Roberts, F.J. (1971) Depression: Defense mechanisms in speech. *Br. J. Psychiatr.* **118**, 471–472. [64]

Hinde, R.A. (1976) The use of differences and similarities in comparative psychopathology. In G. Serban and A. Kling (Eds.), *Animal Models in Human Psychobiology.* Plenum, New York, pp. 187–202. [109]

Hinde, R.A. and McGinnis, L. (1977) Some factors influencing the effects of temporary mother-infant separation. Some experiments with rhesus monkeys. *Psychol. Med.* **7**, 197–212. [132]

Hinde, R.A. and Spencer-Booth, Y. (1970) Individual differences in the responses of rhesus monkeys to a period of separation from their mothers. *J. Child Psychol. Psychiatr.* **11**, 159–176. [140]

Hinde, R.A., Leighton-Shapiro, M.E., and McGinnis, L. (1978) Effects of various types of separation experience on rhesus monkeys 5 months later. *J. Child Psychol. Psychiatr.* **19**, 199–211. [132]

Hintgen, J.N., Smith, J.E., Shea, P.A., Aprison, M.H., and Gaff, T.M. (1976) Cholinergic changes during conditioned suppression in rats. *Science* **193**, 332–334. [141, 275, 364]

Hiroto, D.S. (1974) Locus of control and learned helplessness. *J. Exp. Psychol.* **102**, 187–193. [75]

Hirschfeld, R.M. and Klerman, G.A. (1979) Personality attributes and affective disorders. *Am. J. Psychiatr.* **136**, 67–70. [80]

Hirschfeld, R.M.A. and Cross, C.C. (1982) Epidemiology of affective disorders: Psychosocial risk factors. *Arch. Gen. Psychiatr.* **39**, 35–47. [395]

Hjorth, S., Carlsson, A., Wikstrom, H., Lindberg, P., Sanchez, D., Hacksell, U., Arvidsson, L.-E., Svensson, U., and Nilsson, J.L.G. (1981) 3-PPP, a new centrally acting DA-receptor agonist with selectivity for autoreceptors. *Life Sci.* **28**, 1225–1238. [156, 191]

Hjorth, S., Carlsson, A., Clark, D., and Svensson, K. (1982) Pharmacological manipulation of central dopamine (DA) autoreceptors: Biochemical and behavioral consequences. Paper presented at Symposium on Dopamine Receptor Agonists: Medicinal Chemistry, Pharmacology and Clinial Aspects, Stockholm, Sweden, April 1982. [191]

Ho, B.T. and Huang, J.T. (1975) Role of dopamine in D-amphetamine-induced discriminative responding. *Pharmacol. Biochem. Behav.* **3**, 1085–1092. [182]

Hobson, J.A., McCarley, R.W., Freedman, R., and Pivik, R.T. (1974a) Selective firing by cat pontine brainstem neurons in desynchronized sleep. *J. Neurophysiol.* **37**, 497–511. [212, 213, 278]

Hobson, J.A., McCarley, R.W., Freedman, R., and Pivik, R.T. (1974b) Time course of discharge rate changes by cat pontine brainstem neurons during sleep cycle. *J. Neurophysiol.* **37**, 1297–1309 [212, 213, 278]

Hobson, J.A., McCarley, R.W., and Wyzinski, P.W. (1975) Sleep cycle oscillation: reciprocal discharge by two brain stem neuronal groups. *Science* **189**, 55–58. [205, 224, 271, 377]

Hoch, P.H. and Mauss, W. (1932) Atropin Behandling bei Geisteckvankheiten. *Arch. Gen. Psychiatr.* **97**, 546–552. [269, 283]

Hoebel, B.G. (1976) Brain stimulation reward and aversion in relation to behavior. In A. Wauquier and E.T. Rolls (Eds.), *Brain-Stimulation Reward*. Elsevier, New York, pp. 331–372. [136, 196, 363]

Hoebel, B.G. (1978) The psychopharmacology of feeding. In L.L. Iversen, S.D. Iversen, and S.H. Snyder (Eds.), *Handbook of Psychopharmacology*, Vol. 7. Plenum, New York, pp. 55–128. [302, 303]

Hoebel, B.G. (1979) Hypothalamic self-stimulation and stimulation escape in relation to feeding and mating. *Fed. Proc.* **36**, 2454–2461. [196]

Hoebel, B.G. and Teitelbaum, P. (1962) Hypothalamic control of feeding and self-stimulation. *Science* **135**, 375–377. [135, 196]

Hoebel, B.G., Hernandez, L., McLean, S., Stanley, B.G., Aulissi, E.F., Glimcher, P., and Margolin, D. (1981) Catecholamines, enkephalin and neurotensin in feeding and reward. In B.G. Hoebel and D. Novin (Eds.), *The Neural Basis of Feeding and Reward*. Haer Institute, Brunswick, Me., pp. 465–478. [152, 361, 362]

Hofmann, A. (1970) The discovery of LSD and subsequent investigations on naturally occurring hallucinogens. In F.J. Ayd and B. Blackwell (Eds.), *Discoveries in Biological Psychiatry*. Lippincott, Philadelphia, pp. 93–106. [21]

Hokfelt, T., Lundberg, J.M., Schultzberg, M., Johansson, O., Ljungdahl, A., and Rehfeld, J. (1980) Coexistence of peptides and putative neurotransmitters in neurons. In E. Costa and M. Trabucchi (Eds.), *Neuropeptides and Neuronal Communication*. Raven, New York, pp. 1–23. [259, 358, 370]

Holaday, J.W. and Belenky, G.L. (1980) Opiate-like effects of electroconvulsive shock in rats: A differential effect of naloxone on nociceptive measures. *Life Sci.* **27**, 1929–1938. [367]

Holaday, J.W., Hitzeman, J., Curell, J., Tortella, F.C., and Belenky, G.L. (1983) Repeated electroconvulsive shock or chronic morphine treatment increases the number of [^{3}H]-D-Ala2,D-Leu5-enkephalin binding sites in rat brain membranes. *Life Sci.* **31**, 2359–2362. [367]

Holcomb, H.H., Bannon, M.J., and Roth, R.H. (1982) Striatal dopamine autoreceptors uninfluenced by chronic administration of antidepressants. *Eur. J. Pharmacol.* **82**, 173–178. [185]

Hole, K. and Lorens, S.A. (1975) Response to electric shock in rats: Effects of selective midbrain Raphe lesions. *Pharmacol. Biochem. Behav.* **3**, 95–102. [297]

Hole, K., Fuxe, K., and Jonsson, G. (1976) Behavioral effects of 5,7-dihydroxytryptamine lesions of ascending 5-hydroxytryptamine pathways. *Brain Res.* **107**, 385–399. [294, 296, 297]

Hollister, L.E. (1981) Excretion of 3-methoxy-4-hydroxyphenylglycol in depressed and geriatric patients and normal persons. *Int. Pharmacopsychiatr.* **16**, 138–143. [234]

Hollister, L.E. and Overall, J.E. (1965) Reflections on the specificity of action of anti-depressants. *Psychosomatics* **6**, 361–365. [57, 171]

Hollister, L.E., Overall, J.E., Johnsson, M.H., Shelton, J., Kimbell, J., and Brunse, A. (1966) Amitriptyline alone and combined with perphenazine in newly admitted depressed patients. *J. Nerv. Ment. Disord.* **142**, 460–469. [171]

Hollister, L.E., Overall, J.E., Shelton, J., Pennington, V., Kimbell, J., and Johnson, M. (1967) Drug therapy in depression: Amitriptyline, perphenazine and their combination in different syndromes. *Arch. Gen. Psychiatr.* **17**, 486–493. [171]

Hollister, L.E., Davis, K.L., and Berger, P.A. (1977) Thyrotropin-releasing hormone and psychiatric disorders. In E. Usdin, D.A. Hamburg, and J.D. Barchas (Eds.), *Neuroregulators and Psychiatric Disorders*. Oxford University Press, New York, pp. 250–257. [371]

Hollister, L.E., Davis, K.L., Overall, J.E., and Anderson, T. (1978) Excretion of MHPG in normal subjects. *Arch. Gen. Psychiatr.* **35**, 1410–1415.[226]

Hollister, L.E., Davis, K.D., and Berger, P.A. (1980) Subtypes of depression based on excretion of MHPG and response to nortriptyline. *Arch. Gen Psychiatr.* **37**, 1107–1110. [233]

Hollister, L.E., Johnson, K., Boukhabza, D., and Gillespie, H.K. (1981) Aversive effects of naltrexone in subjects not dependent on opiates. *Drug Alcohol Depend.* **7**, 1–5. [366]

Holsboer, F., Bender, W., Benkert, O., Klein, H.E., and Schmauss, M. (1980) Diagnostic value of dexamethasone suppression test in depression. *Lancet* **1**, 706. [54]

Holsboer, F., Liebl, R., and Hofschuster, E. (1982) Repeated dexamethasone suppression test during depressive illness: Normalization of test result compared with clinical improvement. *J. Affect. Disord.* **4**, 93–101. [53]

Holzman, S.G. (1974) Behavioral effects of separate and combined administration of naloxone and d-amphetamine. *J. Pharmacol. Exp. Ther.* **189**, 51–60. [363]

Homburger, V., Lucas, M., Cantau, B., Barabe, J., Peuit, J., and Bockaert, J. (1980) Further evidence that desensitization of beta-adrenergic sensitive adenylate cyclase proceeds in two steps. *J. Biol. Chem.* **255**, 10436–10444. [257, 259]

Honecker, H., Fahndrich, E., Coper, H., and Helmchen, H. (1981) Serum DBH and platelet MAO in patients with depressive disorders. *Pharmakopsychiatr.* **14**, 10–14. [220, 221]

Hong, J.S., Gillin, J.C., Yang, H.-Y.T., and Costa, E. (1979) Repeated electroconvulsive shocks and the brain content of endorphins. *Brain Res.* **177**, 273–278. [367]

Hornykiewicz, O. (1966) Dopamine (3-hydroxytyramine) and brain function. *Pharmacol. Rev.* **18**, 925–964. [8, 22, 170]

Horovitz, Z.P. (1965) Selective block of rat mouse killing by antidepressants. *Life Sci.* **4**, 1909–1912. [107]

Horovitz, Z.P. (1967) The amygdala and depression. In S. Garattini and M.N.G. Dukes (Eds.), *Antidepressant Drugs*. Excerpta Medica, Amsterdam, pp. 121–129. [113]

Horovitz, Z.P., Piala, J.J., High, J.P., Burke, J.C., and Leaf, R.C. (1966) Effects of drugs on the mouse killing (muricide) test and its relationship to amygdaloid function. *Int. J. Neuropharmacol.* **5**, 405–411. [107, 271, 272, 292]

Horrobin, D.F., Mtabaji, J.P., Karmali, R.A., Manku, M.S., and Nassar, B.A. (1976) Prolactin and mental illness. *Postgrad. Med. J.,* Suppl. 3, 79–85. [166]

Hosobuchi, Y. (1978) Tryptophan reversal of tolerance to analgesia induced by central gray stimulation. *Lancet* **2**, 47. [299]

Hosobuchi, Y., Adams, J.E., and Linchitz, R. (1977) Pain relief by central gray stimulation and its reversal by naloxone. *Science* **197**, 183–186. [359]

Howard, J.L., Soroko, F.E., and Cooper, B.R. (1981) Empirical behavioral models of depression, with emphasis on tetrabenazine antagonism. In S.J. Enna, J.B. Malick, and E. Richelson (Eds.), *Antidepressants: Neurochemical, Behavioral and Clinical Perspectives*. Raven, New York, pp. 107–120. [110, 132]

Howlett, D.R. and Nahorski, S.R. (1980) Quantitative assessment of heterogenous [^{3}H]spiperone binding to rat neostriatum and frontal cortex. *Life Sci.* **26**, 511–517. [190]

Hrdina, P.D., Von Kulmiz, P., and Stretch, R. (1979) Pharmacological modification of experimental depression in infant macaques. *Psychopharmacology* **64**, 89–93. [132]

Huang, W.Y., Chang, R.C., Kastin, A.J., Coy, D.H., and Schally, A.V. (1979) Isolation and structure of pro-methionine-enkephalin: Potential enkephalin precursor from porcine hypothalamus. *Proc. Natl. Acad. Sci. USA* **76**, 6177–6180. [358]

Huang, Y.H. (1979a) Chronic desipramine treatment increases activity of noradrenergic postsynaptic cells. *Life Sci.* **25**, 709–716. [262, 264]

Huang, Y.H. (1979b) Net effect of acute administration of desipramine on the locus coeruleus-hippocampal system. *Life Sci.* **25**, 739–746. [241]

Huang, Y.H., Maas, J.W., and Hu, G. (1980) The time course of noradrenergic pre- and post-synaptic activity during chronic desipramine treatment. *Eur. J. Pharmacol.* **68**, 41–47. [248, 264]

Hudgens, H., Morrison, J., and Barcha, R. (1967) Life events and onset of primary affective disorders. *Arch. Gen. Psychiatr.* **16**, 134–145. [131]

Huesmann, L.R. (1978) Cognitive processes and models of depression. *J. Abnorm. Psychol.* **87**, 194–198. [78, 127]

Hughes, J., Smith, T.W., Kosterlitz, H., Fothergill, L.A., Morgan, B.A., and Morris, H.R. (1975) Identification of two related pentapeptides from the brain with potent opiate agonist activity. *Nature* **258**, 577–579. [358]

Hunt, G.E., Atrens, D.M., Becker, F.T., and Paxinos, G. (1978) Alpha-adrenergic modulation of hypothalamic self-stimulation: Effects of phenoxybenzamine, yohimbine, dexamphetamine and their interactions with clonidine. *Eur. J. Pharmacol.* **53**, 1–8. [199]

Hutchinson, R.R. and Renfrew, J.W. (1978) Functional parallels between the neural and environmental antecedents of aggression. *Neurosci. Biobehav. Rev.* **2**, 33–58. [363]

Hwang, E.C. and Van Woert M.H. (1980) Acute versus chronic effects of serotonin uptake blockers on potentiation of the "serotonin syndrome." *Commun. Psychopharmacol.* **4**, 161–167. [330, 341]

Hytell, J. (1978) Inhibition of [^{3}H]dopamine accumulation in rat striatal synaptosomes by psychotropic drugs. *Biochem. Pharmacol.* **27**, 1063–1068. [181]

Hyttel, J., Overo, K.F., and Arnt, J. (1984) Biochemical effects and drug levels in rats after long-term treatment with the specific 5-HT-uptake inhibitor, citalopram. *Psychopharmacology* **83**, 20–27. [256, 324, 332, 347, 348]

Imura, N., Nakai, Y., and Yoshima, T. (1973) Effect of 5-hydroxytryptophan (5-HTP) on growth hormone and ACTH release in man. *J. Clin. Endocrinol. Metab.* **36**, 204–206. [314]

Innis, R.B. and Snyder, S.H. (1981) Psychotropic drugs and neurotransmitter receptors: (a) Radioreceptor assays for neuroleptics and tricyclic antidepressants; (b) Antidepressants and neurotransmitter receptors; (c) [^{3}H]Imipramine binding sites. In E. Usdin, W.E. Bunney, and J.M. Davis (Eds.), *Neuroreceptors: Basic and Clinical Aspects*. Wiley, New York, pp. 141–164. [14]

Insel, T.R. and Siever, L.J. (1981) The dopamine system challenge in affective disorders: A review of behavioral and neuroendocrine responses. *J. Clin. Psychopharmacol.* **1**, 207–213. [166]

Insel, T.R., Kalin, N.H., Guttmacher, L.B., Cohen, R.M., and Murphy, D.L. (1982) The dexamethasone suppression test in patients with primary obsessive-compulsive disorders. *Psychiatr. Res.* **6**, 153–160. [54]

Inturrisi, C.E., Alexopoulos, G., Lipman, R., Foley, K., and Rossier, J. (1982) Beta-endorphin immmunoreactivity in the plasma of psychiatric patients receiving electroconvulsive treatment. *Ann. N.Y. Acad. Sci.* **398**, 413–422. [367]

Ireson, J.D. (1970) A comparison of the antinociceptive actions of cholinomimetic and morphine-like drugs. *Br. J. Pharmacol.* **40**, 92–101. [276]

Isen, A.M., Shalker, T.E., Clark, M., and Karp, L. (1978) Affect, accessibility of material in memory, and behavior: A cognitive loop? *J. Pers. Soc. Psychol.* **36**, 1–12. [71]

Iversen, L.L. (1964) Inhibition of noradrenaline uptake by sympathomimetic amines. *J. Pharm. Pharmacol.* **16,** 435–437. [8]

Iversen, S.D. (1973) Brain lesions and memory in animals. In J.A. Deutsch (Ed.), *The Physiological Basis of Memory.* Academic, New York, pp. 305–364. [94]

Jablensky, A., Sartorius, N., Gulbinat, W., and Ernberg, G. (1981) Characteristics of depressive patients contacting psychiatric services in four cultures. *Acta Psychiatr. Scand.* **63,** 367–383. [51]

Jackson, R.L., Maier, S.F., and Rapoport, P.M. (1978) Exposure to inescapable shock produces both activity and associative deficits in rats. *Learn. Motiv.* **9,** 69–98. [125, 158]

Jackson, R.L., Maier, S.F., and Coon, D.J. (1979) Long-term analgesic effects of inescapable shock and learned helplessness. *Science* **206,** 91–93. [126, 141, 360, 384]

Jacobs, B.L. and Cohen, A. (1976) Differential behavioral effects of lesions of the medial or dorsal raphe nuclei in rats: Open field and pain-elicited aggression. *J. Comp. Physiol. Psychol.* **90,** 102–108. [295]

Jacobs, B.L. and Klemfuss, H. (1975) Brainstem and spinal cord mediation of a serotonergic behavioral syndrome. *Brain Res.* **100,** 450–457. [288, 289]

Jacobs, B.L., Wise, W.D., and Taylor, K.M. (1974) Differential behavioral and neurochemical effects following lesions of the dorsal or median raphe nuclei in rats. *Brain Res.* **79,** 353–361. [294, 296]

Jacobs, B.L., Trimbach, C., Eubanks, E.E., and Trulson, M. (1975) Hippocampal mediation of raphe lesion- and PCPA-induced hyperactivity in the rat. *Brain Res.* **94,** 253–261. [296]

Jacobs, S.C., Prusoff, B.A., and Paykel, E.S. (1974) Recent life events in schizophrenia and depression. *Psychol. Med.* **4,** 444–453. [397]

Jacobsen, C.F. (1936) Studies of cerebral functions in primates. I. The function of the frontal association areas in primates. *Comp. Psychol. Monogr.* **13,** 1–60. [94]

Jacobsen, E. (1964) The theoretical basis of the chemotherapy of depression. In E.B. Davis (Ed.), *Depression: Proceedings of the Symposium held at Cambridge, September 1959.* Cambridge University Press, New York, pp. 208–213. [6, 8]

Jahoda, M. (1979) The impact of unemployment in the 1930s and the 1970s. *Bull. Br. Psychol. Soc.* **32,** 309–314. [392]

Jain, S., Kyriakides, M,. Silverstone, T., and Turner, P. (1980) The effect of small and moderate doses of D-amphetamine on hunger, mood and arousal in man. *Psychopharmacology* **70,** 109–111. [176]

Jakimow-Venulet, B., Kobrzynska, E., Puzynski, S., and Sulikowski, T. (1981) The pathogenesis of affective disturbances connected with disulfiram therapy. *Psychiatr. Pol.* **15,** 251–256. [230]

Jalowiec, J.E., Panksepp, J., Zolovick, A.J., Najam, N., and Herman, B.H. (1981) Opioid modulation of ingestive behaviour. *Pharmacol. Biochem. Behav.* **15,** 477–484. [362]

Janowsky, A.J., Steranka, L.R., Gillespie, D.D., and Sulser, F. (1982) Role of neuronal signal input in the down-regulation of central noradrenergic receptor function by antidepressant drugs. *J. Neurochem.* **39,** 290–292. [258–260, 262]

Janowsky, D.S. and Risch, S.C. (1984a) Adrenergic-cholinergic balance and affective disorders: A review of clinical evidence and therapeutic implications. In A.J. Rush and K.C. Altschuler (Eds.), *New Advances and Treatment of Depression.* Guilford Press, New York. [279, 281–283, 380]

Janowsky, D.S. and Risch, S.C. (1984b) Cholinomimetic and anticholinergic drugs used to investigate an acetylcholine hypothesis of affective disorders and stress. *Drug Dev. Res.* **4,** 125–142. [254, 277, 281–283, 397]

Janowsky, D.S., El-Yousef, M.K., Davis, K.M., and Serkerke, H.J. (1972a) A cholinergic-adrenergic hypothesis of mania and depression. *Lancet* **2**, 6732–6735. [17, 269, 417]

Janowsky, D.S., El-Yousef, M.K., Davis, J.M., and Serkerke, H.J. (1972b) Cholinergic antagonism of methylphenidate-induced stereotyped behavior. *Psychopharmacology* **27**, 295–303. [269, 379]

Janowsky, D.S., El-Yousef, M.K., Davis, J.M., and Serkerke, H.J. (1973a) Parasympathetic suppression of manic symptoms by physostigmine. *Arch. Gen. Psychiatr.* **28**, 542–547. [267, 281, 282]

Janowsky, D.S., El-Yousef, M.K., Davis, J.M., and Serkerke, H.J. (1973b) Anatagonistic effects of physostigmine and methylphenidate in man. *Am. J. Psychiatr.* **130**, 1370–1376. [23, 267, 269, 281, 282]

Janowsky, D.S., El-Yousef, M.K., and Davis, J.M. (1974) Acetylcholine and depression. *Psychosom. Med.* **36**, 248–257. [281, 282]

Janowsky, D.S., Judd, L., Huey, L., Roitman, N., Parker, D., and Segal, D. (1978) Naloxone effects on manic symptoms and growth hormone levels. *Lancet* **2**, 320. [366]

Janowsky, D.S., Judd, L.L., Huey, L., and Segal, D.S. (1979) Effects of naloxone in normal, manic and schizophrenic patients: Evidence for alleviation of manic symptoms. In E. Usdin, W.E. Bunney, and N.S. Kline (Eds.), *Endorphins in Mental Health Research.* Oxford University Press, New York, pp. 435–447. [366]

Janowsky, D.S., Risch, S.C., Judd, L.L., Parker, D.C., Kalin, N.H., and Huey, L.Y. (1983) Behavioral and neuroendocrine effects of physostigmine in affect disorder patients. In P.J. Clayton and J.E. Barrett (Eds.), *Treatment of Depression: Old Controversies and New Approaches.* Raven, New York, pp. 61–74. [279, 281–283]

Jellinek, T., Gardos, G. and Cole, J. (1981) Adverse effects of antiparkinsonian drug withdrawal. *Am. J. Psychiatr.* **138**, 1567–1571. [284]

Jerussi, T.P. and Glick, S.D. (1974) Amphetamine-induced rotation in rats without lesions. *Neuropharmacology* **13**, 283–286. [96]

Jimerson, D.C., Gordon, E.K., Post, R.M., and Goodwin, F.K. (1975) Central noradrenergic function in man: VMA in CSF. *Brain Res.* **99**, 434–439. [222]

Johansson, C.E. and Uhlenluth, E.H. (1980) Drug preference and mood in humans: D-amphetamine. *Psychopharmacology* **71**, 275–279. [27]

Johansson, F. and Von Knorring, L. (1979) A double-blind controlled study of a serotonin uptake inhibitor (zimelidine) versus placebo in chronic pain patients. *Pain* **7**, 69–78. [298]

Johansson, F., von Knorring, L., Sedvall, G. and Terenius, L. (1980) Changes in endorphins and 5-hydroxyindoleacetic acid in cerebrospinal fluid as a result of treatment with a serotonin uptake inhibitor (zimelidine) in chronic pain patients. *Psychiatr. Res.* **2**, 167–172. [298]

Johnson, D.N., Funderburk, W.H., and Ward, J.W. (1970) Preclinical evaluation of AHR-1118: A potential antidepressant drug. *Curr. Ther. Res.* **12**, 402–413. [106]

Johnson, O. and Crockett, D. (1982) Changes in perceptual asymmetries with clinical improvement of depression and schizophrenia. *J. Abnorm. Psychol.* **91**, 45–54. [90, 91]

Johnson, R.W., Reisine, T., Spotnitz, S., Wiech, N., Ursillo, R., and Yamamura, H. (1980) Effects of desipramine and yohimbine on alpha$_2$- and beta-adrenoceptor sensitivity. *Eur. J. Pharmacol.* **67**, 123–127. [247, 259]

Jones, D.L., Mogenson, G.J., and Wu, M. (1981) Injections of dopaminergic, cholinergic, serotonergic and gabaergic drugs into the nucleus accumbens: Effects on locomotor activity in the rat. *Neuropharmacology* **20**, 29–37. [378, 380]

Jones, F.D., Maas, J.W., Dekirmenjian, H., and Fawcett, J.A. (1973) Urinary catecholamine metabolism during behavioral changes in a patient with manic depressive cycles. *Science* **179**, 300. [225, 226]

Jones, F.D., Maas, J.W., Dekirmenjian, H., and Sanchez, J. (1975) Diagnostic subgroups of affective disorders and their urinary excretion of catecholamine metabolites. *Am. J. Psychiatr.* **132**, 1141–1148. [224–226]

Jones, R.S.G. (1980a) Long-term administration of atropine, imipramine, and viloxazine alters responsiveness of rat cortical neurons to acetylcholine. *Can. J. Physiol.* **58**, 531–535. [285]

Jones, R.S.G. (1980b) Enhancement of 5-hydroxytryptamine-induced behavioral effects following chronic administration of antidepressant drugs. *Psychopharmacology* **69**, 307–311. [330, 341, 350]

Jones, R.S.G. and Roberts, M.H.T. (1977) Effects of viloxazine on cortical neurone responses to monoamines and acetylcholine. *Br. J. Pharmacol.* **59**, 460P. [241]

Jones, R.T. and Herning, R. (1979) Naloxone-induced mood and physiologic changes in normal volunteers. In E. Usdin, W.E. Bunney, and N.S. Kline (Eds.), *Endorphins in Mental Health Research.* Oxford University Press, New York, pp. 484–491. [366]

Jonsson, L.E. (1972) Pharmacological blockade of amphetamine effects in amphetamine dependent subjects. *Eur. J. Clin. Pharmacol.* **4**, 206–211. [173, 233]

Jonsson, L.E., Anggard, E., and Gunne, L.M. (1969) Blockade of intravenous amphetamine euphoria in man. *Clin. Pharmacol Ther.* **12**, 889–896. [27, 173, 233]

Jori, A., Bernardi, D., Muscettola, G., and Garattini, S. (1971) Brain levels of imipramine and desipramine after combined treatment with these drugs in rats. *Eur. J. Pharmacol.* **15**, 85–95. [181]

Jori, A., Dolfini, E., Casati, C., and Argenta, G. (1975) Effect of ECT and impramine treatment on the concentration of 5-hydroxyindoleacetic acid (5-HIAA) and homovanillic acid (HVA) in the cerebrospinal fluid of depressed persons. *Psychopharmacology* **44**, 87–90. [311]

Joseph, M.H. and Kennett, G.A. (1983) Corticosteroid response to stress depends upon increased tryptophan availability. *Psychopharmacology* **79**, 79–81. [299]

Joseph, M.S. and Reus, V.I. (1981) Increased pain sensitivity in depressed patients with hypersecretion of cortisol. *Soc. Neurosci. Abstr.* **7**, 379. [69]

Jouvent, R., Lecrubier, Y., Puech, A.-J., Frances, H., Simon, P., and Widlocher, D. (1977) De l'étude experimentale d'un stimulant beta-adrenergique à la mise en evidence de son activité antidepressive chez l'homme. *L'Encéphale* **3**, 285–293. [232]

Jouvent, R., Lecrubier, Y., Puech, A.-J., Simon, P., and Widlocher, D. (1980) Antimanic effect of clonidine. *Am. J. Psychiatr.* **137**, 1275–1276. [231]

Jouvet, M. (1972) The role of monoamines and acetylcholine-containing neurons in the regulation of the sleep-waking cycle. *Ergeb. Physiol. Biol. Chem. Exp. Pharmakol.* **64**, 166–307. [206]

Jouvet, M. (1975) Cholinergic mechanisms and sleep. In P. Waser (Ed.), *Cholinergic Mechanisms.* Raven, New York, pp. 455–476. [274]

Joyce, E.M. and Iversen, S.D. (1979) The effect of morphine applied locally to mesencephalic dopamine cell bodies on spontaneous locomotor activity in the rat. *Neurosci. Lett.* **14**, 217–212. [151]

Joyce, J.N., Davis, R.E., and Van Hartesfeldt, C.V. (1981) Behavioral effects of unilateral dopamine injection into dorsal or ventral striatum. *Eur. J. Pharmacol.* **72**, 1–10. [159]

Judd, L.L., Janowsky, D.S, Segal, D.S., and Huey, L.L. (1980) Naloxone-induced behavioral and physiological effects in normal and manic subjects. *Arch. Gen. Psychiatr.* **37**, 583–586. [366]

Judd, L.L., Risch, S.C., Parker, D.C., Janowsky, D.S., Segal, D.S., and Huey, L.Y. (1982) Blunted prolactin response: A neuroendocrine abnormality manifested by depressed patients. *Arch. Gen. Psychiatr.* **39**, 1413–1416. [166, 315, 365]

Judd, L.L., Risch, S.C., Janowsky, D.S., Segal, D.S., and Huey, L.Y., (1983) Methadone and metoclopramide may differentially affect prolactin secretion in depressed patients. *Psychopharmacol. Bull.* **19**, 482–485. [315, 365]

Kaada, B.R. (1972) Stimulation and regional ablation of the amygdaloid cortex with reference to functional representations. In B.E. Eleftheriou (Ed.), *The Neurobiology of the Amygdala*. Plenum, New York, pp. 205–282. [197]

Kafka, M.S., Van Kammen, D.P., Kleiman, J.E., Nurnberger, J.I., Siever, L.J., Uhde, T.W., and Polinsky, R.J. (1980) Alpha-adrenergic receptor function in schizophrenia, affective disorders and some neurological diseases. *Commun. Psychopharmacol.* **4**, 477–486. [218, 219]

Kafka, M.S., Wirz-Justice, A., Naber, D., Marangos, P.J., O'Donohue, T.L., and Wehr, T.A. (1982) The effect of lithium on circadian neurotransmitter receptor rhythms. *Neuropsychobiology* **8**, 41–50. [257]

Kafoe, W.F., De Ridder, J.J., and Leonard, B.E. (1976) The effect of a tetracyclic antidepressant compound, Org GB94, on the turnover of biogenic amines in the rat brain. *Biochem. Pharmacol.* **25**, 2455–2460. [249]

Kaiya, H., Namba, M., Yoshida, H., and Nakamura, S. (1982) Plasma glutamate decarboxylase activity in neuropsychiatry. *Psychiatr. Res.* **6**, 335–343. [355, 356]

Kajaczowska, M.N. (1975) Acetylcholine content in the central and peripheral nervous system and its synthesis in the rat brain during stress and post-stress exhaustion. *Acta Physiol. Pol.* **26**, 493–497. [276]

Kalin, N.H., Weiler, S.J., McKinney, W.T., Kraemer, G.W., and Shelton, S.E. (1982) Where is the "lesion" in patients who fail to suppress plasma cortisol concentrations with dexamethasone? *Psychopharmacol. Bull.* **18**, 219–220. [133]

Kalin, N.H., Shelton, S.E., McKinney, W.T., Kraemer, G.W., Scanlon, J., and Suomi, S.J. (1983) Stress alters the dexamethasone suppression test in rhesus monkeys. *Psychopharmacol. Bull.* **19**, 542–544. [133]

Kametani, H., Nomura, S., and Shimizu, J. (1983) The reversal effect of antidepressants on the escape deficit induced by inescapable shock in rats. *Psychopharmacology* **80**, 206–208. [123]

Kamin, L.J. (1957) The retention of an incompletely learned avoidance response. *J. Comp. Physiol. Psychol.* **50**, 457–460. [276]

Kamin, L.J. (1969) Predictability, surprise, attention and conditioning. In B.A. Campbell and R.M. Church (Eds.), *Punishment and Aversive Behaviour*. Appleton-Century-Crofts, New York, pp. 279–296. [204]

Kane, F.J. (1970) Treatment of mania with cinanserin, an antiserotonergic agent. *Am. J. Psychiatr.* **126**, 1020–1023. [318]

Kanfer, R. and Zeiss, A.M. (1983) Depression, interpersonal standard setting, and judgements of self-efficacy. *J. Abnorm. Psychol.* **92**, 319–329. [70]

Kanner, A.D., Coyne, J.C., Schaefer, C., and Lazarus, R.S. (1981) Comparison of two modes of stress measurement: Daily hassles and uplifts versus major life events. *J. Behav. Med.* **4**, 1–39. [80, 214]

Kanof, P.D. and Greengard, P. (1978) Brain histamine receptors as targets for antidepressant drugs. *Nature* **272**, 329–333. [368, 369]

Kaplan, R.D. and Mann, J.J. (1982) Altered platelet serotonin uptake kinetics in schizophrenia and depression. *Life Sci.* **31**, 583–588. [316]

Kaplanski, J. and Smelik, P.G. (1973) Analysis of the inhibition of ACTH release by hypothalamic implants of atropine. *Acta Endocrinol.* **73**, 651–659. [277]

Karczmar, A.G. and Dun, N.J. (1978) Cholinergic synapses: Physiological, pharmacological and behavioral considerations. In M.A. Lipton, A. DiMaschio, and K.F. Killam (Eds.),

Psychopharmacology: A Generation of Progress. Raven, New York, pp. 293–303. [274, 276]

Karczmar, A.G., Scudder, C.L., and Richardson, D.L. (1973) Interdisciplinary approach to the study of behavior in related mice types. In S. Ehrenpreis and I.J. Kopin (Eds.), *Chemical Approaches to Brain Function.* Academic, New York, pp. 159–244. [270, 276]

Karobath, M. (1975) Tricyclic antidepressant drugs and dopamine sensitive adenylate cyclase from rat brain striatum. *Eur. J. Pharmacol.* **30,** 159–163. [182]

Kasa, K., Otsuki, S., Yamamoto, M., Sato, M., Kuroda,H., and Ogawa, N. (1982) Cerebrospinal fluid gamma-aminobutyric acid and homovanillic acid in depressive disorders. *Biol. Psychiatr.* **17,** 877–883. [167, 355]

Kasamatsu, T. (1983) Neuronal plasticity maintained by the central norepinephrine system in the cat visual cortex. In J.M. Sprague and A.N. Epstein (Eds.), *Progress in Psychobiology and Physiological Psychology* Vol. 10. Academic, New York, pp. 1–112. [198, 202]

Kashani, J.H., Husain, A., Shekim, W.O., Hodges, K.K., Cytryn, L., and McKnew, D.H. (1981) Current perspectives on childhood depression: An overview. *Am. J. Psychiatr.* **138,** 143–153. [132, 133]

Kaskey, G.B., Nasr, S., and Meltzer, H.Y. (1980) Drug treatment in delusional depression. *Psychiatr. Res.* **2,** 267–277. [172]

Kasper, S., Moise, H.W., and Beckman, H. (1981) The anticholinerigic biperiden in depressive disorders. *Pharmakopsychiatrie* **14,** 195–198. [283]

Kastin, A.J., Schalch, D.S., Ehrensing, R.H., and Anderson, M.S. (1972) Improvement in mental depression with decreased thyrotropin response after administration of thyrotropin-releasing hormone. *Lancet* **2,** 740–742. [371]

Kastin, A.J., Scollan, E.L., Ehrensing, R.H., Schally, A.V., and Coy, D.H. (1978) Enkephalin and other peptides reduce passiveness. *Pharmacol. Biochem. Behav.* **9,** 515–519. [128, 371]

Katayama, Y., Carlton, S.M., Becker, D.P., and Hayes, R.L. (1982) Behavioral and physiological characterization of non-narcotic analgesia produced by cholinergic microinjection in the parabrachial region of the cat. *Soc. Neurosci. Abstr.* **8,** 619. [276]

Kato, T., Hashimoto, Y., Nagatsu, T., Shimoda, T., Okada, T., Takeuchi, T., and Umeyawa, H. (1980) 24-hour rhythm of human plasma noradrenaline and the effect of fusaric acid, a dopamine-beta-hydroxylase inhibitor. *Neuropsychobiology* **6,** 61–65. [230]

Katz, R.J. (1981a) Animal models and human depressive disorders. *Neurosci. Biobehav. Rev.* **5,** 231–246. [132]

Katz, R.J. (1981b) Animal model of depression: Effects of electroconvulsive shock therapy. *Neurosci. Biobehav. Rev.* **5,** 273–277. [130]

Katz, R.J. (1982) Animal model of depression: Pharmacological sensitivity of a hedonic deficit. *Pharmacol. Biochem. Behav.* **16,** 965–968. [130, 403]

Katz, R.J. and Baldrighi, G. (1982) A further parametric study of imipramine in an animal model of depression. *Pharmacol. Biochem. Behav.* **16,** 969–972. [130]

Katz, R.J. and Carroll, B.J. (1978) Endocrine control of psychomotor activity in the rat: Effects of chronic dexamethasone upon general activity. *Physiol. Behav.* **20,** 25–30. [383]

Katz, R.J. and Hersh, S. (1981) Amitriptyline and scopolamine in an animal model of depression. *Neurosci. Biobehav. Rev.* **5,** 265–271. [130, 270, 271]

Katz, R.J. and Schmaltz, K. (1980) Reduction in opiate activation after chronic electroconvulsive shock: Possible role for endorphins in the behavioral effects of convulsive shock treatment. *Neurosci. Lett.* **19,** 85–88. [367]

Katz, R.J. and Sibel, M. (1982a) Animal model of depression: Tests of three structurally and pharmacologically novel antidepressant compounds. *Pharmacol. Biochem. Behav.* **16,** 973–977. [130]

Katz, R.J. and Sibel, M. (1982b) Further analysis of the specificity of a novel animal model of depression: Effects of an antihistaminic, antipsychotic and anxiolytic compound. *Pharmacol. Biochem. Behav.* **16**, 979–982. [130]

Katz, R.J., Roth, K. A., and Carroll, B.J. (1981a) Acute and chronic stress effects on open field activity in the rat: Implications for a model of depression. *Neurosci. Biobehav. Rev.* **5**, 247–251. [130]

Katz, R.J., Roth, K.A., and Schmaltz, K. (1981b) Amphetamine and tranylcypromine in an animal model of depression: Pharmacological specificity of the reversal effect. *Neurosci. Biobehav. Rev.* **5**, 259–264. [130]

Kaufman, I.C. and Rosenblum, L.A. (1967) The reaction to separation in infant monkeys: Anaclitic depression and conservation-withdrawal. *Psychosom. Med.* **29**, 648–675. [132, 140]

Kaufman, I.C. and Rosenblum, L.A. (1969) The waning of the mother-infant bond in two species of macaque. In B.M. Foss (Ed.), *Determinants of Infant Behaviour,* Vol. 4. Methuen, London, pp. 46–59. [140]

Kaufman, I.C. and Stynes, A.J. (1978) Depression can be induced in a bonnet macaque infant. *Psychosom. Med.* **40**, 71–75. [132, 141]

Kawamura, H., Gunn, C.G., and Frohlich, E.D. (1978) Cardiovascular alteration by nucleus locus coeruleus in spontaneously hypertensive rat. *Brain Res.* **140**, 137–147. [198]

Keehn, J.D., ed. (1979) *Psychopathology in Animals: Research and Clinical Implications.* Academic, New York. [102]

Kellar, K.J. and Bergstrom, D.A. (1983) Electroconvulsive shock: Effects on biochemical correlates of neurotransmitter receptors in rat brain. *Neuropharmacology* **22**, 401–406. [255, 258, 347]

Kellar, K.J., Cascio, C.S., Butler, J.A., and Kurtzke, R.N. (1981a) Differential effects of electroconvulsive shock and antidepressant drugs on serotonin-2 receptors in rat brain. *Eur. J. Pharmacol.* **69**, 515–518. [348, 349]

Kellar, K.J., Cascio, C.S., Bergstrom, D.A., Butler, J.A., and Iadorola, P. (1981b) Electroconvulsive shock and reserpine: Effects on beta-adrenergic receptors in rat brain. *J. Neurochem.* **37**, 830–836. [285]

Kelly, P.H., Seviour, P.W., and Iversen, S.D. (1975) Amphetamine and apomorphine responses in the rat following 6-OHDA lesions of the nucleus accumbens septi and corpus striatum. *Brain Res.* **94**, 507–522. [9, 15, 149, 178, 342]

Kelly, W.F., Checkley, S.A., and Bender, D.A. (1980) Cushing's syndrome, tryptophan and depression. *Br. J. Psychiatr.* **136**, 125–142. [267]

Kelly, W.F., Checkley, S.A., Bender, D.A., and Mashiter, K. (1983) Cushing's syndrome and depression—A prospective study. *Br. J. Psychiatr.* **142**, 16–19. [267, 308, 399]

Kel..ala, S., Jones, D., and Sitaram, N. (1983) Monoamine metabolites as predictors of antidepressant response: A critique. *Prog. Neuropsychopharmacol.* **7**, 229–240. [234]

Kendall, D.A., Duman, R., Slopis, J., and Enna, S.J. (1982a) Influence of adrenocorticotropic hormone and yohimbine on antidepressant-induced declines in rat brain neurotransmitter receptor binding and function. *J. Pharmacol. Exp. Ther.* **222**, 566–571. [259, 267]

Kendall, D.A., Stancel, G.M. and Enna, S.J. (1982b) The influence of sex hormones on antidepressant-induced alterations in neurotransmitter receptor binding. *J. Neurosci.* **2**, 354–360. [348]

Kendell, R.E. (1976) The classification of depressions: A review of contemporary confusion. *Br. J. Psychiatr.* **129**, 15–28. [44, 49, 57, 59]

Kendell, R.E. (1982) The present status of electroconvulsive therapy. *Br. J. Psychiatr.* **139**, 265–283. [89]

Kennett, G.A. and Joseph, M.H. (1981) The functional importance of increased brain tryptophan in the serotonergic response to restraint stress. *Neuropharmacology* **20,** 39–43. [299]

Kesner, R.P. (1981) The role of amygdala within an attribute analysis of behaviour. In Y. Ben-Ari (Ed.), *The Amygdaloid Complex.* Elsevier, New York, pp. 331–342. [197]

Kessler, J.A., Gordon, E.K., Reid, J.L., and Kopin, I.J. (1976a) Homovanillic acid and 3-methoxy-4-hydroxyphenylethyleneglycol production by the monkey spinal cord. *J. Neurochem.* **26,** 1057–1061. [223]

Kessler, J.A., Fenstermacher, J.D., and Patlak, C.S. (1976b) MHPG transport from the spinal cord during subarachnoid perfusion. *Brain Res.* **102,** 131–141 [223]

Kety, S.S. (1972) The possible role of the adrenergic systems of the cortex in learning. *Res. Publ. Assoc. Res. Nerv. Ment. Disord.* **50,** 376–389. [200]

Kiloh, L.G. and Garside, R.F. (1963) The independence of neurotic depression and endogenous depression. *Br. J. Psychiatr.* **109,** 451–463. [50]

Kiloh, L.G., Andrews, G., Nielsen, M., and Bianchi, G.N. (1972) The relationship of the syndromes called endogenous and neurotic depression. *Br. J. Psychiatr.* **121,** 183–196. [57]

Kimura, S., Lewis, R.V., Stern, A.S., Rossier, J., Stein, S., and Udenfried, S. (1977) Probable precursors of [leu]enkephalin and [met]enkephalin in adrenal medulla: Peptides of 3-5 kilodaltons. *Proc. Natl. Acad. Sci. USA* **74,** 1681–1685. [358]

King, B.M., Castellanos, F.X., Kastin, A.J., Berzas, M.C., Mauk, M.D., Olson, G.A., and Olson, R.D. (1979) Naloxone-induced suppression of food intake in normal and hypothalamic obese rats. *Pharmacol. Biochem. Behav.* **11,** 729–732. [362]

Kinnier, W.J., Chuang, D.M., and Costa, E. (1980) Down regulation of dihydroalprenolol and imipramine binding sites in brain of rats repeatedly treated with imipramine. *Eur. J. Pharmacol.* **67,** 289–294. [332]

Kinsbourne, M., ed. (1978a) *Asymmetrical Functions of the Brain.* Cambridge University Press, New York. [85, 90]

Kinsbourne, M. (1978b) The biological determinants of functional bisymmetry and asymmetry. In M. Kinsbourne (Ed.), *Asymmetrical Functions of the Brain.* Cambridge University Press, New York, pp. 3–13. [95]

Kinsbourne, M. (1978c) The evolution of language in relation to lateral action. In M. Kinsbourne (Ed.), *Asymmetrical Functions of the Brain.* Cambridge University Press, New York, pp. 553–565. [95]

Kirkegaard, C., Bjorum, W., Cohn, D., Faber, J., Lauridsen, U.B., and Nerup, J. (1977) Studies on the influence of biogenic amines and psychoactive drugs on the prognostic value of the TRH stimulation test in endogenous depression. *Psychoneuroendocrinology* **2,** 131–136. [372]

Kirkegaard, C., Bjorum, W., Cohn, D., and Lauridsen, U.B. (1978) Thyrotropin-releasing hormone (TRH) stimulation test in manic-depressive illness. *Arch. Gen. Psychiatr.* **35,** 1017–1021. [371, 372]

Kirstein, L. and Bukberg, J. (1979) Temporal disorganization and primary affective disorder. *Am. J. Psychiatr.* **136,** 1313–1316. [74]

Kishimoto, H. and Hama, Y. (1979) The level and diurnal rhythm of plasma tryptophan and tyrosine in manic-depressive patients. *Yokohama Med. Bull.* **27,** 89–97. [164, 222]

Kitada, Y., Miyauchi, T., Satoh, A., and Satoh, S. (1981) Effects of antidepressants in the rat forced swimming test. *Eur. J. Pharamcol.* **72,** 145–152. [128, 158, 272]

Klaiber, E. L., Broverman, D.M., Vogel, W., Kobayashi, Y., and Moriarty, D. (1972) Effects of estrogen therapy on plasma MAO activity and EEG driving response of depressed women. *Am. J. Psychiatr.* **128,** 1492–1498. [221]

Klein, D.C. and Seligman, M.E.P. (1976) Reversal of performance deficits in learned helplessness and depression. *J. Abnorm. Soc. Psychol.* **85**, 11–26. [142]

Klein, D.C., Fencil-Morse, E., and Seligman, M.E.P. (1976) Learned helplessness, depression and attribution of failure. *J. Pers. Soc. Psychol.* **33**, 508–516. [78, 124, 127]

Klein, D.F. (1968) Psychiatric diagnosis and a typology of clinical drug effects. *Psychopharmacology* **13**, 359–386. [46]

Klein, D.F. (1974) Endogenomorphic depression: A conceptual and terminological revision. *Arch. Gen. Psychiatr.* **31**, 447–454. [58, 59, 61, 62, 67, 81, 135, 160, 401]

Klerman, G.L. (1972) Clinical phenomenology of depression: Implications for research strategies in the psychobiology of the affective disorders. In T.A. Williams, M.M. Katz, and J.A. Shield (Eds.), *Recent Advances in the Psychobiology of the Depressive Illnesses.* U.S. Government Printing Office, Washington, D.C., pp. 331–339. [11, 49, 173, 233]

Klerman, G.L. (1978) Long term treatment of affective disorders. In M.A. Lipton, A. DiMascio and K.F. Killam (Eds.), *Psychopharmacology: A Generation of Progress.* Raven, New York, pp. 1303–1312. [410]

Kline, N.S., Sacks, W. and Simpson, G.M. (1964) Further studies on one day treatment of depression with 5-HTP. *Am. J. Psychiatr.* **121**, 379–381. [320]

Kline, N.S., Li, C.H., Lehman, H.E., Lajtha, A., Laski, E., and Cooper, T. (1977) Beta-endorphin-induced changes in schizophrenic and depressed patients. *Arch. Gen. Psychiatr.* **34**, 1111–1113. [366]

Klinger, E. (1975) Consequences of commitment to and disengagement from incentives. *Psychol. Rev.* **82**, 1–24. [68, 134, 405]

Klinger, E., Barta, S.G., and Kemble, E.D. (1974) Cyclic activity changes during extinction in rats: A potential model of depression. *Anim. Learn. Behav.* **2**, 313–316. [134]

Knobloch, L.C., Goldstein, J.R., and Malick, J.B. (1982) Effects of acute and subacute antidepressant treatment on kindled seizures in rats. *Pharmacol. Biochem. Behav.* **17**, 461–465. [108]

Knoll, J. (1983) Satietin. Paper presented to the British Association for Psychopharmacology, London. [303]

Koehn, G.L. and Karczmar, A.G. (1977) The behavioral effects of diisopropyl phosphofluoridate: Interactions with morphine and naloxone in rats. *Pharmacol.* **19**, 141. [276]

Koehn, G.L., Henderson, G., and Karczmar, A.G. (1980) Di-isopropyl phosphofluoridate-induced antinociception: Possible role of endogenous opioids. *Eur. J. Pharmacol.* **61**, 167–173. [276]

Koenig, J.I., Mayfield, M.A., McCann, S.M., and Krulich, L. (1979) Stimulation of prolactin secretion by morphine: Role of the central serotonergic system. *Life Sci.* **25**, 853–863. [315]

Koff, E., Borod, J.C., and White, B. (1983) A left hemispace bias for visualizing emotional situations. *Neuropsychology* **21**, 273–275. [86]

Kohler, C. and Lorens, S.A. (1978) Open field activity and avoidance behavior following serotonin depletion: A comparison of the effects of parachlorophenylalanine and electrolytic midbrain lesions. *Pharmacol. Biochem. Behav.* **8**, 223–233. [294]

Koide, T. and Matsushita, H. (1981a) Influence of a chronic new potential antidepressant, 1-[3-(dimethylamino)propyl]-5-methyl-3-phenyl-1H-indazole (FS32) and its N-desmethylated compound (FS97) treatment on monoaminergic receptor sensitivity in the rat brain. *Neuropharmacology* **20**, 285–292. [190]

Koide, T. and Matsushita, H. (1981b) An enhanced sensitivity of muscarinic cholinergic receptors associated with dopaminergic receptor subsensitivity after chronic antidepressant treatment. *Life Sci.* **28**, 1139–1145. [190, 285, 347]

Koide, T. and Uyemura, K. (1980) Inhibition of [³H]-dopamine uptake into rat brain synaptosomes by the new non-tricyclic antidepressants, FS32 and FS97. *Eur. J. Pharmacol.* **62**, 147–155. [181]

Kokkinidis, L. and Zacharko, R.M. (1980) Response sensitization and depression following long-term amphetamine treatment in a self-stimulation paradigm. *Psychopharmacology* **68**, 73–76. [134]

Kokkinidis, L., Zacharko, R.M., and Predy, P.A. (1980) Post-amphetamine depression of self-stimulation responding from the substantia nigra: Reversal by tricyclic antidepressants. *Pharmacol. Biochem. Behav.* **13**, 379–383. [135, 150]

Koob, G.F., Fray, P.J., and Iversen, S.D. (1978a) Self-stimulation at the lateral hypothalamus and locus coeruleus after specific unilateral lesions of the dopamine system. *Brain Res.* **14**, 123–140. [150]

Koob, G.F., Kelley, A.F., and Mason, S.T. (1978b) Locus coeruleus lesions: Learning and extinction. *Physiol. Behav.* **20**, 709–716. [200]

Koob, G.F., Simon, H., Herman, J.P., and LeMoal, A. (1983) Neuroleptic-like deficits in the conditioned avoidance response require destruction of both the mesolimbic and nigrostriatal dopamine systems. Paper presented to 5th International Catecholamine Symposium, Goteborg, Sweden. [156]

Kopin, I.J. (1978) Measuring turnover of neurotransmitters in the human brain. In M.A. Lipton, A. DiMascio, and K.F. Killam (Eds.), *Psychopharmacology: A Generation of Progress.* Raven, New York, pp. 933–942. [167]

Korf, J., Van Praag, H.M., and Sebens, J.B. (1971) Effect of intravenously administered probenecid in humans on the levels of 5-hydroxy-indole-acetic acid, homovanillic acid and 3-methoxy-4-hydroxy-phenyl-glycol in cerebrospinal fluid. *Biochem. Pharmacol.* **20**, 659–668. [224]

Korf, J., Aghajanian, G.K., and Roth, R.H. (1973a) Increased turnover of norepinephrine in the rat cerebral cortex during stress: Role of the locus coeruleus. *Neuropharmacology* **12**, 933–938. [236]

Korf, J., Aghajanian, G.K., and Roth, R.H. (1973b) Stimulation and destruction of the nucleus coeruleus: Opposite effects on 3-methoxy-4-hydroxyphenylglycol sulfate levels in the rat cerebral cortex. *Eur. J. Pharmacol.* **21**, 305–310. [236]

Korf, J., Roth, R.H., and Aghajanian, G.K. (1973c) Alterations in turnover and endogenous levels of norepinephrine in cerebral cortex following electrical stimulation and acute axotomy of cerebral noradrenergic pathways. *Eur. J. Pharmacol.* **23**, 276–282. [236]

Korf, J., Sebens, J.B., and Postrema, F. (1979) Cyclic AMP in the rat cerebral cortex after stimulation of the locus coeruleus: Decrease by antidepressant drugs. *Eur. J. Pharmacol.* **59**, 23–30. [211, 212]

Kornetsky, C. and Markovitz, R. (1978) Animal models of schizophrenia. In M.A. Lipton, A. DiMascio, and K.F. Killam (Eds.), *Psychopharmacology: A Generation of Progress.* Raven, New York, pp. 583–594. [120]

Kornetsky, C., Esposito, R.U., McLean, S. and Jacobsen, J.O. (1979) Intracranial self-stimulation thresholds: A model for the hedonic effects of drugs of abuse. *Arch. Gen. Psychiatr.* **36**, 289–292. [363]

Kostowski, W. (1971) The effects of some drugs affecting brain 5-HT on electrocortical synchronization following low-frequency stimulation of brain. *Brain Res.* **31**, 151–157. [304]

Kostowski, W. (1975) Brain serotonergic and noradrenergic systems: Fact and hypothesis. In W.B. Essman and L. Valzelli (Eds.), *Current Developments in Psychopharmacology,* Vol. 1. Spectrum, New York, pp. 37–64. [377, 378]

Kostowski, W. (1980) Noradrenergic interactions among central neurotransmitters. In W. Essman (Ed.), *Neurotransmitters, Receptors and Drug Action.* Spectrum, New York, pp. 47–64. [377]

Kostowski, W. (1981) Brain noradrenaline, depression and antidepressant drugs: Facts and hypotheses. *Trends Pharmacol. Sci.* **3**, 314–317. [19]

Kostowski, W. and Gomulka, W. (1974) Injections of some drugs affecting cholinergic and catecholaminergic neurons into the pontine raphe area: Effect on EEG pattern. *Pol. J. Pharmacol. Pharm.* **26**, 351–368. [377]

Kostowski, W. and Malatynska, E. (1983) Antagonism of behavioral depression produced by clonidine in the mongolian gerbil: A potential screening test for antidepressant drugs. *Psychopharmacology* **79**, 203–208. [245, 246]

Kostowski, W., Giacalone, E., Garattini, S., and Valzelli, L. (1969) Electrical stimulation of midbrain raphe: Biochemical, behavioral, and bioelectric effects. *Eur. J. Pharmacol.* **7**, 170–175. [304]

Kostowski, W., Samanin, R., Bareggi, S., Marc, V., Garattini, S., and Valzelli, L. (1974) Biochemical aspects of the interaction between midbrain raphe and locus coeruleus in the rat. *Brain Res.* **82**, 178–182. [377]

Kostowski, W., Jerlicz, M., Bidzinski, A., and Hauptmann, M. (1978) Evidence for the existence of two opposite noradrenergic brain systems controlling behavior. *Psychopharmacology* **59**, 311–312. [376]

Kostowski, W., Plaznik, A., Pucilowski, O. Bidzinski, A., and Hauptman, M. (1981) Lesion of serotonergic neurons antagonizes clonidine-induced suppression of avoidance behavior and locomotor activity in rats. *Psychopharmacology* **73**, 261–264. [377]

Kovacs, G.L., Bohus, B., and Versteeg, D.H.G. (1979) Facilitation of memory consolidation by vasopressin: Mediation by terminals of the dorsal noradrenergic bundle? *Brain Res.* **172**, 73–85. [201]

Kovacs, M. (1980) Efficacy of cognitive and behavior therapies for depression. *Am. J. Psychiatr.* **137**, 1495–1501. [4, 142]

Kowalik, S., Levitt, M., and Barkai, A.I. (1984) Effects of carbamazepine and antidepressant drugs on endogenous catecholamine levels in the cerebroventricular compartment of the rat. *Psychopharmacology* **83**, 169–171. [181]

Kraemer, G.W. and McKinney, W.T. (1979) Interactions of pharmacological agents which alter biogenic amine metabolism and depression. *J. Affect. Disord.* **1**, 33–54. [132, 141, 178, 291]

Kraepelin, E. (1901) *Einführung in die Psychiatrische Klinik*. Joh Ambrosius Barth-Verlag, Leipzig. [358, 366]

Krieger, D.T. (1973) Neurotransmitter regulation of ACTH release. *Mt. Sinai J. Med. N.Y.* **40**, 302–314. [278]

Kronfol, Z., Hamsher, K.de S., Digre, K., and Waziri, R. (1978) Depression and hemispheric functions: Changes associated with unilateral ECT. *Br. J. Psychiatr.* **132**, 560–567. [90, 91]

Krupinski, J., Polke, P., and Stoller, A. (1965) Psychiatric disturbances in attempted and completed suicide in Victoria during 1963. *Med. J. Aust.* **2**, 773. [312]

Kubos, K.L., Pearlson, G.D., and Robinson, R.G. (1982a) Intracortical kainic acid induces an asymmetrical behavioral response in the rat. *Brain Res.* **239**, 303–309. [97]

Kubos, K.L., Pearlson, G.D., and Robinson, R.G. (1982b) Circular cortical knife cuts induce asymmetrical behavior in the rat. *Soc. Neurosci. Abstr.* **8**, 627. [97]

Kugler, J., Seus, R., Krauskopf, R., Brecht, H.M., and Raschig, A. (1980) Differences in psychic performance with guanfacine and clonidine in normotensive subjects. *Br. J. Clin. Pharmacol.* **10**, 71S–80S. [231]

Kuhn, R. (1958) The treatment of depressive states with G22355 (imipramine hydrochloride). *Am. J. Psychiatr.* **115**, 459–464. [3, 368]

Kuiper, N.A. (1978) Depression and causal attributions for success and failure. *J. Pers. Soc. Psychol.* **36,** 236–246. [78]

Kumakura, K., Guidotti, A., and Costa, E. (1980) Modulation of nicotinic receptors by opiate receptor agonists in cultured adrenal chromaffin cells. *Nature* **283,** 489–492. [267]

Kupfer, D.J. (1976) REM latency: A psychobiological marker for primary depressive disease. *Biol. Psychiatr.* **11,** 159–174. [54, 116, 271]

Kupfer, D.J. and Detre, T.P. (1978) Trycyclic and monoamine-oxidase inhibitor antidepressants: Clinical use. In L.L. Iversen, S.D. Iversen, and S.H. Snyder (Eds.), *Handbook of Psychopharmacology,* Vol. 14. Plenum, New York. pp. 199–232. [113, 115]

Kupfer, D.J. and Foster, F.G. (1975) The sleep of psychotic patients: Does it all look alike? In D.X. Freedman (Ed.), *The Biology of the Major Psychoses: A Comparative Analysis.* Raven, New York, pp. 143–159. [54]

Kupfer, D.J. and Thase, M.E. (1983) The use of the sleep laboratory in the diagnosis of affective disorders. *Psychiatr. Clin. North Am.* **6,** 3–25. [54, 55, 278]

Kupfer, D.J., Himmelhoch, J.M., Swartzburg, M., Anderson, C., Byck, R., and Detre, T.P. (1972) Hypersomnia in manic-depressive disease. *Dis. Nerv. Syst.* **33,** 720–724. [46]

Kupfer, D.J., Weiss, B.L., Foster, F.G., Detre, T.P., Delgado, J., and McPartland, R. (1974) Psychomotor activity in affective states. *Arch. Gen. Psychiatr.* **30,** 765–768. [46, 64, 168, 177]

Kupfer, D.J., Foster, F.G., Detre, T.P., and Himmelhoch, J. (1975a) Sleep EEG and motor activity as indicators in affective states. *Neuropsychobiology* **1,** 296–303. [46]

Kupfer, D.J., Pickar, D., Himmelhoch, J.M., and Detre, T.P. (1975b) Are there two types of unipolar depression? *Arch. Gen. Psychiatr.* **32,** 866–871. [46]

Kupfer, D.J., Foster, F.G., Coble, P., McPartland, R.J., Ulrich, R.E., and Hyg, M.S. (1978) The application of EEG sleep for the differential diagnosis of affective disorders. *Am. J. Psychiatr.* **135,** 69–74. [54, 278]

Kupfer, D.J., Spiker, D.G., Rossi, A., Coble, P.A., Ulrich, R., and Shaw, D. (1983) Recent diagnostic and treatment advances in REM sleep and depression. In P.J. Clayton and J.E. Barrett (Eds.), *Treatment of Depression: Old Controversies and New Approaches.* Raven, New York, pp. 31–52. [55, 278]

Kvetansky, R., Mitro, A., Palkowitz, M., Brownstein, M., Torda, T., Vigas, M., and Mikulaj, L. (1976) Catecholamines in individual hypothalamic nuclei in stressed rats. In E. Usdin, R. Kvetansky, anad I.J. Kopin (Eds.), *Catecholamines and Stress.* Pergamon, New York, pp. 39–50. [157]

Laakman, G. (1980) Effect of antidepressants on the secretion of pituitary hormones in healthy subjects, neurotic depressive patients and endogenous depressive patients. *Nervenarzt* **51,** 725–732. [229]

Laakman, G., Dieterle, D., Weiss, L., and Schmauss, M. (1981) Therapeutic and neuroendocrine studies using yohimbine and antidepressants in depressed patients and healthy subjects. In S.Z. Langer, R. Takahashi, T. Segawa, and M. Briley (Eds.), *New Vistas in Depression.* Pergamon, New York, pp. 295–301. [228]

Laborit, H. (1982) Angoisse, depression et pathologie de l'emotion. *L'Encéphale* **8,** 299–314. [383]

Ladisch, W., Steinhauff, N., and Matussek, N. (1969) Chronic administration of electroconvulsive shock and norepinephrine metabolism in the rat brain. *Psychopharmacology* **15,** 296–304. [249]

Lahti, R.A. and Barsuhn, C. (1980) The effect of antidepressants on L-5HTP-induced changes in rat plasma corticosteroids. *Res. Commun. Chem. Pathol. Pharmacol.* **28,** 343–349. [329, 330]

Lahti, R.A. and Maickel, R.P. (1971) The tricyclic antidepressants: Inhibition of norepinephrine uptake as related to potentiation of norepinephrine and clinical efficacy. *Biochem. Pharmacol.* **20**, 482–486. [240]

Lai, J.C.K., Leung, T.K.C., Guest, J.F., Lim, L., and Davison, A.N. (1980) The monamine oxidase inhibitors clorgyline and L-deprenyl also affect the uptake of dopamine, noradrenaline and serotonin by rat brain synaptosomal preparations. *Biochem. Pharmacol.* **29**, 2763–2767. [329]

Lake, C.R., Pickar, D., Ziegler, M.G., Lipper, S., Slater, S., and Murphy, D.L. (1982) High plasma norepinephrine levels in patients with major affective disorders. *Am. J. Psychiatr.* **139**, 1315–1318. [218, 219]

Lal, S., De La Vega, C.E., Sourkes, T.L., and Friesen, H.G. (1972) Effect of apomorphine on human-growth-hormone. *Lancet* **2**, 661. [165]

Lal, S., Tolis, G., Martin, J.B., Brown, G.M., and Guyda, H. (1975) Effect of clonidine on growth hormone, prolactin, luteinizing hormone, follicle-stimulating hormone and thyroid stimulating hormone in the serum of normal men. *J. Clin. Endocrinol. Metab.* **41**, 827–832. [231]

Lal, S., Thavundayil, J., Nair, N.P.V., Etienne, P., Rastogi, R., Schwartz, G., Pulman, J., and Guyda, H. (1981) Effect of sleep deprivation on dopamine receptor function in normal subjects. *J. Neural Trans.* **50**, 39–45. [187]

Lambert, P.-A., Carraz, G., Borselli, S., and Bouchardy, M. (1975) Le dipropylacetamide dans le traitement de la psychose maniaco-depressive. *L'Encéphale* **1**, 25–31. [356]

Lamprecht, F., Ebert, M.H., Tuch, I., and Kopin, I.J. (1974) Serum dopamine-beta-hydroxylase in depressed patients and the effect of electroconvulsive shock treatment. *Psychopharmacology* **40**, 241–248. [220]

Landowski, J. (1977) Kinetics of blood platelet MAO in patients with cylclophrenic depressive syndrome. *Psychiatr. Pol.* **11**, 151–157. [221]

Landowski, J., Lysiak, W., and Angielski, S. (1975) Monoamine oxidase activity in blood platelets from patients with cyclophrenic depressive syndromes. *Biochem. Med.* **14**, 347–354. [221]

Lang, W. and Gershon, S. (1962) Effect of psychoactive drugs on yohimbine-induced responses in conscious dogs. A study of antidepressant drugs. *Med. Exp. (Basel)* **7**, 125–134. [106]

Lang, W. and Gershon, S. (1963) Effects of psychoactive drugs on yohimbine-induced responses in conscious dogs. A proposed screening procedure for anti-anxiety agents. *Arch. Int. Pharmacodyn.* **142**, 457–472. [106]

Langer, G., Heinze, G., Reim, B., and Matussek, N. (1976) Reduced growth hormone responses to amphetamine in "endogenous" depressive patients: Studies in normal, "reactive" and "endogenous" depressive, schizophrenic, and chronic alcoholic subjects. *Arch. Gen. Psychiatr.* **33**, 1471–1475. [165, 229]

Langer, G., Aschauer, H., Konig, G., Resch, F., and Schonbeck, G. (1983) The TSH-response to TRH: A possible predictor of outcome to antidepressant and neuroleptic treatment. *Prog. Neuropsychopharmacol.* **7**, 335–342. [371, 372]

Langer, S.Z. (1977) Presynaptic receptors and their role in the regulation of transmitter release. *Br. J. Pharmacol.* **60**, 481–497. [242]

Langer, S.Z. and Raisman, R. (1983) Binding of [³H]imipramine and [³H]desipramine as biochemical tools for studies in depression. *Neuropharmacology* **22**, 407–413. [249, 316, 333]

Langer, S.Z., Briley, M.S., Raisman, R., Henry, J.-F., and Morselli, P.L. (1980) Specific ³H-imipramine binding in human platelets: Influence of age and sex. *Naunyn Schmiedebergs Arch. Pharmacol.* **313**, 189–194. [316, 332]

Langer, S.Z., Zarifian, E., Briley, M., Raisman, R., and Sechter, D. (1981) High affinity binding of ^{3}H-imipramine in brain and platelets and its relevance to the biochemistry of affective disorders. *Life Sci.* **29**, 211–220. [316, 332]

Langer, S.Z., Briley, M., Raisman, R., Sette, M., and Pimoule, C. (1982a) Specific tricyclic antidepressant binding sites and their relationship with the neuronal uptake of different monoamines. In S.Z. Langer, R. Takahashi, T. Segawa, and M. Briley (Eds.), *New Vistas in Depression.* Pergamon, New York, pp. 21–28. [316]

Langer, S.Z., Zarifian, E., Briley, M., Raisman, R., and Sechter, D. (1982b) High affinity ^{3}H-imipramine binding: a new biological marker in depression. *Pharmakopsychiatrie* **15**, 4–10. [316]

Lansdell, H., and Donnelly, E.F. (1977) Factor analysis of the Wechsler Adult Intelligence Scale subtests and the Halstead-Reitan Category and Tapping tests. *J. Consult. Clin. Psychol.* **45**, 412–416. [90]

Lapin, I.P. (1967) Comparison of antireserpine and anticholinergic effects of antidepressants and of central and peripheral cholinolytics. In S. Garattini and M.N.G. Dukes (Eds.), *Antidepressant Drugs,* International Congress Series, Vol. 122. Excerpta Medica, Amsterdam, pp. 266–278. [271]

Lapin, I.P. (1980) Adrenergic nonspecific potentiation of yohimbine toxicity in mice by antidepressants and related drugs and antiyohimbine action of antiadrenergic and serotonergic drugs. *Psychopharmacology* **70**, 179–185. [106]

Lapin, I.P. and Oxenkrug, G.F. (1969) Intensification of the central serotonergic processes as a possible determinant of the thymoleptic effect. *Lancet* **1**, 132–136. [10, 17, 308, 327]

Lasagna, L., Felsinger, J.M., and Beecher, H.K. (1955) Drug induced mood changes in man. 1. Observations on healthy subjects, chronically ill patients and post-addicts. *J. Am. Med. Assoc.* **157**, 1006–1020. [173]

Lavadas, E., Umilta, C., and Ricci-Bitti, P.E. (1980) Evidence for sex differences in right-hemisphere dominance for emotions. *Neuropsychology* **18**, 361–366. [86]

Lazarus, A.A. (1968) Learning theory and the treatment of depression. *Behav. Res. Ther.* **6**, 83–89. [66]

Lazarus, L.H., Ling, N., and Guillemin, R. (1976) Beta-lipotropin as a prohormone for the morphinomimetic peptides endorphins and enkephalins. *Proc. Nat. Acad. Sci. USA* **73**, 2156–2159. [373, 400]

Le Magnen, J., Marfaing-Jallat, P., Miceli, D., and Devos, M. (1980) Pain modulation and reward systems: A single brain mechanism? *Pharmacol. Biochem. Behav.* **12**, 729–733. [362, 363]

Lebensohn, Z.M. and Jenkins, R.B. (1975) Improvement of Parkinsonism in depressed patients treated with ECT. *Am. J. Psychiatr.* **132**, 283–285. [181]

Lebrecht, V. and Nowak, J.Z. (1980) Effect of single and repeated electroconvulsive shock on serotonergic system in rat brain. II. Behavioral studies. *Neuropharmacology* **19**, 1055–1061. [339, 343]

Leckman, J.F., Charney, D.S., Nelson, J.C., Heninger, G.R., and Bowers, M.B. (1980a) CSF tryptophane, 5-HIAA and HVA in 132 psychiatric patients characterized by diagnosis and clinical state. In B. Angrist, G.D. Burrows, M. Lader, O. Lingjaerde, G. Sedvall, and D. Wheatley (Eds.), *Recent Advances in Neuropsychopharmacology.* Pergamon, New York, pp. 289–297. [312]

Leckman, J.F., Maas, J.W., Redmond, D.E., and Heninger, G.R. (1980b) Effects of oral clonidine on plasma 3-methoxy-4-hydroxyphenethyleneglycol (MHPG) in man: Preliminary report. *Life Sci.* **26**, 2179–2185. [227, 231]

Lecrubier, Y., Puech, A.J., Jouvent, R., Simon, P., and Widlocher, D. (1980) A beta adrenergic stimulant (salbutamol) versus imipramine in depression: A controlled study. *Br. J. Psychiatr.* **136**, 354–358. [232]

Lee, R. and Spencer, P.S.J. (1977) Antidepressants and pain: A review of the pharmacological data supporting the use of certain tricyclics in chronic pain. *J. Int. Med. Res.* **5** (Suppl. 1), 146–156. [367]

Lee, T. and Tang, S.W. (1982) Reduced presynaptic dopamine receptor density after chronic antidepressant treatment in rats. *Psychiatr. Res.* **7**, 111–119. [185]

Leff, M.H., Roatch, J.F., and Bunney, W.E. (1970) Environmental factors preceding the onsets of severe depressions. *Psychiatry* **33**, 293–311. [50]

Leibowitz, S.F. (1975) Catecholaminergic mechanisms of the lateral hypothalamus: Their role in the mediation of amphetamine anorexia. *Brain Res.* **98**, 529–545. [196, 265]

Leibowitz, S.F. (1978) Paraventricular nucelus: A primary site mediating adrenergic stimulation of feeding and drinking. *Pharmacol. Biochem. Behav.* **8**, 163–175. [196, 208]

Leibowitz, S.F. (1980) Neurochemical systems of the hypothalamus in the control of feeding and drinking behaviour and water-electrolyte balance. In P.J. Morgane and J. Panksepp (Eds.), *Handbook of the Hypothalamus,* Vol. 3A. Dekker, New York, pp. 299–437. [196, 208, 211, 303]

Leibowitz, S.F. and Brown, L.L. (1980a) Histochemical and pharmacological analysis of noradrenergic projections to the paraventricular hypothalamus in relation to feeding stimulation. *Brain Res.* **210**, 289–314. [196, 208]

Leibowitz, S.F. and Brown, L.L. (1980b) Histochemical and pharmacological analysis of catecholaminergic projections to the lateral hypothalamus in relation to feeding inhibition. *Brain Res.* **201**, 315–345. [196]

Leibowitz, S.F. and Rossakis, C. (1978a) Pharmacological characterization of perifornical hypothalamic beta-adrenergic receptors mediating feeding inhibition in the rat. *Neuropharmacology* **17**, 691–702. [196]

Leibowitz, S.F. and Rossakis, C. (1978b) Analysis of feeding suppression produced by perifornical hypothalamic injection of catecholamines, amphetamine and mazindol. *Eur. J. Pharmacol.* **53**, 69–81. [265]

Leith, N.J. and Barrett, R.J. (1976) Amphetamine and the reward system: Evidence for tolerance and post-drug depression. *Psychopharmacology* **46**, 19–25. [134, 135]

Leith, N.J. and Barrett, R.J. (1980) Effects of chronic amphetamine or reserpine on selfstimulation: Animal model of depression? *Psychopharmacology* **72**, 9–15. [134, 135]

Lenard, L.G. and Beer, B. (1975) 6-hydroxydopamine and avoidance: Possible role of response suppression. *Pharmacol. Biochem. Behav.* **3**, 873–878. [156]

Lenox, R.H., Van Riper, D.A., Ellis, J. Peyser, J.M., King, J., and Weaver, L.A. (1982) Platelet alpha$_2$ adrenergic receptor activity in clinical studies of depression: A critical perpective. *Abstr. 13th. CINP,* p. 432. [219]

Leonard, B.E. (1982) On the mode of action of mianserin. In E. Costa and G. Racagni (Eds.), *Typical and Atypical Antidepressants: Molecular Mechanisms.* Raven, New York, pp. 301–319. [112, 113, 255, 347]

Leonard, B.E. and Kafoe, W.F. (1976) A comparison of the acute and chronic effects of four antidepressant drugs on the turnover of serotonin, dopamine and noradrenaline in the rat brain. *Biochem. Pharmacol.* **25**, 1939–1942. [182, 183, 240, 329, 334]

Lerer, B., Ebstein, R.P., and Belmaker, R.H. (1981) Subsensitivity of human beta-adrenergic adenylate cyclase after salbutamol treatment of depression. *Psychopharmacology* **75**, 169–172. [256]

Lerer, B., Jabotinsky-Rubin, K., Bannet, J., Ebstein, R.P., and Belmaker, R.H. (1982) Electroconvulsive shock prevents dopamine receptor supersensitivity. *Eur. J. Pharmacol.* **80**, 131–134. [188, 190]

Lerer, B., Stanley, M., and Belmaker, R.H. (1984) ECT and lithium: Parallels and contrasts in receptor mechanisms. In B. Lerer, R.D. Weiner, and R.H. Belmaker (Eds.), *ECT: Basic Mechanisms*. John Libbey, London, pp. 67–78. [285]

Lerner, P., Goodwin, F.K., Van Kammen, D.P., Post, R.M., Major, L.F., Ballenger, J.C., and Lovenberg, W. (1978) Dopamine-beta-hydroxylase in the cerebrospinal fluid of psychiatric patients. *Biol. Psychiatr.* **13,** 685–695. [223]

Lerner, P., Major, L.F., Ziegler, M., Dendel, P.S., and Ebert, M.H. (1980) Central noradrenergic adaptation to long-term treatment with imipramine in rhesus monkeys. *Brain Res.* **200,** 220–224. [249]

Leshner, A.I., Hofstein, R., and Samuel, D. (1978) Intraventricular injection of antivasopressin serum blocks learned helplessness in rats. *Pharmacol. Biochem. Behav.* **9,** 889–897. [371]

Leshner, A.I., Remler, H., Biegon, A., and Samuel, D. (1979) Effects of desmethylimipramine (DMI) on learned helplessness. *Psychopharmacology* **66,** 207–213. [122]

Leshner, A.L. and Potitch, J.A. (1979) Hormonal control of submissiveness in mice: Irrelevance of the androgens and relevance of the pituitary-adrenal hormones. *Physiol. Behav.* **22,** 531–534. [383]

Leshner, A.L., Korn, S.J., Mixon, J.F., Rosenthal, C., and Besser, A.K. (1980) Effects of corticosterone on submissiveness in mice: Some temporal and theoretical considerations. *Physiol. Behav.* **24,** 283–288. [383]

Levi, L.D., Fales, G.H., Stein, M., and Sharp, V.H. (1966) Separation and attempted suicide. *Arch. Gen. Psychiatr.* **15,** 158–164. [395]

Levin, B.E. and Smith, G.P. (1972) Impaired learning of active avoidance responses in rats after lateral hypothalamic injection of 6-hydroxydopamine. *Neurology* **22,** 433. [156]

Levis, D.J. (1976) Learned helplessness: A reply and alternative S-R interpretation. *J. Exp. Psychol: Gen.* **1,** 47–65. [125]

Lewander, T. (1968) Effects of amphetamine on urinary and tissue catecholamines in rats after inhibition of its metabolism with desmethylimipramine. *Eur. J. Pharmacol.* **5,** 1–9. [111]

Lewander, T. (1974) Effects of chronic treatment with central stimulants on brain monoamines and some behavioral and physiological consequences in rats, guinea pigs and rabbits. In E. Usdin (Ed.), *Neuropsychopharmacology of Monoamines and their Regulatory Enzymes*. Raven, New York, pp. 221–239. [150]

Lewinsohn, P.M. (1974) A behavioral approach to depression. In R.J. Friedman and M.M. Katz (Eds.), *The Psychology of Depression: Contemporary Theory and Research*. Winston/Wiley, New York, pp. 157–185. [67, 136]

Lewinsohn, P.M. and Graf, M. (1973) Pleasant activities and depression. *J. Consult. Clin. Psychol.* **41,** 261–268. [67]

Lewinsohn, P.M. and Libet, J. (1972) Pleasant events, activity schedules and depression. *J. Abnorm. Psychol.* **79,** 291–295. [67]

Lewinsohn, P.M. and MacPhillamy, D.J. (1974) The relationship between age and engagement in pleasant activities. *J. Gerontol.* **29,** 290–294. [67]

Lewinsohn, P.M. and Tarkington, J. (1979) Studies on the measurement of unpleasant events and relations with depression. *Appl. Psychol. Meas.* **3,** 83–101. [69]

Lewinsohn, P.M., Weinstein, M.S., and Shaw, D.A. (1969) Depression: A clinical-research approach. In R.D. Rubin and C.M. Franks (Eds.), *Advances in Behavior Therapy 1968*. Academic, New York, pp. 231–240. [66, 67]

Lewinsohn, P.M., Lobitz, C., and Wilson, S. (1973) "Sensitivity" of depressed individuals to aversive stimuli. *J. Abnorm. Psychol.* **81,** 259–263. [69]

Lewinsohn, P.M., Zeiss, A.M., Zeiss, R.A., and Haller, R. (1977) Endogenicity and reactivity as orthogonal dimensions in depression. *J. Nerv. Ment. Disord.* **164**, 327–332. [50, 79, 81, 131]

Lewinsohn, P.M., Youngren, M.A., and Grosscup, S.J. (1979) Reinforcement and depression. In R.A. Depue (Ed.), *The Psychobiology of the Depressive Disorders: Implications for the Effects of Stress.* Academic, New York, pp. 291–316. [67, 136, 139]

Lewinsohn, P.M., Mischel, W., Chaplin, W., and Barton, R. (1980) Social competence and depression: The role of illusory self-perceptions. *J. Abnorm. Psychol.* **90**, 213–219. [70]

Lewinsohn, P.M., Steinmetz, J.L., Larson, D.W., and Franklin, J. (1981) Depression-related cognitions: Antecedent or consequence? *J. Abnorm. Psychol.* **90**, 213–219. [73, 78]

Lewis, A. (1934) Melancholia: A clinical survey of depressive states. *J. Ment. Sci.* **80**, 277–378. [401]

Lewis, D.J. (1979) Psychobiology of active and inactive memory. *Psychol. Bull.* **86**, 1054–1083. [201]

Lewis, J.K. and McKinney, W.T. (1976) Effects of electroconvulsive shock on the behavior of normal and abnormal rhesus monkeys. *Behav. Psychiatr.* **37**, 687–693. [132]

Lewis, J.K., McKinney, W.T., Young, L.D., and Kraemer, G.W. (1976) Mother-infant separation in rhesus monkeys as a model of human depression: A reconsideration. *Arch. Gen. Psychiatr.* **33**, 699–705. [132]

Lewis, J.W., Cannon, J.T. and Liebeskind, J.C. (1980) Opioid and non-opioid mechanisms of stress analgesia. *Science* **208**, 623–625. [360]

Lewis, P.R. and Shute, C.C.D. (1978) Cholinergic pathways in the CNS. In L.L. Iversen, S.D. Iversen, and S.H. Snyder (Eds.), *Handbook of Psychopharmacology,* Vol. 9. Plenum, New York, pp. 315–355. [271, 272]

Leysen, J. (1984) Problems in in vitro receptor binding studies and identification and role of serotonin receptor sites. *Neuropharmacology* **23**, 247–254. [345]

Leysen, J.E., Niemegeers, C.J.E., Tollenaere, J.P., and Laduron, P.M. (1978) Serotonergic component of neuroleptic receptors. *Nature* **272**, 163–166. [345]

Leysen, J.E., Awouters, F., Kennis, L., Laduron, P.M., Vandenberk, J., and Janssen, P.A.J. (1981) Receptor binding profile of R41 468, a novel antagonist at 5-HT$_2$ receptors. *Life Sci.* **28**, 1015–1022. [345]

Leysen, J.E., Niemegeers, C.J.E., Van Nueten, J.M., and Laduron, P.M. (1982) [^{3}H]Ketanserin (R41 468), a selective ^{3}H-ligand for serotonin$_2$ receptor binding sites. Binding properties, brain distribution and functional role. *Mol. Pharmacol.* **21**, 301–314. [330, 331, 345]

Leysen, J.E., Van Gompel, P., Verwimp, M., and Niemegeers, C.J.E. (1983) Role and localization of serotonin$_2$ (S$_2$)-receptor-binding sites: Effects of neuronal lesions. In P. Mandel and F.V. DeFeudis (Eds.), *CNS Receptors: From Molecular Pharmacology to Behavior,* Raven, New York, pp. 373–383. [345]

Li, C.H. and Chung, D. (1976) Isolation and structure of an untriakontapeptide with opiate activity from camel pituitary glands. *Proc. Natl. Acad. Sci. USA* **73**, 1145–1148. [358]

Libet, J. and Lewinsohn, P.M. (1973) The concept of social skill with special reference to the behavior of depressed persons. *J. Consult. Clin. Psychol.* **40**, 304–312. [64]

Liebman, J. (1983) Discriminating between reward and performance: A critical review of self-stimulation methodology. *Neurosci. Biobehav. Rev.* **7**, 45–72. [135, 272]

Liebman, J.M., Fenton, H.M., Gerhardt, S., and Noreika, L. (1982a) The dopamine autoreceptor agoinsts TL-99 and 3-PPP attenuate self-stimulation but not avoidance responding in rats. *Soc. Neurosci. Abstr.* **8**, 469. [156]

Liebman, J.M., Gerhardt, S., and Prowse, J. (1982b) Differential effects of d-amphetamine, pipradrol and buproprion on shuttlebox self-stimulation. *Pharmacol. Biochem. Behav.* **16**, 791–794. [150, 199]

Liebman, J.M., Hall, N., and Prowse, J. (1982c) Effects of various catecholamine receptor antagonists, muscle relaxation and physical hindrance on shuttlebox self-stimulation. *Pharmacol. Biochem. Behav.* **16**, 785–790. [150]

Liebowitz, M.R. and Klein, D.F. (1979) Hysteroid dysphoria. *Psychiatr. Clin. North Am.* **2**, 555–575. [58]

Limbird, L.E. (1981) Activation and attenuation of adenylate cyclase. The role of GTP binding proteins as macromolecular messengers. *Biochem. J.* **195**, 1–13. [256]

Lindsay, P.H. and Norman, D.A. (1971) *Human Information Processing: An Introduction to Psychology.* Academic, New York. [21]

Lindstrom, L.H., Widerlov, W., Gunne, L.M., Wahlstrom, A., and Terenius, L. (1978) Endorphins in human cerebrospinal fluid: Clinical correlations to some psychotic states. *Acta Psychiatr. Scand.* **57**, 153–164. [364]

Lindvall, O. and Bjorklund, A. (1974) The organization of the ascending catecholamine neuron systems in the rat brain as revealed by glyoxylic acid fluorescence method. *Acta Physiol. Scand.*, Suppl. 412, 1–18. [9, 194, 376]

Lindvall, O. and Bjorklund, A. (1978) Organization of catecholamine neurons in the rat central nervous system. In L.L. Iversen, S.D. Iversen, and S.H. Snyder (Eds.), *Handbook of Psychopharmacology,* Vol. 9. Plenum, New York, pp. 139–231. [149, 194]

Lingjaerde, O. (1963) Tetrabenazine (Nitoman) in the treatment of psychoses. *Acta Psychiatr. Scand.* **39** (Suppl. 170), 1–109. [7]

Linkowski, P., Bauman, M., and Mendlewicz, J. (1980a) Growth hormone after TRH in women with depressive illness. *Br. J. Psychiatr.* **137**, 229–232. [372]

Linkowski, P., Brauman, H., and Mendlewicz, J. (1980b) Prolactin secretion in women with unipolar and bipolar depression. *Psychiatr. Res.* **3**, 265–271. [166]

Linnoila, M. (1978) Neuroendocrine dysfunction in depressive disorders. *Acta Endocrinol.* **89** (Suppl. 220), 15. [315]

Linnoila, M., Lamberg, B.A., Rosberg, G., Karonen, S.L., and Welin, M.G. (1979) Thyroid hormones and TSH, prolactin and LH responses to repeated TRH and LRH injections in depressed patients. *Acta Psychiatr. Scand.* **59**, 536–544. [373]

Linnoila, M., Karoum, F., Calil, H.M., Kopin, I.J., and Potter, W.Z. (1982) Alteration of norepinephrine metabolism with desipramine and zimelidine in depressed patients. *Arch. Gen. Psychiatr.* **39**, 1025–1028. [250, 251]

Lints, C.E. and Harvey, J.A. (1976) Altered sensitivity to foot shock and decreased brain content of serotonin following brain lesions in the rat. *J. Comp. Physiol. Psychol.* **67**, 23–31. [297]

Lipsey, J.R., Pearlson, G.D., and Robinson, R.G. (1982) Nortriptyline treatment of post-stroke depressive disorder: A double-blind therapeutic trial. *Soc. Neurosci. Abstr.* **8**, 464. [92, 93]

Lishman, W.A. (1972) Selective factors in memory. *Psychol. Med.* **2**, 248–253. [70, 131]

Lishman, W.A. (1973) The psychiatric sequelae of head injury: A review. *Psychol. Med.* **3**, 304–318. [92]

List, S.J. and Seeman, P. (1981) Resolution of dopamine and serotonin receptor components of ^{3}H-spiperone binding to rat brain regions. *Proc. Natl. Acad. Sci. USA* **78**, 2620–2624. [345]

Litman-Adizes, T. (1978) An attributional model of depression: Laboratory and clinical investigations. Doctoral dissertation, University of California, Los Angeles. [78]

Liuzzi, A., Panerai, A.C., Chiodini, P.G., Sacchi, C., Cocchi, D., Botaila, L., Silvestrini, F., and Muller, E.E. (1976) Neuroendocrine control of growth hormone secretion, experimental and clinical studies. In A. Pecib and E.E. Muller (Eds.), *Proceedings of the Third*

Symposium on Growth Hormone and Related Peptides. Excerpta Medica, Amsterdam, pp. 236–251. [166]

Llorens, C., Martres, M.P., Baudry, M., and Schwartz, J.C. (1978) Hypersensitivity to noradrenaline in cortex after chronic morphine: Relevance to tolerance and dependence. *Nature* **274**, 603–605. [361]

Lloyd, C. (1980a) Life events and depressive disorder reviewed. I. Events as predisposing factors. *Arch. Gen. Psychiatr.* **37**, 529–535. [71, 141, 178, 394, 395]

Lloyd, C., (1980b) Life events and depressive disorders reviewed. II. Events as precipitating factors. *Arch. Gen. Psychiatr.* **37**, 541–548. [101, 141, 178, 392, 397]

Lloyd, G.G. and Lishman, W.A. (1975) The effect of depression on the speed of recall of pleasant and unpleasant experiences. *Psychol. Med.* **5**, 173–180. [70]

Lloyd, K.G., Farley, I.J., Deck, J.H.N., and Hornykiewicz, O. (1974) Serotonin and 5-hydroxyindoleacetic acid in discrete areas of the brainstem of suicide victims and control patients. In E. Costa, G.L. Gessa, and M. Sandler (Eds.), *Serotonin—New Vistas.* Raven, New York, pp. 387–397. [309]

Lloyd, K.G., Garrigou, D., and Broekkamp, C.L.E. (1982) The action of monoaminergic, cholinergic and gabaergic compounds in the olfactory bulbectomized rat model of depression. In S.Z. Langer, R. Takahashi, T. Segawa, and M. Briley (Eds.), *New Vistas in Depression.* Pergamon, New York, pp. 179–186. [112, 113, 271, 292, 354]

Lloyd, K.G., Morselli, P.L., Depoortere, H., Fournier, V., Zivkovic, B., Scatton, B., Broekkamp, P., Worms, P., and Bartholini, G. (1983) The potential use of GABA agonists in psychiatric disorders: Evidence from studies with progabide in animal models and clinical trials. *Pharmacol. Biochem. Behav.* **18**, 957–966. [344, 345]

Lobitz, W.C. and Post, R.D. (1979) Parameters of self-reinforcement and depression. *J. Abnorm. Psychol.* **88**, 33–41. [66]

Loeb, A., Beck, A.T., and Diggory, J. (1971) Differential effects of success and failure on depressed and non-depressed patients. *J. Nerv. Ment. Disord.* **152**, 106–114. [63]

Longoni, R., Mulas, A., Novak, B.O., Pepeu, I.M., and Pepeu, G. (1976) Effect of single and repeated electroshock applications on brain acetylcholine levels and choline acetyltransferase activity in the rat. *Neuropharmacology* **15**, 283–286. [285]

Loomer, H.P., Saunders, J.C., and Kline, N.S. (1957) A clinical and pharmacodynamic evaluation of iproniazid as a psychic energizer. *Psychiatr. Res. Rep. Am. Psychiatr. Assoc.* **8**, 129–141. [3]

Looney, T.A. and Cohen, P.S. (1972) Retardation of jump-up escape responding in rats pretreated with different frequencies of non-contingent shock. *J. Comp. Physiol. Psychol.* **78**, 317–322. [122]

Loosen, P.T. and Prange, A.J. (1980) Thyrotropin releasing hormone (TRH): A useful tool for psychoneuroendocrine investigation. *Psychoneuroendocrinology* **5**, 63–80. [371, 372]

Loosen, P.T. and Prange, A.J. (1982) Serum thyrotropin response to thyrotropin releasing hormone in psychiatric patients: A review. *Am. J. Psychiatr.* **139**, 405–415. [372]

Loosen, P.T., Prange, A.J., and Wilson, I.C. (1978) Influence of cortisol on TRH induced TSH response in depression. *Am. J. Psychiatr.* **135**, 244–246. [372]

Loosen, P.T., Prange, A.J., and Wilson, I.C. (1979) TRH (Proterlin) in depressed alcoholic men: Behavioral changes and endocrine responses. *Arch. Gen. Psychiatr.* **36**, 540–547. [371, 399]

Lopez-Ibor, J.J., Gutierrez, J.J.A., and Iglesias, M.L.M.M. (1976) 5-hydroxytryptophan (5-HTP) and a MAOI (nialamide) in the treatment of depression. A double-blind controlled study. *Intern. Pharmacopsychiatr.* **11**, 8–15. [321]

Lord, J.A.H., Waterfield, A.A., Hughes, J., and Kosterlitz, H. (1977) Endogenous opioid peptides: Agonists and receptors. *Nature* **267**, 495–499. [360]

Lorden, J., Oltmans, G.A., and Margules, D.L. (1976) Central noradrenergic neurons: Differential effects on body weight of electrolytic and 6-hydroxydopamine lesions in rats. *J. Comp. Physiol. Psychol.* **90**, 144–155. [196]

Lorden, J., Richert, E.J., Dawson, R., and Pelleymounter, M.A. (1980) Forebrain norepinephrine and the selective processing of information. *Brain Res.* **190**, 569–573. [204]

Lorens, S.A. and Sainati, S.M. (1978) Naloxone blocks the excitatory effect of ethanol and chlordiazepoxide on lateral hypothalamic self-stimulation behaviour. *Life Sci.* **23**, 1359–1364. [363]

Lorens, S.A., Sorenson, J.P., and Yunger, L.M. (1971) Behavioral and neurochemical effects of lesions in the raphe system of the rat. *J. Comp. Physiol. Psychol.* **77**, 48–52 [295]

Lorens, S.A., Guldberg, H.C., Hole, K., Kohler, C., and Srebro, B. (1976) Activity, avoidance learning and regional 5-hydroxytryptamine following intra-brainstem 5,7-dihydroxytryptamine and electrolytic midbrain raphe lesions in the rat. *Brain Res.* **108**, 97–113. [294]

Louis, W.J., Doyle, A.E., and Anavekar, S.N. (1975) Plasma noradrenaline concentration and blood pressure in essential hypertension, pheochromocytoma and depression. *Clin. Sci. Mol. Med.* **48**, 239S–242S. [218]

Lovinger, R., Holland, J., Kaplan, S., Grumbach, M.M., Boryczka, A.T., Shackleford, R., Salmon, J., Reid, I.A., and Ganong, W.F. (1976) Pharmacological evidence for stimulation of growth hormone secretion by a central noradrenergic system in dogs. *Neuroscience* **1**, 443–450. [228]

Lucki, I. and Frazer, A. (1982) Prevention of the serotonin syndrome in rats by repeated administration of monoamine oxidase inhibitors but not tricyclic antidepressants. *Psychopharmacology* **77**, 205–211. [340, 341, 343, 347, 351]

Ludwig, L.D. (1975) Elation-depression and skill as determinants of desire for excitement. *J. Pers.* **43**, 1–22. [72]

Luria, A.R. (1973) *The Working Brain: An Introduction to Neuropsychology*. Penguin, Harmondsworth. [93]

Lyness, W.H. and Moore, K.E. (1981) Destruction of 5-hydroxytryptaminergic neurons and the dynamics of dopamine in the nucleus accumbens septi and other forebrain regions of the rat. *Neuropharmacology* **20**, 327–334. [378]

Lyness, W.H. and Moore, K.E. (1983) Increased self-administration of d-amphetamine by rats pretreated with metergoline. *Pharmacol. Biochem. Behav.* **18**, 721–724. [302]

Lyness, W.H., Friedle, N.M., and Moore, K.E. (1979) Destruction of dopaminergic nerve terminals in nucleus accumbens: Effect on D-amphetamine self-administration. *Pharmacol. Biochem. Behav.* **11**, 553–556. [152]

Lyness, W.H., Friedle, N.M., and Moore, K.E. (1980) Increased self-administration of d-amphetamine after destruction of 5-hydroxytryptaminergic nerves. *Pharmacol. Biochem. Behav.* **12**, 937–941. [302]

Lyon, M. and Robbins, T. (1975) The action of central nervous stimulant drugs: A general theory concerning amphetamine effects. In W.B. Essman and L. Valzelli (Eds.), *Current Developments in Psychopharmacology,* Vol. 2. Spectrum, New York, pp. 79–164. [158]

Lytle, L.D., Messing, R.B., Fisher, L., and Phebus, L. (1975) Effects of long-term corn consumption on brain serotonin and the response to electric shock. *Science* **190**, 692–694. [297]

Maany, I., Mendels, J., Frazer, A., and Brunswick, D.A. (1979) A study of growth hormone release in depression. *Neuropsychobiology* **5**, 282–289. [165]

Maas, J.W. (1975) Biogenic amines and depression. Biochemical and pharmacological separation of two types of depression. *Arch. Gen. Psychiatr.* **32**, 1357–1361. [17, 322, 417]

Maas, J.W. (1979) Neurotransmitters and depression: Too much, too little or too unstable? *Trends Neurosci.* **2**, 305–307. [16, 260]

Maas, J.W. and Landis, D.H. (1968) In vivo studies of the metabolism of norepinephrine in the central nervous system. *J. Pharmacol. Exp. Ther.* **163**, 147–162. [222, 224]

Maas, J.W. and Landis, D.H. (1971) The metabolism of circulating norepinephrine by human subjects. *J. Pharmacol. Exp. Ther.* **177**, 600–612. [224]

Maas, J.W., Fawcett, J., and Dekirmenjian, H. (1968) 3-methoxy-4-hydroxyphenylglycol (MHPG) excretion in depressive states: A pilot study. *Arch. Gen. Psychiatr.* **19**, 129–134. [8, 13, 224, 225]

Maas, J.W., Dekirmenjian, H., and Fawcett, J.A. (1971) Catecholamine metabolism and stress. *Nature* **230**, 330. [224, 226]

Maas, J.W., Dekirmenjian, H., Garver, D., Redmond, D.E., and Landis, D.H. (1972a) Catecholamine metabolite excretion following intraventricular injection of 6-OH-dopamine. *Brain Res.* **41**, 507–511. [224]

Maas, J.W., Fawcett, J.A., and Dekirmenjian, H. (1972b) Catecholamine metabolism, depressive illness and drug response. *Arch. Gen. Psychiatr.* **26**, 252–262. [233, 250, 251]

Maas, J.W., Dekirmenjian, H., and Jones, F.D. (1973) The identification of depressed patients who have a disorder of norepinephrine metabolism and/or disposition. In E. Usdin and S. Snyder (Eds.), *Frontiers in Catecholamine Research.* Pergamon, New York, pp. 1091–1096. [224]

Maas, J.W., Kocsis, J.H., Bowden, C.L., Davis, J.M., Redmond, D.E., Hanin, I., and Robins, E. (1982) Pre-treatment neurotransmitter metabolites and response to imipramine or amitriptyline treatment. *Psychol. Med.* **12**, 37–43. [223, 235, 310, 322]

Maayani, S., Hough, L.B., Weinstein, H., and Green, J.P. (1982) Response of the histamine H_2-receptor in brain to antidepressant drugs. In E. Costa and G. Racagni (Eds.), *Typical and Atypical Antidepressants: Molecular Mechanisms.* Raven, New York, pp. 133–147. [368, 369]

Mack, G. and Mandel, P. (1976) Inhibition du comportement muricide du rat par la taurine, le GABA et ses analogues. *CR Acad. Sci. D (Paris)* **283**, 361–362. [354]

Mack, G., Simler, S., and Mandel, P. (1975) Système inhibiteur GABA-nergique dans l'agressivité interspecifique rat-souris. *J. Physiol. (Paris)* **71**, 162A. [354]

MacLennan, A.J., Jackson, R.L., and Maier, S.F. (1980) Conditioned analgesia in the rat. *Bull. Psychonom. Soc.* **15**, 387–390. [359]

MacLennan, A.J., Drugan, R.C., Hyson, R.L., Maier, S.F., Madden, J., and Barchas, J.D. (1982) Corticosterone: A critical factor in an opioid form of stress-induced analgesia. *Science* **215**, 1530–1532. [126, 276, 360]

MacLennan, A.J., Drugan, R.C., Hyson, R.L., Maier, S.F., Madden, J., and Barchas, J.D. (1983) Dissociation of long-term analgesia and the shuttle box escape deficit caused by inescapable shock. *J. Comp. Physiol. Psychol.* **96**, 904–912. [276, 360]

MacNiell, D.A. and Gower, M. (1982) Do antidepressants induce dopamine autoreceptor subsensitivity? *Nature* **298**, 302. [180]

MacRae-Deguerce, A., Berod, B., Mermet, A., Keller, A., Chouvet, G., Joh, T., and Pujol, J. (1982) Alterations in tyrosine hydroxylase activity elicited by raphe nuclei lesions in the rat locus coeruleus: Evidence for the involvement of serotonin afferents. *Brain Res.* **235**, 285–301. [377]

Madden, J., Akil, H., Patrick, R.L., and Barchas, J.D. (1977) Stress-induced parallel changes in central opioid levels and pain responsiveness in the rat. *Nature* **265**, 358–360. [359]

Maddison, D. and Walker, W.L. (1967) Factors affecting the outcome of conjugal bereavement. *Br. J. Psychiatr.* **113**, 1057–1067. [66]

Maeda, H. and Mogenson, G.J. (1982) Effects of peripheral stimulation on the activity of neurons in the ventral tegmental area. *Brain Res. Bull.* **8**, 7–14. [155]

Maeda, K., Kato, Y., Ohgo, S., Chihara, K., Yoshimoto, Y., Tamaguchi, N., Kuromaru, S., and Imura, H. (1975) Growth hormone and prolactin release after injection of thyrotropin-releasing hormone in patients with depression. *J. Clin. Endocrinol. Metab.* **40**, 501–505. [166, 315]

Maggi, A. and Enna, S.J. (1980) Regional alterations in rat brain neurotransmitter systems following chronic lithium treatment. *J. Neurochem.* **34**, 888–892. [257, 346]

Maggi, A., U'Prichard, D.C., and Enna, S.J. (1980) Differential effects of antidepressant treatment on brain monaminergic receptors. *Eur. J. Pharmacol.* **61**, 91–98. [240, 241, 251, 266, 285, 347, 348]

Mah, C., Suissa, A., and Anisman, H. (1980) Dissociation of antinociception and escape deficits induced by stress in mice. *J. Comp. Physiol. Psychol.* **94**, 1160–1171. [126]

Maier, S.F. (1970) Failure to escape traumatic shock: Incompatible skeletal motor response or learned helplessness? *Learn. Motiv.* **1**, 157–170. [125]

Maier, S.F. and Jackson, R.L. (1979) Learned helplessness: All of us were right (and wrong): Inescapable shock has multiple effects. In G. Bower (Ed.), *The Psychology of Learning and Motivation,* Vol. 13. Academic, New York, pp. 155–218. [126]

Maier, S.F. and Seligman, M.E.P. (1976) Learned helplessness: Theory and evidence. *J. Exp. Psychol.: Gen.* **1**, 3–46. [121, 122, 125]

Maier, S.F. and Testa, T.J. (1975) Failure to learn to escape by rats previously exposed to inescapable shock is partly produced by associative interference. *J. Comp. Physiol. Psychol.* **88**, 554–564. [125, 129]

Maier, S.F., Anderson, C., and Lieberman, D.A. (1972) Influence of control of shock on subsequent shock-elicited aggression. *J. Comp. Physiol. Psychol.* **81**, 94–100. [123]

Maier, S.F., Coon, D.J., McDaniel, M.A., Jackson, R., and Grau, J. (1979) The time course of learned helplessness, inactivity, and nociceptive deficits in rats. *Learn. Motiv.* **10**, 467–487. [360]

Maier, S.F., Davies, S., Grau, J.W., Jackson, R.L., Morrison, D.H., Moye, T., Madden, J., and Barchas, J.D. (1980) Opiate antagonists and the long-term analgesic reaction induced by inescapable shock. *J. Comp. Physiol. Psychol.* **94**, 1172–1183. [359, 360]

Maier, S.F., Drugan, R., Grau, J.W., Hyson, R., MacLennan, A.J., Moye, T., Madden, J., and Barchas, J.D. (1983) Learned helplessness, pain inhibition, and the endogenous opiates. In M.D. Zeiler and P. Harzem (Eds.), *Advances in Analysis of Behaviour,* Vol. 3. Wiley, New York, pp. 275–325. [361]

Maitre, L., Waldmeier, P.C., Greengrass, P.M., Jaeckel, J., Sedlucek, S., and Delina-Stula, A. (1975) Maprotiline—Its position as an antidepressant in the light of recent neuropharmacological and neurobiochemical findings. *J. Int. Med. Res.* **3** (Suppl. 2), 2–15. [234]

Maitre, L., Baumann, P.A., Jaeckel, J., and Waldmeier, P.C. (1982) 5-HT uptake inhibitors: Psychopharmacological and neurobiological criteria of selectivity. In B.T. Ho, J.C. Schoolar, and E. Usdin (Eds.), *Serotonin in Biological Psychiatry.* Raven, New York, pp. 229–246. [233, 240, 322, 328, 329]

Maj, J., Sowinska, H., Baran, L., Ganarczyk, L., and Rawlow, A. (1978) The central antiserotonergic action of mianserin. *Psychopharmacology* **59**, 79–84. [350]

Maj, J., Mogilnicka, E., and Klimek, V. (1979a) The effect of repeated administration of antidepressant drugs on the responsiveness of rats to catecholamine agonists. *J. Neural Trans.* **44**, 221–235. [188, 253]

Maj, J., Mogilnicka, E., and Kordecka, A. (1979b) Chronic treatment with antidepressant drugs: Potentiation of apomorphine-induced aggressive behaviour in rats. *Neurosci. Lett.* **13**, 337–341. [253]

Maj, J., Palinder, W., and Rawlow, A. (1979c) Trazodone, a central serotonin antagonist and agonist. *J. Neural Trans.* **44**, 237–248. [318]

Maj, J., Mogilnicka, E., and Kordecka-Magiera, A. (1980) Effects of chronic administration of antidepressant drugs on aggressive behaviour induced by clonidine in mice. *Pharmacol. Biochem. Behav.* **13**, 153–154. [253]

Maj, J., Mogilnicka, E., Klimek, V., and Kordecka-Magiera, A. (1981) Chronic treatment with antidepressants: Potentiation of clonidine-induced aggression in mice via noradrenergic mechanism. *J. Neural Trans.* **52**, 189–197. [253]

Maj, J., Rogoz, Z., Skuza, G., and Sowinska, H. (1982) Effects of chronic treatment with antidepressants on aggressiveness induced by clonidine in mice. *J. Neural Trans.* **55**, 19–25. [253, 254]

Maj, J., Gorka, Z., Melzacka, M., Rawlow, A., and Pilc, A. (1983) Chronic treatment with impramine: Further functional evidence for the enhanced noradrenergic transmission in flexor reflex activity. *Naunyn Schmiedebergs Arch. Pharmacol.* **322**, 256–260. [253, 255]

Major, L.F., Murphy, D.L., Gershon, E.S., and Brown, G.L. (1979a) The role of plasma amine oxidase, platelet monoamine oxidase, and red cell catechol-O-methyl transferase in severe behavioral reactions to disulfiram. *Am J. Psychiatr.* **136**, 679–684. [221, 230]

Major, L.F., Lake, C.R., Lipper, S., Lerner, P., and Murphy, D.L. (1979b) The central noradrenergic system and affective response to MAO inhibitors. *Prog. Neuropsychopharmacol.* **3**, 535–542. [222, 251]

Major, L.F., Lerner, P., Dendel, P.F., and Post, R.M. (1981) Dopamine-beta-hydroxylase in cerebrospinal fluid: A possible indicator of central noradrenergic activity. In J.H. Wood (Ed.), *The Neurobiology of Cerebrospinal Fluid,* Vol. 2. Plenum, New York, pp. 179–196. [219]

Makanjuola, R.O.A. and Ashcroft, G.W. (1982) Behavioural effects of electrolytic and 6-hydroxydopamine lesions of the accumbens and caudate-putamen nuclei. *Psychopharmacology* **76**, 333–340. [149]

Makanjuola, R.O.A., Dow, R.C., and Ashcroft, G.W. (1980) Behavioural responses to stereotaxically controlled injections of monoamine neurotransmitters into the accumbens and caudate-putamen nuclei. *Psychopharmacology* **71**, 227–235. [149]

Malick, J.B. (1981) Yohimbine potentiation as a predictor of antidepressant action. In S.J. Enna, J.B. Malick, and E. Richelson (Eds.), *Antidepressants: Neurochemical, Behavioral and Clinical Perspectives.* Raven, New York, pp. 141–155. [106, 271]

Malmgren, R., Asberg, M., Olsson, P., Tornling, G., and Unge, G. (1981) Defective serotonin transport mechanism in platelets from endogenously depressed patients. *Life Sci.* **29**, 2649–2658. [316]

Mandel, P., and De Feudis, F.V., eds. (1979) *GABA: Biochemistry and CNS Function.* Plenum, New York. [354]

Mandel, P., Mack, G., Kempf, E., Ebel, A., and Simler, S. (1978) Molecular aspects of a model of aggressive behavior. In S. Garattini, J.F. Pujol, and R. Samanin (Eds), *Interactions between Putative Neurotransmitters in the Brain.* Raven, New York, pp. 285–302. [354]

Mandell, A.J. and Knapp, S. (1979) Asymmetry and mood, emergent properties of serotonin regulation: A proposed mechanism of action of lithium. *Arch. Gen. Psychiatr.* **36**, 909–916. [99]

Mandler, G. (1975) *Mind and Emotion.* Wiley, New York. [29, 120]

Mandler, G. (1983) Consciousness: Its function and construction. Technical Report No. 117, Centre for Human Information Processing, University of California, San Diego. [27]

Manier, D.H., Okada, F., Janowsky, A.J., Steranka, L.R., and Sulser, F. (1983) Serotonergic denervation changes binding characteristics of beta-adrenoceptors in rat cortex. *Eur. J. Pharmacol.* **86**, 137–139. [260]

Manly, P.C., McMahon, R.J., Bradley, C.F., and Davidson, P.O. (1982) Depressive attributional style and depression following childbirth. *J. Abnorm. Psychol.* **91**, 245–254. [78]

Mann, L. (1979) Altered platelet monoamine oxidase activity in affective disorders. *Psychol. Med.* **9**, 729–736. [165]

Manto, P.G. (1967) Blockade of epinephrine-induced decrement in activity by scopolamine. *Psychonom. Sci.* **7**, 203–204. [277]

Mao, C.C. and Costa, E. (1978) Biochemical pharmacology of GABA transmission. In M.A. Lipton, A. DiMascio, and K.F. Killam (Eds.), *Psychopharmacology: A Generation of Progress.* Raven, New York, pp. 307–318. [355]

Marangos, P.J., Campbell, I.C., Schmechel, D.E., Murphy, D.L., and Goodwin, F.K. (1980) Blood platelets contain a neuron-specific enolase subunit. *J. Neurochem.* **34**, 1254–1258. [315]

Maranon, G. (1924) Contribution a l'étude de l'áction emotive de l'adrénaline. *Rev. Fr. Endocrinol.* **2**, 301–325. [28]

Marczynski, T.J. and Burns, L.L. (1976). Reward contingent positive variation (RCPV) and post-reinforcement EEG synchronization (PRS) in the cat: Physiological aspects, the effects of morphine and LSD-25, and a new interpretation of cholinergic mechanisms. *Gen. Pharmacol.* **1**, 211–221. [273]

Margules, D.L. (1971) Localization of antipunishment actions of norepinephrine and atropine in amygdala and entopeduncular nucleus of rats. *Brain Res.* **35**, 177–184. [275]

Margules, D.L., Moisset, B., Lewis, M.J., Shuberg, H., and Pert, C.B. (1978) Beta-endorphin is associated with overeating in genetically obese mice (ob/ob) and rats (fa/fa). *Science* **202**, 988–991. [362]

Mark, V.H. and Ervin, F.R. (1970) *Violence and the Brain.* Harper & Row, New York. [197]

Markianos, M., and Lykouras, L. (1981) Circadian rhythms of dopamine-beta-hydroxylase and c-AMP in plasma of controls and patients with affective disorders. *J. Neural Trans.* **50**, 149–155. [220]

Markianos, M., Varsou, E., Evangelou, E., and Bistolaki, E. (1982) Neurotransmitter parameters in plasma and urine of affective patients in depression and in normothymia after drug treatment. *Pharmakopsychiatrie* **15**, 61–64. [220, 310]

Marko, E.J. and Meek, J.L. (1979) The effects of antidepressants on serotonin turnover in discrete regions of rat brain. *Naunyn Schmiedebergs Arch. Pharmacol.* **306**, 75–79. [329, 334]

Marks, I.M., Stern, R., Mawson, D.J., Cobb, J., and McDonald, R. (1980) Chlorimipramine and exposure for obsessive-compulsive rituals. *Br. J. Psychiatr.* **136**, 1–25. [229]

Marks, P.C., O'Brien, M., and Paxinos, G. (1978) Chlorimipramine inhibition of muricide: The role of the ascending 5-HT projection. *Brain Res.* **149**, 270–273. [291]

Marsden, C.A. and Curzon, G. (1976) Studies on the behavioural effects of tryptophan and p-chlorophenylalanine. *Neuropharmacology* **15**, 165–171. [294]

Marshall, J.F. (1979) Somatosensory inattention after dopamine-depleting intracerebral 6-OHDA injections: Spontaneous recovery and pharmacological control. *Brain Res.* **177**, 311–324. [158]

Martensen-Larsen, O. (1951) Psychotic phenomenon provoked by tetraethylthiuram disulfide. *Q. J. Stud. Alcohol* **12**, 206–216. [230]

Martin, I. and Rees, L. (1966) Reaction times and somatic reactivity in depressed patients. *J. Psychosom. Res.* **9**, 375–382. [64]

Martin, J.B., Reichlin, S., and Brown, G.M. (1977) *Clinical Neuroendocrinology.* F.A. Davis, Philadelphia. [372]

Martin, J.B., Brazeau, P., Tannenbaum, G.S., Willoughby, J.O., Epelbaum, J., Terry, L.C., and Durand, D. (1978) Neuroendocrine organization of growth hormone regulation. In S. Reichlin, R. Baldessarini, and J.B. Martin (Eds.), *The Hypothalamus*. Raven, New York, pp. 329–355. [228]

Martin, J.L., Spatz, H., Abdala, N.E., and Basombrio, J. (1980) Clinical, biochemical, and pharmacological correlations in patients with depressive symptomatology. *Acta Psyquiatr. Psicol. Am. Lat.* **26**, 13–25. [233, 310]

Martin, L.L. and Sanders-Bush, E. (1982) Comparison of the pharmacological characteristics of 5-HT$_1$ and 5-HT$_2$ binding sites with those of serotonin autoreceptors which modulate serotonin release. *Naunyn Schmiedebergs Arch. Pharmacol.* **321**, 165–170. [344]

Martin, M., Ward, J.C., and Clark, D.M. (1983) Neuroticism and the recall of positive and negative personality information. *Behav. Res. Ther.* **21**, 495–503. [70]

Martinez, J.L., Jensen, R.A., and McGaugh, J.L. (1981) Attenuation of experimentally-induced amnesia. *Prog. Neurobiol.* **16**, 155–186. [201]

Martorana, P.A. and Nitz, R.E. (1979) The new antidepressant pirlindone: A comparison with imipramine and tranylcypromine. *Arzneim. Forsch.* **29**, 946–949. [127]

Maruta, T., Swanson, D.W., and Swenson, W.M. (1976) Pain as a psychiatric symptom: Comparison between low back pain and depression. *Psychosomatics* **17**, 123–127. [69]

Marwaha, J. and Prasad, K.N. (1981) Hypothyroidism elicits electrophysiological noradrenergic subsensitivity in rat cerebellum. *Science* **214**, 675–677. [373]

Marx, J.H. Learning and behavior. II. The hypothalamic peptides. *Science* **190**, 544–545. [373]

Maser, J.D. and Gallup, G.G. (1974) Tonic immobility in the chicken: Catalepsy potentiation by uncontrollable shock and alleviation by imipramine. *Psychosom. Med.* **36**, 199–205. [124]

Maser, J.D. and Seligman, M.E.P., eds. (1977) *Psychopathology: Experimental Models*. Freeman, San Francisco. [102]

Mason, S.T. (1981) Noradrenaline in the brain: Progress in theories of behavioral function. *Prog. Neurobiol.* **16**, 263–303. [199, 200, 202, 204]

Mason, S.T. and Angel, A. (1983) Behavioural evidence that chronic treatment with the antidepressant desipramine causes reduced functioning of brain noradrenaline systems. *Psychopharmacology* **81**, 73–77. [263, 265]

Mason, S.T. and Angel, A. (1984) Chronic and acute administration of typical and atypical antidepressants on activity of brain noradrenaline systems in the rat thiopentone anaesthesia model. *Psychopharmacology* (in press). [263, 265]

Mason, S.T. and Fibiger, H.C. (1979a) Noradrenaline, fear and extinction. *Brain Res.* **165**, 47–56. [203]

Mason, S.T. and Fibiger, H.C. (1979b) Noradrenaline and avoidance behavior in the rat. *Brain Res.* **161**, 321–333. [203]

Mason, S.T. and Fibiger, H.C. (1979c) Noradrenaline and selective attention. *Life Sci.* **25**, 1949–1956. [204]

Mason, S.T. and Iversen, S.D. (1977a) Effects of selective noradrenaline loss on behavioral inhibition in the rat. *J. Comp. Physiol. Psychol.* **91**, 165–173. [203]

Mason, S.T. and Iversen, S.D. (1977b) Behavioral basis of the dorsal bundle extinction effect. *Pharmacol. Biochem. Behav.* **7**, 373–379. [203]

Mason, S.T. and Iversen, S.D. (1978) The dorsal noradrenergic bundle, extinction and non-reward. *Physiol. Behav.* **21**, 1043–1045. [203]

Mason, S.T. and Iversen, S.D. (1979) Theories of the dorsal bundle extinction effect. *Brain Res. Rev.* **1**, 107–137. [202, 204]

Mason, S.T., Beninger, R.J., Fibiger, H.C., and Phillips, A.G. (1980) Pimozide-induced suppression of responding: Evidence against a block of food reward. *Pharmacol. Biochem. Behav.* **12**, 917–923. [153]

Massingham, R., Dubocovitch, M.L., Shepperson, N.B., and Langer, S.Z. (1981) In vivo selectivity of prazosin but not of WB 4101 for postsynaptic alpha$_1$-adrenoceptors. *J. Pharmacol. Exp. Ther.* **217**, 467–474. [255]

Mathew, R.J., Largen, J., and Claghorn, J.L. (1979) Biological symptoms of depression. *Psychosom. Med.* **41**, 439–443. [407]

Mathew, R.J., Ho, B.T., Kralik, P., Taylor, D., and Kralik, J.L. (1980) MAO, DBH and COMT: The effect of anxiety. *J. Clin. Psychiatr.* **41** (12) (Sec.2), 25–28. [221]

Mathew, R.J., Ho, B.T., Davis, C., Taylor, D., and Rech, J. (1981) Depression, antidepressants and plasma DBH. *Psychiatr. Res.* **5**, 331–334. [220]

Matousek, M., Capone, C., and Okawa, M. (1981) Measurement of the interhemispheral differences as a diagnostic tool in psychiatry. *Adv. Biol. Psychiatr.* **6**, 76–80. [88]

Matthews, R.T. and German, D.C. (1982) Electrophysiological evidence for morphine excitation of ventral tegmental dopamine neurons. *Soc. Neurosci. Abstr.* **8**, 777. [151]

Mattson, B., Mjordal, T., Oreland, L., and Perris, C. (1974) Catechol-O-methyltransferase and plasma monoamine oxidase in patients with affective disorders. *Acta Psychiatr. Scand.* (Suppl. 255), 187–197. [220]

Matussek, N., Ackenheil, M., Hippius, H., Muller, F., Schroder, H.T., Schultes, H., and Wasilewski, B. (1980) Effect of clonidine on growth hormone release in psychiatric patients. *Psychiatr. Res.* **2**, 25–36. [228, 229, 231]

Matussek, P., Soldner, M., and Nagel, D. (1981) Identification of the endogenous depressive syndrome based on the symptoms and the characteristics of the course. *Br. J. Psychiatr.* **138**, 361–372. [50, 51]

Matussek, P., Luks, O., and Nagel, D. (1982) Depression symptom patterns. *Psychol. Med.* **12**, 765–773. [51, 57]

Matuzas, W., Meltzer, H.Y., Uhlenluth, E.H., Glass, R.M. and Tong, C. (1982) Plasma dopamine-beta-hydroxylase in depressed patients. *Biol. Psychiatr.* **17**, 1415–1424. [220]

Mavroidis, M.L., Kanter, D.R., Greenblum, D.N. and Garver, D.L. (1984) Adrenergic-receptor desensitization and course of clinical improvement with desipramine treatment. *Psychopharmacology* **83**, 295–296. [246]

Maxwell, D.R. and Palmer, H.T. (1961) Demonstration of anti-depressant or stimulant properties of imipramine in experimental animals. *Nature* **191**, 84–85. [110, 159]

Mayer, D.J. and Hayes, R.L. (1975) Stimulation-produced analgesia: Development of tolerance and cross-tolerance to morphine. *Science* **188**, 941–943. [359]

Maynert, E.W., Marczynski, T.J., and Browning, R.A. (1975) The role of the neurotransmitters in the epilepsies. *Adv. Neurol.* **13**, 79–147. [273]

McAdoo, B.C., Doering, C.H., Kraemer, H.C., Dessert, N., Brodie, H.K.H., and Hamburg, D.A. (1978) A study of the effects of gonadotropin releasing hormone on human mood and behavior. *Psychosom. Med.* **40**, 199–209. [373]

McCarley, R.W. (1982) REM sleep and depression: Common neurobiological control mechanisms. *Am. J. Psychiatr.* **139**, 565–570. [271, 278, 381, 382]

McCord, P.R. and Wakefield, J.A. (1981) Arithmetic achievement as a function of introversion-extraversion and teacher-presented reward and punishment. *Pers. Individ. Differ.* **2**, 145–152. [80]

McCormick, D.A., and Thompson, R.F. (1982) Locus coeruleus lesions and resistance to extinction of a classically conditioned response: Involvement of the neocortex and hippocampus. *Brain Res.* **245**, 239–249. [204]

McDowell, F., Markham, C., Lee, J., Treciokas, L., and Ansel, R. (1971) The clinical use of levodopa in the treatment of Parkinson's disease. In F. McDowell and C. Markham (Eds.), *Recent Advances in Parkinson's Disease*. Blackwell, Oxford, pp. 175–201. [170]

McEntee, W.J. and Mair, R.G. (1978) Memory impairment in Korsakoff's psychosis: A correlation with brain noradrenergic activity. *Science* **202**, 905–907. [207]

McEntee, W.J. and Mair, R.G. (1980) Korsakoff's amnesia: A noradrenergic hypothesis. *Psychopharmacol. Bull.* **16**, 22–24. [207]

McEwen, B.S., Weiss, J.M., and Schwartz, L.S. (1969) Uptake of corticosterone by rat brain and its concentration by certain limbic structures. *Brain Res.* **16**, 227–241. [383]

McGaugh, J.L. (1966) Time-dependent processes in memory storage. *Science* **153**, 1351–1358. [201]

McGaugh, J.L., Gold, P.E., Handwerker, M.J., Jensen, R.A., Martinez, J.L,. Meligeni, J.A., and Vasquez, B.J. (1979) Altering memory by electrical and chemical stimulation of the brain. In M.A. Brazier (Ed.), *Brain Mechanisms in Learning and Memory*, Vol. 4. Raven, New York, pp. 151–164. [201]

McGinty, D.J. and Harper, R.M. (1976) Dorsal raphe neurons: Depression of firing during sleep in cats. *Brain Res.* **101**, 569–575. [377, 383]

McKay, J.M. and Horn, G. (1971) Effects of LSD on single cells in the lateral geniculate nucleus of the cat. *Nature* **229**, 347–349. [21]

McKenzie, G.M. (1974) The effects of catechol-O-methyltransferase inhibitors on behavior and dopamine metabolism. In E. Usdin (Ed.), *Neuropsychopharmacology of Monoamines and their Regulatory Enzymes*. Raven, New York, pp. 339–351. [165]

McKinney, W.T. and Bunney, W.E. (1969) Animal model of depression: Review of evidence and implications for research. *Arch. Gen. Psychiatr.* **21**, 240–248. [101, 108, 132]

McKinney, W.T. and Kane, F.J. (1967) Depression with the use of alpha-methyldopa. *Am. J. Psychiatr.* **124**, 80–81. [170]

McKinney, W.T., Young, L.D., and Suomi, S.J. (1973) Chlorpromazine treatment of disturbed monkeys. *Arch. Gen. Psychiatr.* **29**, 490–494. [132]

McKnew, D.H. and Cytryn, L. (1979) Urinary metabolites in chronically depressed children. *J. Am. Acad. Child Psychiatr.* **18**, 608–615. [225]

McKnew, D.H. and Cytryn, L. (1973) Historical background in children with affective disorders. *Am. J. Psychiatr.* **130**, 1278–1280. [133]

McLean, P.D. and Hakstian, L. (1979) Clinical depression: Comparative efficacy of outpatient treatments. *J. Consult. Clin. Psychol.* **47**, 818–836. [411]

McLeod, W.R. and McLeod, M.F. (1972) Indoleamines and the cerebrospinal fluid. In B.M. Davis, B.J. Carroll, and R.M. Mowbray (Eds.), *Depressive Illness: Some Research Studies*. Charles C Thomas, Springfield, Ill., pp. 209–225. [311]

McMillen, B.A., Warnack, W., German, D.C. and Shore, P.A. (1980) Effects of chronic desipramine treatment on rat brain noradrenergic responses to alpha-adrenergic drugs. *Eur. J. Pharmacol.* **61**, 239–246. [241, 244, 248]

McNair, D.M., Kahn, R.J., Frankenthaler, L.M., and Faldetta, L.L. (1984) Amoxapine and amitriptyline. I. Relative speed of antidepressant action. *Psychopharmacology* **83**, 129–133. [235]

McNamara, J.O., Pepeu, A.M., and Patrone, V. (1980) Repeated seizures induce long-term increase in hippocampal benzodiazepine receptors. *Proc. Natl. Acad. Sci. USA* **77**, 3029–3032. [356]

McNaughton, N. and Mason, S.T. (1980) The neuropsychology and neuropharmacology of the dorsal ascending noradrenergic bundle—A review. *Prog. Neurobiol.* **14**, 157–219. [198, 199]

McNitt, P.C. and Thornton, D.W. (1978) Depression and perceived reinforcement: A reconsideration. *J. Abnorm. Psychol.* **87,** 137–140. [76]

McRaven, D.R., Kroetz, F.W., Kioschos, J.M., and Kirkendall, W.M. (1971) The effect of clonidine on hemodynamics in hypertensive patients. *Am. Heart J.* **81,** 482–489. [231]

McWilliam, J.R., Meldrum, B.S., and Checkley, S.A. (1981) Enhanced growth hormone response to clonidine after repeated electroconvulsive shock in a primate species. *Psychoneuroendocrinology* **6,** 77–79. [252]

McWilliam, J.R., Meldrum, B.S. and Checkley, S.A. (1982) Changes in noradrenergic responses following repeated seizures and the mechanism of action of ECT. *Psychopharmacology* **77,** 53–57. [252, 258]

McWilliam, J.R., Meldrum, B.S., and Checkley, S.A. (1983) Changes in the sensitivity of the central alpha- and beta-adrenergic systems during desmethylimipramine tretment as assessed by plasma growth hormone response in the baboon. *Psychopharmacology* **80,** 263–266. [252, 258]

Meares, R., Grimwade, J., and Wood, C. (1976) A possible relationship between anxiety in pregnancy and puerperal depression. *J. Psychosom. Res.* **20,** 605–610. [70]

Meco, G., Casacchia, M., Boni, B., Falaschi, P., and Rocco, A. (1981) Prolactin and GH response to DA-agonist drugs before and after ECT. Paper presented to 3rd. World Congress of Biological Psychiatry, Stockholm, Sweden. [187, 188]

Meddis, R. (1977) *The Sleep Instinct.* Routledge & Kegan Paul, London. [402]

Meek, J. and Werdinius, B. (1970) 5-Hydroxytryptamine turnover decreased by the antidepressant drug chlorimipramine. *J. Pharm. Pharmacol.* **22,** 141–143. [334]

Melamed, E. and Larsen, B. (1977) Regional cerebral blood flow during voluntary conjugate eye movements in man. *Acta Neurol. Scand.* (Suppl. 64), 530–531. [89]

Melgar, R. and Lazzari, A. (1975) Ensayo doble ciego cruzado entre un nuevo antidepressivo (Viloxazina) ICI 58, 834 versus Imipramina en depresiones moderadas. *Sermona Medica (Buenos Aires)* **147,** 633. [235]

Meligeni, J.A., Ledergerber, S.A., and McGaugh, J.L. (1978) Norepinephrine attenuation of amnesia produced by diethyldithiocarbamate. *Brain Res.* **149,** 155–164. [201]

Mellerup, C., Plenge, P., and Rosenberg, R. (1982) ^{3}H-Imipramine binding sites in platelets from psychiatric patients. *Psychiatr. Res.* **7,** 221–227. [316]

Mellgren, R.L. and Ost, J.W.P. (1971) Discriminative stimulus pre-exposure and learning of an operant discrimination in the rat. *J. Comp. Physiol. Psychol.* **77,** 179–187. [204]

Meltzer, H.Y. and Arora, R.C. (1980) Skeletal muscle MAO activity in the major psychoses. *Arch. Gen. Psychiatr.* **37,** 333–339. [221]

Meltzer, H.Y., Cho, H.W., Carroll, B.J., and Russo, P. (1976) Serum dopamine-beta-hydroxylase activity in the affective psychoses and schizophrenia. *Arch. Gen. Psychiatr.* **33,** 585–591. [220]

Meltzer, H.Y., Piyakalmala, S., Schyve, P., and Fang, V.S. (1977) Lack of effect of tricyclic antidepressants on serum prolactin level. *Psychopharmacology* **51,** 185–187. [187]

Meltzer, H.Y., Arora, R.C., Baber, R., and Tricou, B.J. (1981a) Serotonin uptake in blood platelets of psychiatric patients. *Arch. Gen. Psychiatr.* **38,** 1322–1326. [316, 333]

Meltzer, H.Y., Simonovic, M., Sturgeon, R.D., and Fang, V.S. (1981b) Effect of antidepressants, lithium and electroconvulsive shock treatment on rat serum prolactin levels. *Acta Psychiatr. Scand.* **63** (Suppl. 290), 100–121. [329, 330, 338]

Meltzer, H.Y., Arora, R.C., and Goodnick, P. (1983a) Effect of lithium carbonate on serotonin uptake in blood platelets of patients with affective disorders. *J. Affect. Disord.* **5,** 215–221. [333]

Meltzer, H.Y., Uberkoman-Wiita, B., Robertson, A., Tricou, B.J., and Lowy, M. (1983b) Enhanced serum cortisol response to 5-hydroxytryptophan in depression and mania. *Life Sci.* **33**, 2541–2549. [314]

Meltzer, H.Y., Arora, R.C., Robertson, A., and Lowy, M. (1984) Platelet ^{3}H-imipramine binding and platelet 5-HT uptake in affective disorders and schizophrenia. *Clin. Neuropharmacol.* **7** (Suppl. 1), 320–321. [333]

Mena, I., Court, J., and Cotzias, G.C. (1971) Levadopa, involuntary movements and fusaric acid. *J. Am. Med. Assoc.* **218**, 1829–1830. [230]

Mendels, J. (1976) Lithium in the treatment of depression. *Am. J. Psychiatr.* **133**, 373–378. [46]

Mendels, J. and Cochrane, C. (1968) The nosology of depression: The endogenous-reactive concept. *Am. J. Psychiatr.* **124**, 1–11. [49, 57]

Mendels, J. and Frazer, A. (1974) Brain biogenic amine depletion and mood. *Arch. Gen. Psychiatr.* **30**, 447–451. [169, 399]

Mendels, J., Frazer, A., Fitzgerald, R.G., Ramsey, T.A., and Stokes, J.W. (1972) Biogenic amine metabolites in cerebrospinal fluid of depressed and manic patients. *Science* **175**, 1380–1382. [17, 167, 311–313, 417]

Mendels, J., Frazer, A., and Carroll, B. (1974) Growth hormone responses in depression. *Am. J. Psychiatr.* **131**, 1154–1155. [164]

Mendlewicz, J. (1982) Biological factors in affective disorders and their relevance to lithium prophylaxis. *Pharmakopsychiatria* **15**, 11–18. [166]

Mendlewicz, J. and Fliess, J.L. (1974) Linkage studies with X-chromosome markers in bipolar (manic-depressive) and unipolar (depressive) illness. *Biol. Psychiatr.* **9**, 261–294. [45]

Mendlewicz, J. and Youdim, M.B.H. (1980) Antidepressant potentiation of 5-hydroxytryptophan by l-deprenyl in affective illness. *J. Affect. Disord.* **2**, 137–146. [321]

Mendlewicz, J., Linkowski, P., and Brauman, H. (1977) Growth hormone and prolactin response to levodopa in affective illness. *Lancet* **2**, 652–653. [164]

Mendlewicz, J., Linkowski, P., and van Cauter, E. (1979a) Some neuroendocrine parameters in bipolar and unipolar depression. *J. Affect. Disord.* **1**, 25–32. [166]

Mendlewicz, J., Linkowski, P., and Brauman, H. (1979b) TSH response to TRH in women with unipolar and bipolar depression. *Lancet* **2**, 1079–1080. [372]

Mendlewicz, J., Charles, G., and Frankson, J.M. (1982a) The dexamethasone suppression test in affective disorder: Relationship to clinical and genetic subgroups. *Br. J. Psychiatr.* **141**, 464–470. [53, 54]

Mendlewicz, J., Pinder, R.M., Stulemeijerm, S.M., and Van Dorth, R. (1982b) Monoamine metabolites in cerebrospinal fluid of depressed patients during treatment with mianserin or amitriptyline. *J. Affect. Disord.* **4**, 219–226. [235, 251, 322, 333]

Menkes, D.B. and Aghajanian, G.K. (1981) Alpha$_1$-adrenoceptor-mediated responses in the lateral geniculate nucleus are enhanced by chronic antidepressant treatment. *Eur. J. Pharmacol.* **74**, 27–35. [242, 253, 285, 335, 336]

Menkes, D.B., Aghajanian, G.K., and McCall, R.B. (1980) Chronic antidepressant treatment enhances alpha-adrenergic and serotonergic responses in the facial nucleus. *Life Sci.* **27**, 45–55. [242, 253, 330, 335, 336]

Menkes, D.B., Aghajanian, G.K., and Gallager, D.W. (1983) Chronic antidepressant treatment enhances agonist affinity of brain alpha$_1$-adrenoceptors. *Eur. J. Pharmacol.* **87**, 35–41. [255]

Menzel, E.W., Davenport, R.K., and Rogers, C.M. (1963) Effects of environmental restriction upon the chimpanzee's responsiveness to objects. *J. Comp. Physiol. Psychol.* **56**, 78–85. [132]

Mereu, G., Serra, G., and Gessa, G.L. (1982) Repeated electroconvulsive shock prevents apomorphine-induced EEG synchronization. *Ann. Ist. Super. Sanita* **18**, 23–26. [183]

Messing, R.B., Phebus, L., Fisher, L.A., and Lytle, L.D. (1975) Analgesic effect of fluoxetine hydrochloride (Lilly 110140), a specific inhibitor of serotonin uptake. *Psychopharmacol. Commun.* **1**, 511–521. [297]

Messing, R.B., Fisher, L.A., Phebus, L., and Lytle, L.D. (1976) Interaction of diet and drugs in the regulation of brain 5-hydroxyindoles and the response to painful electric shock. *Life Sci.* **18**, 707–714. [297]

Metys, J., Wagner, N., Metysova, J., and Herz, A. (1969) Studies on the central antinociceptive action of cholinomimetic agents. *Int. J. Neuropharmacol.* **8**, 413–425. [276]

Metz, A., Stump, K., Cowen, P.J., Elliott, J.M., Gelder, M.G. and Grahame-Smith, D.G. (1983) Changes in platelet alpha$_2$-adrenoceptor binding post-partum: Possible relation to maternity blues. *Lancet* **1**, 495–498. [219, 237]

Metz, J.A., Halter, J.B., Porte, D., and Robertson, R.D. (1978) Suppression of plasma catecholamines and flushing by clonidine in man. *J. Clin. Endocrinol. Metab.* **46**, 83–90. [231]

Meyerson, L.R., Wennogle, L.P., Anel, M.S., Coupet, J., Lippa, A.S., Rauh, C.E., and Beer, B. (1982) Human brain receptor alterations in suicide victims. *Pharmacol. Biochem. Behav.* **17**, 159–163. [279, 316]

Miach, P.J., Dausse, J.-P., Cardot, A., and Meyer, P. (1980) ^{3}H-Prazosin binds specifically to alpha$_1$-adrenoceptors in rat brain. *Naunyn Schmiedebergs Arch. Pharmacol.* **312**, 23–26. [255]

Micco, D.J., McEwen, B.S., and Shein, W. (1979) Modulation of behavioral inhibition in appetitive extinction following manipulation of adrenal steroids in rats: Implications for involvement of the hippocampus. *J. Comp. Physiol. Psychol.* **93**, 323–329. [383]

Mikuni, M., Stoff, D.M., and Meltzer, H.Y. (1983) Effects of combined administration of imipramine and chlorpromazine on beta- and alpha$_2$-adrenergic receptors in rat cerebral cortex. *Eur. J. Pharmacol.* **89**, 313–316. [247]

Miller, I.W., Klee, S.H., and Norman, W.H. (1982) Depressed and nondepressed patients' cognitions of hypothetical events, experimental tasks and stressful life events. *J. Abnorm. Psychol.* **91**, 78–81. [127]

Miller, N.E. (1951) Learnable drives and rewards. In S.S. Stevens (Ed.), *Handbook of Experimental Psychology*. Wiley, New York, pp. 435–472. [362]

Miller, N.E. and Weiss, J.M. (1969) Effects of somatic or visceral responses to punishment. In B.A. Campbell and R.M. Church (Eds.), *Punishment and Aversive Behavior*. Appleton, New York, pp. 343–372. [125]

Miller, R.R. and Springer, A.D. (1973) Implications of recovery from experimental amnesia. *Psychol. Rev.* **81**, 470–473. [201]

Miller, W.R. (1974) Learned helplessness in depressed and non-depressed students. *Diss. Abstr.* **35**, 192–193. [64]

Miller, W.R. (1975) Psychological deficit in depression. *Psychol. Bull.* **82**, 238–260. [64, 65, 159]

Miller, W.R. and Seligman, M.E.P. (1975) Depression and learned helplessness in man. *J. Abnorm. Psychol.* **84**, 228–238. [124]

Miller, W.R., Rosellini, R.A., and Seligman, M.E.P. (1977) Learned helplessness and depression. In J.D. Maser and M.E.P. Seligman (Eds.), *Psychopathology: Experimental Models*. Freeman, San Francisco, pp. 104–130. [121, 122, 126]

Milner, B. (1964) Some effects of frontal lobectomy in man. In J.M. Warren and K. Akert (Eds.), *The Frontal Granular Cortex and Behavior*. McGraw-Hill, New York, pp. 313–334. [93]

Milner, B. (1967) Discussion of the paper: Experimental analysis of cerebral dominance in man. In C.H. Millikan and F.H. Darley (Eds.), *Brain Mechanisms Underlying Speech and Memory.* Grune & Stratton, New York, pp. 177–184. [91]

Milner, B. (1971) Interhemispheric differences in the localization of psychological processes in man. *Br. Med. Bull.* **27,** 272–277. [94]

Milner, B. (1982) Some cognitive effects of frontal lobe lesions in man. *Philos. Trans. Roy. Soc. Lond. B* **298,** 211–226. [94]

Minchin, M.C.W., Williams, J., Bowdler, J.M., and Green, A.R. (1983) The effect of electroconvulsive shock on the uptake and release of noradrenaline and 5-hydroxytryptamine in rat brain slices. *J. Neurochem.* **40,** 765–768. [328, 332]

Minkoff, K., Bergman, E., Beck, A.T., and Beck, R. (1973) Hopelessness, depression and attempted suicide. *Am. J. Psychiatr.* **130,** 455–459. [72]

Minneman, K.P., Wolfe, B.B., and Molinoff, P.B. (1982) Selective changes in the density of beta$_1$-adrenergic receptors in rat striatum following chronic drug treatment and adrenalectomy. *Brain Res.* **252,** 309–314. [258, 266, 267]

Mirkin, A.M. and Coppen, A. (1980) Electrodermal activity in depression: Clinical and biochemical correlates. *Br. J. Psychiatr.* **137,** 93–97. [316]

Misanin, J.R., Miller, R.R., and Lewis, D.J. (1968) Retrograde amnesia induced by electroconvulsive shock after reactivation of a consolidated memory. *Science* **160,** 554–555. [201]

Mishra, R., Janowsky, A., and Sulser, F. (1979) Subsensitivity of the NE receptor coupled adenylate cyclase system in rat brain. Effects of nisoxetine or fluoxetine. *Eur. J. Pharmacol.* **60,** 379–382. [256, 257]

Mishra, R., Janowsky, A., and Sulser, F. (1980) Action of mianserin and zimelidine on the norepinephrine receptor coupled adenylate cyclase system in brain: Subsensitivity without reduction in beta-adrenergic receptor binding. *Neuropharmacology* **19,** 983–987. [256, 257]

Mishra, R., Gillespie, D.D., Lovell, R., Robson, R.D., and Sulser, F. (1982) Oxaprotiline: Induction of central noradrenergic subsensitivity to its (+)-enantiomer. *Life Sci.* **30,** 1747–1755. [259]

Mittelman, G. and Valenstein, E.S. (1982) Mesostriatal dopamine systems and eating and drinking evoked by hypothalamic stimulation: Differences between the dominant and non-dominant hemispheres. *Soc. Neurosci. Abstr.* **8,** 894. [96]

Miyauchi, T., Kitada, Y., and Satoh, S. (1981) Effects of acutely and chronically administered antidepressants on the brain regional 3-methoxy-4-hydroxyphenylethyleneglycol sulfate in the forced swimming rat. *Life Sci.* **29,** 1921–1928. [211, 212]

Mobley, P.L. and Sulser, F. (1980a) Adrenal corticoids regulate sensitivity of noradrenaline receptor coupled adenylate cyclase in brain. *Nature* **286,** 608–609. [267]

Mobley, P.L. and Sulser, F. (1980b) Adrenal steroids affect norepinephrine sensitive adenylate cyclase system in rat limbic forebrain. *Eur. J. Pharmacol.* **65,** 321–323. [267]

Modai, I., Apter, A., Golomb, M., and Wijsenbeek, H. (1979) Response to amitriptyline and urinary MHPG in bipolar depressed patients. *Neuropsychobiology* **5,** 181–184. [235]

Modestin, J.J., Hunger, J., and Schwartz, R.B. (1973a) Über die depressogene Wirkung von Physostigmine. *Arch. Psychiatr. Nervenkr.* **218,** 67–77. [282]

Modestin, J.J., Schwartz, R.B., and Hunger, J. (1973b) Zur Frage der Beinflussung schizophrener Symptome Physostigmine. *Pharmakopsychiatrie* **9,** 300–304. [282]

Modigh, K. (1973) Effects of L-tryptophan on motor activity in mice. *Psychopharmacology* **30,** 123–134. [302]

Modigh, K. (1974) Functional aspects of 5-hydroxytryptamine turnover in the central nervous system. *Acta Physiol. Scand.,* Suppl. 403, 1–56. [302]

Modigh, K. (1975) Electroconvulsive shock and postsynaptic catecholamine effects: Increased psychomotor stimulant effect of apomorphine and clonidine in reserpine pretreated mice by repeated ECS. *J. Neural Trans.* **36**, 19–32. [159, 188, 191, 252]

Modigh, K. (1976) Long-term effects of electroconvulsive shock therapy on synthesis, turnover and uptake of brain monoamines. *Psychopharmacology* **49**, 179–185. [183, 249]

Modigh, K. (1979) Long lasting effects of ECT on monoaminergic mechanisms. In B. Saletu, P. Berner, and L. Hollister (Eds.), *Neuropsychopharmacology*. Pergamon, Oxford, pp. 11–20. [188, 189]

Modigh, K. (1984) Increased responsiveness of dopamine receptors after electroconvulsive therapy: A review of experimental and clinical evidence. In B. Lerer, R.D. Weiner, and R.H. Belmaker (Eds.), *ECT: Basic Mechanisms.* John Libbey, London, pp. 18–27. [188]

Mogenson, G.J. (1981) Studies on the nucleus accumbens and its mesolimbic dopaminergic afferents in relation to ingestive behaviours and reward. In B.G. Hoebel and D. Novin (Eds.), *The Neural Basis of Feeding and Reward.* Haer Institute, Brunswick, Me., pp. 275–288. [155]

Mogenson, G.J. and Yim, C.Y. (1981) Electrophysiological and neuropharmacological-behavioral studies of the nucleus accumbens: Implications for its role as a limbic-motor interface. In R.B. Chronister and J.F. DeFrance (Eds.), *The Neurobiology of the Nucleus Accumbens.* Haer Institute, Brunswick, Me., pp. 210–229. [155]

Mogenson, G.J., Takigawa, M., Robertson, A., and Wu, M. (1979) Self-stimulation of the nucleus accumbens and ventral tegmental area of Tsai attenuated by microinjections of spiroperidol into the nucleus accumbens. *Brain Res.* **171**, 247–259. [150, 151]

Mogenson, G.J., Jones, D.L., and Yim, C.Y. (1980) From motivation to action: Functional interface between the limbic system. *Prog. Neurobiol.* **14**, 69–97. [155]

Mogilnicka, E. (1981) REM sleep deprivation changes behavioral response to catecholaminergic and serotonergic receptor activation in rats. *Pharmacol. Biochem. Behav.* **15**, 149–151. [343]

Mogilnicka, E. (1982) The effect of acute and repeated treatment with salbutamol, a beta-adrenoceptor agonist, on clonidine-induced hypoactivity in rats. *J. Neural Trans.* **53**, 117–126. [245, 258]

Mogilnicka, E. and Klimek, V. (1979a) Effect of chronic administration of antidepressant drugs on the noradrenaline disappearance induced by FLA-63 in the rat brain. *Pol. J. Pharmacol. Pharm.* **31**, 139–147. [249, 250]

Mogilnicka, E. and Klimek, V. (1979b) Mianserin, danitracen and amitriptyline withdrawal increases the behavioral responses of rats to L-5-HTP. *J. Pharm. Pharmacol.* **31**, 704–705. [341]

Mogilnicka, E. and Pilc, A. (1981) Rapid eye movement sleep deprivation inhibits clonidine-induced sedation in rats. *Eur. J. Pharmacol.* **71**, 123–126. [245, 247]

Mogilnicka, E., Arbilla, S., Depoortere, H., and Langer, S.Z. (1980) Rapid-eye-movement sleep deprivation decreases the density of ^{3}H-dihydroalprenolol and ^{3}H-imipramine binding sites in the rat cerebral cortex. *Eur. J. Pharmacol.* **65**, 289–292. [257, 332]

Moleman, P. and Bruinvels, J. (1976) Differential effect of morphine on dopaminergic neurons in frontal cortex and striatum in the rat. *Life Sci.* **19**, 1277–1282. [151]

Moleman, P. and Bruinvels, J. (1979) Morphine-induced striatal dopamine efflux depends on the activity of nigrostriatal dopamine neurons. *Nature* **281**, 686–687. [151]

Molinoff, P.B. and Axelrod, J. (1971) Biochemistry of catecholamines. *Ann. Rev. Biochem.* **40**, 465–500. [9]

Moller, S.E., Kirk, L., and Fremming, K.H. (1976) Plasma amino acids as an index for subgroups in manic depressive psychosis: Correlation to effect of tryptophan. *Psychopharmacology* **49**, 205–213. [308]

Moller, S.E., Kirk, L., and Honore, P. (1980) Relationship between plasma ratio of tryptophan to competing amino acids and the response to L-tryptophan treatment in endogenously depressed patients. *J. Affect. Disord.* **2**, 47–59. [319]

Monnier, M., Sauer, R., and Hatt, A.M. (1970) The activating effect of histamine on the central nervous system. *Neurobiology* **12**, 265–305. [368]

Monroe, S.M., Imhoff, D.F., Wise, B.D., and Harris, J.E. (1983) Prediction of psychological symptoms under high-risk psychosocial circumstances: Life-events, social support, and symptom specificity. *J. Abnorm. Psychol.* **92**, 338–350. [67]

Montgomery, A. and Burton, M.J. (1983) The effects of flavour on 5HT-induced dipsogenesis. *Neurosci. Lett.*, Suppl. 14, S253. [301]

Montgomery, A. and Willner, P. (1980) Effects of subchronic desmethylimipramine (DMI) treatment on the classically conditioned eyeblink response in rabbits. *Commun. Psychopharmacol.* **4**, 519–525. [159, 262–265]

Montgomery, S.A. (1980) Maprotiline, nomifensine, mianserin, zimelidine: A review of antidepressant efficacy in in-patients. *Neuropharmacology* **19**, 1185–1190. [235]

Montgomery, S.A. (1982) The nonselective effect of selective antidepressants. In E. Costa and G. Racagni (Eds.), *Typical and Atypical Antidepressants: Clinical Practice.* Raven, New York, pp. 49–55. [414]

Montgomery, S.A. and Montgomery, D.B. (1982) Pharmacological prevention of suicidal behaviour. *J. Affect. Disord.* **4**, 291–298. [312]

Montgomery, S.A., McAuley, R., Rani, S.J., Roy, D., and Montgomery, D.B. (1981) A double blind comparison of zimelidine and amitriptyline in endogenous depression. *Acta Psychiatr. Scand.* **63** (Suppl. 290), 314–327. [323]

Moore, K.E. and Kelly, P.H. (1978) Biochemical pharmacology of mesolimbic and mesocortical dopaminergic neurons. In M.A. Lipton, A. DiMascio, and K.F. Killam (Eds.), *Psychopharmacology: A Generation of Progress.* Raven, New York, pp. 221–234. [188]

Moore, K.E., Demarest, K.T., and Johnston, C.A. (1980) Influence of prolactin on dopaminergic neuronal systems in the hypothalamus. *Fed. Proc.* **39**, 2912–2916. [165, 187]

Morgan, M.J., Einon, D.F., and Nicholas, D. (1975) The effects of isolation rearing on behavioural inhibition in the rat. *Q. J. Exp. Psychol.* **27**, 615–634. [115]

Morley, J.E. and Levine, A.S. (1982) Opiates, dopamine and feeding. In B.G. Hoebel and D. Novin (Eds.), *The Neural Basis of Feeding and Reward.* Haer Institute, Brunswick, Me., pp. 499–506. [362]

Morpurgo, C. and Theobald, W. (1965) Effect of imipramine-like compounds and chlorpromazine on reserpine-hypothermia in mice and amphetamine-hyperthermia in rats. *Med. Pharmacol. Exp.* **2**, 226–232. [111]

Morris, J.B. and Beck, A.T. (1974) The efficacy of antidepressant drugs: A review of research 1958–1972. *Arch. Gen. Psychiatr.* **30**, 667–674. [11]

Morris, M.J., Elghozi, J.-L., Dausse, J.-P., and Meyer, P. (1981) Alpha-1 and alpha-2 adrenoceptors in rat cerebral cortex: Effect of frontal lobotomy. *Naunyn Schmiedebergs Arch. Pharmacol.* **316**, 42–44. [246]

Morris, R.G.M. and Black, A.H. (1978) Hippocampal electrical activity and behavior elicited by nonreward. *Behav. Biol.* **22**, 524–532. [203]

Morrison, J.H., Molliver, M.E., and Grzanna, R. (1980) Noradrenergic innervation of cerebral cortex: Widespread effects of local cortical lesions. *Science* **205**, 313–316. [194]

Morselli, P.L., Bossi, L., Henry, J.F., Zarifian, E., and Bartholini, G. (1980) On the therapeutic action of SL 76002, a new GABA-mimetic agent: Preliminary observations in neuropsychiatric patients. *Brain Res. Bull.* **5** (Suppl.2), 411–414. [355]

Morselli, P.L., Henry, J.F., Macher, J.P., Bottin, P., Huber, J.P., and Van Landeghem, V.H. (1981) Probagide and mood. In C. Perris, G. Struwe, and B. Jansson (Eds.), *Biological Psychiatry, 1981*. Elsevier, Amsterdam, pp. 440–443. [355]

Moses, S.G. and Robins, E. (1975) Regional distribution of norepinephrine and dopamine in brains of depressive suicides and alcoholic suicides. *Psychopharmacol. Commun.* **1**, 327–337. [164]

Moye, T.B., Coon, D.J., Grau, J.W., and Maier, S.F. (1981) Therapy and immunization of long-term analgesia in rats. *Learn. Motiv.* **12**, 133–148. [360]

Moyer, J.A., Greenberg, L.M., Frazer, A., Brunswick, D., Mendels, J., and Weiss, B. (1979) Opposite effects of acute and repeated administration of desmethylimipramine on adrenergic responsiveness in rat pineal gland. *Life Sci.* **24**, 2237–2246. [261–263]

Moyer, J.A., Greenberg, L.H., Frazer, A., and Mendels, J. (1981) Subsensitivity of the beta-adrenergic receptor-linked system of the rat pineal gland following repeated treatment with desmethylimipramine and nialamide. *Mol. Pharmacol.* **19**, 187–193.

Mueller, P.S., Heninger, G.R., and McDonald, R. (1969) Insulin tolerance test in depression. *Arch. Gen. Psychiatr.* **21**, 587–594. [261]

Muller, E.E., Brambilla, E., Cavagnini, F., Perachi, M., and Paneri, A. (1974) Slight effect of l-tryptophan on growth hormone release in normal human subjects. *J. Clin. Endocrinol. Metab.* **39**, 1–5. [314]

Murphy, D.L. (1972) L-dopa, behavioral activation and psychopathology. *Res. Publ. Assoc. Res. Nerv. Ment. Disord.* **50**, 472–493. [173, 177]

Murphy, D.L. (1976) The neuropharmacology of depression. In L. Simpson (Ed.), *The Use of Psychotherapeutic Drugs in the Treatment of Mental Illness*. Raven, New York, pp. 109–125. [177]

Murphy, D.L. and Donnelly, C. (1974) Monoamine oxidase in man: Enzyme characteristics in platelets, plasma, and other human tissues. In E. Usdin (Ed.), *Neuropsychopharmacology of Monoamines and their Regulatory Enzymes*. Raven, New York, pp. 71–85. [313]

Murphy, D.L. and Redmond, D.E. (1975) The catecholamines: Possible role in affect, mood and emotional behavior in man and animals. In A.J. Friedhoff (Ed.), *Catecholamines and Behavior*, Vol. 2. Plenum, New York, pp. 73–117. [176]

Murphy, D.L. and Weiss, R. (1972) Reduced monoamine oxidase activity in blood platelets from bipolar depressed patients. *Am. J. Psychiatr.* **128**, 1351–1357. [165, 221]

Murphy, D.L. and Wyatt, R.J. (1975) Neurotransmitter-related enzymes in the major psychiatric disorders. I. COMT, MAO in the affective disorders, and factors affecting some behaviorally correlated enzyme activities. In D.X. Freedman (Ed.), *Biology of the Major Psychoses*. Raven, New York, pp. 277–288. [221]

Murphy, D.L., Colbourn, R.W., Davis, J.M., and Bunney, W.E. (1969) Stimulation by lithium of monoamine uptake in human platelets. *Life Sci.* **8**, 1187–1193. [316]

Murphy, D.L., Brodie, H.K.H., Goodwin, F.K., and Bunney, W.E. (1971) Regular induction of hypomania by L-dopa in "bipolar" manic-depressive patients. *Nature* **229**, 135–136. [46]

Murphy, D.L., Baker, M., Goodwin, F.K., Miller, H., Kotin, J., and Bunney, W.E. (1974a) L-tryptophan in affective disorders: Indoleamine changes and differential clinical effects. *Psychopharmacology* **34**, 11–20. [320]

Murphy, D.L., Belmaker, R., and Wyatt, R.J. (1974b) MAO in schizophrenia and other behavioral disorders. *J. Psychiatr. Res.* **11**, 221–247. [221]

Murphy, D.L., Donnelly, C., and Moskovitz, J. (1974c) Catecholamine receptor function in depressed patients. *Am. J. Psychiatr.* **131**, 1389–1391. [219]

Murphy, D.L., Campbell, I., and Costa, E. (1978a) Current status of the indoleamine hypothesis of affective disorders. In M.A. Lipton, A. DiMascio, and K.F. Killam (Eds.),

Psychopharmacology: A Generation of Progress. Raven, New York, pp. 1235–1248. [177, 181]

Murphy, D.L., Shiling, D.J., and Murray, R.M. (1978b) Psychoactive drug responder subgroups: Possible contributions to psychiatric classification. In M.A. Lipton, A. DiMascio, and K.F. Killam (Eds.), *Psychopharmacology: A Generation of Progress.* Raven, New York, pp. 807–820. [322]

Murphy, D.L., Lipper, S., Pickar, D., Jimerson, D., Cohen, R.M., Garrick, N.A., Alterman, I.S., and Campbell, I.C. (1981) Selective inhibition of monoamine oxidase type A. Clinical antidepressant effects and metabolic changes in man. In M.B.H. Youdim and E.S. Paykel (Eds.), *Monoamine Oxidase Inhibitors—The State of the Art.* Wiley, Chichester, pp. 189–205. [329]

Murphy, G.E., Woodruff, R.A., Herjanic, M., and Fischer, J.R. (1974) Validity of the diagnosis of primary affective illness: A prospective study with a five-year follow-up. *Arch. Gen. Psychiatr.* **30**, 751–756. [47]

Musacchio, J.M., Joulou, L., Kety, S.S., and Glowinski, J. (1969) Increase in brain tyrosine hydroxylase activity produced by electroconvulsive shock. *Proc. Natl. Acad. Sci. USA* **63**, 1117–1119. [210, 249]

Myers, R.D., Evans, J.E., and Yaksh, T.L. (1972) Ethanol preference in the rat: Interactions between brain serotonin and ethanol, acetaldehyde, paraldehyde, 5-HTP and 5-HTOL. *Neuropharmacology* **11**, 539–549. [301, 351]

Myslobodsky, M., Mintz, M., and Tomer, R. (1979) Asymmetric reactivity of the brain and components of hemispheric imbalance. In J.H. Gruzelier and P. Flor-Henry (Eds.), *Hemispheric Asymmetries of Function and Psychopathology.* Elsevier, Amsterdam, pp. 125–148. [98, 99]

Nadel, L. and O'Keefe, J. (1974) The hippocampus in pieces and patches: An essay on modes of explanation in physiological psychology. In R. Bellairs and E.G. Gray (Eds.), *Essays on the Nervous System: A Festschrift for Professor J.Z. Young.* Clarendon, Oxford, pp. 367–390. [26]

Nadi, N.S., Nurnberger, J.I., and Gershon, E.S. (1984) Investigations of muscarinic receptors in skin fibroblasts from manic-depressive patients. *Clin. Neuropharmacol.* **7** (Suppl. 1), 192–193. [279, 281]

Nagi, T., Kimura, H., Maeda, T., McGeer, P.L, Peng, F., and McGeer, E.G. (1982) Cholinergic projections from the basal forebrain of rat to the amygdala. *J. Neurosci.* **2**, 513–520. [275]

Nagayama, H., Hintgen, J.N., and Aprison, M.H. (1980) Pre- and postsynaptic serotonergic manipulations in an animal model of depression. *Pharmacol. Biochem. Behav.* **13**, 575–579. [111, 300, 330]

Nagayama, H., Hintgen, J.N., and Aprison, M.H. (1981) Postsynaptic action by four antidepressive drugs in an animal model of depression. *Pharmacol. Biochem. Behav.* **15**, 125–130. [111, 300, 330]

Nagel, E. (1961) *The Structure of Science.* Routledge & Kegan Paul, London. [24, 29]

Nagy, A. (1977) Blood and brain concentrations of imipramine, clomipramine and their monomethylated metabolites after oral and intramuscular administration in rats. *J. Pharm. Pharmacol.* **29**, 104–107. [128]

Nagy, J.I., Lee, T., Seeman, P., and Fibiger, H.C. (1978) Dopamine receptor binding in brain: Direct evidence for presynaptic and postsynaptic receptors. *Nature* **274**, 278–281. [185, 190]

Nakaya, K. (1976) Serum free tryptophan concentration—The effects on the brain serotonin metabolism and its relationship to the mental diseases. *Psychiatr. Neurol. Jpn.* **78**, 119–132. [308]

Narabayashi, M. (1972) Stereotaxic amygdalaotomy. In B.E. Eleftheriou (Ed.), *The Neurobiology of the Amygdala.* Plenum, New York, pp. 459–483. [197]

Nasr, S., Daiguji, M.D., Tong, C., and Meltzer, H.Y. (1980) Comparison of midday serum dopamine-beta-hydroxylase activity in depressed patients and normal controls. *Commun. Psychopharmacol.* **4**, 263–267. [220]

Nassif, S., Kempf, E., Cardo, B., and Velley, L. (1983) Neurochemical lesion of the locus coeruleus of the rat does not suppress the sedative effect of clonidine. *Eur. J. Pharmacol.* **91**, 69–76. [243]

Natale, M. (1977) Effects of induced elation-depression on speech in the initial interview. *J. Consult. Clin. Psychol.* **45**, 45–52. [68, 73]

Neal, H. and Bradley, P.B. (1979) Electrocortical changes in the encéphale isole cat following chronic treatment with antidepressant drugs. *Neuropharmacology* **18**, 611–615. [192]

Neeley, S.P. and Stellar, J.R. (1983) Reward and aversive effects of lateral hypothalamic stimulation in rats measured by a modified runway and reward summation technique. *Physiol. Behav.* **31**, 657–662. [362]

Neff, N.H. and Costa, E. (1967) Effect of tricyclic antidepressants and chlorpromazine on brain catecholamine synthesis. In S. Garattini and M.N.G. Dukes (Eds.), *Antidepressant Drugs.* Excerpta Medica, Amsterdam, pp. 28–34. [183]

Neill, D.B. (1982) Problems of concept and vocabulary in the anhedonia hypothesis. *Behav. Brain Sci.* **5**, 70. [154]

Neill, D.B. and Justice, J.B. (1981) An hypothesis for a behavioral function of dopaminergic transmission in nucleus accumbens. In R.B. Chronister and J.F. DeFrance (Eds.), *The Neurobiology of the Nucleus Accumbens.* Haer Institute, Brunswick, Me., pp. 343–350. [154, 155]

Neill, D.B., Boggan, W.B. and Grossman, S.P. (1974) Impairment of avoidance performance by intrastriatal administration of 6-OHDA. *Pharmacol. Biochem. Behav.* **2**, 97–103. [156]

Nelson, D.L., Herbet, A., Enjalbert, A., Bockaert, J., and Hamon, M. (1980a) Serotonin-sensitive adenylate cyclase and [³H]serotonin binding sites in the CNS of the rat. I. Kinetic parameter and pharmacological properties. *Biochem. Pharmacol.* **29**, 2445–2453. [345]

Nelson, O.L., Herbet, A., Adrien, J., Bockaert, J., and Hamon, M. (1980b) Serotonin-sensitive adenylate cyclase and [³H]serotonin binding sites in the CNS of the rat. II. Respective regional and subcellular distributions and ontogenetic developments. *Biochem. Pharmacol.* **29**, 2455–2463. [345]

Nelson, J.C. and Bowers, M.B. (1978) Delusional unipolar depression: Description and drug response. *Arch. Gen. Psychiatr.* **35**, 1321–1328. [52]

Nelson, J.C. and Charney, D.S. (1981) The symptoms of major depression. *Am. J. Psychiatr.* **138**, 1–13. [51, 52, 57, 63, 66, 81, 113, 123, 124, 130, 131, 135, 160, 192, 226, 406, 407]

Nelson, J.C., Charney, D.S., and Quinlan, D.M. (1981) Evaluation of the DSM-III criteria for melancholia. *Arch. Gen. Psychiatr.* **38**, 555–559. [51]

Nelson, R.E. and Craighead, W.E. (1977) Selective recall of positive and negative feedback, self-control behaviors, and depression. *J. Abnorm. Psychol.* **86**, 379–388. [66, 70]

Nemeroff, C.B. and Prange, A.J. (1978) Peptides and psychoneuroendocrinology: A perspective. *Arch. Gen. Psychiatr.* **35**, 999–1010. [370]

Ng, L., Chase, T.N., Colburn, R.W., and Kopin, I.J. (1971) L-dopa induced release of cerebral monoamines. *Science* **170**, 76–77. [177]

Nielsen, E.B., Nielsen, M., Ellison, G., and Braestrup, C. (1980) Decreased spiroperidol and LSD binding in rat brain after continuous amphetamine. *Eur. J. Pharmacol.* **66**, 149–154. [348]

Nielsen, J.A. and Moore, K.E. (1982) Measurement of metabolites of dopamine and 5-hydroxytryptamine in cerebroventricular perfusates of unanesthetized, freely moving rats: Selective effects of drugs. *Pharmacol. Biochem. Behav.* **16,** 131–137 [309]

Nielsen, M. (1975) The influence of desipramine and amitriptyline on the accumulation of [^{3}H]noradrenaline and its two major metabolites formed from [^{3}H]tyrosine in the rat brain. *J. Pharm. Pharmacol.* **27,** 206–208. [241]

Nielsen, M. and Braestrup, C. (1977) Desipramine and some other antidepressant drugs decrease the major norepinephrine metabolite 3,4-dihydroxy-phenylglycol-sulphate in the rat brain. *Naunyn Schmiedebergs Arch. Pharmacol.* **300,** 93–99. [241, 248–250]

Nielsen, M., Eplov, L., and Scheel-Kruger, J. (1975) The effect of amitriptyline, desipramine and imipramine on the in vivo brain synthesis of ^{3}H-noradrenaline from ^{3}H-L-dopa in the rat. *Psychopharmacology* **41,** 249–254. [241]

Niemegeers, C.J.E., Verbruggen, F.J., and Janssen, P.A.J. (1969) The influence of various neuroleptic drugs on shock avoidance responding in rats. *Psychopharmacology* **16,** 161–174. [155, 156]

Nieoullon, A., Cheramy, A., and Glowinski, J. (1977) Nigral and striatal dopamine release under sensory stimuli. *Nature* **269,** 340–342. [99]

Nies, A., Robinson, D.S., Ravaris, C.L., and Davis, J.M. (1971) Amines and monoamine oxidase in relation to aging and depression in man. *Psychosom. Med.* **33,** 470. [221]

Nies, A., Robinson, D.S., Lambourn, K.R., and Lampert, R.P. (1973) Genetic control of platelet and plasma monoamine oxidase activity. *Arch. Gen. Psychiatr.* **28,** 834–838. [221]

Nies, A., Robinson, D.S., Harris, L.S., and Lambourn, K.R. (1974) Comparison of monoamine oxidase substrate activities in twins, schizophrenics, depressives and controls. In E. Usdin (Ed.), *Neuropsychopharmacology of Monoamines and Their Regulatory Enzymes.* Raven, New York, pp. 59–70. [221]

Nilsson, L. and Smith, G.J.W. (1965) Optical analysis of EEG changes during ECT and imipramine treatment. *Acta Psychiatr. Scand.* **41,** 141–156. [88, 89]

Nimgaonkar, V.L., Green, A.R., Cowen, P.J., Heal, D.J., Grahame-Smith, D.G., and Deakin, J.F.W. (1983) Studies on the mechanisms by which clenbuterol, a beta-adrenoceptor agonist, enhances 5-HT-mediated behaviour and increases metabolism of 5-HT in the brain of the rat. *Neuropharmacology* **22,** 739–749. [343]

Nishikawa, T., Tanaka, M., Tsuda, A., Kohno, Y., and Nagasaki, N. (1983) Differential effects of clonidine on alpha$_1$ and alpha$_2$-adrenoceptors in footshock-induced jumping behavior. *Eur. J. Pharmacol.* **88,** 399–401. [211]

Niskanen, P., Huttunen, M., Tamminen, T., and Jaaskelainen, J. (1976) The daily rhythm of plasma tryptophan and tyrosine in depression. *Br. J. Psychiatr.* **128,** 67–73. [308]

Nobrega, J.N. and Coscina, D.V. (1981) Effects of chronic antidepressant treatment on feeding behavior in rats. In B.G. Hoebel and D. Novin (Eds.), *The Neural Basis of Feeding and Reward.* Haer Institute, Brunswick, Me., pp. 525–534. [159]

Nomra, M., Colmenares, J., and Wurtman, R.J. (1977) Effect of dietary protein on urinary 5-hydroxyindoleacetic acid levels. *J. Neurochem.* **29,** 267–271. [310]

Nomura, A., Shimizu, J., Kamateni, H., Kinjo, M., Watanabe, M., and Nakazawa, T. (1982) Swimming mice: In search of an animal model for human depression. In S.Z. Langer, R. Takahashi, T. Segawa, and M. Briley (Eds.), *New Vistas in Depression.* Pergamon, New York, pp. 203–210. [129]

Nordin, C., Ottoson, J.O., and Roos, B.E. (1971) Influence of convulsive therapy on 5-hydroxyindoleacetic acid and homovanillic acid in cerebrospinal fluid in endogenous depression. *Psychopharmacology* **20,** 315–320. [167, 334]

Nordin, C., Siwers, B., and Bertilsson, L. (1981) Bromocryptine treatment of depressive disorders. *Acta Psychiatr. Scand.* **64,** 25–33. [167, 174, 177]

Noreika, L., Pastor, G., and Liebman, J. (1981) Delayed emergence of antidepressant efficacy following withdrawal in olfactory bulbectomized rats. *Pharmacol. Biochem. Behav.* **15,** 393–398. [112, 114, 350, 351]

Norman, T.R., Burrows, G.D., Marriott, P.E., McIntyre, I.M., Davies, B.D., and Moore, R.G. (1983) Zimelidine: a placebo controlled trial in depression. *Psychiatr. Res.* **8,** 95–103. [323]

Nottebohm, F. (1971) Neural lateralization of vocal control in a Passerine bird. I. Song. *J. Exp. Zool.* **177,** 229–262. [97]

Nottebohm, F. (1977) Asymmetries in neural control of vocalization in the canary. In S. Harnad, R.W. Doty, L. Goldstein, J. Jaynes, and G. Krauthamer (Eds.), *Lateralization in the Nervous System.* Academic, New York, pp. 23–44. [97]

Nowak, J.Z., Bielkiewicz, B., and Lebrecht, U. (1979) Dimaprit-induced hypothermia in normal rats: Its attenuation by cimetidine and by tricyclic antidepressant drugs. *Neuropharmacology* **18,** 783–789. [369]

Nuller, J.L. and Ostroumova, M.N. (1980) Resistance to inhibiting effect of dexamethasone in patients with endogenous depression. *Acta Psychiatr. Scand.* **61,** 169–177. [54]

Nurnberger, J., Gershon, E.S., Sitaram, N., Gillin, J.C., Brown, G., Ebert, M., Gold, P., Jimerson, D., and Kessler, L. (1982) Dextroamphetamine and arecoline as pharacogenetic probes in normals and remitted bipolar patients. *Psychopharmacol. Bull.* **17,** 80–82. [280–282]

Nutt, D.J., Cowen, P.J. and Green, A.R. (1980a) On the measurement in rats of the convulsant effects of drugs and the changes which follow electroconvulsive therapy. *Neuropharmacology* **19,** 1017–1023. [339]

Nutt, D.J., Green, A.R., and Grahame-Smith, D.G. (1980b) Enhanced 5-hydroxytryptamine and dopamine-mediated behavioural responses following convulsions. I. The effects of single and repeated bicuculline-induced seizures. *Neuropharmacology* **19,** 897–900. [357]

Nyback, H.V., Walters, J.R., Aghajanian, G.K., and Roth, R.H. (1975) Tricyclic antidepressants: Effects on the firing rate of brain noradrenergic neurons. *Eur. J. Pharmacol.* **32,** 302–312. [241]

O'Keefe, J. and Nadel, L. (1978) *The Hippocampus as a Cognitive Map.* Clarendon, Oxford. [273, 274]

O'Neill, K.A. and Valentino, D. (1982) Escapability and generalization: Effect on behavioral despair. *Eur. J. Pharmacol.* **78,** 379–380. [129]

Oatley, K. and Dickinson, A. (1970) Air drinking and the measurement of thirst. *Anim. Behav.* **18,** 259–269. [402]

Ogren, S.-O. and Fuxe, K. (1977) The role of brain noradrenaline and the pituitary-adrenal system in learning. *Brain Res.* **127,** 372–373. [203]

Ogren, S.-O. and Holm, A.-C. (1980) Test-specific effects of the 5-HT reuptake inhibitors alaproclate and zimelidine on pain sensitivity and morphine analgesia. *J. Neural Trans.* **47,** 253–271. [297]

Ogren, S.-O. and Fuxe, K., Agnati, L.F., Gustafsson, J.A., Jonsson, G., and Holm, A.C. (1979) Reevaluation of the indoleamine hypothesis of depression. Evidence for a reduction of functional activity of central 5-HT systems by antidepressant drugs. *J. Neural Trans.* **46,** 85–103. [329–331, 342, 345]

Ogren, S.-O., Holm, A.C., Renyi, A.L., and Ross, S.B. (1980) Anti-aggressive effect of zimelidine in isolated mice. *Acta Pharmacol. Toxicol.* **47,** 71–74. [295]

Ogren, S.-O., Fuxe, K., Archer, T., Hall, H., Holm, A.-C., and Kohler, C. (1981a) Studies on the role of central 5-HT neurons in avoidance learning: A behavioral and biochemical analysis. In B. Haber, S. Gabay, M.I. Issidorides, and G.A. Alivisatos (Eds.), *Serotonin: Current Aspects on Neurochemistry and Function* Plenum, New York, pp. 681–705. [296]

Ogren, S.-O., Ross, S.B., Hall, H., Holm, A.-C., and Renyi, A.L. (1981b) The pharmacology of zimelidine: A 5-HT selective reuptake inhibitor. *Acta Psychiatr. Scand.* **63** (Suppl. 290), 127–151. [331, 332]

Ogren, S.-O., Fuxe, K., Archer, T., Johansson, G., and Holm, A.C. (1982) Behavioral and biochemical studies on the effects of acute and chronic administration of antidepressant drugs on central serotonergic receptor mechanisms. In S.Z. Langer, R. Takahashi, T. Segawa, and M. Briley (Eds.), *New Vistas in Depression*. Pergamon, New York, pp. 11–19. [329, 340–342]

Oishi, R. and Ueki, S. (1980) Facilitation of muricide by dorsal norepinephrine bundle lesions in olfactory bulbectomized rats. *Pharmac. Biochem. Behav.* **8**, 133–136. [292]

Okada, F., Manier, D.H., Janowsky, A.J., Steranka, L.R., and Sulser, F. (1982) Role of aminergic neuronal input in the down-regulation by desipramine (DMI) of the norepinephrine (NE) coupled adenylate cyclase system in rat cortex. *Soc. Neurosci. Abstr.* **8**, 659. [258]

Oke, A., Keller, R., Mefford, I., and Adams, R.N. (1978) Lateralization of norepinephrine in human thalamus. *Science* **200**, 1411–1414. [98]

Okuma, T., Kishimoto, A., and Inone, K. (1973) Antimanic and prophylactic effects of carbamazepine (Tegretol) on manic depressive psychoses: A preliminary report. *Folia Psychiatr. Neurol. Jpn* **27**, 283–297. [356]

Olds, J. (1956) Pleasure centres in the brain. *Sci. Am.* **195**, 2–7. [150]

Olds, J. (1958) Effects of hunger and male sex hormone on self-stimulation of the brain. *J. Comp. Physiol. Psychol.* **51**, 320–324. [135, 196]

Olds, M.E. and Ho, M. (1973) Noradrenergic and cholinergic action on neuronal activity during self-stimulation behavior in the rat. *Neuropharmacology* **12**, 525–539. [271]

Olds, M.E. and Olds, J. (1963) Approach-avoidance analysis of the rat diencephalon. *J. Comp. Physiol. Psychol.* **120**, 259–295. [362, 363]

Oleson, T.D., Twombley, D.A., and Liebeskind, J.C. (1978) Effects of pain-attenuating brain stimulation and morphine on electrical activity in the raphe nuclei of the awake rat. *Pain* **4**, 211–230. [299]

Olianas, M., Oliver, A.P., and Neff, N.H. (1982) Biochemical and electrophysiological studies on the mechanism of action of typical and atypical antidepressants on the H₂-histamine receptor complex. In E. Costa and G. Racagni (Eds.), *Typical and Atypical Antidepressants: Molecular Mechanisms*. Raven, New York, pp. 149–156. [369]

Oliveras, J.L., Hosobuchi, Y., Redjemi, F., Guilbaud, G., and Besson, J.M. (1977) Opiate antagonist, naloxone, strongly reduces analgesia induced by stimulation of a raphe nucleus (centralis inferior). *Brain Res.* **120**, 221–230. [359]

Oliveras, J.L., Hosobuchi, Y., Guilbaud, G., and Besson, J.M. (1978) Analgesia by electrical stimulation of the feline nucleus raphe magnus: development of tolerance and its reversal by 5-HTP. *Brain Res.* **146**, 404–409. [299]

Olpe, H.R. (1981) Differential effect of chlorimipramine and clorgyline on the sensitivity of cortical neurons to serotonin. *Eur. J. Pharmacol.* **69**, 375–377. [335, 337, 351]

Olpe, H.R. and Schellenberg, A. (1980) Reduced sensitivity of neurons to noradrenaline after chronic treatment with antidepressant drugs. *Eur. J. Pharmacol.* **63**, 7–13. [253, 262, 264, 356]

Olpe, H.R. and Schellenberg, A. (1981) The sensitivity of cortical neurons to serotonin: Effect of chronic treatment with antidepressants, serotonin-uptake inhibitors and monoamine-oxidase-blocking drugs. *J. Neural Trans.* **51**, 233–244. [335, 337, 343, 356]

Olpe, H.R., Jones, R.S.G., and Steinmann, M.W. (1983) The locus coeruleus: Actions of psychoactive drugs. *Experientia* **39**, 242–249. [381]

Oltman, J.E., McGarry, J.J., and Friedman, S. (1952) Parental deprivation and the "broken home" in dementia praecox and other mental disorders. *Am. J. Psychiatr.* **108,** 685–694. [395]

Oltmans, G.A., Lorden, J.F., and Margules, D.L. (1977) Food intake and body weight: Effects of specific and non-specific lesions in the midbrain path of the ascending noradrenergic neurons of the rat. *Brain Res.* **128,** 293–303. [196]

Onodera, K., Ogura, Y., and Kisara, K. (1981) Characteristics of muricide induced by thiamine deficiency and its suppression by antidepressants or intraventricular serotonin. *Physiol. Behav.* **27,** 847–853. [291]

Oppenheimer, G., Ebstein, R., and Belmaker, R. (1979) Effects of lithium on the physostigmine-induced behavioral syndrome and plasma cyclic GMP. *J. Psychiatr. Res.* **14,** 133–138. [282]

Oreland, L., Wiberg, A., Asberg, M., Traskman, L., Sjostrand, L., Thoren, P., Bertilsson, L., and Tybring, G. (1981) Platelet MAO activity and monoamine metabolites in cerebrospinal fluid in depressed and suicidal patients and in healthy controls. *Psychiatr. Res.* **4,** 21–29. [221, 313]

Orsulak, P.J., Schildkraut, J.J., Schatzberg, A.F., and Herzog, J.M. (1978) Differences in platelet monoamine oxidase activity in subgroups of schizophrenic and depressive disorder. *Biol. Psychiatr.* **13,** 637–647. [221]

Ortmann, R., Martin, S., Radeke, E., and Delina-Stula, E. (1981) Interaction of beta-adrenoceptor agonists with the serotonergic system in rat brain. A behavioral study using the 5-HTP syndrome. *Naunyn Schmiedebergs Arch. Pharmacol.* **316,** 225–230. [343]

Ostrowsky, N.L., Foley, T.L., Lind, M.D., and Reid, L.D. (1980) Naloxone reduced fluid intake: Effects of food and water deprivation. *Pharmacol. Biochem. Behav.* **12,** 431–435. [362]

Overall, J.E., Hollister, L.E., Johnson, M., and Pennington, V. (1966) Nosology of depression and differential response to drugs. *J. Am. Med. Assoc.* **195,** 946–948. [171]

Overmeier, J.B. and Seligman, M.E.P. (1967) Effects of inescapable shock upon subsequent escape and avoidance learning. *J. Comp. Physiol. Psychol.* **78,** 340–343. [121]

Oxenkrug, G.F. (1979) The content and uptake of 5-HT by blood platelets in depressive patients. *J. Neural Trans.* **45,** 285–289. [315]

Padfield, M. (1976) The comparative effects of two counselling approaches on the intensity of depression among rural women of low socioeconomic status. *J. Couns. Psychol.* **23,** 209–214. [67]

Palkovits, M., Brownstein, M., Kizer, J.S., Saavedra, J.M. and Kopin, I.J. (1976) Effect of stress on serotonin and tryptophan hydroxylase activity of brain nuclei. In E. Usdin, R. Kvetnansky, and I.J. Kopin (Eds.), *Catecholamines and Stress.* Pergamon, New York, pp. 51–59. [289]

Palkovits, M., Zaborsky, L., Feminger, A., Mezey, E., Fekete, M.I.K., Herman, J.P., Kanyicska, B., and Szabo, D. (1980) Noradrenergic innervation of the rat hypothalamus: Experimental biochemical and electron microscopic studies. *Brain Res.* **191,** 161–171. [196, 198, 228]

Pandey, G.N., Dysken, M.W., Garver, D.L., and Davis, J.M. (1979a) Beta-adrenergic receptor function in affective illness. *Am. J. Psychiatr.* **136,** 675–678. [218]

Pandey, G.N., Heinze, W.J., Brown, B.D., and Davis, J.M. (1979b) Electroconvulsive shock treatment decreases beta-adrenergic receptor sensitivity in rat brain. *Nature* **280,** 234–235. [257]

Pandey, G.N., Sudershan, P., and Davis, J.M. (1982) Antidepressant treatment and central adrenergic and histamine receptors. *Psychopharmacol. Bull.* **18,** 147–150. [369]

Panksepp, J. (1981) Hypothalamic integration of behavior: Rewards, punishments and related psychological processes. In P.J. Morgane and J. Panksepp (Eds.), *Handbook of the Hypothalamus*, Vol. 3B, Dekker, New York, pp. 289–431. [401]

Panksepp, J., Herman, B.H., Connor, R., Bishop, P., and Scott, J.P. (1978) The biology of social attachments: Opiates alleviate separation distress. *Biol. Psychiatr.* **13**, 607–618. [363, 386]

Panksepp, J., Herman, B.H., Vilberg, T., Bishop, T., and DeEskinazi, F.G. (1980) Endogenous opioids and social behavior. *Neurosci. Biobehav. Rev.* **4**, 473–487. [363, 386]

Papakostas, Y., Lee, J., Johnson, L., and Fink, M. (1980) Neuroendocrine effects of ECT. *Sci. Proc. Soc. Biol. Psychiatr., Abstr.* (3), 35. [53, 54]

Papeschi, R. (1977) The functional pool of brain catecholamines: Its size and turnover rate. *Psychopharmacology* **55**, 1–7. [175]

Papeschi, R. and McClure, D.J., (1971) Homovanillic and 5-hydroxyindoleacetic acid in cerebrospinal fluid of depressed patients. *Arch. Gen. Psychiatr.* **25**, 354–358. [167, 311, 333]

Pare, C.M.B. (1963) Potentiation of monoamine-oxidase inhibitors by tryptophan. *Lancet* **2**, 527–528. [319]

Pare, C.M.B. and Sandler, M. (1959) A clinical and biochemical study of a trial of iproniazid in the treatment of depression. *J. Neurol. Neurosurg. Psychiatr.* **22**, 247–251. [321]

Pare, C.M.B., Young, D.P.H., Price, L., and Stacey, R.S. (1969) 5-hydroxytryptamine, noradrenaline, and dopamine in brainstem, hypothalamus and caudate nucleus of controls and patients committing suicide by coalgas poisoning. *Lancet* **2**, 133–135. [164, 222, 309]

Parkes, C.M. (1972) *Bereavement: Studies of Grief in Adult Life*. International University Press, New York. [81, 133, 141, 392, 397]

Parrott, A.C. and Kentridge, R. (1982) Personal constructs of anxiety under the 1,5-benzodiazepine derivative clobazam related to trait-anxiety levels of the personality. *Psychopharmacology* **78**, 353–357. [27]

Parry, B.L. and Rush, A.J. (1979) Oral contraceptives and depressive symptomatology: Biologic mechanisms. *Compr. Psychiatr.* **20**, 347–358. [267, 308, 399]

Pasahow, R.J. (1980) The relation between an attributional dimension and learned helplessness. *J. Abnorm. Psychol.* **89**, 358–367. [78]

Passarelli, F. and Scotti de Carolis, A. (1982) Effects of chronic treatment with imipramine on the behavioral and electroencephalographic modifications induced by clonidine in the rat. *Neuropharmacology* **21**, 591–593. [245]

Passarelli, F. and Scotti de Carolis, A. (1983) Effects of chronic treatment with imipramine, trazodone and electroshock on the behavioral and electroencephalographic modifications induced by clonidine in the rat. *Neuropharmacology* **22**, 785–789. [245]

Paul, S.M. and Skolnick, P. (1978) Rapid changes in brain benzodiazepine receptors after experimental seizures. *Science* **202**, 892–894. [356]

Paul, S.M., Rehavi, M., Skolnick, P., Ballenger, J.C., and Goodwin, F.K. (1981) Depressed patients have decreased binding of tritiated imipramine to platelet serotonin "transporter". *Arch. Gen. Psychiatr.* **38**, 1315–1317. [316]

Paull, W.K., Scholer, J., Arimura, A., Meyers, C., Chang, J.K., Chang, D., and Shimizu, M. (1982) Immunocytochemical localization of CRF in the ovine hypothalamus. *Peptides* **1**, 183–191. [195]

Pawlowski, L., Stach, R., and Kacz, D. (1982) Chronic treatment with amitriptyline and zimelidine: Attenuation of serotonin-induced changes in the light-evoked responses from the occipital cortex. In S.Z. Langer, R. Takahaski, T. Segawa, and M. Briley (Eds.), *New Vistas in Depression*. Pergamon, New York, pp. 73–80. [337]

Paykel, E.S. (1971) Classification of depressed patients: A cluster analysis derived grouping. *Br. J. Psychiatr.* **118**, 275–288. [57, 124]

Paykel, E.S. (1972) Depressive typologies and response to amitriptyline. *Br. J. Psychiatr.* **120**, 147–156. [11]

Paykel, E.S. (1979a) Predictors of treatment response. In E.S. Paykel and A. Coppen (Eds.), *Psychopharmacology of Affective Disorders.* Oxford University Press, Oxford, pp. 193–220. [58]

Paykel, E.S. (1979b) Recent life events in the development of the depressive disorders. In R.A. Depue (Ed.), *The Psychobiology of the Depressive Disorders: Implications for the Effects of Stress.* Academic, New York, pp. 245–265. [50, 79, 81, 131]

Paykel, E.S. and Coppen, A. (Eds.) (1979) *Psychopharmacology of Affective Disorders.* Oxford University Press, Oxford. [105]

Paykel, E.S., Myers, J., Dienelt, M., Klerman, G., Lindenthal, J.J., and Pepper, M.P. (1969) Life events and depression: A controlled study. *Arch. Gen. Psychiatr.* **21**, 753–760. [50, 392]

Paykel, E.S., Parker, R.R., Penrose, R.J., and Rassaby, E.R. (1979) Depressive classification and prediction of response to phenelzine. *Br. J. Psychiatr.* **134**, 572–581. [221]

Paykel, E.S., Parker, R.R., Rowan, R.R., Rao, B.M., and Taylor, C.N. (1983a) Nosology of atypical depression. *Psychol. Med.* **13**, 131–139. [57]

Paykel, E.S., Rowan, P.R., Rao, B.M., and Bhat, A. (1983b) Atypical depression: Nosology and response to antidepressants. In P.J. Clayton and J.E. Barrett (Eds.), *Treatment of Depression: Old Controversies and New Approaches.* Raven, New York, pp. 247–252. [57, 58]

Payne, R.W. and Hewlett, J.H.G. (1960) Thought disorder in psychotic patients. In H.J. Eysenck (Ed.), *Experiments in Personality,* Vol. 2. Routledge & Kegan Paul, London, pp. 3–104. [64]

Pearce, J.B. (1973) Fenfluramine in mania. *Lancet* **1**, 427. [322]

Pearce, J.B. (1981) Drug treatment of depression in children. *Acta Paedopsychiatr.* **46**, 317–328. [132]

Pearlson, G.D. and Robinson, R.G. (1981) Suction lesions of the frontal cerebral cortex in the rat induce asymmetrical behavioral and catecholaminergic responses. *Brain Res.* **218**, 233–242. [97, 98]

Pearlson, G.D., Kubos, K.L., and Robinson, R.G. (1982) Novel cortical localization of a lateralized behavior in the rat: Relationship to noradrenergic innervation. *Soc. Neurosci. Abstr.* **8**, 894. [97, 98]

Pearse, A.S. (1977) The diffuse neuroendocrine system and the apud concept: related "endocrine" peptides in brain, intestine, pituitary, placenta and anuran cutaneous glands. *Med. Biol.* **55**, 115–125. [370]

Pederson, O.L., Kragh-Sorensen, P., Bjerre, M., Overo, K.F., and Gram, L.F. (1982) Citalopram, a selective serotonin reuptake inhibitor: Clinical antidepressive and long-term effect—A phase II study. *Psychopharmacology* **77**, 199–204. [323]

Pedigo, N.W. and Dewey, W.L. (1981) Comparison of the antinociceptive activity of intraventricularly administered acetylcholine to narcotic antinociception. *Neurosci. Lett.* **26**, 85–90. [276]

Pedigo, N.W., Dewey, W.L., and Harris, L.S. (1975) Determination and characterization of the anti-nociceptive activity of intraventricularly administered acetylcholine in mice. *J. Pharmacol. Exp. Ther.* **193**, 845–852. [276]

Penn, P.E., McBride, W.J., Hintgen, J.N., and Aprison, M.H. (1977) Differential uptake, metabolism and behavioral effects of the D and L isomers of 5-hydroxytryptophan. *Pharmacol. Biochem. Behav.* **7**, 515–518. [301]

Peroutka, S.J. and Synder, S.H. (1980a) Long-term antidepressant treatment decreases spiroperodol-labelled serotonin receptor binding. *Science* **210**, 88–90. [190, 255, 257, 266, 285, 347, 348]

Peroutka, S.J. and Synder, S.H. (1980b) Regulation of serotonin$_2$ (5-HT$_2$) receptors labelled with [^{3}H] spiroperidol by chronic treatment with the antidepressant amitriptyline. *J. Pharmacol. Exp. Ther.* **215**, 582–586. [247, 257, 348]

Peroutka, S.J. and Synder, S.H. (1981a) Interactions of antidepressants with neurotransmitter receptor sites. In S.J. Enna, J.B. Malick, and E. Richelson (Eds.), *Antidepressants: Neurochemical, Behavioral and Clinical Perspectives*. Raven, New York, pp. 75–90. [242, 284, 368]

Peroutka, S.J. and Synder, S.H. (1981b) Two distinct serotonin receptors: Regional variations in receptor binding in mammalian brain. *Brain Res.* **208**, 339–347. [330, 344]

Peroutka, S.J. and Synder, S.H. (1982) Recognition of multiple serotonin receptor binding sites. In B.T. Ho, J.C. Schoolar, and E. Usdin (Eds.), *Serotonin in Biological Psychiatry*. Raven, New York, pp. 155–172. [330, 331, 344, 345]

Peroutka, S.J., Lebovitz, R.M., and Synder, S.H. (1981) Two distinct central serotonin receptors with different physiological functions. *Science* **212**, 827–829. [330, 345]

Perris, C. (1966) A study of bipolar (manic-depressive) and unipolar recurrent depressive psychoses. *Acta Psychiatr. Scand.* **42**, (Suppl. 194), 1–188. [45]

Perris, C. (1975) The bipolar-unipolar dichotomy and the need for a consistent terminology. *Neuropsychology* **1**, 65–69. [47]

Perris, C. and Monakhov, K. (1979) Depressive symptomatology and systemic structural analysis of the EEG. In J.H. Gruzelier and P. Flor-Henry (Eds.), *Hemispheric Asymmetries of Function and Psychopathology*. Elsevier, Amsterdam, pp. 223–236. [88]

Perris, C., Jacobsson, L, Von Knorring, L., Oreland, L., Perris, H., and Ross, S.B. (1980) Enzymes related to biogenic amine metabolism and personality characteristics in depressed patients. *Acta Psychiatr. Scand.* **61**, 477–484. [313]

Perry, E.K., Gibson, P.H., Blessed, G., Perry, R.H., and Tomlinson, B.E. (1977) Neurotransmitter enzyme abnormalities in senile dementia: Choline acetyltransferase and glutamic acid decarboxylase activities in necropsy brain tissue. *J. Neurol. Sci.* **34**, 247–265. [355]

Perry, E.K., Marshall, E.F., Blessed, G., Tomlinson, B.E., and Perry, R.H. (1983) Decreased imipramine binding in the brains of patients with depressive illness. *Br. J. Psychiatr.* **142**, 188–192. [315, 317]

Perry, G.F., Fitzsimmons, B., Shapiro, L., and Irwin, P. (1978) Clinical study of mianserin, imipramine and placebo in depression: Blood level and MHPG correlations. *Br. J. Clin. Pharmacol.* **5**, 35S–41S. [250, 251]

Pert, C. and Synder, S. (1973) Opiate receptor: Demonstration in nervous tissue. *Science* **179**, 1011–1014. [360]

Peselow, E.D., Fieve, R.R., Goldring, N., Wright, R., and Deutsch, S.I. (1983a) The DST and clinical symptoms in predicting response to tricyclic antidepressants. *Psychopharmacol. Bull.* **19**, 642–645. [237]

Peselow, E.D., Goldring, N., Fieve, R.R., and Wright, R. (1983b) The dexamethasone suppression test in depressed outpatients and normal control subjects. *Am. J. Psychiatr.* **140**, 245–247. [54]

Peterfy, G., Pinter, E.J., and Pattee, C.J. (1976) Psychosomatic aspects of catecholamine depletion: Comparative aspects of metabolic, endocrine and affective changes. *Psychoneuroendocrinology* **1**, 243–253. [110, 169]

Petersen, M.R., Beecher, M.D., Zoloth, S.R., Moody, D.B., and Stebbins, W.C. (1978) Neural lateralization of species-specific vocalizations by Japanese macaques (Macaca fuscata). *Science* **202**, 324–327. [97]

Peterson, C., Luborsky, L., and Seligman, M.E.P. (1983) Attributions and depressive mood shifts: A case study using the symptom-context method. *J. Abnorm. Psychol.* **92**, 96–103. [78]

Petrides, M. and Milner, B. (1982) Deficits on subject-ordered tasks after frontal- and temporal-lobe lesions in man. *Neuropsychology* **20**, 249–262. [93]

Petrie, W.M., Maffucci, R.J., and Woolsley, R.L. (1982) Propranolol and depression. *Am. J. Psychiatr.* **139**, 92–94. [231]

Petty, F. and Schlesser, M.A. (1981) Plasma GABA in affective illness: A preliminary investigation. *J. Affect. Disord.* **3**, 339–343. [355]

Petty, F. and Sherman, A.D. (1980) Reversal of learned helplessness by imipramine. *Commun. Psychopharmacol.* **3**, 371–373. [122]

Petty, F. and Sherman, A.D. (1981) GABAergic modulation of learned helplessness. *Pharmacol. Biochem. Behav.* **15**, 567–570. [654]

Petty, F. and Sherman, A.D. (1983) Learned helplessness induction decreases in vivo cortical serotonin release. *Pharmacol. Biochem. Behav.* **18**, 649–650. [290]

Peyrin, L. and Pequignot, J.M. (1983) Free and conjugated 3-methoxy-4-hydroxyphenylglycol in human urine: Peripheral origin of glucuronide. *Psychopharmacology* **79**, 16–20. [224, 226, 227]

Pfaffman, C. (1960) The pleasures of sensation. *Psychol. Rev.* **67**, 253–268. [402]

Pfohl, B., Vasquez, N., and Nasrullah, H. (1982) Unipolar versus bipolar mania: A review of 247 patients. *Br. J. Psychiatr.* **141**, 453–458. [45]

Phillips, A.G. and LePiane, F.G. (1980) Reinforcing effects of morphine microinjection into the ventral tegmental area. *Pharmacol. Biochem. Behav.* **12**, 965–968. [361]

Phillips, A.G., Carter, D.A., and Fibiger, H.C. (1976a) Dopaminergic substrates of intracranial self-stimulation in the caudate-putamen. *Brain Res.* **104**, 221–232. [150]

Phillips, A.G., Carter, D.A., and Fibiger, H.C. (1976b) Differential effects of para-chlorophenylalanine on self-stimulation in caudate-putamen and lateral hypothalamus. *Psychopharmacology* **49**, 23–28. [304]

Phillips, A.G., Van Der Kooy, D., and Fibiger, H.C. (1977) Maintenance of intra-cranial self-stimulation in hippocampus and olfactory bulb after regional depletion of noradrenaline. *Neurosci. Lett.* **4**, 77–84. [199]

Phillips, A.G., Spyraki, C., and Fibiger, H.C. (1982) Conditioned place preference with amphetamine and opiates as reward stimuli: Attenuation by haloperidol. In B.G. Hoebel and D. Novin (Eds.), *The Neural Basis of Feeding and Reward.* Haer Institute, Brunswick, Me., pp. 455–464. [361]

Physicians Desk Reference, 36th ed. (1982). Medical Economics, Oradell, N. J. [105]

Pickar, D., Sweeney, D.R., Maas, J.W., and Heninger, G.R. (1978) Primary affective disorder, clinical state change, and MHPG excretion: a longitudinal study. *Arch. Gen. Psychiatr.* **35**, 1378–1383. [225]

Pickar, D., Cohen, R.M., Murphy, D.L., and Fried, D. (1979) Tyramine infusions in bipolar illness: Behavioral effects and longitudinal changes in pressor sensitivity. *Am. J. Psychiatr.* **136**, 1460–1463. [218]

Pickar, D., Cutler, N.R., Naber, D., Post, R.J., Pert, C.B., and Bunney, W.E. (1980a) Plasma opioid activity in manic-depressive illness. *Lancet* **1**, 937. [364]

Pickar, D., Lake, C., Cohen, M., Jimerson, D.C., and Murphy, D.L. (1980b) Alterations in noradrenergic function during clorgyline treatment. *Commun. Psychopharmacol.* **4**, 379–386. [254]

Pickar, D., Davis, G.C., Schultz, S.C., Extein, I., Wagner, R., Naber, D., Gold, P.W., van Kammen, D.P., Goodwin, F.K., Wyatt, R.J., Li, C.H., and Bunney, W.E. (1981) Behavioral and biological effects of acute beta-endorphin injection in depressed and schizophrenic patients. *Am. J. Psychiatr.* **138**, 160–166. [365]

Pickar, D., Cohen, M.R., Naber, D., and Cohen, R.M. (1982a) Clinical studies of the endogenous opioid system. *Biol. Psychiatr.* **17**, 1243–1276. [364–366]

Pickar, D., Extein, I., Gold, P.W., Naber, D., Summers, R.S., and Goodwin, F.K. (1982b) Endorphins in affective disorders. In N.S. Shah and A.G. Donald (Eds.), *Endorphins and Opiate Antagonists in Psychiatric Illness*. Plenum, New York, pp. 375–397. [366]

Pickar, D., Naber, D., Post, R.M., van Kammen, D., Kaye, W., Rubinow, D.R., Ballenger, J.C., and Bunney, W.E. (1983) Endorphins in the cerebrospinal fluid of psychiatric patients. *Ann. N.Y. Acad. Sci.* **398**, 399–411. [364]

Pijnenburg, A.J.J. and Van Rossum, J.M. (1973) Stimulation of locomotor activity following injection of dopamine into the nucleus accumbens. *J. Pharm. Pharmacol.* **25**, 1003–1004. [149]

Pilc, A. and Rokosz-Pelc, A. (1983) The attenuation by chronic electroconvulsive treatment of hypothermia induced by histamine H_2-receptor stimulants in rats. *Eur. J. Pharmacol.* **88**, 255–257. [369]

Pilc, A. and Vetulani, J. (1982) Attenuation by chronic imipramine treatment of [^{3}H] clonidine binding to cortical membranes and of clonidine-induced hypothermia: The influence of central chemosympathectomy. *Brain Res.* **238**, 499–504. [244, 247]

Pilowsky, I. and Bassett, D.L. (1982) Pain and depression. *Br. J. Psychiatr.* **141**, 30–36. [69]

Pimoule, C., Briley, M.S., Gay, C., Loo, H., Sechter, D., Zarifian, E., Raisman, R., and Langer, S.Z. (1983) ^{3}H-rauwolscine binding in platelets from depressed patients and healthy volunteers. *Psychopharmacology* **79**, 308–312. [219, 248]

Pinder, R.M., Brogden, R.N., Speight, T.M., and Avery, G.S. (1977) Viloxazine: A review of its pharmacological properties and therapeutic efficacy in depressive illness. *Drugs* **13**, 401–421. [235]

Pinto-Hamuy, T. and Linck, P. (1965) Effect of frontal lesions on performance of sequential tasks by monkeys. *Exp. Neurol.* **12**, 96–107. [94]

Pirch, J.H. (1969) Behavior "recovery" during chronic reserpine treatment: Effect of dose of reserpine. *Psychopharmacology* **16**, 253–260. [169]

Pisa, M. and Fibiger, H.C. (1980) Noradrenaline and discrimination learning: Failure to support the attentional hypothesis. *Soc. Neurosci. Abstr.* **6**, 724. [204]

Pisa, M., Martin-Iverson, M.T., and Fibiger, H.C. (1981) Noradrenaline, extinction, and spatial alternation learning. *Soc. Neurosci. Abstr.* **7**, 342. [204]

Platt, J.E. and Stone, E.A. (1982) Chronic restraint stress elicits a positive antidepressant response on the forced swim test. *Eur. J. Pharmacol.* **82**, 179–181. [210, 412]

Plaznik, A., Danysz, W., Kostowski, W., Bidzinski, A., and Hauptmann, M. (1983) Interaction between noradrenergic and serotonergic brain systems as evidenced by behavioral and biochemical effects of microinjections of adrenergic agonists and antagonists into the median raphe nucleus. *Pharmacol. Biochem. Behav.* **19**, 27–32. [377]

Plenge, P. and Mellerup, E.T. (1982) ^{3}H-Imipramine high-affinity sites in rat brain. Effects of imipramine and lithium. *Psychopharmacology* **77**, 94–97. [332]

Pletscher, A. and Gey, K.F. (1963) The effect of a new decarboxylase inhibitor on endogenous and exogenous monoamines. *Biochem. Pharmacol.* **12**, 223–228. [301]

Pletscher, A., Shore, P.A., and Brodie, B.B. (1956) Serotonin as a mediator of reserpine action in the brain. *J. Pharmacol.* **116**, 84–89. [9]

Pohl, W. (1973) Dissociation of spatial discrimination deficits following frontal and parietal lesions in monkeys. *J. Comp. Physiol. Psychol.* **82**, 227–239. [94]

Polivy, J. and Doyle, C. (1980) Laboratory induction of mood states through the reading of self-referent mood statements: Affective changes or demand characteristics. *J. Abnorm. Psychol.* **89**, 286–290. [72]

Pollard, H., Llorens-Cortes, C., and Schwartz, J.C. (1977) Enkephalin receptors on dopaminergic neurones in rat striatum. *Nature* **268**, 745–747. [361]

Polleri, A., Murialdo, G., and Masturzo, P. (1979) Spontaneous prolactin secretory pattern in depressive patients. In E.E. Muller and A. Agnoli (Eds.), *Neuroendocrine Correlates in Neurology and Psychiatry.* Elsevier, Amsterdam, pp. 255–261. [166]

Pope, B., Blass, T., Siegman, A.W., and Raher, J. (1970) Anxiety and depression in speech. *J. Consult. Clin. Psychol.* **35**, 128–133. [64]

Popper, K.R. and Eccles, J.C. (1977) *The Self and Its Brain.* Springer, New York. [28]

Porsolt, R.D. (1981) Behavioral despair. In S.J. Enna, J.B. Malick, and E. Richelson (Eds.), *Antidepressants: Neurochemical, Behavioral and Clinical Perspectives.* Raven, New York, pp. 121–139. [127–129, 212, 290]

Porsolt, R.D., Bertin, A., and Jalfre, M. (1977a) Behavioral despair in mice: A primary screening test for antidepressants. *Arch. Int. Pharmacodyn.* **229**, 327–336. [127, 128, 213]

Porsolt, R.D., LePichon, M., and Jalfre, M. (1977b) Depression: A new animal model sensitive to antidepressant treatment. *Nature* **266**, 730–732. [127, 128, 213]

Porsolt, R.D., Anton, G., Blavet, N., and Jalfre, M. (1978a) Behavioral despair in rats, a new model sensitive to antidepressant treatments. *Eur. J. Pharmacol.* **47**, 379–391. [127, 290]

Porsolt, R.D., Bertin, A., and Jalfre, M. (1978b) Behavioral despair in rats and mice: Strain differences and the effects of imipramine. *Eur. J. Pharmacol.* **51**, 291–294. [127, 140]

Porsolt, R.D., Bertin, A., Blavet, M., Deniel, M., and Jalfre, M. (1979) Immobility induced by forced swimming in rats: Effects of agents which modify central catecholamine and serotonin activity. *Eur. J. Pharmacol.* **57**, 201–210. [127, 128, 157, 211, 212, 290]

Poschel, B.P.H. and Ninteman, F.W. (1968) Excitatory effects of 5-HTP on intracranial self-stimulation following MAO blockade. *Life Sci.* **7**, 317–323. [304]

Poschel, B.P.H. and Ninteman, F.W. (1971) Intracranial reward and the forebrain's serotonergic mechanism: Studies employing para-chloro-phenyl-alanine and para-chloroamphetamine. *Physiol. Behav.* **7**, 39–46. [301]

Post, R.M. and Goodwin, F.K. (1974) Effects of amitriptyline and imipramine on amine metabolites in the cerebrospinal fluid of depressed patients. *Arch. Gen. Psychiatr.* **30**, 234–239. [333]

Post, R.M. and Goodwin, F.K. (1978) Approaches to brain amines in psychiatric patients: A reevaluation of cerebrospinal fluid studies. In L.L. Iversen, S.D. Iversen, and S.H. Snyder (Eds.), *Handbook of Psychopharmacology*, Vol. 13. Plenum, New York, pp. 147–185. [322]

Post, R.M. and Uhde, T.W. (1982) Biological relationships between mania and melancholia. *L'Encéphale* **8**, 213–228. [355, 356]

Post, R.M., Gordon, E.K., Goodwin, F.K., and Bunney, W.E. (1973a) Central norepinephrine metabolism in affective illness: MHPG in the cerebrospinal fluid. *Science* **179**, 1002–1003. [222]

Post, R.M., Goodwin, F.K., Gordon, E.K., and Watkin, D.M. (1973b) Amine metabolism in human cerebrospinal fluid: Effects of cord transection and spinal fluid block. *Science* **179**, 897–899. [223]

Post, R.M., Kotin, J., Goodwin, F.K., and Gordon, E.K. (1973c) Psychomotor activity and cerebrospinal fluid amine metabolites in affective illness. *Am. J. Psychiatr.* **130**, 67–72. [168, 176, 311]

Post, R.M., Stoddard, F.J., Gillin, J.C., Buchsbaum, M., Runkle, D.C., Black, K.E., and Bunney, W.E. (1977) Slow and rapid alterations in motor activity, sleep, and biochemistry in a cycling manic-depressive patient. *Arch. Gen. Psychiatr.* **34,** 470–477. [225, 226]

Post, R.M., Gerner, R.H., Carman, J.S., Gillin, J.C., Jimerson, D.C., Goodwin, F.K., and Bunney, W.E. (1978a) Effects of a dopamine agonist piribedil in depressed patients. *Arch. Gen. Psychiatr.* **35,** 609–615. [174, 177]

Post, R.M., Lake, C.R., Jimerson, D.C., Bunney, W.E., Wood, J.H., Ziegler, M.G., and Goodwin, F.K. (1978b) CSF norepinephrine in affective illness. *Am. J. Psychiatr.* **135,** 907–917. [223]

Post, R.M., Ballenger, J.C., Hare, T.A., Goodwin, F.K., Lake, C.R., Jimerson, D.C., and Bunney, W.E. (1980a) Cerebrospinal fluid GABA in normals and patients with affective disorders. *Brain Res. Bull.* **5,** 755–759. [355, 357]

Post, R.M., Jimerson, D.C., Bunney, W.E., and Goodwin, F.K. (1980b) Dopamine and mania: Behavioral and biochemical effects of the dopamine blocker pimozide. *Psychopharmacology* **67,** 297–305. [191]

Post, R.M., Ballenger, J.C., Jimerson, D.C., Gold, P.W., Goodwin, F.K., Rubinow, D.R., and Bunney, W.E. (1981a) Cerebrospinal fluid amines and peptides in affective illness. In B. Angrist, G.D. Burrows, M. Lader, O. Lingjaerde, G. Sedvall, and D. Wheatley (Eds.), *Recent Advances in Neuropsychopharmacology.* Pergamon, New York, pp. 275–282. [223, 227, 236]

Post, R.M., Bunney, W.E., Van Kammen, D.P., Ballenger, J.C., Lake, C.R., Lerner, P., Sternberg, D.E., Uhde, T.W., and Goodwin, F.K. (1981b) Cerebrospinal fluid norepinephrine and dopamine-beta-hydroxylase in affective illness and schizophrenia. In B. Angrist, G.D. Burrows, M. Lader, O. Lingjaerde, G. Sedvall, and D. Wheatley (Eds.), *Recent Advances in Neuropharmacology.* Pergamon, Oxford, pp. 283–287. [223]

Post, R.M., Ballenger, J.C., Uhde, T.W., Smith, C., Rubinow, D.R., and Bunney, W.E. (1982) Effect of carbamazepine on cyclic nucleotides in CSF of patients with affective illness. *Biol. Psychiatr.* **17,** 1037–1045. [355]

Post, R.M., Uhde, T.W., Rubinow, D.R., Ballenger, J.C., and Gold, P.W. (1983) Biochemical effects of carbamazepine: Relationship to its mechanisms of action in affective illness. *Prog. Neuropsychopharmacol.* **7,** 263–271. [355]

Potter, C.D., Borer, K.T., and Katz, R.J. (1982) Opiate-receptor blockade reduces voluntary running but not self-stimulation in hamsters. *Soc. Neurosci. Abstr.* **8,** 777. [363]

Potter, W.Z., Calil, H.M., Extein, I., Gold, P.W., Wehr, T.A., and Goodwin, F.K. (1981) Specific norepinephrine and serotonin uptake inhibitors in man: A crossover study with pharmacokinetic, biochemical, neuroendocrine and behavioral parameters. *Acta Psychiatr. Scand.* **63,** (suppl. 290), 152–165. [251]

Poznanski, E.O. (1982) The clinical phenomenology of childhood depression. *Am. J. Orthopsychiatr.* **52,** 308–313. [133]

Pozuelo, J. and Kerr, F.W.L. (1972) Suppression of craving and other signs of dependence in morphine-addicted monkeys by administration of alpha-methyl-para-tyrosine. *Mayo Clin. Proc.* **47,** 621–628. [151]

Pradhan, S.N. and Bose, S. (1978) Interactions among central neurotransmitters. In M.A. Lipton, A. DiMascio, and K.F. Killam (Eds.) *Psychopharmacology: A Generation of Progress.* Raven, New York, pp. 271–291. [377, 379, 380]

Pradhan, S.N. and Dutta, S.N. (1971) Central cholinergic mechanisms and behavior. *Int. Rev. Neurobiol.* **14,** 173–231. [271]

Prange, A.J. (1977) Patterns of pituitary responses to thyrotropin-releasing hormone in depressed patients: A review. In W.E. Fann, A. Kazacan, and N.L. Pokorny (Eds.), *Phenomenology and Treatment of Depression.* Spectrum, New York, pp. 1–15. [372]

Prange, A.J., McCurdy, R.L., and Cochrane, C.M. (1967) The systolic blood pressure response of depressed patients to infused norepinephrine. *J. Psychiatr. Res.* **5**, 1–13. [218]

Prange, A.J., Wilson, I.C., Lana, P.P., Alltop, L.B., and Breese, G.R. (1972) Effects of thyrotropin-releasing hormone in depression. *Lancet* **2**, 999–1002. [371]

Prange, A.J., Wilson, I.C., Lynn, C.W., Alltop, L.B., and Stikeleather, R.A. (1974) L-tryptophan in mania. *Arch. Gen. Psychiatr.* **30**, 56–62. [17, 320, 417]

Prange, A.J., Wilson, I.C., Breese, G.R., and Lipton, M.A. (1976) Hormonal alteration of imipramine response: A review. In E.J. Sachar (Ed.), *Hormones, Behavior and Psychopathology.* Raven, New York, pp. 41–67. [371, 373]

Premack, D. (1959) Toward empirical behavioral laws: I. Positive reinforcement. *Psychol. Rev.* **66**, 219–233. [402]

Pribram, K.H. and Tubbs, W.E. (1967) Short-term memory, parsing, and the primate frontal cortex. *Science* **156**, 1765–1767. [94]

Pribram, K.H., Ahmuda, A., Hartog, J., and Ross, L. (1964) A progress report on the neurological processes disturbed by frontal lesions in primates. In J.M. Warren and K. Akert (Eds.), *The Frontal Granular Cortex and Behavior.* McGraw-Hill, New York, pp. 28–55. [94]

Pribram, K.H., Plotkin, H.C., Anderson, R.M., and Leong, D. (1977) Information sources in the delayed alternation task for normal and "frontal" monkeys. *Neuropsychology* **15**, 329–340. [94]

Price, J. (1967) The dominance hierarchy and the evolution of mental illness. *Lancet* **2**, 243–246. [214]

Price, J.L. and Amaral, D.G. (1981) An autoradiographic study of the projections of the central nucleus of the monkey amydala. *J. Neurosci.* **1**, 1242–1259. [196]

Price, K.P., Tryon, W.W., and Raps, C.S. (1978) Learned helplessness and depression in a clinical population: a test of two behavioral hypotheses. *J. Abnorm. Psychol.* **87**, 113–121. [76, 126]

Prien, R.F., Caffey, E.M. (1977) Long-term maintenance in drug therapy in recurrent affective illness: Current status and issues. *Dis. Nerv. Syst.* **38**, 981–992. [46]

Prociuk, T.J., Breen, L.J., and Lussier, R.J. (1976) Hopelessness, internal-external locus of control, and depression. *J. Clin. Psychol.* **32**, 299–300. [72]

Prosen, M., Clark, D.C., Harrow, M., and Fawcett, J. (1983) Guilt and conscience in major depressive disorders. *Am. J. Psychiatr.* **140**, 839–840. [63]

Proudfit, H.K. and Anderson, E.G. (1975) Morphine analgesia: Blockade by raphe magnus lesions. *Brain Res.* **98**, 612–618. [299, 359]

Przegalinski, E., Kordecka-Magiera, A., Mogilnicka, E., and Maj, J. (1981) Chronic treatment with some atypical antidepressants increases the brain level of 3-methoxy-4-hydroxyphenylglycol (MHPG) in rats. *Psychopharmacology* **74**, 187–190. [249, 250]

Przegalinski, E., Baran, L., and Siwanowicz, J. (1983) The effect of chronic treatment with antidepressant drugs on salbutamol-induced hypoactivity in rats. *Psychopharmacology* **80**, 355–359. [258]

Psychoyos, S. (1981) Antidepressant inhibition of H_1- and H_2-histamine-receptor-mediated adenylate cyclase in (2-^{3}H)adenine-prelabelled vesicular preparations from guinea pig brain. *Biochem. Pharmacol.* **30**, 2182–2185. [369]

Puhringe, W., Wirz-Justice, A., Graw, P., Lacoste, V., and Gastpar, M. (1976) Intravenous L-5-hydroxytryptophan in normal subjects: An interdisciplinary precursor preloading study. I. Implications of reproducible mood elevation. *Pharmakopsychiatria.* **9**, 260–268. [320]

Puzynski, S., Bidzinski, A., Hauptmann, M., Rode, A., Jakimov-Venulet, B., and Zaluska, M. (1979) Peripheral metabolism of indoleamines and catecholamines in endogenous depressive syndrome. *Aggressologie* **20,** 245–251. [310]

Puzynski, S., Bidzinski, A., and Hauptmann, M. (1980) Correlations between the urinary levels of biogenous amines and their metabolites in patients with endogeous depression before and after treatment. *Psychiatr. Pol.* **14,** 457–463. [224, 225]

Puzynski, S., Rode, A., and Zaluska, M. (1983a) Studies on biogenic amine metabolizing enzymes (DBH, COMT, MAO) and pathogenesis of affective illness. I. Plasma dopamine-beta-hydroxylase activity in endogenous depression. *Acta Psychiatr. Scand.* **67,** 89–95. [220]

Puzynski, S., Bidzinski, A., Mrozek, S., and Zaluska, M. (1983b) Studies on biogenic amine metabolizing enzymes (DBH, COMT, MAO) and pathogenesis of affective illness. II. Erythrocyte catechol-O-methyltransferase activity in endogenous depression. *Acta Psychiatr. Scand.* **67,** 96–100. [220, 221]

Puzynski, S., Hauptmann, M., and Zaluska, M. (1983c) Studies on biogenic amine metabolizing enzymes (DBH, COMT, MAO) and pathogenesis of affective illness. III. Platelet monoamine oxidase activity in endogenous depression. *Acta Psychiatr. Scand.* **67,** 101–108. [221]

Quineaux, N., Scuvee-Moreau, J., and Dresse, A. (1982) Inhibition of in vitro and ex vivo uptake of noradrenaline and 5-hydroxytryptamine by five antidepressants: Correlation with reduction of spontaneous firing rate of central monaminergic neurons. *Naunyn Schmiedebergs Arch. Pharmacol.* **319,** 66–70. [241, 329]

Quinton, R.M. (1963) The increase in the toxicity of yohimbine induced by imipramine and other drugs in mice. *Br. J. Pharmacol.* **21,** 51–66. [106]

Quitkin, F., Rifkin, A., and Klein, D.F. (1979) Monoamine oxidase inhibitors: A review of antidepressant effectiveness. *Arch. Gen. Psychiatr.* **36,** 749–760. [57, 221]

Quitkin, F.M., Schwartz, D., Liebowitz, M.R., Stewart, J.R., McGrath, P.J., Harrison, W., Halpern, F., Puig-Antoch, K., Tricamo, E., Sachar, E.J., and Klein, D.F. (1983) Atypical depressives: A preliminary report of antidepressant response, sleep patterns, and cortisol secretion. In P.J. Clayton and J.E. Barrett (Eds.), *Treatment of Depression: Old Controversies and New Approaches.* Raven, New York, pp. 253–263. [57]

Racagni, G., Moccetti, I., Calderini, G., Battistella, A., and Brunello, N. (1983) Temporal sequence of changes in rat central noradrenergic system of rat after prolonged antidepressant treatment: Receptor desensitization and neurotransmitter interactions. *Neuropharmacology* **22,** 415–424. [249, 250, 332]

Rackensperger, W., Fritsch, W., Schwartz, D., Stutte, K.H., and Von Zerssen, D. (1976) Wirkung des Beta-Rezeptoren-Blockers Propranolol auf Manie. *Arch. Psychiatr. Nervenkr.* **222,** 223–243. [356]

Radulovacki, M. and Micovic, N. (1982) Effects of REM sleep deprivation and desipramine on beta-adrenergic binding sites in rat brain. *Brain Res.* **235,** 393–396. [257]

Raichle, M.E., Hartman, B.K., Eichling, J.O., and Sharpe, L.G. (1975) Central noradrenergic regulation of cerebral blood flow and vascular permeability. *Proc. Natl. Acad. Sci. USA* **72,** 3726–3730. [198]

Raisman, R., Briley, M., and Langer, S.Z. (1979a) High affinity ^{3}H-imipramine binding in rat cerebral cortex. *Eur. J. Pharmacol.* **54,** 307–308. [249, 316]

Raisman, R., Briley, M., and Langer, S.Z. (1979b) Specific tricyclic antidepressant binding sites in rat brain. *Nature* **281,** 148–150. [249, 316]

Raisman, R., Briley, M.S., Bouchami, F., Sechter, D., Zarifian, E., and Langer, S.Z. (1982) ^{3}H-imipramine binding and serotonin uptake in platelets from untreated patients and control volunteers. *Psychopharmacology* **77,** 332–335. [316]

Raiteri, M., Maura, G., and Versace, P. (1983a) Functional evidence for two stereochemically different alpha$_2$-adrenoceptors regulating central norepinephrine and serotonin release. *J. Pharmacol. Exp. Ther.* **224,** 679–684. [252]

Raiteri, M., Marchi, M., and Maura, G. (1983b) Chronic drug treatments induce changes in the sensitivity of presynaptic autoreceptors but not of presynaptic heteroreceptors. *Eur. J. Pharmacol.* **91,** 141–142. [244, 249, 252, 280]

Ramsey, T.A. and Mendels, J. (1981) Lithium ion as an antidepressant. In S.J. Enna, J.B. Malick, and E. Richelson (Eds.), *Antidepressants: Neurochemical, Behavioral and Clinical Perspectives.* Raven, New York, pp. 175–182. [191, 332, 343]

Randic, M. and Yu, H.H. (1976) Effects of 5-hydroxytryptamine and bradykinin in cat dorsal horn neurones activated by noxious stimuli. *Brain Res.* **111,** 197–203. [298]

Randrup, A. and Braestrup, C. (1977) Uptake inhibition of biogenic amines by newer antidepressant drugs: Relevance to the dopamine hypothesis of depression. *Psychopharmacology* **53,** 309–314. [181, 233, 240, 328, 329]

Randrup, A., Munkvad, J., Fog, R., Gerlach, J., Molander, L., Kjellberg, B., and Scheel-Kruger, J. (1975) Mania, depression and brain dopamine. In W.B. Essman and L. Valzelli (Eds.), *Current Developments in Psychopharmacology,* Vol. 2. Spectrum, New York, pp. 206–248. [9, 17, 163, 167, 170–173, 181, 417]

Raps, C.S., Reinhard, K.E., and Seligman, M.E.P. (1980) Reversal of cognitive and affective deficits associated with depression and learned helplessness by mood elevation in patients. *J. Abnorm. Psychol.* **89,** 342–349. [68, 76, 126]

Raps, C.S., Peterson, C., Reinhard, K.E., Abramson, L.Y., and Seligman, M.E.P. (1982) Attributional style among depressed patients. *J. Abnorm. Psychol.* **91,** 102–108. [78]

Raskin, A. and Crook, T.H. (1976) The endogenous-neurotic distinction as a predictor of response to antidepressant drugs. *Psychol. Med.* **6,** 59–70. [57, 171]

Raskin, A., Schulterbrandt, J.G., Reatig, N., and McKeon, J.J. (1970) Differential response to chlorpromazine, imipramine and placebo—A study of subgroups of hospitalized patients. *Arch. Gen. Psychiatr.* **23,** 164–173. [171]

Rausch, J., Janowsky, D., Risch, S.C., Huey, L., and Swanson, G. (1982) Physostigmine effect on platelet serotonin uptake. In B.T. Ho, J.C. Schoolar, and E. Usdin (Eds.), *Serotonin in Biological Psychiatry.* Raven, New York, pp. 326–327. [315, 325]

Ravaris, C.L., Nies, A., Robinson, D.S., Ives, J.O., Lambourn, K.R., and Korson, L. (1976) A multiple dose, controlled study of phenelzine in depression anxiety states. *Arch. Gen. Psychiatr.* **33,** 347–350. [11, 221]

Ravaris, C.L., Robinson, D.S., Ives, J., Nies, A., and Bartlett, D. (1980) Phenelzine and amitriptyline in the treatment of depression. *Arch. Gen. Psychiatr.* **37,** 1075–1080. [58]

Reader, T.A., Ferron, A., Descarries, L, and Jasper, H.H. (1979) Modulatory role for biogenic amines in the cerebral cortex: Microiontophoretic studies. *Brain Res.* **160,** 217–229. [381]

Reches, A., Wagner, H.R., Barkai, A.I., Jackson, V., Yablouskaya-Alter, E., and Fahn, S. (1984) Electroconvulsive treatment and haloperidol: Effects on pre- and post-synaptic dopamine receptors in rat brain. *Psychopharmacology* **83,** 155–158. [185, 190]

Redmond, D.E., Maas, J.W., Kling, A., and Dekirmenjian, H. (1971) Changes in primate social behavior after treatment with alpha-methyl-para-tyrosine. *Psychosom. Med.* **33,** 97–113. [291]

Redmond, D.E., Huang, Y.H., Snyder, D.H., and Maas, J.W. (1976) Behavioral effects of stimulation of the nucleus locus coeruleus in the stump-tailed monkey (Macaca arctoides). *Brain Res.* **116,** 502–510. [203]

Reebye, P.N. Yiptong, C., Samsoon, J., Schulzinger, F., and Fabricius, J. (1982) A controlled double-blind study of femoxetine and amitriptyline in patients with endogenous depression. *Pharmakopsychiatria* **15,** 164–169. [323]

Rees, L., Butler, B.W.P., Gosling, C., and Besser, G.M. (1970) Adrenergic blockade and the corticosteroid and growth hormone responses to methylamphetamine. *Nature* **228,** 565–566. [229]

Rehavi, M., Paul, S.M., Skolnick, P., and Goodwin, F.K. (1980a) Demonstration of high affinity binding sites for ^{3}H-imipramine in human brain. *Life Sci.* **26,** 2273–2279. [316]

Rehavi, M., Ramot, O., Yavetz, B., Pert, A., and Bunney, W.E. (1980b) Amitriptyline: Long-term treatment elevates alpha-adrenergic and muscarinic receptor binding in mouse brain. *Brain Res.* **194,** 443–453. [190, 255, 285]

Rehavi, M., Skolnick, P., Brownstein, M.J. and Paul, S.M. (1982) High-affinity binding of [^{3}H]desipramine to rat brain: A presynaptic marker for NA uptake sites. *J. Neurochem.* **38,** 889–895. [249]

Rehavi, M., Skolnick, P., and Paul, S.M. (1983) Subcellular distribution of high affinity [^{3}H]imipramine binding and [^{3}H]serotonin uptake in rat brain. *Eur. J. Pharmacol.* **87,** 335–339. [316]

Rehm, L.P. (1978) Mood, pleasant events and unpleasant events: Two pilot studies. *J. Clin. Consult. Psychol.* **46,** 854–859. [67–69, 81]

Reichlin, S. (1975) Regulation of the hypophysiotropic secretions of the brain. *Arch. Intern. Med.* **135,** 1350–1361. [372]

Reid, L.D. and Bozarth, M.A. (1978) Addictive agents and pressing for intracranial stimulation (ICS): The effects of various opioids on pressing for ICS. In L.S. Harris (Ed.), *Problems of Drug Dependence.* National Institute on Drug Dependence, Washington, D.C., pp. 729–741. [362]

Reinhard, J.F., Bannon, M.J., and Roth, R.H. (1982) Acceleration by stress of dopamine synthesis and metabolism in prefrontal cortex: Antagonism by diazepam. *Naunyn Schmiedebergs Arch. Pharmacol.* **318,** 374–377. [157]

Reis, D.J., Joh, T.H., Ross, R.A., and Pickel, V.M. (1974) Reserpine selectively inceases tyrosine hydroxylase and dopamine-beta-hydroxylase enzyme protein in central noradrenergic neurones. *Brain Res.* **81,** 380–386. [210]

Reisine, T. and Soubrie, P. (1982) Loss of rat cerebral cortex opiate receptors following chronic desipramine treatment. *Eur. J. Pharmacol.* **77,** 39–44. [367]

Reisine, T.D., U'Prichard, D.C., Wiech, N.L., Ursillo, R.C., and Yamamura, H.I. (1980) Effects of combined administration of amphetamine and iprindole on brain adrenergic receptors. *Brain Res.* **188,** 587–592. [247, 255]

Reite, M., Short, R., Seiler, C., and Pauley, J.D. (1981) Attachment, loss and depression. *J. Child Psychol. Psychiatr.* **22,** 141–169. [132]

Renfordt, E., Busch, H., Fahndrich, E., and Muller-Oerlinghausen, B. (1976) Untersuchung einer neuen antidepressiven Substanz (Viloxazin) mit Hilfe der Zert-Reiten-Analysis TV-gespeichereter Interviews. *Arzneim. Forsch.* **26,** 1114–1116. [235]

Renyi, L. (1984) Blockade of the serotonin syndrome induced by 5-methoxy-*N,N*-dimethyl-tryptamine after repeated treatment of rats with amiflamine and some other monoamine oxidase inhibitors. *Abstr. 14th CINP,* Florence, p. 409. [341, 343, 351]

Reus, V.I., Silberman, E., Post, R.M., and Weingartner, H. (1979) D-Amphetamine: Effects on memory in a depressed population. *Biol Psychiatr.* **14,** 345–356. [207]

Reus, V.I., Buchsbaum, M.S., and Post, R.M. (1979) D-Amphetamine: Differential effects on right and left hemispheres. In J.H. Gruzelier and P. Flor-Henry (Eds.), *Hemispheric Asymmetries of Function and Psychopathology.* Elsevier, Amsterdam, pp. 329–338. [99]

Reus, V.I., Lake, C.R., and Post, R.M. (1980) Effect of piribedil (ET-495) on plasma norepinephrine: Relationship to antidepressant response. *Commun. Psychopharmacol.* **4,** 207–213. [174]

Reynolds, D.V. (1969) Surgery in the rat during electrical analgesia induced by focal brain stimulation. *Science* **64,** 444–445. [298, 359]

Richards, G.E., Holland, F.J., Aubert, M.L., Ganong, W.F., Kaplan, S.L., and Grumbach, M.M. (1980) Regulation of prolactin and growth hormone secretion. Site and mechanism of action of thyrotropin-releasing hormone, L-dopa and L-5-hydroxytryptophan in unanesthetized dogs. *Neuroendocrinology* **30,** 139–143. [314]

Richelson, E. (1981) Tricyclic antidepressants: Interactions with histamine and muscarinic acetylcholine receptors. In S.J. Enna, J.B. Malick, and E. Richelson (Eds.), *Antidepressants: Neurochemical, Behavioral and Clinical Perspectives.* Raven, New York, pp. 53–73. [284, 367–370]

Ridges, A.P., Bishop, F.M., and Goldberg, I.J. (1980) Urinary amine metabolites in depression: A combined biochemical and general practice study. II. Biochemical aspects. *J. Int. Med. Res.* **8,** (Suppl. 3), 37–44. [234]

Rie, H.E. (1966) Depression in childhood: a survey of some pertinent contributions. *J. Am. Acad. Child. Psychiatr.* **5,** 653–685. [133]

Riederer, P., Birkmayer, W., Neumayer, E., Ambozi, L., and Linauer, W. (1974) The daily rhythm of HVA, VMA, (VA) and 5-HIAA in depressionsyndrom. *J. Neural Trans.* **35,** 23–45. [310]

Riederer, P., Birkmayer, W., Seemann, D., and Wuketich, S. (1980) 4-hydroxy-3-methoxy-phenylglycol as an index of brain noradrenaline turnover in endogenous depression. *Acta Psychiatr. Scand.* **61,** (Suppl. 280), 251–257. [222]

Riley, G.J. and Shaw, D.M. (1976) Total and non-bound tryptophan in unipolar illness. *Lancet* **2,** 1249. [308]

Rimon, R., Terenius, L., and Kampman, R. (1980) Cerebrospinal fluid endorphins in schizophrenia. *Acta Psychiatr. Scand.* **61,** 395–403. [364]

Risch, S.C. (1982) Beta-endorphin hypersecretion in depression: Possible cholinergic mechanisms. *Biol. Psychiatr.* **17,** 1071–1079. [364]

Risch, S.C., Cohen, P.M., Janowsky, D.S., Kalin, N.H., Insel, T.R., and Murphy, D.L., (1981a) Physostigmine induction of depressive symptomatology in normal volunteer subjects. *J. Psychiatr. Res.* **4,** 89–94. [281, 282]

Risch, S.C., Janowsky, D.S., and Huey, L.Y. (1981b) Plasma levels of tricyclic antidepressants and clinical efficacy. In S.J. Enna, J.B. Malick, and E. Richelson (Eds.), *Antidepressants: Neurochemical, Behavioral and Clinical Perspectives.* Raven, New York, pp. 183–207. [12]

Risch, S.C., Kalin, N.H., and Janowsky, D.S. (1981c) Cholinergic challenges in affective illness: Behavioral and neuroendocrine correlates. *J. Clin. Psychopharmacol.* **1,** 185–192. [281–283]

Risch, S.C., Kalin, N.H., and Murphy, D.L. (1981d) Neurochemical mechanisms in the affective disorders and neuroendocrine correlates. *J. Clin. Psychopharmacol.* **1,** 180–185. [14, 195]

Risch, S.C., Janowsky, D.S., Siever, L.J., Judd, L.L., Huey, L.Y., Beckman, K.A., Cohen, R.M., and Murphy, D.L. (1982a) Cholinomimetic-induced co-release of prolactin and beta-endorphin in man. *Psychopharmacol. Bull.* **18,** 21–25. [279, 300, 361, 364]

Risch, S.C., Janowsky, D.S., Judd, L.L., and Huey, L.Y. (1982b) Elevated plasma beta-endorphin concentrations in depression and cholinergically supersensitive release mechanisms. *Psychopharmacol. Bull.* **18,** 211–216. [279]

Risch, S.C., Janowsky, D.S., Kalin, N.E., Cohen, R.M., Aloi, J.A., and Murphy, D.L. (1983) Cholinergic beta-endorphin hypersensitivity in association with depression. In I. Hanin and E. Usdin (Eds.), *Biological Markers in Psychiatry and Neurology.* Pergamon, Oxford, pp. 269–278. [279]

Ritter, R.C. and Epstein, A.N. (1975) Control of meal size by central noradrenergic action. *Proc. Natl. Acad. Sci. USA* **72,** 3740–3743. [208]

Ritter, S. and Ritter, R.C. (1977) Protection against stress-induced brain norepinephrine depletion after repeated 2-deoxy-D-glucose administration. *Brain Res.* **127**, 179–184. [210]

Ritter, S., Pelzer, N.L., and Ritter, R.C. (1978) Absence of glucoprivic feeding after stress suggests impairment of noradrenergic neuron function. *Brain Res.* **149**, 399–411. [211]

Rivot, J.P., Chaouch, A., and Besson, J.M. (1979) The influence of naloxone on the C fibre response of dorsal horn neurons and their inhibitory control by raphe magnus stimulation. *Brain Res.* **176**, 355–364. [298]

Rizley, R. (1978) Depression and distortion in the attribution of causality. *J. Abnorm. Psychol.* **87**, 32–48. [76, 78, 126]

Robbins, T.W. (1975) The potentiation of conditioned reinforcement by psychomotor stimulant drugs: A test of Hill's hypothesis. *Psychopharmacol.* **45**, 103–114. [153]

Robbins, T.W. (1976) Relationship between reward-enhancing and stereotypical effects of psychomotor stimulant drugs. *Nature* **264**, 57–59. [153]

Robbins, T.W., Watson, B.A., Gaskin, M., and Ennis, C. (1983) Contrasting interactions of pipradrol, D-amphetamine, cocaine, cocaine analogues, apomorphine and other drugs with conditioned reinforcement. *Psychopharmacology* **80**, 113–119. [153]

Roberts, D.C.S. and Koob, G.F. (1982) Disruption of cocaine self-administration following 6-hydroxydopamine lesions of the ventral tegmental area in rats. *Pharmacol. Biochem. Behav.* **17**, 901–904. [152]

Roberts, D.C.S., Price, M.T.C., and Fibiger, H.C. (1976) The dorsal tegmental noradrenergic projection: Analysis of its role in maze learning. *J. Comp. Physiol. Psychol.* **90**, 363–372. [203]

Roberts, D.C.S., Corcoran, M.E., and Fibiger, H.C. (1977) On the role of the ascending catecholaminergic systems in intravenous self-administration of cocaine. *Pharmacol. Biochem. Behav.* **6**, 615–620. [152]

Roberts, D.C.S., Koob, G.F., Klonoff, P., and Fibiger, H.C. (1980) Extinction and recovery of cocaine self-administration following 6-hydroxydopamine lesions of the nucleus accumbens. *Pharmacol. Biochem. Behav.* **12**, 781–787. [152]

Roberts, D.C.S., Segal, D.S., Vickers, G.J., and Pappas, B.A. (1981) Evidence for recovery of function following 6-hydroxydopamine lesions of the dorsal tegmental noradrenergic bundle. *Soc. Neurosci. Abstr.* **7**, 41. [243]

Roberts, J. (1959) Prognostic factors in the electro-shock treatment of depressive states. II. The application of specific tests. *J. Ment. Sci.* **105**, 703–713. [173]

Robertson, J. and Bowlby, J. (1952) Responses of young children to separation from their mothers. *Cour Cent. Int. Enfance* **2**, 131–142. [133]

Robertson, M.M. and Trimble, M.R. (1981) Neuroleptics as antidepressants. *Neuropharmacology* **20**, 1335–1336. [171, 172]

Robertson, M.M. and Trimble, M.R. (1982) Major tranquillizers used as antidepressants: A review. *J. Affect. Disord.* **4**, 173–193. [171, 172]

Robichaud, R.C. and Sledge, K.L. (1969) The effects of p-chlorophenylalanine on experimentally induced conflict in the rat. *Life Sci.* **8**, 965–969. [294]

Robins, A.H. (1976) Depression in patients with Parkinsonism. *Br. J. Psychiatr.* **128**, 141–145. [22, 170]

Robins, E. and Guze, S.B. (1972) Classification of affective disorders: The primary-secondary, the endogenous-reactive and the neurotic-psychotic concepts. In T.A. Williams, M.M. Katz, and J.A. Shields (Eds.), *Recent Advances in the Psychobiology of the Depressive Illness*. U.S. Government Printing Office, Washington, D.C., pp. 283–293. [47]

Robinson, D.S., Nies, A., Ravaris, C.L., and Lambourn, K.R. (1973) The monoamine oxidase inhibitor phenelzine in the treatment of depressive anxiety states: A controlled clinical trial. *Arch. Gen. Psychiatr.* **29,** 407–413. [11, 221]

Robinson, R.G. and Bloom, F.E. (1977) Pharmacological treatment following experimental cerebral infarction: Implications for understanding psychological symptoms of human stroke. *Biol. Psychiatr.* **12,** 669–680. [98]

Robinson, R.G. and Coyle, J.T. (1980) The differential effect of right versus left hemispheric cerebral infarction on catecholamines and behavior in the rat. *Brain Res.* **188,** 63–78. [97, 98]

Robinson, R.G. and Stitt, T.G. (1981) Intracortical 6-hydroxydopamine induces an asymmetrical behavioral response in the rat. *Brain Res.* **213,** 387–395. [98]

Robinson, R.G. and Szetela, B. (1981) Mood changes following left hemispheric brain injury. *Ann. Neurol.* **9,** 447–453. [91, 92]

Robinson, R.G., Kubos, K.L., Starr, L.B., and Price, T.R. (1982) Cortical localization for control of affect in humans. *Soc. Neurosci. Abstr.* **8,** 626. [92]

Robinson, S.E. (1983) Effect of specific serotonergic lesions on cholinergic neurons in the hippocampus, cortex, and striatum. *Life Sci.* **32,** 345–353. [383]

Robinson, T.E. and Becker, J.B. (1982) Functional asymmetry in the nigrostriatal dopamine system. *Soc. Neurosci. Abstr.* **8,** 895. [96]

Roccatagliata, G., Albano, C., and Abbruzzese, G. (1981) CSF-MHPG in depressive syndromes: Basal values and imipramine-induced modifications. *Neuropsychobiology* **7,** 169–171. [234, 251]

Rochat, C., Cervo, L., Romandini, S., and Samanin, R. (1982) Differences in the effects of D-fenfluramine and morphine on various responses of rats to painful stimuli. *Psychopharmacology* **76,** 188–192. [298]

Rockhold, R.W. and Caldwell, R.W. (1980) Cardiovascular effects following clonidine microinjection into the nucleus tractus solitarii of the rat. *Neuropharmacology* **19,** 919–922. [228]

Rockman, G.E., Amit, Z., Carr, G., Brown, Z.W., and Ogren, S.-O. (1979a) Attenuation of ethanol intake by 5-hydroxytryptamine uptake blockade in laboratory rats. I. Involvement of brain 5-hydroxytryptamine in the mediation of the positive reinforcing properties of alcohol. *Arch. Int. Pharmacodyn.* **241,** 245–259. [301, 350, 351]

Rockman, G.E., Amit, Z., Carr, G., and Ogren, S.-O. (1979b) Attenuation of ethanol intake by 5-hydroxytryptamine uptake blockade in laboratory rats: II. Possible interaction with brain noradrenaline. *Arch. Int. Pharmacodyn.* **241,** 260–265. [301, 350, 351]

Rockman, G.E., Amit, Z., Bourque, C., Brown, Z.W., and Ogren, S.-O. (1980) Reduction of voluntary morphine consumption following treatment with zimelidine. *Arch. Int. Pharmacodyn.* **244,** 123–129. [350, 351, 386]

Rodbell, M. (1980) The role of hormone receptors and GTP-regulatory proteins in membrane transduction. *Nature* **284,** 17–22. [256]

Roffler-Tarlov, S., Schildkraut, J.J., and Draskoczy, P.R. (1973) Effects of acute and chronic administration of desmethylimipramine on the content of norepinephrine and other monoamines in the rat brain. *Biochem. Pharmacol.* **22,** 2923–2926. [249]

Roffman, M., Kling, M.A., Cassens, G., Orsulak, P.J., Reigle, T.G., and Schildkraut, J.J. (1977) The effects of acute and chronic administration of tricyclic antidepressants on MHPG-SO$_4$ in rat brain. *Psychopharmacol. Commun.* **1,** 195–206. [241, 248–250]

Rogers, L.J. and Anson, J.M. (1980) Lateralization of function in the chicken fore-brain. *Pharmacol. Biochem. Behav.* **10,** 679–686. [97]

Rogers, T.B., Kuiper, N.A., and Kirker, W.S. (1977) Self-reference and the encoding of personal information. *J. Pers. Soc. Psychol.* **35,** 677–688. [74]

Rolls, E.T. (1982) Feeding and reward. In B.G. Hoebel and D. Novin (Eds.), *The Neural Basis of Feeding and Reward.* Haer Institute, Brunswick, Me., pp. 323–337. [196, 197, 303, 362, 385]

Romano, J.A. and King, J.M. (1980) Benactyzine-induced reversal of physostigmine and cold-water analgesia. *Soc. Neurosci. Abstr.* **6**, 432. [276]

Romano, J.A. and King, J.M. (1981) Naloxone differentially affects the analgetic actions of physostigmine on three behavioral measures of antinociception. *Soc. Neurosci. Abstr.* **7**, 879. [276]

Romano, J.A. and King, J.M. (1982) The effects of adrenalectomy and dexamethasone on the antinociceptive effects of physostigmine using the rat tail flick test. *Soc. Neurosci. Abstr.* **8**, 621. [276]

Romano, J.A. and Shih, T.-M. (1983) Cholinergic mechanisms of analgesia produced by physostigmine, morphine and cold water swimming. *Neuropharmacol.* **22**, 827–833. [276]

Roos, B.-E. and Sjostrom, R. (1969) 5-hydroxyindoleacetic acid (and homovanillic acid) levels in the CSF after probenecid application in patients with manic-depressive psychosis. *Pharmacol. Clin.* **1**, 153–155. [167, 311, 312]

Rosellini, R.A. (1978) Inescapable shock interferes with the acquisition of a free appetitive operant. *Anim. Learn. Behav.* **6**, 155–159. [123]

Rosellini, R.A. and DeCola, J.P. (1981) Inescapable shock interferes with the acquisition of a low-activity response in an appetitive context. *Anim. Learn. Behav.* **9**, 487–490. [123]

Rosellini, R.A. and Seligman, M.E.P. (1975) Learned helplessness and escape from frustration. *J. Exp. Psychol: Anim. Behav. Proc.* **1**, 149–158. [122]

Rosenbaum, A.R., Schatzberg, A.F., Maruta, T., Orsulak, P.J., Cole, J.O., Grab, E.L., and Schildkraut, J.J. (1980) MHPG as a predictor of antidepressant response to imipramine. *Am. J. Psychiatr.* **137**, 1090–1092. [233, 234]

Rosenblatt, J.E., Pert, C.E., Tallman, J.F., Pert, A., and Bunney, W.E. (1979) The effect of imipramine and lithium on alpha- and beta-receptor binding in rat brain. *Brain Res.* **160**, 186–191. [190, 255, 257]

Rosenblatt, S., Chanley, J.D., Sobotka, H., and Kaufman, M.R. (1960) Interrelationships between electro-shock, the blood-brain barrier, and catecholamines. *J. Neurochem.* **5**, 172–176. [6]

Rosenblatt, W.H., Hutchins, K., and Sinnamon, H.M. (1979) Pimozide's effects on ICSS depend on the interaction of reward and effort. *Soc. Neurosci. Abstr.* **5**, 350. [155]

Rosenkilde, C.E. (1979) Functional heterogeneity of the prefrontal cortex in the monkey: A review. *Behav. Neural Biol.* **25**, 301–345. [94]

Rosenthal, N.E., Davenport, Y., Cowdry, R.W., Webster, M., and Goodwin, F.K. (1980) Monoamine metabolites in cerebrospinal fluid of depressed subgroups. *Psychiatr. Res.* **2**, 113–119. [312]

Rosenthal, S.H. and Klerman, G.L. (1966) Content and consistency in the endogenous depressive pattern. *Br. J. Psychiatr.* **112**, 471–484. [49]

Rosenthal, T.L., Akiskal, H.S., Scott-Strauss, A., Rosenthal, R.H., and David, M. (1981) Familial and developmental factors in characterological depressions. *J. Affect. Disord.* **3**, 183–192. [56, 58, 395]

Rosloff, B.N. and Davis, J.M. (1974) Effect of iprindole on norepinephrine turnover and transport. *Psychopharmacology* **40**, 53–64. [240, 250]

Rosloff, B.N. and Davis, J.M. (1978) Decrease in brain NE turnover after chronic DMI treatment: No effect with iprindole. *Psychopharmacology* **56**, 335–341. [241, 248, 250]

Ross, E.D. and Mesulam, M.M. (1979) Dominant language functions of the right hemisphere? Prosody and emotional gesturing. *Arch. Neurol.* **36**, 144–148. [86]

Ross, S.B. (1979) Interactions between reserpine and various compounds on the accumulation of (^{14}C) 5-hydroxytryptamine and (^{3}H) noradrenaline in homogenates from rat brain hypothalamus. *Biochem. Pharamacol.* **28**, 1085–1088. [323]

Ross, S.B. and Renyi, A.L. (1969) Inhibition of the uptake of tritiated 5-HT in brain tissue. *Eur. J. Pharmacol.* **4**, 270–277. [336]

Ross, S.B. and Renyi, A.L. (1975) Tricyclic antidepressant agents. I. Comparison of the inhibition of uptake of ^{3}H-noradrenaline and ^{14}C-5-hydroxytryptamine in slices and crude synaptosome preparations of the midbrain-hypothalamus region of rat brain. *Acta Pharmacol. Toxicol.* **36**, 382–392. [322, 323]

Ross, S.B., Ogren, S.-O., and Renyi, A.L. (1976) (Z)-Dimethylamino-I-(4-bromophenyl)-1-(3-pyridyl) propene (H102/09), a new selective inhibitor of the neuronal 5-hydroxytryptamine uptake. *Acta Pharmacol. Toxicol.* **39**, 152–166. [323]

Ross, S.B., Aperia, B., Beck-Friis, J., Jansa, S., Wetterberg, L., and Aberg, A. (1980) Inhibition of 5-hydroxytryptamine uptake in human platelets by antidepressant agents in vivo. *Psychopharmacology* **67**, 1–7. [333]

Ross, S.B., Hall, H., Renyi, A.L., and Westerlund, D. (1981) Effects of zimelidine on serotonergic and noradrenergic neurons after repeated administration in the rat. *Psychopharmacology* **72**, 219–225. [329, 334]

Rossi, G.F. and Rossadini, G. (1967) Experimental analysis of cerebral dominance in man. In C.H. Millikan and F.L. Darley (Eds.), *Brain Mechanisms Underlying Speech and Language*. Grune & Stratton, New York, pp. 166–184. [91]

Rossi, J., Zolovick, A.J., Davies, R.F., and Panksepp, J. (1982) The role of norepinephrine in feeding behavior. *Neurosci. Biobehav. Rev.* **6**, 195–204. [208]

Rossier, J., French, E., Guillemin, R., and Bloom, F.E. (1980) On the mechanisms of the simultaneous release of immunoreactive beta-endorphin, ACTH and prolactin by stress. In E. Costa and M. Trabucchi (Eds.), *Neural Peptides and Neuronal Communication*. Raven, New York, pp. 363–376. [299, 364]

Rossor, M., Garret, N., and Iversen, L. (1980) No evidence for lateral asymmetry of neurotransmitters in postmortem human brain. *J. Neurochem.* **35**, 743–745.

Roth, D. and Rehm, L.P. (1980) Relationships among self-monitoring processes, memory and depression. *Cogn. Ther. Res.* **4**, 149–158. [99]

Roth, K.A. and Katz, R.J. (1981) Further studies on a novel animal model of depression: Therapeutic effects of a tricyclic antidepressant. *Neurosci. Biobehav. Rev.* **5**, 253–258. [70]

Roth, R.H. (1979) Dopamine autoreceptors: Pharmacology, function and comparison with post-synaptic dopamine receptors. *Commun. Psychopharmacol.* **3**, 429–445. [130]

Roth, R.H., Murrin, L.C., and Walters, J.R. (1976) Central dopaminergic neurons: Effects of alterations in impulse flow on the accumulation of dihydroxyphenylacetic acid. *Eur. J. Pharmacol.* **36**, 163–171. [185]

Roth, S. and Kubal, L. (1976) The effects of noncontingent reinforcement on tasks of differing importance: Facilitation and learned helplessness effects. *J. Pers. Soc. Psychol.* **32**, 680–691. [75]

Roth, S.R., Sterman, M.B., and Clemente, C.D. (1967) Comparison of EEG correlates of reinforcement, internal inhibition and sleep. *Electroencephalogr. Clin. Neurophysiol.* **23**, 509–520. [304]

Rothschild, A.J., Schatzberg, A.F., Rosenbaum, A.H., Stahl, J.B., and Cole, J.O. (1982) The dexamethasone suppression test as a discriminator among subtypes of psychotic patients. *Br. J. Psychiatr.* **141**, 471–474. [54]

Rowe, D. (1978) *The Experience of Depression*. Wiley, Chichester. [35]

Rowland, N., Antelman, S.M., Chiodo, L.A., DeGiovanni, L., and Kocan, D. (1982) Differences among serotonergic anorectics and interactions with stress and antidepressants.

In B.T. Ho, J.C. Schoolar, and E. Usdin (Eds.), *Serotonin in Biological Psychiatry*. Raven, New York, pp. 318–319. [341]

Rowntree, D.W., Neven, S., and Wilson, A. (1950) The effects of diisopropylfluorophosphate in schizophrenia and manic-depressive psychosis. *J. Neurol. Neurosurg. Psychiatr.* **13**, 47–62. [269, 281]

Rozensky, R.H., Rehm, L.P., Pry, G., and Roth, D. (1977) Depression and self-reinforcement behavior in hospitalized patients. *J. Behav. Ther. Exp. Psychiatr.* **8**, 35–38. [66]

Rubin, R.T., Miller, R.G., Clark, B.R., Poland, R.E., and Arthur, R.J. (1970) The stress of aircraft carrier landings. II. 3-methoxy-4-hydroxyphenylglycol excretion in naval aviators. *Psychosom. Med.* **32**, 589–596. [226]

Rubovits, R. and Klawans, H.L. (1972) Implications of amphetamine-induced stereotyped behavior as a model for tardive dyskinesias. *Arch. Gen. Psychiatr.* **27**, 502–507. [16]

Rudorfer, M.V., Hwu, H.G. and Clayton, P.J. (1982) Dexamethasone suppression test in primary depression: Significance of family history and psychosis. *Biol. Psychiatr.* **17**, 41–48. [53]

Rumelhart, D.W. and Ortony, A. (1977) The representation of knowledge in memory. In R. Anderson and W. Montague (Eds.), *Schooling and the Acquisition of Knowledge*. Erlbaum, Hillsdale, N. J., pp. 99–135. [74]

Rush, A.J., Giles, D.E., Roffwarg, H.P., and Parker, C.R. (1982) Sleep EEG and dexamethasone suppression test findings in outpatients with unipolar major depressive disorders. *Biol. Psychiatr.* **17**, 327–341. [54, 55]

Russell, P.N. and Beekhuis, M.E. (1976) Organization in memory: A comparison of psychotics and normals. *J. Abnorm. Psychol.* **85**, 527–534. [65]

Russell, R.W. (1964) Extrapolation from animals to man. In H. Steinberg (Ed.), *Animal Behaviour and Drug Action*. Churchill, London, pp. 410–418. [103]

Ruther, E., Ackenheil, M., and Matussek, N. (1966) Beitrag zum Noradrenalin und Serotonin Stoffwechsel im Rattenhirn nach Stresszustanden. *Arneim. Forsch.* **16**, 261–263. [289]

Sacchetti, E., Allaria, E., Negri, F., Biondi, P.A., Smeraldi, E., and Cazzullo, C.L. (1979) 3-methoxy-4-hydroxyphenylglycol and primary depression: Clinical and pharmacological considerations. *Biol. Psychiatr.* **14**, 473–484. [225, 234, 235]

Sachar, E.J., Finkelstein, J., and Hellman, L. (1971) Growth hormone responses in depressive illness. I. Responses to insulin tolerance test. *Arch. Gen. Psychiatr.* **25**, 263–269. [229]

Sachar, E.J., Mushrush, G., Perlow, M., Weitzman, E.D., and Sassin, J. (1972) Growth hormone responses to L-dopa in depressed patients. *Science* **178**, 1304–1305. [165]

Sachar, E.J., Frantz, A.B., Altman, N., and Sassin, J. (1973a) Growth hormone and prolactin in unipolar and bipolar depressed patients: Responses to hypoglycemia and L-dopa. *Am. J. Psychiatr.* **130**, 1362–1367. [165, 166]

Sachar, E.J., Hellman, L., Roffwarg, H., Halpern, F.S., Fukushima, D., and Gallagher, T. (1973b) Disrupted 24-hour patterns of cortisol secretion in psychotic depression. *Arch. Gen. Psychiatr.* **28**, 19–24. [113]

Sachar, E.J., Altman, N., Gruen, P.H., Glassman, A., Halpern, F.S., and Sassin, J. (1975) Human growth hormone response to L-dopa in relation to menopause, depression and plasma level of L-dopa. *Arch. Gen. Psychiatr.* **32**, 502–503. [165, 166, 229]

Sachar, E.J., Asnis, G., Nathan, R.S., Halbreich, U., Tabrizi, M.A., and Halpern, F.S. (1980) Dextroamphetamine and cortisol in depression: Morning plasma cortisol levels suppressed. *Arch. Gen. Psychiatr.* **37**, 755–757. [229]

Sackheim, H.A. and Gur, R.C (1978) Lateral asymmetry in intensity of emotional expression. *Neuropsychology* **16**, 473–481. [87]

Sackheim, H.A., Gur, R.C., and Saucy, M.C. (1978) Emotions are expressed more intensely on the left side of the face. *Science* **202**, 434–435. [87]

Sackheim, H.A., Greenberg, M.S., Weiman, A.L., Gur, R.C., Hungerbuhler, J.P., and Geschwind, N. (1982) Hemispheric asymmetry in the expression of positive and negative emotions. *Arch. Neurol.* **19**, 210–218. [91]

Sacks, O. (1973) *Awakenings*. Duckworth, London. [156]

Safer, M.A. and Leventhal, H. (1977) Ear differences in evaluation of emotional tones of voice and verbal content. *J. Exp. Psychol.: Hum. Percept. Performance* **3**, 75–82. [86]

Sagen, J. and Proudfit, H.K. (1981) Identification of noradrenergic neurons projecting to medullary nuclei involved in the modulation of pain. *Soc. Neurosci. Abstr.* **7**, 880. [197]

Sahakian, B.J. and Robbins, T.W. (1977) Isolation-rearing enhances tail pinch-induced oral behavior in rats. *Physiol. Behav.* **18**, 53–58. [292]

Sahakian, B.J., Robbins, T.W., Morgan, M.J., and Iversen, S.D. (1975) The effects of psychomotor stimulants on stereotypy and locomotor activity in socially deprived and control rats. *Brain Res.* **84**, 195–205. [114]

Sahakian, B.J., Robbins, T.W., and Iversen, S.D. (1977) The effects of isolation rearing on exploration in the rat. *Anim. Learn. Behav.* **5**, 193–198. [114]

Saito, H., Morita, A., Miyazaki, I., and Takagi, K. (1976) Comparison of the effects of various stresses on biogenic amines in the central nervous system and animal symptoms. In E. Usdin, R. Kvetansky, and I.J. Kopin (Eds.), *Catecholamines and Stress*. Pergamon, Oxford, pp. 95–103. [276]

Sakai, Y. and Deguchi, T. (1980) Effects of mianserin on functions of ascending and descending monoaminergic systems using experimental models. *Folia Pharmacol. Jpn.* **76**, 213–225. [330]

Saletu, B., Schjerue, M., Grunberger, J., Schanda, H., and Arnold, O.H. (1977) Fluvoxamine: A new serotonin uptake inhibitor: First clinical and psychometric experiences in depressed patients. *J. Neural Trans.* **41**, 17–36. [323]

Samanin, R., Bendotti, C., Bernasconi, S., Borroni, E., and Garattini, S. (1977) Role of brain monoamines in the anorectic activity of mazindol and d-amphetamine in the rat. *Eur. J. Pharmacol.* **43**, 117–124. [265]

Sandberg, D.E. and Segal, M. (1978) Pharmacological analysis of analgesia and self-stimulation elicited by electrical stimulation of catecholamine nuclei in the rat brain. *Brain Res.* **152**, 529–542. [197]

Sangdee, C. and Franz, D.N. (1979) Enhancement of central norepinephrine and 5-hydroxytryptamine transmission by tricyclic antidepressants: A comparison. *Psychopharmacology* **62**, 9–16. [242, 330]

Sangdee, C. and Franz, D.N. (1980) Lithium enhancement of central 5-HT transmission induced by 5-HT precursors. *Biol. Psychiatr.* **15**, 59–75. [343]

Sanghera, M.K., Rolls, E.T., and Roper-Hall, A. (1979) Visual responses of neurons in the dorsolateral amygdala of the alert monkey. *Exp. Neurol.* **63**, 610–626. [197]

Sanghvi, I. and Gershon, S. (1969) The evaluation of central nervous system stimulants in a new laboratory test for antidepressants. *Life Sci.* **8**, 449–457. [107]

Sanghvi, I., Bindler, E., and Gershon, S. (1969) The evaluation of a new animal method for the prediction of clinical antidepressant activity. *Life Sci.* **8**, 99–106. [104, 106, 107]

Sanghvi, I., Geyer, H., and Gershon, S. (1976) Exploration of the antidepressant potential of iprindole. *Life Sci.* **18**, 569–574. [106]

Santos, R. and Carlini, E.A. (1983) Serotonin receptor activation in rats previously deprived of REM sleep. *Pharmacol. Biochem. Behav.* **18**, 501–507. [343]

Sarai, K., Nakahara, T., Nakagawa, K., and Yoshihara, S. (1982) Lymphocytic beta-adrenergic receptor function in affective disorders. In S.Z. Langer, R. Takahashi, T. Segawa, and M. Briley (Eds.), *New Vistas in Depression*. Pergamon, New York, pp. 161–165. [218, 219]

Satoh, M., Kawajiri, S., Yamamoto, M., Makino, H., and Takagi, H. (1979) Reversal by naloxone of adaptation of rats to noxious stimuli. *Life Sci.* **24,** 685–690. [359]

Savage, D.D., Frazer, A., and Mendels, J. (1979) Differential effects of monoamine oxidase inhibitors and serotonin reuptake inhibitors on ^{3}H-serotonin receptor binding in rat brain. *Eur. J. Pharmacol.* **58,** 87–88. [347]

Savage, D.D., Mendels, J., and Frazer, A. (1980) Monoamine oxidase inhibitors and serotonin uptake inhibitors: Differential effects on [^{3}H]serotonin binding sites in rat brain. *J. Pharm. Exp. Ther.* **212,** 259–263. [347]

Savard, R.J., Rey, A.C., and Post, R.M. (1980) Halstead-Reitan category test in bipolar and unipolar affective illness. Relationship to age and place of illness. *J. Nerv. Ment. Disord.* **168,** 297–304. [90]

Sawa, Y., Odo, S., and Nakazawa, T. (1980) Growth hormone secretion by tricyclic and non-tricyclic antidepressants in healthy volunteers and depressives. In S.Z. Langer, R. Takahashi, T. Segawa, and M. Briley (Eds.), *New Vistas in Depression*. Pergamon, New York, pp. 309–315. [229]

Sawchenko, P.E. (1982) Anatomic relationships between the paraventricular nucleus of the hypothalamus and visceral regulatory mechanisms: Implications for the control of feeding behavior. In B.G. Hoebel and D. Novin (Eds.), *The Neural Basis of Feeding and Reward*. Haer Institute, Brunswick, Me., pp. 259–274. [195]

Scarf, M. (1980) Women and depression. *New Republic* **183,** 25–29. [405]

Schachter, S. and Singer, J.E. (1962) Cognitive, social and physiological determinants of emotional state. *Psychol. Bull.* **69,** 379–399. [28, 176, 283]

Schaefer, G.J. and Holzman, S.G. (1979) Free-operant and auto-titration brain self-stimulation procedures in the rat: A comparison of drug effects. *Pharmacol. Biochem. Behav.* **10,** 127–135. [154]

Schaefer, G.J. and Michael, R.P. (1980) Acute effects of neuroleptics on brain self-stimulation thresholds in rats. *Psychopharmacology* **67,** 9–25. [154]

Schaefer, G.J. and Michael, R.P. (1981) Threshold differences for naloxone and naltrexone in the hypothalamus and midbrain using fixed ratio brain self-stimulation. *Psychopharmacology* **74,** 17–22. [362, 363]

Schaffer, C.B., Donlon, P.T., and Bittle, R.M. (1980) Chronic pain and depression: A clinical and family history survey. *Am. J. Psychiatr.* **137,** 118–120. [69]

Schaffer, C.E., Davidson, R.J., and Saron, C. (1983) Frontal and parietal electroencephalogram asymmetry in depressed and nondepressed subjects. *Biol. Psychiatr.* **18,** 753–762. [88]

Schanberg, S.M., Breese, G.R., Schildkraut, J.J., Gordon, E.K., and Kopin, I.J. (1968) 3-methoxy-4-hydroxyphenylglycol sulfate in brain and cerebrospinal fluid. *Biochem. Pharmacol.* **17,** 2006–2008. [222]

Schatzberg, A.F. (1978) Classification of depressive disorders. In J.O. Cole, A.F. Schatzberg, and S.H. Frazier (Eds.), *Depression: Biology, Psychodynamics and Treatment*. Plenum, New York, pp. 13–40. [49]

Schatzberg, A.F., Orsulak, P.J., Rosenbaum, A.H., Maruta, T., Kruger, E.R., Cole, J.O., and Schildkraut, J.J. (1980) Towards a biochemical classification of depressive disorders. IV. Pretreatment urinary MHPG levels as predictors of antidepressant response to imipramine. *Commun. Psychopharmacol.* **4,** 441–445. [233]

Schatzberg, A.F., Rosenbaum, A.H., Orsulak, P.J., Rohde, W.A., Maruta, T., Kruger, E.R., Cole, J.O., and Schildkraut, J.J. (1981) Towards a biochemical classification of depressive disorders. III. Pretreatment urinary MHPG levels as predictors of response to treatment with maprotiline. *Psychopharmacology* **75,** 34–38. [234]

Schatzberg, A.F., Orsulak, P.J., Rosenbaum, A.H., Toshihiko, M., Kruger, E.R., Cole, J.O., and Schildkraut, J.J. (1982) Towards a biochemical classification of depressive disorders. V. Heterogeneity of unipolar depressions. *Am. J. Psychiatr.* **139**, 471–475. [225]

Schechter, M.D. (1980) Effects of neuroleptics and tricyclic antidepressants upon D-amphetamine discrimination. *Pharmacol. Biochem. Behav.* **12**, 1–5. [182]

Schechter, M.D. and Chance, W.T. (1979) Non-specificity of "behavioral despair" as an animal model of depression. *Eur. J. Pharmacol.* **60**, 139–142. [127, 128]

Schechter, M.D. and Cook, P.G. (1975) Dopaminergic mediation of the interoceptive cue produced by D-amphetamine in rats. *Psychopharmacology* **42**, 183–193. [182]

Scheckel, C.L. and Boff, E. (1964) Behavioral effects of interacting imipramine and other drugs with d-amphetamine, cocaine and tetrabenazine. *Psychopharmacology* **5**, 198–208. [111]

Schershlicht, R., Polc, P., Schneeberger, J., Steiner, M., and Haefely, W. (1982) Selective suppression of rapid eye movement sleep (REMS) in cats by typical and atypical antidepressants. In E. Costa and G. Racagni (Eds.), *Typical and Atypical Antidepressants: Molecular Mechanism.* Raven, New York, pp. 359–364. [116]

Schick, J.F.E., Smith, D.E., and Wesson, D.R. (1973) An analysis of amphetamine toxicity and patterns of use. In D.E. Smith and D.R. Wesson (Eds.), *Uppers and Downers.* Prentice Hall, Englewood Cliffs, N.J., pp. 23–61. [135, 399]

Schildkraut, J.J. (1965) The catecholamine hypothesis of affective disorders: A review of supporting evidence. *Am. J. Psychiatr.* **122**, 509–522. [6, 8, 17, 168, 217, 239, 260, 261, 268, 417]

Schildkraut, J.J. (1973) Neuropharmacology of the affective disorders. *Ann. Rev. Pharm.* **13**, 427–454. [222, 223]

Schildkraut, J.J. (1974) Catecholamine metabolism and affective disorders. In E. Usdin and S. Synder (Eds.), *Frontiers in Catecholamine Research.* Pergamon, New York, pp. 1165–1171. [226, 235]

Schildkraut, J.J. (1975) Norepinephrine metabolism after short- and long-term administration of tricyclic antidepressant drugs and electroconvulsive shocks. In A.J. Mandell (Ed.), *Neurobiological Mechanisms of Adaptation and Behavior.* Raven, New York, pp. 137–153. [249]

Schilkdraut, J.J. (1978) Current status of the catecholamine hypothesis of affective disorders. In M.A. Lipton, A. DiMascio and K.F. Killam (Eds.), *Psychopharmacology: A Generation of Progress.* Raven, New York, pp. 1223–1234. [181]

Schildkraut, J.J., Winokur, A., Draskoczy, P.R., and Hensle, J.H. (1971) Changes in norepinephrine turnover during chronic administration of imipramine and protriptyline: A possible explanation for the delay in onset of clinical antidepressant effects. *Am. J. Psychiatr.* **127**, 72–79. [12, 249]

Schildkraut, J.J., Keeler, B.A., Papousek, M., and Hartmann, E. (1973) MHPG excretion in depressive disorders: Relation to clinical subtypes and desynchronized sleep. *Science* **181**, 762–764. [224–226]

Schildkraut, J.J., Roffman, M., Orsulak, P.J., Schatzberg, A.F., Kling, M.A., and Reigle, T.G. (1976) Effects of short- and long-term administration of tricyclic antidepressants and lithium on norepinephrine turnover in brain. *Pharmakopsychiatria* **9**, 193–202. [241]

Schildkraut, J.J., Orsulak, P.J., Gudeman, J.E., Schatzberg, A.F., Rohde, W.A., Labrie, R.A., Cahill, J.F., Cole, J.O., and Frazier, S.F. (1978) Norepinephrine metabolism in depressive disorders: Implications for a biochemical classification of depressions. In J.O. Cole, A.F. Schatzberg, and S.H. Frazier (Eds.), *Depression: Biology, Psychodynamics and Treatment.* Plenum, New York, pp. 75–101. [224–226]

Schildkraut, J.J., Orsulak, P.J., Schatzberg, A.F., Cole, J.O., and Rosenbaum, A.H. (1981) Possible pathophysiological mechanisms in subtypes of unipolar depressive disorders based on differences in urinary MHPG levels. *Psychopharmacol. Bull.* **17**, 90–91. [225, 234, 237]

Schless, A.P., Schwartz, L., Goetz, C., and Mendels, J. (1974) How depressives view the significance of life events. *Br. J. Psychiatr.* **125**, 406–410. [69]

Schlesser, M.A., Winokur, G., and Sherman, B.M. (1980) Hypothalamic-pituitary-adrenal axis activity in depressive illness: Its relationship to classification. *Arch. Gen. Psychiatr.* **37**, 737–743. [54]

Schlicker, E., Gothert, M., and Clausing, R. (1982) Acute or chronic changes of noradrenergic transmission do not affect the alpha-adrenoceptor-mediated inhibition of ^{3}H-serotonin release in the cerebral cortex. *Naunyn Schmiedebergs Arch. Pharmacol.* **320**, 38–44. [252, 377]

Schlienger, J.L., Kapfer, M.T., Singer, L., and Stephan, F. (1980) Differential effects of tricyclic (clomipramine and amitriptyline) and tetracyclic (maprotiline) antidepressors on the release of thyroid stimulating hormone, prolactin and growth hormone to thyrostimulating releasing hormone in patients with psychoaffective disorders. *Acta Psychiatr. Belg.* **80**, 584–599. [372]

Schmale, A.H. (1973) Adaptive role of depression in health and disease. In J.P. Scott and E. Senay (Eds.), *Separation and Depression.* Am. Assoc. Adv. Sci., Washington, D.C., pp. 187–214. [133, 384, 405]

Schneider, E., Jacobi, P., Maxion, H., and Fischer, P.-A. (1975) Neuropsychologische Untersuchungen zur Kurzzeitwirkung von Biperiden (Akineton) beim Parkinsonsyndrom. *Arch. Psychiatr. Nervenkr.* **221**, 15–28. [284]

Schneider, K. (1958) *Psychopathic Personalities* (M.W. Hamilton, Trans.). Cassell, London. [58]

Schubert, H., Fleischhacker, W.W., and Demel, I. (1982) Bromocriptyn bei organische Depressionen. *Pharmakopsychiatria* **15**, 133–135. [174]

Schulterbrandt, J.G. and Raskin, A., eds. (1977) *Depression in Childhood: Diagnosis, Treatment and Conceptual Models.* Raven, New York. [133]

Schultz, H. and Trojan, B. (1979) A comparison of eye movement density in normal subjects and in depressed patients before and after remission. *Sleep Res.* **8**, 49. [279]

Schultz, J. (1976) Psychoactive drug effects on a system which generates cyclic AMP in brain. *Nature* **261**, 417–418. [257]

Schultz, J.E., Siggins, G.R., Schocker, F.W., Turck, M., and Bloom, F.E. (1981) Effects of prolonged treatment with lithium and tricyclic antidepressants on discharge frequency, norepinephrine respones and beta receptor binding in rat cerebellum: Electrophysiological and biochemical comparison. *J. Pharmacol. Exp. Ther.* **216**, 28–38. [241, 253, 262, 264, 356]

Schuster, C.R. (1975) Drugs as reinforcers in monkeys and man. *Pharmacol. Rev.* **27**, 511–521. [302]

Schutz, R.A., Schutz, M.T.B., Orsingher, O.A., and Izquierdo, I. (1979) Brain dopamine and noradrenaline levels in rats submitted to four different aversive tasks. *Psychopharmacology.* **63**, 289–292. [157, 208, 209]

Schwaber, J.S., Kapp, B.S., Higgins, G.A., and Rapp, P.R. (1982) Amygdaloid and basal forebrain direct connections with the nucleus of the solitary tract and the dorsal motor nucleus. *J. Neurosci.* **2**, 1424–1438. [197]

Schwartz, G.E., Davidson, R.J., and Maer, F. (1975) Right hemisphere lateralization for emotion in the human brain: Interactions with cognition. *Science* **190**, 286–288. [89]

Schwartz, G.E., Ahern, G.L., and Brown, S.-L. (1979) Lateralized facial muscle response to positive and negative emotional stimuli. *Psychophysiology* **16**, 561–571. [87]

Schwartz, J.-C., Barbin, G., Baudry, M., Garbarg, M., Martres, M.P., Pollard, H., and Ver-
diere, M. (1979) Metabolism and functions of histamine in the brain. In W.B. Essman
and L. Valzelli (Eds.), *Current Developments in Psychopharmacology,* Vol. 5. Spectrum,
New York, pp. 173–261. [367, 368]

Schweitzer, J.W., Schwartz, R., and Friedhoff, A.J. (1979) Intact presynaptic terminals required for beta-adrenergic receptor regulation by desipramine. *J. Neurochem.* **33,**
377–379. [258]

Schweitzer, L. (1979) Differences of cerebral lateralization among schizophrenic and depressed patients. *Biol. Psychiat.* **14,** 721–733. [89]

Schweitzer, L., Becker, E., and Welsh, H. (1978) Abnormalities of cerebral lateralization
in schizophrenic patients. *Arch. Gen. Psychiatr.* **35,** 982–985. [89]

Sclafani, A., Aravich, P.F., and Xenakis, S. (1982) Dopaminergic and endorphinergic mediation of a sweet reward. In B.G. Hoebel and D. Novin (Eds.), *The Neural Basis of
Feeding and Reward.* Haer Institute, Brunswick, Me., pp. 507–515. [362]

Scott, M., Reading, H.W., and Loudon, J.B. (1979) Studies on human blood platelets in
affective disorder. *Psychopharmacology* **50,** 131–135. [316, 333]

Scuvee-Moreau, J.J. and Dresse, A.E. (1979) Effect of various antidepressant drugs on the
spontaneous firing rate of locus coeruleus and dorsal raphe neurons in the rat. *Eur. J.
Pharmacol.* **57,** 219–225. [241, 329]

Sechter, D., Poirier, M.F., and Loo, H. (1984) Clinical studies with indalpine: A critical
review. *Clin. Neuropharmacol.* **7,** (Suppl. 1), 870–871. [323, 324]

Sedvall, G., Fyro, B., Gullberg, B., Nyback, H., Wiesel, F.-A., and Wode-Helgodt, B. (1980)
Relationships in healthy volunteers between concentrations of monoamine metabolites
in cerebrospinal fluid and family history of psychiatric morbidity. *Br. J. Psychiatr.* **136,**
366–374. [313]

Seeman, P. (1980) Dopamine receptors. *Pharmacol. Rev.* **32,** 229–313. [149, 150]

Segal, D.S. (1975) Behavioral and neurochemical correlates of repeated d-amphetamine
administration. In A.J. Mandell (Ed.), *Neurobiological Mechanisms of Adaptation and
Behavior.* Raven, New York, pp. 247–262. [150]

Segal, D.S., Knapp, S., Kuczenski, R., and Mandell, A.J. (1973) The effects of environmental
isolation on behavior and regional rat brain tyrosine hydroxylase and tryptophan hydroxylase activities. *Behav. Biol.* **8,** 47–53. [291]

Segal, D.S., Kuczenski, R., and Mandell, A.J. (1974) Theoretical implications of drug-induced adaptive regulation for a biogenic amine hypothesis of affective disorder. *Biol.
Psychiatr.* **9,** 147–159. [12, 13, 15, 17, 101, 238, 239, 248, 256, 260, 261, 268, 313, 418]

Segal, M. and Bloom, F.E. (1976a) The action of norepinephrine in the rat hippocampus.
III. Hippocampal cellular responses to locus coeruleus stimulation in the awake rat.
Brain Res. **107,** 499–511. [199, 206]

Segal, M. and Bloom, F.E. (1976b) The action of norepinephrine in the rat hippocampus.
IV. The effects of locus coeruleus stimulation on evoked hippocampal unit activity. *Brain
Res.* **107,** 513–525. [206]

Segal, M. and Edelson, A. (1978) Effect of priming stimulation of catecholamine nuclei in
the rat brain. *Brain Res.* **123,** 369–372. [201]

Segawa, T., Mizuta, T., and Nomura, T. (1979) Modification of central 5-hydroxytryptamine
binding sites in synaptic membranes from rat brain after long-term administration of
tricyclic antidepressants. *Eur. J. Pharmacol.* **58,** 75–83. [347]

Segawa, T., Mizuta, T., and Uehara, M. (1982) Role of the central serotonergic system as
related to the pathogenesis of depression: Effect of antidepressants on rat central serotonergic activity. In S.Z. Langer, R. Takahashi, T. Segawa, and M. Briley (Eds.), *New
Vistas in Depression.* Pergamon, New York, pp. 3–10. [291, 332, 347]

Seligman, M.E.P. (1975) *Helplessness: On Depression, Development and Death.* Freeman, San Francisco. [74, 79, 121, 123–125, 142]

Seligman, M.E.P. (1978) Comment and integration. *J. Abnorm. Psychol.* **87,** 165–179. [75, 76, 79, 124]

Seligman, M.E.P. and Beagley, G. (1975) Learned helplessness in the rat. *J. Comp. Physiol. Psychol.* **88,** 534–541. [122, 123, 129, 290]

Seligman, M.E.P., Maier, S.F., and Geer, J. (1968) The alleviation of learned helplessness in the dog. *J. Abnorm. Soc. Psychol.* **73,** 256–262. [142]

Seligman, M.E.P., Rosellini, R.A., and Kozak, M. (1975) Learned helplessness in the rat: Reversibility, time course and immunization. *J. Comp. Physiol. Psychol.* **88,** 542–547. [124, 142]

Seligman, M.E.P., Abramson, L.Y., Semmel, A., and Von Baeyer, C. (1979) Depressive attributional style. *J. Abnorm. Psychol.* **88,** 242–247. [78]

Sellinger-Barnette, M.D., Mendels, J., and Frazer, A. (1980) The effects of psychoactive drugs on beta-adrenergic binding sites in rat brain. *Neuropharmacology* **19,** 447–454. [257, 266]

Selye, H. (1952) *The Story of the Adaptation Syndrome.* Acta, Montreal. [305]

Sem-Jacobsen, C.W. (1976) Electrical stimulation and self-stimulation in man with chronic implanted electrodes. Interpretation and pitfalls of results. In A. Wauquier and E.T. Rolls (Eds.), *Brain-Stimulation Reward.* North Holland/American Elsevier, New York, pp. 508–520. [136]

Semmes, J., Weinstein, S., Ghent, L., and Teuber, H.L. (1963) Correlates of impaired orientation in personal and extrapersonal space. *Brain* **86,** 747–772. [94]

Serban, G. and Kling, A., eds. (1976) *Animal Models in Human Psychobiology.* Plenum, New York. [102]

Serra, G., Argiolas, A., Klimek, V., Fadda, F., and Gessa, G.L. (1979) Chronic treatment with antidepressants prevents the inhibitory effect of small doses of apomorphine on dopamine synthesis and motor activity. *Life Sci.* **25,** 415–424. [183, 185, 188]

Serra, G., Argiolas, A., Fadda, F., Melis, M.R., and Gessa, G.L. (1981a) Repeated electroconvulsive shock prevents the sedative effect of small doses of apomorphine. *Psychopharmacology* **73,** 194–196. [183, 185, 189]

Serra, G., Melis, M.R., Argiolas, A., Fadda, F., and Gessa, G.L. (1981b) REM sleep deprivation induces subsensitivity of dopamine receptors mediating sedation in rats. *Eur. J. Pharmacol.* **72,** 131–135. [184, 185]

Sessions, G.R., Kant, G.J., and Koob, G.F. (1976) Locus coeruleus lesions and learning in rats. *Physiol. Behav.* **17,** 853–859. [200]

Sette, M., Raisman, R., Briley, M.S., and Langer, S.Z. (1981) Localization of tricyclic antidepressant binding sites on serotonin nerve terminals. *J. Neurochem.* **37,** 40–42. [316]

Shallice, T. (1978) The dominant action system: An information-processing approach to consciousness. In K.S. Pope and J.L. Singer (Eds.), *The Stream of Consciousness: Scientific Investigations into the Flow of Human Experience.* Plenum, New York, pp. 137–168. [27]

Shallice, T. (1982) Specific impairments of planning. *Philos. Trans. Roy. Soc. Lond., Ser. B* **298,** 199–209. [93, 95]

Sharman, D.F. (1973) The catabolism of catecholamines. *Br. Med. Bull.* **29,** 110–115. [5]

Sharp, F.R. and Schwartz, W.J. (1977) Proposed effects of brain noradrenaline on neuronal activity and cerebral blood flow during REM sleep. *Experientia* **33,** 1618–1619. [198]

Sharpless, N.S. (1977) Determination of 3-methoxy-4-hydroxyphenylglycol in urine and the effect of diet on its excretion. *Res. Comm. Chem. Pathol. Pharm.* **18,** 257–273. [225]

Shaw, D.M., Camps, F.E., and Eccleston, E.G., (1967) 5-hydroxytryptamine in the hindbrain of depressive suicides. *Br. J. Psychiatr.* **113**, 1407–1411. [309]

Shaw, D.M., Johnson, A.L., and MacSweeney, D.A. (1972) Tricyclic antidepressants and tryptophan in unipolar affective disorder. *Lancet* **2**, 1245. [319]

Shaw, D.M., O'Keefe, R., MacSweeney, D.A., Brooksbank, B.W.L., Noguera, R., and Coppen, A. (1973) 3-methoxy-4-hydroxy-phenylglycol in depression. *Psychol. Med.* **3**, 333–336. [222, 273]

Shaw, D.M., MacSweeney, D.A., Hewland, R., and Johnson, A. (1975) Tricyclic antidepressants and tryptophan in unipolar depression. *Psychol. Med.* **5**, 276–278. [319]

Shaw, D.M., Riley, G., Tidmarsh, S., and Blazek, R. (1976) Unipolar affective illness. *Lancet* **1**, 363–364. [308]

Sheard, M.H. (1963) The influence of doctor's attitude on the patient's response to anti-depressant medication. *J. Nerv. Ment. Disord.* **136**, 555–560. [176]

Sheard, M.H. and Davis, M. (1976) Shock elicited fighting in rats: importance of intershock interval upon effect of p-chlorophenylalanine (PCPA). *Brain Res.* **111**, 433–437. [295]

Sheffield, F.D. and Roby, T.B. (1950) Reward value of a nonnutritive sweet taste. *J. Comp. Physiol. Psychol.* **43**, 471–481. [402]

Sheffield, F.D., Wulff, J.J, and Backer, R. (1951) Reward value of copulation without sex drive reduction. *J. Comp. Physiol. Psychol.* **44**, 3–8. [402]

Shepard, R.N. (1980) Multidimensional scaling, tree fitting and clustering. *Science* **210**, 390–398. [27]

Sherman, A. (1979) Time course of the effects of antidepressants on serotonin in rat neo-cortex. *Commun. Psychopharmacol.* **3**, 1–5. [334]

Sherman, A.D. and Petty, F. (1980) Neurochemical basis of the action of antidepressants on learned helplessness. *Behav. Neur. Biol.* **30**, 119–134. [290, 292, 354]

Sherman, A.D., Allers, G.L., Petty, F., and Henn, F.A. (1979) A neuropharmacologically relevant animal model of depression. *Neuropharmacology* **18**, 891–893. [123]

Sherman, A.D., Sacquitne, J.L., and Petty, F. (1982) Specificity of the learned helplessness model of depression. *Pharmacol. Biochem. Behav.* **16**, 449–454. [122]

Sherman, G.F. and Galaburda, A.M. (1982) Cortical volume asymmetry and behavior in the albino rat. *Soc. Neurosci. Abstr.* **8**, 627. [97]

Sherman, G.F., Garbanati, J.A., Rosen, G.D., Yutzey, D.A., and Denenberg, V.H. (1980) Brain and behavioral asymmetries for spatial preference in rats. *Brain Res.* **192**, 61–67. [97]

Sherman, J.E. and Liebeskind, J.D. (1980) An endorphinergic, centrifugal substrate of pain modulation: Recent findings, current concepts, and complexities. In J.J. Bonica (Ed.), *Pain.* Raven, New York, pp. 191–204. [359]

Sheu, Y., Nelson, J.P., and Bloom, F.E. (1974) Discharge patterns of cat raphe neurons during sleep and waking. *Brain Res.* **73**, 263–276. [377, 383]

Shields, P.J. (1972) Effects of electroconvulsive shock on the metabolism of 5-hydroxytrypt-amine in the rat brain. *J. Pharm. Pharmacol.* **24**, 919–920. [328]

Shipley, J.E., Kupfer, D.J., Spiker, D.G., Shaw, D.H., Coble, P.A., Neil, J.F., and Cofsky, J. (1981) Neuropsychological assessment and EEG sleep in affective disorders. *Biol. Psychiatr.* **16**, 907–918. [90]

Shizgal, P. and Matthews, G. (1977) Electrical stimulation of the rat diencephalon: Differential effects of interrupted stimulation on ON- and OFF-responding. *Brain Res.* **129**, 319–333. [362]

Shopsin, B. (1976) Tryptophan and allopurinol in the treatment of depression. *Lancet* **1**, 1186. [320]

Shopsin, B. and Gershon, S. (1978) Dopamine receptor stimulation in the treatment of depression: Piribedil (ET-495). *Neuropsychobiology* **4**, 1–14. [174]

Shopsin, B., Freedman, L.S., Goldstein, M., and Gershon, S. (1972) Serum dopamine-beta-hydroxylase (DBH) activity and affective states. *Psychopharmacology* **27**, 11–16. [220]

Shopsin, B., Wilk, S., Suthananthan, G., Gershon, S., and Davis, K. (1974) Catecholamines and affective disorders revisited: A critical assessment. *J. Nerv. Ment. Disord.* **158**, 369–383. [10]

Shopsin, B., Friedman, E., Goldstein, M., and Gershon, S. (1975a) The use of synthesis inhibitors in defining a role for biogenic amines during imipramine treatment in depressed patients. *Psychopharmacol. Commun.* **1**, 239–249. [317]

Shopsin, B., Janowsky, D.S., Davis, J.M., and Gershon, S. (1975b) Rebound phenomena in manic patients following physostigmine. *Neuropsychobiology* **1**, 180–187. [282]

Shopsin, B., Friedman, E., and Gershon, S. (1976) Parachlorophenylalanine reversal of tranylcypromine effects in depressed patients. *Arch. Gen. Psychiatr.* **33**, 811–819. [317]

Shopsin, B., Cassano, G.B., and Conti, L. (1981) An overview of new "second generation" antidepressant compounds: Research and treatment implications. In S.J. Enna, J.B. Malick, and E. Richelson (Eds.), *Antidepressants: Neurochemical, Behavioral and Clinical Perspectives*. Raven, New York, pp. 219–251. [113, 235, 323, 324]

Shore, P.A. (1962) Release of serotonin and catecholamines by drugs. *Pharmacol. Rev.* **14**, 531–550. [7]

Shulman, R., Griffiths, J., and Diewold, P. (1978) Catechol-O-methyltransferase activity in patients with depressive illness and anxiety states. *Br. J. Psychiatr.* **132**, 133–138. [220]

Shur, E. and Checkley, S. (1982) Pupil studies in depressed patients: An investigation of the mechanism of action of desipramine. *Br. J. Psychiatr.* **140**, 181–184. [254, 285]

Shur, E., Checkley, S., and Delgado, I. (1983) Failure of mianserin to affect autonomic function in the pupils of depressed patients. *Acta Psychiatr. Scand.* **67**, 50–55. [254]

Sicuteri, F., Anselmi, B., and Fanciullacci, M. (1970) A therapeutic trial in migraine with parachlorophenylalanine, a specific serotonin depletor. *Headache* **10**, 124–125. [317]

Siegel, R.A., Andersson, K., Fuxe, K., Eneroth, P., Lindbom, L.-O., and Agnati, L.F. (1983) Rapid and discrete changes in hypothalamic catecholamine nerve terminal systems induced by audiogenic stress, and their modulation by nicotine: Relationship to neuroendocrine function. *Eur. J. Pharmacol.* **91**, 49–56. [198, 208]

Siegfried, B. and Bures, J. (1979) Conditioning compensates the neglect due to unilateral 6-OHDA lesions of substantia nigra in rats. *Brain Res.* **167**, 139–155. [158]

Siever, L., Insel, T., and Uhde, T. (1981a) Noradrenergic challenges in the affective disorders. *J. Clin. Psychopharmacol.* **1**, 193–206. [218, 219]

Siever, L.J., Risch, S.C., and Murphy, D.L. (1981b) Possible concurrence of cholinergic receptor hypersensitivity and adrenergic receptor hyposensitivity in affective disorders. *Psychiatr. Res.* **5**, 108–109. [381]

Siever, L.J., Cohen, R.M., and Murphy, D.L. (1981c) Antidepressants and alpha$_2$-adrenergic autoreceptor desensitization. *Am. J. Psychiatr.* **138**, 681–682. [246]

Siever, L.J., Uhde, T.W., Insel, T.R., Roy, B.F., and Murphy, D.L. (1982a) Growth hormone responses to clonidine unchanged by chronic clorgyline treatment. *Psychiatr. Res.* **7**, 139–144. [252]

Siever, L.J., Uhde, T.W., Silberman, E.K., Jimerson, D.C., Aloi, J.A., Post, R.M., and Murphy, D.L. (1982b) Growth hormone response to clonidine as a probe of noradrenergic receptor responsiveness in affective disorder patients and controls. *Psychiatr. Res.* **6**, 171–183. [228–230]

Siever, L.J., Insel, T.R., Jimerson, D.C., Lake, C.R., Uhde, T.W., Aloi, J., and Murphy, D.L. (1983a) Growth hormone response to clonidine in obsessive-compulsive patients. *Br. J. Psychiatr.* **142**, 184–187. [229]

Siever, L.J., Kafka, M.S., Insel, T.R., Lake, C.R., and Murphy, D.L. (1983b) Effect on long-term clorgyline administration on human platelet alpha-adrenergic receptor binding and platelet cyclic AMP responses. *Psychiatr. Res.* **9**, 37–44. [218, 219, 248]

Siever, L.J., Murphy, D.L., Slater, S., De La Vega, E., and Lipper, S. (1984) Plasma prolactin changes following fenfluramine in depressed patients compared to controls: An evaluation of central serotonergic responsivity in depression. *Life Sci.* **34**, 1029–1039. [315]

Sigg, E.B. and Hill, R.T. (1967) The effect of imipramine on central adrenergic mechanisms. In H. Brill (Ed.), *Neuro-Psycho-Pharmacology*. Excerpta Medica, Amsterdam, pp. 367–372. [106, 110, 271]

Sigg, E.B., Gyermek, L., and Hill, R.T. (1965) Antagonism to reserpine induced depression by imipramine, related psychoactive drugs and some autonomic agents. *Psychopharmacology* **7**, 144–149. [110]

Silberman, E.K., Vivaldi, E., Garfield, J., McCarley, R.W., and Hobson, J.A. (1980) Carbachol triggering of desynchronized sleep phenomena: Enhancement via small volume infusions. *Brain Res.* **191**, 215–224. [278]

Silberman, E.K., Reus, V.I., Jimerson, D.C., Lynott, A.M., and Post, R.M. (1981) Heterogeneity of amphetamine response in depressed patients. *Am. J. Psychiatr.* **138**, 1302–1307. [173, 176]

Silverman, P.B. and Ho, B.T. (1977) Characterization of discriminative stimulus control by psychomotor stimulants. In H. Lal (Ed.), *Discriminative Stimulus Properties of Drugs*. Plenum, New York, pp. 107–119. [152]

Silverstone, T. (1978) Dopamine, mood and manic-depressive psychosis. In S. Garattini (Ed.), *Depressive Disorders*. F.K. Schattauer Verlag, Stuttgart, pp. 419–430. [174]

Silvestrini, B. (1982) Trazodone—A new type of antidepressant: A discussion of pharmacological data and their clinical implications. In E. Costa and G. Racagni (Eds.), *Typical and Atypical Antidepressants: Molecular Mechanisms*. Raven, New York, pp. 327–340. [106, 110, 111, 243]

Simantov, R. (1981) Localization and modulation of enkephalins, endorphins and opiate receptors in the CNS and the pituitary gland. In H.M. Emrich (Ed.), *The Role of Endorphins in Neuropsychiatry: Modern Problems of Pharmacopsychiatry*. Karger, Basel, pp. 38–48. [358, 359]

Simon, H., LeMoal, M. and Calas, A. (1979) Efferents and afferents of the ventral tegmental A10 region studied after local injections of [^{3}H]-leucine and horseradish peroxidase. *Brain Res.* **178**, 17–40. [148]

Simon, P., Lecrubier, Y., Jouvent, R., Puech, A.J., Allilaire, J.F., and Widlocher, D. (1978) Experimental and clinical evidence of the antidepressant effect of a beta-adrenergic stimulant. *Psychol. Med.* **8**, 335–338. [232]

Simonson, M. (1964) Phenothiazine depressive reaction. *J. Neuropsychiatr.* **5**, 259–265. [171]

Simpson, D.M. and Annau, Z. (1977) Behavioral withdrawal following several psychoactive drugs. *Pharmacol. Biochem. Behav.* **7**, 59–64. [134]

Sinden, J.D. and Atrens, D.M. (1983) Dopaminergic and noradrenergic inhibition of hypothalamic self-stimulation: Differentiation of reward and performance effects. *Eur. J. Pharmacol.* **86**, 237–246. [199]

Sinnamon, H.M. (1982) The reward-effort model: An economic framework for examining the mechanism of neuroleptic action. *Behav. Brain Sci.* **5**, 73–75. [154]

Sirota, A.D. and Schwartz, G.E. (1982) Facial muscle patterning and lateralization during elation and depression imagery. *J. Abnorm. Psychol.* **91**, 25–34. [87]

Sitaram, N., Wyatt, R.J., Dawson, S., and Gillin, J.C. (1976) REM sleep induction by physostigmine infusion during sleep. *Science* **191**, 1281–1283. [278]

Sitaram, N., Mendelson, W.B., Wyatt, R.J., and Gillin, J.C. (1977) Time dependent induction of REM sleep and arousal by physostigmine infusion during normal human sleep. *Brain Res.* **122**, 562–567. [278]

Sitaram, N., Moore, A.M., and Gillin, J.C. (1978a) The cholinergic induction of dreaming in man. *Arch. Gen. Psychiatr.* **35**, 1239–1242. [278]

Sitaram, N., Moore, A.M., and Gillin, J.C. (1978b) Induction and resetting of REM sleep rhythm in normal man by arecoline: Blockade by scopolamine. *Sleep* **1**, 83–90. [278]

Sitaram, N., Nurnberger, J.I., Gershon, E.S., and Gillin, J.C. (1980) Faster cholinergic REM induction in euthymic patients with primary affective illness. *Science* **208**, 200–202. [279]

Sitaram, N., Nurnberger, J.I., Gershon, E.S., and Gillin, J.C. (1982) Cholinergic regulation of mood and REM sleep: Potential model and marker of vulnerability to affective disorder. *Am. J. Psychiatr.* **139**, 571–576. [279]

Sitaram, N., Jones, D., Kelwala, S., Bell, J., Stevenson, J., and Gershon, S. (1983) Pharmacology of the human iris: Development and use of challenge strategies in the study of the antidepression response. *Prog. Neuropsychopharmacol.* **7**, 273–286. [285]

Siviy, S.M., Calcagnetti, D.J., and Reid, L.D. (1982a) A temporal analysis of naloxone's suppressive effect on drinking. *Pharmacol. Biochem. Behav.* **16**, 173–175. [362]

Siviy, S.M., Calcagnetti, D.J., and Reid, L.D. (1982b) Opioids and palatability. In B.G. Hoebel and D. Novin (Eds.), *The Neural Basis of Feeding and Reward.* Haer Institute, Brunswick, Me., pp. 517–524. [362]

Siwers, B., Ringberger, V.A., Tuck, J.R., and Sjoqvist, F. (1977) Initial clinical trial based on biochemical methodology of zimelidine (a serotonin uptake inhibitor) in depressed patients. *Clin. Pharmacol. Ther.* **21**, 194–200. [251, 323, 333]

Sjostrom, R. (1973) 5-hydroxyindoleacetic acid and homovanillic acid in cerebrospinal fluid in manic-depressive psychosis and the effect of probenecid treatment. *Eur. J. Clin. Pharmacol.* **6**, 75–80. [167, 311]

Sjostrom, R. and Roos, B.-E. (1972) 5-hydroxyindoleacetic acid and homovanillic acid in cerebrospinal fluid in manic depressive psychosis. *Eur. J. Clin. Pharmacol.* **4**, 170–176. [168, 169, 311–313]

Sjostrom, R., Ekstedt, J., and Anggard, E. (1975) Concentration gradients of monoamine metabolites in human cerebrospinal fluid. *J. Neurol. Neurosurg. Psychiatr.* **38**, 666–668. [223]

Skirboll, L.R., Grace, A.A., and Bunney, B.S. (1979) Dopamine auto- and postsynaptic receptors: Electrophysiological evidence for differential sensitivity to dopamine agonists. *Science* **206**, 80–82. [183, 184]

Slade, A.P. and Checkley, S.A. (1980) A neuroendocrine study of the mechanism of action of ECT. *Br. J. Psychiatr.* **137**, 217–221. [186, 252]

Small, I.F., Small, J.G., Milstein, V., and Moore, J.E. (1972) Neuropsychological observations with psychosis and somatic treatment. *J. Nerv. Ment. Disord.* **155**, 6–13. [90]

Smeraldi, E., Negri, F., and Melica, A.M. (1977) A genetic study of affective disorders. *Acta Psychiatr. Scand.* **56**, 382–398. [45]

Smilde, J. (1963) Risks and unexpected reactions in disulfiram therapy of alcoholism. *Q. J. Stud. Alcohol.* **24**, 489–494. [230]

Smith, A.D. and Winkler, H. (1972) Fundamental mechanisms in the release of catecholamines. In H. Blaschko and E. Muscholl (Eds.), *Catecholamines: Handbook of Experimental Pharmacology*, Vol. 33. Springer, Berlin, pp. 538–617. [220]

Smith, C.B., Garcia-Sevilla, J.A., and Hollingsworth, P.J. (1981) Alpha$_2$-adrenoreceptors in rat brain are decreased after long-term tricyclic antidepressant drug treatment. *Brain Res.* **210,** 413–418. [247, 248]

Smith, C.B., Hollingsworth, P.J., Garcia-Sevilla, J.A., and Zis, A.P. (1983) Platelet alpha$_2$ adrenoceptors are decreased in number after antidepressant therapy. *Prog. Neuropsychopharmacol.* **7,** 241–247. [219, 248]

Smith, C.M., Semple, S.A., and Swash, M. (1982) Effects of physostigmine on responses in memory tests in patients with Alzheimer's disease. In S. Corkin, K. Davis, J. Growdon, E. Usdin, and R. Wurtman (Eds.), *Alzheimer's Disease: A Report of Progress*. Raven, New York, pp. 405–411. [281]

Smith, D.E., King, M.B., and Hoebel, B.G. (1970) Lateral hypothalamic control of killing: Evidence for a cholinoceptive mechanism. *Science* **167,** 900–901. [271]

Smith, G.P. and Gibbs, J. (1979) Postprandial satiety. In J.M. Sprague and A.N. Epstein (Eds.), *Progress in Psychobiology and Physiological Psychology*, Vol. 8. Academic, New York, pp. 180–242. [303]

Smith, J.A. (1980) Abuse of antiparkinsonian drugs: A review of the literature. *J. Clin. Psychiatr.* **41,** 351–354. [284]

Smith, J.E. and Lane, J.D. (1983) Brain neurotransmitter turnover correlated with morphine self-administration. In J.E. Smith and J.D. Lane (Eds.), *The Neurobiology of Opiate Reward Processes*. Elsevier, New York, pp. 361–402. [386]

Smith, J.E., Hintgen, J.N., Lane, J.D., and Aprison, M.H. (1976) Neurochemical correlates of behavior. Content of tryptophan, 5-hydroxytryptophan, serotonin, 5-hydroxyindoleacetic acid, tyrosine, dopamine and noradrenaline in four brain parts of the pigeon during behavioral depression following an injection of tryptophan. *J. Neurochem.* **26,** 537–541. [301]

Smith, J.E., Co, C., Freeman, M.E., Sands, M.P., and Lane, J.D. (1980) Neurotransmitter turnover in rat striatum is correlated with morphine self-administration. *Nature* **287,** 152–154. [151]

Smith, J.R. and Simon, E.J. (1980) Selective protection of stereospecific enkephalin and opiate binding against inactivation by N-ethylmaleimide: Evidence for two classes of opiate receptor. *Proc. Natl. Acad. Sci. USA* **77,** 281–284. [358]

Smith, R.F. (1979) Mediation of footshock sensitivity by serotonergic projection to hippocampus. *Pharmacol. Biochem. Behav.* **10,** 381–388. [297]

Smith, S.G. and Davis, W.M. (1973) Haloperidol effects on morphine self-administration: Testing for pharmacological modification of the primary reinforcement mechanism. *Psychol. Rec.* **23,** 215–221. [151]

Smith, S.R., Bledsoe, T., and Chhetri, M.K. (1975) Cortisol metabolism and the pituitary-adrenal axis in adults with protein-calorie malnutrition. *J. Clin. Endocrinol. Metab.* **40,** 43–52. [53]

Smotherman, W.P., Hunt, L.E., McGinnis, L.M., and Levine, S. (1979) Mother-infant separation in group-living rhesus macaques: A hormonal analysis. *Dev. Psychobiol.* **12,** 211–217. [133]

Sneddon, J.N. (1973) Blood platelets as a model for monoamine-containing neurons. *Prog. Neurobiol.* **2,** 151–198. [316]

Snodgrass, S.R., Hedley-White, E.T., and Lorenzo, A.V. (1973) GABA transport by nerve ending fractions of cat brain. *J. Neurochem.* **20,** 771–782. [357]

Snyder, S.H. and Yamamura, H.I. (1977) Antidepressants and the muscarinic acetylcholine receptor. *Arch. Gen. Psychiatr.* **34,** 236–239. [284]

Snyder, S.H., U'Prichard, D.C., and Greenberg, D.A. (1978) Neurotransmitter receptor binding in the brain. In M.A. Lipton, A. DiMascio, and K.F. Killam (Eds.), *Psychopharmacology: A Generation of Progress*. Raven, New York, pp. 361–370. [14]

Soblosky, J.S. and Thurmond, J.B. (1982) Tricyclic antidepressants and serotonin manipulations in an animal model of depression utilizing chronic intermittent stress. *Soc. Neurosci. Abstr.* **8**, 464. [130]

Sofia, R.D. (1969a) Effects of centrally active drugs on experimentally-induced aggression in rodents. *Life Sci.* **8**, 705–716. [107, 114, 291]

Sofia, R.D. (1969b) Structural relationship and potency of agents which selectively block mouse killing (muricide) behavior in rats. *Life Sci.* **8**, 1201–1210. [107]

Sokoloff, L. (1977) Relation between physiological function and energy metabolism in the nervous system. *J. Neurochem.* **29**, 13–26. [97]

Sorbi, S., Amaducci, L., Albanese, A., and Gainotti, G. (1980) Biochemical differences between the left and right hemispheres? Preliminary observations on choline acetyltransferase (CAT) activity. *Boll. Soc. Ital. Biol. Sper.* **56**, 226–227. [99]

Sourkes, T.L. (1973) On the origin of homovanillic acid (HVA) in the cerebrospinal fluid. *J. Neural Trans.* **34**, 153–157. [167, 175]

Sourkes, T.L. (1980) The mind-body problem: A neurochemists view. In D. Bindra (Ed.), *The Brain's Mind: A Neuroscience Perspective on the Mind-Body Problem*. Gardner, New York, pp. 53–68. [19]

Sourkes, T.L., Murphy, G.F., Chavez, B., and Zielinski, M. (1961) The action of some alpha-methyl and other amino acids on cerebral catecholamines. *J. Neurochem.* **8**, 109–115. [169]

Spano, P.F., Andreoli, V., Tonon, G.C., and Sirtori, C.R. (1975) Plasma tryptophan transport in normal and depressed subjects. *Med. Biol.* **53**, 489–492. [308]

Spector, S., Hirsch, C.W., and Brodie, B.B. (1963) Association of behavioral effects of pargyline, a non-hydrazide MAO inhibitor with increase in brain norepinephrine. *Int. J. Neuropharmacol.* **2**, 81–93. [7, 10]

Spencer-Booth, Y. and Hinde, R.A. (1971) The effects of 13 days' maternal separation on infant rhesus monkeys compared with those of shorter and repeated separations. *Anim. Behav.* **19**, 595–605. [141]

Spiker, D.G., Edwards, D., Hanin, I., Neil, J.F., and Kupfer, D.J. (1980) Urinary MHPG and clinical response to amitriptyline in depressed patients. *Am. J. Psychiatr.* **137**, 1183–1187. [235]

Spitz, R. (1946) Anaclitic depression. *Psychoanal. Stud. Child.* **2**, 113–117. [133]

Spitzer, R.L. and Williams, J.W.B. (1980) Classification of mental disorders and DSM-III. In H.I. Kaplan, A.M. Freedman, and B.J. Sadock (Eds.), *Comprehensive Textbook of Psychiatry*, Vol. 1, 3rd ed. Williams and Wilkins, Baltimore, pp. 1035–1072. [41]

Spitzer, R.L., Endicott, J., and Robins, E. (1978) Research diagnostic criteria. Rationale and reliability. *Arch. Gen. Psychiatr.* **35**, 773–782. [41, 47, 48, 50, 59]

Spyraki, C. and Fibiger, H. (1980) Functional evidence for subsensitivity of noradrenergic alpha-$_2$ receptors after chronic desipramine treatment. *Life Sci.* **27**, 1863–1867. [245]

Spyraki, C. and Fibiger, H.C. (1981) Behavioral evidence for supersensitivity of postsynaptic dopamine receptors in the mesolimbic system after chronic administration of desipramine. *Eur. J. Pharmacol.* **74**, 195–206. [184, 188]

Spyraki, C., Fibiger, H.C., and Phillips, A.G. (1982) Dopaminergic substrates of amphetamine-induced place preference conditioning. *Brain Res.* **235**, 185–193. [152]

Spyraki, C., Fibiger, H.C., and Phillips, A.G. (1983) Attenuation of heroin reward in rats by disruption of the mesolimbic dopamine system. *Psychopharmacol.* **79**, 278–283. [151]

Squires, R.F. (1974) Hyperthermia and L-tryptophan-induced increases in serotonin turnover in rat brain. *Adv. Biochem. Psychopharmacol.* **10**, 207–211. [289]

Squires, R.F. and Braestrup, C. (1977) Benzodiazepine receptors in the rat brain. *Nature*, **266**, 732–734. [20]

Srebo, B. and Lorens, S.A. (1975) Behavioral effects of selective midbrain raphe lesions in the rat. *Brain Res.* **89**, 303–325. [294, 296]

Stahl, S.M. and Meltzer, H.Y. (1978a) A kinetic and pharmacological analysis of 5-hydroxytryptamine transport by human platelets and platelet storage granules: Comparison with central serotonergic neurons. *J. Pharmacol. Exp. Ther.* **205**, 118–132. [316]

Stahl, S.M. and Meltzer, H.Y. (1978b) The human platelet as a model for the dopaminergic neuron: Kinetic and pharmacological properties and the role of the amine storage granules. *Exp. Neurol.* **59**, 1–15. [164]

Standage, K.F. (1979) The use of Schneider's typology for the diagnosis of personality disorder: An examination of reliability. *Br. J. Psychiatr.* **135**, 238–242. [58]

Stanford, S.C. and Nutt, D.J. (1982) Comparison of the effects of repeated electroconvulsive shock on alpha$_2$- and beta-adrenoceptors in different regions of rat brain. *Neuroscience* **7**, 1753–1757. [247, 257, 258]

Stanford, C., Nutt, D.J., and Cowen, P.J. (1983) Comparison of the effects of chronic desmethylimipramine administration on alpha$_2$- and beta-adrenoceptors in different regions of rat brain. *Neuroscience* **8**, 161–164. [247, 258]

Stanley, M., Virgilio, J., and Gershon, S. (1982) Tritiated imipramine binding sites are decreased in the frontal cortex of suicides. *Science* **216**, 1337–1339. [316]

Stanley, M., Mann, J.J., and Gershon, S. (1983) Alterations in pre- and postsynaptic serotonergic neurons in suicide victims. *Psychopharmacol. Bull.* **19**, 684–687. [315, 316]

Stapleton, J.M., Merriman, V.J., Coogle, C.L., Gelbard, S.D., and Reid, L.R. (1979) Naloxone reduces pressing for intracranial stimulation of sites in the periaqueductal gray area, accumbens nucleus, substantia nigra and lateral hypothalamus. *Physiol. Psychol.* **7**, 427–436. [362]

Stark, P. and Boyd, E.S. (1963) Effects of cholinergic drugs on hypothalamic self-stimulation rates in dogs. *Am. J. Physiol.* **205**, 745–748. [271]

Stark, P. and Hardison, C.D. (1984) A composite view of fluoxetine: A new alternative in the treatment of major depressive disorder. *Abstr. 14th CINP*, Florence, p. 1152. [323]

Starke, K. and Altman, K.P. (1973) Inhibition of adrenergic neurotransmission by clonidine: An action of prejunctional alpha-receptors. *Neuropharmacology* **12**, 339–347. [231]

Starke, K., Endo, T., and Taube, H.D. (1975) Relative pre- and postsynaptic potencies of alpha-adrenoceptor agonists in the rabbit pulmonary artery. *Naunyn Schmiedebergs Arch. Pharmacol.* **291**, 55–78. [211, 253]

Starke, K., Taube, H.D., and Borowski, E. (1977) Presynaptic receptor systems in catecholaminergic transmission. *Biochem. Pharmacol.* **26**, 259–268. [185, 199, 211, 228, 242]

Steel, J.M. and Briggs, W. (1972) Withdrawal depression in obese patients after fenfluramine treatment. *Br. Med. J.* **3**, 26. [322, 399]

Stein, G., Milton, F., Bebbington, P., Wood, K., and Coppen, A. (1976) Relationship between mood disturbances and free and total plasma tryptophan in postpartum women. *Br. Med. J.* **2**, 457. [308]

Stein, L. (1962) New methods for evaluating stimulants and antidepressants. In J.H. Nodine and J.H. Moyer (Eds.), *The First Hahnemann Symposium on Psychosomatic Medicine.* Lea and Fibiger, Philadelphia, pp. 297–301. [111, 136]

Stein, L. (1968) Chemistry of reward and punishment. In D.H. Efron (Ed.), *Psychopharmacology: A Review of Progress, 1957–1967.* U.S. Government Printing Office, Washington, D.C., pp. 105–123. [199, 363]

Stein, L. and Belluzi, J.D. (1978) Brain endorphins and the sense of well-being. In E. Costa and M. Trabucchi (Eds.), *The Endorphins.* Raven, New York, pp. 299–311. [362, 363]

Stein, L. and Seifter, J. (1961) Possible mode of antidepressive action of imipramine. *Science* **134**, 286–287. [111]

Stein, L., Belluzi, J.D., and Wise, C.D. (1975a) Memory enhancement by central administration of norepinephrine. *Brain Res.* **84**, 329–335. [201]

Stein, L., Wise, C.D., and Belluzi, J.D. (1975b) Effects of benzodiazepines on central serotonergic mechanisms. In E. Costa and P. Greengard (Eds.), *Mechanism of Action of Benzodiazepines.* Raven, New York, pp. 29–44. [293]

Steinbook, R.M., Jacobsen, A.F., Weiss, B.L., and Goldstein, D.J. (1979) Amoxapine, imipramine and placebo: A double-blind study with pretherapy urinary 3-methoxy-4-hydroxyphenylglycol levels. *Curr. Ther. Res.* **26**, 490–496. [233]

Steiner, J.A. and Grahame-Smith, D.G. (1980a) The effect of repeated electroconvulsive shock on corticosterone responses to centrally acting pharmacological stimuli in the male rat. *Psychopharmacology* **71**, 205–212. [252, 285, 338]

Steiner, J.A. and Grahame-Smith, D.G. (1980b) Central pharmacological control of corticosterone secretion in the intact rat. Demonstration of cholinergic and serotonergic facilitatory and alpha-adrenergic inhibitory mechanisms. *Psychopharmacology* **71**, 213–217. [285]

Steinfels, G.F., Strecker, R.E., Heym, J., and Jacobs, B.L. (1982) Correlations of dopaminergic unit activity with feeding and other behaviors in freely moving cats. In B.G. Hoebel and D. Novin (Eds.), *The Neural Basis of Feeding and Reward.* Haer Institute, Brunswick, Me., pp. 391–404. [199]

Steriade, M. and Hobson, J.A. (1976) Neuronal activity during the sleep-waking cycle. *Prog. Neurobiol.* **6**, 155–376. [205, 212, 213, 228, 274, 278, 381]

Stern, L.D. (1981) Theories of amnesia. *Mem. Cogn.* **9**, 247–262. [207]

Sternbach, H., Gerner, R.H., and Gwirtsman, H.E. (1982) The thyrotropin releasing hormone stimulation test: A review. *J. Clin. Psychiatr.* **43**, 4–6 [371]

Sternbach, H.A., Kirstein, L., Pottash, A.L.C., Gold, M.S., Extein, I., and Sweeney, D.R. (1983) The TRH test and urinary MHPG in unipolar depression. *J. Affect. Disord.* **5**, 233–237. [372]

Sternberg, D.E. and Jarvik, M.E. (1976) Memory functions in depression. *Arch. Gen. Psychiatr.* **32**, 219–224. [65]

Stille, G., Lauener, H., Eichenberger, E., Matussek, N, and Poldinger, W. (1968) Observations concerning adrenergic functions and antidepressant activity. *Pharmakopsychiatr. Neuropsychopharmakol.* **1**, 123–135. [106]

Stilwell, D.J., Levitt, R.A., Horn, C.A., Irvin, M.D., Gross, K., Parsons, D.S., Scott, R.H., and Bradley, E.L. (1980) Naloxone and shuttlebox self-stimulation in the rat. *Pharmacol. Biochem. Behav.* **13**, 739–742. [363]

Stokes, P.E., Stoll, P.M., Mattson, M.R., and Sollod, R.N. (1976) Diagnosis and psychopathology in psychiatric patients resistant to dexamethasone. In E.J. Sachar (Ed.), *Hormones, Behavior and Psychopathology.* Raven, New York, pp. 225–229. [54]

Stolz, J.F. and Marsden, C.A. (1982) Withdrawal from chronic treatment with metergoline, dl-propranolol and amitriptyline enhances serotonin receptor mediated behavior in the rat. *Eur. J. Pharmacol.* **79**, 17–22. [341]

Stolz, J.F., Marsden, C.A., and Middlemiss, D.N. (1983) Effect of chronic antidepressant treatment and subsequent withdrawal on [^{3}H]-5-hydroxytryptamine and [^{3}H]-spiperone binding in rat frontal cortex and serotonin receptor mediated behavior. *Psychopharmacology* **80**, 150–155. [340, 341, 347–349]

Stone, E.A. (1975) Stress and catecholamines. In A.J. Friedhoff (Ed.), *Catecholamines and Behavior*, Vol. 2. Plenum, New York, pp. 31–72. [210, 236]

Stone, E.A. (1979) Subsensitivity to norepinephrine as a link between adaptation to stress and antidepressant therapy: An hypothesis. *Res. Commun. Psychol. Psychiatr. Behav.* **4**, 241–255. [412]

Stone, E.A. and McCarty, R. (1983) Adaptation to stress: Tyrosine hydroxylase activity and catecholamine release. *Neurosci. Biobehav. Rev.* **7**, 29–34. [210]

Strahlendorf, J.C.R., Goldstein, F.J., Rossi, G.V., and Malseed, R.T. (1982) Differential effects of LSD serotonin and 1-tryptophan on visually evoked responses. *Pharmacol. Biochem. Behav.* **16**, 51–55. [21]

Strandman, E., Wetterberg, L., Perris, C., and Ross, S.B. (1978) Serum dopamine-beta-hydroxylase in affective disorders. *Neuropsychobiologoy* **4**, 248–255. [220]

Strombom, U. (1977) Antagonism by haloperidol of locomotor depression induced by small doses of apomorphine. *J. Neural Trans.* **40**, 191–194. [183]

Strombom, U., Svenssonn, T.H., Jackson, D.M., and Engstrom, G. (1977) Hyperthyroidism: Specifically increased response to central NA-(alpha-) receptor stimulation and generally increased monoamine turnover in brain. *J. Neural Trans.* **41**, 73–92. [373]

Stromgren, L.S. (1977) The influence of depression on memory. *Acta Psychiatr. Scand.* **56**, 108–128. [65]

Su, Y.F., Harden, T.K., and Perkins, J.P. (1980) Catecholamine-specific desensitization of adenylate cyclase. *J. Biol. Chem.* **255**, 7410–7419. [257, 259]

Suberi, M. and McKeever, W.F. (1977) Differential right hemispheric memory storage of emotional and non-emotional faces. *Neuropsychology* **15**, 757–768. [86]

Subramanyam, S. (1975) Role of biogenic amines in certain pathological conditions. *Brain Res.* **87**, 355–362. [167, 222, 311]

Sugrue, M.F. (1980a) Effects of acutely and chronically administered desipramine and mianserin on the clonidine-induced decrease in rat brain 3-methoxy-4-hydroxyphenylethyleneglycol sulphate content. *Br. J. Pharmacol.* **69**, 299. [241]

Sugrue, M.F. (1980b) The inability of chronic mianserin to block central alpha$_2$-adrenoceptors. *Eur. J. Pharmacol.* **68**, 377–380. [240, 244, 250]

Sugrue, M.F. (1980c) Changes in rat brain monoamine turnover following chronic antidepressant administration. *Life Sci.* **26**, 423–429. [182, 183, 248–250, 334]

Sugrue, M.F. (1981) Effects of acutely and chronically administered antidepressants on the clonidine-induced decrease in rat brain 3-methoxy-4-hydroxyphenylethyleneglycol sulphate content. *Life Sci.* **28**, 377–384. [244, 250]

Sugrue, M.F. (1982a) Effect of chronic antidepressants on rat brain alpha$_2$-adrenoceptor sensitivity. In G. Racagni and E. Costa (Eds.), *Typical and Atypical Antidepressants: Molecular Mechanisms.* Raven, New York, pp. 55–62. [244, 248]

Sugrue, M.F. (1982b) A study of the sensitivity of rat brain alpha$_2$-adrenoceptors during chronic antidepressant treatments. *Naunyn Schmiedebergs Arch. Pharmacol.* **320**, 90–96. [244, 247, 248, 257]

Sugrue, M.F. (1983) Some effects of chronic antidepressant treatments on rat brain monoaminergic systems. *J. Neural Trans.* **57**, 281–295. [344]

Sugrue, M.F. and McIndewar, I. (1976) Effect of blockade of 5-hydroxytryptamine reuptake on drug-induced antinociception in the rat. *J. Pharm. Pharmacol.* **28**, 447–448. [297]

Sullivan, J.L., Cevenar, J.O., Maltbie, A., and Stanfield, C. (1977a) Plasma MAO activity predicts response to lithium in manic-depressive illness. *Lancet* **2**, 1325–1327. [221]

Sullivan, J.L., Dackis, C., and Stanfield, C. (1977b) In vivo inhibition of platelet MAO activity by tricyclic antidepressants. *Am. J. Psychiatr.* **134**, 188–190. [221]

Sulser, F. (1978) New perspectives on the mode of action of antidepressant drugs. *Trends Pharmacol. Sci.* **1**, 92–94. [15, 17, 260, 418]

Sulser, F. (1982) Antidepressant drug research: Its impact on neurobiology and psychobiology. In E. Costa and G. Racagni (Eds.), *Typical and Atypical Antidepressants: Molecular Mechanisms.* Raven, New York, pp. 1–20. [260]

Sulser, F. and Mishra, R. (1982) Regulation of central noradrenergic receptor function and its relevance to the therapy of depression. In S.Z. Langer, R. Takahashi, T. Segawa, and M. Briley (Eds.), *New Vistas in Depression*. Pergamon, New York, pp. 37–47. [267]

Sulser, F. and Sanders-Bush, E. (1971) Effects of drugs on amines in the CNS. *Ann. Rev. Pharmacol.* **11**, 209–230. [173]

Sulser, F., Bickel, M.H., and Brodie, B.B. (1964) The action of desmethylimipramine in counteracting sedation and cholinergic effects of reserpine-like drugs. *J. Pharmacol. Exp. Ther.* **144**, 321–330. [7, 110]

Sulser, F., Owens, M.L., and Dingell, J.V. (1966) On the mechanism of amphetamine potentiation by desipramine. *Life Sci.* **5**, 2005–2010. [111]

Sulser, F., Vetulani, J. and Mobley, P.L. (1978) Mode of action of antidepressant drugs. *Biochem. Pharmacol.* **27**, 257–261. [101, 239]

Sulser, F., Janowsky, A.J., Okada, F., Manier, D.H., and Mobley, P.L. (1983) Regulation of recognition and action function of the norepinephrine (NE) receptor-coupled adenylate cyclase system in brain: Implications for the therapy of depression. *Neuropharmacology* **22**, 425–431. [259]

Suomi, S.J. (1976) Factors affecting responses to social separation in rhesus monkeys. In G. Serban and A. Kling (Eds.), *Animal Models in Human Psychobiology*. Plenum, New York, pp. 9–26. [132, 142]

Suomi, S.J. and Harlow, H.F. (1975) The role and reason of peer relationships in rhesus monkeys. In M. Lewis and L.A. Rosenblum (Eds.), *Friendship and Peer Relations*. Wiley, New York, pp. 153–185. [141]

Suomi, S.J., Harlow, H.F., and Domek, C.J. (1970) Effect of repetitive infant-infant separation of young monkeys. *J. Abnorm. Psychol.* **76**, 161–172. [132, 178]

Suomi, S.J., Collins, M.L., and Harlow, H.F. (1976) Effect of maternal and peer separations on young monkeys. *J. Child Psychol. Psychiatr.* **17**, 101–112. [132]

Suomi, S.J., Seaman, S.F., Lewis, J.K., De Lizio, R.B., and McKinney, W.T. (1978) Effects of imipramine treatment on separation-induced social disorders in rhesus monkeys. *Arch. Gen. Psychiatr.* **35**, 321–325. [101, 132]

Sutherland, R.J., Kolb, B., Becker, J.B., and Wishaw, I.Q. (1981) Neonatal 6-hydroxydopamine administration eliminates sparing of function after neonatal frontal cortex damage. *Soc. Neurosci. Abstr.* **7**, 41. [202]

Sved, F.F., Fernstrom, J.D., and Wurtman, R.J. (1979) Tyrosine administration reduces blood pressure and enhances brain norepinephrine release in spontaneously-hypertensive rats. *Proc. Natl. Acad. Sci. USA* **76**, 3511–3514. [232]

Svensson, L. and Ahlenius, S. (1983) Suppression of exploratory locomotor activity in the rat by the local application of 3-PPP enantiomers into the nucleus accumbens. *Eur. J. Pharmacol.* **88**, 393–397. [156]

Svensson, T.H. (1978) Attenuated feedback inhibition of brain serotonin synthesis following chronic administration of imipramine. *Naunyn Schmiedebergs Arch. Pharmacol.* **302**, 115–118. [334]

Svensson, T.H. (1980) Effect of chronic treatment with tricyclic antidepressant drugs on identified brain noradrenergic and serotonergic neurons. *Acta Psychiatr. Scand.* **61** (Suppl. 280), 121–131. [244, 331]

Svensson, T.H. and Usdin, T. (1978) Feedback inhibition of brain noradrenaline neurons by tricyclic antidepressants: Alpha-receptor mediation. *Science* **202**, 1089–1091. [16, 227, 241, 244, 248]

Svensson, T.H., Bunney, B.S., and Aghajanian, G.K. (1975) Inhibition of both noradrenergic and serotonergic neurons in brain by the alpha-adrenergic agonist clonidine. *Brain Res.* **92**, 291–306. [377]

Svensson, T.H., Dahlof, C., Engberg, G., and Hallberg, H. (1981) Central pre- and postsynaptic monoamine receptors in antidepressant therapy. *Acta Psychiatr. Scand.* **63** (Suppl. 290), 67–78. [250, 260]

Swanson, L.W. and Mogenson, G.J. (1981) Neural mechanisms for functional coupling of autonomic, endocrine and skeletomotor responses in adaptive behaviour. *Brain Res. Rev.* **3**, 1–34. [155]

Swanson, L.W., Connelly, M.A., and Hartman, B.K. (1977) Ultrastructural evidence for central monoaminergic innervation of blood vessels in the paraventricular nucleus of the hypothalamus. *Brain Res.* **136**, 166–173. [198]

Sweeney, D.R., Maas, J.W., and Heninger, G.R. (1978a) State anxiety, physical activity, and urinary 3-methoxy-4-hydroxyphenethylene glycol excretion. *Arch. Gen. Psychiatr.* **35**, 1418–1423. [226]

Sweeney, D.R., Nelson, C., Bowers, M., Maas, J., and Heninger, G. (1978b) Delusional versus non-delusional depression: Neurochemical differences. *Lancet* **2**, 100–101. [168]

Swensson, R.M. and Vogel, W.H. (1983) Plasma catecholamine and corticosterone as well as brain catecholamine changes during coping in rats exposed to stressful footshock. *Pharmacol. Biochem. Behav.* **18**, 689–693. [208, 209]

Syvalahti, E., Kangasniemi, P., and Ross, S.B. (1979a) Migraine headache and blood serotonin levels after administration of zimelidine, a selective inhibitor of serotonin uptake. *Curr. Ther. Res* **25**, 299–310. [298]

Syvalahti, E., Nagy, A., and Van Praag, H.M. (1979b) Effects of zimelidine, a selective 5-HT uptake inhibitor, on serum prolactin levels in man. *Psychopharmacology* **64**, 251–253. [337]

Szabadi, E., Bradshaw, C.M., and Besson, J.A.O. (1976) Elongation of pause-time in speech: A simple objective measure of motor retardation in depression. *Br. J. Psychiatr.* **129**, 592–597. [64]

Szerb, J.C. (1967) Cortical acetylcholine release and electro-encephalographic arousal. *J. Physiol. (Lond.)* **192**, 329–343. [273]

Szewczak, M.R., Fielding, S., and Cornfeldt, M. (1982) Rat internal capsule lesion: Further characterization of antidepressant screening potential. *Soc. Neurosci. Abstr.* **8**, 465. [135]

Takahashi, R., Tateishi, T., Yoshida, H., and Hironaka, I. (1982) Effects of chronic treatment with antidepressant drugs on serotonergic receptor binding activity in normal and tetrabenazine depression rat. In S.Z. Langer, R. Takahashi, T. Segawa, and M. Briley (Eds.), *New Vistas in Depression.* Pergamon, New York, pp. 29–36. [347]

Takahashi, S., Kondo, H., Yoshimura, M., Ochi, Y., and Yoshimi. T. (1973) Growth hormone responses to administration of L-5-hydroxytryptophan (l-5-HTP) in manic-depressive psychoses. *Folia Psychiatr. Neurol. Jpn.* **27**, 187–206. [314]

Takahashi, S., Yamane, H., Kondo, H., Tani, N., and Kato, N. (1974) CSF monoamine metabolites in alcoholism: A comparative study with depression. *Folia Psychiatr. Neurol. Jpn.* **28**, 347–354. [167]

Tamminga, C.A. (1981) Tardive dyskinesia and the dopamine receptor. In E. Usdin, W.E. Bunney, and J.M. Davis (Eds.), *Neuroreceptors: Basic and Clinical Aspects.* Wiley, New York, pp. 231–240. [16]

Tamminga, C.A., Smith, R.C., Change, S., Haraszti, J.S., and Davis, J.M. (1976) Depression associated with oral choline. *Lancet* **2**, 905. [281]

Tamminga, C.A., Smith, R.C., Pandey, G., Frohman, L.A., and Davis, J.M. (1977) A neuroendocrine study of supersensitivity in tardive dyskinesia. *Arch. Gen. Psychiatr.* **34**, 1199–1203. [186]

Tang, S.W. and Seeman, P. (1980) Effect of antidepressant drugs on serotonergic and adrenergic receptors. *Naunyn Schmiedebergs Arch. Pharmacol.* **311**, 255–261. [190, 242, 330]

Tang, S.W., Helmeste, D.M., and Stancer, H.C. (1978) The effect of acute and chronic desipramine and amitriptyline on rat brain total 3-methoxy-4-hydroxyphenylglycol. *Naunyn Schmiedebergs Arch. Pharmacol.* **305**, 207–211. [244, 248, 250]

Tang, S.W., Helmeste, D.M., and Stancer, H.C. (1979) Interaction of antidepressants with clonidine on rat brain total 3-methoxy-4-hydroxyphenylglycol. *Can. J. Physiol. Pharmacol.* **57**, 435–437. [248, 249]

Tang, S.W., Seeman, P., and Kwan, S. (1981) Differential effect of chronic imipramine and amitriptyline treatment on rat brain adrenergic and serotonergic receptors. *Psychiatr. Res.* **4**, 129–138. [190, 348]

Tanner, J., Weissman, M., and Prusoff, B. (1975) Social adjustment and clinical relapse in depressed outpatients. *Compr. Psychiatr.* **16**, 547–556. [67]

Targum, S.D. (1983a) Application of serial neuroendocrine challenge studies in the management of depressive disorders. *Biol. Psychiatr.* **18**, 3–19. [53]

Targum, S.D. (1983b) Reported weight loss and the dexamethasone suppression test. *Psychiatr. Res.* **9**, 173–174. [53]

Targum, S.D., Sullivan, A.C., and Byrnes, S.M. (1982) Neuroendocrine interrelationships in major depressive disorder. *Am. J. Psychiatr.* **139**, 282–286. [372]

Taube, S., Kirstein, L.S., Sweeney, D.R., Heninger, G.R., and Maas, J.W. (1978) Urinary 3-methoxy-4-hydroxyphenylglycol and psychiatric diagnosis. *Am. J. Psychiatr.* **135**, 78–82. [225]

Taylor, D.C. (1975) Factors influencing the occurrence of schizophrenia-like psychoses in patients with temporal lobe epilepsy. *Psychol. Med.* **5**, 249–254. [92]

Taylor, D.P., Allen, L.E., Ashworth, E.M., Becker, J.A., Hyslop, D.K., and Riblet, L.A. (1981) Treatment with trazodone plus phenoxybenzamine accelerates development of decreased type 2 serotonin binding in rat cortex. *Neuropharmacology* **20**, 513–516. [248]

Taylor, M.A. and Abrams, R. (1980) Reassessing the bipolar-unipolar dichotomy. *J. Affect. Disord.* **2**, 195–217. [45, 46]

Taylor, M.A., Greenspan, B., and Abrams, R. (1979) Lateralized neuropsychological dysfunction in affective disorder and schizophrenia. *Am. J. Psychiatr.* **136**, 1031–1034. [90]

Taylor, M.A., Abrams, R., and Hayman, M.A. (1980) The classification of affective disorder—A reassessment of the unipolar-bipolar dichotomy. A clinical, laboratory, and family study. *J. Affect. Disord.* **2**, 95–109. [45]

Taylor, M.A., Redfield, J., and Abrams, R. (1981) Neuropsychological dysfunction in schizophrenia and affective disease. *Biol. Psychiatr.* **16**, 467–478. [90]

Teasdale, J.D. (1983) Affect and accessibility. *Philos. Trans. Roy. Soc. Lond., Ser. B* **302**, 403–412. [71]

Teasdale, J.D. and Fogarty, S.J. (1979) Differential effects of induced mood on retrieval of pleasant and unpleasant events from episodic memory. *J. Abnorm. Psychol.* **88**, 248–257. [71, 72]

Teasdale, J.D. and Taylor, R. (1981) Induced mood and accessibility of memories: An effect of mood state or of induction procedure? *Br. J. Clin. Psychol.* **20**, 39–48. [71]

Teasdale, J.D., Taylor, R., and Fogarty, S.J. (1980) Effects of induced elation-depression on the accessibility of memories of happy and unhappy experiences. *Behav. Res. Ther.* **18**, 339–346. [71]

Telner, J., Lepore, F., and Guillemot, J.-P. (1979) Effects of serotonin content on pain sensitivity in the rat. *Pharmacol. Biochem. Behav.* **10**, 657–661. [297]

Tenen, S.S. (1967) The effects of p-chlorophenylalanine, a serotonin depletor, on avoidance acquisition, pain sensitivity and related behavior in the rat. *Psychopharmacology* **10**, 204–219. [294, 296, 297]

Tenen, S.S. (1968) Antagonism of the analgesic effect of morphine and other drugs by p-chlorophenylalanine, a serotonin depletor. *Psychopharmacology* **12**, 278–285. [299]

Tennant, C., Bebbington, P., and Hurry, J. (1981) The role of life events in depressive illness: Is there a substantial causal connection? *Psychol. Med.* **11**, 379–389. [131, 392, 396]

Tennant, C., Hurry, J., and Bebbington, P. (1982) The relation of childhood separation experiences to adult depressive and anxiety states. *Br. J. Psychiatr.* **141**, 475–482. [395]

Tepper, J.M., Nakamura, S., Spanis, C.W., Squire, L.R., Young, S.J., and Groves, P.M. (1982) Subsensitivity of catecholaminergic neurons to direct acting agonists after single or repeated electroconvulsive shock. *Biol. Psychiatr.* **17**, 1059–1070. [184]

Terenius, L. (1973) Characteristics of the "receptor" for narcotic analgesics in a synaptic plasma membrane fraction from rat brain. *Acta Pharmacol. Toxicol.* **33**, 377–384. [358]

Terenius, L. (1980) Opiate receptors: Problems of definition and characterization. *Adv. Biochem.* **21**, 321–358. [358]

Terenius, L., Wahlstrom, A., Lindstrom, L., and Widerlov, E. (1976) Increased CSF levels of endorphins in chronic psychoses. *Neurosci. Lett.* **3**, 157–162. [364]

Terenius, L., Wahlstrom, A., and Agren, H. (1977) Naloxone treatment in depression: Clinical observations and effects on CSF endorphins and monoamine metabolites. *Psychopharmacology* **54**, 31–33. [366]

Terry, L.C. and Martin, J.B. (1981) Evidence for alpha-adrenergic regulation of episodic growth hormone and prolactin secretion in the undisturbed male rat. *Endocrinology* **108**, 1869–1873. [228]

Terzian, H. (1964) Behavioral and EEG effects of intracarotid sodium amytal injection. *Acta Neurochir.* **12**, 230–239. [91]

Teuber, H.L. and Mishkin, M. (1954) Judgement of visual and postural vertical after brain injury. *J. Psychol.* **36**, 161–175. [94]

Theobald, W., Buch, O., Kunz, H., Morpurgo, C., Stenger, E.G., and Wilhelmi, G. (1964) Comparative pharmacological studies with Tofranil, Pertofran and Ensidon. *Arch. Int. Pharmacodyn. Ther.* **148**, 560–569. [110]

Theohar, C., Fischer-Cornelsson, K., Akesson, H.O., Ansari, J., Gerlach, G., Ohman, R., Ose, E., and Steglink, A.J. (1981) Bromocryptine as antidepressant: Double-blind comparative study with imipramine in psychogenic and endogenous depression. *Curr. Ther. Res.* **30**, 830–842. [174]

Thesleff, S. (1960) Effects of motor innervation on the chemical sensitivity of skeletal muscle. *Physiol. Rev.* **40**, 734–752. [15]

Thiebot, M.H., Jobert, A., and Soubrie, P. (1980) Conditioned suppression of behavior: Its reversal by intra-raphe microinjection of chlordiazepoxide and GABA. *Neurosci. Lett.* **16**, 213–217. [294]

Thierry, A.M., Javoy, F., Glowinski, J., and Kety, S.S. (1968) Effects of stress on the metabolism of norepinephrine, dopamine and serotonin in the central nervous system of the rat. *J. Pharmacol. Exp. Ther.* **163**, 163–171. [289]

Thoa, N.B., Tizabi, Y., and Jacobowitz, D.M. (1977) The effect of isolation on catecholamine concentration and turnover in discrete regions of rat brain. *Brain Res.* **131**, 259–269. [291]

Thoenen, H. (1970) Induction of tyrosine hydroxylase in peripheral and central adrenergic neurones by cold-exposure of rats. *Nature* **228**, 861–862. [210]

Thompson, C., Checkley, S.A., Corn, T., Franey, C., and Arendt, J. (1983) Down-regulation at pineal beta-adrenoceptors in depressed patients treated with desipramine? *Lancet* **1,** 1101. [262, 263]

Thompson, J., Rankin, H., Ashcroft, G.W., Yates, C.M., McQueen, J.K., and Cummings, S.W. (1982) The treatment of depression in general practice: A comparison of L-tryptophan, amitriptyline, and a combination of L-tryptophan and amitriptyline with placebo. *Psychol. Med.* **12,** 741–751. [319]

Thompson, R.W. and Nielson, C. (1972) The effect of scopolamine on the Kamin effect: A test of a parasympathetic overreaction hypothesis. *Psychonom. Sci.* **28,** 140–142. [277]

Thomson, R. (1982) Side effects and placebo amplification. *Br. J. Psychiatr.* **140,** 64–68. [284]

Thoren, P., Asberg, M., Bertilsson, L., Mellstrom, B., Sjoqvist, F., and Traskman, L. (1980) Clomipramine treatment of obsessive-compulsive disorder. II. Biochemical aspects. *Arch. Gen. Psychiatr.* **37,** 1289–1294. [229, 312]

Thornton, E.W. and Goudie, A.J. (1978) Evidence for the role of serotonin in the inhibition of specific motor responses. *Psychopharmacology* **60,** 73–79. [294]

Thornton, J.W. and Jacobs, P.D. (1972) The facilitating effects of prior inescapable/unavoidable stress on intellectual performance. *Psychonom. Sci.* **26,** 185–187. [75]

Toates, F.M. (1981) The control of ingestive behaviour by internal and external stimuli: A theoretical review. *Appetite* **2,** 25–50. [196, 362, 363]

Tolman, E.C. (1932) *Purposive Behaviour in Animals and Men.* Century, New York. [25]

Tombaugh, T.N., Anisman, H., and Tombaugh, J. (1980) Extinction and dopamine receptor blockade after intermittent reinforcement in training: Failure to find functional equivalence. *Psychopharmacology* **70,** 19–28. [153]

Tombaugh, T.N., Grandmaison, L.J., and Zito, K.A. (1982a) Establishment of secondary reinforcement in sign tracking and place preference tests following pimozide treatment. *Pharmacol. Biochem. Behav.* **17,** 665–670. [153]

Tombaugh, T.N., Pappas, B.A., Roberts, D.C.S., Vickers, G.J., and Szostak, C. (1982b) Failure to replicate the dorsal bundle extinction effect: Telencephalic norepinephrine depletion does not reliably increase resistance to extinction but does augment gustatory neophobia. *Soc. Neurosci. Abstr.* **8,** 309. [204]

Trabucchi, M., Cheney, D.L., Racagni, G., and Costa, E. (1975) In vivo inhibition of striatal acetylcholine turnover by L-dopa, apomorphine and (+)-amphetamine. *Brain Res.* **85,** 130–134. [379]

Tran, B.T., Chang, R.D.L., and Snyder, S.H. (1978) Histamine H_1 receptors identified in mammalian brain membranes with [^{3}H]mepyramine. *Proc. Natl. Acad. Sci. USA* **75,** 6290–6294. [368]

Traskman, L., Asberg, M., Bertilsson, L., Cronholm, B., Mellstrom, B., Neckers, L.M., Sjoqvist, F., Thoren, P., and Tybring, G. (1979) Plasma levels of chlorimipramine and its desmethyl metabolite during treatment of depression. *Clin. Pharmacol. Ther.* **26,** 600–610. [251, 323, 333]

Traskman, L., Tybring, G., Asberg, M., Bertilsson, L., Lantto, O., and Schalling, D. (1980) Cortisol in the CSF of depressed and suicidal patients. *Arch. Gen. Psychiatr.* **37,** 761–767. [53, 314]

Traskman, L., Asberg, M., Bertilsson, L., and Sjostrand, L. (1981) Monoamine metabolites in CSF and suicidal behaviour. *Arch. Gen. Psychiatr.* **38,** 631–636. [167, 222]

Traskman-Bendz, L., Asberg, M., and Bertilsson, L. (1981) Serotonin and noradrenaline uptake inhibitors in the treatment of depression—Relationship to 5-HIAA in spinal fluid. *Acta Psychiatr. Scand.* **63** (Suppl. 290), 209–218. [251, 323]

Treiser, S. and Kellar, K.J. (1979) Lithium effects on adrenergic receptor supersensitivity in rat brain. *Eur. J. Pharmacol.* **58,** 85–86. [257]

Treiser, S. and Kellar, K.J. (1980) Lithium: Effects on serotonin receptors in rat brain. *Eur. J. Pharmacol.* **64**, 183–185. [346]

Tricklebank, M.D., Drewitt, P.N., and Curzon, G. (1980) The effect of L-tryptophan on motor activity and its prevention by an extracerebral decarboxylase inhibitor and by 5-HT receptor blockers. *Psychopharmacology* **69**, 173–177. [302]

Trimble, M.R. and Robertson, M.M. (1983) Flupenthixol in depression: A study of serum levels and prolactin response. *J. Affect. Disord.* **5**, 81–89. [171]

Trimble, M.R., Chadwick, D., Reynolds, E.H., and Marsden, C.D. (1975) L-5-hydroxytryptophan and mood. *Lancet* **1**, 583. [320]

Trulson, M.E. and Jacobs, B.L. (1979a) Long-term amphetamine treatment decreases brain serotonin metabolism: Implications for theories of schizophrenia. *Science* **205**, 1295–1297. [150]

Trulson, M.E. and Jacobs, B.L. (1979b) Raphe unit activity in freely moving cats: Correlation with level of behavioral arousal. *Brain Res.* **163**, 135–150. [377, 383]

Tsuang, M.T. (1978) Familial subtyping of schizophrenia and affective disorders. In R.L. Spitzer and O.L. Klein (Eds.), *Critical Issues in Psychiatric Diagnosis*. Raven, New York, pp. 203–211. [45]

Tsubokawa, T., Katayama, Y., Kondo, T., Ueno, Y., Hayashi, N., and Moriyasu, N. (1980) Changes in local cerebral blood flow and neuronal activity during sensory stimulation in normal and sympathectomized cats. *Brain Res.* **190**, 51–65. [199]

Tsunoda, T. and Oka, M. (1976) Lateralization for emotion in the human brain and auditory cerebral dominance. *Proc. Jpn. Acad.* **52**, 528–531. [91]

Tucker, D.M. (1981) Lateral brain function, emotion, and conceptualization. *Psychol. Bull.* **89**, 19–46. [86, 365, 408]

Tucker, D.M. and Williamson, P.A. (1984) Asymmetric neural control systems in human self-regulation. *Psychol. Rev.* **91**, 185–215. [99]

Tucker, D.M., Watson, R.T., and Heilman, K.M. (1977) Discrimination and evocation of affectively intoned speech in patients with right parietal disease. *Neurology* **27**, 947–950. [86]

Tucker, D.M., Stenslie, C.E., Roth, R.S., and Shearer, S.L. (1981) Right frontal lobe activation and right hemisphere performance decrement during a depressed mood. *Arch. Gen. Psychiatr.* **38**, 169–174. [87, 90]

Tucker, J.E. and Spielberg, M.J. (1958) Bender-Gestalt test correlates of emotional depression. *J. Consult. Psychol.* **22**, 56. [64]

Tufik, S. (1981) Increased responsiveness to apomorphine after REM sleep deprivation: Supersensitivity of dopamine receptors or increase in dopamine turnover. *J. Pharm. Pharmacol.* **33**, 732–733. [188]

Tufik, S., Lindsey, C.J., and Carlini, E.A. (1978) Does REM sleep deprivation induce a supersensitivity of dopaminergic receptors in the rat brain? *Pharmacology* **16**, 98–105. [188, 189]

Tuomisto, J. and Tukainen, E. (1976) Decreased uptake of 5-hydroxytryptamine in blood platelets from depressed patients. *Nature* **262**, 596–598. [316]

Tuomisto, J., Tukainen, E., and Ahlfors, U.G. (1979) Decreased uptake of 5-hydroxytryptamine in blood platelets from patients with endogenous depression. *Psychopharmacology* **65**, 141–147. [316, 333]

Turner, C., Davenport, R., and Rogers, C. (1969) The effect of early deprivation on the social behaviour of adolescent chimpanzees. *Am. J. Psychiatr.* **125**, 1531–1536. [132]

Turner, W.J. and Merlis, S. (1964) A clinical trial of pargyline and DOPA in psychotic subjects. *Dis. Nerv. Syst.* **25**, 538–546. [8]

Tye, N.C., Everitt, B.J., and Iversen, S.D. (1977) 5-Hydroxytryptamine and punishment. *Nature* **268**, 741–742. [293, 295]

Tyrer, P. (1976) Towards rational therapy with monoamine oxidase inhibitors. *Br. J. Psychiatr.* **128**, 354–360. [221]

Tyrer, P. (1979) Clinical use of monoamine oxidase inhibitors. In E.S. Paykel and A. Coppen (Eds.), *Psychopharmacology of Affective Disorders.* Oxford University Press, Oxford, pp. 159–178. [11, 57, 113]

Tyrer, P. and Alexander, J. (1979) Classification of personality disorders. *Br. J. Psychiatr.* **135,** 163–167. [58]

Tyrer, P. and Lader, M. (1974) Response to propranolol and diazepam in somatic and psychic anxiety. *Br. Med. J.* **2,** 13–15. [204]

U'Prichard, D.C., Greenberg, D.A., and Snyder, S.H. (1977) Binding characteristics of radiolabelled agonists and antagonists at central nervous system alpha noradrenergic receptors. *Mol. Pharmacol.* **13,** 454–473. [246]

U'Prichard, D.C., Greenberg, D.A., Sheehan, P.P., and Snyder, S.H. (1978) Tricyclic antidepressants: Therapeutic properties and affinity for alpha-noradrenergic receptor binding sites in the brain. *Science* **199,** 197–198. [241]

U'Prichard, D.C., Bechtel, W.D., Rouot, B.M., and Snyder, S.H. (1979) Multiple apparent alpha-noradrenergic receptor binding sites in rat brain: Effect of 6-hydroxydopamine. *Mol. Pharmacol.* **16,** 47–60. [246]

U'Prichard, D.C., Daiguji, M., Tong, C., Mitrius, J.C., and Meltzer, H.Y. (1982) Alpha$_2$-adrenergic receptors: Comparative biochemistry of neural and non-neural receptors, and in vivo analysis in psychiatric patients. In E. Usdin and I. Hanin (Eds.), *Biological Markers in Psychiatry and Neurology.* Pergamon, New York, pp. 205–217. [248]

Ueki, S. (1982) Mouse-killing behaviour (muricide) in the rat and the effect of antidepressants. In S.Z. Langer, R. Takahashi, T. Segawa, and M. Briley (Eds.), *New Vistas in Depression.* Pergamon, New York, pp. 187–194. [107, 113]

Uhde, T.W., Post, R.M., Siever, L.J., and Buchsbaum, M.S. (1980) Clonidine and psychophysical pain. *Lancet* **2,** 1375. [223, 231]

Ungerstedt, U. (1971) Stereotaxic mapping of the monoamine pathways in the rat brain. *Acta Physiol. Scand.* (Suppl. 367), 1–48. [9, 149, 193, 194]

Ungerstedt, U. (1979) Central dopamine mechanisms and behavior. In A.S. Horn, J. Korf, and B.H.C. Westerink (Eds.), *The Neurobiology of Dopamine.* Academic, New York, pp. 577–596. [149]

Usdin, E. and Bunney, W.E., eds. (1975) *Pre- and Postsynaptic Receptors.* Dekker, New York. [16, 171]

Valenstein, E.S. (1973) *Brain Control: A Critical Examination of Brain Stimulation and Psychosurgery.* Wiley, New York. [136]

Valero, I., Stewart, J., McNaughton, N., and Gray, J.A. (1977) Septal driving of the hippocampal theta rhythm as a function of frequency in the male rat: Effects of adreno-pituitary hormones. *Neuroscience* **2,** 1029–1032. [383]

Valzelli, L. and Bernasconi, S., (1971) Psychoactive drug effects on behavioral changes induced by prolonged socio-environmental deprivation in rats. *Psychol. Med.* **6,** 271–276. [114, 291]

Valzelli, L., Consolo, S., and Morpurgo, C. (1967) Influence of imipramine-like drugs on the metabolism of amphetamine. In S. Garattini and M.N.G. Dukes (Eds.), *Antidepressant Drugs.* Excerpta Medica, Amsterdam, pp. 61–69. [111]

Valzelli, L., Garattini, S., Bernasconi, S., and Sala, A. (1981) Neurochemical correlates of muricidal behavior in rats. *Neuropsychobiology* **7,** 172–178. [291]

Van Cauter, E. and Mendlewicz, J. (1978) 24-hour dopamine-beta-hydroxylase pattern: A possible biological index of manic-depression. *Life Sci.* **22**, 147–156. [220]

Van der Kooy, D., LePianne, F.G., and Phillips, A.G. (1977) Apparent independence of opiate reinforcement and electrical self-stimulation systems in rat brain. *Life Sci.* **20**, 981–986. [363]

Van Hiele, L.J. (1980) L-5-hydroxytryptophan in depression: The first substitution therapy in psychiatry? The treatment of 99 out-patients with "therapy-resistant" depressions. *Neuropsychobiology* **6**, 230–240. [320]

Van Kammen, D.P. and Murphy, D.L. (1978) Prediction of imipramine antidepressant response by a one-day d-amphetamine trial. *Am. J. Psychiatr.* **135**, 1179–1184. [233]

Van Kammen, D.P., Bunney, W.E., Docherty, J.P., Jimerson, D.C., Post, R.M., Siris, S., Ebert, M., and Gillin, J.C. (1977) Amphetamine-induced catecholamine activation in schizophrenia and depression: Behavioral and physiological effects. In E. Costa and G.L. Gessa (Eds.), *Non-Striatal Dopamine Neurons.* Raven, New York, pp. 655–659. [233]

Van Praag, H.M. (1977) Significance of biochemical parameters in the diagnosis, treatment and prevention of depressive disorders. *Biol. Psychiatr.* **12**, 101–131. [322]

Van Praag, H.M. (1978) Amine hypotheses of affective disorders. In L.L. Iversen, S.D. Iversen, and S.H. Snyder (Eds.), *Handbook of Psychopharmacology*, Vol. 13. Plenum, New York, pp. 187–297. [318]

Van Praag, H.M. (1980) Central monoamine metabolism in depression. I. Serotonin and related compounds. *Compr. Psychiatr.* **21**, 30–43. [319]

Van Praag, H.M. (1982a) Depression, suicide and the metabolism of serotonin in the brain. *J. Affect. Disord.* **4**, 275–290. [310, 312]

Van Praag, H.M. (1982b) Serotonin precursors in the treatment of depression. In B.T. Ho, J.C. Schoolar, and E. Usdin (Eds.), *Serotonin in Biological Psychiatry.* Raven, New York, pp. 259–286. [319–321]

Van Praag, H.M. (1983) In search of the mode of action of antidepressants: 5-HTP/tyrosine mixtures in depressions. *Neuropharmacology* **22**, 433–440. [320, 321]

Van Praag, H.M. and De Haan, S. (1979) Central serotonin metabolism and frequency of depression. *Psychiat. Res.* **1**, 219–224. [313]

Van Praag, H.M. and De Haan, S. (1980) Depression vulnerability and 5-hydroxytryptophan prophylaxis. *Psychiatr. Res.* **3**, 75–83. [322]

Van Praag, H.M. and De Haan, S. (1981) Chemoprophylaxis of depressions. An attempt to compare lithium with 5-hydroxytryptophan. *Acta Psychiatr. Scand.* **63** (Suppl. 290), 191–201. [322]

Van Praag, H.M. and Korf, J. (1971a) Endogenous depressions with and without disturbances in the 5-hydroxytryptamine metabolism: A biochemical classification? *Psychopharmacology* **25**, 14–21. [311]

Van Praag, H.M. and Korf, J. (1971b) Retarded depression and the dopamine metabolism. *Psychopharmacology* **19**, 199–203. [167, 168]

Van Praag, H.M. and Korf, J. (1975) Central monoamine metabolism in depression: Causative or secondary phenomenon. *Pharmakopsychiatria* **8**, 321–326. [11, 172, 177]

Van Praag, H.M., Korf, J., and Puite, J. (1970) 5-hydroxyindoleacetic acid levels in the cerebrospinal fluid of depressive patients treated with probenecid. *Nature* **225**, 1259–1260. [311]

Van Praag, H.M., Korf, J., Dols, L.C.W., and Schut, T. (1972) A pilot study of the predictive value of the probenecid test in application of 5-hydroxytryptophan as an antidepressant. *Psychopharmacology* **25**, 14–21. [320, 321]

Van Praag, H.M., Korf, J., and Schut, D. (1973) Cerebral monoamines and depression: An investigation with the probenecid technique. *Arch. Gen. Psychiatr.* **28**, 827–831. [167, 168, 310, 311]

Van Praag, H.M., Van Den Burg, W., Bos, E.R.H., and Dols, L.C.W. (1974) 5-hydroxytryptophan in combination with clomipramine in "therapy-resistant" depression. *Psychopharmacology* **38**, 267–269 [321]

Van Praag, H.M., Korf, J., Lakke, J.P.W.F., and Schut, T. (1975) Dopamine metabolism in depressions, psychoses and Parkinson's disease: The problem of the specificity of biological variables in behavior disorders. *Psychol. Med.* **5**, 138–146. [168]

Van Riezen, H. (1972) Different central effects of the 5-HT antagonists mianserin and cyproheptadine. *Arch. Int. Pharmacodyn. Ther.* **198**, 256–269. [110, 111]

Van Riezen, H., Behagel, H., and Chafik, M. (1975) Development of psychotropic drugs. *Psychopharmacol. Bull.* **11**, 10–15. [106, 107]

Van Riezen, H., Schnieden, H., and Wren, A.F. (1977) Olfactory bulb ablation in the rat: Behavioral changes and their reversal by antidepressant drugs. *Br. J. Pharmacol.* **60**, 521–528. [113]

Van Scheyen, J.D. (1975) Manie als complicatie bij behandeling van unipolaire vitale depressies. *Ned. Tijdschr. Geneeskd.* **119**, 1567–1571. [413]

Van Scheyen, J.D., Van Praag, H.M., and Korf, J. (1977) Controlled study comparing nomifensine and chlomipramine in unipolar depression, using the probenecid technique. *Br. J. Clin. Pharmacol.* **4**, 179S–184S. [173, 174, 177, 323]

Van Wijk, M., Meisch, J.J., and Korf, J. (1977) Metabolism of 5-hydroxytryptamine and levels of tricyclic antidepressant drugs in rat brain after acute and chronic treatment. *Psychopharmacology* **55**, 217–223. [329, 334]

Van Woert, M.H., Rosenbaum, D., Howieson, J., and Bowers, M.B. (1977) Long-term therapy of myoclonus and other neurologic disorders with L-5-hydroxytryptophan and carbidopa. *New Engl. J. Med.* **296**, 70–75. [320]

Vanderheyden, J.-E., Noel, G., and Mendlewicz, J. (1981) Biogenic amine disturbances in cerebrospinal fluid in Parkinsonism and unipolar depression: Use of the probenecid method. *Neuropsychobiology* **7**, 137–151. [311]

Vanderwolf, C.H., Kramis, R., Gillespie, L.A., and Bland, B.H. (1975) Hippocampal rhythmical slow activity and neocortical low voltage fast activity: Relationship to behavior. In R.L. Isaacson and K.H. Pribram (Eds.), *The Hippocampus*, Vol. 2, *Neurophysiology and Behavior*. Plenum, New York, pp. 101–128. [273, 274]

Vanderwolf, C.H., Kramis, R., and Robinson, T.E. (1978) Hippocampal activity during waking behavior and sleep: Analyses using centrally acting drugs. In K. Elliott and J. Whelan (Eds.), *Functions of the Septo-Hippocampal System*. Elsevier, Amsterdam, pp. 199–221. [273, 274]

Velley, L., Kempf, E., and Cardo, B. (1982) Locomotor activity of rats after stimulation of the nucleus locus coeruleus region or after lesion of the dorsal noradrenergic bundle: Effects of clonidine, prazosin and yohimbine. *Psychopharmacology* **78**, 239–244. [243]

Velten, E. (1968) A laboratory task for the induction of mood states. *Behav. Res. Ther.* **6**, 473–482. [68, 71, 72]

Vergnes, M. and Penot, C. (1976a) Aggression intraspécifique induite par chocs électriques et reactivité apres lésion du raphe chez le rat: Effets de la physostigmine. *Brain Res.* **104**, 107–119. [295]

Vergnes, M. and Penot, C. (1976b) Effets comportmenteaux des lésions du raphe chez des rats privés du septum. *Brain Res.* **115**, 154–159. [295, 296]

Vergnes, M., Mack, G., and Kempf, E. (1974) Controle inhibiteur du comportement d'agression interspécifique du rat. Système serotonergique du raphe et afférences olfactives. *Brain Res.* **70**, 481–491. [292]

Vernon, R.E. (1963) *Personality Assessment: A Critical Survey*. Methuen, London. [120]

Vertes, R.P. (1977) Selective firing of rat pontine gigantocellular neurons during movement and REM sleep. *Brain Res.* **128**, 146–152. [274]

Vertes, R.P. and Miller, N.E. (1976) Brain stem neurons that fire selectively to a conditioned stimulus for shock. *Brain Res.* **103**, 229–242. [213, 275]

Vestergaard, P., Sorensen, T., Hoppe, E., Rafaelsen, O.J., Yates, C.M., and Nicolaou, N. (1978) Biogenic amine metabolites in cerebrospinal fluid of patients with affective disorders. *Acta Psychiatr. Scand.* **58**, 88–96. [167, 168, 225]

Vetulani, J. (1984) Changes in responsiveness of central aminergic structures after chronic ECS. In B. Lerer, R.D. Weiner, and R.H. Belmaker (Eds.), *ECT: Basic Mechanisms*. John Libbey, London, pp. 33–45. [369]

Vetulani, J. and Sulser, F. (1975) Action of various antidepressant treatments reduces reactivity of noradrenergic cyclic AMP generating system in limbic forebrain. *Nature* **257**, 495–496. [15, 256]

Vetulani, J., Stawarz, R.J., Dingell, J.V., and Sulser, F. (1976a) A possible common mechanism of action of antidepressant treatments. *Naunyn Schmiedebergs Arch. Pharmacol.* **293**, 109–114. [256, 260, 262]

Vetulani, J., Stawarz, R.J., and Sulser, F. (1976b) Adaptive mechanisms of the noradrenergic cyclic AMP generating system in the limbic forebrain of the rat: Adaptation to persistent changes in the availability of norepinephrine (NE). *J. Neurochem.* **27**, 661–666. [256, 259]

Vetulani, J., Antkiewicz-Michaluk, L., Golembiowska-Nikitin, K., Michaluk, J., Pilc, A., and Rokosz, A. (1980) The effect of multiple imipramine administration on monoaminergic systems of the rat brain. *Pol. J. Pharm. Pharmacol.* **32**, 523–530. [247, 255]

Vetulani, J., Lebrecht, U., and Nowak, J.Z. (1981) Enhancement of responsiveness of the central serotonergic system and serotonin-2 receptor density in rat frontal cortex by electroconvulsive shock treatment. *Eur. J. Pharmacol.* **81**, 85. [339, 348, 349]

Visi, E.S. (1980) Modulation of cortical release of acetylcholine by noradrenaline released from nerves arising from the rat locus coeruleus. *Neuroscience* **5**, 2139–2144. [381]

Vivaldi, E., McCarley, R.W., and Hobson, J.A. (1980) Evocation of desynchronized sleep signs by chemical microstimulation of the pontine brain stem. In J.A. Hobson and M.A. Brazier (Eds.), *The Reticular Formation Revisited*. Raven, New York, pp. 513–529. [381]

Viveros, O.H., Argueros, L., and Kirshner, N. (1968) Release of catecholamines and dopamine-beta-hydroxylase from the adrenal medulla. *Life Sci.* **7**, 609–618. [220]

Vogel, G.W. (1975) A review of REM sleep deprivation. *Arch. Gen. Psychiatr.* **32**, 749–761. [116, 381, 413]

Vogel, G.W. (1983) Evidence for REM sleep deprivation as the mechanism of action of antidepressant drugs. *Prog. Neuropsychopharmacol.* **7**, 343–349. [343, 412]

Vogel, G.W., Vogel, F., McAbee, R.S., and Thurmond, R.J. (1980) Improvement of depression by REM sleep deprivation. *Arch. Gen. Psychiatr.* **37**, 247–253. [116]

Vogel, J.R. and Hambrich, D.R. (1973) Chronic administration of electroconvulsive shock: Effects on mouse killing activity and brain monoamines in rats. *Physiol. Behav.* **11**, 725–728. [107]

Vogt, M. (1974) The effect of lowering the 5-hydroxytryptamine content of the rat spinal cord on analgesia produced by morphine. *J. Physiol.* **236**, 483–498. [299]

Von Knorring (1975) *The experience of pain in patients with depressive disorders. A clinical and experimental study*. Umea University Medical Dissertations, Umea, Sweden. [69]

Von Voigtlander, P.F., Triezenberg, H.J., and Losey, E.G. (1978) Interaction between clonidine and antidepressant drugs: A method for identifying antidepressant-like agents. *Neuropharmacology* **17**, 375–381. [264–266]

Waal, H.J. (1967) Propranolol-induced depression. *Br. Med. J.* **11**, 50. [231]

Wada, J. and Rasmussen, T. (1960) Intracarotid injection of sodium amytal for the localization of cerebral speech dominance. *J. Neurosurg.* **17**, 266–282. [91]

Waehrens, J. and Gerlach, J. (1981) Bromocryptine and imipramine in endogenous depression: A double-blind controlled trial in out-patients. *J. Affect. Disord.* **3**, 193–202. [174]

Wagner, H.M., Burns, D.H., Dannals, R.F., Wong, D.F., Langstrom, B., Duelfer, T., Frost, J.J., Ravert, H.T., Links, J.M., Rosenbloom, S.B., Lucas, S.E., Kramer, A.V., and Kuhlar, M.J. (1983) Imaging dopamine receptors in the human brain by positron tomography. *Science* **221**, 1264–1266. [98]

Wagner, H.R. and Davies, J.N. (1980) Decreased beta-adrenergic responses in the female brain are eliminated by ovariectomy: Correlation of [³H]-dihydroalprenolol binding and catecholamine stimulated cyclic AMP levels. *Brain Res.* **201**, 235–239. [267]

Wagner, H.R., Hall, T.L., and Cote, I.L. (1977) The applicability of inescapable shock as a source of animal depression. *J. Gen. Psychol.* **96**, 313–318. [123]

Wagner, H.R., Crutcher, K.A., and Davies, J.N. (1979) Chronic estrogen treatment decreases beta-adrenergic responses in rat cerebral cortex. *Brain Res.* **171**, 147–151. [267]

Waldmeier, P.C., Baumann, P., Greengrass, P.M., and Maitre, L. (1976) Effects of clomipramine and other tricyclic antidepressants on biogenic amine uptake and turnover. *Postgrad. Med. J.* **52** (Suppl. 3), 33–39. [234]

Waldmeier, P.C. (1981) Noradrenergic transmission in depression: Under or overfunction? *Pharmakopsychiatria* **14**, 3–9. [16, 260]

Waldmeier, P.C., Feluer, A.E., and Maitre, L. (1981) Long term effects of selective MAO inhibitors on MAO activity and amine levels. In M.B.H. Youdim and E.S. Paykel (Eds.), *Monoamine Oxidase Inhibitors: The State of the Art.* Wiley, London, pp. 87–102. [334]

Walinder, J., Skott, A., Carlsson, A., Nagy, A., and Roos, B.-E. (1976) Potentiation of the antidepressant action of clomipramine by tryptophan. *Arch. Gen. Psychiatr.* **33**, 1384–1389. [319]

Walinder, J., Carlsson, A., and Persson, R. (1981) 5-HT reuptake inhibitors plus tryptophan in endogenous depression. *Acta Psychiatr. Scand.* **63** (Suppl. 290), 179–190. [319]

Wallach, M.D. and Hedley, L.R. (1979) The effects of antihistamines in a modified behavioral despair test. *Commun. Psychopharmacol.* **3**, 35–39. [127, 128]

Wang, R.Y. (1981) Dopaminergic neurons in the rat ventral tegmental area. II. Evidence for autoregulation. *Brain Res. Rev.* **3**, 141–151. [156, 183]

Wang, R.Y. and Aghajanian, G.K. (1980) Enhanced sensitivity of amygdaloid neurons to serotonin and norepinephrine after chronic antidepressant treatment. *Commun. Psychopharmacol.* **4**, 83–90. [253, 335, 336]

Wang, Y.C., Pandey, G.N., Mendels, J., and Frazer, A. (1974) Platelet adenylate cyclase responses in depression: Implications for a receptor deficit. *Psychopharmacology* **36**, 291–300. [219]

Warbritton, J.D., Stewart, R.M., and Baldessarini, R.J. (1978) Decreased locomotor activity and attenuation of amphetamine hyperactivity with intraventricular infusion of serotonin in the rat. *Brain Res.* **143**, 373–382. [378]

Warburton, J.W. (1967) Depressive symptoms in patients referred for thalamotomy. *J. Neurol. Neurosurg. Psychiatr.* **30**, 360–370. [170]

Ward, C.H., Beck, A.T., Mendelsohn, M., Mock, J.E., and Erbaugh, J.K. (1962) The psychiatric nomenclature. Reasons for diagnostic disagreement. *Arch. Gen. Psychiatr.* **7**, 198–205. [41]

Warnke, E. and Hoefke, W. (1977) Influence of central pretreatment with 6-hydroxydopamine on the hypotensive effect of clonidine. *Arzneim. Forsch.* **27**, 2311–2313. [228]

Warsh, J.J. and Stancer, H.C. (1976) Brain and peripheral metabolism of 5-hydroxytryptophan-^{14}C following peripheral decarboxylase inhibition. *J. Pharmacol. Exp. Ther.* **197**, 545–555. [301]

Watanabe, S., Isheno, H., and Otsuki, S. (1975) Double-blind comparison of lithium carbonate and imipramine in treatment of depression. *Arch. Gen. Psychiatr.* **32**, 659–668. [46]

Watanabe, S., Inoue, M., and Ueki, S. (1970) Effects of psychotropic drugs injected into the limbic structures on mouse-killing behaviour in the rat with olfactory bulb ablation. *Jpn. J. Pharmacol.* **29**, 493–496. [113]

Waterhouse, B.D. and Woodward, D.J. (1980) Interaction of norepinephrine with cerebrocortical activity evoked by stimulation of somatosensory afferent pathways in the rat. *Exp. Neurol.* **67**, 11–34. [206]

Waterhouse, B.D., Moises, H.C., and Woodward, D.J. (1981) Alpha-receptor-mediated facilitation of somatosensory cortical neuronal responses to excitatory synaptic inputs and iontophoretically applied acetylcholine. *Neuropharmacology* **20**, 907–920. [206]

Watson, R., Hartman, E., and Schildkraut, J.J. (1972) Amphetamine withdrawal: Affective state, sleep patterns and MHPG excretion. *Am. J. Psychiatr.* **129**, 263–269. [135, 399]

Watson, S.J. (1977) Hallucinogens and other psychotomimetics: Biological mechanisms. In J.D. Barchas, P.A. Berger, R.D. Ciaranello, and G.R. Elliott (Eds.), *Psychopharmacology: From Theory to Practice.* Oxford University Press, New York, pp. 341–354. [21]

Wauquier, A. (1976) The influence of psychoactive drugs on brain self-stimulation in rats: A review. In A. Wauquier and E.T. Rolls (Eds.), *Brain Stimulation Reward.* North Holland, Amsterdam, pp. 123–171. [135]

Wauquier, A., Niemegeers, C.J.E., and Lal, H. (1974) Differential antagonism by naloxone of inhibitory effects of haloperidol and morphine on brain self-stimulation. *Psychopharmacology* **37**, 303–310. [363]

Wehr, T.A. and Wirz-Justice, A. (1982) Circadian rhythm mechanisms in affective illness and in antidepressant drug action. *Pharmakopsychiatria* **15**, 31–39. [116]

Wei, E. and Loh, H. (1976) Physical dependence on opiate-like peptides. *Science* **193**, 1262–1263. [359]

Weinberg, V.E., Lewis, J.W., Cannon, J.T., and Liebeskind, J.C. (1981) Evidence for the involvement of central cholinergic mechanisms in opioid stress analgesia. *Soc. Neurosci. Abstr.* **7**, 879. [276]

Weiner, R.D., Rogers, H.J., Welch, C.A., Davidson, J.R.T., Miller, R.D., Weir, D., Cahill, J.F., and Squire, L.R. (1984) ECT stimulus parameters and electrode placement: Relevance to therapeutic and adverse effects. In B. Lerer, R.D. Weiner, and R.H. Belmaker (Eds.), *ECT: Basic Mechanisms.* John Libbey, London, pp. 139–147. [89]

Weiner, W.J., Goetz, C., Westheimer, R., and Klawans, H.L. (1973) Serotonergic and antiserotonergic influences on amphetamine-induced stereotyped behaviour. *J. Neurol. Sci.* **20**, 373–379. [378]

Weingartner, H. and Silberman, E. (1982) Models of cognitive impairment: Cognitive change in depression. *Psychopharm. Bull* **18**, 27–42. [65, 82, 115, 129, 159]

Weingartner, H., Cohen, R.M., Martello, J.D.I., and Gerdt, C. (1981) Cognitive processes in depression. *Arch. Gen. Psychiatr.* **38**, 42–47. [68]

Weinstock, M., Speiser, Z., and Ashkenazi, R. (1976) Biochemical and pharmacological studies on an animal model of hyperactivity states. In E.S. Gershon, R.H. Belmaker, S.S. Kety, and M. Rosenbaum (Eds.), *The Impact of Biology on Modern Psychiatry.* Plenum, New York, pp. 149–161. [114]

Weinstock, M., Speiser, Z., and Ashkenazi, R. (1978) Changes in brain catecholamine turnover and receptor sensitivity induced by social deprivation in rats. *Psychopharmacology* **56**, 205–209. [114]

Weiss, B. and Laties, V.G. (1962) Enhancement of human performance by caffeine and amphetamines. *Pharmacol. Rev.* **14**, 1–36. [173]

Weiss, B., Heydorn, W., and Frazer, A. (1982) Modulation of the beta-adrenergic receptor-adenylate cyclase system following acute and repeated treatment with antidepressants. In E. Costa and G. Racagni (Eds.), *Typical and Atypical Antidepressants: Molecular Mechanisms.* Raven, New York, pp. 37–53. [262, 263]

Weiss, B.L., Kupfer, D.J., Foster, F.G., and Delgado, J. (1974) Psychomotor activity, sleep and biogenic amine metabolites in depression. *Biol. Psychiatr.* **9**, 45–54. [311]

Weiss, J.M. (1968) Effects of coping responses on stress. *J. Comp. Physiol. Psychol.* **65**, 251–260. [75, 123]

Weiss, J.M., Stone, E.A., and Harrell, N. (1970) Coping behavior and brain norepinephrine level in rats. *J. Comp. Physiol. Psychol.* **72**, 153–160. [208, 210]

Weiss, J.M., Glazer, H.I., Pohorecky, L.A., Brick, J., and Miller, N.E., (1975) Effects of chronic exposure to stressors on avoidance-escape behavior and on brain norepineph-rine. *Psychosom. Med.* **37**, 522–534. [209–212, 412]

Weiss, J.M., Glazer, H.I., and Pohorecky, L.A. (1976) Coping behaviour and neurochemical changes: An alternative explanation for the original "learned helplessness" experiments. In G. Serban and A. Kling (Eds.), *Animal Models in Human Psychobiology.* Plenum, New York, pp. 141–173. [122, 125, 208–210]

Weiss, J.M., Bailey, W.H., Pohorecky, L.A., Korzeniowski, D., and Grillione, G. (1980) Stress-induced depression of motor activity correlates with regional changes in brain norepinephrine but not in dopamine. *Neurochem. Res.* **5**, 9–22. [157]

Weiss, J.M., Goodman, P.A., Losito, B.G., Corrigan, S., Charry, J.M., and Bailey, W.H. (1981) Behavioral depression produced by an uncontrollable stressor: Relationship to nore-prinephrine, dopamine, and serotonin levels in various regions of rat brain. *Brain Res. Rev.* **3**, 167–205. [129, 157, 208–210, 213, 214, 289]

Weiss, J.M., Bailey, W.H., Goodman, P.A., Hoffman, L.J., Ambrose, M.J., Salman, S., and Charry, J.M. (1982) A model for neurochemical study of depression. In M.Y. Spiegelstein and A. Levy (Eds.), *Behavioral Models and the Analysis of Drug Action.* Elsevier, Amsterdam, pp. 195–223. [123, 129, 208–210, 212–215, 397]

Weiss, J.M., Goodman, P.A., Ambrose, M.J., Webster, A., and Hoffman, L.J. (1984) Neurochemical basis of behavioral depression. In E. Katkin and S. Manuck (Eds.), *Advances in Behavioral Medicine*, Vol. 1. JAI Press, Greenwich, Conn. [123, 129, 212, 214]

Weissman, M.S. and Paykel, E.S. (1974) *The Depressed Woman: A Study of Social Relationships.* University of Chicago Press, Chicago. [267, 405]

Weissman, M.S., Pottenger, M., Kleber, H., Ruben, H.L., Williams, D., and Thompson, W.D. (1977) Symptom patterns in primary and secondary depression: A comparison of primary depressives with depressed opiate addicts, alcoholics and schizophrenics. *Arch. Gen. Psychiatr.* **34**, 854–862. [47]

Welch, J., Kim, H., Fallon, S., and Liebman, J. (1982) Do antidepressants induce dopamine autoreceptor subsensitivity? *Nature* **298**, 301–302. [184]

Weller, M.P.I. (1981) Travel induced disturbances in circadian rhythms as precipitants of affective illness. Paper presented at 3rd World Congress of Biological Psychiatry, Stockholm, June–July 1981. [400]

Wener, A.E. and Rehm, L.P. (1975) Depressive affect: A test of behavioral hypotheses. *J. Abnorm. Psychol.* **84**, 221–227. [70]

West, C.H.K., Schaeffer, G.J., and Michael, R.P. (1983) Increasing the work requirements lowers the threshold of naloxone for reducing self-stimulation in the midbrain of rats. *Pharmacol. Biochem. Behav.* **18**, 705–710. [362]

West, E.D. and Dally, P.J. (1959) Effect of iproniazid in depressive syndromes. *Br. Med. J.* **1**, 1491–1494. [11]

Westenberg, H.G.M., Van Praag, H.M., De Jong, J.T.V.M., and Thijssen, J.H.H. (1982) Postsynaptic serotonergic activity in depressive patients: Evaluation of the neuroendocrine strategy. *Psychiatr. Res.* **7**, 361–371. [314]

Westfall, T.C. (1977) Local regulation of adrenergic neurotransmission. *Physiol. Rev.* **57**, 659–728 [242]

Wetterberg, L., Aberg, H., Ross, S.B., and Froden, O. (1972) Plasma dopamine-beta-hydroxylase activity in hypertension and various neuropsychiatric disorders. *Scand. J. Clin. Lab. Invest.* **30**, 283–289. [220]

Wexler, B. and Heninger, G. (1979) Alterations in cerebral lateralization in acute psychotic illness. *Arch. Gen. Psychiatr.* **36**, 278–284. [90, 91]

Whishaw, I.Q. (1972) Hippocampal electroencephalographic activity in the Mongolian gerbil during natural behaviors and in wheel running and conditioned immobility. *Can. J. Physiol.* **26**, 219–239. [273]

Whitaker, P.M., Warsh, J.J., Stancer, H.C., Perzad, E., and Vint, C.K. (1984) Seasonal variations in platelet ^{3}H-imipramine binding: Comparable values in control and depressed populations. *Psychiatr. Res.* **11**, 127–131. [316]

White, D.K. and Barrett, R.J. (1981) The effects of electroconvulsive shock on the discriminative stimulus properties of D-amphetamine and apomorphine: Evidence for dopamine receptor alteration subsequent to ECS. *Psychopharmacology* **73**, 211–214. [188]

White, H.L., McLeod, M.N., and Davidson, J.R.T. (1976) Catechol-O-methyltransferase in red blood cells of scizophrenic, depressed and normal human subjects. *Br. J. Psychiatr.* **128**, 184–187. [220]

White, K., Shih, J., Fong, T., Young, H., Gelfand, R., Boyd, J., Simpson, G., and Sloane, R.B. (1980) Elevated plasma monoamine oxidase activity in patients with non-endogenous depression. *Am. J. Psychiatr.* **137**, 1258–1259. [221]

White, N., Brown, Z., and Yachnin, M. (1978) Effects of catecholamine manipulations on three different self-stimulation behaviors. *Pharmacol. Biochem. Behav.* **9**, 273–278. [196]

Whybrow, P.C., Prange, A.J., and Treadway, C.R. (1969) Mental changes accompanying thyroid gland dysfunction. *Arch. Gen. Psychiatr.* **20**, 48–63. [399]

Wiberg, A., Gottfries, C.G., and Oreland, L. (1977a) Low platelet monoamine oxidase activity in human alcoholics. *Med. Biol.* **55**, 181–186. [221]

Wiberg, A., Wahlstrom, S., and Oreland, L. (1977b) Brain monoamine oxidase activity after chronic ethanol treatment of rats. *Psychopharmacology* **52**, 111–113. [221]

Widerlov, E., Wide, L., and Sjostrom, R. (1978) Effects of tricyclic antidepressants on human plasma levels of TSH, GH and prolactin. *Acta Psychiatr. Scand.* **58**, 449–456. [187]

Widlocher, D., Simon, P., Allilaire, J.F., Jouvent, R., Lecrubier, Y., and Puech, A.-J. (1978) Une nouvelle approche dans le traitement des états dépressifs: Le salbutamol. *Ann. Med. Interne* **129**, 419–422. [232]

Wiech, N.L. and Ursillo, R.C. (1980) Acceleration of desipramine-induced decrease of rat corticocerebral beta-adrenergic receptors by yohimbine. *Commun. Psychopharmacol.* **4**, 95–100. [259]

Wielosz, M. (1981) Increased sensitivity to dopaminergic agonists after repeated electroconvulsive shock (ECS) in rats. *Neuropharmacology* **20**, 941–945. [188, 189, 191]

Wielosz, M. and Kleinrok, Z. (1979) Lithium-induced head twitches in rats. *J. Pharm. Pharmacol.* **31**, 410–411. [339]

Wilk, S., Shopsin, B., Gershon, S., and Suhl, M. (1972) Cerebrospinal fluid levels of MHPG in affective disorders. *Nature* **235**, 440–441. [167, 222, 223]

Williams, A.W., Ware, J.E., and Donald, C.A. (1981) A model of mental health, life events, and social supports applicable to general populations. *J. Health Soc. Behav.* **22**, 324–336. [393]

Williams, J.H. and Azmitia, E.C. (1981) Hippocampal serotonin reuptake and nocturnal locomotor activity after microinjections of 5,7-DHT in the fornix-fimbria. *Brain Res.* **207**, 95–107. [296]

Williams, J.L. and Maier, S.F. (1977) Transituational immunization and therapy of learned helplessness in the rat. *J. Exp. Psychol.: Anim. Behav. Proc.* **3**, 240–252. [360]

Williams, J.M., Hamilton, L.W., and Carlton, P.L. (1974) Pharmacological and anatomical dissociation of two types of habituation. *J. Comp. Physiol. Psychol.* **87**, 724–732. [274, 294]

Williams, L.T., Lefkowitz, R.J., Watanabe, A.M., Hathaway, D.R., and Besch, H.R. (1977) Thyroid hormone regulation of beta-adrenergic receptor number. *J. Biol. Chem.* **252**, 2787–2789. [373]

Willis, M.H. and Blaney, P.H. (1978) Three tests of the learned helplessness model of depression. *J. Abnorm. Psychol.* **87**, 131–136. [76, 126]

Willis, W.D. (1981) Effects of peripherally and centrally administered serotonin on primate spinothalamic neurons. In B. Haber, S. Gabay, M.R. Issidorides, and G.A. Alivisatos (Eds.), *Serotonin: Current Aspects on Neurochemistry and Function.* Plenum, New York, pp. 681–705. [298]

Willner, P. (1983) A conceptual framework for psychobiological synthesis. *Biol. Psychiatr.* **18**, 1447–1450. [22]

Willner, P. (1984a) The validity of animal models of depression. *Psychopharmacology* **83**, 1–16. [137]

Willner, P. (1984b) Drugs, biochemistry and subjective experience: Towards a theory of psychopharmacology. *Perspect. Biol. Med.* **28**, 49–64. [21, 22, 27]

Willner, P. (1984c) The ability of antidepressant drugs to desensitize beta-adrenergic receptors is not correlated with their clinical potency. *J. Affect. Disord.* **7**, 53–58. [265, 266]

Willner, P. (1984d) Cognitive functioning in depression: A review of theory and research. *Psychol. Med.* **14**, 807–823. [62]

Willner, P. and Clark, D. (1978) A reappraisal of the interaction between tricyclic antidepressants and reserpine-like drugs. *Psychopharmacology* **58**, 55–62. [110]

Willner, P. and Montgomery, A. (1980a) Drugs, neurotransmitters and depression: Too much, too little, too unstable—Or not unstable enough? *Trends Neurosci.* **3**, 201. [16, 260]

Willner, P. and Montgomery, A. (1980b) Attenuation of amphetamine anorexia in rats following subchronic treatment with a tricyclic antidepressant. *Commun. Psychopharmacol.* **4**, 101–106. [263, 265]

Willner, P. and Montgomery, A. (1981) Behavioural changes during withdrawal from the tricyclic antidepressant desmethylimipramine (DMI). I. Interactions with amphetamine. *Psychopharmacology* **75**, 54–59. [188, 189, 263, 265]

Willner, P. and Towell, A. (1982a) Evidence suggesting that DMI-induced resistance to extinction is not mediated by the dorsal noradrenergic bundle. *Brain Res.* **238**, 251–253. [264]

Willner, P. and Towell, A. (1982b) The effects of chronic tricyclic antidepressant treatment on anorexia mediated by presynaptic dopamine receptors. *Soc. Neurosci. Abstr.* **8**, 358. [184]

Willner, P., Montgomery, A., and Bird, D. (1981a) Behavioural changes during withdrawal from the tricyclic antidepressant desmethylimipramine (DMI). II. Increased resistance to extinction. *Psychopharmacology* **75**, 60–64. [262, 264, 265]

Willner, P., Theodorou, A., and Montgomery, A. (1981b) Subchronic treatment with the tricyclic antidepressant DMI increases isolation-induced fighting in rats. *Pharmacol. Biochem. Behav.* **14**, 475–479. [159]

Willner, P., Towell, A., and Montgomery, A. (1984) Changes in amphetamine-induced anorexia and stereotypy during chronic treatment with antidepressant drugs. *Eur. J. Pharmacol.* **98**, 397–406. [188, 189, 263, 265]

Willoughby, J.O., Menadue, M., and Jervois, P. (1982) Function of serotonin in physiologic secretion of growth hormone and prolactin: Action of 5,7-dihydroxytryptamine, fenfluramine and p-chlorophenylalanine. *Brain Res.* **249**, 291–299. [314]

Wilson, M.C. and Schuster, C.R. (1973) Cholinergic influence on intravenous cocaine self-administration by rhesus monkeys. *Pharmacol. Biochem. Behav.* **1**, 643–649. [380]

Winokur, A., Amsterdam, J., Caroff, S., Snyder, P.J., and Brunswick, D. (1982) Variability of hormonal responses to a series of neuroendocrine challenges in depressed patients. *Am. J. Psychiatr.* **139**, 39–44. [315, 372]

Winokur, G. (1972) Family history studies. 8. Secondary depression is alive and well and ... *Dis. Nerv. Syst.* **33**, 94–99. [47]

Winokur, G. (1975) The Iowa 500: Heterogeneity and course in manic-depressive illness (bipolar). *Compr. Psychiatr.* **16**, 125–131. [45]

Winokur, G. (1979) Unipolar depression: Is it divisible into autonomous subtypes? *Arch. Gen. Psychiatr.* **36**, 47–57. [58]

Winokur, G. and Bagchi, S.P. (1974) Effects of bufotenine and p-chlorophenylalanine on reactivity to footshock. *Physiol. Psychol.* **2**, 75–79. [294]

Winokur, G. and Morrison, J. (1973) The Iowa 500: Following of 225 depressives. *Br. J. Psychiatr.* **123**, 543–548. [47]

Winokur, G., Cadoret, R., and Dorzab, J. (1971) Depressive disease. A genetic study. *Arch. Gen. Psychiatr.* **24**, 135–144. [58, 325]

Winter, J.C. (1978) Drug-induced stimulus control. In D.E. Blackman and D.J. Sanger (Eds.), *Contemporary Research in Behavioral Pharmacology*. Plenum, New York, pp. 209–238. [152]

Wirz-Justice, A., Puhringer, W., Hole, G., and Menzi, R. (1975) Monoamine oxidase and free tryptophan in human plasma: Normal variations and their implications for biochemical research in affective disorders. *Pharmakopsychiatria* **8**, 310–317. [308]

Wirz-Justice, A., Puhringer, W., Lacoste, P., Graw, P., and Gastpar, M. (1976) Intravenous L-5-hydroxytryptophan in normal subjects: An interdisciplinary precursor preloading study. III. Neuroendocrinological and biochemical changes. *Pharmakopsychiatria* **9**, 277–288. [314]

Wirz-Justice, A., Krauchi, K., Lichtsteiner, M., and Feer, H. (1978) Is it possible to modify serotonin receptor sensitivity? *Life Sci.* **23**, 1249–1254. [247]

Wirz-Justice, A., Arendt, J., and Marston, A. (1980) Antidepressant drugs elevate rat pineal and plasma melatonin. *Experientia* **36**, 442–444. [262, 263]

Wise, C.D., Berger, B.D., and Stein, L. (1973) Evidence of alpha-noradrenergic reward receptors and serotonergic punishment receptors in the rat brain. *Biol. Psychiatr.* **6**, 3–21. [294]

Wise, R.A. (1978) Catecholamine theories of reward: A critical review. *Brain Res.* **152**, 215–247. [200]

Wise, R.A. (1982) Neuroleptics and operant behaviour: The anhedonia hypothesis. *Behav. Brain Sci.* **5**, 39–87. [150, 152, 153]

Wise, R.A., Spindler, J., and Legault, L. (1978a) Major attenuation of food reward with performance-sparing doses of pimozide in the rat. *Can. J. Psychol.* **32**, 77–85. [151]

Wise, R.A., Spindler, J., De Wit, H., and Gerber, G.J. (1978b) Neuroleptic-induced "anhedonia" in rats: Pimozide blocks reward quality of food. *Science* **201**, 262–264. [151]

Wojcik, W.J. and Radulovacki, M. (1981) Selective increase in brain dopamine metabolism during REM sleep rebound in the rat. *Physiol. Behav.* **27**, 305–312. [183]

Wolfe, D.B., Harden, T.K., Sporn, J.R., and Molinoff, P.B. (1978) Presynaptic modulation of beta adrenergic receptors in rat cerebral cortex after treatment with antidepressants. *J. Pharmacol. Exp. Ther.* **207**, 446–457. [256, 258, 259]

Wood, D., Othmer, S., Reich, T., Viesselman, J., and Rutt, C. (1977) Primary and secondary affective disorder. I. Past social history and current episodes on 92 depressed inpatients. *Compr. Psychiatr.* **18**, 201–210. [47]

Wood, K. and Coppen, A. (1982) Peripheral alpha-adrenergic activity in the affective disorders. In E. Costa and G. Racagni (Eds.), *Typical and Atypical Antidepressants: Clinical Practice*. Raven, New York, pp. 13–19. [219]

Wood, K. and Coppen, A. (1983) Prophylactic lithium treatment of patients with affective disorders is associated with decreased platelet [^{3}H]dihydroergocryptine binding. *J. Affect. Disord.* **5**, 253–258. [219, 248]

Wood, K., Harwood, J., and Coppen, A. (1978) The effect of antidepressant drugs on plasma kynurenine in depressed patients. *Psychopharmacology* **59**, 263–266. [308]

Woodruff, R.A., Murphy, G.A., and Herjanic, M. (1967) The natural history of affective disorders. I. Symptoms of 72 patients at the time of index hospitalization. *J. Psychiatr. Res.* **5**, 255–263. [47]

Woods, J.H. and Tessel, R.E. (1974) Fenfluramine: Amphetamine congener that fails to maintain drug-taking behavior in the rhesus monkey. *Science* **185**, 1066–1070. [302]

Wortman, C.B. and Dintzer, L. (1978) Is an attributional analysis of the learned helplessness phenomenon viable?: A critique of the Abramson-Seligman-Teasdale reformulation. *J. Abnorm. Psychol.* **87**, 75–90. [78, 126, 127]

Wurtman, J.J. and Wurtman, R.J. (1979) Fenfluramine and other serotoninergic drugs depress food intake and carbohydrate consumption while sparing protein consumption. *Curr. Med. Res. Opin.* **6** (Suppl. 1), 28–33. [301]

Wurtman, R.J., Larin, F., Mostafour, S., and Fernstrom, J.D. (1974) Brain catechol synthesis: Controlled by brain tyrosine concentrations. *Science* **185**, 183–184. [172]

Wyatt, R.J. and Murphy, D.L. (1975) Neurotransmitter-related enzymes in the major psychiatric disorders. II. MAO and DBH in schizophrenia. In D.X. Freedman (Ed.), *The Biology of the Major Psychoses: A Comparative Analysis*. Raven, New York, pp. 289–296. [221]

Wyatt, R.J., Portnoy, B., Kupfer, D.J., Snyder, F., and Engelman, K. (1971) Resting plasma catecholamine concentrations in patients with depression and anxiety. *Arch. Gen. Psychiatr.* **24**, 65–70. [218]

Xenakis, S. and Sclafani, A. (1982) The dopaminergic mediation of a sweet reward in normal and VMH hyperphagic rats. *Pharmacol. Biochem. Behav.* **16**, 293–302. [152]

Yaksh, T.L. and Rudy, T.A. (1978) Narcotic analgetics: CNS sites and mechanisms of action revealed by intracerebral injection techniques. *Pain* **4**, 299–359. [299]

Yaksh, T.L. and Wilson, P.R. (1979) Spinal serotonin system mediates antinociception. *J. Pharm. Exp. Ther.* **208**, 446–453. [297]

Yaksh, T.L., Du Chateau, J., and Rudy, T.A. (1976) Antagonism by methysergide and cinanserin of the antinociceptive action of morphine administered into the periaqueductal gray. *Brain Res.* **104**, 367–372. [299]

Yaksh, T.L., Plant, R.L., and Rudy, T.A. (1977) Studies of the antagonism by raphe lesions of the antinociceptive action of systemic morphine. *Eur. J. Pharmacol.* **41**, 399–408. [299, 359]

Yanai, J. and Sze, P.Y. (1983) Isolation reduces midbrain tryptophan hydroxylase activity in mice. *Psychopharmacology* **80**, 284–285. [291]

Yim, G.K.W., Lowy, M.T., Davis, J.M., Lamb, D.R., and Malven, P.V. (1982) Opiate involvement in glucoprivic feeding. In B.G. Hoebel and D. Novin (Eds.), *The Neural Basis of Feeding and Reward*. Haer Institute, Brunswick, Me., pp. 485–498. [362]

Yokel, R.A. and Wise, R.A. (1976) Attenuation of intravenous amphetamine reinforcement by central dopamine blockade in rats. *Psychopharmacology* **48**, 311–318. [153]

Young, G.C.D. and Martin, M. (1981) Processing of information about self by neurotics. *Br. J. Clin. Psychol.* **20**, 205–212. [70]

Young, S.N. and Gauthier, S. (1981a) Tryptophan availability and the control of 5-hydroxytryptamine and tryptamine synthesis in human CNS. *Adv. Exp. Med. Biol.* **133**, 221–230. [309]

Young, S.N. and Gauthier, S. (1981b) Effect of tryptophan administration on tryptophan, 5-hydroxyindoleacetic acid and indoleacetic acid in human lumbar and cisternal cerebrospinal fluid. *J. Neurol. Neurosurg. Psychiatr.* **44**, 323–328. [309]

Young, S.N. and Sourkes, T.L. (1977) Tryptophan in the central nervous system: Regulation and significance. *Adv. Neurochem.* **2**, 133–191. [319]

Youngren, M.A. and Lewinsohn, P.M. (1980) The functional relation between depression and problematic interpersonal behaviour. *J. Abnorm. Psychol.* **89**, 333–341. [66]

Yozawitz, A., Bruder, G., Sutton, S., Sharpe, L., Gurland, B., Fliess, J., and Costa, L. (1979) Dichotic perception: Evidence for right hemisphere dysfunction in affective psychosis. *Br. J. Psychiatr.* **135**, 224–237. [89]

Yu, P.H., O'Sullivan, K.S., Keegan, D., and Boulton, A. (1980) Dopamine-beta-hydroxylase and its apparent endogenous inhibitory activity in the plasma of some psychiatric patients. *Psychiatr. Res.* **3**, 205–210. [220]

Yunger, L.M. and Harvey, J.A. (1976) Behavioral effects of L-5-hydroxytryptophan after destruction of ascending serotonergic pathways in the rat: The role of catecholaminergic neurons. *J. Pharm. Exp. Ther.* **196**, 307–315. [297]

Yuwiler, A., Geller, E., and Eidusin, S. (1957) Studies on 5-hydroxytryptophan decarboxylase. I. In vitro inhibition and substrate interaction. *Arch. Biochem.* **80**, 162–173. [321]

Zabik, J.E. and Roache, J.D. (1983) 5-hydroxytryptophan-induced conditioned taste aversion to ethanol in the rat. *Pharmacol. Biochem. Behav.* **18**, 785–790. [302]

Zacharko, R.M., Bowers, W.J., Kokkinidis, L., and Anisman, H. (1982) Alteration of intracranial self-stimulation in mice following inescapable stress. *Soc. Neurosci. Abstr.* **8**, 898. [123, 363, 385]

Zacharko, R.M., Bowers, W.J., Kokkinidis, L., and Anisman, H. (1983) Region-specific reductions of intracranial self-stimulation after uncontrollable stress: Possible effects on reward processes. *Behav. Brain Res.* **9**, 129–141. [123, 363, 385]

Zarevics, P. and Setler, P.E. (1979) Simultaneous rate-independent and rate-dependent assessment of intracranial self-stimulation: Evidence for direct involvement of dopamine in brain reinforcement mechanisms. *Brain Res.* **169**, 499–512. [154]

Zebrowska-Lupina, I. (1980) Presynaptic alpha-adrenoceptors and the action of tricyclic antidepressant drugs in behavioral despair in rats. *Psychopharmacology* **71**, 169–172. [188, 212]

Zebrowska-Lupina, I. and Kozyrska, C. (1980) The studies on the role of brain dopamine in the action of antidepressant drugs. *Naunyn Schmiedebergs Arch. Pharmacol.* **313** (Suppl. 80), R20. [183]

Zeiss, A.M., Lewinsohn, P.M., and Munoz, R.F. (1979) Nonspecific improvement effects in depression using interpersonal skills training, pleasant activity schedules, or cognitive training. *J. Consult. Clin. Psychol.* **45**, 543–551. [411]

Zelger, K.D. and Carlini, E.A. (1982) The persistence of hyperresponsiveness to apomorphine in rats following REM sleep deprivation and the influence of housing conditions. *Eur. J. Pharmacol.* **80**, 99–104. [189]

Ziegler, M.G., Wood, J.H., Lake, C.R., and Kopin, I.J. (1977) Norepinephrine and 3-methoxy-4-hydroxyphenyl glycol gradients in human cerebrospinal fluid. *Am. J. Psychiatr.* **134**, 565–568. [223]

Zigmond, M. and Harvey, J. (1970) Resistance to central norepinephrine depletion and decreased mortality in rats chronically exposed to electric foot shock. *J. NeuroVisc. Relat.* **31**, 373–381. [210]

Zigmond, R.D. (1979) Tyrosine hydroxylase activity in noradrenergic neurons of the locus coeruleus after reserpine administration: Sequential increase in cell bodies and nerve terminals. *J. Neurochem.* **32**, 23–29. [210]

Zimmerberg, B., Glick, S.D., and Jerussi, T.P. (1974) Neurochemical correlates of a spatial preference in rats. *Science* **185**, 623–625. [96, 99]

Zis, A.P. and Goodwin, F.K. (1979) Novel antidepressants and the biogenic amine hypothesis of depression. The case for iprindole and mianserin. *Arch. Gen. Psychiatr.* **36**, 1097–1107. [12, 329]

Zis, A.P., Fibiger, H.C., and Phillips, A.G. (1974) Reversal by L-dopa of impaired learning due to destruction of the dopaminergic nigroneostriatal projection. *Science* **185**, 960–962. [156]

Zubin, J. (1967) Classification of the behavior disorders. *Ann. Rev. Psychol.* **18**, 373–407. [41]

INDEX

effects on receptor function, 15, 183,
188-189, 191, 243, 245, 343
neurochemical effects, 15, 177, 183,
Social dominance, 214-215, 383, 397, 405
Social isolation:
as animal model of depression, 114-115,
117, 138
physiological consequences, 291-293,
295, 378, 386
Socially dependent personality, 81, 405,
419
Social reinforcement, 393, 397-398,
405-406, 409-410, 419
physiological mechanisms, 363-364,
386-387, 406, 419
Social skills, 67, 93, 393, 411, 419
Social support, 66-67, 293, 393-394,
396-398, 400, 407, 409-411, 414,
419
Somatostatin, 371
Speech pause time, increase in depression,
64
Spinothalamic tract, 298
Spiroperidol, 151
as ligand in receptor binding
experiments, 190, 330-331, 345
State dependent learning, 71
Stereotyped behavior, 149, 153, 158,
187-189, 378-379
Stimulant drugs:
effects in animal models of depression,
106-107, 110-111, 122, 128, 130,
409
rewarding effects, 152, 302
self-administration of, 152-153, 302, 380
Stimulation produced analgesia, 298-299,
359-360
Strain, as precipitant of depression, 80,
131, 214, 392-393, 395-396, 397,
400, 418
Stress:
adaptation to, 210-211, 214, 305, 382,
411-412
in animal models of depression, 115,
128, 130-131, 138-139, 214,
270-271
as antidepressant, 412
chronic, 130-131, 139, 214, 270-271, 384,
392, 396, 405, 408
individual differences in response to,
214, 392, 397
as precipitant of depression, 50, 67,
80-81, 131, 139, 214, 392, 396,

398, 400, 407, 418
role of ACh, 213, 375, 382, 384, 387, 396,
403, 418
role of endorphins, 359-361, 365
role of 5-HT, 289-290, 299-300, 305
role of NA, 198, 208, 236, 382, 384, 387,
396, 403, 411-412, 418
and social status, 214, 397
suppression of reward mechanisms by,
403, 418
uncontrollability of and learned
helplessness, 74-75
Striatum, 148-149, 152, 156, 158, 164,
182-183, 190, 288, 345, 357, 376,
378-379
Subaffective dysthymic disorder, 57-59
Subjective experience:
analysis of, 27, 29
and cognitive processes, 21, 26-28, 120
of depression, 19, 35-40, 62, 400
drug effects on, 27-28, 176
relationship to psychobiology, 19-22
Substantia innominata, 385
Substantia nigra, 148, 184-185, 378, 385
Suicide, 41-42, 169, 395, 407, 409
and 5-HT, 309, 311-316, 325, 356,
406-407, 419
other physiological correlates, 164,
222-223, 279, 356, 365
Swimming test, 127
Switch from depression to mania, *see*
Mania

Tail pressure, 185
Tardive dyskinesias, 15, 281-282
Tetrabenazine, 7, 109, 211-212
Thiamine deficiency, 291
Thiopentone anesthesia, effects of
antidepressants, 265
Thioridazine, 171
Thyroid function and depression, 399
Thyroid stimulating hormone (TSH),
371-372
releasing hormone (TRH), 314-315,
337-338, 371-372
as antidepressant, 371, 373
Tofenacin, 263
Tranylcypromine, 11, 188, 339
effects in animal models of depression,
127, 130, 135, 350
interaction with muscarinic receptors,
285
interactions with 5-HT, 317-318, 348